Divination and Prediction in Early China and Ancient Greece

Divination was an important and distinctive aspect of religion in both early China and ancient Greece, and this book will provide the first systematic account and analysis of the two side by side. Who practiced divination in these cultures and who consulted it? What kind of questions did they ask, and what methods were used to answer those questions? As well as these practical aspects, Lisa Raphals also examines divination as a subject of rhetorical and political narratives, and its role in the development of systematic philosophical and scientific inquiry. She explores too the important similarities, differences, and synergies between Greek and Chinese divinatory systems, providing important comparative evidence to reassess Greek oracular divination.

LISA RAPHALS is Professor of Chinese and Comparative Literature at the University of California, Riverside, and Visiting Professor in the Department of Philosophy, National University of Singapore. She is the author of *Knowing Words: Wisdom and Cunning in the Classical Traditions of China and Greece* (1992), *Sharing the Light: Representations of Women and Virtue in Early China* (1998), and many scholarly articles. Her research interests include comparative philosophy (China and Greece), the history of science, religion, gender, and science fiction studies.

Divination and Prediction in Early China and Ancient Greece

LISA RAPHALS

CAMBRIDGE
UNIVERSITY PRESS

CAMBRIDGE
UNIVERSITY PRESS

University Printing House, Cambridge CB2 8BS, United Kingdom

Published in the United States of America by Cambridge University Press, New York

Cambridge University Press is part of the University of Cambridge.

It furthers the University's mission by disseminating knowledge in the pursuit of education, learning, and research at the highest international levels of excellence.

www.cambridge.org
Information on this title: www.cambridge.org/9781107010758

First published 2013

Printed in the United Kingdom by TJ International Ltd. Padstow Cornwall

A catalogue record for this publication is available from the British Library

Library of Congress Cataloging in Publication data
Raphals, Lisa Ann, 1951–
Divination and prediction in early China and ancient Greece / Lisa Raphals.
pages cm
Includes bibliographical references and index.
ISBN 978-1-107-01075-8
1. Divination – China. 2. Divination – Greece. I. Title.
BL613.R37 2013
292.3′2–dc23

2012036781

ISBN 978-1-107-01075-8 Hardback

To Michael Loewe
whose knowledge of this field is unique and whose
contributions deserve far more recognition than can be given
here in gratitude for years of rigor, generosity, kindness

and to Sara Susan Raphals (1920–2013)

Contents

Figures

Maps

Reference tables

Acknowledgments

This book is an exploration of divination and prediction in Chinese and Greek antiquity, but it is also a part of two ongoing interdisciplinary and intercultural explorations that have informed my scholarly work. One is the engagement between the disciplines of philosophy and history from a perspective also informed by anthropology. The other is the comparative study of Chinese and Greek antiquity from a shifting viewpoint informed by all three disciplines. This approach began with my first book, *Knowing Words: Wisdom and Cunning in the Classical Traditions in China and Greece*, and has continued through most of my scholarly work and teaching. This approach is not well recognized in the contemporary academy, and for this reason I shall always be indebted to the teachers, both formal and informal, who informed and encouraged it in diverse ways: A. C. Graham, Sir Geoffrey Lloyd, Michael Loewe, Gregory Nagy, A. K. Ramanujan, Stephen Toulmin, and Anthony Yu. These debts can never be repaid; their example can only be emulated.

Several colleagues have read all or part of the manuscript at various stages: Lothar von Falkenhausen, Stephen Field, Michael Lackner, Geoffrey Lloyd, Poo Mu-chou, Michael Nylan, David Pankenier, Michael Puett, Francesca Rochberg, Richard Smith, and three anonymous readers from Cambridge University Press. I am particularly indebted to the expertise and encouragement of Richard Smith, Poo Mu-chou, and Marc Kalinowski. I also wish to express heartfelt thanks to the three anonymous readers from Cambridge University Press, to Michael Sharp for editorial direction through a complex project, to Elizabeth Davey and Elizabeth Hanlon for help in many aspects of production, to Jael Peh Chieh Yin and John Moffett for reading of the Chinese, and to Nigel Hope for more than exemplary copy-editing of the manuscript.

This project has benefited from residential fellowships and financial support from several institutions. The initial version of the manuscript was written during a visiting fellowship from the Centre for Cross-Cultural Studies at City University of Hong Kong (2002–3), and I am grateful to Zhang Longxi for the invitation that made this possible.

I have received ongoing support from the University of California, Riverside. A Mellon Foundation Workshop Grant for the series "Divination, Prediction and the Very Idea of the Future" (2004–5) provided a rubric for discussions with colleagues and graduate students, especially Chai Jie and Liu Chun. A President's Research Fellowship in the Humanities from the University of California (2005–6) and a grant from the National Endowment for the Humanities and the American Council of Learned Societies for research in China (2006) provided invaluable time for complete revision and expansion of the original manuscript. (Any views, findings, conclusions, or recommendations expressed in this book do not necessarily reflect those of the National Endowment for the Humanities.) My department chair, Thomas Scanlon, has helped me in innumerable ways, and has been an ongoing and important conversation partner. The heroic librarians at the Interlibrary Loan department have been a lifeline over many years.

I am also grateful to the National University of Singapore. An Isaac Manasseh Meyer Fellowship supported a brief residence there in 2006. As a faculty member I have received generous research support, including for expenses associated with preparation of the manuscript of this book. Less tangible but equally important is a collegial department of philosophical conversation partners, especially Tan Sor Hoon, Loy Hui-chieh, and Saranindranath Tagore.

The international research consortium "Fate, Freedom and Prognostication: Strategies for Coping with the Future in East Asia and Europe" at the University of Erlangen-Nürnberg has provided a unique opportunity to work with colleagues engaged in similar research, especially Anne Cheng, Dimitri Drettas, Albert Galvany, Marc Kalinowski, Michael Lackner, Zhou Qi, and Richard Smith. Several portions of this book were presented at conferences there in 2009, 2010, and 2011.

Much of this book has been presented at conference talks and invited lectures over several years, beginning with a panel at the Association for Asian Studies (1998), the Beijing Forum, Beijing Normal University, Bowdoin College, Chinese University of Hong Kong, City University of Hong Kong, Fudan University, Hong Kong University, Hong Kong Baptist University, C.N.R.S., École Normale Supérieure, Emory University, the International Congress on Traditional Asian Medicine (2002), the International Convention of Asia Scholars (2003), the International Society for Chinese Philosophy (2005), the International Congress of the History of Science (2005), Ludwig-Maximilians-Universität (Munich), National Central University (Taiwan), the Needham Research Institute and Cambridge

University, Peking University, Shanghai Jiao Tong University, Stanford University, UCLA, the University of California, Irvine, the University of Chicago, the University of Glasgow, the University of Granada, the University of Oregon, the Wellcome Trust (London), Wuhan University, and the University of Zurich. The ideas in this book are informed by the ideas of many scholars at all these institutions. Finally, I have benefited from discussions and correspondence with colleagues and friends: Sarah Allan, Timothy Brook, Marcello Carastro, Alan Chan, Karine Chemla, Persi Diaconis, Mark Elvin, David Glidden, Christoph Harbsmeier, Donald Harper, Christian Jacob, Julia Kindt, Vivienne Lo, John Moffett, Alicia Eleta Relinque, Julia Strauss, Robin Yates, Zhang Wei, and Zhou Yiqun. Responsibility for all errors and omissions is, of course, my own.

This project could not have been completed without the aid of my family, especially my husband John Baez. Them I thank for everything.

Notes on conventions, editions, and transcriptions

With the exception of a handful of people, at least half this book will be unfamiliar to at least half its readership, including orthography and standard reference conventions.

All dates are given using the Western calendar. They correspond approximately to the luni-solar calendars used in early China.

Detailed material is reserved for appendices, at both the ends of chapters and the end of the volume. Material pertinent to a single chapter is included in an appendix immediately following it. These appendices are numbered 2.1, 6.2, etc. Material of recurring interest appears in six appendices at the end of the volume, lettered A through F.

Chinese

The Pinyin transliteration system is used throughout, including in quoted text, except for the names of authors who use non-Pinyin spellings for their own names and for terms that are well known in a Latinate version (e.g. Confucius).

Chinese characters are included in the text for translated passages and where immediate reference is especially convenient. All Chinese characters are given in traditional form.

Chinese translations are my own unless otherwise indicated. Existing translations of Chinese texts are included for reference and referred to by name (e.g. Biot 1.409), rather than by name and date.

Greek and Latin

In most cases, Latin transliteration is used for Greek names and places mentioned in the text (e.g. Calchas, Chaerophon) because it is more likely to be familiar to the non-specialist. I follow the *Oxford Classical Dictionary* (e.g. Claros, rather than Clarus). Greek transliteration is used for Greek words quoted in Greek and for names that are particularly obscure. A few inscriptions are given in Greek in the footnotes.

Unless otherwise indicated, Greek and Latin texts and translations are from the Loeb Classical Library, sometimes with slight modifications, with the translator indicated by name (e.g. Perrin). Translations from the Homeric poems are modified from Richmond Lattimore's translations of the *Iliad* and *Odyssey*. Other translations are my own.

Abbreviations for Greek and Latin texts follow the *Oxford Classical Dictionary*. References to Greek translations are provided for texts unavailable through the Loeb Classical Library editions. Most abbreviations used are listed below, for the convenience of the non-specialist reader.

Certain key terms only lose by translation, or worse, the short-cut of translation introduces confusion by force of habit. Therefore, I have chosen to leave certain key words as they are. These include the Chinese terms *dao* (familiar to some as *tao*), *qi*, and *yin* and *yang*. Greek examples include *mantis* (plural *manteis*) rather than seer, polis (plural *poleis*) rather than state, and *tekhnē* (art or science). In translating certain Chinese terms I have aimed for renderings that are more clear, if sometimes less familiar, for example mantic astrolabe (rather than diviner's board). In other cases, I have retained Chinese titles, for example for the *Zuo zhuan* (Zuo Transmissions).

I use the term "state" as a term of convenience to comprehend what are in actuality a wide range of communities and authorities. In a Chinese context it includes the domains of the Shang kings (*wang* 王), the dukes in charge of the states (*guo* 國) of the Warring States period, and in the Qin and Han periods the rulers (*di* 帝) of those empires. In a Greek context it includes *poleis*, but also communities such as colonies and other groups, such as the many smaller groups that questioned Delphi. In Macedonian and Roman contexts it refers to those respective empires.

Chinese texts and journals

Unless otherwise indicated, references to the Chinese Thirteen Classics are to the *Shisan jing zhushu* edition of Ruan Yuan (1815, facsimile edition, Taipei: Yiwen jushu, 1980). They and other texts using premodern pagination are cited with colons separating *juan* or *pian* and page number (e.g. *LJ* 13.7b). For the *Zuo zhuan* the modern edition of Yang Bojun (1991) is used because of its availability, convenience, and widespread use by other scholars. In this and other editions that use modern pagination, references give page number, followed by section or subsection (e.g. Zuo, 849 (Cheng 10.4)).

Chinese Standard Histories are from the Zhonghua shuju series (Beijing, 1959–), and are cited by chapter and page number (e.g. *Han shu* 30.1772). Other early Chinese primary texts are cited from the *Xinbian zhuzi jicheng* or *Sibu beiyao* editions. Periods are used to separate chapter and section in texts where a chapter-and-verse or section reference style is conventional (e.g. the *Shi jing*, *Analects*, and *Mencius*).

Premodern texts, excavated texts, and archaeological monographs without individual authors are cited by title. Short archaeological reports without individual authors are cited by journal (e.g. from *Wen wu*: e.g. *WW* 1995: 1: 37–43).

The following abbreviations are used for major Chinese primary and secondary texts and journals. Full entries are found in the bibliography.

AM	*Asia Major*
Baoshan	*Baoshan Chu jian*
BEFEO	*Bulletin de l'École Française d'Extrême-Orient* (Paris)
BHT	*Baihu tong*
BIHP	*Bulletin of the Institute of History and Philology* (Taiwan)
BMFEA	*Bulletin of the Museum of Far Eastern Antiquities* (Stockholm)
BSOAS	*Bulletin of the School of Oriental and African Studies* (London)
CS	*Chinese Science*
DJ	*Daojia wenhua yanjiu* (Shanghai)
EASTM	*East Asian Science, Technology and Medicine*
EC	*Early China*
ECTBG	Loewe (1993)
EO	*Extrême-Orient, Extrême-Occident: Cahiers de recherches comparatives* (Paris)
Guodian	*Guodian Chu mu zhujian*
GY	*Guo yu*
Heji	*Jiaguwen heji*
HHS	*Hou Han shu*
HJAS	*Harvard Journal of Asiatic Studies*
HNZ	*Huainanzi*
HS	*Han shu*
HSBZ	*Han shu bu zhu*
JA	*Journale Asiatique*
JAS	*Journal of Asian Studies*
JAOS	*Journal of the American Oriental Society*

JCR	*Journal of Chinese Religions*
JHKG	*Jianghan Kaogu*
Jiudian	*Jiudian Chu mu*
KGXB	*Kaogu xuebao*
LH	*Lun heng*
LJ	*Li ji*
LNZ	*Lienü zhuan jiao zhu*
LS	*Huangdi neijing lingshu*
LSCQ	*Lü shi chunqiu*
MS	*Monumenta Serica*
MWD	*Mawangdui Han mu boshu*
NN	*Nan Nü* (Leiden)
PEW	*Philosophy East & West*
SBBY	*Sibu beiyao*
SBCK	*Sibu congkan* [*Collected Publications from the Four Categories*]
SHD	*Shuihudi Qin mu zhujian*
SJ	*Shi ji*
SKQS	*Siku quanshu*
SSJZS	*Shisan jing zhushu*
SW	*Huangdi neijing suwen*
TP	*T'oung-pao*
Wangshan	*Jiangling Wangshan Shazhong Chu mu*
WW	*Wen wu*
XBZZJC	*Xinbian Zhuzi jicheng*
Yinwan	*Yinwan Han mu jian du*
YL	*Yi li*
ZJS	*Zhangjiashan Han mu zhujian*
ZJT	*Guanju Qin Han mu jiandu*
ZL	*Zhou li*
Zuo	*Zuo zhuan*
ZY	*Zhou yi zhengyi*
ZZJC	*Zhuzi jicheng*

Greek texts, inscriptions, and journals

The following abbreviations are used for Greek inscriptions, journals, and major reference works. Full references are given in the bibliography.

AGIBM	*The Collection of Ancient Greek Inscriptions in the British Museum*

AJPh	*American Journal of Philology*
BCH	*Bulletin de Correspondance Hellénique*
BE	*Bulletin épigraphique* (1852–84)
BICS	*Bulletin of the Institute of Classical Studies* (London)
C	Carapanos (1878)
CA	*Classical Antiquity*
CDV	Christidis, Dakaris, and Vokotopoulou (1999)
CPh	*Classical Philology*
CQ	*Classical Quarterly*
CR	*Classical Review*
DCV	Dakaris, Christidis, and Vokotopoulou (1993)
DI	*Didyma: Die Inschriften*
Dind.	Dindorff
EE	Edelstein and Edelstein, *Asclepius: A Collection and Interpretation of the Testimonies*
Ep. Chron.	*Ἠπειρωτικὰ Χρονικα* (Epeirotika Chronika, Ioannina)
FD	*Fouilles de Delphes*
Font.	Fontenrose (1978)
G&R	*Greece & Rome*
GRBS	*Greek, Roman and Byzantine Studies*
HPhQ	*History of Philosophy Quarterly*
HR	*History of Religions*
HSPh	*Harvard Studies in Classical Philology*
IC	*Inscriptiones Creticae*
IG	*Inscriptiones Graecae*. Academicia Litterarum Borussica, 1873–
IGUR	*Inscriptiones Graecae Urbis Romae*
IM	*Die Inschriften von Magnesia am Maeander*
JHS	*Journal of Hellenic Studies*
KW	Kekule von Stradonitz and Winnefeld (1909)
OCD[3]	S. Hornblower and A. Spawforth, *Oxford Classical Dictionary* (3rd edn., rev. 2003)
PAAH	*Praktika tes en Athenais Archaiologikes Hetaireias*
Parke	Parke (1957)
PCPhS	*Proceedings of the Cambridge Philological Society*
PW	Parke and Wormell, *The Delphic Oracle*
REG	*Revue des Études Grecques*
RO	Rhodes and Osborne, *Greek Historical Inscriptions, 404–323 BC*
SEG	*Supplementum Epigraphicum Graecum* (1923–)

SGDI	Hoffman (1899)
SIG[3]	*Supplementum Inscriptionum Graecarum*
SVF	*Stoicorum Veterum Fragmenta*. Ed. von Arnim, H. 1903–24. Leipzig.
TAPhA	*Transactions of the American Philological Association*
Tod	Tod, *Greek Historical Inscriptions*
V	Vokotopoulou (1992)

Quotations from major Greek and Latin authors are from standard editions and line numbers are given whenever possible. Editions and translations available through the Loeb Classical Library are not referenced individually. A few less familiar texts and translations are listed in the bibliography.

Abbreviations for Greek and Latin texts follow the *Oxford Classical Dictionary* and the Liddell and Scott *Greek–English Lexicon*.

Ael.	Aelian
VH	*Varia Historia*
Aesch.	Aeschylus
Ag.	*Agamemnon*
Cho.	*Choephoroe* (Libation Bearers)
Eum.	*Eumenides* (Kindly Ones)
PV	*Prometheus Vinctus* (Prometheus Bound)
Sept.	*Septem contra Thebas* (Seven against Thebes)
Apol. Rhod. *Argon.*	Apollonius Rhodius, *Argonautica*
Apollod.	Apollodorus
Bibl.	*Bibliotheca* (Library)
Epit.	*Epitome*
Apul.	Apuleius
De Dog. Plat.	*De dogmate Platonis*
Arist.	Aristotle
An. Pr.	*Analytica Priora*
Ath. Pol.	*Athēnaiōn Politeia* (Constitution of the Athenians)
Div. somn.	*De divinatione per somnia* (On Divination through Dreams)
HA	*Historia animalium* (History of Animals)
Insom.	*De insomniis* (On Dreams)
Metaph.	*Metaphysica*
PA	*De partibus animalium* (Parts of Animals)
Physiogn.	*Physiognomonica*
Rh.	*Rhetorica* (Rhetoric)

Aristid. *Panath.*	Aristides, *Panathenaica*
Aristoph. *Nub.*	Aristophanes, *Nubes* (Clouds)
Arr.	Arrian
Artem.	Artemidorus Daldianus
Ath.	Athenaeus
Cic.	Cicero
Div.	*De divinatione*
Fat.	*De fato*
Leg.	*Laws*
Nat. Deor.	*De natura deorum*
Clem. Al.	Clemens Alexandrinus
Strom.	*Strōmateis*
Curt.	Curtius Rufus
Dem.	Demosthenes
Dio Chrys.	Dio Chrysostom
Diod.	Diodorus Siculus
Diog. Laert.	Diogenes Laertius
DK	Hermann Diels and Walter Kranz, eds. *Die Fragmente der Vorsokratiker* (6th edn., 1966)
Ep.	*Epitome* (Extracts)
Eur.	Euripides
Bacch.	*Bacchae*
Hel.	*Helena*
IT	*Iphigenia Taurica* (Iphigenia in Tauris)
Med.	*Medea*
Or.	*Orestes*
Phoen.	*Phoenissae* (The Phoenician Women)
Eus. *Praep. Evang.*	Eusebius, *Praeparatio Evangelica*
Fr.	Fragment
Hdt.	Herodotus
Hes.	Hesiod
Dies	*Opera et Dies* (Works and Days)
Theog.	*Theogony* (Birth of the Gods)
Hippoc.	Hippocrates (all texts from Littré edn.)
Acut.	*De Victur Ratione in morbis acutis* (On Regimen in Acute Diseases)
Aer.	*De aera, aquis, locis* (Airs, Waters, and Places)

Art.	*De articulis* (On the Articulations)
De arte	*On the Art* (*Peri Tekhnēs*)
Ep.	*Epistulae* (Letters)
Morb. sacr.	*De morbo sacro* (On the Sacred Disease)
Prorrh.	*Prorrheticum* (Prorrhetic)
Vict.	*De Victus Ratione* (On Regimen)
Hom.	Homer
Il.	*Iliad*
Od.	*Odyssey*
Hygin. *Fab.*	Hyginus, *Fabulae*
Iambl.	Iamblichus
Eur.	*Vita Euripidis*
Myst.	*De mysteriis*
Pyth.	*Vita Pythagorae*
Joseph. *Hypomn.*	Josephus, *Hypomnemata*
Jul. *Or.*	Julian, *Orationes*
Just.	Justinus
Epit.	*Epitome* (of Pompeius Trogus)
L	E. Littré, *Œuvres complètes d'Hippocrate*. 10 vols. Paris, 1844, rpt. Amsterdam: Hakkert, 1962
LS	H. G. Liddell and R. Scott, *Greek–English Lexicon* (7th edn., 1883)
Lycurg. *Leoc.*	Lycurgus, *Against Leocrates*
Paus.	Pausanias
Philostr.	Philostratus
Phld.	Philodemus
Mus.	*De Musica* (On Music)
Phlegon	
Ol.	*Olympiads*
Phot.	Photius
Lex.	*Lexicon*
Pind.	Pindar
Ol.	*Olympians*
Pyth.	*Pythians*
Pl.	Plato
Ap.	*Apologia*
Euth.	*Euthydemus*

Grg.	*Gorgias*
Leg.	*Laws*
Phdr.	*Phaedrus*
Rep.	*Republic*
Symp.	*Symposium*
Theag.	*Theages*
Pliny, NH	Pliny the Elder, *Natural History*
Plut.	Plutarch
Alex.	*Alexander*
Arist.	*Aristides*
Cic.	*Cicero*
Cim.	*Cimon*
Comm. not.	*De communibus notitiis adversos Stoicos* (Common Conceptions against the Skeptics)
Def. or.	*De Defectu oraculorum* (On the Obsolescence of Oracles)
Dem.	*Demosthenes*
E apud Delph.	*De E apud Delphos* (*On the E at Delphi*)
Mor.	*Moralia* (Philosophical Essays)
Nic.	*Nicias*
Per.	*Pericles*
Pyth. Orac.	*De Pythiae oraculis* (On the Pythian Oracle)
Quaest. conv.	*Quaestiones convivales*
Thes.	*Theseus*
Porph. *Plot.*	Porphyry, *Vita Plotini*
PW	H. W. Parke and D. E. W. Wormell, *The Delphic Oracle II: The Oracular Responses* (Blackwell, 1956)
Schol.	scholiast or scholia
Serv. *Aen.*	Servius, *Ad Aeneidem*
Socr. *Hist eccl.*	Socrates, *Historia ecclesiastica*
Soph.	Sophocles
Ant.	*Antigone*
OC	*Oedipus Colonus* (Oedipus at Colonus)
OT	*Oedipus Tyrannus* (Oedipus the King)
Stob.	Stobaeus
Ecl.	*Eklogoi* (Selections)
Strab. *Geog*	Strabo, *Geographica*
Suda	Greek Lexicon formerly known as *Suidas*

Suet.	Suetonius
Nero	*Nero*
Tzetzes	
Chil.	*Chiliades*
Thuc.	Thucydides
Xen.	Xenophon
An.	*Anabasis* (Persian Expedition)
Ap.	*Apologia Socratis*
Cyr.	*Cyropaedia*
Hell.	*Hellenica* (History of Greece)
Hipparch.	*Hipparchus* (On the Cavalry General)
Lac.	*Respublica Lacedaemoniorum* (On the Constitution of the Lacedaimonians)
Mem.	*Memorabilia Socratis*
Oec.	*Oeconomicus* (Economics)
Zen.	Zenobius
Zon. *Hist.*	Zonaras (twelfth century CE) *Epitome Historiarum* (Extracts)

Reference tables

Comparative time line (dates BCE unless otherwise indicated)

China	Greece
10,000–*c.* 2100 Neolithic Period	
1700–*c.* 1100 **Shang 商 Dynasty** *c.* 1500–1300 bronze casting *c.* 1400–1200 Chinese script	1700–1100 late **Bronze Age**; Mycenaean culture
c. 1100–256 **Zhou 周 Dynasty**	1200–800 **Dark Age**
c. 1100–771 Western Zhou 西周 King Wu 武王 r. 1045–1043	settlement of Aegean Islands and coast of Asia Minor
770–256 Eastern Zhou 東周	750–594 **Aristocratic Age**
770–475 Spring and Autumn 春秋	composition of Homeric poems (750–700?) Hesiod eighth–seventh century seventh–sixth-century emergence of polis
Zhou power eclipsed by Warring States	561–507 Age of Athenian tyrants 561 Peisistratus seizes power 507 Athenian democracy restored fifth-century emergence of democracies
475–222 Warring States 戰國	490–479 Persian Wars 478–445 Rise of Athenian Empire 431–404 Peloponnesian War
Confucius *c.* 500 Mozi *c.* 470–390	Aeschylus 525–456, Sophocles 495–405 Euripides 480–406, Herodotus *c.* 484–425 404–371 supremacy of Sparta Socrates 469?–399, Aristophanes *c.* 450–*c.* 385
Mencius 372–328 Xunzi *c.* 310–237 Lü Buwei *c.* 239 Han Fei d. 233	Xenophon 430–354 Plato 428–347 Aristotle 384–322

China	Greece
221–209 **Qin 秦 Dynasty**	359–323 Rise of Macedon 323–146 **Hellenistic Period**
206 BCE–220 CE **Han 漢 Dynasty** 206 BCE–9 CE Western (Former) Han 漢	323 death of Alexander
Liu Xin 劉歆 46 BCE–23 CE	146–44 Greece a province of Roman Republic Apollodorus *c.* 180, Cicero 106–43, Lucretius (99–*c.* 55), Diodorus Siculus (*c.* 80–20) Roman Republic to 44
9–23 CE Xin 新 Dynasty Wang Mang 王莽 25–220 CE Eastern (Later) Han 後漢	**Roman Empire** 31 on Strabo (64 BCE–*c.* 25 CE), Pliny (23–79 CE) Plutarch *c.* 45–*c.* 125 CE, Arrian *c.* 87–145 CE Pausanias 115–18 CE

Chinese dynasties (all dates BCE unless indicated)

Shang 1700–*c.* 1100 BCE
Zhou *c.* 1100–256 BCE
  c. 1100–771 Western Zhou BCE
  770–256 Eastern Zhou BCE
    770–475 Spring and Autumn BCE
    475–222 Warring States BCE
Qin 221–209 BCE
Western (Former) Han 206 BCE–9 CE
Xin Wang Mang 9–23
Eastern (Later) Han 25–220
Three Kingdoms 220–65
Six Dynasties 220–589
  Jin 265–420
Northern Dynasties 386–581
Sui 581–618
Tang 618–907
Five Dynasties (north) 907–60
Ten Kingdoms (south) 907–79
Liao 907–1279
Song 960–1279
  Northern Song 960–1127

Southern Song 1127–1279
Jin 1115–1234
Yuan 1271–1368
Ming 1368–1644
Qing 1644–1911
Republic of China 1912–49
People's Republic of China 1949–

Dukes of Lu in the *Zuo zhuan*

Duke	Reign
Yin 隱	722–712
Huan 桓	711–694
Zhuang 莊	693–662
Min 閔	661–660
Xi 僖	659–627
Wen 文	626–609
Xuan 宣	608–591
Cheng 成	590–573
Xiang 襄	572–542
Zhao 昭	541–510
Ding 定	509–495
Ai 哀	494–467
[Dao 悼	466–429]

1 Introduction

> Now I am aware of no people, however refined and learned or however savage and ignorant, which does not think that signs are given of future events, and that certain persons can recognize those signs and foretell events before they occur.
>
> Cicero, *De Divinatione* 1.2

We live today in an intellectual climate of particularism. In an effort to focus on the unique features of individual cultures, we tend to reject the idea of cultural universals as products of an imperialistic age, in which hegemonic cultures painted the canvas of the world with their own values in the guise of universalism. Nonetheless, one of the few things that can still stand as a human universal is concern about the future (however understood), as Cicero put it two millennia ago. And divination has been an important manifestation of that concern from the earliest times to the present day. Divination is a deliberate search for understanding of the *hidden* significance of events in the future, present, or past. (If it were obvious, there would be no need to divine.) In some cases it involves two parties: a diviner (with particular gifts, training, or even lack of training) and some kind of extra-human contact that makes divination possible. This may be a god, spirit, or ancestor, or (and there is argument about this point) a cosmic pattern without deliberative divine agency. The contact might be indirect, mediated by a system of signs requiring interpretation, for example when questions are put to signs present in nature, but perceptible only to those with appropriate gifts.

Scholars use the term "divination" in different ways, to refer to a range of interpretive activities. At one end are deliberate queries; at the other end are spontaneous natural phenomena that are visible to all. Some such events, eclipses for example, are so visible and unusual as to demand explanation. Others are unremarkable, save for those who can "read" their hidden significance. But whether predicting the future or interpreting events or signs in the past or present, divination purports to interpret the hidden significance of events.

Some scholars restrict the term "divination" to deliberate activities. Divination can be characterized as a deliberate search for answers, and linked to the production of artificial signs. In this sense it contrasts with oracles that refer to signs already inherent in nature (and interpreted by specialists). It also contrasts with omens: natural phenomena that are visible to all and significant enough to demand explanation.[1] I use the terms divination and mantic activity inclusively to refer to activities seeking to find the meaning of hidden phenomena, objects or events in the past, present, or future, whether or not divinatory signs are understood as direct or indirect communications by a divine entity directly addressed. Divination thus overlaps with prognostication, which also is concerned with predicting both future events and good and ill auspice. Some modes of divination presuppose a diviner and a topic of inquiry. It may, but need not, involve interaction with a god or other extra-human contact. Or divination may rely entirely on a hermeneutic system of signs, with no divine agency implied. It is also necessary to consider a range of textual genres that deal with divination in very different ways.[2] Divination thus may, but need not, involve prediction. Depending on its predictive methods – its use of observation, search for regularity, etc. – it may or may not be science or proto-science.

Because the term "divination" may be culturally specific, I prefer the term "mantic activity" in a comparative context and prognostication (*zhanbu* 占卜) in a specifically Chinese context (of activities concerned with prediction).[3] Nonetheless, at times I use "divination" for ease of expression, familiarity, or for consistency with other scholarship. The term "oracle" is sometimes used to refer to all mantic practice, but I use it in the specific sense of a shrine of one or more deities who spoke "through" an oracle. I use the term "spirit medium" for practitioners who are possessed by gods or spirits, as distinct from shamans, who actively engage in spirit journeys in order to encounter gods and spirits. In a Greek context I use the term primarily to refer to the seer or *mantis* (plural *manteis*), but also for oracles, temples (primarily of Zeus, Apollo, and Asclepius) which provided divinatory information to local and sometimes non-local consultors.

1 This is the distinction used in Michael Loewe's pioneering study (1981: 38–39).

2 For recent uses of the term "divination" that focus on its hermeneutic aspects, rather than explicit interactions with a "divinity," see Flad 2008: 403–37. For approaches to divination as a form of risk management, see Fiskesjö 2001: 154–57 and Eidinow 2007a.

3 In its earliest uses, the term *bu* 卜 referred specifically to pyromantic "cracking," but the term later came to be used of all mantic activity.

Where do the signs come from? They have been variously understood as the will of the gods, fate, and patterns of nature or cosmic principles. In contexts where divination took the form of communication with divine agencies, there is a fine line between asking about a future outcome ("Will it rain on Tuesday?") and requesting it ("May it rain on Tuesday!").

Mantic activity concerns the future, either as direct prediction or because patterns in the past and present have future ramifications. To what extent does the notion of predictability imply that events are necessary, inevitable, or predetermined? Reflection on this implication became an important element in debates about divination.[4] For example, knowledge of our individual genetic predispositions does not predetermine our futures or life spans. It does tell us governing tendencies we may choose to encourage or minimize.

Another view is that the codes of divination are direct communications from benevolent gods, and are best understood as straightforward, useful instructions, like a railway timetable or a cookbook, which we read for limited and useful purposes, to optimize our behavior to conform to the way the world works. A railway timetable does not make the train arrive (and has nothing to do with causation); it does allow one to be on the platform on time.[5] We do not consult the *Joy of Cooking* to change the cooking time of bread or rice, but to make sure it will be ready in time for supper.

Divination, rationality, and modernity

As a mode of prediction, divination has typically been regarded as primitive superstition (religious or otherwise) or as a pseudoscience to be disparaged and debunked. That situation changed with the work of Bronislav Malinowski and Claude Lévi-Strauss, who in very different ways explored the rationality of magic and myth.[6] A series of studies over the past two decades have focused on important sociological and epistemological dimensions of divination, both in antiquity and in the present. It emerges as a set of coherent technologies for predicting (and potentially controlling) the future, and as a set of social practices whose importance extended far beyond telling the future.

Several studies of divination in Greco-Roman antiquity (or "Classical antiquity," usually meaning the ancient Mediterranean) have examined the

[4] This issue is discussed in Chapter 9. [5] I take this example from Denyer 1985: 4.
[6] E.g. Malinowski 1954, Lévi-Strauss 1963.

mutual influences of divination practices in Greece, Rome, and Etruria, with some attention to possible Egyptian and Babylonian influences. The first of these was Auguste Bouché-Leclercq's (1842–1923) *Histoire de la divination dans l'antiquité*, a monumental study of divination in the Hellenic, Etrurian, and Roman worlds. Meanwhile, the study of mantic practices in China has been transformed over the course of the twentieth century: first by the recognition of the true nature of the so-called "oracle bone" inscriptions of the Shang dynasty and more recently by the ongoing excavation of a wide variety of texts, instruments, and other material evidence of Chinese divination practices. (Dates of dynasties and important figures are given in the Reference Tables.)

The entire problem of divination was reconsidered in Jean-Pierre Vernant's landmark volume, *Divination et rationalité* (1974), which focused on the rationality and coherence of divination and its significance in the formation of social institutions. Vernant approached divination in its dual role as both a set of mental attitudes and a set of social institutions.[7] The project of *Divination et rationalité* was to show how the symbolic operations of diviners and the rational system behind them imposed their rationality and legitimacy on the intellectual and social fabric of those societies. What kind of rationality expresses itself in the play of divinatory procedures, oracular symbolisms, and the classificatory systems they employ to manipulate and interpret information? What is the place and function of this oracular knowledge in a given society? Recognition of the importance of the social role of divination invites many other questions. What domains of society were under the authority of divination, and where were diviners in the hierarchy of members of a society who wield the power of decision, such as kings, priests, or judges? The possibility and act of prophecy themselves created important choices that determined decisions on both public and private matters. In the Homeric world, divination was a craft or metier; the diviner was a worker for the public good (*demiourgos*) like the carpenter or physician.[8] Vernant emphasized the "normalcy" of both aspects of divination in civilizations where it was central. It was not an isolated mentality, opposed to such "ordinary" social practices as law, medicine, or administration, but rather a coherent part of social thought (like consulting a physician or a stockbroker). By contrast, despite its actual popularity, divination has the character of a marginal aberrance in societies where it is not prominent (such as ours), and it could be argued that this marginality is a hallmark of modernity. Anthony Giddens adopts a similar perspective

[7] Vernant 1974b: 9. [8] Cf. *Od.* 17.382–85. See Vernant 1974b: 12.

in his distinction between "modern" notions of risk and earlier notions of fate, fortune, and divine intervention.[9]

Several collected studies have begun to address mantic activity in cross-cultural perspective. Two French collections, the third issue of the journal *Kernos* (1990; articles cited under their authors) and *Oracles et Prophéties dans l'Antiquité* (1997), addressed highly focused aspects of divination across Classical antiquity. Initial comparative studies, reflecting this focus on Classical antiquity, compared Greek oracular divination with oracles in several African societies without extensive written traditions of reflective thought that provided textual counterparts to the Greek textual record. André Caquot and Marcel Leibovici's more ambitious study, *La Divination: Études recueillies* (Divination: Collected Studies, 1968), published under the aegis of the French Centre National de la Recherche Scientifique (CNRS), surveyed divination in both the ancient and modern world: Pharaonic Egypt, Babylonia, and Israel; India and Iran; Greece, Etruria, and Rome; the Celts, Germans, and Slavs; ancient China, Peru, and North America; modern Mexico and the Maya; the Arctic, Central Asia, and the Turks; sub-Saharan and South Africa, Madagascar, and contemporary Afro-American and French practices, including thematic studies on psychoanalysis and geomancy. Michael Loewe and Carmen Blacker's edited volume *Oracles and Divination* (1981) provides greater Asian focus, with essays on divination in China, Japan, and Tibet. But because each volume assigns one chapter to a culture or civilization, the chapters are necessarily general. Leo Howe and Alan Wain's edited volume, *Predicting the Future* (1993), takes a different approach, and includes essays by contemporary practitioners of prediction, including scientists, economists, and physicians. These essays suggest that predictions are the products of elites. They are normative and reflect the worldviews and cultures from which they arise.[10]

There are several reasons for the choice of China and Greece as comparanda. They begin with comparability of intellectual productions and social institutions. By such measures as textual production, evidence of intellectual debate and self-reflection, state formation, or technological advancement, China was of comparable or greater sophistication to Greece, a point that was first argued by the Jesuit Matteo Ricci in his journals from his mission to China in the sixteenth century.[11] Comparison of China and Greece has an important twentieth-century history in the work of Vernant,

[9] Giddens 1990: 29–31. [10] For further discussion see Morrison 1993.
[11] Ricci (1910–13), 1.5.22 and 1.10.85–86.

Finley, and Detienne; and several contemporary scholars engage in comparison of this kind.[12] The study of Classical antiquity is also beginning to emerge as a discipline in China.[13] Second, an important intellectual advantage of such comparison is that one historical and philosophical context effectively "parochializes" the other.[14] Third, comparison can show what elements are constant across divination methods and cultures. Comparative studies of divination by Classicists have focused on African oracles, with little attention to the Chinese evidence, which is textually and materially rich. Chinese material may shed light on phenomena that in the Greek context are fragmented or that only appear in literary sources. Fourth, Greek classifications have been constitutive of understandings of what divination is and how it should be classified. (This point is discussed at length in Chapter 3.) Fifth, both the Chinese and Greek materials present the problem of reconciling the received textual tradition with the evidence of archaeology. In summary, scholars of Chinese and Greek divination have much to learn from each other.

Systematic studies of Chinese mantic activity are far fewer than for Greco-Roman antiquity. An exception is Richard J. Smith's *Fortune-tellers and Philosophers* (1991), which demonstrates both the antiquity and pervasiveness of mantic practices in Chinese culture, and argues that its continuing popularity and prevalence is in part due to its links with the past, and with fundamental elements in Chinese culture. In the brief comparative reflections that conclude the book, he notes that modern Western comparative works on divination tend to focus on "dead" divinations such as ancient Greece or Mesopotamia, or on "primitive" or "occult" marginalized countercultures.[15] An eponymous successor to *Divination et rationalité* applies the agenda of Vernant's original volume to early China.[16]

Both the universality of the problem of the future and the diversity of ways of gauging it invite comparison of Chinese and Greek mantic practices and theories, which emerge early in the extensive textual traditions of both societies. Both societies present a wide range of evidence of the origins, techniques, and social and intellectual contexts of mantic activity. Their differences partake of broad problems of cultural commensurability that are

[12] See Finley 1975, Vernant 1974a, and Detienne 2000, 2001, and 2002, all discussed in Chapter 3. The work of Geoffrey Lloyd (1996, 1999a, 1999b, 2002, 2007; Lloyd and Sivin 2002) is also especially important. For a recent review of comparative studies of Greece and China see Tanner 2009.

[13] Peking University inaugurated a Center for [Greco-Roman] Classical Studies in November 2011, the first institution of its kind in China.

[14] For this point see Lloyd 1996.

[15] R. J. Smith 1991: 271–81.

[16] Chemla, Harper, and Kalinowski 1999.

matters of heated debate across several scholarly disciplines. All these add to the challenge, and interest, of finding a framework within which to consider divination across cultures.

Nor has our rationalist age made divination obsolete. Even if it is not quite respectable, it is immensely popular. Horoscopes appear on the pages of many, but not all, newspapers and magazines. We find them in the *New York* or *Los Angeles Times*, but not in the *Wall Street Journal*; in magazines aimed at women and young people, but not in *Nature* or *Scientific American*.[17] A variety of polls attest to the ongoing popularity of astrology. During the real-estate boom of the past years, some knowledge of the Chinese geomantic techniques of *feng shui* 風水 (literally "wind and water") became a practical necessity for real-estate brokers in major American cities. And in the current financial decline, fortune-tellers of various kinds continue to do a brisk business. The methods used today may differ from those used in antiquity, but divination is alive and well.

The apparatus of mantic practice is equally visible in Asian cosmopolitan cities. In Hong Kong, fortune-tellers are to be found near any temple. Mantic texts are for sale in street markets, in both modern paperbacks and real or pseudo-antique editions. Divination software sits side by side with Microsoft (and may be equally reliable). Marriages may be made, prevented, or ruined by it, even among young urban professionals. Science fiction and popular cinema abound with images of destiny and attempts to foreknow or forestall it.

By contrast, the People's Republic of China has tried to suppress divination under the rubric of "superstition" (*mi xin* 迷信). Although the Chinese Constitution guarantees freedom of religion, this protection is limited to the five officially recognized religions (Buddhism, Catholicism, Daoism, Protestantism, and Islam). In some cases, divination is specifically prohibited, for example in a Shanghai ordinance against divination, fortune-telling, and other similar practices in places of religious worship.[18] Campaigns in the 1950s and 1960s and most recently in 1991 attacked the use of the *Yi jing* for divination.[19] Nevertheless, fortune-telling is widely practiced in contemporary China. Diviners are found on the streets and, as in Western cities, take advantage of popular tourist sites (Figures 1.1–1.3).

[17] For an excellent treatment of the broad history of astrology, with focus on Greco-Roman antiquity, see Barton 1994a and 1994b.

[18] Article 28, Regulations from the Shanghai Religious Affairs Bureau, Standing Committee of the 10th People's Congress of Shanghai, December 1995 (Spiegel 1997 and Human Rights Watch Asia 1997: 94). According to Human Rights Watch, the government is more tolerant of geomancy and fortune-telling than of divination, palm-reading, or casting lots, but the degree of censure varies by locale. For more on "feudal superstition" in China see Feuchtwang 1989.

[19] Foreign Broadcast Information Service (China), 9 Oct. 1991 and 22 Dec. 1995.

Figure 1.1 Mantic practitioners: Mount Song (Henan, 2010).

Figure 1.2 Mantic practitioners: Shanghai, 2010.

Figure 1.3 Mantic practitioners: Paris, 2009.

Bookstores abound with mantic texts. Even venues with limited shelf space, such as airport book stalls, sell them in abundance.

Intellectual contexts

What were the key intellectual contexts for the mantic arts of early China and Greece? What beliefs about the world made it possible? Cross-cultural study reveals the extent to which divination is an artificial category. The diversity of mantic practice and belief in both cultures makes it difficult to introduce one definition, because divination simply was not a unified concept in either culture.

What major principles and beliefs governed Chinese and Greek divination practices? One aspect of this question is the changing religious, philosophical, or cosmological principles that informed mantic practices during different historical periods. Another is the nature and degree of self-conscious reflection about mantic activity and its preconditions. A third is how the Greeks and Chinese themselves classified, discussed, or debated their own mantic beliefs. Assumptions about epistemological and ethical aspects of divination reflect their views on such questions as: the extent to which the future is determined, the possibility of foreknowledge, the transparency of the cosmos, the nature of the gods (or ancestors), their degree of interest in human affairs, and their accessibility to human intercession.

Several beliefs and assumptions informed the history of Chinese divination.

(1) Auspicious Times. The notion of good and ill auspice (*ji xiong* 吉凶), that certain times were propitious or inauspicious for certain activities, was central to Chinese mantic and ritual practice. Techniques to identify the best time for important activities remain in use in the present day. Textual records attest to the importance attached to the selection of auspicious times for both state and private activities. Calendric texts were used to determine auspicious days for state ritual activities such as sacrifice, warfare, royal marriages, and beginning the construction of a new palace or capital. Archaeological evidence from recently discovered manuscripts excavated from tombs underscores the ritual character of a wide variety of governmental activity, including the daily functioning of court, law cases, and administration. An important aspect of all these activities was the determination of auspicious times to conduct them. Similarly, warfare was considered a ritual activity, and divination was used both to select an auspicious time to initiate military activity and to gauge its chances of success. As mantic techniques proliferated among the broader population, almanac texts, in the form of daybooks and calendric tables, were used to select auspicious times for marriage, construction, travel, or beginning medical treatment. (The importance of selecting an auspicious day for a high religious or political occasion is by no means unique to the Chinese mantic traditions. The first Queen Elizabeth is said to have consulted the astrologer and polymath John Dee to determine an auspicious date for her coronation.)

(2) Systematic Thought and Cosmology. Another aspect of Chinese mantic thinking was the possibility that a sage "reader" could perceive pervasive connections and systematic correspondences between aspects of a cosmos in constant change.[20] Several concepts are important here. First is the idea of interactions of time and space (*yu zhou* 宇宙), especially the correlation of areas of the world to the seasons of the year and periods of time such as the sexagenary cycle (*ganzhi* 干支, the combinations of Ten Heaven Stems and Twelve Earth Branches). Second is the idea of a cosmos composed of *qi* 氣. Third is an understanding of cosmic change, based on the interactions of *yin* and *yang* 陰陽 and the Five Agents (*wuxing* 五行), and interactions between

[20] Kaltenmark and Ngo Van Xuyet 1966: 334–37.

heaven, earth, and humanity.[21] Such notions of cosmic unity underline cleromantic techniques such as *Yi* divination, in which the random manipulation of milfoil (yarrow) stalks revealed the underlying patterns of *yin* and *yang* manifest at the time and place of the procedure. In this case a cleromantic procedure was used to select a text for interpretation. Later techniques such as divining rods operated on the same principle, as did the Western medieval customs of divining by Virgil's *Aeneid* or the *Diwan* of Hafiz. Another aspect of early Chinese cosmologies was belief in the transparency of the world in the sense that correspondences and signs were consistent and did not lie.

(3) Number, Calculation, and Chance. Some mantic techniques used "calculation" in the sense that the "texts" they interpret or manipulate are numbers. The linking of divinatory formulae with sequences of numbers dates back to the Shang oracle bones. Many techniques share the premise that events can be interpreted, not through the reading of signs, but through the understanding, or manipulation, of numbers based on events. Some methods are based on the experience of time, quantified by calendrics. Horoscopes are the most well known, and occur in both China and Greece. Recently excavated archaeological texts provide evidence for distinctively Chinese fate calculation methods. Daybooks (*rishu* 日書) indicate what kinds of activities are auspicious or inauspicious for the days of the month. Several systems are based on the calendrics of the sexagenary cycle, for example the "Sanctions and Virtues" texts from Mawangdui and Shuihudi, mantic astrolabes (also known as diviner's boards), and other representations of the sexagenary cycle. Other methods use numbers to calculate auspicious configurations of space or dispositions of the body (as in physiognomy).[22]

Greek divination had its own distinct set of epistemological presuppositions. Perhaps the most philosophically powerful fruits of that reflection were Greek ideas of fate and necessity that have so influenced Western cultures

[21] Between the fourth and second centuries the meanings of *wuxing* included (depending on context) Five Courses (of planets), Five Materials, Five Powers, Five Modes of Conduct, etc. At some point in the Han it acquired the meaning of Five Phases, referring specifically to the transformations of *qi* in correlative cosmology, but when this usage began is a matter of debate. Following Graham (1991: 225–30) and Nylan (2010: esp. 403), I use the term Five Agents when context requires translation, and reserve the term Five Phases for Eastern Han and later contexts when the term clearly refers to the Five Phases of correlative cosmology (see Chapter 9 for further discussion).

[22] These issues are discussed in Chapter 9.

that they are all too easily taken as universal or inevitable. One purpose of the present study is to reconsider the cultural peculiarity or specificity of Greek notions of fate that were closely connected with the practice of divination.

(1) Omniscient Gods. Greek texts are explicit about the existence of gods who knew the future and might be persuaded to share their knowledge with humans. The gods were also assumed to have some benevolent interest in humanity, and to manifest their will (and eventually ethical notions of justice and retribution) through divination. Cicero (*Div.* 1.5) notes that, with the exception of Xenophanes (*c.* 560–*c.* 478) and Epicurus (341–270), all the ancient philosophers approved of and believed in divination. Both exceptions are significant: Epicurus because he considered the gods remote from human concerns, and Xenophanes as the first to criticize belief in omnipresent, anthropomorphic, accessible gods.[23]

(2) Semiosis. The belief that the gods used signs to communicate knowledge about the future to humans. Greek (and Roman) divination consistently implied and involved the gods, even if the communication occurs indirectly through a semiotic system. The hermeneutics of early divination assumed the existence of gods (or their intermediaries) who communicated signs about future events to humans, sometimes (but not always) in response to deliberate questions. Such communication was lubricated by economies of prayer and sacrifice managed through ritual. In later and more naturalistic worldviews, cosmic patterns functioned independently of immediate divine will and the decoding of signs revealed the workings of an impersonal order of nature. The nature (or absence) of human–divine communication helps us understand tacit theories of the production and interpretation of divinatory signs and the rituals through which they occur. The problem for any consideration of the semiotics of divination is how human audiences judge the relevance and meaning of signs consistently and correctly; in other words, how we construct divinatory systems in which signifiers consistently point to their signifieds.[24]

[23] See Defradas 1968.

[24] Signifiers and signifieds: according to the Prague School, the process of signification is twofold. A sender creates and transmits a sign or coded message, which combines a signified and a signifier. Only after such a message has been sent can a recipient decode the sign and interpret the meaning of the message. The process of signification thus falls into two distinct halves. The first is the production, encoding, and transmission of the sign; the second is its reception and interpretation. See Hollman 2005: esp. 281–82 and Burkert 2005: 31–35.

(3) Fate or Necessity. While concern *about* the future may be universal, cultural understandings of the nature of time and causation vary widely.[25] Corollary to the Greek idea that the future was knowable was the idea that it was predetermined. As early as the Homeric poems, Greek assumptions about the future consistently combined some sense that it was given or predetermined, with extraordinary concern for the implications and potential contradictions of a future determined by fates or lots (*moira*). These agencies were first understood as gods who determined human destinies, but as early as the Homeric poems, the three fates or Moirai stood in a complex relation to the plan of Zeus. The implication was that some events were fated even beyond the power of the king of the gods to control. The determinist tendency in Greek notions of fate may arise from the Greek tendency to focus on the logical implications and preconditions of the notions of the future and of fate. By contrast, Chinese debates about fate were pragmatic, and assumed a flexible future that was constrained but not rigidly determined. Later philosophical reflection subsumed *moira* under a more abstract notion of necessity. Heraclitus spoke of Fate and Necessity (DK 22A8) and the Pythagorean Philolaus of Necessity (DK 44A1–2), while the Stoics provided elaborate philosophic theories of determinism.[26]

Form of the inquiry

The present study began as a chapter in a comparative study of Chinese and Greek ideas on fate and fatalism. The chapter got out of hand, less because of the diversity of techniques than because of the comparative problems that divination illuminates. For example, the evidence of mantic activity suggests that philosophers were far more engaged with the religious values of their societies than secular humanist constructions of ancient China or Greece tend to credit. Although the mantic arts were thoroughly integrated in ancient societies in diverse and complex ways, their role as a fundamental constituent of the "rationalism" of those societies tends to be overlooked in modern accounts.

There are already a number of detailed anthologies of aspects of divination in both China and Greece, as well as comparative anthologies that

[25] See Lloyd 2007: 108–30 for a review of some of these differences.

[26] See Bouché-Leclercq 1879–82: 1.62.

present ancient and modern divination in comparative perspective. Many are specialist studies of particular texts, locales, or archaeological sites. Most of the anthologies include only single-chapter accounts of divination in each society or period considered. A more nuanced and detailed comparative study of divination in two of the hegemonic civilizations of the ancient world may offer new insights on the roles of divination in society, and bring to light broad problems in the comparative study of culture and the nature of the comparative process.

Previous studies of divination underscore the need to approach cross-cultural study through the comparison of contexts, rather than isolated ideas or techniques. I have attempted to balance the strengths and risks of a comparative approach. The organization of material through a pervasively comparative framework risks several kinds of misrepresentation. It can obscure key issues, micro-historical and otherwise, within a tradition or local tradition, if they do not fit well under the aegis of the comparative structure. It also risks compressing historical and local variation, and thus losing detail and grounding in specific events. For this reason I have opted to present what I think are key issues and problems in each tradition separately, before engaging in comparative discourse. In this way it becomes possible to highlight internal tensions and problems that may bear on, or be aided by, the comparative process.

The present volume surveys the historical development of mantic practices in China and Greece before the advent of Buddhism (in the Chinese case) and Christianity (in the Greek). The Chinese context for this inquiry is from the earliest times through the Han dynasty, with the exception of the occasional divagation into a later period to help clarify an earlier text. I begin with the language used to classify and describe mantic activity and the fundamental principles by which it operated. These included early cosmological speculation, the notion of good and ill auspice, and the role of gods and ancestors in both determining human fate and vouchsafing human knowledge about it. The Greek context begins with the Homeric poems, continues through the "Classical" period of the fifth and fourth centuries, and then into Hellenistic Greece, with occasional forays into later periods. Similarly, Babylonian, Etrurian, and Roman divination are beyond the scope of this inquiry, except for specific commentary on Greek sources. It includes the rich vocabulary of Greek natural and technical divination and the assumptions and principles by which it operated. The comparative study of Greek oracles raises particular questions about the authenticity of oracles as texts and as performances. Who were the diviners of early China and Greece, and what methods did they use? In what social domains did divination operate; what was the place of the diviner in society? Which individuals and groups availed of divination and what questions did they ask? Finally, how did early mantic activity affect the development of systematic thought and cosmology in China and Greece?

If divination was a coherent and normal element of social practice, access to it was an important matter. How controlled was mantic knowledge and access to those who had it? Which personnel performed divination and how were they trained? Were they specialized by technique, gender, or social class? How was their knowledge transmitted or constrained? To what extent was divination an aspect of specialist domains of knowledge, such as architecture, law, medicine, or military strategy? Similarly, who consulted diviners? Was consultation restricted to state or religious institutions, or were the same techniques used by private individuals to resolve mundane and quotidian concerns? How accessible was divination throughout society? Was access to divination gendered? Was divination available to commoners? How did it inform political and social life? China and Greece show very different historical patterns in access of the overall population to divination techniques, which reflect their profoundly different social structures.

In China the expansion of the mantic arts beyond royal and elite ritual contexts led to an ongoing increase of access to divination methods at all levels of society. In Greece the institutionalization of divination through oracles created a mixed result. Oracles remained available for both private and state consultation (and, as with contemporary software licenses, individual use was far cheaper than group access). The remote locations of some Greek oracular sanctuaries helped maintain their neutrality, but it also restricted non-local private access to elites who could afford the cost of travel and oracular fees. Other non-oracular techniques proliferated that were amenable to private use by individuals without specialist training.

Chinese and Greek mantic techniques changed considerably over time and were subject to many regional variations. Both scholarly literatures abound with detailed and particular studies of these changes through the study of individual texts, techniques, archaeological sites, and highly focused philological or historical discussions. Any historical overview must identify both social and institutional contexts that can serve as comparative frameworks and also must take into account indigenous Chinese and Greek categories and classificatory paradigms.

Plan of the book

I begin with the contexts for the comparative study of Chinese and Greek divination. Chapter 2 provides a critical overview of the sources for both Chinese and Greek divination: material, manuscript, and transmitted. Chapter 3 takes up the ways in which divination has been theorized in both Classical and Sinological scholarship. It reviews the history of the classification of divination, beginning with a passing remark by Plato and a rubric introduced by Cicero that persists to the present day. The study of Greek divination also forms part of an ongoing engagement between the disciplines of Classics and anthropology. The history of debates about Greek divination is diverse and theoretically sophisticated. Chinese theories of the history of divination draw on far richer data, but have tended to engage with, or be co-opted by, nationalist histories.

Next I turn to Chinese and Greek mantic specialists and the methods they used. Chapter 4 introduces the range of mantic practitioners and their intellectual and social contexts. In both China and Greece, there were significant and comparable differences between independent practitioners and "official" divination: court mantic officials in China and oracles in Greece. These two types of practitioner differed in construction of authority and in the relations with clientele.

Chapter 5 surveys the range of methods at the disposal of diviners. Divination is a hermeneutic system of great potential diversity, since anything can be a sign. Greek divinatory hermeneutics stressed the act of communication between gods and humans. Chinese divination stressed the nature of the system itself, with less emphasis on the source or nature of the message.

Chapter 6 surveys changing topics of state and private consultation. Despite their differences of emphasis, both state and private Chinese and Greek divination topics are strikingly similar. In both cases, there is a distinction between predictive questions and questions that seek to enhance the "wellbeing" of consultors in their relation to the cosmo-moral order, understood as the goodwill of the gods, or as harmony with *dao*. (For example, "will X occur?" is a predictive question. "To whom should I pray and sacrifice for X?" is a question about wellbeing.)

The opposite side of the coin from wellbeing is risk. The questions addressed to mantic expertise indicate what areas of life consultors considered full of danger and risk. Chapter 6 also takes up questions posed by private consultors as indicators of perceptions of risk by ordinary individuals, and how they used the mantic arts to manage risk in daily life. Explicit topics of risk are very similar, but the articulation of specific dangers and problems is very different.

Chapter 7 turns to consultors and mantic access: the question of who had access to mantic expertise and what kind, including the question of how gender affected mantic access. The analogy between Greek and Chinese "independent" and "official" practitioners of the mantic arts does not extend to consultation and mantic access because Chinese "official" prognostication was controlled by and reserved for state use. By contrast, all Greek consultors, in principle, had access to both oracles and independent practitioners. There are, however, points of comparability in the one mode of consultation common to both: private consultation of independent practitioners.

Divination was a powerful potential source of legitimation, authority, and consensus for any state, and it has been argued, on the model of African divination, that Greek states used divination in this way. Chapter 7 takes up some of these questions from a Chinese comparative perspective.

Chapters 6 and 7 are focused on mantic questions and responses that are historically factual or probable. (In particular, I distinguish a narrow set of clearly historical queries at Delphi from a broad set of quasi-historical queries.) Chapter 8 turns to mantic narratives with significant didactic, literary, or ideological content, which cannot be read as transparent accounts. Here I take up the possibility of a topos or genre of mantic narratives in both early Chinese and Greek historical texts, drawing on the *Zuo Transmissions* (*Zuo zhuan*), Chinese dynastic histories, and the histories of Herodotus and Plutarch.

There were major differences between Chinese and Greek perceptions of divination as a hermeneutic system. Chapter 9 examines the contributions of Chinese and Greek divination to systematic inquiry in philosophy and science. As already indicated in Chapter 5, Chinese divination was based on the assumption of a cosmological system, though it is easy to overstate this by anachronistically applying Han dynasty systematic cosmologies to earlier periods. Pre-Han "systematic" elements include: (1) the early articulation of a cosmic *yin–yang* polarity, (2) the abstraction of patterns of change into a discrete number of types, represented by numbers, and (3) the early articulation of the sixty-four hexagrams as a complex and nuanced model of cosmic change, based on the combinatorics of *yin* and *yang*. Greek mantic hermeneutics focused, by contrast, on divination as a communication from the gods, with implications for both morality and ritual. The important role of divination as the impetus for Hellenistic debates about causality also arose out of a moral problem: the issue of choice and responsibility.

In both China and Greece the evidence for understanding mantic activity is immense, diverse, and unsystematic. The nature of the difficulties varies from source to source and period to period, but several points can be made about both China and Greece. First, the available evidence spans a wide variety of sources and genres, and in no way respects the contemporary academic specializations that study these genres. Thus evidence must come from history, philosophy, the history of science, rhetorical practices, epigraphy, and several literary genres. Other important evidence comes from the material and manuscript tradition. This diversity requires a compromise between detailed attention to historical context and the insights gained by seeking a wide range of sources. This situation is particularly acute in the case of Chinese archaeology and recently excavated texts that, not only have not been translated, but within a Chinese context remain largely the preserve of epigraphers and highly technical specialists.

Second, this study is a deliberately limited comparison. Other evidence could be adduced from historical or anthropological studies of other societies. In restricting myself to these periods in the history of early China and ancient Greece, I hope to avoid the worst errors of misjudgment or ignorance. In engaging in comparison at all I hope to benefit from the many parallels and differences between various aspects of Chinese and Greek divination. In particular, since the Chinese evidence is vastly more substantial than the Greek, but not widely familiar outside specialist circles, I hope to use comparative evidence from China to help enrich our understanding of Greek divination.

Third, because the Chinese evidence is so much more substantial, equal treatment is not possible in all cases. Also, since in some cases detail is necessary to any understanding of the matter in question, I must ask the reader's patience. Even within the limited time frame under discussion, the present study cannot hope to be comprehensive, and must of necessity select from representative genres and types of source material. These are discussed in the next chapter.

2 Sources

This chapter describes the textual, material, and manuscript sources for Greek and Chinese mantic activity and the genres and interpretive problems associated with each. Detailed references are reserved for later chapters. In both contexts there is tension between the received textual tradition and archaeological and material evidence, but the sources and problems are very different. These diverse sources need to be viewed within the context of their respective genres. Insofar as texts within a given genre have common subject matters and sets of concerns, they tend to focus on similar areas of experience and belief, and to exclude others. As a result, different genres' treatment of ideas may be profoundly different, or even contradictory, and any account of cultural change that draws on different genres and different historical periods must take this issue into account.[1]

Within each tradition, I begin with transmitted textual traditions. Next I turn to the discovered (rather than transmitted) evidence in manuscripts and inscriptions, as well as indirect material evidence such as decorative motifs, instruments, and implements. After reviewing the kinds of sources for Greek and Chinese evidence, I then turn to a comparative survey of sources: archival records of instances of divination and its results and interpretations; factual accounts; rhetorical accounts; and methods, rules, and procedures. The latter include hermeneutic guides to the interpretation of mantic signs; prescriptions for ritual; and legal and administrative procedures associated with divination. Detailed examples and accounts of sources are reserved for later chapters.

Greek sources

Textual, inscriptional, and material evidence of Greek mantic activity spans the historical record (see Appendix 2.1). The nature of the sources varies considerably by period, and the evidence is strongest between roughly 800 and 300.

[1] On this issue see Parker 1983: 13–17.

The literary tradition

Accounts of mantic activity first appear in the Homeric poems. They are prominent in the writings of some historians (Herodotus, Xenophon, and Plutarch, especially). They appear in passing in philosophical literature, and are a major element in both tragedy and comedy. Literary accounts of mantic activity include legends of the births and exploits of mantic gods and the establishment of oracular sites. Accounts of legendary *manteis* such as Cassandra, Tiresias, and Mopsus include descriptions of their lineages and how they acquired their gifts. Accounts of historical mantic figures appear across the genres of Greek literature, and include descriptions of their sacrificial and ritual activities. All these texts use divination for their own purposes, so a major interpretive problem is to distinguish factual accounts from rhetorical anecdotes. The latter may be valuable as guides to attitudes, even if they cannot be taken as historically factual or transparent accounts of it.

It is striking that, as early as the Homeric poems, there are descriptions of most major forms of Greek divination. These include the flight of birds (ornithoscopy), by weather, by dreams (oneiromancy), by the appearance of the entrails of sacrificial animals (hieroscopy), by casting lots (cledonomancy), and by invoking the dead (necromancy).[2] These legendary accounts attest to the antiquity of certain practices and attitudes toward divination. They also serve as the oldest textual baseline both for linguistic usage and for references to particular modes of divination, by what they do, and do not, include (though the latter is not an argument for absence). For example, Homer refers to the oracle of Zeus at Dodona, but not to Delphi.

The *Histories* of Herodotus is both the best known and the most extensive source for divination narratives, including consultation of both the oracle of Apollo at Delphi and individual *manteis*. Herodotus documents a range of attitudes toward oracles, with a particular interest in ambiguous oracles and their misinterpretation. There are also many accounts of military divination, for example his detailed account of the skills, background, and activities of Tisamenus of Elis. Herodotus also makes his own use of the Delphic oracle, especially in the story of Croesus. Oracles purport to convey divine authority, but they also reflect the voice of the historian. By contrast, Thucydides refers to divination only in passing and never mentions a *mantis* by name.[3]

[2] For details see Appendix 5.6. For technical terms connected with divination see the Glossary and Chapter 5.

[3] Herodotus and the Croesus cycle are discussed in Chapter 8. Thucydides: 3.20.1, 5.54.2, 5.55.3, 5.116, and 6.69.1–2. See Powell 1979 and Hornblower 1992.

A very different account of mantic practice comes from Xenophon, who describes his own experiences, frequently in a military context. The *Anabasis* provides eyewitness accounts of divination, including his own consultation of the Delphic oracle on whether to accompany Cyrus the younger in his attempt to become king of Persia in 401.[4]

Divination figures prominently in Plutarch's *Lives*, especially the *Lives* of Alexander, Cimon, Nicias, and Pericles. These accounts cannot be taken at face value because of the literary and rhetorical role of misguided or unheeded divinations as a narrative element in his biographies. Plutarch, himself a Delphic priest of Apollo, also wrote several texts on Delphi, including *On the Pythian Oracle* (*De Pythiae oraculis*), *On the Decline of Oracles* (*De defectu oraculorum*), and *On the E at Delphi* (*De E apud Delphi*). These reflected practices in his own time, and his speculations about the past. Briefer accounts of divination appear in many other texts. Arrian gives useful details of military divination. Other accounts appear in the writings of Apollodorus, Diodorus Siculus, Lucretius, Strabo, Pliny, and Pausanias.[5]

All these texts present interpretive problems: some because they use divination as a literary motif, others because of their lack of interest in historical matters. Even in these cases, historical sources can indicate the kind of everyday concerns that were referred to mantic consultation, for example lack of children (including royal heirs), concerns about wellbeing, relief from illness, decisions about travel, migration, and financial matters, and lost or stolen items, money, or even persons (especially women). Other topics include the interpretation of dreams and omens and questions on how best to sacrifice to the gods. Finally, historical texts indicate the popularity and activity of oracles such as Delphi, Dodona, Didyma, and Ammon.

Divination is also a prominent and dangerous theme in Greek tragedy. Fate becomes a tragic motif in the hands of Aeschylus and Sophocles, most famously in Sophocles' *Oedipus Tyrannus*, but also in Aeschylus' *Agamemnon* and *Seven against Thebes*.[6] Aeschylus and Sophocles rework mythological narratives in ways that prominently feature divination,

[4] Xen. *An.* books 4, 5, 6, and 7, discussed further in Chapters 4–7.

[5] Arrian: see Appendix 2.1 and Chapter 8. Plutarch: discussion in Chapters 4, 5, 6, and 8.

[6] E.g. Soph. *OT* 711–25, 790–93; Aesch. *Sept.* 742–57. The plot of the *Agamemnon* is driven by predictions by Calchas (29–30, 104–5, 264–67, 320–40) and Cassandra (1072–1330). The *Libation Bearers* (*Cho.* 269–96, 555–59, 1029–33) and Orestes (971–80) are driven by oracles of Apollo. For the *Oresteia* see D. H. Roberts (1984). See Staehlin 1912 for a comprehensive list of instances of divination in Greek and Roman drama.

oracles, and prophecies. Sophocles in particular turns oracles and oracular knowledge into objects of contest and debate.

Although tragic treatments of divination tend to be destructive and sinister, the utterances of mantic figures are typically proven to be accurate. The oracle of Apollo at Delphi is indirectly responsible for the deaths of Laius, Jocasta, and Oedipus in *Oedipus Tyrannus*, and for the persecution of Orestes in the *Libation Bearers*. Similarly, the predictions of such figures as Amphiaraus and Tiresias tend to be proven right. By contrast, diviners and chresmologues (oracle interpreters, discussed on page 109) are frequent objects of derision in comedy; thus their predictions are typically proved wrong.[7]

References to divination in Presocratic fragments are scattered, but divination becomes a topic of philosophical speculation in very different ways for Plato, Aristotle, and the Stoics. It also becomes an important site of philosophical debate in Hellenistic Greece. The Platonic Socrates respects and at times recommends both divination and the oracle of Apollo at Delphi.[8] Plato discusses divination at several points, in ways that are part of his own philosophical agenda, including what became a definitive (if misguided) distinction between inspired and technical divination.[9]

Aristotle takes up the question of oneiromancy in "On Divination through Dreams" (*De divinatione per somnia*). However, his enduring influence on the philosophical history of divination came through his emphasis on the importance of choice as central to human responsibility, and Hellenistic debates about determinism and freedom began as reactions to his analysis of choice and responsibility. Divination thus became an important topic in late Greek debates on fate, necessity, and causality. The only systematic philosophical account of divination in Greco-Roman antiquity is Cicero's *De Divinatione*, written in two books as a dialogue between Cicero and his brother Quintus. The first presents a Stoic defense of divination by Quintus, the second a refutation by Cicero himself.

In summary, much of the textual history of divination and oracles must be read with care. The evidence for archaic oracles in the Homeric poems is a fragmentary product of oral tradition, and correspondingly difficult to assess. Sources from the classical period are more diverse in content and genre, but they present their own problems, especially accounts of the Delphic oracle, which may say more about a history of narrative modes than a history of

[7] On this point see Flower 2008: 18–20. [8] Oracle to Chaerophon: Pl. *Ap.* 22c, Xen. *An.* 3.1.

[9] Inspired and technical divination: Pl. *Phdr.* 224a–e, discussed in Chapter 3; consultation of Delphi: Pl. *Rep.* 427b, *Leg.* 738b–d.

divination. Such depictions reflect both the beliefs of individual authors and the conventions of the genres in which they wrote. To be plausible to their intended audiences, such depictions must reflect prevailing attitudes and practices, but there is a large gap for invention. Thus, to a point, it is possible to use literary texts as evidence for attitudes toward divination and prediction. Instances where divination comes up in passing in a legal or administrative context, and is not itself the focus of interest, may be less biased, for example, passing references in speeches by Demosthenes and others.

Material and manuscript

Oracular sanctuaries first rose to prominence in several Greek locales in the eighth century. The preeminent sites were associated with two gods: Zeus, the king of the gods, and Apollo, the god of oracular divination. The most important (and rival) Greek oracular sites were the oracles of Zeus at Dodona, Olympia, and Ammon, in Libya, and the oracles of Apollo at Delphi and Didyma (near Miletus). Beginning in the late fifth or fourth century, temples of the healer god Asclepius spread throughout the Greek world. The most important was at Epidaurus, but they came to span the Greek world, outstripping the oracles of Apollo (Map 2.1). Other, lesser-known oracles include the oracle of Mopsus at Claros (near Colophon). Most oracles left little in the way of material remains, and this limits our knowledge of oracular procedures.

Despite the prevalence of divination in the Greek world, epigraphic evidence is fairly sparse. Over fifty oracular sites have been identified in the Greco-Roman world, but most have left no inscriptional or manuscript remains.[10] Most procedures did not leave material remains, and much of what does remain consists of inscriptions concerning oracular consultation. Some preserve only the questions posed by consultors, others only the answers.

Early accounts of oracular responses at Dodona describe interpretation of the rustling of the leaves of the oak tree, the cooing of doves, or the ringing of metal tripods. By the sixth century, oracular responses were recorded on lead tablets. The site of Dodona was first explored by the Greek archaeologist Constantin Carapanos, who uncovered over 150 texts engraved on bronze, copper, and lead, dating from the sixth or fifth century to the destruction of the temple in 88, including oracular texts engraved on lead tablets (Figure 6.1). Subsequent excavations yielded additional tablets, and the corpus now consists of some 167 divination inscriptions, the largest

[10] For a comprehensive list of some fifty oracular sites in ancient Greece see Curnow 2004.

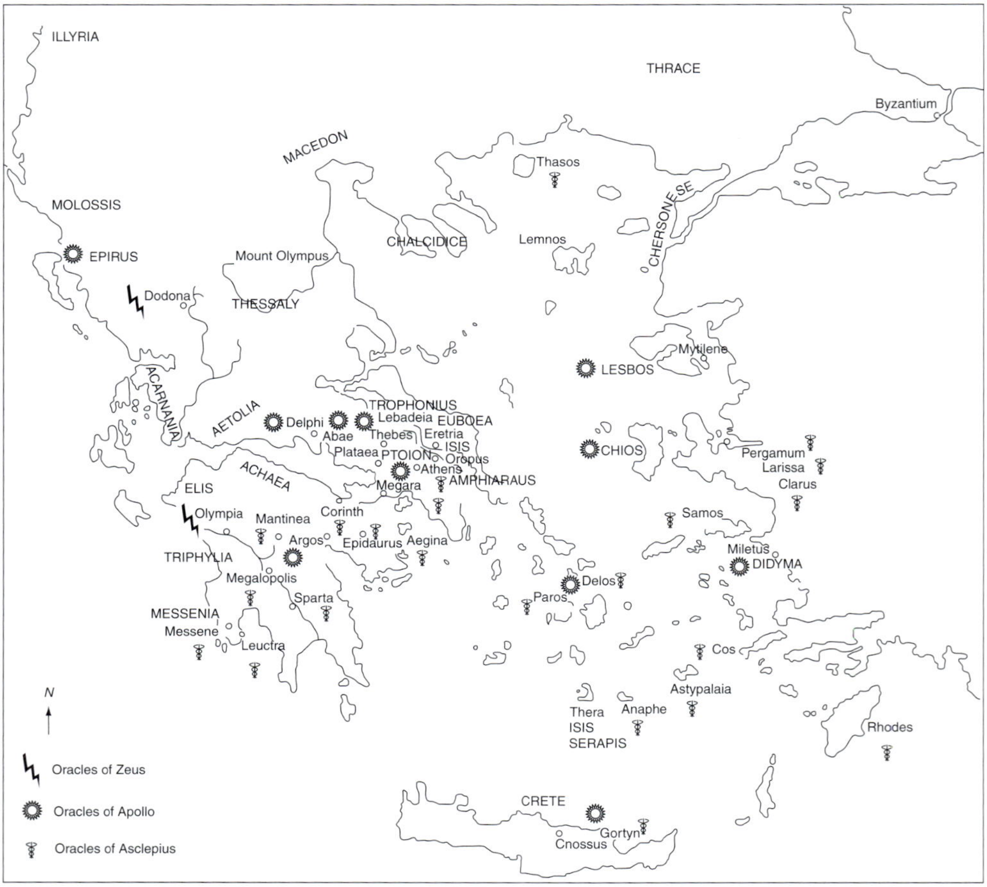

Oracles of Zeus

1. Dodona
2. Olympia

Oracles of Apollo

3. Abae
4. Argos
5. Chios
6. Delos
7. Delphi
8. Didyma
9. Epirus
10. Lesbos
11. Ptoion
12. Thebes

Temples of Asclepius

13. Aegina
14. Anaphe
15. Astypalaia
16. Athens
17. Clarus
18. Corinth
19. Cos
20. Delos
21. Epidaurus
22. Gortyn
23. Larissa
24. Leuctra
25. Mantinea
26. Megalopolis
27. Messene
28. Oropus
29. Paros
30. Pergamum
31. Rhodes
32. Samos
33. Sparta
34. Thasos

Other

35. Lebadeia, Trophonius
36. Thera, Isis, Serapis
37. Eretria, Isis
38. Oropus, Amphiaraus

Map 2.1 Major Greek oracular sites.

extant corpus of oracular consultations.[11] They include both state and private queries, many from local residents. Both sides of many of the tablets are inscribed, and some are in poor condition. Other texts include bronze

[11] Carapanos 1878, followed by E. S. Roberts 1880 and 1881, Merriam 1884, summarized in Parke 1967. Additional inscriptions: Evangelidis 1935 and 1952 (some tablets are still unpublished), Dakaris 1993, Christidis et al. 1997 and 1999, L'Hôte 2006, Eidinow 2007a, which includes a useful introduction (esp. 269 n. 51) and an extensive study of the corpus. The history of Dodona is discussed further in Chapter 4.

votive inscriptions and bronze or copper inscriptions recording contracts, decrees of citizenship, and deeds of manumission.[12]

The shrine of Zeus at Dodona was the most widely sought sanctuary of Zeus in the ancient world because it offered oracular consultation, but the cult of Zeus was centered on Olympia, the site of the Olympic Games. There was an oracle of Zeus at Olympia, but little is known of its procedures, and it is not a significant source for evidence on divination.[13]

The most famous oracle of the ancient world was the oracle of Apollo at Delphi, yet no direct archaeological evidence of divination procedures remains there. Few extant accounts of divinations at Delphi come from inscriptional sources (Appendix A), and of these, only eight are from Delphi itself. There is a great deal of epigraphic material from Delphi, but it concerns the bureaucracy of consultation, not its results. For example, there are over 600 grants of priority of access (*promanteia*) to states and individuals. Other inscriptions record dedications, thank-offerings, names of contributors, and accounts of funds received, for example an inscription from 361 or 360 listing contributions by *poleis* and individuals (including several women) toward rebuilding the temple.[14] Other inscriptions record agreements with different *poleis* on the cost of state and private consultations. By contrast, oracular responses tend to be preserved in the home locales of consultors. Examples include a treaty between Chalcidia and Macedon (preserved in Macedon) and the Sacred Orgas decree (preserved in Athens).

After Delphi, the oracle of Apollo at Didyma near Miletus in Ionia may have been the most renowned oracle in the Greek world. According to Herodotus, both the shrine and its priestly lineage, the Branchidae, predated the arrival of the Ionian Greeks.[15] Most are state queries, and many are historically dubious.[16]

Asclepian sanctuaries first appeared in the Mediterranean in the sixth century, but their growth as healing centers dates from the fifth and fourth centuries. The most important were at Epidaurus and Cos. The temple at

[12] There are also deeds of *proxenia* conferred on individuals and in one case a whole community, a contract establishing the right of intermarriage, a gift of land and property, and a contract for the purchase of a slave. *Proxenia* and *promanteia* are discussed further in Chapter 5. Some inscriptions are discussed in detail in Chapter 6.

[13] Paus. 5.15.10, Weniger 1915, Sinn 1991, discussed in Chapter 4.

[14] Dedications: Athenian portico (*SEG* 39.473); thank-offering for Persian War victors engraved on "serpent column" at Delphi (*SEG* 14.412; 22.458; 16.337). Temple contributors and accounts: *FD* 3 5.3, 5.23 (RO no. 45). Fines to Delphi: *FD* 3 5.14 (Tod 1 Nos. 18, 19; 2 Nos. 140, 169, 172).

[15] The Branchidae were a male priestly lineage in charge of the temple of Apollo at Didyma until its destruction by the Persians in 494. They claimed descent from Branchos, a youth dear to Apollo. Hdt. 1.157.3 (cf. 1.46, 1.92, 2.159); Paus. 7.2.6. See Hammond 1998.

[16] Fontenrose 1988, based on an unpublished dissertation (1933), includes a detailed catalog of responses from Didyma. It is more extensive than the brief catalog in Fontenrose 1978.

Epidaurus was extensively developed during the fourth century and remained prosperous throughout the Hellenistic period. It contains four late fourth-century stelae recording some seventy cures, including details and names of consultors.[17] These records, however, cannot be taken at face value. As Rhodes and Osborne point out in their commentary on the first stele, the records seem to be rhetorical in tone, giving the god a personality and linking successful cure to faith, moral uprightness, and prompt payment.[18] They emphasize the god's powers, and include straightforward accounts of faith and cure, cases of skepticism or failure to reward the god, and examples of punishment for failure to make votive offerings.

A marble stele at Amphiaraus, Oropus (386–374) specifies the times of operation of the sanctuary, the fees for consultations, and duties of the priests.[19]

Another source for passing references to divination consists of the Greek magical papyri: a group of papyri from Greco-Roman Egypt from the second century BCE to the fifth century CE.[20] Although literary sources indicate the existence of many collections of magical spells in late antiquity, systematic destruction and suppression have destroyed most, and those that survived did so in the collections of philosophers, alchemists, astrologers, and theologians. These texts include divinatory spells, procedures for revealing the future, and memory spells to help recall what is said. Some spells are "oracles" connected with specific gods or legendary figures (Chronos, Sarapis, even Homer). They also include procedures for dream divination, saucer and lamp divination, and spells for divination using a child as a spirit medium. They also contain astrocalendric information such as listings of days and hours for divination, an astrological calendar, and horoscopes.

These examples suggest the diffusion and difficulty of tracing manuscript sources relevant to divination, many of which are reproduced in multiple journals or held in museums scattered around the world. Recently developed databases and concordances have done much to make these materials more accessible.

The oracle at Delphi provides additional material evidence, both from the shrine itself and from the many offerings dedicated there. There is evidence of Mycenaean settlement in the area of Delphi, but no evidence of sanctuary activity before 800 and no evidence of oracular activity there before the eighth century. Mythological accounts of the antiquity of the shrine are of

[17] *IG* 4^2, 1.121–24. The first two are translated in Edelstein and Edelstein 1945: 221–37 and RO no. 102, esp. 540–42. They and the entire corpora of *IG* can be accessed electronically at www.epigraphy.packhum.org/inscriptions/main.

[18] RO no. 102, 541. [19] *IG* 7.235; *SIG*^{3} 1004, RO no. 27.

[20] Preisendanz and Henrichs 1973–74. Translation and history: Betz 1986.

late date.[21] The site was only excavated in 1892, by a French team, after an earthquake devastated the village of Kastri, which was built above the ruins of the temple.

A Sacred Way runs up the mountain from the main gate of the sanctuary of Apollo Pythios to the temple of Apollo, from there to the sanctuary theater, and finally to the stadium of Delphi, where the Pythian Games were held every four years, starting in 582. It was lined on both sides by votive monuments and treasuries, in which client *poleis* placed dedicatory offerings. Extant remains begin with the bronze Bull of Corcyra (dedicated by the Corcyreans about 580), followed by dedications from the Arcadians, Spartans, Athenians, Argives, Tarentines, Boeotians, Plataeans, Chians, Aetolians, and Messenians. These are followed by the Treasuries of the Sicyonians, the Siphnians, the Megarians, the Thebans, the Athenians, the Syracusans, the Clazomenians, the Cyrenaeans, and the Corinthians. There are also dedications by individuals, but few bear inscriptions that could explain purpose or context. The surviving temple was the third built in historical times, and dates from the fourth century. It was extensively damaged by both earthquakes and later occupants.

Despite this wealth of dedicatory offerings, there are no records of divinations or other evidence of the divination process. In particular, there is no extant evidence of the *adyton*, the chamber where the Pythia delivered her responses, or the vapor-emitting chasm over which her tripod was said to have been placed. Most accounts of consultations come from literary sources.[22]

Depictions of mantic consultation provide a different kind of material evidence. Perhaps most famous is a scene from an Athenian vase ascribed to the Codrus painter (*c.* 440) depicting the legendary king Aegeus consulting Themis, depicted as the Pythia of youthful age, sitting on the tripod (Figure 2.1). Other fifth-century vase paintings show many images of Pythian Apollo, and also show images of divination by professional *manteis* and others.[23]

[21] In particular Apollodorus (*c.* 180 CE), Diodorus Siculus (*c.* 80–20), and Pausanias (second century CE). See Appendix 2.1 as well as Fontenrose 1959, Sourvinou-Inwood 1987, Catherine Morgan 1990: 107–8 and 148–49.

[22] Fontenrose (1978) in particular gives no credence to any accounts of the chasm. De Boer et al. (2001) have argued for the existence of chthonic vapors, based on seasonal chemical changes in the limestone strata beneath Delphi. This issue is discussed in detail in Chapter 4.

[23] Bowden 2005: 58–63, Flower 2008: 28 (Melampus), 41 (mantis on the pediment of the temple of Zeus at Olympia), 98 (grave stele of the mantis Cleobulus), 163 and 164 (depictions of military *manteis*).

Figure 2.1 Themis as Pythia seated on the tripod. Codrus painter (*c.* 440).

In summary, there is relatively little material evidence directly connected with divination. There are archaeological remains of the sanctuaries, of the treasuries at Delphi, and of dedicatory offerings. There are also depictions in vase paintings and sculpture of divinities associated with divination, and even of the consultation process, but not of divination instruments or implements, with the exception of a few *astralagoi* (knuckle-bones used as dice). An obvious reason for this is that most Greek mantic procedures did not require specific implements. In a broader Mediterranean context, this lacuna is especially striking compared to the ample evidence of Babylonian mantic activity and its instruments.[24] It also contrasts with the wealth of Chinese archaeological evidence.

Modern compendia

In addition to the ancient sources themselves, two compendia of Delphic oracles based on both literary and manuscript traditions have greatly enhanced the systematic study of divination at Delphi: a compendium of

[24] Brown 2000; Rochberg 2004.

615 Greek responses by H. W. Parke and D. E. Wormell (1956) and a compendium of 535 oracles collected and translated by Joseph Fontenrose (1978). Both editors were faced with the problem of grouping the oracles; some questions were not preserved, so it was possible that several responses might answer the same question. Several interpretations account for differences between the two collections. They also faced a second problem that remains hotly debated: the question of authenticity. What counts as an authentic response or a "genuine" oracle?

Parke and Wormell grouped the oracles into fourteen categories based on the date of alleged utterance, using standard periods of Greek and Roman history. Nine additional categories addressed thematic content. These criteria allowed them to assess oracles as genuine, historical, authentic, legendary, fictional, dubious, or spurious. They defined "historical" oracles by absence of the supernatural. Their criterion of authenticity was that the reported words of the Pythia be established as her exact words.[25]

Fontenrose classified oracles under four headings: legendary (pre-eighth century or timeless), fictional (the literary inventions of poets, dramatists, etc.), quasi-historical (from historical times, but attested after the events described), and historical. He considered as historical only oracles recorded during the lifetime of the first writer to attest them, or contemporary to inscriptions recording them. Fontenrose did not attempt to judge authenticity, but he considered "historical responses" the most likely to be authentic because their shorter time of transmission would leave less time for alteration or forgery.

By these criteria some half of known Delphic oracles are quasi-historical, mostly from the works of Herodotus, Plutarch, and Pausanias. Many differ in style and content from Fontenrose's "historical" oracles, which give straightforward advice on a limited number of choices. Quasi-historical oracles, by contrast, often use ambiguity and, as Julia Kindt argues, share features with "legendary" responses.[26]

Several scholars question this approach. For example, Lisa Maurizio argues that these criteria apply to written texts, and that oracles should be regarded as oral literature and judged by the very different criteria developed by scholars of oral traditions. She argues that oracles were primarily transmitted orally, "performed" when delivered to consultors, and in many cases reperformed in consultors' home locales. Jon Mikalson argues that Fontenrose's criteria beg

[25] Thus a response could be authentic but not historical. As Kindt points out (2003: 9–10), this assessment relied on subjective judgments, and labeled many responses with a "strong mythic tenor" as authentic and wholly or partially historical.

[26] Fontenrose 1978: 7–9 and 240–416.

the important question of whether Greeks of the time considered oracles recorded by Herodotus and others to be authentic, and there is very good evidence that they did.[27] Other studies take other directions.[28]

Chinese sources

Chinese evidence for mantic practices is vastly greater than the Greek in both content and types of extant document, including mantic texts, procedures and methods, narrative accounts (which may be factual or rhetorical in nature), and collected records.

Most important are mantic texts, by which I mean texts that provide guidance in interpreting mantic signs and allow a (usually) skilled interpreter to offer guidance to consultors. They appear in both textual and manuscript traditions. Some are comprehensive and systematic; for example, the *Zhou yi* 周易 (*Zhou Changes*) provides interpretive guidance on the sixty-four hexagrams of the text in a systematic order.[29] Daybooks such as those excavated from Shuihudi 水虎地 link auspicious days for some types of activities to the calendar, but do not give recommendations for all days or day types, or cover a full range of activities.[30] Mantic texts also include technical treatises on particular and specialized aspects of divination, including astronomical, meteorological, and calendric texts.

Prescriptive procedural texts provide other kinds of guidance. For example, the *Li ji* 禮記 (*Book of Rites*) describes the correct performance of rituals that include divination. (See Appendix 2.3 for approximate dates for this and other texts mentioned below.) Administrative and legal texts describe the duties, aptitudes, or selection and training of officials connected with divination. The *Zhou li* 周禮 (*Rites of Zhou*) describes the titles and duties of several officials concerned with divination and the specialists they supervised.[31]

[27] Maurizio 1997; Mikalson 2003: 56–58.

[28] Some focus on the influence of oracles on Greek politics (Crahay 1956, 1974, Parker 2000a, Bowden 2005). Others explore the literary dimensions of fictional oracles, especially in tragedy and comedy (e.g. Vellacott 1964, Dodds 1966, Kane 1975, Burkert 1991, for *Oedipus Rex*). Yet other scholars study (usually Delphic) oracles as a coherent body of texts and mode of reflection (Dougherty 1992, 1993, 1994; Kindt 2003, 2006, 2007, 2008; Maurizio 1993, 1995, 2001).

[29] The *Zhou yi* and its relation to the *Yi jing* 易經 (*Classic of Change*) is discussed in Chapters 5 and 9.

[30] The Shuihudi daybooks are discussed in detail in Chapters 6 and 9.

[31] Similarly, the *Shi lü* 史律 section of the legal statutes excavated from Zhangjiashan 張家山 gives instructions for the training and appointment of *shi*. See *ZJS* 203–4.

A third type of text purports to describe incidents of prognostication and divination. Such accounts occur in several genres of text, including historical narratives, biographies, poems, philosophical works, and in legal and administrative records. They vary in length, detail, and complexity from brief passages to systematic compendia. For example, the *Zuo zhuan* 左傳 (*Zuo Transmissions*) abounds with accounts of divinations of all kinds, including divinations about battle, marriage and progeny, dreams, and portents. Accounts of divination also appear in philosophical "Masters texts" (*zi* 子, discussed below), including the *Analects* of Confucius (*Lun yu* 論語), *Mencius* (*Mengzi* 孟子), and *Zhuangzi* 莊子, among others. Some are part of a historical narrative in which so-and-so performed a divination. Others occur in philosophical debates about the value of mantic knowledge or the nature of fate, for example the "Against Physiognomy" (Fei xiang 非相) chapter of the *Xunzi* 荀子.

A fourth type of text records instances of divination and their interpretation. These occur in legal or administrative records and in texts excavated from tombs. An interpretive issue here is the circumstances under which they were assembled. Even in cases where the selection was made at or near the time divinations were performed, the basis of selection is not always clear. In other cases, "archives" are a matter of what archaeologists have happened to find, and do not necessarily reflect the priorities of practitioners or consultors. The divination archive materials in excavated texts have no real counterparts in the received tradition. By contrast ostensive accounts of individuals performing divination abound throughout the received tradition, especially in the genres of History and Masters texts. Some provide evidence of divination as a factor in the growth of self-conscious critical thought, systematic inquiry, and the development of science and philosophy.

Finally, divination or prognostication may appear as a category of classification in bibliographies, encyclopedias, and other compendia. A useful guide to accounts of mantic activity within the textual tradition is the categories of the bibliographic chapter of the *Standard History of the Western Han*, the *Han shu* 漢書 Bibliographic Treatise (*Yiwenzhi* 藝文志). This chapter lists titles in the imperial library under six categories in an explicitly descending hierarchy, and created the paradigm by which subsequent compendia classified texts.[32] Many titles listed in the Treatise

[32] *HS* 30.1701–84. It was compiled by Ban Gu (32–92 CE). The first three categories were based on compilations by the Han exegete Liu Xiang 劉向 (79–78 BCE) and on his son Liu Xin's 劉歆 (46 BCE–23 CE) description of the imperial library. The last three were compiled by three technical experts: the military official Ren Hong 任宏, a Colonel of Foot Soldiers under Han Cheng Di; the *Taishi* (Director of Astronomy) Yin Xian 尹咸; and the imperial physician Li

are no longer extant, but the Treatise provides a guide to the categories of knowledge used by Han thinkers. The first three categories, Six Arts (*Liuyi* 六藝), Masters (*Zhuzi* 諸子, the texts equated with Warring States philosophy), and Poetry (*Shifu* 詩賦), contain mantic materials, but are generalist in focus. The last three categories are technical: Military Works (*Bingshu* 兵書), Numbers and Techniques (*Shushu* 數術), and Recipes and Methods (*Fangji* 方技). "Numbers and Techniques" is particularly concerned with mantic texts, most of which are no longer extant.[33]

Chinese transmitted texts

The Six Arts category is based, not on the Six Arts, but on the Five Classics (*Wu jing* 五經): the Classic of Change (*Yi jing* 易經), Documents (*Shu jing* 書經, also known as the *Shang shu* 商書 or Venerated Documents), Odes (*Shi jing* 詩經), Ritual (*Li jing* 禮經), and the Spring and Autumn Annals (*Chunqiu* 春秋), supplemented by the Zuo Transmissions (*Zuo zhuan* 左傳).[34] All were significantly concerned with divination.

Most important is the *Yi jing*, a mantic text in form and probably in original use, perhaps the best known text in the world associated with divination. In its present form it consists of the *Zhou Changes* (*Zhou yi*) and seven commentaries. The *Zhou yi* consists of sixty-four hexagrams and statements related to them. A hexagram (*gua* 卦) is a vertical sequence (from bottom to top) of six "lines" (*yao* 爻), each of which is understood as representing either a number or a *yin* or *yang* line. The sixty-four possible combinations of six such lines make up the hexagrams. The *Zhou yi* probably dates to the ninth century, and consisted of the hexagram images, the hexagram names (*gua ming* 卦名), the explanations to each hexagram (the hexagram statements or *gua ci* 卦辭), and the 384 line statements

Zhuguo 李柱國 (*HS* 30.1701). Later rubrics use a simpler classification of: Classics (*jing* 經), Histories (*shi* 史), Masters (*zi* 子), and Collections (*ji* 集). An example is the "four treasuries" (*siku* 四庫) of the *Siku quanshu* 四庫全書 or "Complete Library of the Four Treasuries," compiled under the command of the Qianlong emperor between 1773 and 1782.

33 For divination in the *Han shu* Bibliographic Treatise see Raphals 2008–9.

34 The Six Arts were Ritual, Music, Archery, Charioteering, Calligraphy, and Mathematics. The *Yi*, *Shi*, and *Shu* date from the Western Zhou (1045–771). The *Yi* and *Shu* were subject to later interpolation, but scholars have attempted to identify the original layers of both texts. A sixth "classic," the *Yue ji* 樂記 (*Record of Music*), is no longer extant, but may correspond to a chapter of the *Li ji* of the same title. All were closely associated with Confucius. In 136, Han Wu Di 漢武帝 (r. 141–87) restricted officially appointed academicians to chairs in the five classical traditions. In 124, he founded the Taixue 太學 academy, an imperial academy with regular instruction in these works. Authorship, history, and dating: ECTBG and Nylan 2001a. Imperial academy: Twitchett and Loewe 1986: 756–58.

(*yao ci* 爻辭) for each of the six lines of every hexagram.[35] The commentaries are ascribed by tradition to Confucius, but probably date from the mid third to early second century. Most important is the Great Treatise (*Da zhuan* 大傳, also called the Commentary on the Appended Phrases or *Xi ci* 繫辭).

In traditional accounts, the *Zhou yi* was created by King Wen (文王, r. 1099–1050) and the Duke of Zhou (周公, d. 1032), who modified and expanded an earlier Shang dynasty mantic system called the *Guicang* 歸藏 (Returning to the Treasury). They created the hexagram and line statements, and rearranged the order of the hexagrams to start with *Qian* 乾.[36] Gu Jiegang 顧頡剛 and other revisionist early twentieth-century scholars argued against traditional accounts of the origins of the *Yi*.[37] The archaeological evidence of the last several decades has considerably nuanced their insights by providing evidence of its complex evolution. In addition to the received versions of the *Zhou yi* and its commentaries, there are now four versions excavated from tombs.[38]

The *Shu jing* also contains accounts of prognostication.[39] Of particular interest is the "Great Plan" (*Hongfan* 洪範) chapter, attributed to the reign of King Wu 武王 (r. 1049 or 1045–1043) but probably dating to the

[35] *Yi jing*: Shaughnessy 1983, 1996, ECTBG: 216–28. Important studies: Gao Heng 1947, 1979; Li Jingchi 1978: 407–21; Li Xueqin 1992; R. J. Smith 2008. Origins of milfoil divination: Li Ling 1993: 64–68. Translations: Wilhelm 1950, Lynn 1994, Schilling 2009.

[36] The *Zhou yi* was considered the third of "Three *Changes*" (*San yi* 三易): three pre-Han systems of naming and ordering the hexagrams. The earliest system, "Linked Mountains" (*Lian shan* 連山 or *Lie shan* 烈山), was attributed to the Xia dynasty, but to date there is no archaeological evidence for its existence.

[37] Gu Jiegang et al. 1926–41 (vol. 3). Modern Chinese historiography begins in a series of studies published between 1920 and 1940 by Gu Jiegang (1893–1980) and his followers, known as *Gushibian* 古史辯 or Debates on Ancient History, discussed further in Chapter 3.

[38] The oldest is the so-called Shanghai Museum text: fragments of thirty-four hexagrams on bamboo slips. Most complete is the Mawangdui *Zhou yi*, which includes the *Xi ci* and other commentaries. A third version, the so-called Fuyang *Zhou yi*, was excavated from the tomb of the lord of Ruyin 汝陰, Xiahou Zao 夏侯灶 (d. 165), at Shuanggudui (Fuyang, Anhui) Tomb 1 in 1977. The fourth is the *Guicang Yi* text from Wangjiatai Tomb 15. See Chapter 9 and Raphals 2008–9: 51–54. Revisionist scholarship: see Chapter 3.

[39] It purports to record events from 2500 to 500, mostly in records of speeches in highly ritual form. Of the fifty chapters, twenty-nine are considered pre-Han. Modern scholars group the text into four sections based on grammar and style: (1) the "Five Proclamations," early Western Zhou: the Great Proclamation (*Da gao* 大誥), Proclamation to Kang (*Kang gao* 康誥), Proclamation on Wine (*Jiu gao* 酒誥), Proclamation at Luo (*Luo gao* 洛誥), and Proclamation at Shao (*Shao gao* 召誥); (2) eighteen chapters, late Western or Eastern Zhou, including the Great Plan (*Hongfan* 洪範) and Metal Coffer (*Jinteng* 金縢); (3) six chapters, shortly before (or after) the Qin unification, including the Canon of Yao, the Tribute of Yu, and Counsels of Gao Yao; (4) twenty-one chapters, considered late compilations, dating up to the early fourth century CE. See ECTBG 376–89 and Nylan 2001a: 120–67, esp. 132–36. Translation: Karlgren 1950a.

Warring States. It describes the use of turtle and milfoil to resolve doubts as one of nine components of the "Great Plan" granted to Yu by heaven. Sections that date to later periods are valuable as guides to attitudes toward divination, even if they cannot be taken as historically transparent accounts. Two other passages, one probably pre-Qin and the other clearly not, prescribe methods for using turtle and milfoil. They are of particular comparative interest because they outline methods for achieving social consensus, managing risk, and preventing the kind of open-ended inquiry that *Yi* divination tends to promote.

The *Shi jing* is not primarily concerned with prognostication, but several poems refer briefly to it and its practitioners. They mention prognostication before founding a capital and the consultation of dream diviners. These poems show glimpses of mantic practices at both the state and popular level. Other poems are strongly rhetorical, and lament the failure of court diviners to predict and address problems that afflict the people.[40]

A now lost *Classic of Rites* (*Li jing*) was replaced by three later texts on ritual: the *Rites of Zhou* (*Zhou li* 周禮, also known as the *Zhou guan* 周官 or "Offices of Zhou"), the *Record of Rites* (*Li ji* 禮記), and the *Ceremonials* (*Yi li* 儀禮). All three contain prescriptive sections on prognostication, and together they underscore the prestige of divination and its use in creating consensus and establishing authority. They differ in the techniques they privilege and in attitudes toward combined divination methods as a source of reassurance or potential conflict. The *Zhou li* describes the offices and officials of an idealized Zhou bureaucracy, including an extensive listing of officials concerned with prognostication and ritual.[41] It provides the oldest known classification of these activities. There is considerable doubt about the existence of these offices, but for purposes of the present discussion, the *Zhou li* offers a view into an early Chinese mental universe, based on distinct theories of cosmology, number, and ritual.[42] The *Li ji* and *Yi li* indicate procedures for particular circumstances, especially the correct use of turtle

40 *Shi jing*: ECTBG 415–23, Nylan 2001a: 202–52. Translation: Karlgren 1950b.

41 Considerable controversy surrounds the dating of these three ritual texts. The Eastern Han commentator Zheng Xuan (127–200 CE) ascribed them to the Duke of Zhou, arguing that, taken together, they described a complete ritual system, which addressed all aspects of life from daily courtesies to the highest rituals of state, prominently including prognostication. Some contemporary scholars date the *Zhou li* to the Han dynasty and consider it the work of the Liu Xin and Wang Mang 王莽; others date it to the late Warring States. Jin Chunfeng (1993) considers it to reflect Qin practices and beliefs, based on systematic comparison to Qin excavated (Shuihudi) and transmitted texts (*Shangjun shu*, *Lü shi chunqiu*). Dating and authorship: ECTBG 24–32, Nylan 2001a: 82–85.

42 On this point see Lewis 1999: 42–48.

and milfoil. (Despite the importance ascribed to dream divination in the *Zhou li*, it receives little attention.) The *Yi li* gives an idealized description of major rituals performed by officials of the *shi* 士 rank, some of which involve divination.[43] The *Li ji* addresses the theory of ritual and many details of its practice.[44] It also prescribes which types of question should be resolved by turtle shell and which by milfoil for both state and family matters such as marriages and funerals. Eastern Han sources also address the use of turtle and milfoil. The *Comprehensive Discussions in White Tiger Hall* (*Baihu tong* 白虎通, *c.* 79 CE) describes a hierarchy of mantic practitioners from the ruler down to officials of the *shi* rank, with different grades of materials reserved for each. It also specifies how to use turtle and milfoil to resolve questions of imperial succession and to interpret anomalies.

The *Zuo zhuan* is sometimes seen as the major commentary to the fifth classic, the *Spring and Autumn Annals* (*Chunqiu*), a chronicle of events in the state of Lu over a 250-year period between 722 and 481.[45] Its rich narratives describe many types of mantic activity, including weather divination, turtle and milfoil, dream divination, physiognomy, and omens. Its narratives also suggest what topics were viewed as appropriate matters for consultation. Divination topics in the *Zuo zhuan* include battle, marriage and progeny, dreams, and portents. Some passages, especially accounts of *Yi* and dream divination, are quite suspect as historical descriptions, but give valuable information about attitudes and practices nonetheless.

The *Zuo zhuan* is also the first recorded mention (in the received tradition) of several techniques, including divination by clouds and vapors (*yunqi* 雲氣) and physiognomy. The wide range of methods mentioned in the *Zuo zhuan* also attests to their early use by elites and (in some cases) commoners. These accounts also underscore the importance of prognostication in resolving doubts and creating social stability; they show less concern with prediction, accuracy, or the verification of prognostications.

The eight sections of the Masters category include most of the texts of early Chinese philosophy.[46] Our access to these texts comes through the eyes of Han anthologists and commentators. A partial exception is the

[43] They are: (1) the capping ceremony that initiates a young man into adulthood, (2) betrothal and marriage, (3) visits between ordinary officials, (4) district symposia and feasts held by the district officer, (5) district archery contests, (6) formal banquets held by a duke for his officers, (7) the Capital archery contest, and (8) the preparation and conduct of missions of state. Dating and authorship: ECTBG 34–43. Contents: Nylan 2001a: 178–81.

[44] Dating and authorship: ECTBG 293–97. Contents: Nylan 2001a: 185–88.

[45] *Zuo*: ECTBG 67–76, Nylan 2001a: 253–89.

[46] They are grouped under the rubrics of: "Ru" (*Ru jia* 儒家, often mistranslated as "Confucian"), Daoists (*Dao jia* 道家), *Yin–yang* (*Yinyang jia* 陰陽家), Legalists (*Fa jia* 法家), Names (*Ming jia*

discovery of excerpts from Masters texts in several tombs, the most important being Guodian 郭店 and the Shanghai Museum texts. Debates about divination appear in texts traditionally classified as both Ru 儒 ("Confucian" or textualist) and Daoist, and also in technical texts classed as Miscellaneous.[47]

Accounts of divination in Masters texts indicate active competition between the textual specialists of the Masters schools and mantic experts. This competition involved career choice, patronage, students, and the status of genres and modes of knowledge; discourse on prognostication was a part of that intellectual milieu. Most Masters texts seem to have approved of divination. A few represent vignettes of "masters" such as Confucius and Mencius practicing it.[48] The Mohists advocate prognostication in military affairs. The *Guanzi* 管子 (fourth century) recommends it to protect rulers. By contrast, the legalist Han Fei 韓非 (*c.* 280–*c.* 233) considered trust in prognostication to be one of the causes of the ruin of a state. Other texts criticize it for a variety of reasons, including claims that it is an inferior mode of knowledge. The Masters category includes two texts that are important sources for astronomic and astrocalendric materials on divination: the *Huainanzi* 淮南子 of Liu An 劉安 (*c.* 180–122) and *Springs and Autumns of Master Lü* (*Lü shi chunqiu* 呂氏春秋, *c.* 239) of Lü Buwei 呂不韋. Other Masters texts are little concerned with divination, for example the titles in the *Yin–yang* group.

Prognostication is an important theme in Han dynasty *fu* 賦 poetry (rhymprose), and narratives of mantic failure are a significant theme in this genre. *Fu* draws on the lament tradition of the *Songs of Chu*

名家), Mohists (*Mo jia* 墨家), vertical and horizontal alliances (*Zongheng jia* 縱橫家), Miscellaneous (*Za jia* 雜家), the school of Shen Nong (*Shen Nong jia* 神農家), and Smaller Teachings (*Xiao Shuo* 小說). These classifications also appear in the postface to the *Shi ji* (130.3288–92). Discussion: K. Smith 2003, Csikszentmihalyi and Nylan 2003. Masters also became the third of the four headings of traditional Chinese bibliography (Classics, Histories, Masters, and [Literary] Collections). The contents of Masters texts spans a wide range of time and subject matter, from the Spring and Autumn period (the *Analects*) to the Eastern Han (Wang Chong). Most are effectively anthologies attributed to an eponymous author. Details of many can be found in ECTBG.

47 The term *Ru*, traditionally translated as "Confucian," has been reconsidered in recent years, in the light of increasing debate about the origins of a "Confucian" school. The term has also been translated as "classicist" (e.g. Nylan and Loewe 2010: esp. 4–5), though it could be objected that the term is too broad, and includes individuals who were in no sense members of a Confucian school. The question of the origins and identity of the Ru in early China is complex and controversial (Zufferey 1998 and 2003; Csikszentmihalyi 2004: 19–27). Guodian: *Guodian Chu mu zhu jian*. Shanghai: Ma Chengyuan et al. 2001–8.

48 Detailed discussion of these and other passages is reserved for later chapters.

(*Chu ci* 楚辭), which repeatedly laments the inadequacy of divination.[49] Accounts of failed divination resemble poems in the *Shi jing*, and continue what was clearly a powerful mode of remonstrance.[50] The theme of failed divination remains a subject for *fu* poetry long after the Han.

Many of the texts in the last three categories are no longer extant, but the titles listed give an indication of their concerns. Military Works includes a section titled *Yin–yang*, which mentions astrocalendric techniques, the use of mantic astrolabes (diviner's boards), and the consultation of spirits.[51] The listing of mantic texts in the Bibliographic Treatise is richest in the six sections of the fifth category, "Numbers and Techniques" (*Shushu*). It is here that we find the greatest number of what appear to be hermeneutic texts and collections of mantic records. Mantic texts are a significant lacuna in the transmitted textual record, and most of these titles are no longer extant, but some do have equivalents in excavated texts.[52]

The Celestial Patterns (*Tianwen* 天文) section concerned divination by the stars and weather phenomena such as clouds, mists, and *qi* configurations, as well as mapping of the constellations. They refer to stars, the *qi* of the sun, moon and stars, clouds and rain, various types of star divination, and the Twenty-eight Lunar Lodges (*xiu* 宿). A section titled Calendars and Chronologies (*Lipu* 歷譜) dealt with calendric computations and the movements of the heavenly bodies. Its titles refer to calendars, the movements of the heavens, moon, and stars, and methods of calculation. It also included astronomical calculations through gnomon shadow measurements, as well as genealogies and chronologies. The third section, *Wuxing* 五行 (Five Agents), dealt with *yin–yang* and *wuxing* divination, including portents, baleful omens (*zaiyi* 災異), hemerology, the winds, and divination by pitch pipes.[53] Titles in this group mention arts associated with recipe masters (*fangshi* 方士) and *fang* arts, such as Wind Horns (*Feng jiao* 風角),

49 Poems concerned with divination include the *Li sao* 離騷 ("Encountering Sorrow"), "Summoning the Soul" (*Zhao hun* 招魂), the Nine Songs (*Jiu ge* 九歌), "Great Director of Destinies" (*Da Si Ming* 大司命), and "Divination" (*Bu ju* 卜居). The *Li sao* is partially structured around two failed divinations, in which the consultor cannot get a mantic response (*Chu ci bu zhu*, 36–42 ("Li sao" 1), trans. Hawkes 1985: 75–77, lines 257–334). In "Summoning the Soul," the spirit medium Wu Yang 巫陽 tries unsuccessfully to perform both milfoil and dream divination on the narrator's behalf (*Chu ci bu zhu*, 197–98 ("Zhao hun" 9), Hawkes 1985: 224, lines 7–15).

50 For example, the *Shi jing* poem "Xiao min" 小旻 (Mao 195) begins: "Our turtle shells are exhausted but tell us no plans" 我龜既厭、不我告猶.

51 The first two include *Sunzi's Art of War* and the *Weiliaozi*, both actively hostile to prognostication in military matters. See Yates 1988: esp. 214–15, 231 and 2005.

52 See Li Ling 1993: 19–27; Kalinowski 2004: 225–28; Raphals 2008–9.

53 "Hemerology" refers to a variety of techniques used to determine auspicious and inauspicious times for different types of activity.

Dunjia 遁甲 (Hidden Stems or Hidden Cycles), and Orphans and Voids (*Guxu* 孤虛).[54] Other titles refer to methods for using mantic astrolabes (*shi* 式, also known as diviner's boards).[55] These topics are addressed in excavated texts and in the astronomical treatises of the *Han shu* and later standard histories.

The fourth section, Milfoil and Turtle Shells (*Shigui* 蓍龜), includes titles on turtle shell, milfoil, and *Yi* divination, including its use in guessing games.[56] This distinction suggests the existence of milfoil methods that did not use the *Yi* as a hermeneutic text. It is also noteworthy that the *Zhou yi* is placed in a different category than the *Yi jing*.

The Miscellaneous Divination (*Zazhan* 雜占) section begins with two titles on dream divination, the only reference to it in the Treatise. There follow texts on physiognomy, bird cries, anomalies (*bian guai* 變怪), prayers and exorcism (including prayers for rain or its absence), and agricultural applications of physiognomy. They are thus distinct in subject matter from the military physiognomy text that appeared earlier in the section and from additional physiognomy titles that appear in the next section.[57]

The Morphoscopy section (*Xingfa* 刑法) gives titles on topomancy and on state or military physiognomy.[58] Its three physiognomy titles – Physiognomizing People (*Xiang ren* 相人), Physiognomizing Precious Swords and Knives (*Xiang bao jian dao* 相寶劍刀), and Physiognomizing the Six Kinds of Domestic Animal (*Xiang liu xu* 相六畜) – suggest government, military, and agricultural uses of physiognomy, and indicate its practical and technical uses. Physiognomy could be used to assess

[54] *HHS* 82A.2703. Wind Horns used the eight directional winds to predict military victory or political prosperity. *Dunjia* (Hidden Stems or Hidden Cycles) and Orphans and Voids (*Guxu*) were mantic astrolabe techniques for avoiding inauspicious days. See Ngo Van Xuyet 1976: 23–27; DeWoskin 1983: 22–29, 43–45; and Ho Peng Yoke 2003: 83–112.

[55] *HS* 30.1769, *HSBZ* 30.72a, cf. *SJ* 6.251 and 28.1367.

[56] *HS* 30.1770–71; for example, Shooting Riddles by the Sui System of the Zhou Changes (*Zhou yi Sui qu she ni* 周易隨曲射匿) referred to the game of *shefu* 射覆, a guessing game. See *HSBZ* 30.73b.

[57] *HS* 30.1772–73. A few examples include: Wu Jin's Physiognomy of Clothing and Equipment (*Wu Jin xiang yi qi* 武禁相衣器); Miscellaneous Prognostications from Sneezing and Tinnitus (*Ti er ming za zhan* 嚏耳鳴雜占); Changes and Anomalies in Humans, Ghosts, Monsters, and the Six Domestic Animals (*Ren gui jing wu liuchu bian guai* 人鬼精物六畜變怪); Invoking Rain and Stopping Rain (*Qing yu zhi yu* 請雨止雨); Teachings of Shen Nong on Fields, Physiognomizing the Earth, and Cultivation (*Shen Nong jiao dian xiang tu gengzhong* 神農教田相土耕種); and Planting Trees, Storing Fruit, and Physiognomizing Silkworms (*Zhongshu zang guo xiang can* 種樹臧果相蠶).

[58] *HS* 30.1774. Topomancy titles address the three different contexts of natural geography, the reigning dynasty, and habitations. It includes the Classic of Mountains and Seas (*Shanhai jing* 山海經), the only title from the entire *Shushu* section extant in the received tradition.

the economic worth of objects (clothing, equipment, swords), animals (domestic animals, silkworms), and people. Excavated texts on physiognomy also emphasize these practical contexts, for example a text from Yinqueshan 銀雀山 (Linyi, Shandong, 140–111) on physiognomizing dogs, a Han sword physiognomy text from Juyan 居延, and a text on the physiognomy of horses from Mawangdui 馬王堆 (Changsha, Hunan, 168).

The Recipes and Methods (*Fangji*) category includes the *Huangdi neijing* (Inner Classic of the Yellow Lord, first century), the preeminent medical work from the Han and pre-Han periods.[59] It contains some materials on prognostication, for example instructions for medical prognostication based on the directional winds.[60] This category also includes the titles of medical works concerned with physical cultivation, health, and longevity.

History is not a category in the Bibliographic Treatise. The most authoritative genre of historical text comprised the standard histories. For the period under consideration these are the *Standard History of the [Western] Han* (*Han shu* 漢書) and *Standard History of the Later [Eastern] Han* (*Hou Han shu* 後漢書). Much of the formal template of the standard histories comes from the *Historical Records* (*Shi ji* 史記) of Sima Qian 司馬遷 (*c.* 145 or 135–86). In some cases, standard histories from later dynasties throw light on procedures or accounts that are fragmentary in manuscript sources.

Standard histories contain several kinds of text relevant to divination. Many are purported accounts of mantic activity in transmissions (especially in administrative contexts) and biographies. Some collected biographies are based on mantic expertise, for example the Collected Biographies of Diviners of Auspicious Days (*SJ* 127) and the Collected Biographies of Mantic Experts (*HHS* 82A).[61] The standard histories also contain technical treatises, which provide information on the use of astrocalendrics and pitch pipes for mantic purposes.

Several other important sources appear under the bibliographic rubric of history. The *Zuo zhuan* is the beginning of the historical narrative genre of "transmissions" (*zhuan* 傳), an important source for information on

59 It contained four sections: Medical Classics (*Yi jing* 醫經); Classical Recipes (*Jing fang* 經方) referring to *fangshi* texts; Sexual Arts (*Fang zhong* 房中); and Immortality Practices (*Shen xian* 神僊).

60 Sources of the *Huangdi neijing*: Yamada Keiji 1979: 67–89, Keegan 1988, Unschuld 2003.

61 *SJ* 128 contains an addendum to 127, attributed to Chu Shaosun 褚少孫 (*c.* 105–30), a near contemporary of Sima Qian. There are doubts about the authenticity of both *Shi ji* chapters. See Pokora 1987 and Schaab-Hanke 2003–4.

divination.[62] For example, the *Lives of Exemplary Women* (*Lienü zhuan* 列女傳) includes accounts of women as mantic practitioners, interpreters, and consultors not found elsewhere.[63] The rhetorical force of this text is the importance of female virtue to a ruler and a state, and prognostication is not contested territory. Although some accounts are of legendary women for whom we have little in the way of direct historical sources, its accounts of divination per se are not suspect.

Other compendia provide valuable information on divination, for example a new Eastern Han textual genre of "apocrypha" (*chen wei* 讖緯, literally "prophecy and weft").[64] The *Compendium on the Five Phases* (*Wuxing dayi* 五行大義) of Xiao Ji 蕭吉 (late sixth century CE) links Han mantic techniques with those of the Tang and later dynasties.[65] Ming and Qing compendia include biographies of mantic experts, organized by technique. For example, the Qing dynasty *Gujin tushu jicheng* 古今圖書集成 (Complete Collection of Past and Present Illustrations and Writings, 1726) classifies mantic practices under five headings, most of which date to the Eastern Zhou or Western Han.[66]

Material and manuscript sources

Material and manuscript sources (discovered rather than transmitted) provide additional information on mantic activity. It is immediately striking that they are found throughout China (Map 2.2 and Appendix 2.2), and are not restricted to any one area, though the greatest concentrations are in south China, in an area identified with the state of Chu (Map 2.3). Many of these tombs have been discovered through archaeological surveys undertaken as a legal requirement for construction. These tombs contain the oldest form of Chinese "book": texts written on silk or bound bamboo slips. These excavated texts have prompted a reconsideration of early Chinese history, especially since they do not reflect any process of official selection.

62 Closely related to the *Zuo zhuan* is the *Guo yu* or *Tales of the States*. It too contains many accounts of divination and is subject to many of the same interpretive problems as the *Zuo zhuan*. See ECTBG 263–68.

63 Dating and discussion: Raphals 1998a.

64 These texts probably date from the Western Han, but were collected and promulgated during the Eastern Han. Apocrypha: Zhong Zhaopeng 1993: 77–86.

65 The *Wuxing dayi* uses several numeric schemata to relate the Five Phases (*wuxing*) and their correlates to the sexagenary cycle, *yin* and *yang*, the trigrams of the *Yi jing*, etc. Translation and commentary: Kalinowski 1991.

66 Turtle and Milfoil, Astrology (*xingming* 星命), Physiognomy (*xiangshu* 相術), Geomancy (*kanyu* 堪輿, literally canopy of heaven and chariot of earth), and Numbers and Techniques (*shushu*). See *Qin ding gu jin tu shu ji cheng* 47.5681–7854 (Yishu), cf. R. J. Smith 1991: 262–63, 290 n. 6.

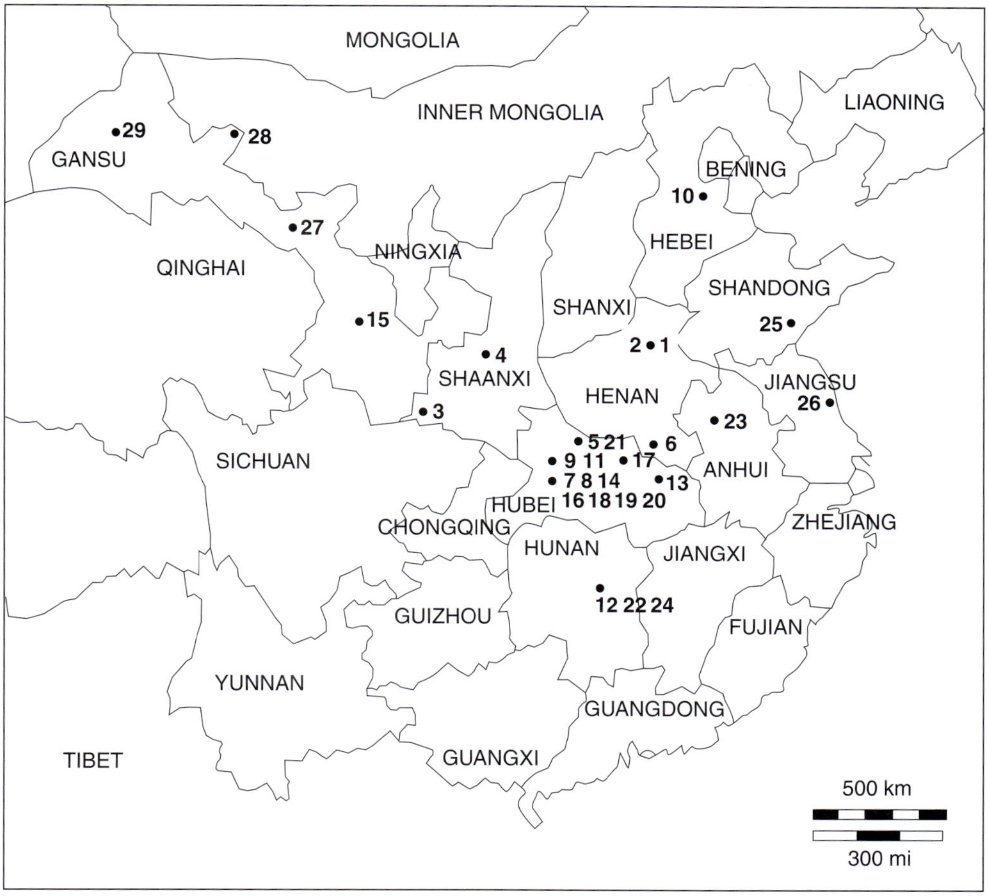

1. Xiaotun 小屯 (Anyang 安陽, Henan)
2. Sipanmo 四盤磨
3. Qishan 岐山 (Shaanxi)
4. Zhangjiapo 張家坡 (Xi'an, Shaanxi)
5. Leigudun 擂鼓墩 (Suizhou 隨州, Hubei)
6. Caigeling 蔡葛陵 (Xinxian, Henan)
7. Tianxingguan 天星觀 (Jiangling, Hubei)
8. Yutaishan 雨臺山 (Jiangling, Hubei)
9. Baoshan 包山 (Jingmen, Hubei)
10. Zhongshan 中山 (Pingshan, Hebei)
11. Guodian 郭店 (Jingmen, Hubei)
12. Chu Silk MS (Zidanku 子彈庫, Changsha)
13. Wangshan 望山 (Hubei)
14. Jiudian 九店 (Jiangling, Hubei)
15. Fangmatan 放馬灘 (Tianshui, Gansu)
16. Wangjiatai 王家台 (Jiangling, Hubei)
17. Shuihudi 睡虎地 (Yunmeng, Hubei)
18. Zhoujiatai 周家台 (Guanju, Shashi, Hubei)
19. Zhangjiashan 張家山 (Jiangling, Hubei)
20. Fenghuangshan 鳳凰山 (Jiangling, Hubei)
21. Kongjiapo 孔加坡 (Suizhou, Hubei)
22. Mawangdui 馬王堆 (Changsha, Hunan)
23. Shuanggudui 雙古堆 (Fuyang, Anhui)
24. Huxishan 虎溪山 (Yuanling, Hunan)
25. Yinqueshan 銀雀山 (Shandong)
26. Yinwan 尹灣 (Liangyungang, Jiangsu)
27. Mozuizi 磨嘴子 (Wuwei, Gansu)
28. Juyan 居延 (Gansu)
29. Dunhuang 敦煌 (Gansu)

Map 2.2 Chinese archaeological sites for mantic materials.

5. Leigudun 擂鼓墩 (Suizhou 隨州, Hubei)
7. Tianxingguan 天星觀 (Jiangling, Hubei)
8. Yutaishan 雨臺山 (Jiangling, Hubei)
9. Baoshan 包山 (Jingmen, Hubei)
11 Guodian 郭店 (Jingmen, Hubei)
12 Chu Silk MS (Zidanku 子彈庫, Changsha)
13 Wangshan 望山 (Hubei)
14 Jiudian 九店 (Jiangling, Hubei)
16 Wangjiatai 王家台 (Jiangling, Hubei)
17 Shuihudi 睡虎地 (Yunmeng, Hubei)
18 Zhoujiatai 周家台 (Guanju, Shashi, Hubei)
19 Zhangjiashan 張 Wangjiatai 王家台 (Jiangling, Hubei)
20 Fenghuangshan 鳳凰山 (Jiangling, Hubei)
21 Kongjiapo 孔加坡 (Suizhou, Hubei)
22 Mawangdui 馬王堆 (Changsha, Hunan)
23 Shuanggudui 雙古堆 (Fuyang, Anhui)
24 Huxishan 虎溪山 (Yuanling, Hunan)

Map 2.3 Detail of Chu sites.

Many concern divination in various aspects. Other relevant excavated objects include astronomical instruments, dice and other materials used in divination, and objects bearing decorative motifs of mantic significance.

The oldest divination records are the Shang oracle bone inscriptions (*jiaguwen* 甲骨文) from Anyang (Henan). First discovered in 1898 by villagers in Xiaotun 小屯 near Anyang in north Henan province, they were sold as "dragon bones" (*longgu* 龍骨), a traditional ingredient in Chinese medicine. In 1899 the paleographer Wang Yirong 王懿榮 (1845–1900) discovered that bones purchased as part of a medical prescription were inscribed with ancient writing. They are the most ancient Chinese writing known today. Official excavations were conducted in Xiaotun from 1928 through 1937 under the auspices of the newly formed Academia Sinica. In 1936 a pit was discovered containing some 17,000 pieces of inscribed turtle plastrons. (In 1937, the Japanese invasion of China forced the evacuation of the site.) Since then, some 200,000 oracle bone inscriptions on bones and turtle shells have been reproduced and published.[67] Most are from Anyang, and date from the reigns of the last nine Shang kings, but oracle bones have been unearthed throughout China. The inscriptions reflected the concerns of the Shang and Western Zhou courts. Modern scholars have classified them into five periods on the basis of preferred topics, styles of formulating questions, calligraphy, and other considerations.[68] They are artifacts of divination by bones (osteomancy) that had been "cracked" by the application of heat (pyromancy). The crack could then be interpreted as the answer to a query. Inscriptions on the bones record the time, personnel, query, result, and, at times, verification of the prognostication. The largest collection is the *Jiaguwen heji*, a thirteen-volume collection edited by Guo Moruo and Hu Houxuan.[69] Additional finds from the 1950s, 1970s, and 1980s include "cracked" but uninscribed Shang bones and shells and inscribed bones and shells from the Western and Eastern Zhou, discovered in Henan and Shandong. Some bear distinctive numerical inscriptions; they are of both late Shang and Western Zhou provenance, and have been found at Sipanmo 四盤磨 (Anyang, Henan) and at Qishan 岐山 (Shaanxi, the so-called Zhouyuan oracle bones).

67 For this story and its variants see Allan 1991: 1 and 177 n. 1. Excavation: Bagley in Loewe and Shaughnessy 1999: esp. 126–31; oracle bone inscriptions: Keightley 1999b.

68 The last nine Shang kings were Wu Ding 武丁 (1324–1265) through Di Xin 帝辛 (d. *c.* 1045). Periods: Period 1 (to 1180), Period 2 (1180–1151), Period 3 (1150–??), Period 4 (??–1106), Period 5 (1105–1045). See Keightley 1997: 18.

69 Guo Moruo and Hu Houxuan 1978–82, cited by *Heji* number. The other major collection is Yao Xiaosui and Xiao Ding's *Xiaotun nan di jiagu* (1985), cited with the prefix T.

Most Warring States sites are in south China in the area of present-day Wuhan. The tomb of Marquis Yi of Zeng (Zeng Hou Yi 曾侯乙) at Leigudun 擂鼓墩 (Suizhou 隨州, Hubei, *c.* 433) contains the oldest known representation of the stars surrounding the North Pole or Dipper. This was the area of the sky that was most important for later hemerology.[70]

Mid- and late fourth-century Warring States tombs contain records of prognostications on behalf of the tombs' occupants and boards for playing the game *liubo* 六博, which was probably also used for divination. The oldest records are from Tianxingguan 天星觀 (Jiangling, Hubei, *c.* 340), which also contained a *liubo* board.[71] (These sites are described in more detail in Appendix 2.2.) A very well-preserved *liubo* board was also excavated from Yutaishan 雨臺山 (Jiangling, Hubei), which also contained the oldest known set of pitch pipes, made of nodeless bamboo. It is not known whether they were used for divination. A late fourth-century board was found in the tomb of King Cuo of Zhongshan (Pingshan, Hebei, d. 313). It is unusual for its carving in softer stone, and for its elaborate compositions of interlacing snakes.[72]

A set of extensive and well-preserved prognostication records was recovered from Baoshan 包山 (Jingmen, Hubei, *c.* 316). The tomb was discovered in the village of Wangchangcun at Baoshan Hill in April 1986 by archaeologists working in conjunction with the construction of the Jingmen–Shashi railroad, in an area rich in Chu burial sites. The tomb contained inscribed bamboo slips recording grave inventory lists, legal or administrative documents, and prognostications over the last three years of the life of the tomb's occupant, a high official of the state of Chu. A slightly later site, Wangshan 望山 (Hubei, *c.* 309–278), also contains prognostications on behalf of the tomb's occupant.[73]

A second type of mantic text first recovered from tombs are "daybooks" (*rishu*), and other hemerological texts that provided guidance for selecting auspicious times for a range of activities. The oldest known hemerological text, the Chu Silk Manuscript from Zidanku, Changsha (*Changsha Zidanku Chu boshu* 長沙子彈庫楚帛書, *c.* 300, discussed in Chapter 9), is not strictly a

[70] Tomb reports: Wang Jianmin and Liang Zhu 1979: 41 and *Zenghou Yi mu* in Tan Weisi 2003.

[71] "Jiangling Tianxingguan yihao Chu mu" in *Kaogu xuebao* 1982.1:71–116, esp. 109–10. According to the archaeological reports, the tomb contained bamboo slips with over 2,700 characters, most concerned with "Year" and "Illness" divinations (discussed in Chapters 4 and 9), as well as queries about change of residence. Tianxingguan Tomb 2: *WW* 2001.9: 4–21, *Jingzhou Tianxingguan erhao Chu mu* 2003.

[72] Yutaishan: *Jiangling Yutaishan Chu mu* 1984: 103–4.

[73] Baoshan archaeological report: *Baoshan Chu mu* 1991; transcription: *Baoshan Chu jian* 1991 (*Baoshan*). Wangshan: *Jiangling Wangshan sha zhong Chu mu* 1996 (*Wangshan*). Of the 167 slips transcribed, about a third are fragmentary and contain only a brief phrase.

daybook. The oldest extant daybooks have been found at Jiudian 九店 (Jiangling, Hubei, *c.* 330–270) and Fangmatan 放馬灘 (Tianshui, Gansu, *c.* 230–220). A third type comprises four early versions of the *Zhou yi*. The oldest is part of a trove of 1,200 bamboo slips in Chu script from a Warring States tomb, purchased in Hong Kong by the Shanghai Museum in 1994. The tomb had been looted and extensively damaged, and the texts are still being published.[74]

A significant number of Qin and Han tombs contain texts and instruments of increasing sophistication. The major Qin sites are Shuihudi 睡虎地 (Yunmeng 雲夢, Hubei, 217), Wangjiatai 王家台 (Jiangling 江陵, Hubei, 278–207), and Zhoujiatai 周家台 (Guanju 關沮, Hubei, 213–209). The Shuihudi tombs contain two sets of well-preserved daybooks comprising some 425 slips, as well as two *liubo* sets, each containing six counting rods. The Wangjiatai tomb is unusual for the variety of materials it contains, including a version of the *Guicang Yi* text, other hexagram texts (divinatory texts that collected groups of hexagrams together under summary headings, discussed below), daybooks, a mantic astrolabe, and dice. Daybooks and boards for playing the game of *liubo*, which was also used in divination, have been excavated from Zhoujiatai (discovered in 1993), as well as an illustrated text that discusses the use of the mantic astrolabe.[75]

Eastern Han tombs also contain a variety of mantic material, including hexagram texts, mantic astrolabes of several kinds (discussed in Chapter 5), and *liubo* boards. A second-century site at Yinqueshan contained calendric texts and fragmentary materials on *yin–yang* and wind divination. Many of the Yinqueshan slips were in poor condition and they have been grouped into texts by the editors. Another site at Zhangjiashan 張家山 (Jiangling, Hubei, 186) has yielded legal texts that include instructions for the appointment of diviners. A *liubo* set has been excavated from Fenghuangshan 鳳凰山 (Jiangling, Hubei, *c.* 179–141), along with six counting rods and an eighteen-sided die marked with numbers. A diagram of the divinatory uses of a *liubo* board has been excavated from a Han site at Yinwan 尹灣 (Jiangsu 江蘇, 15–10).[76]

But by far the most important Western Han excavation comes from Mawangdui (Changsha, Hunan, 168 BCE). This tomb is best known for two

74 Ma Chengyuan et al. 2001–8. The others are from Wangjiatai, Fuyang, and Mawangdui. They are discussed in detail in Chapter 9.

75 Initial publication and archaeological reports: Shuihudi: *Yunmeng Shuihudi Qin mu* 1981; transcription of texts: *Shuihudi Qin mu zhujian* 1990 (*SHD*). Wangjiatai: *WW* 1995.1: 37–43; Zhoujiatai: *WW* 1999.6: 26–32 and 42–47.

76 Yinqueshan: Transcribed in Wu Jiulong 1985. Zhangjiashan: *Zhangjiashan Han mu zhujian* 2001 (*ZJS*). Fenghuangshan: *WW* 1974.6: 50–51. Yinwan: *Yinwan Han mu jiandu* 1977 (*Yinwan*).

versions of the *Daodejing* and an important trove of medical texts written on silk. However, the Mawangdui tombs also contained an early version of the *Zhou yi*, important charts and diagrams on cloud divination and physiognomy, and a *liubo* set.[77] Another early version of the *Zhou yi* was excavated from Shuanggudui 雙古堆 (Fuyang 阜陽, Anhui, 165). In addition to the so-called Fuyang *Zhou yi*, this tomb contained a text on physiognomy, daybooks, and other hemerological texts and divination instruments. Other hemerological materials have been excavated from a Western Han tomb at Mozuizi 磨嘴子 (Wuwei 武威, Gansu, first century CE).[78]

Indirect material evidence

The oldest material evidence are bones and plastrons used for pyromancy. There is also archaeological evidence of pyromancy without written records, including 300 inscribed and 17,000 non-inscribed Shang-Zhou fragments excavated from Shaanxi and eight Shang plastrons from Daxinzhuang 大辛莊, Shandong.[79] Other non-inscribed oracle bones have been excavated from the areas of present-day Chongqing, Chengdu, and the Three Gorges. The importance of these finds is their clear geographic and cultural distance from the Shang or Zhou courts of north China. Non-inscribed turtle plastrons have been excavated from a salt production site at Zhongba 中壩 (Zhongxian 忠線) near present-day Chongqing. This area was culturally separate from the Shang court at Anyang, but was a tribute source for turtles. The Zhongba materials contain 453 divination marks, each presumably a query.[80] To these we can add mantic astrolabes, *liubo* boards, dice, and divining rods.

Warring States and Han tombs have also yielded non-textual evidence that, carefully used, may provide further context for mantic procedures or the assumptions behind them. For example, a lacquer clothing case from the tomb of Marquis Yi of Zeng clearly shows the Dipper (*Beidou* 北斗) surrounded by the Twenty-eight Lunar Lodges. Warring States and Han artifacts display designs such as the so-called "cord and hook" pattern and the "TLV" motif found on *liubo* boards and bronze mirrors.[81] Other tombs contained

[77] Mawangdui original reports: Tomb 1: *Changsha Mawangdui yi hao Han mu* 1973. Tombs 2 and 3: *WW* 1974.7: 39–48; *Kaogu* 1975.1: 47–61, *Changsha Mawangdui er, san hao Han mu* 2004. Tomb 3: Fu Juyou and Chen Songchang 1992. Transcription: *Mawangdui Han mu boshu* 1980– (*MWD*).

[78] Shuanggudui: Wang Xiangtian and Han Ziqiang 1978; Hu Pingsheng 1998. Wuwei: *Wuwei Han jian* 1964.

[79] See Bagley 2004: 199–200. Shaanxi fragments: Qiu Xigui 2000: 68–69. Daxinzhuang: *Kaogu* 2003.6: 3–6.

[80] For photographs and descriptions of the marks see Flad 2004: 746–65.

[81] Bronze mirrors first became common in Warring States tombs and have been excavated from tombs as late as the Tang. The cord and hook pattern and TLV motif are discussed in Chapter 9.

divinatory charts or diagrams that connected visual patterns with mantic procedures, for example the Chu Silk Manuscript from Changsha, Hunan (*c.* 300), an illustrated text on the use of the mantic astrolabe from Zhoujiatai, and several diagrams from Mawangdui. One, a text titled "Miscellaneous Prognostications by Celestial Patterns and Qi Images" (*Tianwen qixiang zazhan*) by modern editors, illustrates objects visible in the sky that were influenced by *qi* and had mantic significance, including clouds, stars, constellations, and what is probably the oldest representation of comets. (The twenty-nine entries on comets include the comet's name, accounts of its appearance, and general prognostications about likely events, especially military prognostications.)[82] There is also a diagram for predicting a newborn child's fortune. (The Shuihudi daybooks include a similar diagram in a better state of preservation, discussed in Chapters 6 and 9.)

Sources compared

The foregoing review of Chinese and Greek textual and material evidence allows us to begin to compare sources for four kinds of text: (1) narrative accounts of divination, (2) mantic texts, either hermeneutic guides or technical treatises on other aspects of mantic expertise, (3) procedures and methods, including prescriptive texts for the correct performance of sacrifices and other rituals and administrative and legal texts, and (4) records of mantic queries.

Narratives

Nominally historical anecdotes about divination provide some parity between Greek and Chinese sources. Yet neither Chinese nor Greek "historical" accounts of divination can be read as transparent elements in a history of divination. Both must be considered as literary narratives, with their own goals and perspectives (discussed in Chapter 8). In both traditions there is a wealth of such accounts, but both contexts offer similar grounds for caution. First, Greek and Chinese sources contain many accounts of mantic consultation by states or elites, but accounts of private consultation, especially by commoners, are few and far between.

Second, if Greek and Chinese mantic narratives are colored by the aims of their authors, we can usefully compare those aims, but with several cautions in mind. One is the important differences between authors within each tradition, for example the very different treatments of divination and oracles

[82] See "The Han View of Comets" in Loewe 1994: esp. 61–67.

by Herodotus, Thucydides, and Xenophon, or the very different accounts of mantic activity selected for inclusion in Han histories by Sima Qian in the *Shi ji* and Ban Gu 班固 (32–92 CE) in the *Han shu*. For example, the *Han shu* does not include the *Shi ji*'s long account of the marketplace diviner Sima Jizhu (discussed in Chapter 4).

Third, in reading Chinese and Greek historical accounts, it is possible and important to distinguish evidence for the historicity of particular divinations from evidence for attitudes toward divination and prediction. Historically problematic accounts remain important evidence for: (1) attitudes toward mantic activity, (2) descriptions of mantic procedures and the circumstances of consultation, and (3) what topics were considered appropriate for mantic consultation. For example, passages that are widely believed to be interpolated, such as many *Zuo zhuan* accounts of *Yi jing* divination and accounts of oracular consultation in Herodotus, would only be credible or rhetorically useful if they portrayed incidents that were believable to contemporary audiences of those texts.

Fourth, texts where divination is not a central concern may present more reliable information. Narratives in which divination accounts are "loaded" as signposts of character (of individuals) or where predictions (usually fulfilled) advance the purposes of the narrative must be viewed with particular caution. At the same time, divination narratives only "work" to the extent that they are credible to their intended audience. In this sense, such narratives in both traditions present valuable information on attitudes toward oracles.

Mantic texts

Mantic texts allow a (usually) skilled interpreter to offer guidance to consultors. Here the Chinese evidence is far richer than the Greek. While there are abundant descriptive accounts of individual mantic interpretations, and a few late texts on physiognomy and dream interpretation, I know of no Greek text on the interpretation of mantic signs, though there are passing references to Greek *manteis* who owned "books" that may have provided some systematic information.

By contrast, three distinct kinds of Chinese mantic text occur in both the received tradition and in excavated texts. Most important is the *Zhou yi*, the divinatory core of the *Yi jing*.

A second type of mantic text falls under the broad rubric of almanacs. In the strict sense, an almanac is a text that presents monthly sections that give the locations of each planet in the zodiac throughout the year.[83] However, the term can be more generally used to refer to systems that combine cosmological and calendric principles. In the received tradition we find Monthly Ordinances (*Yue ling* 月令). These texts prescribe particular activities for the months of the year. They appear in the late Warring States and Western Han as chapters in the *Guanzi*, *Lüshi chunqiu*, and *Huainanzi*. During the Eastern Han, they were incorporated into the *Li ji* and thereby raised to the status of state ritual.[84] They also appear in excavated texts. A text from Yinqueshan titled "Prohibitions" (*Jin* 禁) provides seasonal prohibitions linked to the calendar and four of the Five Agents (*wuxing*). Broadly almanac texts also have been excavated from Warring States, Qin, and Han tombs. The oldest is a calendric diagram known as the Chu Silk Manuscript, excavated from a tomb near Changsha, Hunan and dated to about 300.

Finally, daybooks have been excavated from some twenty tombs.[85] (Most recently, daybook material and other mantic manuscripts are among the bamboo slips purchased by Peking University.) Daybooks are not almanacs in the strict sense because they are not organized around systematic coverage of the days of the calendar. Daybook contents are of two kinds, and some do cover the entire calendar. One type is represented by the *jianchu* 建除 system (discussed in Chapter 9), which classifies all the days of the year according to the Twelve Earth Branches and gives auspices for each (which change with each month). In this sense, the *jianchu* system does cover the whole calendar year.[86] Although daybooks are not systematic in their treatment of the calendar, they attempt a theoretical account of time insofar as they present cycles of day types. They organize time into types of day, but never refer to any actual days or particular consultation.

The daybooks also contain texts arranged by topic. These offer information on auspicious times for such activities as travel, marriage, building a house, hunting, business, etc. They could also be used to avoid inauspicious

[83] E.g. Rochberg 2004: 153. The *Oxford English Dictionary* defines an almanac as an annual table or book of tables with a monthly calendar of days, with astronomical data and astrological and astrometeorological forecasts. Modern almanacs also contain calculations, anniversaries, and other useful information.

[84] *HNZ* 5 (*Shixiun*), trans. Major 1993: 217–68; *LJ* 14 and 15, trans. Legge 1885: 1.249–310, Couvreur 1.330–411. Cf. Bodde 1975: 16 and Loewe 1994: 184, 223–24, 228.

[85] Summarized in Kalinowski 2010: 353–59, appendix 1. Full information regarding the mantic manuscripts now in the possession of Peking University was not available while this book was under preparation and in press. Preliminary reports: *WW* 2011.6, Li Ling 2011.

[86] Different daybooks use different calendric principles, including the sexagenary cycle of Ten Heaven Stems and Twelve Earth Branches (*ganzhi* 干支), the so-called *jianchu* 建除 (Establishment and Removal) series, and cycles of "Sanctions and Virtues" (*xingde* 刑德).

situations, such as vulnerability to robbery or illness. In addition to entire texts organized around mantic techniques, less systematic passages appear both in excavated texts and in the received tradition. For example, the texts excavated from Mawangdui include a fragmentary text on cloud divination that correlates the cloud images of animals (pig, horse, ox, etc.) with military prognostications. There is also a fragmentary text on horse physiognomy.

A third type of Chinese mantic text are technical treatises, which discuss prognostication in specialized contexts such as astronomy, the observation of winds, clouds, and other subcelestial phenomena, physiognomy, and medicine. Technical treatises first appear in the *Shi ji*, which describes them as *shu* 書 or documents; most important for present purposes are the Treatises on the Pitch Pipes, the Calendar, and the Offices of Heaven (*SJ* 25–27).[87] The Treatise on the Pitch Pipes contains detailed discussions of the use of pitch pipes and the interpretation of clouds and winds. The Treatise on the Calendar describes the legendary history of the invention of the calendar, and more technical aspects of calendrics, including a set of notations for the years 104 to 29 BCE. (These must have been added after Sima Qian's time, since the *Shi ji* was completed by about 90 BCE.) The Treatise on the Offices of Heaven has several sections on prognostication by the sun, moon (including eclipses of both), various stars, and clouds and mists, as well as prognostications about harvests.[88] Technical treatises also appear in the first two standard histories: the *Han shu* and *Hou Han shu*, which describe them as *zhi* 志. *Han shu* treatises include chapters on the Pitch Pipes, the Calendar, the Patterns of Heaven, Five Agents (*wuxing*), and the Bibliographic Treatise.[89] The treatises in the *Hou Han shu* – the *Xu Han zhi* 續漢志 – appear after the collected biographies, and were compiled by Sima Biao 司馬彪 (*c.* 240–*c.* 306 CE, rather than Fan Ye). They include treatises on the Pitch Pipes, the Calendar, the Patterns of Heaven, and Five Phases (*wuxing*).[90]

The treatises are also important for records of the observation of astronomical or subcelestial anomalies. These are not divination records in that no

[87] *SJ* 25.1239–54 (*Lü shu* 律書), Chavannes 3.293–319, cf. Needham and Wang Ling 1962: 173–75; *SJ* 26.1255–88 (*Li shu* 曆書), Chavannes 3.320–38; *SJ* 27.1331–42 (*Tianguan shu* 天官書), Chavannes 3.339–412.

[88] Questions have been raised about the authenticity of the treatises on the pitch pipes and calendar, but they are not relevant to the present inquiry. Both have been attributed to Chu Shaosun. It has been claimed that the pitch pipes treatise may have been a replacement for a lost military treatise (Chavannes 1.ccv–ccvii), and the dates of the calendar treatise are fifty years past Sima Qian's lifetime (Chavannes 3.293 n. 1 and 332 n. 4).

[89] *HS* 21.955–1026 (*Lüli zhi* 律曆志 parts 1 and 2), 26.1273–1314 (*Tianwen zhi* 天文志), 27.1315–50 (*Wuxing zhi* 五行志), 30.1701–84 (*Yiwen zhi*).

[90] *HHS*: *Lüli zhi* (zhi 1–3), 2999–3100; *Tianwen zhi* (zhi 10–12), 3213–64; *Wuxing zhi* (zhi 13–18), 3265–3384.

divination was performed, but the results of these observations became objects of mantic interpretation. These events included eclipses, falling stars, comets, and terrestrial phenomena such as floods and drought. They also included terrestrial anomalies such as locusts and abnormal births, etc. Accounts of them appear in the Patterns of Heaven and *Wuxing* treatises, where they are arranged by topic and chronologically. They are most detailed in the Patterns of Heaven chapters (*Shi ji* 27, *Han shu* 26), and include falling stars, irregular movement of planets, obscurity of the sun or the moon, and unusual cloud formations. The *Wuxing* treatises are concerned with the reportage of terrestrial omens and portents. The authorship and authenticity of the accounts in both standard histories are firmly attributed, but interpretive problems remain, in part because of the intensely political character of Han astronomy. Accounts of anomalies also appear in Annals (*benji*, chapters 1–12), where they are recorded in chronological order, along with political information. Here there are important differences between the Annals chapters of the *Shi ji* and *Han shu*. Although they cover parallel periods, the *Han shu* reports many more anomalies than does the *Shi ji*.[91]

Finally, instructions for medical prognostication based on the directional winds appear in several of the *Taisu* chapters of the *Huangdi neijing*.[92] They link seasonal winds and diseases associated with them to transits of the star god Taiyi. Other passages contain fragmentary instructions for interpreting divinatory dreams, for example a brief typology in the *Zhou li*.

Of this diverse literature, only calendric texts have any Greek equivalent, and that a slight one.

Procedures and methods

As with mantic texts, Greek accounts of mantic procedures are late, few, and unsystematic. They can be considered under three headings: accounts of the origin of mantic gifts, oracular procedures, and prescriptive texts. Beginning with Homer, the *mantis* appears as a ruler or priest gifted with prophetic wisdom or as a military commander or professional diviner from a lineage of diviners. Accounts of legendary *manteis* such as Tiresias and Mopsus include their lineages and descriptions of how they acquired their gifts. There is no account of their training, and their activities resist easy classification.

An even more glaring silence is our ignorance of oracular procedures, especially at Delphi. Plutarch provides some information about procedures in his own time. Documentary evidence attests to detailed procedures for

[91] Eberhard 1957: 42. [92] *Lingshu* 43, 58, and 77, *Suwen* 3, 4, 17, 35, 42, all discussed in Chapter 9.

the management of consultation (such as *promanteia*) and the procedures by which an official envoy (*theōros*) delivered a Delphic oracle to his home state. There are many literary accounts of the procedures of the Pythia, but no archaeological evidence to back them up, and the lacuna has created a veritable industry of explanation. Prescriptive knowledge on mantic activity clearly existed, whether in the management of oracular consultation or in sacrificial procedures used by military *manteis*, but it has not been transmitted in extant texts. An exception is the Greek magical papyri, which do give detailed instructions for mantic procedures, including preparations, purification rituals, sacrifices, and spells to be recited.

If Greek procedural texts are a famine, Chinese accounts of mantic procedures are a feast, even if we ignore the procedures of contemporary practitioners. Chinese procedures and methods include instructions for the selection of auspicious times for ritual activities, how or when to perform divination rituals, what sacrifices to make and to whom, and what method to use. There are also guides for the selection and training of personnel. Ritual texts such as the *Li ji* and *Yi li* give detailed and comprehensive accounts of procedures and methods. By contrast, excavated texts mention such matters only in passing.

The notion of good and ill auspice, that certain times were propitious or ill-omened for certain activities, was central to Chinese mantic activity and many aspects of ritual.[93] Prognostication was used to select auspicious times for state activities, such as sacrifice, warfare, royal marriages, and beginning the construction of a new palace or capital. It was also used for family matters, such as marriages, funerals, and changes of residence. Excavated texts also underscore the ritual character of many government activities, including the daily functioning of court, law cases, and administration (and determining auspicious times to conduct them). Warfare was also considered a ritual activity; divination determined an auspicious time to initiate military activity and also sought to gauge its chances of success.

Different kinds of procedural text regulated these activities. Monthly Ordinances prescribed appropriate times for state activities, and daybooks were implicitly prescriptive. Other texts specified the choice of method for particular circumstances. The *Li ji* and *Yi li* (and to a lesser extent, the *Zhou li*) prescribe methods for particular types of question. They authorize the combined and often complementary use of turtle and milfoil for family matters such as marriages and funerals, and for matters of state. Prognostication records from Baoshan, Tianxingguan, and Wangshan included instructions for sacrifice, including detailed lists of the divinities and ancestors who should

[93] Chinese and Greek notions of good and ill auspice are compared in Chapter 9.

receive it and the quantity and even color of the sacrificial animals, typically pigs, cows, sheep, and goats. Finally, procedural directions appear in legal statutes: in the *Han shu* and in legal statutes from Shuihudi and Zhangjiashan.

Notions of good and ill auspice were also central to some areas of Greek mantic practice, but with different significance. *Manteis* especially used bird divination and hieroscopy to determine good or ill auspices for planned events. (These notions were less central to oracular divination.) But an important difference between Chinese and Greek notions of good and ill auspice was that the former were closely linked to cosmic models and regular cycles of time, whereas the latter were understood as the goodwill of the gods. In this sense, the former were closely linked to prediction in ways the latter were not. (This issue is discussed at length in Chapter 9.)

Divination records

The final grouping to consider is records of divinations, either deliberately assembled or collected ex post facto. However, it is not easy to establish the purpose of records or collections of mantic queries in either tradition. As Rosalind Thomas has pointed out, Greek texts were created for a wide range of purposes, and documentary practices varied in what was written down, how it was arranged, and how used.[94]

Collections of Greek mantic records are few and far between. In particular, we do not find records or archives at oracular sanctuaries. Although inscriptions have survived at Dodona, Didyma, and Epidaurus, in each case there are difficulties in describing these materials as deliberately compiled records or archives. The Dodona tablets record questions but not answers, which were presumably given to the consultors. Both sides of many tablets are inscribed, some seem to have been reused, and others are in poor condition. Not all are complete or legible, and the dating of many of the inscriptions is problematic. In short, there is little evidence to suggest a deliberate collection. The four surviving stelae at the temple of Asclepius at Epidaurus (late fourth century) present a different problem. They record cures ostensibly performed at the temple for illnesses such as blindness, parasites, paralysis, and failure to become pregnant. Although individual inscribed accounts of cures at healing sanctuaries are common, collected testimonies are unique to sanctuaries of Asclepius. But the veracity of these accounts is open to question. They conspicuously record successful cures,

[94] R. Thomas 1992: 93–94. For example, Sparta kept few records, whereas under the Athenian democracy inscriptional records proliferated extravagantly.

and effectively advertise the powers of Asclepius. In a few cases they record punishments meted out to those who did not pay the temple fees. Rhodes and Osborne's commentary to one of the stelae points out that the ordering of the cures is not random. Their rhetorical effect is to link prospects for cure with moral uprightness and faith in Asclepius. So they too cannot be considered a systematic record or archive.[95] There are other collections of cures at Asclepain sanctuaries at Lebena (near Gortyn in Crete) and on Tiber island at Rome. Of some fifty known consultations at Didyma, fewer than half are from inscriptional sources.[96] These too are not systematic and show no evidence of deliberate compilation. Nor is there evidence of Delphi attempting to maintain archives in any sense.

Did state consultors preserve records or archives? We know that consultors generally preserved responses in their own locales. Herodotus refers to collections of oracles at Athens and elsewhere. One foretold that the Spartans would be injured by the Athenians. According to Herodotus, it was brought to Sparta by Cleomenes from the acropolis at Athens and had previously been in the possession of the Pisistratids. Hugh Bowden has argued that oracles were consulted regularly by the Athenian Assembly, both for direction in the appropriate performance of sacrifice, and for political purposes.[97] However, many references to discussion of oracles refer to one or several prophecies, not to an explicit collection of them.

A third possible source is the oracle collections of chresmologues or "oracle interpreters." According to Plato (*Rep.* 364e): "They hold in readiness a din (ὅμαδον) of books of Musaeus and Orpheus, the offspring of the Moon and of the Muses, as they say, and go about their sacrifices according to them [these books]." Herodotus mentions two such "collectors." Onomacritus of Athens was associated with the oracles of Musaeus, and Herodotus (7.6.3) reports that he was exiled for attempting to interpolate an oracle into that collection. Antichares of Eleon was associated with oracles of Laius (5.43.1).

Chinese divination records are from three major sources: Shang and Western Zhou oracle bone inscriptions and prognostication records excavated from Warring States tombs. The oracle bone inscriptions are widely described as archives, but there are unresolved questions whether the term is apt. David Keightley has argued that several problems complicate this view. The bones are secondary rather than primary sources, presumably

95 Stelae: *SEG*^{3} 1168, *IG* 4^2, 1 121; Herzog 1931: 8–16; EE no. 423, RO no. 102. Pausanias (2.27.3) records that six stelae survived in his time and that more had existed in the past.

96 *IC* 1.17.8–12; *IGUR* 1.148; Fontenrose 1978: 417–29.

97 Athens: Hdt. 5.90.2, cf. 5.92B.3. He also describes two oracles of Bacis (8.77.1–2, 9.43.2). Bowden 2003: esp. 264–70.

derived from some kind of "diviners' notebooks" or intermediate recording that has not survived. Some burials were clearly storage pits that had been converted to caches for oracle bones, possibly set up in a way that prevented consultation of older layers of inscribed material.[98] All this suggests that the oracle bone inscriptions may not have been intended as documents in the modern sense of an archive intended for ongoing consultation. The distinction is an important one. Keightley argues that the bones were not buried with any intent of retrieval, and therefore resists the tendency to describe them as archives.[99] He speculates that the bones may have "lost" their efficacy after a certain period, possibly after the death of the king on whose behalf the divinations were performed. At that point a "used" archive may have been disposed of by burial.

Warring States tombs from Baoshan, Tianxingguan, and Wangshan contain records of prognostications performed on behalf of the tombs' occupants. They have no equivalent in the received textual tradition. They use formulaic language and attempt to predict success over a given year, or address presumably unexpected health problems. The most extensive are from Baoshan. There are many unanswered questions about these records. We do not know why they were placed in the tomb, and can only speculate from what records they were copied, and by whom. They clearly were not intended for ongoing consultation by the living. Nonetheless we may be tempted to consider them archives insofar as they were deliberately assembled collections of mantic queries.

In summary, no systematic Greek divination records remain, although there is evidence that they might once have existed. They may have been compiled for subsequent advice, but there is little evidence of attempting to verify predictions or the quality of advice given. By contrast, some oracle bone inscriptions provide verifications of predictions made, as do the Baoshan divinations. (The Wangshan and Tianxingguan records are too fragmentary to assess.)

Conclusion

This brief comparative overview of sources for Chinese and Greek mantic activity suggests several useful areas for comparison. In most areas, Chinese sources are far more extensive, especially in the areas of mantic and procedural texts. This evidence may seem to offer little to the Hellenist,

[98] Keightley 2006: 4–8. [99] Cf. Postgate et al. 1995; Djamouri 1999.

since Greek mantic expertise seems not to have been transmitted in textual form. (Nor is there an obvious Chinese equivalent to the use of divination in Greek tragedy.) But to look for strictly comparable textual genres may be to ask the wrong question. The extensive Chinese materials add to our understanding of the intellectual attitudes and social practices that underlie divination. The plethora of textual evidence (both manuscript and received) puts the Chinese evidence in a unique position to contribute to the anthropological orientation of contemporary classical scholarship on divination.

In some areas, the textual genres and interpretive problems are comparable, especially in assessing historical narratives and philosophical debates about divination, and the value of these narratives as indirect sources. Here, methods developed in one tradition may benefit the other. The compendia of Delphic responses and the debates on authenticity that arose from their publication have no equivalent in Chinese scholarship, and might have much to offer to Chinese historiography and the legacy of Gu Jiegang 顧頡剛 and the *Gushibian* 古史辯 (Debates on Ancient History) school that largely defined twentieth-century Chinese historiography. These issues are discussed in detail in Chapter 3.

Appendix 2.1: Greek sources for divination

Apollodorus

- *Epit.* 5.23, 6.3–4
- *Lib.* 1.9.11, 2.8.2, 3.6.5–7, 3.7.2, 3.15.6

Arrian

- Divination by Alexander: 3.3–4, 3.4.5, 3.9.6, 4.9.9, 7.8.3, 7.26.2, 7.29.3

Diodorus Siculus

- Alexander: 17.93
- Delphi: 4.66.1, 8.8.2, 8.17.1, 8.21.3, 8.23.2.1, 9.5.2, 11.45.8, 12.35.3, 15.8.4, 15.13.4, 15.49.1, 16.27.1, 16.91.2, 17.10.3, 17.51, 22.9.5, 34/35.13

Herodotus

- Delphi: 1.19, 1.46–48, 1.53–54, 1.66–68, 1.87, 1.91, 1.167, 1.174, 2.134, 3.57, 4.15, 4.150, 4.156–57, 4.161, 5.63, 5.66–69, 5.82, 5.89–90, 5.92, 6.66, 6.75, 6.86, 6.123,

6.135, 6.139, 7.142, 7.148, 7.169, 8.36, 8.122; corruption of Pythia: 5.63, 6.66; Croesus: 1.46–55, 1.85; Wooden Wall: 7.139–43

- Didyma: 1.46, 1.92, 1.157, 2.159, 5.36, 6.18–21
- Military divination and military *manteis*: 2.49, 2.83, 5.44, 6.76, 7.219, 7.221, 7.228, 9.33, 9.37, 9.42, 9.61–62, 9.93–94
- Oracle collections: 5.43, 7.6
- Oracles of Bacis: 8.77, 9.43

Pausanias

- Delphi: 1.32.5, 2.33.2, 3.11.6, 3.19.12, 4.9.4, 4.12.1, 4.12.4, 4.16.7, 4.21.7–8, 4.24.2, 4.32.3–5, 5.4.6, 6.3.8, 6.9.8, 7.1.8, 7.3.1–2, 7.17.6, 8.7.6, 8.9.4, 9.23.3, 9.33.2, 9.37.4, 10.14.4, 10.22.12, 10.37.6, 19.2–31
- Didyma: 7.2.6
- Dodona: 8.11
- Military *manteis*: 3.11.5–6, 3.12.9, 10.9.7
- Olympia: 5.27.1–2

Pliny

- Delphi: *NH* 7.46.151–47.152, 34.12.26, 36.4.10

Plutarch

- Delphi: *Alex.* 3.1, 14.4, 37.1; *Arist.* 11.3, 20.4; *Cic.* 5.1; *Cim.* 8.6; *Dem.* 19.1, 20.1; *Mor.* 76e, 271c, 310b, 315, 386ef, 403b, 404a, 579bd; *Nic.* 13.6; *Solon* 12.1–4; *Thes.* 3.5, 36.1
- *Manteis* and military divination: *Alex.* 25.1–3, *Arist.* 17–18, *Cim.* 18, *Per.* 6.2
- Siwa: *Alex.* 6.19.4, 27.4, 27.7

Strabo

- Olympia: 8.3.30
- Siwa: 17.1.43

Thucydides

- Delphi: 1.25.1, 1.103.2, 1.118.3, 123.1, 1.126.4, 1.134.4, 2.17.1, 2.54.4, 3.92.5, 3.104, 5.1, 5.16.2, 5.16.12, 5.32.1, 8.108.4
- Military divination: 3.20.1, 5.54.2, 5.55.3, 5.116, 6.69.1–2

Xenophon

- Delphi: *An.* 3.1.5–8, 6.1.22; *Ap.* 14 (Chaerophon); *Cyr.* 7.2.20; *Hell.* 4.7.2, 6.4.30; *Lac.* 8.5
- Military divination: *An.* 4.3.17–19, 4.5.2–4, 5.4.2–3, 5.5.1–4, 6.4.13–27, 7.8.1–6; *Hell.* 2.4.19, 3.1.17, 3.5.7, 4.7.2, 4.7.7, 5.4.47, 6.4.16; *Hipparch.* 9.8–9; *Lac.* 13; *Mem.* 1.1.9; *Oec.* 5.19–20
- Physiognomy: *Mem.* 3.10.5

Appendix 2.2: Chinese excavated texts

Shang

1. Xiaotun 小屯 (Anyang 安陽, Henan), *c.* 1324–1045. 20,000 oracle bone pieces.
2. Sipanmo 四盤磨 (Anhui), late Shang.
3. Qishan 岐山 (Shaanxi), Zhouyuan oracle bones, early W. Zhou. 17,000 oracle bones, 300 inscribed.
4. Zhangjiapo 張家坡 (Xi'an, Shaanxi), late W. Zhou.

Spring and Autumn

5. Leigudun 擂鼓墩 (Suizhou 隨州, Hubei), *c.* 433. Zeng Hou Yi 曾侯乙.
6. Caigeling 蔡葛陵 (Xinxian, Henan), also called Xin Cai 新蔡, 500–223. 1,500 bamboo slips.

Warring States

7. Tianxingguan 天星觀 (Jiangling, Hubei) T. 1, *c.* 340. Pan Cheng 槃秤, Lord of Diyang.
8. Yutaishan 雨臺山 (Jiangling, Hubei) T. 21, mid-fourth century.
9. Baoshan 包山 (Jingmen, Hubei) T. 2, *c.* 316. Shao Tuo, Zuoyin of Chu.
10. Zhongshan 中山 (Pingshan, Hebei), 313. King Cuo of Zhongshan.
11. Guodian 郭店 (Jingmen, Hubei) T. 1, 310–300.
12. Chu Silk Manuscript (Zidanku 子彈庫, Changsha), *c.* 300.
13. Wangshan 望山 (Hubei), *c.* 309–278.
14. Jiudian 九店 (Jiangling, Hubei) T. 56, *c.* 330–270.
15. Fangmatan 放馬灘 (Tianshui, Gansu) T. 1, *c.* 269–221.
16. Wangjiatai 王家台 (Jiangling, Hubei) T. 15, 278–221.
    - Shanghai Museum, Chu bamboo slips (provenance unknown), Warring States.

Qin

17. Shuihudi 睡虎地 (Yunmeng, Hubei) T. 11, 217. A foreman clerk named Xi.
18. Zhoujiatai 周家台 (Guanju, Shashi, Hubei) T. 30, 209. Minor official aged under 30.

Western Han

19. Zhangjiashan 張家山 (Jiangling, Hubei) T. 127 (*c.* 194–188), 247 (186) and 249 (early W. Han).
20. Fenghuangshan 鳳凰山 (Jiangling, Hubei) T. 8, 9, 10, *c.* 179–141, W. Han emperors Wen and Jing (T. 8).
21. Kongjiapo 孔加坡 (Suizhou, Hubei) T. 8, *c.* 179–141.
22. Mawangdui 馬王堆 (Changsha, Hunan) T. 1, 2, 3, 168, Li Cang, chancellor of Changsha, Marquis of Dai (T. 2), his wife Xin Zhuyi (T. 1), their son (T. 3).
23. Shuanggudui 雙古堆 (Fuyang 阜陽, Anhui) T. 1, 165, Xiahou Zao, marquis of Ruyin.
24. Huxishan 虎溪山 (Yuanling, Hunan).
25. Yinqueshan 銀雀山 (Shandong) T. 1 and 2, 140–120.
26. Yinwan 尹灣 (Liangyungang, Jiangsu) T. 6, 10, a scribe and his wife.
    - Peking University, Western Han bamboo slips (provenance unknown), Warring States.

Eastern Han

27. Mozuizi 磨嘴子 (Wuwei, Gansu) T. 6, first century CE, Wang Mang reign.
28. Juyan 居延 (Gansu), W. to E. Han.
29. Dunhuang 敦煌 (Gansu), W. to E. Han.

Appendix 2.3: Chinese transmitted texts

Most pre-Han texts are of multiple authorship, and considerable scholarly debate surrounds their dating. The following dates (based on ECTBG and Nylan 2001a) are provided for general guidance.

Western Zhou *c.* 1100–771

Zhou yi 周易, late ninth century.

Eastern Zhou 770–256

Chunqiu 春秋 (*Spring and Autumn Annals*), comp. fifth century.

Warring States 475–222

Mengzi 孟子 [*Mencius*] (372–289).
Guanzi 管子, contents fourth–second century, comp. second–first century.
Zhuangzi 莊子 (fourth century), comp. second–first century BCE.
Xunzi 荀子 (*c.* 312–230), *c.* 239.
Han Feizi 韓非子 (*c.* 280–*c.* 233).
Lü shi chunqiu 呂氏春秋 (*Springs and Autumns of Master Lü* [Buwei]), *c.* 239.
Huang di nei jing 黃帝內經 (*Inner Classic of the Yellow Lord*), contents late Warring States–early Han, comp. first century BCE.

Qin 221–209 BCE

Western Han 206 BCE–9 CE

Yi jing 易經 (*Classic of Change*), comp. mid-third–early second century.
Shi jing 詩經 (*Book of Odes*), contents 1000–600 BCE.
Shu jing 書經 (*Classic of Documents*), contents W. Zhou–W. Han.
Lun yu 論語 (*Analects* of Confucius).
Mozi 墨子, contents fifth–second century.
Zuo zhuan 左傳 (*Zuo Transmissions*), comp. fourth–second century.
Zhou li 周禮 (*Rites of Zhou*), comp. late Warring States to mid-second century.
Yi li 儀禮 (*Record of Ceremonials*).
Huainanzi 淮南子, comp. Liu An 劉安 (*c.* 180–122).
Chu ci 楚辭 (*Songs of Chu*), comp. second–first century BCE.
Li ji 禮記 (*Book of Rites*), comp. first century BCE.

Eastern Han 25–220

Han shu 漢書 (*Standard History of the [W.] Han*), comp. Ban Gu 班固 (32–92 CE).
Baihu tong 白虎通 (*Comprehensive Discussions in White Tiger Hall*), *c.* 79 CE.
Lun heng 論衡 (*Weighing Discourses*), Wang Chong 王充 (27–97).

Six Dynasties 220–589

Hou Han shu 後漢書 (*Standard History of the Later [E.] Han*), by Fan Ye 范曄 (398–445).

3 Theorizing divination

> The greatest of good things come to us through madness, when sent as a gift of the gods. For when mad, the *prophētis* [Pythia] at Delphi and the priestesses at Dodona have conferred many great benefits on Greece in both private and in public matters, but, when sane, little or none.
>
> (Pl. *Phdr.* 244a–b)

> The ancients all bear witness that, just as much as the mantic art is superior and more honored than augury in name and deed, by so much is divine madness superior to human sanity.
>
> (Pl. *Phdr.* 244d)

Many classifications of divination still in use begin with Plato. In the *Phaedrus* Socrates argues that madness (*mania*) is beneficial as long as it comes from the gods. His example is the madness of Sibyls and Pythias, which he considered the true mantic art (*mantikē*). He contrasts it with *tekhnē*: studying signs of future events by the flight of birds and other methods (*Phdr.* 244a–e). This distinction is part of Plato's broader epistemological agenda: to contrast the self-conscious reflection of the philosopher with the inferior, unreflective activity of the seer and bard. Socrates plays on this distinction in his account of the oracle given to Chaerophon (that no man is wiser than Socrates) in the *Apology*, and argues that inspired seers and bards work not by wisdom (*sophia*) but by nature (*phusis*).[1] They are ignorant of what they create; they can describe sword and shield, but cannot wield them. Plato needs to deny *manteis* and bards self-conscious reflection about their art in order to reserve this ability for philosophers. For Plato inspired divination is unlearned (*adidaktos*) and without skill (*atekhnos*), while technical divination is both learned (*entekhnos*) and skilled (*tekhnikos*).

Plato's distinction reappears in the oldest Western comparative study of divination: Cicero's *De Divinatione*. According to Cicero, there is a

[1] Pl. *Ap.* 22c. In the *Ion* (533e, cf. 534b–d) Socrates argues that epic and lyric poets create "not from *tekhnē*, but by being inspired and possessed" by the Muse (*ouk ek tekhnēs all' entheoi ontes kai katekhomenoi*).

"consensus of antiquity" that there are two kinds of divination: by nature (*natura*) and by technical expertise (*ars*).[2] For Cicero as for Plato, natural divination came from the gods and was the highest form of the mantic art. It came "without reason or consciousness" (*sine ratione et scientia*) and was inspired by frenzy or dreams.[3] It occurred either when the soul was free of the body (in dreams or to those approaching death) or when the soul's natural power of prediction became overdeveloped, manifesting as frenzy or inspiration (as in the case of Cassandra).[4] He explicitly excluded from natural divination both the use of reason and prediction by "natural law," for example the predictions of physicians, pilots, or farmers.[5]

Thus, for both Plato and Cicero, the power of prediction was a universal human potential, but was only realized fully in limited circumstances: in the grip of divine possession or when the soul was loosened from the hold of the body. Prediction was only subject to study or mastery in the inferior form of technical divination by signs.

This chapter addresses how divination and prognostication have been theorized by contemporary scholars, Western and Chinese. It is important to appreciate that Plato and Cicero's view of divination has informed (and possibly distorted) the entire history of the subject. I now turn to the recent history of classical scholarship on divination and the intellectual and political contexts for Chinese scholarship on the mantic arts. I conclude with the question of how Greek and Chinese theorizing about divination might enrich each other.

For purposes of this discussion I use the terms "Classics" and "Classicist," with some reluctance, as a convenient way to refer to scholars of ancient Greece and Rome. The term could equally refer to the scholarship of Classical Chinese or, more narrowly, to Ru or literati (introduced in Chapter 2).

Divination, Classics, and the social sciences

The modern study of Greek divination takes place in a history of interactions between the discipline of Classics and anthropology, archaeology, and

2 Cic. *Div.* 1.6.12 (cf. 1.33.72–1.36.79). See Beard 1986. 3 Cic. *Div.* 1.2.4 (cf. 1.32.68).

4 Dreams: Cic. *Div.* 1.20.39–1.28.59. Sleep: 1.29.60–1.30.63. Approach of death: 1.30.64. Inherent power of prediction: 1.30.65–1.31.66. Frenzy and inspiration: 1.19.38, 1.31.66. Disassociation from the body: 1.113–15. Cassandra: 1.31.66 and 1.40.89.

5 Cic. *Div.* 1.49.111–1.50.112. He mentions Thales' prediction of an eclipse and Anaximander's prediction of an earthquake.

the history of religions. It also partakes of debates on the use of comparative methods, including the vexed question of how "other" the Greeks were, and who, if anyone, should be compared to them. Sally Humphreys, Ian Morris, Marcel Detienne, and others have given detailed accounts of the history of these disciplinary interactions.[6] My interest here is the place of the study of divination within that history.

Evolutionist frameworks

Starting in the mid-nineteenth century, classicists turned to anthropology to reconstruct the origins of Greek and Roman society. Central to the evolutionist models they used was the view that societies evolved in stages from the "primitive" to the "rational." Key in that evolution was the passage of ancient Greece "from myth to reason": a triumphal progress that included philosophy, historiography, medicine, technology, and several sciences.[7]

Here, Plato and Cicero's classification took on a life of its own. It informs the structure of Auguste Bouché-Leclercq's monumental history of divination in Greco-Roman antiquity as a distinction between "intuitive" (inspired) and "inductive" (technical) divination. His influence in turn propagated this dichotomy among later scholars.[8] In an evolutionist framework, intuitive divination became "primitive" and "inductive" divination became "rational" proto-science. Under the influence of Friedrich Schlegel, Erwin Rohde, and Friedrich Nietzsche, opposition between Greek reason and "barbarian" Asian mystery cults became a philosophical dogma.[9] Some German scholars even used this dichotomy to create boundaries between Greeks (or at worst, Indo-Europeans) and other Mediterraneans: Egyptians,

[6] Classics and anthropology: Humphreys 1974. Archaeology: Cartledge 1994. Greek ritual: Morris 1993. Classics and comparison: Detienne 2001.

[7] The phrase comes from Wilhelm Nestle's *Vom Mythos zum Logos: die Selbstentfaltung des griechischen Denkens von Homer bis auf die Sophistik* (Stuttgart: A. Kröner, 1940). Bruno Snell used it as the title of a chapter in *Die Entdeckung des Geistes* (1948), translated into English as *The Discovery of the Mind* (1953). In his *Myth and Reason* (1953), W. K. C. Guthrie described Greek philosophy as evolving from the "mythopoeic" to the "rational." See Buxton 1999: 4–5.

[8] W. R. Halliday's (1913: 55–57) still influential study adopts Bouché-Leclercq's language outright. More recent French studies by Robert Flacelière (1965: 7 and passim) and Raymond Bloch (1984: 9) use the terms inspired prophecy and inductive divination. By contrast a comparative volume edited by André Caquot and Marcel Leibovici (1968: v–xix) acknowledges this system, but the editors do not impose systematic terminology or categories on their contributors.

[9] As Dietrich (1992: 45–58) remarks, in this historically incorrect view, Dionysian cults introduced inspirational divination to an older Apolline oracle. But the Nietzschean antipathy between Apollonian and Dionysian modes is a modern perception that had no basis in the cults of Apollo and Dionysus or in their coexistence at Delphi.

Babylonians, and "Semites" of all kinds.[10] The distinction between inspiration and technical expertise continues to reappear in general discussions of the history of divination.[11] This typology reifies and attempts to universalize culturally specific categories derived from a particularly Greek mode of divination: oracular consultation, especially of Apollo at Delphi.

In *Theories of the Sign in Classical Antiquity* Giovanni Manetti considers divination as a hermeneutic process, and argues against the evolutionist move of creating a binary opposition between a "divinatory paradigm" and a "scientific paradigm."[12] Drawing on Carlo Ginzburg's insight that the relationship is more complex (and more advantageous to the divinatory paradigm), Manetti examines the logic of Mesopotamian divination and its extension from divination to medicine, law, and eventually all knowledge. Unlike Greek logical inference, Mesopotamian inference was linked to the content of predictions, rather than their form. Manetti also notes the crucial importance of writing as the model for a series of intellectual activities that included mantic hermeneutics. He contrasts the Babylonian use of writing, and its independence from oral language, with the oral bias of Greek divination. The Babylonian emphasis on writing had several important implications: it provides mental training and makes possible subtle webs of relationships.

The sociological turn

The engagement between Classics and the social sciences continued to affect the study of divination in three areas. The first is the study of ritual. Drawing on Karl Marx's arguments that social institutions determined intellectual structures, fundamentalist and Marxist historians argued that ritual behavior was a reflection of underlying social structure, starting with the publication of *La Cité Antique* by Fustel de Coulanges in 1864. Émile Durkheim's *Elementary Models of Religious Life*, published in 1912, argued

[10] The Mediterranean context: Burkert 1992: 1–4.

[11] For example, the entry on divination in the *Encyclopedia Britannica* distinguishes between inspired "intuitive divination" and set or flexible procedures for technical divination. "Inductive" divination uses completely set procedures (such as Chinese practices of using natal horoscopes to predict, and ensure, marital compatibility) while "interpretive" divination allows for the special insights of the diviner (such as contemporary Mayan medical diviners in Guatemala). See Park and Gilbert 2003. In the *Encyclopedia of Religion*, the distinction is between technical "wisdom" divination and two varieties of inspired divination. Here "wisdom" divination decodes impersonal patterns of reality. "Intuitive" divination is spontaneous, whereas in "possession" divination, the diviner is a passive vehicle for divine communication. See Zuesse 1987.

[12] Manetti 1993: 1–5, cf. Bottéro 1974 and Ginzburg 1979. Mesopotamian divination is discussed further below.

that rituals created social order and were in this sense far more important than individual belief. The views of Marx and Durkheim also affected Chinese theorizing about divination during the 1920s through their influence on the *Gushibian* school (discussed below).[13]

During the interwar years, Classics as a discipline became increasingly specialized, treating politics, economics, law, religion, literature, and philosophy as separate fields. In this framework, religion and ritual were artificially separated from politics and the rest of society.[14] This atmosphere did not encourage interactions with the social sciences, and Durkheimian sociology was negatively associated with the "Cambridge school."[15] A major exception, the Durkheimian French Classicist Louis Gernet, was relegated to a position in Algeria. But while Classics was contracting, anthropologists such as Bronislav Malinowski and Claude Lévi-Strauss were exploring the rationality of magic and myth. Divination entered debates about the "irrational" in anthropology, philosophy, and psychology; and the anthropological studies addressed the social contexts in which divination took place.[16]

The second key element was a renewed interest in anthropology and comparison. Anthropology reentered Classics in the work of Moses Finley and Louis Gernet. Finley was trained in Weberian historical sociology and the economic anthropology of Karl Polanyi. He shifted attention toward the radical otherness of the Greeks, and the "logic of institutions" such as marriage, slavery, and citizenship.[17] Gernet returned to Paris in 1947. One of his few students, Jean-Pierre Vernant, combined Durkheimian sociology with the structuralism of Lévi-Strauss. Vernant began a comparativist

[13] Classics and anthropology: Humphreys 1974: 17–19. De Coulanges argued that family and property were the pillars of European civilization. The implicit argument, that the Greeks were like us, became enormously important.

[14] Humphreys 1974: 19–20, J.-P. Vernant 1977: 9–10, Morris 1993. These artificial separations introduced categories of analysis that would have been meaningless to the Greeks themselves, such as "sacred and secular" (Morris 1993: 23, Connor 1988). The period was marked by isolated studies of late cults and creeds, and did not lead to useful methods for the study of ancient religion or comparisons across time periods.

[15] The Cambridge school, associated with Jane Harrison, Francis Cornford, and Gilbert Murray, advanced archaeological, anthropological, and comparative interests that challenged the ideas of the previous generation, especially Max Müller. Cambridge school: Finley 1975: 102–3, Morris 1993: 21–22. Gernet: Humphreys 1978: 76–106, J.-P. Vernant 1981.

[16] L. Gernet 1955, 1981. Myth: Malinowski 1954, Lévi-Strauss 1963. Rationality: Dodds 1951, Moore 1957, Park 1963, Hollis and Lukes 1982.

[17] Finley: Humphreys 1974: 24–26, Cartledge 1994: 4. Major publications: *The World of Odysseus* (1954), *The Ancient Greeks* (1963), *Aspects of Antiquity* (1972), *The Ancient Economy* (1973), *The Use and Abuse of History* (1975, including the 1972 Jane Harrison Memorial Lecture), *Economy and Society in Ancient Greece* (1980), *Politics in the Ancient World* (1983), *Ancient History: Evidence and Models* (1985).

seminar (initially at the Center for Marxist Research and Studies) and in 1965 established the Center for Comparative Research on Ancient Societies at the École Pratique des Hautes Études. Its membership included Classicists, anthropologists, and scholars of Assyria, Egypt, India, China, and Africa. It became a focal point for comparative history, but slowly, and to the regret of Vernant himself, the focus of the center shifted toward the Classical world. Ten years later, it had become a center for the study of Greek and Roman antiquity.[18] With Vernant's new methods came a renewed interest in purely Greek categories, expressed in Greek words. As Detienne describes it, the Greeks ceased to be "other" and again became our closest neighbors, now cut off from comparison by a new "anthropology" of ancient Greece.[19] Comparativism had become a thing of the past, and Greek and Greek categories drove out all others.

A third key framework was the efforts of "new archaeology" to extend and complement the limited resources provided by the textual tradition. Starting in the 1970s, Anthony Snodgrass and other Classical archaeologists began to adopt functionalist theories to the study of the Bronze Age and prehistoric Greece. Snodgrass and his students viewed changes in eighth-century sanctuaries, hero cults, and burials as reflections of the rise of the polis.[20] The work of Catherine Morgan in particular introduced a sociological view of the Delphic oracle. Morgan argued that Delphi probably arose as a panhellenic site because the existing mechanisms of consultor states were inadequate to address new problems created by social change in the eighth century, when emerging *poleis* were vulnerable to crises in authority caused by such problems. Such an oracle would need a home, and an existing sanctuary would have been a practical solution. Delphi was especially suitable because it was located beyond the boundaries or control of any one consultor state. Morgan argued that the real significance of the rise of the Delphic oracle is that it is the beginning of state domination of a sanctuary that had previously served the personal interests of the elite.[21] Sociological approaches also informed accounts of the "decline of oracles" (Appendix A).

[18] Detienne 2001: 104–5, Murray 2007. Vernant and his students, especially Marcel Detienne, Pierre Vidal-Naquet, and Nicole Loraux created a new "Paris school." Vernant left the center in 1975 for the Collège de France.

[19] Detienne 2001, cf. J.-P. Vernant 1991: 305–14.

[20] Cartledge 1994. New archaeology: Snodgrass 1971, 1980, 1986, 1987. His students include Catherine Morgan (1988, 1990, 2001), Ian Morris (1987, 1989, 1992, 1993, esp. 25), and Robin Osborne (1989, 1991, 1997).

[21] Catherine Morgan 1990.

Finally, anthropological methods also informed a growing literature on indigenous Greek notions of ethnicity or cultural identity, and the role of myth in creating regional and eventually panhellenic identities, including the rise of a panhellenic oracle at Delphi.[22] The point for the present discussion is that it is very problematic to speak of early Greek practices in terms of cultural unity, which came gradually and relatively late.[23] Nonetheless, we *can* speak of regional practices as evidenced by archaeological sites and the combined evidence of archaeological and textual traditions.

In summary, all these studies abandoned psychologically and individually oriented studies of Greek ritual and asked instead how rituals maintained social power. The "sociological turn" in the study of Greek religion and ritual substantially informed the study of divination at panhellenic sites, of which the most important was the shrine of Apollo at Delphi.[24]

Sociological analysis was also applied to the question of how responses were used by consultor states. The argument was advanced that the most important functions of oracles were political and rhetorical. Oracles could sanction decisions already taken by community leaders, provide legitimacy and authority, confer consensus, mollify the powerful, and deflect potential blame from individual opinion. In this view, consultation was not an open-ended inquiry. The most common form of question was a simple statement to be affirmed or denied, or a request for a preference between two alternatives.[25] Open-ended questions or predictions of the future were rare; despite the oracle's literary reputation for ambiguity, most responses were straightforward. Even ambiguous responses could have the practical effect of forcing consultor states to reconsider issues that admitted no straightforward answer.[26] In practical terms, no state would leave itself open to unsolicited or problematic directives that might ignore the original problem.

[22] *Ethnē* and ethnic groups: Hall 1997: 34–43, 2002: 5–6, 2003a, 2003b; Konstan 2001: 31–32; Catherine Morgan 2001: 76–78.

[23] Hall 1997, 2002, 2003a. On China see Nylan 2005.

[24] Since the mid-1980s, a new, broadly "cultural" direction has emerged. Morris (1993) links this direction to a shift of dominance in theoretical studies from anthropology to literary theory and the rise of poststructuralism. It is linked to the influence of Michel Foucault, Jean-François Lyotard, and Clifford Geertz and the methods of poststructuralist analysis. It has moved toward decentering subjects of analysis, toward isolating local knowledges and private worlds, and to more sophisticated approaches to representation.

[25] Fontenrose 1978: 24–35, Parker 2000a: 77–79.

[26] Some ambiguities involve morality tales and structuring devices, for example in the *Histories* of Herodotus. An example of an oracle that forced reconsideration by consultors is Herodotus' (7.140–43) account of the Athenian response to the threat of a Persian invasion, which forced the Athenian assembly to reconsider the best defense and reach an independent decision. See Parker 2000a: 80; cf. Fontenrose 1978: 123–28.

Other scholars have examined the reasons for the creation of treasure houses (*thēsauroi*), the temple-like structures Greek *poleis* built at Delphi and Olympia to house their citizens' dedications to the god.[27] These studies also address divination as a set of social institutions. They view oracles as sources of consensus whose function was neither to predict future events nor to bestow divine authority on rulers or elites. In this view, the function of oracles was to resolve doubt, mediate disputes, establish consensus, and legitimate difficult group decisions that had been made before oracular consultation occurred.[28]

The "received opinion" of the sociological role of oracles has been challenged explicitly in a recent study of the role of divination in Athenian democracy by Hugh Bowden, who argues that concern to understand and follow the will of the gods was an important factor in Athenian decisions. In other words, consultations of the oracle were genuine attempts to ascertain the will of the gods, rather than mere sanctions for human political decisions. Bowden in particular raises objections to what he considers reliance on unreliable literary evidence, Herodotus especially.[29] But more generally, he disagrees with a modern tendency to downplay the effects of oracles on Greek communities. He argues that Greek states consulted oracles on matters of major import that they could not resolve by debate, and made every effort to get, and follow, unambiguous advice. Bowden's skepticism about accounts of oracles in Herodotus points to the status of divination accounts as a narrative genre.

Divination and comparison

When Vernant's Center for Comparative Research shifted from comparativism to Hellenism, as Detienne puts it, "the Greeks gobbled up sacrifice," but the study of divination remained comparative under the influence of Vernant. The result was *Divination et rationalité* (discussed in Chapter 1). Two points are particularly important. First, the book focuses equally on mental attitudes and social institutions. Vernant thus diverged from the thread of social theory that privileged social over intellectual institutions, and stressed the need to study both. The second point is that the project was thoroughly comparative. Although the ancient Mediterranean received more "space" than other areas,

27 Neer 2001, 2004. Their construction, beginning in the late seventh century, coincides with the heyday of Greek *poleis*.

28 Parke 1967, Parker 2000a, Catherine Morgan 1989: 17 and passim, 1990: 153.

29 Bowden 2005: 1–5, cf. Price 1985, Parker 2000a, Catherine Morgan 1989, 1990.

and the New World was not included, contributions addressed divination in Greece, Rome, Assyria, and China.[30]

Subsequent studies have focused on important sociological and epistemological dimensions of divination, both in antiquity and in the present. Divination extended to a wide range of activities and its importance was not limited to predicting future or hidden events. It had profound effects on the development of medicine, law, philosophy, politics, and science. Geoffrey Lloyd suggests that the hope of being able to foretell the future or to know hidden truths may be a strong incentive to intellectual activities such as experimentation, analysis, and research. In this sense, divination may be a positive influence on the growth of systematic inquiry, rather than an impediment to it.[31]

Vernant's key insight that divination must be studied through the dual aspects of intellectual and social operations arose through comparative study, and specifically through the study of African divination.[32] From the evidence of African oracles it was argued that divination was used to support authority. Community authorities typically formulated desirable solutions before consulting an oracle, which in turn approved their decisions, with social or divine sanctions to preclude improper subjects or modes of inquiry. These comparisons have focused on spirit mediums and "ordeal" oracles, almost all oral.[33] Comparison between the Delphic oracle and the Azande poison oracle was used to show similar attitudes toward divination and common topics of consultation such as illness, warfare, matters of state, and questions of family welfare.[34]

This use of comparative evidence has been challenged on several fronts. Lisa Maurizio argues that C. R. Whittaker, in his initial comparative studies,

[30] J.-P. Vernant 1974a. Contributors include Jean-Pierre Vernant, Luc Brisson, and Roland Crahay (Greece), Jean Bottéro (Mesopotamia), Jacques Gernet and Léon Vandermeersch (China), Denise Grodzynski (Rome), and Anne Retel-Laurentin (Africa).

[31] Lloyd 2002: 23.

[32] Whittaker 1965, Bowden 2005: 28–33. African oracles: Jules-Rosette 1978, Peek 1991, Johnston in Johnston and Struck 2005: 1–5, esp. 3 n. 5.

[33] The most detailed example is the Azande "poison" oracle studied by Evans-Pritchard (1976: esp. 159) in the 1920s, in which poison was administered to a chicken, whose death or survival would recommend or countermand a proposed course of action. A second question would confirm the results of the first.

[34] Illness included both plague and individual conditions. Other topics included exile or change of residence by individuals or groups; crime and guilt; war or *casus belli*; problems of rulership, communal welfare, and interstate relations; desire for marriage, children, or knowledge of one's children's future; death or disappearance; change of career or a contemplated enterprise; desire for reward or wellbeing by individuals, families, or states; and questions of cult and religion, including even testing the oracle itself. Evans-Pritchard 1976: 122, Fontenrose 1978: 442–44, Bowden 2005: 29–30.

only turned to African evidence after addressing problems in the history of Delphi that had no counterpart in comparative sources. As a result, his African evidence shed no new insight on Delphi and did not affect any of his preexisting views. Rather it "simply supplies exotic parallels to conclusions he has already reached."[35] Esther Eidinow has pointed out that comparisons with the Azande poison oracle fail to address equivalent uses of oracles across cultures. State consultations at Delphi are not equivalent to oracles used by individuals, such as the Azande poison oracle.[36] Eidinow argues that sociological studies of divination based on panhellenic oracles blur the distinction between public and private queries. They tend to overlook the roles of divination in the lives of ordinary individuals and the concerns that motivated them to consult divinatory expertise. Eidinow takes a very original approach to divination as a way to mitigate risk and uncertainty in everyday life. She juxtaposes two genres not typically considered together: oracular consultation and curse tablets (*katadesmoi*), juxtaposing the lead question tablets from Dodona with curse tablets from the sixth to the first centuries, on the grounds that both were strategies for the management of risk in everyday life by ordinary people. Taken together, she argues, they provide an index of aspects of risk and uncertainty in ancient Greek culture.[37]

Other studies have returned to Vernant's emphasis on divination as a set of mental attitudes, and address issues of hermeneutics and semiosis, questions of genre. Another seminal work from the Paris school, Marcel Detienne's *The Invention of Mythology*, reexamines received notions of genre and discourse, with particular attention to the categories of "myth," "history," and the ambiguous territory that lies between them. Other studies reassess literary genres, with an ear to indigenous categories of enunciation

35 Maurizio 1995: 72; cf. Whittaker 1965: 30. Comparisons with African oracles: Whittaker 1965, comments by Parker 2000a, and Catherine Morgan 1989, 1990.

36 Eidinow 2007a: 239 n. 9; cf. Price 1985: 143.

37 Eidinow 2007a: 3–5 and 20–22 draws on the theory that risk is socially constructed. The question of what areas of life are viewed as dangerous or "risky" is part of culturally specific views of agency and the nature of "luck" and misfortune. The Greek term that best expresses the contemporary notion of "risk" is *kindunos* ("risk," "threat," "danger"). Curses were typically used in agonistic relationships (athletes, litigants, lovers, rival tradesmen, etc.). Curse tablets were aggressive moves in competition, by which the otherwise "weaker" party sought to avoid defeat. It is unusual to explore divination in conjunction with curse-writing, perhaps because of a historiographical legacy which at least partially legitimated oracular consultation, but which has tended to ignore curses until a recent upsurge of interest in magical studies. Consultors of oracles were uncertain about a course of action, and sought assurances that their choices were the best ones. Curses were used by individuals already in what they perceived as a dangerous situation. They sought to limit their vulnerability at the hands of a competitor or enemy. In this sense, we might perceive oracles as a form of "insurance" and curses as as a defense against misfortune (and an explanation of it). See Eidinow 2007b.

and reception. One of their foci is Herodotus and his central and problematic role as a source for many accounts of Delphic consultation. The Herodotean enterprise has been described as a movement from epic and *mythos* to history and *logos*, and that movement includes a new use of oracular rhetoric. Studies by Gregory Nagy, François Hartog, and Julia Kindt have examined the genesis of the authority of the historian, its complex relation to epic and the authority of the bard, and the status of "divination narratives" as a distinct genre.[38]

The Mediterranean context

Claims for the unique character of Greek science and philosophy tend to downplay connections between the Greek world and the ancient Mediterranean and Near East. A different theoretical turn has been to compare Greek and Mesopotamian divination from several different perspectives. One is to look for interactions between Mesopotamian and Greek diviners or other evidence of influence. This is not a purely empirical problem, since Classics as a discipline has gone through a series of cycles of receptivity and hostility toward claims for parallels between, interactions with, and borrowings from other cultures, especially "Eastern" ones.[39] A wide variety of evidence from the archaeology and art history of Asia Minor, Mycenae, archaic Greece, and Mesopotamia suggests resemblances, but actual connections are harder to establish.

Geoffrey Lloyd takes the comparison in a different direction, contrasting the different stances of Greek and Babylonian divination toward systematic inquiry and their relations to the history of science. Lloyd argues that any Mediterranean account must touch on Mesopotamian divination, both because of its antiquity and extent and because it differed from Greek practices in important ways. One way in which it differed was the extent of royal patronage and control. Astronomical and meteorological study was originally undertaken for practical and political purposes, closely linked to the welfare of the king and the state, and many aspects of Mesopotamian divination were under the direct control of the king and the officials who

[38] Detienne 1981. Genre: Calame 1996: 46–55, 2003: 1–34. Authority of the historian: Nagy 1990, Hartog 1999: esp. 186. Nagy (1990: 329) describes two parallel appropriations of the authority of epic: the lyric "authoritative speech" (*ainos*) of Pindar and the *historia* of Herodotus. Herodotus combines prose and the "poetry of oracles" to convey the same kind of message as Pindaric lyric.

[39] Ken Dowden summarizes some of this history in a review article in *JHS* 121 (2001): 167–75.

reported to him.[40] Sustained Babylonian interest in the study of the heavens begins in the seventh century. Its original goal was the prediction of good and ill auspice, but the perception of the regular behavior of the sun, moon, and planets led to a new and different kind of interest in the study of celestial phenomena. The accumulation of astronomical data may have been stimulated by the desire to predict the future, but new astronomical knowledge led to further study for several hundred years, undertaken by specialist officials financed and controlled by kings.[41]

Babylonian divination records present no divide between "irrational" pursuits based on omens and "rational" mathematics and astronomy. As Francesca Rochberg has argued at length, Babylonian divination thus challenges taxonomies based on Greek practices, even within the ancient Mediterranean.[42] It is also relevant to any comparison with China because, like Chinese materials, the predictions of Babylonian diviners were logically complex. For example, there is a vast literature of medical and astronomical omens, often in the form of conditional statements of the form: If X [a sign] then Y [a "verdict"]. Each statement linked a sign in the protasis with an anticipated outcome in the apodosis. Signs could include medical symptoms, but also circumstances (such as an individual's physiognomy, the flight of a bird, or the presence of an insect). In medical predictions typical verdicts were prognostications about life or death, possibly identifying a god or demon responsible for the illness. Other predictions addressed the state of mind of the patient ("knowing tears," "good morale," "anxious") and the duration or difficulty of the ailment.[43]

Babylonian astronomical diviners developed sophisticated arithmetical models for astronomical phenomena. Major developments in astronomical divination took place around the seventh century, when there was a shift in both the substance of predictions and the level of confidence in their

[40] These included "astrologer-scribes" (*ṭupšarru*), "haruspex diviners" (*barû*), "exorcist magicians" (*āšipu*), "physicians" (*asû*), and "dream interpreters" (*šā'ilu*). For these translations see Parpola 1993: xiii, Lloyd 2002: 24–25, and Rochberg 2000: 44–49.

[41] And in the Achaemenid period (*c.* 550–330) by temples. It continued through a series of major political upheavals, including conquest by the Assyrians in the late eighth century, Babylonian destruction of the Assyrian empire at the end of the seventh century, and the Persian conquest of Babylonia in 539. Relevant history of European Classicism: Burkert 1992: 1–6. Overlap of Babylonian "science" and "religion": Rochberg 2004: 15–29.

[42] Rochberg 2004.

[43] Description: Bottéro 1974, Rochberg 2000: 49–54. Medical examples: Labat 1951: 7–19, 25–31, 33–35, 41–43, 55–57, 69–79, 83–87, 105, 115–21, 151–59, 173. Astronomy: Neugebauer 1975, Swerdlow 1998, Reiner and Pingree 1975, Brown 2000. The *Enima Anu Enlil* was probably compiled between 1500 and 1200 from earlier material. Predictions in the "Venus tablet" (*c.* 1600) record information about the appearances of Venus.

accuracy.[44] Signs (in the protases of texts) were classified more rigorously and more empirically. These included such measurements as the length of the month (measured by the appearance of the new moon), the phases of the planets (measured relative to the sun and stationary points), and lunar and solar eclipses. The possibility of detailed and exact predictions about such phenomena as the appearance of a planet or the occurrence of an eclipse offered a new kind of prognostication. In addition to general prediction based on good or ill auspice, it became possible to make precise predictions about celestial phenomena themselves. In particular, scribes were able to make more precise predictions about eclipses, which were considered especially inauspicious. This enabled rulers to take ritual precautions to divert the worst effects, typically by substituting a false "king" to attract and thereby neutralize the impending misfortune.[45]

In summary, although several recent studies have distanced themselves from purely functionalist accounts of divination, other approaches have not coalesced around any systemic theoretical consensus. An important casualty of the sociological view of divination has been at least some aspects of the comparative agenda that originally motivated it. What happened?

A partial answer is flagged in Detienne's account of the encounters of Classics, history, and anthropology: an effect of the "return" of Classical scholarship to the perceived cultural specificity of the Greeks in the late 1970s. The Greeks as "Others" had offered the possibility of a comparative approach, but unlike the "otherness" of China or India, the Greek version came stamped with the more prestigious seal of European cultural beginnings. The result was the paradox of a comparativism that was based on cultural particularism but did not construct "comparables" to address the cultural specificity of the comparanda.[46] By contrast, under Jean-Paul Vernant, the study of divination remained comparative. That aegis included comparative work in psychology by his brother Jacques Vernant and collaborations with the sinologist Léon Vandermeersch and the Assyriologist Jean Bottéro.[47] Here the Greeks were again a non-privileged minority among other minorities. Hellenists had never studied relations between divination and society or rationality, and the "comparables" were "waiting to be constructed."[48]

[44] The main source of evidence for this shift is the "Letters and Reports," mostly composed between 680 and 650 by officials reporting to the Assyrian Kings at Nineveh.

[45] See Bottéro 1992: 138–55. [46] Detienne 2001: 108–9. [47] Jacques Vernant 1948.

[48] Detienne 2001: 112; cf. J.-P. Vernant 1974a.

Theories of divination in China

I now turn to a "comparable" of a different order. Early Chinese divination offers a rich array of sources, a long history, a vast range of methods, types of question, relation to political power, and intellectual complexity. That richness, however, has historically tended to be pursued in relative isolation, for several reasons.

Several historiographic approaches (by both Chinese and Western historians) affect the study of the Chinese mantic arts. One is the ongoing influence of the *Gushibian* school that largely defined historiography in twentieth-century China. It stands in contrast to a second, older paradigm of dynastic and cultural unity grounded in an idealized image of the founding culture heroes of ancient China. A third is a very different, but also politically motivated, view of ancient China as a rational or "secular humanist" state, which inherently excludes divination as irrational or primitive.

Gushibian historiography

The development of modern methods of historiography in China began with the research of Gu Jiegang and his followers. Gu Jiegang, a student of Hu Shi 胡適 (1891–1962), was responding to the effects on their own discipline of the intellectual crises caused by the confrontation with Western modernity and the challenges it offered to traditional intellectual practices. Their approach derives from writings known as *Gushibian* 古史辯 or Debates on Ancient History. The *Gushibian* scholars used the methods of their immediate predecessors, the Qing dynasty School of Evidential Research (*Kaozheng xue* 考證學), who attempted to accurately date classical texts and to distinguish authentic passages from forgeries and later interpolations. But although *kaozheng* scholarship brought about a revolution in discourse, its motivations were traditional: to eliminate the corrupting effects of some elements of Neo-Confucianism and to restore learning to an earlier and more positive form. As On-cho Ng notes, the main goal of Qing *kaozheng* scholarship was to "sharpen the philological tools for philosophical arguments"; their battles were fought "with reference and in deference to the classics."[49] The *Gushibian* scholars took

[49] Ng 2003: 49; cf. Elman 1984 and Wang Aihe 2000a, esp. 370–74. Its avowed motive was to eliminate the corrupting effects of Ming Neo-Confucianism and to restore learning to an earlier, more pristine form.

these methods in a new direction: from philosophy to historiography. As self-professed "doubters of the ancients" (*yigupai* 疑古派), they began to question not only the content of classical texts, but the dating and authenticity of traditional historiography and its accounts of antiquity. They tried to demonstrate the mythological (rather than historical) origins of the culture heroes of Chinese history.[50] Gu argued that the "earliest" figures appeared in relatively late texts. He used careful chronologies of early texts to claim that the culture heroes of early China were creations of Warring States and Han authors. Gu also claimed that the sources for these legends were oral myths, in which the "sages" were gods.[51] It is important to note that Gu Jiegang did not seem to have access to a crucial piece of historical evidence unavailable to the *kaozheng* scholars: the discovery of the Shang oracle bones.[52]

In the latter half of the twentieth century, the focus of Chinese historiography as practiced by Chinese scholars shifted from questions of authenticity or antiquity to new reconstructions of antiquity, including a revival of the notion of a "static continuity" in Chinese culture. For example, the contemporary archaeologist Pang Pu makes the problematic claim that, "before the May Fourth Movement, the structure of Chinese indigenous culture was based on *yin–yang* and *wuxing*."[53] Lothar von Falkenhausen formulates the problem another way: "Nowhere else in the world is archaeology as closely enmeshed in a millennia-old living tradition of national history."[54] There are many reasons for this. Historiography and the creation of official (standard) history have always been linked to state power. Archaeology as a discipline is closely linked to history. Most Chinese universities offer it within history departments. (A few place it in anthropology, but even here it falls squarely within the social sciences.) The exception is the prehistoric Paleolithic, which is taught under the rubric

50 Gu Jiegang et al. 1926–41, esp. 1.43. *Yigupai* has sometimes been translated as "the skeptical school."

51 Gu Jiegang et al. 1926–41, 1:105–50 and Gu's preface (1:52). Yang Kuan 楊寬 in particular tried to reconstruct these mythical sources. See Gu Jiegang et al. 1926–41, 7A (1942): 65–421, esp. 189–93 (*Zhongguo shanggushi daolun* 中國上古史導論). This issue is reviewed in Puett 2001: 95–96.

52 The first volume of the *Gushibian* was published in 1926. Though Gu Jiegang was familiar with the discovery of Neolithic sites early in the twentieth century, there seems to be no evidence that the first oracle bone discoveries influenced his thinking. The excavation of the Shang capital at Yinxu took place from 1928 to 1937. See Su Rongyu 2004.

53 一般都承认，"五四"以前的中国固有文化，是以阴阳五行作为骨架的。 He goes on to argue that this structure has never gone through fundamental change or destructive breaks. Pang Pu 1988: 355; cf. Wang Aihe 2000a.

54 Falkenhausen 1993a: 839.

of the natural sciences. But historical scholarship became more conservative after the Second World War, and "doubting the ancients" went out of fashion. Within the People's Republic of China, archaeology (like astronomy in ancient China!) has both benefited and suffered from state sponsorship. In particular, state sponsorship of archaeology required it (like other branches of scholarship) to validate Marxist ideology. In addition, archaeology was expected to enhance the legitimacy and prestige of the state by fostering patriotism and national prestige, both at home and abroad.[55] Much of this attitude could be summed up by Mao Zedong's slogan of "using the past to serve the present" (*gu wei jin yong*古為今用).

Nationalism and cultural unity

Accounts of the nature and practice of mantic activity are central elements in Chinese narratives of cultural unity. In legendary accounts, Fu Xi's invention of the trigrams of the *Yi jing* was an important element of the founding of civilization. Central to these narratives is an idealized view of the Zhou dynasty and its differences from the Shang and Xia, views held by both the Zhou conquerors and modern Chinese scholars. Both the *Gushibian* scholars and Western scholars of Chinese mythology (such as Henri Maspéro, Jacques Gernet, and Bernhard Karlgren) argued that Warring States and Han accounts of the Xia and Shang dynasties are probably Western Zhou fabrications.[56] These accounts attacked the "fatalist" beliefs of the Shang rulers in accounts that emphasized the intellectual and moral weakness of the Zhou's conquered predecessors.[57]

A number of twentieth-century Chinese scholars, several associated with the "New Confucianism" movements of the mid-twentieth century and the 1990s, also attributed fatalism to a primitive or superstitious element in Shang or Xia culture.[58] Nonetheless, archaeological evidence indicates

55 These developments are reviewed in Falkenhausen 1993a.

56 Maspéro 1924: 1–11, Gu Jiegang et al. 1926–41, Chang 1980: 350, Allan 1991: 63f., Chen Ning 1997: 141. As Michael Puett (2001: 92–95) points out, the *Gushibian* scholars, Maspéro, and other twentieth-century scholars all tried to use anthropological and mythological models to reconstruct a lost Bronze Age mythology.

57 The "Against Fatalism" (*Fei ming* 非命) chapter of the Mohist canon critically attributes belief in "fixed fate" to the vicious last rulers of the Xia and Shang dynasty: Jie of the Xia and Zhou of the Shang. The *Lü shi chunqiu* (ch. 20, Zhi fen, 7a) contains several narratives that also attribute belief that human life was fated to the sage king Yu, the legendary founder of the Xia dynasty, and to the Xia king Kong jia (*LSCQ*, ch. 6, Yin chu, 5a).

58 Chan 1967: 286–302; Xu Fuguan 1963: 154–55; Tang Junyi 1957: 17–18, as T'ang Chün-i 1962 and 1963. This topic is discussed further in n. 69. Needless to say, there are important differences between the "New Confucians" of the 1950s and the Confucians of the 1990s, such as Tu

the continuity of bone and shell divination from the Shang to the Zhou (discussed in Chapter 9). The Shang kings used prognostication, prayer, and sacrifice to influence and negotiate with royal ancestors through an economy of sacrifice, and this power legitimated their role within the state. David Keightley argues that divination validated the offering of large (and expensive) sacrifices, legitimated the king's leadership, and provided a form of ratification for policy choices. This institutionalized divination was an important Shang legacy that was continued by the Zhou state.[59] Archaeological evidence for the Shang as a bureaucratic, rationalized, and orderly state contrasts to attempts to link Shang mantic practices to shamanism or spirit mediumship.[60] Advocates of both views of Shang religion disagree on the primary mode of mantic activity and on the character of the Shang state. They agree, however, on the religious and even theocratic character of Shang divination. Both views attest to the close connection between divination, royal power, and the legitimation of the state. For purposes of the present discussion, their agreements are more important than their disagreements.

A nationalist framework continues to emphasize the antiquity, unity, and continuity of Chinese civilization. There is a political dimension to the mononuclear model of Chinese culture and its interpretation of transmitted texts. Mao Zedong promoted theories of indigenous evolution and cultural diffusion according to which culture and writing spread outward from the Central Plains. Under Mao, a state-sponsored, nationalist archaeology consistently privileged the role of the Central Plains and Han ethnicities.[61] Li Ling too has argued that the combined force of traditional historiography and nationalist priorities has affected the course of contemporary archaeology in China. Both privilege the Central Plains as the origin of "Chinese civilization," to the detriment of archaeology in other areas. As a result, artifacts from other areas are taken as derivative, assuming one-way cultural influence from the north (especially Henan and Shaanxi provinces).[62]

Since Mao, archaeology has begun to move away from these monocultural, mononuclear theories. The late Harvard archaeologist K. C. Chang from Taiwan argued for a "Chinese Interaction Sphere," in which several distinct regional cultures in north and south China became interconnected in about 4000. This more egalitarian view of the Chinese past was motivated in

Wei-ming and Yu Ying-shih. Their activities occurred some twenty years after the "Criticize Lin Biao and Confucius" (*Pi Lin pi Kong* 批林批孔) campaign of the 1970s.

[59] Keightley 1998: 797. These arguments are also developed in Keightley 1978a.

[60] Shamanism: Chen Mengjia 1936; Chang 1983; Keightley 1998. Overview of debates: Poo 1998; Puett 2002: 32–40.

[61] Tong Enzheng 1995. [62] Li Ling 2000a.

part by new discoveries, especially in the state of Chu (Map 2.3). A new "regionalist paradigm" of interaction reflects greater decentralization since the reforms of Deng Xiaoping. This trend incorporates a much larger part of the country into the "foundation" of Chinese civilization, and creates a different narrative of unity than its centralist predecessors.[63] Li Ling also has urged archaeologists to emphasize the contexts of excavation as well as its results, partly in order to deprivilege transmitted texts. One effect would be a reassessment of the role of non-Han peoples in Chinese antiquity.[64] In summary, the ongoing political role of archaeology especially introduces difficulties that, at the present time, have no equivalent in Classical scholarship.

Religion and philosophy

Another element in Chinese historiography that has complicated the understanding of divination is a traditional separation between "philosophical schools" (*jia* 家) and religious teachings or sects (*jiao* 教). An example is the traditional distinction between the "philosophical" Daoism (*Dao jia* 道家) of the *Daodejing* and *Zhuangzi* and the "religious" Daoism (*Dao jiao* 道教) of longevity practices and popular religion. In Western historiographies of China a paradigm of secular humanism has de-emphasized religious and ritual aspects of Warring States and Han intellectual and social practices, including mantic activity. European notions of "secular" Chinese religion begin with the first Jesuit missions to China. Matteo Ricci described Confucius and the sages of ancient China as rational and humanist. They considered reason (*la ragione*) to have been received from heaven and the books of their ancient philosophers were full of piety and advice on the conduct of human life and the acquisition of virtue.[65] For a time, these favorable views influenced European philosophers to portray China as a nation organized on reason and virtue. Confucius became a veritable patron saint of the eighteenth-century Enlightenment, largely as a foil for criticism of European political institutions.[66]

63 Chinese Interaction Sphere: Chang 1986: 241, cf. Su Bingqi 1983: 34. Regionalist paradigm: Falkenhausen 1995b, which contains an excellent account of this history.

64 Li Ling 2000a.

65 *Pieni di molta pietà e buoni avisi per la vita humana et acquistare le virtù.* Ricci, *Opere storiche*, vol. 1 bk. 10: 86.

66 Examples include Montaigne (1533–92), Leibniz (1646–1716), and Voltaire (1694–1778). See Zhang Longxi 1988: esp. 117–19, Spence 1990: esp. 1–18, and Raphals 2009.

Max Weber invoked "secular" China to explain the non-emergence of capitalism there. For Weber, the Chinese "lacked the *central*, religiously determined, and rational method of life which came from within *and* which was characteristic of the classical puritan."[67] For the puritan, economic success was not an end but a means for serving God. By contrast, Confucians viewed self-cultivation as an end in itself. The Weberianism that entered China through discourses on modernization implied that Confucianism and Daoism directly impeded the development of capitalism in China (and by implication, modernization).[68] But not all post-May Fourth Chinese intellectuals embraced modernization wholeheartedly. Others, especially thinkers associated with "New Confucianism," sought a specifically Chinese modernity and emphasized the religious dimensions of Confucianism.[69]

In summary, these elements have combined in ways that artificially separate "Chinese philosophy" (or "Chinese thought") from religious practices. Within indigenous Chinese historiography, both Confucian and nationalist priorities have marginalized practices and entire geographical regions that do not fit into dynastic, Confucian, or modernizing histories. Western historiographies of China have their own reasons for separating philosophy from religion: to create a "rational" state, a liberal "Confucian humanism," or a modern secular state.

Nonetheless, several recent studies have combined sociological and philosophical approaches, and have addressed the intellectual and social contexts for divination. One example is the work of Richard J. Smith, which considers mantic practices both in the Qing dynasty and as a global phenomenon in the contemporary world.[70]

Other studies have drawn on tremendous advances in archaeology in China, especially Li Ling's *Zhongguo fang shu kao* (*A Study of the Occult Arts of China*, 1993) and a supplementary volume in 2000, revised in 2006. Li's approach of showing the complex interactions between philosophers and

[67] Weber 1951: 50. [68] See Dirlik 1995: 233–35.

[69] Although May Fourth intellectuals attacked Confucianism, their positions were not unified. Some embraced Westernization wholeheartedly; others questioned unreflective emulation of the West and attempted to reconcile "Western" and "Chinese" values. An important product of these efforts was the "New Confucianism" of Fung Yu-lan 馮友蘭 (1895–1990), Mou Tsung-san 牟宗三 (1909–95), and Tang Junyi 唐君毅 (1909–78), which questioned the positivism of scientific modernization. Other important figures attached to this movement include Xiong Shili 熊十力 (1885–1968), Liang Shuming 梁漱溟 (1893–1968), Qian Mu 錢穆 (1895–1990), Zhang Junmai 张君劢, also known as Carsun Chang (1886–1969), and Xu Fuguan 徐復觀 (1902 or 1903–82). See Furth 1976, esp. 276–302 (Chang Hao) and 242–75 (Tu Wei-ming), and Liu Shu-hsien (1991).

[70] R. J. Smith 1991: 271–81 and 2008.

technical experts has also been reflected in important studies by Donald Harper, Mark Kalinowski, and Mu-chou Poo.[71]

Finally, it must be pointed out that differences in early Chinese sources may also have indicated different attitudes toward the mantic arts by their authors. For example, the *Shi ji* chapter on mantic practitioners includes a detailed account of the marketplace diviner Sima Jizhu (discussed in Chapter 4). The *Han shu*, by contrast, never mentions him. It is not impossible that this was a deliberate omission and reflected very different attitudes toward the mantic arts by Sima Qian and Ban Gu, respectively.

Comparing comparables

What can we gain from comparing Chinese and Greek historiographies and theories of divination? In some areas, the two are similar. In others, one effectively parochializes the other. The historiographies of divination in China and Greece seem to have nothing in common. Why should we compare them and what can we learn from them? What can Classicists learn from a comparison with Chinese divination? What can sinologists learn from the study of Greek divination?

In a changing and complex history, recent engagement between Classics, sociology, and anthropology, and in particular the influence of the Paris school and recent archaeology, has revolutionized the discipline in ways that the foregoing discussion has only touched upon. The result is a wealth of theoretical perspectives. For the study of divination, the work of Vernant is particularly important, and his emphasis on the need to explore both mental attitudes and social institutions has informed most work on the subject ever since.[72] By contrast, systematic interpretive studies of Chinese divination are less common than those covering Greco-Roman antiquity. There are several possible reasons for this. On the one hand, long-standing traditions of *Yi jing* hermeneutics do not take an interest in expertise traditions. Much of the important archaeological evidence is fairly recent, and many studies of Chinese mantic texts excavated from tombs are paleographical or otherwise highly specialized. The wealth of different methods, and the healthy debate about methodology that has characterized recent Classical scholarship on Greek and Roman divination, has much to offer.

[71] Harper 1997, 1999b, 2001; Kalinowski 2004, 2005; Chemla, Harper, and Kalinowski 1999; Poo 1998.

[72] For example, the introduction to Johnston and Struck 2005 is organized around this dichotomy.

As yet, however, these issues and debates have not engaged historians of early China in China or the West. For example, Chinese scholarship occasionally cites Jean-Pierre Vernant (Wei Ernan 維爾南), but primarily for his work on slavery. I can find no Chinese citation of his work on divination.

Vernant's work on divination has been applied to Chinese sources in a major way in an eponymous volume titled *Divination et Rationalité en Chine Ancienne* in the French journal *Extrême-Orient Extrême-Occident*, which explicitly pursues the agenda of the original volume.[73] It investigates how the elements of divination constituted and were constituted by the historical processes of Chinese scientific thought in the Shang, Zhou, Warring States, and Han periods. These essays show that in China, as in Greece, divination extended to a wide range of activities and its importance was not limited to predicting future or hidden events. In both China and Greece, it had profound effects on the development of medicine, law, philosophy, politics, and science. The volume concludes with a brief comparison of the roles of Chinese and Greek divination in the development of self-conscious reflection and methods of scientific inquiry.

Why should Classicists study Chinese divination? There is an inherent difficulty, because of the unique position of Greece and Rome in European and more broadly "Western" history. To quote Detienne again:

> by insisting on the otherness of the Greeks or the Roman citizens and putting them into perspective by employing a comparative approach, you are directly threatening the cultural heritage of which the ancients are the surest value. When the heritage is in danger, just look how the old nations begin to tremble and foam at the mouth.[74]

Why, after such an auspicious beginning under Vernant, did Classicists abandon comparative study? Detienne notes that part of the problem was the state of an earlier "dialogue" between Classics and an anthropology that restricted itself to the study of small, self-contained groups without writing or history.[75] This point was originally made by Moses Finley in his Jane Harrison Memorial Lecture of 1972. Finley proposed what he considered appropriate comparanda for Classics. Taking anthropology rather than sociology as a model, he advocated the creation of a third discipline: the comparative study of literate, "post-primitive," pre-industrial, historical societies.[76] Detienne does not agree with Finley on all points, but in *comparer l'incomparable* and several subsequent papers, Detienne defends

[73] Chemla, Harper, and Kalinowski 1999. [74] Detienne 2001: 102. [75] Finley 1975: 106.

[76] He identified pre-Maoist China, pre-colonial India, medieval Europe, pre-revolutionary Russia, and medieval Islam. Finley 1975: 118–19; cf. Detienne 2001: 105–6.

a "constructive" comparativism between historians and anthropologists, with a specific view to establishing "comparables" (*comparables*), without regard to the limits of time and space.[77]

Comparisons used by Classicists to understand oracular divination have been limited to African oracles, but are these the best comparanda? With few exceptions, this comparative turn has not extended to China, and this is a lost opportunity.[78] The diversity and rich textual and material history of early Chinese divination offer a nuanced comparative context for many issues, including functionalist arguments and the Greek distinction between inspired and technical divination. For example, Lisa Maurizio argues that Plato's distinction between inspired divination and spirit possession may be useful for ancient Greece, but it cannot be applied to cultures in which diviners combine spirit possession with technical methods such as bird divination (ornithomancy) or casting lots (cleromancy).[79] She offers an alternative typology of divination based on contemporary Chinese practices.[80] Her point is that such comparisons can show what elements are constant across divination methods and cultures. As the ensuing chapters will show, early Chinese divination practices present a wide range of techniques, most of which do not involve spirit possession.

The Chinese evidence may also contribute to ongoing debates on sociological accounts of Greek divination. Sociological explanations partially preclude two other possible functions of divination: predicting the future and ascertaining the will of the gods. The goals of accurate prediction and social consensus are partially at odds. The goal of prediction is to reveal future events or explain past or present ones. By contrast, social consensus is not concerned with whether any given prediction proves accurate or not.

Finally, comparison may provide new perspectives for Classicists on a philosophical problem closely related to divination: namely attitudes toward fate and fatalism. Here Mesopotamian evidence is also instructive, since the assumption of divine intervention did not deter interest in prediction. Although a god might cure or kill, Babylonian diviners still sought to predict the course of illnesses, and the systematic observation that went with that effort. As in the case of Hippocratic physicians, who also believed

[77] Detienne 2000, 2001, and 2002.

[78] Significant exceptions are Maurizio 1995, Johnston 2001 (citing Maurizio), Lloyd 1999a, 1999b, 2002, and Lloyd and Sivin 2002.

[79] Maurizio 1995: 80–81.

[80] Emily Ahern (1981: 51–63) focuses on the presence (interpersonal) or absence (non-interpersonal) of communication within the divination process. Non-interpersonal knowledge systems include physiognomy or horoscopes. According to Maurizio, Ahern's schema corresponds closely to Zuesse 1987, but is based on comparative evidence.

that not all illnesses were curable, the ability to prognosticate the course of an illness accurately increased the authority of the physician. Patients' confidence might in turn improve their prospects for recovery.

In summary, Greek classifications have been constitutive of understandings of what divination is and how it should be classified, but scholars of Chinese and Greek divination have much to learn from each other. It is particularly striking that in both cases there is a history of dissonance between received textual traditions and archaeology. How to combine the use of archaeological and textual sources is clearly an important methodological issue for both. Equally striking are the very different methods used and questions asked.

4 Practitioners

吾聞古之聖人，不居朝廷，必在卜醫之中。

I have heard that the sages of antiquity did not reside at court, but were surely to be found among the turtle shell diviners and physicians.[1]

Who were the mantic experts in China and Greece? What did they do and how did they become practitioners of mantic arts? In China we can distinguish court officials from independent practitioners, who might specialize in one method or who might be competent in several, but that distinction is nuanced in several important ways. In Greece, the major division was between temple oracles and independent practitioners. The *prophētēs* (feminine *prophētis*) officiated at an oracular shrine; the *mantis* (plural *manteis*) was an independent diviner, sometimes itinerant, who developed his own practice and clientele. Some individual *manteis* "inherited" their expertise within family lineages; others gained it or were selected for training for other reasons. *Manteis* coexisted with oracles, and also competed with other technical experts. I compare Chinese and Greek mantic practitioners from three perspectives.

The first perspective looks at differences between official and independent mantic practitioners. John Dillery has observed that the main difference between the *prophētēs* and the *mantis* was that the *prophētēs* was a "dependent diviner" associated with a particular god and cult while a *mantis* was "independent" of both place and cult.[2] In both Greece and China there was a strong distinction between "official" personnel dependent on a particular oracle (Greece) or court (China) and practitioners who retained independence of employment. Needless to say, the nature of official employment differed significantly between Chinese courts and Greek oracular shrines. Both Chinese and Greek mantic officials participated in state ritual and interpreted signs arising from sacrifice. They were also called upon to interpret the significance of dreams, omens, and other spontaneous occurrences. Chinese

[1] *SJ* 127.3215. Sima Qian attributes this remark to the great Han poet and statesman Jia Yi 賈誼 (201–169).

[2] Dillery 2005: 171.

officials were also centrally concerned with creating and preserving calendars and written records.

Chinese and Greek official diviners also differed in their relation to political authority. Chinese mantic officials drew their authority as well as employment from the state, but independence from political authority contributed to the authority and prestige of Delphi in particular. Greek "official" diviners were employed by, and drew their authority from, temples, in each case a specific cult of a particular god.

Chinese independent practitioners used some of the same methods as their official counterparts, including turtle shell, milfoil, and mantic astrolabes (diviner's boards), but did not enjoy the same status. Greek independent practitioners used other methods than oracles, and also held lower status (with the partial exception of military *manteis*). Yet both Chinese and Greek independent practitioners enjoyed lower prestige than official divination.

The second perspective is the importance of mantic lineages. Descent from a mantic family was an important qualification for both oracular and independent Greek diviners. It was an important factor in an independent *mantis*' ability to attract clientele. Oracular sites depended on the family lineages of the (male) priestly clans that managed them. There is also some evidence that descent was a factor in the appointment of priestesses. Lineage was also important for Chinese official and independent practitioners. Mantic offices (like many others) may have been hereditary. There is evidence that Chinese independent practitioners also passed down their skills through family lineages. The collected biographies of a particular type of mantic expert (the *fang* 方 arts, discussed below) suggest that membership in a family was not the major source of mantic expertise.

The benefits of mantic lineages did not necessarily extend to women, who were largely excluded from the Greek independent competitive milieu and the Chinese official one. Can we account for these differences by the competitiveness of Greek professional life or the lack of state patronage of the mantic arts?

A third perspective is the role of competition, control, and charisma. In *The Seer in Ancient Greece*, Michael Flower has argued that independence of employment was an important difference between itinerant Greek *manteis* and their Mesopotamian counterparts.[3] They needed different skills from those of Mesopotamian mantic officials, and relied on oral knowledge and charisma to master their craft and to attract and retain clientele. Flower

[3] Flower 2008.

describes a transition from one cultural context to another and the transformation of a science into a performance. Flower's contrast may help explain differences between Chinese and Greek mantic practice.

Vernant, Lloyd, and others have argued for a Greek penchant for intense political and intellectual competition; and have even linked the rise of Greek science to the availability of debate and competition.[4] Did an analogous competition extend to the mantic arts?

Mantic competition took its own form in China. The Warring States period was a time of unprecedented social mobility and political change. The Zhou court had been displaced from its original capital, and local rulers and smaller states fought internally and externally for hegemony. There was internal and external competition across society. Warfare was transformed by the creation of infantry armies and new disciplines of military strategy. With these arose new modes of discourse and power relations, and a reconfiguration of the relations between political power, knowledge, and authority, including divination and knowledge of Heaven and the gods. By the third century, several major social groups had claimed various aspects of divine knowledge and authority. Most important were technical specialists: ritualists, physicians, and astrocalendric specialists, a group whose importance has been noted by a wide range of scholars.[5] Their expertise preceded and paralleled that of the textual specialists of the philosophical traditions, with whom they competed for patronage and clientele.

Chinese mantic experts

The earliest evidence for Chinese mantic practices concerns court officials. It is possible that mantic expertise diffused outward from courts to elites, to the broader population, but this picture may reflect the limitations of the evidence.

Court officials

We can historicize important changes in the organization and practices of court mantic officials by considering evidence from Shang mantic practices, Warring States testimony from the *Zhou li* and excavated texts, and institutional developments in the Western and Eastern Han.

[4] Vernant 1982, 1983; Lloyd 1979, 1987, 1990, 1996, 2002; Vidal-Naquet 1986.

[5] A. C. Graham (1986: 1–2) credited them with the development of Five-phase cosmology. Cf. Ngo Van Xuyet 1976, Li Ling 1993 and 2000a.

Figure 4.1 Turtle plastron, from Anyang (*c.* 1300–1046).

The oracle bone inscriptions (Figure 4.1) name some 120 diviners, but named mantic officials are most prominent in the earlier records. Later inscriptions increasingly specify that the king read and interpreted the cracks.[6] Given the limitations of the Shang evidence, we do not know whether Shang diviners were court officials or independent practitioners. There is also archaeological evidence of turtle and possibly milfoil divination at the Western Zhou court (discussed further in Chapter 9).

Turtle and milfoil diviners also appear in the bamboo slip texts from Baoshan (*c.* 316), which provide late fourth-century accounts of prognostications on behalf of the tomb's occupant, a high official in the state of Chu.[7] The queries are personal in nature, and concern his official prospects and health. We know no details of the staff that served him, including whether the diviners he consulted were part of his household or official staff or independent practitioners consulted at need. The records name twelve mantic specialists and the method each used.[8] Each appears to specialize in turtle or milfoil and to use one instrument, which is also named. Most

[6] E.g. 甲申卜殻貞 "Crack making on *jiashen*, Que prognosticated" (*Heji* 1400 正). Other inscriptions refer to prognostications by Bin 賓, Zheng 爭 (Period 1, before 1180); Da 大, Lü 旅, Xing 行, Ji 即, Yin 尹, Chu 出 (Period 2, 1180–1151); and He 何 (Period 3, 1150–?). By Periods 4 (?–1106) and 5 (1105–1045), the king seems to have performed both prognostication and interpretation. Dong Zuobin 1965: 116 and 1967–68; Keightley 1978b: 31–35, 1997: 30–41.

[7] *Baoshan Chu jian* 1991. Studies: Li Ling 1990, 1993: esp. 271–86; Chen Wei 1996, 1997, 1999; Harper 1998, 1999b, 2001; Weld 1999; Raphals 2004, 2005; Cook 2006. Translations: Raphals 2005 (partial) and Cook 2006 (full).

[8] The shell names: Li Ling 1990: 81 and 1993: 263, 280–82. The Baoshan materials are discussed in Chapter 9.

records include both methods, but no two sequences are the same. The majority are turtle shell procedures (sixteen out of twenty-two). Most records include a man named Gu Ji 盬吉, who begins the sequence and prognosticates in all three years recorded. It is possible that he was part of a permanent staff, and that other specialists were brought in for individual consultations. Prognostications and their associated sacrifices were also "transferred" from one diviner to another, sometimes after a specific instruction to do so in a previous procedure. The Baoshan evidence does indicate that turtle shell was the dominant procedure and that turtle and milfoil specialists worked in conjunction.

A detailed if perhaps hypothetical description of Eastern Zhou court mantic officials appears in the *Zhou li*. The text probably dates to the late third century, and may be a partly ideal account of third-century offices, deliberately ascribed to the Zhou. There is considerable doubt about the existence of the offices it describes, but for purposes of the present discussion, it offers a Warring States Chinese perspective on how mantic officials should be organized. The *Zhou li* locates three mantic offices in the Offices of Spring (*Chun guan* 春官), the bureaucracy concerned with ancestral sacrifice. The Director of Divination (*Taibu* 大卜), the Director of Incantation (*Taizhu* 大祝), and the Director of Astronomy (*Taishi* 大史) worked in conjunction. Diviners (*bu*) prognosticated, incantators (*zhu*) invoked the spirits, and recording officials (*shi*) recorded and preserved the results. Each had a large and complex staff of junior officers, scribes, and assistants (described in Appendix 4.1).

The Director of Divination was in charge of turtle shell diviners, milfoil specialists, and dream prognosticators, which suggests the early importance of these three methods. Shell cracking and stalk casting were often done together in highly ritual circumstances. Dream diviners questioned the ruler about his dreams at the end of winter and offered new grain to the four directions for the spirits who send evil dreams.

The Director of Incantation was in charge of several types of incantator as well as spirit mediums (*wu* 巫, less correctly called *wu*-shamans), both male and female, who were not themselves diviners but who worked with them.[9] There seems to have been some initial redundancy between the two groups. Participation in state ritual distinguished *wu* officials from non-official spirit mediums and other independent practitioners.[10]

9 *ZL* 17:13b–14b (Biot 1.409); cf. 25:5b–19a (Biot 2.85–104). Incantators: Falkenhausen 1995a: 280–89.

10 Loewe 1994: 165–67. As Zeng Qinliang observes (1993: 4), if they could serve the gods by singing poems they became musicians. If they could deliver invocations, they became incantators.

In the oracle bone and bronze inscriptions, scribes (*shi* 史) were officials charged with writing who recorded and preserved texts, prominently including mantic records. At some point, these duties expanded to astronomical matters, including regulation of the calendar and the selection of auspicious days.[11]

The *Zhou li* describes the *Taishi* as an astronomical official responsible for astrocalendric and textual aspects of ritual, including the identification of auspicious days. He maintained records, regulated the calendar, announced the first day of the new moon, and advised the sovereign whenever an intercalary month was impending. His ritual duties included determining auspicious days for grand sacrifice and participating in funerals. During sacrifice he accompanied the officials in charge and regulated the proceedings by "reading his ritual texts." At assemblies of state he advised the sovereign on accepting tribute. At conclaves of the army, he was responsible for bringing the calendar. He studied the designs for any change of the capital and inspected arrangements for state funerals. At the funeral of an emperor, he read the elegy.[12] The *Zhou li* describes the *Taishi* as performing astronomical observations, but he was not an astrologer; the primary purpose of astronomical observation was the regulation of the calendar. The *Zhou li* also mentions several other specifically astronomical officials.[13]

Another section of the *Zhou li* describes an official called the *fangxiangshi* 方相氏, possibly a spirit medium responsible for exorcisms. This official may be a predecessor of the *fangshi* ("recipe masters") of the Qin and Han courts (discussed below). This office was located in the Offices of Summer (*Xia guan* 夏官), concerned with military affairs. It may have been understood as distinct from the ritual concerns of the Offices of Spring.[14]

The classification of the *Zhou li* reflects changes in the relative status of different officials as the overlapping functions of diviner, incantator, and

[11] See Xu Fuguan 1980.

[12] *ZL* 26:11a–16b (Biot 2.104–10). Taishi's staff: 17:14b (Biot 1.413). Reading ritual texts (*Du li shu* 讀禮書): 26:14a–b (Biot 2.107–10). In addition, scribes (*shi*) appear as part of the attendant staff of high offices, including those specifically connected with divination and incantation, for example the *Taizai* (1:5b–7b), *Tai Situ* (9:1b–2a), *Tai Zongbo* (17:3a–b), and *Tai Siguan* (34:1b–2a).

[13] Ministry of Spring: the Royal Astronomer (*Fengxiangshi* 馮相氏) made observations in the *Lingtai* hall (*ZL* 26:17a–20b). The Guardian of Celestial Manifestations (*Baozhangshi* 保章氏) recorded them (*ZL* 26:20b–24a). The Observer of Encroachments (*Shijin* 眡祲) observed weather and eclipses (*ZL* 25:4a–5b; "encroachments" refer to *yin* and *yang*). The Ministry of Spring also included a Supervisor of Water Clocks (*Qiehushi* 挈壺氏, *ZL* 30:15a–16b). See Needham 1959: 189–91 for these officials.

[14] *ZL* 31:12a. Major divisions of the *Zhou li*: ECTBG. It is dangerous to jump to conclusions on this point. Other classificatory systems such as the *Han shu* Bibliographic Treatise show considerable overlaps in their distribution of material. Examples: Kalinowski 2004, Yates 1994.

spirit medium differentiated under the pressures of new bureaucratic forms of government in the Warring States and Western Han. It has been speculated that, as the older theocratic state system collapsed and formerly religious ceremonies became secularized, the originally equal status of incantators and spirit mediums transformed. The status of incantators rose and that of spirit mediums fell; incantators came to hold high positions and spirit mediums became low-level officials. There is also evidence that mantic offices were hereditary.[15]

Important institutional changes occurred during the Western Han. The officials in charge of sacrifice, prognostication, astronomy, and record-keeping were placed under the authority of the Minister of Ceremonial (*Taichang* 太常), the foremost of the Nine Ministers of State. The *Taichang* ministry, which approximately corresponded to the *Zhou li* Offices of Spring, was in charge of prognostication and sacrifice, including ceremonies in the imperial ancestral temples and the worship of Heaven and Earth (see Appendix 4.2). The *Taibu ling* 太卜令 (Grand Diviner) was responsible for prognostication. The *Taizhu ling* 太祝令 (Grand Incantator) read incantations and welcomed and sent off the spirits. The *Taishi ling* 太史令 (Grand Scribe or Grand Astronomer), the office held by Sima Qian and Sima Tan 司馬談, was in charge of astronomy, astrology, calendrics, record-keeping, the choice of auspicious days, and other ritual matters, including expiatory sacrifices and prayers for rain. All this parallels the structure of the *Zhou li*, where astronomical expertise was located in the Offices of Spring, which, like the *Taichang* ministry, was concerned with ritual and ancestral sacrifice.[16]

In the Eastern Han, the management of turtle and milfoil was transferred to the *Taishi ling*, who thus gained far-reaching authority over astronomical and meteorological observation, calendrics, and records concerning disasters and portents.[17] The effect was to further consolidate power in the

[15] The *Zuo zhuan* mentions a request for prognostication by the official diviner's father (263, Min 2.4, Legge 128–29). Other passages suggesting the hereditary nature of prognostication: Zuo, 629 (Wen 18.1, Legge 281) and 1263 (Zhao 5.1, Legge 603). Sima Qian provides a lineage of his own office at *SJ* 130.3285–95.

[16] *Taichang* ministry: *HS* 19A.726–27. Office of *Taibu ling*: *SJ* 127.3215, which states that this office existed from the beginning of the Western Han. See Goh Thean Chye [Wu Tiancai] 1967: 47–52, 84–94; Eberhard 1957: esp. 46; Bielenstein 1980: 17–23; Loewe 1994: 166–67 and 2006: 24–25; and Kalinowski 2010: 340.

[17] The enhanced role of the office of the *Taishi ling* is also evident in the structure of the *Han shu* Bibliographic Treatise, which gives priority to astrocalendric texts. Other late Western Han ritual and doctrinal reforms also enhanced the importance of astrocalendric ideas and practices. See *HHS* 25.3574; Kalinowski 2004 (esp. 225–28) and 2010.

Astronomical Bureau.[18] Major foci of court astronomy were the calendar and the observation, recording, and explanation of portents: celestial events such as eclipses, supernovae, planetary conjunctions, and comets.[19]

Other Western Han officials performed subcelestial observation and prognostication by "wind horns" (*fengjiao* 風角) and by pitch pipes. The *Shi ji* Treatise on the Pitch Pipes (*SJ* 25) describes their use to observe the otherwise imperceptible movements of *qi* and in the yearly cycle of *yin* and *yang* (discussed in detail in Chapter 5). The *Taishi ling*'s staff included officials in charge of observing *qi* (*hou qi* 候氣 or *wang qi* 望氣).[20] The Astronomical Treatise (*SJ* 27) discusses wind divination after the observation of clouds and vapors (which are, of course, moved by the winds). Wind divination was used to predict the nature of the harvest, based on directional winds. In the Eastern Han, there may have been an official specifically charged with watching them.[21] Subsequently, winds and clouds were increasingly associated with military prognostication.

How were these offices filled? There is at least some evidence that the office of the *Taishi ling* was hereditary. Sima Qian inherited his office from his father Sima Tan. In addition, mechanisms developed during the Western Han for recruiting talent would also have applied to mantic officials. Legal statutes excavated from Shuihudi (217) and Zhangjiashan (186) provide some information on this point, as well as on the selection duties and official status of prognosticators and scribes. The Shuihudi text now known as "Eighteen Qin Statutes" (*Qin lü shiba zhong* 秦律十八種) indicates the status of diviners and scribes as government employees. One specifies the daily food rations for officials without aristocratic rank, including diviners, scribes, chief coachmen, attendants, and storehouse keepers: one *dou* (one pint) of grain, vegetable soup, and a small measure of salt.[22] Statutes from Zhangjiashan on scribes and diviners prove that, by the early

[18] There were also conflicts between different groups of mantic officials, for example Eastern Han conflicts between factions promoting the techniques and authority of the office of the *Taishi ling* and practitioners of non-official, occult arts (often vaguely described as *fangshi*). See Kalinowski 2010: 351. *Fangshi*: Li Ling 1995. On the terms *fangshi*, *boshi*, and *Ru*: Zufferey 1998: 962–63; Cheng 2001: 109–14.

[19] Additional accounts of portents and abnormal natural phenomena appear in the *Han shu* Annals (1–12) and the Treatise on the Five Agents (*Wuxing zhi*, *HS* 27). See Dubs 1958, Nakayama 1966.

[20] *SJ* 25.1243 (Chavannes 3.300–14). See Bodde 1959, Vogel 1994, and Huang Yi-Long and Chang Chih-Ch'eng 1996.

[21] *SJ* 27.1340 (Chavannes 3.397); *HHS* 25.3572n2, Loewe 1994: 197–208.

[22] *SHD* (Statutes) 60, slip 182; Hulsewé 1985: 85. A passage from the section "Answers to Questions on the Qin Statutes" (*Qin lü da wen* 秦律答問) asks about diviners' and scribes' servants with beards shaved off. These officials, when convicted of a crime, could be demoted to servants of their former office (139, slip 194; Hulsewé 1985: 176). See also Yates 1995.

Western Han, official rules governed the careers of specialists in sacrifice and prognostication at the court, commandery, and county levels. The *Han shu* Bibliographic Treatise and the "Statutes and Ordinances of the Second Year" (*Er nian lü ling* 二年律令) from Zhangjiashan specify the responsibilities of the *Taibu* and *Taishi* for testing students for those offices. For example, the *Taibu* was responsible for testing the writing abilities of student candidates for scribal positions. They were graded, and appointed appropriately as clerks or copyists within the central government.[23] The section titled "Statutes on Scribes" (*Shi lü* 史律) gives instructions for the training and appointment of scribes and diviners.[24]

Independent practitioners: marketplace diviners and *fangshi*

By the Western Han, we find evidence of the popularity of mantic practices across the social spectrum, and some consensus that humans could understand patterns of change in the universe. Independent mantic experts "sold prognostication in the marketplace."[25] They are the focus of *Shi ji* 127, the collected biographies of "Diviners of auspicious and inauspicious days" (*rizhe* 日者). This chapter describes an independent diviner named Sima Jizhu 司馬季主, a native of Chu who practiced his art in the Eastern Market of Chang'an. One day the erudite Jia Yi 賈誼 (206–169) and the palace counselor Song Zhong 宋忠 decided to test a saying that the sages of antiquity were to be found not in the courts, but prognosticating in the marketplace.

They encounter Sima Jizhu on a rainy day with few people about, giving instruction to several students. The two officials are treated to a discourse on heaven and earth, the cycles of the sun, moon, stars, and constellations, benevolence and righteousness, and how to distinguish signs of good and ill auspice.[26] Startled, they ask why Sima engages in such a low occupation. He turns the tables on his visitors by inquiring into their own values and priorities. They look down on diviners who exaggerate their predictions to appeal to clientele and extort money, but corrupt court officials take public money for private profit and twist the law to oppress the people. By contrast:

今夫卜者，必法天地，象四時，順於仁義，分策定卦，旋式正棋，然後言天地之利害，事之成敗。

[23] *HS* 30.1720–21; cf. Hulsewé 1990: 219–22.

[24] *ZJS* 203–4, slips 474–86. Context: Li Xueqin and Xing Wen 2001.

[25] *Mai bu yu shi* 賣卜於市, cf. *HHS* 63.2089–90 and 81.2689. The *Hou Han shu* also refers to diviners who "sold prognostications to provide the necessities of life" (*mai bu zi feng* 賣卜自奉, 30B.1053) and "sold prognostications to eat" (*mai bu ji shi* 賣卜給食, 53.1750).

[26] *SJ* 127.3215–20. Discussion: Loewe 1994: 170–71. Translation: Pokora 1987.

Now the diviner of necessity takes heaven and earth as his model and the four seasons as his image. He conforms to benevolence and righteousness; he divides the milfoil stalks and establishes the hexagram. He revolves the mantic astrolabe [*shi*] and rectifies the mantic chessboard [*qi*]. Only afterward does he speak of benefit and harm in heaven and earth or [predict] whether undertakings will result in success or failure.[27]

He argues that their activities create social order, cure the sick, avoid disaster, arrange marriages, and bring human plans to fruition. He portrays diviners as generalists who know how to use turtle, milfoil, *Yi jing* trigrams, and mantic astrolabes. He adds:

今夫卜筮者之為業也，積之無委聚，藏之不用府庫，徙之不用輜車，負裝之不重，止而用之無盡索之時。

Now as to the livelihood of the turtle or milfoil diviner, accumulating [equipment] is not a care, and storing it requires no state repository. His migrations require no baggage cart; it is light enough to bear on his shoulders. When he stops and uses it there is no limit of time.[28]

The rhetorical force of this passage is to praise the ethics and skill of the marketplace diviners over those of their court counterparts (presumably including the office of Sima Qian himself). His emphasis on portability and freedom of time or season suggests that some diviners were itinerant.

The *Han shu* describes a second independent mantic expert in the person of Yan Junping 嚴君平 (83 BCE–10 CE), a Daoist scholar who made his living at prognostication in the Chengdu marketplace. After earning enough for his daily needs, he would close his shop and teach the *Laozi* and *Zhuangzi*. He gave this explanation for his way of life:

卜筮者賤業，而可以惠人。有邪惡非正之問，則依蓍龜為言利害。 與人子言依於孝，與人弟言依於順，與人臣言依於忠，各因勢導之以善，從吾言者，已過半矣。

Turtle and milfoil prognostication is a low occupation, but it can benefit people nonetheless. If the questions are about what is wicked or not upright, I use turtle and milfoil to speak of benefit and harm. To a son I speak of filiality; to a younger brother I speak of deference; to a subject I speak of loyalty. Each according to situation, I lead them toward being good, and the majority follow my words.[29]

[27] *SJ* 127.3218, based on Pokora 1987: 221–22. [28] *SJ* 127.3219.

[29] *HS* 72.3056. Yan (for Zhuang 莊) Zun 嚴遵 (style name Junping 君平) was a teacher of the great Ru exegete Yang Xiong (53 BCE–18 CE). See Farmer 2001: 79–81.

Neither Sima Jizhu nor Yan Junping report in detail what their clients consulted them about. In each case, the rhetorical point is to praise the scholar-diviner and to show that he was a type of sage who used the need for making a living to help and improve the people who clearly did consult him. Jia Yi's visit to "Diviners Market" (*bu si* 卜肆) also makes it clear that the court was aware of, and not overly interested in, marketplace diviners. There seems to be no paranoia over their predictions, or any suggestion that predictive techniques diffused through the population undermined imperial authority.[30]

The *fangshi* were a second group of independent diviners who became an important force in the Han court during the reign of Han Wu Di.[31] Most came from outlying regions, and gained influence for their skills in prediction, healing, and omen interpretation (all linked to the growth of science in early China). They used magico-medical practices to maintain the health and vitality of the emperor and also introduced standardized measurement of time, space, weight, and musical pitch.

Collected biographies of *fangshi* appear in the *Hou Han shu* under the heading "Fang Techniques" (*fang shu* 方術). According to the preface, *fang* fate calculation techniques included mantic astrolabes, milfoil, mantic texts, stem-branch analysis, communication with spirits, and prognostication based on clouds, winds, birdcalls, dreams, physiognomy, and writing.[32] They could interpret the *Yi jing*, the River diagram, and the meaning of anomalies. They could heal and had magical powers; they could act at a distance and revive the dead. Predictions attributed to them included eclipses, the time of their own deaths, and the future generally. They were also credited with expertise in classical texts and in Huang-Lao and Daoist lore. Several were wind prognosticators.

[30] The third figure, Lang Zong 郎宗 (style name Zhong Sui 仲綏), the father of the great Eastern Han omen interpreter Lang Yi 郎顗 (fl. 133 CE), receives only a passing reference. According to the *Hou Han shu* (30B.1053) he "had studied Master Jing's 'Changes.' He was good at Wind Horns, star calculations (*xing suan* 星筭), and Six Days and Seven Parts 六日七分. He knew how to observe *qi* and prognosticate good and ill auspice, and he often sold prognostications in order to support himself 常賣卜自奉. Lang Yi: de Crespigny 1976: 98, n. 88.

[31] Their origins are probably much older. They are mentioned in the *Zhou li*, and references to "esoteric books" (*fangshu* 方書) and "esoteric theories" (*fangshuo* 方說) begin to appear in Warring States texts. Practices attributed to the *fangshi* have clear antecedents in Warring States sources such as the *Zhuangzi* and the *Neiye*. They first appear in a court context in references to their presence in the court of Qin Shihuang 秦始皇 (259–210), who ruled Qin from 246 to 221 and promulgated the Qin dynasty in 221. They remained influential to the early part of the Six Dynasties (to the fourth century CE).

[32] *HHS* 82A and 82B. Most of these techniques date from the late Zhou. See Li Ling 1995 and Kalinowski 2010: esp. Appendix 2.

Several were officials who used their mantic skills to predict and prevent disasters. For example, in the midst of a drought, the wind diviner Ren Wengong 任文公 (fl. 5 CE) predicted an impending flood. He built boats and persuaded others to do so; but he could not persuade the governor, and hundreds of people died in the flood. Another wind diviner named Liao Fu 廖扶 (fl. 110 CE) predicted a failed harvest; he stored grain against it and even paid for the burial of the dead whose own families could not.[33]

After the creation of chairs in the Classics, many Eastern Han mantic specialists were educated Ru (introduced in Chapter 2), in some cases even members of the Academy (*bo shi* 博士). Their biographies also indicate textual lineages passed on through family lineages. For example, the *Hou Han shu* biography of Yang Hou 楊厚 (fl. 109–49 CE) indicates that training in omenology went back three generations in his family, in part through a collection of occult writings from his grandfather's Western Han ancestors.[34]

Physiognomy was particularly important because of its practical applications. The oldest account of it is in the *Zuo zhuan*:

公孫敖聞其能相人也，見其二子焉。叔服曰，穀也食子，難也收子，穀也豐下，必有後於魯國。

Gongsun Ao had heard that Shu Fu was a master of physiognomy and introduced his two sons to him. Shu Fu said: "Gu will feed you, Nuo will bury you. The lower part of Gu's face is large, he will have posterity in the state of Lu."[35]

Chinese accounts of physiognomy refer to three distinct kinds of prediction or assessment: (1) predictive judgments based on physical features of animate beings (bone structure, color, particular physical features such as moles or other distinguishing marks), (2) the application of these principles to non-animate beings, such as swords and knives, and (3) physiognomic predictions based on non-observable features, for example predictions about a future birth. Physiognomy thus includes a spectrum of abilities that range from the strict sense of predicting a person's future from his or

[33] *HHS* 82A.2707–21. They include Ren Wengong 任文公 (2707), Xie Yiwu 謝夷吾 (2713), Yang You 楊由 (2716), Li Nan 李南, Duan Yi 段翳, and Liao Fu 廖扶 (2719), and Fan Ying 樊英 (2721).

[34] Lang Yi 郎顗 is probably another example. His biography is followed by those of his father Yang Tong 楊統 and his grandfather Yang Chunqing 楊春卿: *HHS* 30A.1047. See Kalinowski 2010. The term Ru is introduced in Chapter 2.

[35] Zuo, 510 (Wen 1.1), trans. Legge 229. Wen Gong's reign began in 725.

her bone structure or coloring to the more extended sense of the ability to judge character from stance or physical presence.[36]

The *Zuo zhuan*, *Guo yu*, and *Shi ji* describe the use of physiognomy to predict the character of potential heirs. Several of these accounts involve women. The *Zuo zhuan* and *Guo yu* recount physiognomic assessments of newborn sons by the mother of the Jin 晉 statesman Shu Xiang 叔向 (d. 528 BCE). The *Shi ji* also describes king Jianzi of Zhao (d. 475 BCE) consulting a physiognomist to assess his grown sons as potential heirs.[37] The *Shi ji* and *Han shu* also describe two verified predictions by the second-century woman physiognomist Xu Fu 許負 (fl. 200 BCE), the grandmother of the physiognomist Guo Jie 郭解 (d. 126–124). She predicted a princess would give birth to Han Gaozu's 漢高祖 (r. 202–195) son, the future emperor Han Wendi 漢文帝 (r. 180–157, for which she was given a title of nobility in her own right). She also predicted (from the lines converging at the corner of the mouth) that the official Zhou Yafu 周亞夫 would attain high rank but would die of starvation.[38] Another *Shi ji* narrative describes the female physiognomist Tang Ju 唐舉 of Liang (fl. 250) predicting the rise of Li Si 李斯 of Qin (discussed in Chapter 7).

Excavated texts on physiognomy include a horse physiognomy text from Mawangdui and physiognomy texts on dogs (Yinqueshan) and swords (Juyan). Some dozen mostly undated manuscripts discovered at Dunhuang provide important additional information, including five texts attributed to Xu Fu and twelve other experts, most of whose names appear in Han, Later Han, and Three Kingdoms accounts.[39]

Several make an analogy between character and the configuration of the body, but these brief accounts give little detail of the methods used. More extensive accounts come from physiognomy manuals from later periods, especially the Ming dynasty *Shenxiang quanbian* 神相全編 (Complete Account of Spirit Physiognomy).[40] Another physiognomic specialty was

[36] This distinction between divination and other modes of prediction is not uniquely Chinese; Cicero (*Div*. 1.34) makes an analogous distinction in *De Divinatione* when Quintus distinguishes between "natural" divination and the "skillful" diviners who learn what is known by observation and deduce the unknown from it.

[37] For references and translations see Chapter 7.

[38] Guo Jie: *SJ* 124.3185, *HS* 92.3701. Han Gaozu: *SJ* 49.1970–71, *HS* 97A.3941, cf. *LH*, 117, 120, and 126 ("Gu xiang" 3.2, Forke 1.308–9) and *Qianfu lun* 27.311. Zhou Yafu: *SJ* 57.2073–74, *HS* 40.2057, cf. Loewe 2000: 618.

[39] Three (P2572, P2797r, and P3589v) are in the Bibliothèque Nationale. Two (S5969 and C117v) are in the British Library. The most complete is P2572. See Despeux 2003. These texts are discussed further in Chapters 5 and 7.

[40] It was compiled by the Ming physiognomist Yuan Zhongche 袁忠徹 (1367–1458), based on transmissions from his father, the physiognomist Yuan Liuzhuang 袁柳莊 (1335–1410). It is

the assessment of horses. Several brief accounts mention horse and also dog physiognomists. The most famous horse physiognomist was the seventh-century figure Sun Yang 孫陽, also known as Bo Le 伯樂 (after the constellation believed to control heavenly horses). According to the *Lü shi chunqiu*, he was able to instantly assess the potential of a horse from its bone structure and the size and shape of parts of its body.[41] Another *Lü shi chunqiu* passage describes the techniques of the ten most famous horse physiognomists. Some used different aspects of the head (the mouth, teeth, lips, forehead, eyes, whiskers), others the torso (rump, chest, and ribs), others the limbs, and still others the front and rear view.[42]

What then were the qualifications for practicing as an independent diviner? One was lineage. Mantic knowledge seems to have been transmitted in families, usually from father to son but sometimes from father to daughter. The necessary aptitudes depended on specialty. Turtle and milfoil diviners were praised for wisdom and a strongly moral outlook. But such a practitioner would also need to be able to communicate effectively with both hierarchical superiors and inferiors, as Sima Jizhu clearly did. By contrast, accounts of (human) physiognomists emphasize skills practiced either within the household (as by the mother of Shu Xiang) or by itinerant practitioners who may not have had ongoing relations with their clients. A few accounts mention physiognomy by convicts. For example, the *Lun heng* 論衡 (*Weighing Discourses*) of Wang Chong 王充 (27–97 CE) describes a convict physiognomizing the Han general Wei Qing 衛青 (d. 106 BCE) as an infant.[43] The skills of horse physiognomists are portrayed differently; they are described as technical specialists pure and simple. But any physiognomist would need keen powers of perception to excel at the art, even if it was learned through family training. (Observation need not be by sight, as some physiognomists were blind.)

We can also understand who mantic experts were by understanding who they were not. They shared expertise or competed with other technical experts, especially physicians, spirit mediums (*wu*), Ru, and other textual specialists. Anecdotes in the *Zuo zhuan* describe a range of technical experts serving the nobility, and the *Li ji* classifies incantators, diviners, and

reprinted in the *Gujin tushu jicheng* (chapters 631–44) and there is a Taiwan edition by Liang Xangrun 梁湘潤 (Taipei: Hungye, 1980). For a study of this text see Kohn 1986.

41 *LSCQ*, 507 ("Jing tong" 精通 9.5), cf. Knoblock and Riegel 2000: 220. Stories about Bo Le: Hong Anquan 1990. The constellation may be the Lunar Lodge Wei, near Scorpio.

42 *LSCQ*, 1414 ("Guan biao" 觀表 20.8). This passage is translated in Chapter 5.

43 *LH*, 117 ("Gu xiang" 3.2), Forke 1.308.

physicians among the hundred craftsmen who "practice a skill to serve their superiors."[44]

Turtle and milfoil diviners, astrologers, physicians, and spirit mediums (*wu*) were all consulted to interpret troublesome dreams. An example is the *Zuo zhuan* account of the death of Duke Huan of Jin. In 581, after a disturbing dream, he consults both a spirit medium and a physician from Qin. Both interpret his dreams and both predict his death within the year.[45]

Physicians, spirit mediums (*wu*), diviners, and *fangshi* all gave medical advice; and *fang* expertise included pharmacological and mantic knowledge. Physicians may have adopted and modified the language of prognostication. For example, the biography of the Han physician Chunyu Yi 淳于意 represents him as infallible in predicting life or death, a prominent concern of iatromancy. Chunyu claims that these predictions determined whether or not he intervened in medical cases on which he was consulted. He also repeatedly claims that his predictions are superior to those of competing physicians. He effectively uses mantic rhetoric to argue his own skill as a physician, both in his apologia to Han Wendi and to posterity.[46]

In summary, the social functions and expertise of physicians, diviners, and *fangshi* formed a fluid continuum and they fulfilled overlapping social functions. Spirit mediums present a more complicated problem because of the many questions about their roles in early Chinese society.[47] After the Western Zhou, the political roles of *wu* seem to have declined. They remained important as experts in magic, functioned as exorcists in rituals designed to bring rain and ward off calamity, and practiced medicine and

[44] *Yi shi shang zhe* 以事上者, *LJ* 13.7b. Technical experts: Zuo, 1217–23 (Zhao 1.2, Legge 575–76) and 1289–90 (Zhao 7.7, Legge 619); *GY* 3.141 (Zhou yu xia) and 5.201 and 213 (Lu yu xia); cf. K. Smith 1989: 424–41.

[45] Zuo, 849 (Cheng 10.4, cf. Legge 372–74), discussed in Appendix 7.1.

[46] *SJ* 105.2805–7, trans. Bridgman 1955: 26–45. One diagnosis (Po Shi, the Inner Attendant of Qi) may reflect knowledge of hemerological iatromancy (Harper 2001: 117–19, and Chapters 5 and 9). Chunyu also predicts the death of a female slave, skilled in *fang* techniques, whose arts allow her to conceal the gravity of her condition. Chunyu's historical context: Loewe 1997.

[47] Chen Mengjia (1936: esp. 533) argued that the practice of *wu* techniques (*wu shu* 巫術) was the basis of Shang religion. K. C. Chang (1982, 1983, 1994) drew on this idea to argue for the fundamental importance of spirit mediumship (*wu*-shamanism) to Chinese culture and to claim that the Shang kings used mantic skills to communicate with royal ancestors and gods, mediating between the divine and secular worlds. Alternatively, David N. Keightley (1983, 1984, 1988, 1998) has argued that divination was less the source of Shang royal power than a means to consolidate and legitimate it. See also Poo 1998: 23–27, Boileau 2002: 350–52, Tong Enzheng 2002. For discussion of the entire controversy see Puett 2002: 33–35 and Falkenhausen 2004. As Falkenhausen points out (personal communication), K. C. Chang's main argument is not about *wu* but about the unique role of the Shang kings in their kinship relations to the ancestors, to whom they alone had access.

healing.[48] According to the *Zhou li*, male *wu* were responsible for sacrifices to departed spirits, which included calling them to the locale by their honorific titles. They were also responsible for winter offerings in the great temple and spring rituals for protecting the country from disease. They preceded the king in visits of condolence (along with incantators). Female *wu* performed ablutions and anointing during regular exorcistic ceremonies. They performed dances to bring rain during drought; preceded the queen in visits of condolence (along with female incantators); and sang, wailed, and prayed during great calamities of the state.[49]

During the Warring States period, divination emerged as one of several livelihoods and social roles offered by literacy and the mastery of a textual tradition. Like physicians and technical experts in military strategy, mantic experts could enter into state service as officials, put their knowledge at the service of a lord in return for patronage, or sell their expertise in the marketplace.[50] But whichever path they chose, literacy and textual mastery was a significant aspect of their expertise and livelihood. During this period a new option emerged: participation in the philosophical textual traditions and teaching lineages of the Masters traditions. The option of teaching for pay became particularly associated with Confucian schools. Archaeological evidence from Warring States and Han tombs provides a fuller picture of the literary culture of the administrators who employed Masters textualists and technical experts.[51] A significant number of the texts excavated from their tombs concern mantic expertise.

Competition between these textualist groups forced them to develop arguments for the efficacy of their texts and knowledge, and profoundly affected the course of Warring States intellectual history. The textualist groups also interacted with each other, and Masters texts may have incorporated ideas and specific vocabulary from the technical experts. Philosophical schools also borrowed imagery from mantic or medical traditions, such as *wuxing* or the image of the body as a bellows. But the

48 Rain: Zuo, 1382 (Zhao 16.6, Legge 665) and *LSCQ*, 478–80 ("*Shun min*" 順民 9.2). Calamity: Zuo, 1394 (Zhao 18.1, Legge 671). Healing: Zuo, 849 (Cheng 10.4, cf. Legge 372–74).

49 *ZL* 26: 9a–11a, Biot 2: 103–4.

50 E.g. the Mawangdui text "Ten Questions" (*Shi wen*) depicts the physician Wen Zhi in an audience with King Wei of Qi (r. 357–320), the founder of the Jixia academy. Wen Zhi specifically mentions his expertise at textual medical knowledge. *Mawangdui Hanmu boshu* 4.150–51 and *LSCQ*, 578 ("*Zhi zhong*" 至忠 11.2), cf. Zhou Yimou 1994: 239–46.

51 Li Ling 1993; Harper 1995, 1999b; Lewis 1999: 53–97, esp. 72–79; Falkenhausen 2003, 2006. Lewis argues against the earlier view that the Warring States "schools" emerged to meet a need to train administrative experts. He notes that none of these textual specialists gained significant office and that the schools were opponents of the state, rather than training grounds for its administrators. Bellows: Harper 1995.

textual record and recent archaeology underscore the differences between the expertise, textual mastery, and basic interests of the Masters traditions and technical experts, who, in modern terms, might be termed experts on nature.

Several noteworthy contrasts present themselves between Chinese and Greek attitudes toward texts and argumentation. The public nature of Greek intellectual competition and the corresponding importance of rhetoric have been widely noted, as has their importance for the development of Greek philosophy and science. By contrast, rhetoric is virtually absent in China as a means of specifically public persuasion. This is not to say that Chinese experts did not compete with or belittle their opponents; they did so in the milieu of texts. By contrast, Greek intellectual and philosophical arguments do not focus on the transmission or priority of written texts. But a different Greek "absence" has been less widely remarked upon. In Greece we do not see arguments for the efficacy or choice of particular texts for exegesis or interpretation, perhaps because of an underlying bias toward orality and oral, rather than textual, argumentation. A second contrast concerns naturalistic thinking and the inquiry into nature. In the Greek world, that inquiry was led by the philosophers and especially the *physiologoi*. In early China technical experts, rather than Masters textualists, cultivated that expertise.[52]

It is difficult to draw hard and firm distinctions between different types of mantic specialist in early China. A distinction can be made between official and independent practitioners (whether in the marketplace or as clients of powerful families), but it is important to note that both groups had access to the same techniques. They all used turtle and milfoil, astrocalendric techniques, dream divination, and physiognomy, although with different emphases.

In summary, there is evidence that Chinese mantic officials served the Shang, Zhou, Qin, and Han courts. Their duties changed with time, but included: (1) preparation of materials, (2) creating and preserving calendars and written records, (3) participating in state ritual occasions, and (4) offering advice on the interpretation of divinatory sacrifices, spontaneous dreams, omens, prodigies, and other matters. Three points are noteworthy. First, Chinese official divination was highly bureaucratic in the sense that it involved combinations of skilled experts working in tandem within and

[52] According to the *Shi ji* (87.2546), Qin Shihuang banned the books of the "hundred schools," but made an exception for technical works on medicine, prognostication, agriculture, and forestry.

between offices. Second, insofar as we can judge by extant evidence, state patronage focused on some practices and marginalized others. Most important were astrocalendrics (including the observation of subcelestial phenomena) and the ongoing use of prognostication to determine auspicious times for important activities. By contrast, oneiromancy and physiognomy were not objects of extensive bureaucracy. (*Fang* arts were patronized under some rulers, notably Han Wu Di.) State patronage may have been instrumental in the development of complex astronomical instrumentation, beginning with mantic astrolabes, but eventually including the armillary sphere and imperial observatories. Third, Chinese official divination was closely connected with writing and record-keeping.

Greek mantic experts

The Greek distinction is between two types of mantic practice: the activities of individual *manteis* and oracular consultation. Their social roles and modes of expertise were very different, and there seems to be no movement from one group to another.

The *mantis*

The Liddell and Scott Greek lexicon glosses *mantis* and *promantis* as a diviner, seer, or prophet, male or female (but with important differences between the two). Plato considered *mantis* to derive from *mania* (madness), and this etymology was accepted throughout antiquity. Contemporary scholars derive it from the Indo-European root *men (to think, to be in a special mental state). Michel Casevitz proposes a Greek etymology based on *mēnuō* (to reveal), since from Homer to Plato the term *mantis* connoted knowledge, whether of a seer who observes signs (in compounds like *iatromantis*) or knowledge from direct inspiration.[53] This view stresses the semantic unity of *mantis*, and de-emphasizes a distinction between two modes of divination.

The earliest accounts of *manteis* come from the Homeric poems. Some were priests of Apollo and ritualists who interpreted the results of sacrifice and determined auspicious times for important actions. The *mantis* was often a military figure, closely associated with kings and often from a royal

[53] Liddell and Scott 1883: 920–21 and Chantraine 1974–80: 3.665 (μάντις). Cf. Roth 1982: 9–18 and 1984, Nagy 1990, Casevitz 1992: esp. 11, Maurizio 1995: 70, Dillery 2005: 168–69, Flower 2008: 23.

or mantic lineage. The paradigmatic Homeric example is Calchas, who appears in *Iliad* 1, after Apollo had sent a plague on the Achaeans. Achilles proposes to "ask some *mantis* or priest, or some dream interpreter (*oneiropolos*), for a dream is also from Zeus, someone who might say why Phoebus Apollo is so angry" (1.60–67).

> And there rose up Calchas the son of Thestor, far the best of the bird interpreters, who knew the present, the future, and the past, and who had the knowledge to lead the ships to Troy by the mantic arts he owed to Phoebus Apollo.[54]

In the debates that follow, Odysseus reminds the Greek forces how Calchas used his foresight (*manteuetai*) when the Achaean ships were detained at Aulis (2.300). During the sacrifice, a snake darted from under the altar, fell upon on a sparrow and her eight fledglings, devoured them all, and was turned to stone. After a terrible portent during sacrifice, Calchas prophesied to the assembly (*theopropeōn agoreue*) that since the snake had eaten eight fledglings and their mother, the Achaeans would fight nine years at Troy, but win victory in the tenth (2.321–29).

This incident illustrates several important aspects of Homeric divination. The incident occurred spontaneously in the midst of a sacrifice. It involved both a sign (*sēma*, the serpent eating the sparrows) and an ominous portent (*pelōr*, Zeus turning the serpent to stone). It did not take place at an oracular site or involve a deliberate consultation. Finally, Calchas interpreted what he had witnessed in his own voice and person, in clear speech that required no further interpretation.

Calchas was an aristocrat and a military commander in the service of a ruler. His opposite number, the Trojan *mantis* Helenus, was a prince. Both indicate the elite status of the Homeric *mantis*, but also show him as a gifted or even charismatic individual who speaks directly and persuasively.[55] Throughout the *Iliad*, signs are recognized by Calchas, Nestor, Hector, Polydamas, and, in one case, by the entire Argive host. Calchas, Nestor, and Odysseus are military leaders, renowned for their wisdom. Hector is not, and he misreads omens consistently. Polydamas claims that any *mantis* would agree with his interpretation.

In the *Odyssey*, Telemachus consults two *manteis*. Halitherses (like Calchas) could see both past and future (*hora prossō kai opissō*, 24.452) and surpassed all in his knowledge of birds and fate-laden mantic pronouncements (*ornithas*

[54] *Il.* 1.68–72, trans. after Lattimore.

[55] *Manteis*: Bouché-Leclercq 1879–82: 2.9–61, Halliday 1913: 54–98. Recent studies: Bremmer 1993 and 1996, Flower 2008, Johnston 2008: esp. 18–19 on Halliday.

gnōnai kai enaisima muthēsasthai, 2.159). Theoclymenus, the first to predict Odysseus' return to Ithaca (*Od.* 17.150–60), came from a mantic lineage; he was the son of the *mantis* Polyphides and the grandson of Melampus (20.350–58). These references include accounts of the lineages of these *manteis* and descriptions of how they acquired their gifts, but not of their training.

The other paradigmatic legendary *mantis* was the blind and long-lived Theban Tiresias. In *Odyssey* 11, Odysseus performs necromantic rituals in Hades to consult Tiresias' ghost about his own homecoming. Tiresias' daughter Manto and her son Mopsus also became famous *manteis*. When the Epigoni attacked Thebes, they captured Manto and brought her to Delphi as a war prize. According to Diodorus Siculus,

> she was no less knowing of the mantic arts than her father, and during her stay at Delphi she augmented her art still further. Because of natural talent, she took the lead in oracular responses and wrote [oracles] of every sort. And they say that the poet Homer took many of her words and made them out to be his own. Because she was often inspired (*entheazousēs*) when she delivered oracles, they say that she was called Sibylla.[56]

Pausanias reports that Apollo sent her to found a colony. She and her companions crossed to Asia by ship. In Claros they were captured and brought before king Rhacius, who married Manto and accepted her people as citizens of Claros. These accounts together emphasize several points. The first is the combination of Manto's inherent gifts and developed technical abilities: the combination of qualities that would predispose success in an itinerant *mantis*. The second is her itinerant life: from her home in Thebes to Delphi, as a colonist to Claros, and as an eventual citizen of the Cretan colony at Claros as the wife of Rhacius.

Apollodorus also recounts a divination contest between Calchas and Manto's son Mopsus, who mocks his rival for inferior descent:

> Calchas' divination is the reverse of exact (*akribous manteias apenantios*); but I, as a son of Apollo and Manto, am extremely rich in the sharp sight which comes of exact divination (*akribous manteias tēn oxudorkian*).[57]

Calchas dies of a broken heart after Mopsus more accurately named the number of figs on a tree and predicted the number, sex, and time of birth of a sow's litter.

[56] Diod. 4.66.5–6. Capture of Manto: Apollod. *Bibl.* 3.7.4.

[57] Apollod. *Epit.* 6.3–4, cf. 5.23. Pausanias (7.3.2.1–3 and 9.33.2) names the father of Mopsus as Rhacius. Other late sources (Hygin. *Fab.* 190) create a mantic lineage for Calchas, as the brother of Theoclymenus, Leucippe (a priestess of Apollo), and the female *mantis* Theonoe.

The Homeric poems also suggest that mantic expertise was not restricted to elite specialists. The *Odyssey* especially mentions independent diviners of lesser pedigree. For example, Telemachus mentions Penelope summoning a *theopropos* to the house (*Od.* 1.415–16). The swineherd Eumaius refers to *manteis*, builders, and physicians as "workers for the public good (*dēmioergoi*) who were welcome everywhere" (17.382–85). Other mantic functions were performed by anyone who ventured to do so. We all experience dreams, the flight of birds, and the weather. Interpretations of these phenomena are ascribed to a wide range of individuals. Dream epiphanies of Athena appear to Penelope and Nausicaa. The entire Greek army recognizes a bird omen in *Iliad* 8; other bird signs are interpreted by Polydamas and Helen. Weather omens are interpreted by Nestor and Hector; and "words of good omen" are interpreted by both Odysseus and Penelope.[58]

Cicero remarks that in the ancient world rulers controlled augury and divination was associated with wisdom and kingship (*Div.* 1.88–90). The legendary *manteis* Amphilochus and Mopsus were kings; Amphiaraus and Tiresias were also highborn. But the Homeric poems also show the potential for conflict between royal and mantic authority. Although Homeric diviners worked closely with kings, they also came into conflict with authority.

Classical myths of legendary *manteis* introduce several changes from their representation in the Homeric poems. One is the introduction of myths of the acquisition of mantic gifts through contact with Apollo and other mantic gods. Aeschylus attributes the mantic arts to Prometheus. Hesiod describes Melampus learning the art of divination either from Apollo or from snakes licking his ears.[59] The other consists of accounts of female *manteis*, including the transformation of the Trojan princess Cassandra from the twin sister of the *mantis* Helenus to an inspired and tragic figure who speaks directly in the voice of Apollo. Priestesses are notable for their absence in the Homeric poems. At the end of the sixth century, Heraclitus (fr. B92) speaks of the Sibyl as "prophesying with a raving mouth." The figure of Cassandra as an inspired priestess first appears in the mid-fifth century in the *Agamemnon* of Aeschylus (1072–1263). These figures seem linked with the rise of Apolline divination. By contrast, according to Herodotus, Melampus "acquired the mantic arts by himself" (2.49) and extispicy (entrail divination) was brought to Greece from Egypt, as was the cult of Zeus at Dodona (2.57).

[58] Dreams: Penelope: *Od.* 4.884–946; Nausicaa: *Od.* 6.5–20. Bird omens: Greek army: *Il.* 8:245–55; Polydamas: *Il.* 12:200–25; Helen: *Od.* 15:160–80. Weather omens: Nestor: *Il.* 2:353; Hector: *Il.* 9:236–40. Words: Odysseus: *Od.* 20:105–25; Penelope: *Od.* 17.541–51. See Appendix 5.6.

[59] Prometheus: Aesch. *PV* 477, 484. Melampus: *Hes.* fr. 261 West, Apollod. *Bibl.* 1.9.11.

It is also worth noting the central roles of *manteis* in mythic cycles, where they outnumber bards, physicians, or magicians. We find Calchas and Tiresias in Homeric poems, Melampus and Amphiaraus in Hesiod, and Prometheus as the transmitter of the mantic arts in Aeschylus. Tiresias is central to four tragedies concerned with Thebes.[60]

In summary, in legendary accounts, both heroic *manteis* and anonymous, itinerant diviners interpreted signs and portents arising from both deliberate questions and spontaneous events. While both kinds of *mantis* did the same kinds of things, legendary accounts differ on how they became *manteis*. Heroic legendary *manteis* attained their gifts and status through membership in mantic lineages but also through talent. In classical myths, they also acquired their gifts from the gods or their animal intermediaries. They advised rulers on military and other matters, and at times came into conflict with political authority. We know less about how non-heroic, anonymous, independent itinerant diviners attained their competence.

Historical accounts from the sixth through the fourth centuries show military *manteis* serving tyrants, kings, and *poleis*. Military divination was a preeminent role of historic *manteis*, often as generals in the field. They are especially prominent in Herodotus and Xenophon. Questions on whether to go to war were referred to Delphi, but divinations about immediate battlefield decisions were performed by military *manteis*. Their expertise included reading bird, weather, and entrail omens, but also strategy and military command. Their high status came from their official function as the heads of armies; they were considered indispensable in obtaining victory in battle. Some were from elite mantic lineages, but even a non-elite *mantis* could achieve significant rewards for success. An example is the fifth-century Iamid *mantis* Tisamenus of Elis. According to Herodotus (9.33–35), he won five battles for Sparta during the Persian War; both he and his brother were granted full citizenship for his services. Other rewards to successful *manteis* included civic honors, huge sums of money, land, and first fruits of victory. For example, Croton granted land to Callias of Elis where his descendants lived, even in Herodotus' time. Callias had initially served the tyrant Telys of Sybaris, but fled to Croton about 510, when Telys attacked Croton without favorable omens (Hdt. 5.44).

Independence of employment was central to the role of the *mantis*. As the example of Callias vividly demonstrates, they freely changed employment and allegiance. Some became an advisor (*sunēthēs*) to a particular ruler or general. For example, the fifth-century Iamid *mantis* Hegesias became

[60] Aesch. *Sept.*; Soph. *OT*, *Ant*; Eur. *Bacch.*

associated with Hieron of Syracuse.[61] Others were itinerant, unattached to any locale and not part of a local power constituency.[62]

An important role of the military *mantis* was prebattle sacrifice in order to obtain favorable signs indicating divine approval.[63] Xenophon recounts many examples, including several he performed himself. Sacrifices were performed frequently on the march and before major actions such as building a fort or attacking a town, up to three victims a day. The results determined whether to encounter the enemy at any particular place and time. A final sacrifice was performed immediately before the battle itself. Xenophon notes the disastrous errors that could result from proceeding in the face of unfavorable signs, and there are many accounts of protracted delays awaiting favorable ones.[64]

Modern commentators have noted the Greeks' adherence to these signals and the rarity of incidents where the gods' advice proved false or was ignored.[65] (We are at the mercy of our sources here, and this consistency may result from selective recording.) Yet the search for divine approval was problematic. Favorable omens did not guarantee victory. The gods might encourage both parties, but warfare is a zero sum game that offers victory to only one side.

A second and distinct mantic role was healing. The legendary models for this kind of healer-*mantis* (*iatromantis*) are Calchas and Melampus.[66] Historical accounts indicate that some itinerant *manteis* specialized in

[61] Pind. *Ol.* 6.80–84; 93–100. Other such associations include the *mantis* Astyphilus of Poseidonia and Cimon (Plut. *Cim.* 18) and the *mantis* Lampon and Pericles (e.g. Plut. *Per.* 6.2). In a somewhat different example, Pisistratus granted Athenian citizenship to the Acarnanian chresmologue Amphilytus, who had prophecied victory at Marathon and had helped him take Athens (Hdt. 1.6.4, Pl. *Theag.* 124d).

[62] For scholarly disagreements on this point see Pritchett 1973–79: 3.52–53. On historical and itinerant *manteis*: Flower 2008.

[63] *Kala ta hiera* or *kallierein*. According to Pausanias (9.13.4) Spartan kings took flocks of sheep on military expeditions for this purpose. Prebattle sacrifice is described by Herodotus, Thucydides, Xenophon, Plutarch, Polyaenus, Diodorus, and Arrian. See Pritchett 1974: esp. 114, Table 2; Jameson 1991: 197–99; and further discussion below in Chapters 5 and 7.

[64] Xen. *An.* 3.1.7 (whether to accompany the forces of Cyrus). Sacrifice: 2.2.4 (by Clearches), 3.5.18 (by the generals), 4.3.9 (after a dream by Xenophon), 5.4.2, 5.5.3, 6.1.22 (whether to take supreme command), 6.2.16 (whether to continue or leave the army), 6.4.9 (whether to engage in a military expedition), 6.4.25 (an improvised *sphagia* sacrifice in a disastrous battle), and 7.8.1 (in gratitude for safe return). Xenophon comments on the sacrifice of Cyrus' diviner Silanus (5.6.17). Specific examples of *sphagia* include *An.* 4.3.19 and 6.5.8. Xenophon also gives examples of omens from sneezing (3.2.10) and bird omens (6.1.23). See Jameson 1991: 198–99.

[65] Lonis 1979: 102–3, Popp 1957: 39–73.

[66] Robert Parker (1983: 209–10) argues that an archaic role of healer-*mantis*-purifier over time developed into two distinct roles: the *iatromantis* and the purifier, who used magical techniques to cure disease without undue interest in its cause.

healing and purification. For example, the "Purifications" of the Presocratic philosopher Empedocles begins with a claim to be in high demand everywhere for mantic and healing expertise.[67] Plato reports that Athens retained the *mantis* Epimenides of Crete to purify the city during an outbreak of plague in 596. Plutarch adds that, after their own *manteis* had failed to cure the plague, Athens consulted the Delphic oracle and was advised to bring in Epimenides from Crete. According to Diogenes Laertius, Epimenides attributed the cause of the plague to pollution caused by the ghosts of murdered men, and devised an exorcistic cure, involving sacrifice to the relevant gods.[68]

There is some evidence for the existence of itinerant female *manteis*. One account comes from the Platonic Socrates, who explains his instruction by Diotima of Mantinea (Socrates' mentor in the *Symposium*) on grounds that she was wise (*sophē*) in matters of Eros but also in many other things. Socrates adds that her advice helped the Athenians delay the onset of the plague in Athens for ten years by offering the correct sacrifices. Whether or not Diotima existed, she could only have been effective in the *Symposium* by representing a recognizable type of individual whose authority the Athenians recognized.[69] But such a figure would be less likely to be mentioned by historians because she was not a military *manteis*.

Edmond Lévy has argued that differences of semantic usage imply distinct attitudes toward male and female *manteis*.[70] Herodotus preserves the names, specialties, and descent of male *manteis*, whose high social status arose from their official function, especially at the head of an army, where *manteis* were considered indispensable in obtaining victory in battle. Names like Hegesistratus and Hippomachus encoded this expectation of military victory. By contrast, Herodotus almost never mentions Pythias by name or

[67] Fr. 112 DK: "Some seeking mantic arts (*mantosuneōn kekhrōmenoi*), others seeking to hear healing oracular speech (*eputhonto kluein euēkea baxin*) for all kinds of diseases."

[68] Pl. *Leg.* 642d–643, cf. Arist. *Rh.* 3.17, 1418a23–26. Plut. *Solon* 12.1–4, Diog. Laert. 1.110, discussed further in Chapter 7. It is worth noting that in the poem *Cretica* Epimenides asserts that all Cretans are liars, and he is a Cretan. The point is neither a general claim about Cretans nor a logical paradox. Rather, Epimenides contests the claim of Minos (a Cretan) that Zeus was mortal. Thus this is not a version of the "liar's paradox" (a Cretan claiming that all Cretans are liars) and there is no reason to doubt his veracity as a *mantis* because of it.

[69] Pl. *Symp.* 201d. A late fifth-century grave stele from Mantinea shows a woman holding a liver, presumably a practitioner of hepatoscopy. See Flower 2008: 211–15.

[70] Lévy (1997: esp. 347–48, 352–56) argues that Herodotus uses the terms *mantis*, *mantikē*, and *manteuesthai* of male seers, but reserves the term *khrān* (to possess) and derivatives (e.g. *khrēsmos*, *khrēstērion*, *khrēstēriazein*, and *khrēsmologos*) for the priestesses at Dodona and Delphi. In this verbal picture, only female *manteis* are objects of direct (or even invasive) possession. In his view, these lexical differences distinguish male self-possessed conscious consultation from female spirit mediumship (discussed further in Chapter 7).

distinct personality. One significant exception is two references to corruption of the Pythia Perialla. A second exception not discussed by Lévy is the Pythia Aristonikē, named by Herodotus as the source of the "Wooden Wall" oracle to Athens.[71]

What made a *mantis*? Myths of the acquisition of mantic gifts derive these talents from contact with Apollo and other mantic gods. Some mantic figures (Cassandra, Helenus, Melampus) had their ears licked by snakes, also associated with Apollo. Others received the gift as a mark of divine favor (Branchus, Cassandra) or in compensation for blindness (Euenius, Tiresias). Otherwise, in both legendary and historic accounts, membership in a mantic lineage (by actual birth, adoption, or creative fiction) was an essential aspect of mantic authority. There is some historical evidence that in both Greece and the ancient Mediterranean generally *manteis* were organized in quasi-familial groups.[72] The most important lineages (and eponymous ancestors) were the Clytiads, Iamids, Melampodids, and Telliads. All came from Elis except the Melampodids, who claimed descent from Melampus. His legendary descendants include Amphiaraus, Amphilochus, Polypheides, his son Theoclymenus, and Clytius, the eponymous ancestor of the Clytiads. Historical Melampodids included the Acarnanian *mantis* Megistias who died at Thermopylae, after sending his son to safety.

The Iamids, who claimed descent from Apollo's son Iamus, included Hagesias of Syracuse (the *mantis* of the tyrant Hieron), Callias of Elis (given land by Croton), and Tisamenus of Elis, who was given citizenship by Sparta and whose descendants continued to practice there as *manteis*. According to Pindar, Apollo gave Iamus the gift of divination and caused him to establish the oracle of Zeus at Olympia. Through the third century, they shared stewardship of Olympia with the Clytiads. According to later sources, they practiced pyromantic divination by examining burnt cracks in the skins of sacrificial animals.[73] The Telliads included the Elean *mantis* Tellias and Hegesistratus, the *mantis* of Mardonius at Plataea.

Descent from a mantic lineage had several implications, beginning with the presumption of inherited aptitude. More realistic was the opportunity

[71] Names: Hdt. 9.37, 38. Perialla: Hdt. 6.63, 66. Aristonikē: Hdt. 7.140–41.

[72] Melampus: Schol. Apol. Rhod. *Argon.* 1.118, cf. Plin. *Nat. Hist.* 10.137. Helenus and Cassandra: Schol. Hom. *Il.* 7.44, cf. Aesch. *Ag.* 1198–1212 (favor of Apollo). Branchus: Callimachus fr. 229. Tiresias: Apollod. *Bibl.* 3.6.5–7. Euenius: Hdt. 9.93–94. Mediterranean context: Burkert 1992: 41–46.

[73] Pind. *Ol.* 6.57–74. Iamids: Bouché-Leclercq 1879–82: 2.59–69, Weniger 1915: 66–76, Parke 1967: 174–78 and 184–85, Flower 2008: 39–40.

for training or apprenticeship within one's own family. Anyone could attempt to interpret dreams or signs from the gods (as Xenophon did in the *Anabasis*), but a recognized professional *mantis* needed the knowledge to make fine distinctions and the ability and flexibility to recognize and interpret spontaneous signs as they occurred.[74] All this presumably required an excellent and vivid memory, since Greek *manteis* did not have access to written records or compendia of signs or omens. Finally, along with the imprimatur of mantic descent, successful *manteis* required persuasiveness and charisma to inspire confidence in their pronouncements.

Several other mantic figures that overlap with the *mantis* must be distinguished. Most important is the *khrēsmologos* or chresmologue. Chresmologues collected, amalgamated, and interpreted oracles. They had considerable influence on public opinion in the fifth century, but were ridiculed by Aristophanes. Thucydides (8.1.1) describes how, after the defeat of the Sicilian expedition in 413, the Athenians turned against the "chresmologues and *manteis*" who had advocated it. Chresmologues have acquired a bad reputation, but their role may have overlapped that of the *mantis*. At issue is the boundary between passively "purveying" oracles and expounding or interpreting them. In one passage, Pausanias credits chresmologues with uttering inspired oracles and relegates *manteis* to their interpretation; a few texts apply both terms to the same individual. Thus some scholars consider chresmologues "speakers" of oracles and thus closer to the *mantis*.[75] According to Plato, the *exēgētēs* or "expounder" of sacred matters (today's exegete) at Athens was responsible for the interpretation of sacred law (*Euth.* 4c).

Sibyls (and their less important male counterparts the Bacis) were isolated female mantic figures, recorded throughout antiquity in Greece, Asia Minor, and southern Italy. Sibylline divination probably originated in Asia Minor, and may date from the religious movements of the eighth century. They were not associated with sanctuaries but were considered priestesses of Apollo nonetheless. Unlike the Pythias, they spoke in their own voices. The "rock of the Sibyl" at Delphi commemorated the first Sibyl Herophila, a contemporary of the earliest Pythias. Heraclitus speaks of the Sibyl with respect. Twelve sibyls are known from the Roman period.[76] When an

[74] Jameson 1991: 60–61 and Flower 2008: 53–58 point to additional evidence from scenes on vase paintings of warriors examining livers and other entrails of sacrificial victims.

[75] Paus. 1.34.4. See Dillery 2005: 169–71 and Eidinow 2007a: 26–28.

[76] Varro lists ten in chronological order, of whom the first was Persian, the second Libyan, and the third the Delphic sibyl described by Chrysippus. Parke 1988: 30 and 100–25.

Apolline priesthood took charge of Delphi, previously independent sibyls became Pythias controlled by the temple officials.

Finally, a range of magical practitioners (*magi*) were itinerant "freelance" ritual specialists who addressed the quotidian problems of arousing love, cursing enemies, curing illnesses, and divining the future. They traveled according to the needs of their clientele, and improvised rituals accordingly, for example creating consecrated spaces in open-air locations.[77]

Oracles of Zeus at Dodona and Olympia

Oracles were specific locales that offered divination and omen interpretation. Most famous was the sanctuary of Apollo at Delphi, and the image of the Pythia seated on her tripod is perhaps the prevailing stereotype of Greek divination. Unlike *manteis* or sibyls, who moved about at will and used a range of methods, each oracle was the shrine of a particular god in a particular locale, typically with at least one charter myth to explain how it came to be there.

Many were in remote locations, far from the centers of power. The type of consultation offered was limited by personnel, method, and in some cases the calendar. For example, at Delphi, consultation was restricted to the seventh day of each month, nine months of the year, excluding the three months of winter. These constraints may have restricted most oracular consultation to local residents. Private individuals consulted oracles on personal matters such as wealth and prosperity, marriage, children, travel, livelihood, citizenship, illness, and questions of prayer and sacrifice. A few oracles gained panhellenic prominence, and were consulted by *poleis* and other groups on religious cult and political matters such as divine sanction to found colonies, victory in warfare, and release from evils such as plague or famine.

The oldest was the oracle of Zeus at Dodona. Most famous was the oracle of Apollo at Delphi. Other important centers included the oracle of Zeus at Olympia, the oracle of Apollo at Didyma (near Miletus, also called Branchidae), the oracle of Mopsus at Claros (near Colophon), and the shrines of Asclepius at Epidaurus and elsewhere (Map 2.1).

Oracles typically employed both priestesses and male priestly lineages such as the Selloi of Dodona and the Branchidae of Didyma. There were important differences in their responsibilities and training. Priestesses typically performed divination, possibly as spirit mediums. Priests managed the temples and played some role in the interpretation and transmission of oracles.

[77] Johnston 2001: 100. Other magi were "truth-seekers" whose goals and practices were personal and private by nature, and did not involve the public practice of the mantic arts.

An initial problem is that the Greek terminology for these roles is imprecise, especially the relationship between the terms *mantis*, *prophētēs* (feminine *prophētis*, the modern "prophet"), *hiereus* ("priest"), and *hosios* ("holy one"). *Prophētēs* or *prophētis* referred to a spokesperson (male or female) for the god. Derived from *phē ("to speak"), it refers to one who makes a public proclamation. The problem was that "spokesperson" had a wide range of meanings, from the *mantis* or even Apollo himself, down to more indirect representatives who managed or assisted in the consultation process. A few examples illustrate these ambiguities. Both the Pythia and Apollo are described as *mantis* and *prophētēs* or *prophētis*. Herodotus (2.55.3) uses the term *hiereus* (fem. *hiereia*) to describe the priestesses of Zeus at Dodona.[78] Thus the roles of *prophētēs* and *mantis* overlapped; the difference is that the *prophētēs* was typically responsible for communicating the will of a particular god at a particular cult site, while a *mantis* was independent and connected to no particular cult.[79] Male priests at Delphi are described as *prophētēs*, *hiereus*, and *hosios*.[80] Despite these ambiguities, it does seem clear that *mantis* and *prophētēs* were separate roles that could (but need not) be performed by the same person.

Dodona was revered in antiquity as the most ancient of the oracles, the seat of "Pelasgian" Zeus.[81] Dodona is located in northwest Greece in Epirus, near the contemporary city of Ioannina and the Adriatic Sea. Inhabitation

[78] Pythia: *mantis*: Aesch. *Eum.* 29 and 33; *promantis*: Hdt. 6.66, 7.111 and 141; Thuc. 5.16.2; Plut. Alex. 14; *prophētis*: Eur. Ion. 42, 321, and 1322; Pl. *Phdr.* 244b; IG 12^3 863; Strabo 9.3.5; Diod. 14.13.3 and 16.26.4; Plut. *Mor.* 414b. Herodotus (Hdt. 9.93) describes her as both (pro)*mantis* and *prophētis*. Aeschylus describes Apollo both as a truthful *mantis* (*Cho.* 559, *Eum.* 18) and as the *prophētēs* of Zeus (*Eum.* 19). See Maurizio 1995: 83–84. In cases where the two roles are separate, it is tempting (but also problematic) to compare this relationship to that of the Incantator, the *Zhou li* divinatory official responsible for calling up the spirits, and the *wu*, the spirit medium through whom the spirits manifested.

[79] Dillery 2005: 171–72. *Hiereiai*: from *hieraomai*, to be a priest or priestess (LS 695a).

[80] *Hiereus* and *prophētēs* may have referred to the same office, with *hiereus* as a general term and *prophētēs* referring to the same individual participating in a consultation. Plutarch describes five *hosioi* participating in preliminary rites (*Mor.* 292d, 365a, 437a, 438b) and also refers to *hiereus* (*Mor.* 437a). Inscriptional evidence from Delphi refers to *hosioi* but never to *prophētēs*. See Fontenrose 1978: 219 n. 32 and 216 and Maurizio 1995: 83–84.

[81] *Il.* 16.233–34 describes Zeus as lord of "Pelasgian Dodona." Odysseus (*Od.* 14.316 and 327–28 and 19.287) consults the oracle of Zeus at Dodona to find the quickest way back to Ithaca. A Hesiodic fragment (319.1) refers to Dodona as *Pelasgōn hedranon*, "the seat of the Pelasgians." A Sophoclean fragment (Schol. in Sophoclem *Trach.* 1167.12) describes how Zeus loved the city of Dodona and appointed it to be his oracle, honored by mortals (*khrēstērion einai timion anthrōpois*). Doves lived in the hollow of an oak from which mortals bore away all kinds of prophecies (*manteia*), and whoever went there to question the deathless god would return with gifts of good auspice (*oiōnois agathoisin*). Herodotus (2.52) also describes Dodona as a Pelasgian oracle. For the history of the oracle see Nicol 1958.

seems to have been pre-Dorian and prehistoric. According to Strabo (7.5.6–12), the area was peopled by Chaonians, Molossians, Thesprotians, and other *ethnē*. A Molossian dynasty acquired Dodona from the Thesprotians about 400. It is not clear when Dodona began to function as an oracular site. A temple of Zeus was erected by the end of the fifth century, and there is evidence that space near it was left for a sacred oak.[82] The temple was enlarged in the mid-fourth century. The Aitolians sacked it in 219. It was rebuilt, expanded, and later sacked by the Romans in 167 and by the Thracians in 88.

In historic times, divination at Dodona was performed by hereditary priests (*tomouroi*) and priestesses (*peleiades*). Herodotus (2.55–57) suggests that there was a confusion between doves (*peleiai*) and the female priestesses of the temple, who may have been foreigners sold as slaves to Thesprotians, and whose foreign speech at first was incomprehensible (e.g. sounded like birds) but later became intelligible after they learned to speak Greek. The important point is that there is no suggestion of trance or possession in these accounts, in contrast with literary accounts of the Pythia at Delphi. Dodona continued to be consulted by *poleis* in classical times, especially when the objectivity of Delphi came into question during the Peloponnesian War.[83]

There are few descriptions of personnel and methods at the Oracle of Zeus at Olympia. It no longer functioned in Pausanias' time, and he mentions only an official in charge of sacrifices (*theokolos*) who holds the office a month each year, assisted by *manteis* and other officials.[84] There is evidence that mantic activities connected with Zeus Olympios continued through the military activities of mantic lineages outside Olympia itself. *Manteis* descended from the Iamid and Clytiad lineages accompanied several Greek military campaigns. Iamids and Clytiads were present at many decisive Greek battles, and reports of their activities continue into the late Hellenistic period.[85] Consultation of *manteis* of these lineages is always military in nature; the *manteis* of Zeus Olympios apparently enjoyed particular status as advisors in military matters.

[82] History and archaeology: Archaeological reports: Evangelidis 1929, 1931, 1932, 1935, 1952, 1958, 1965, 1967, 1968, 1973 in PAAH; Nicol 1958; Dakaris 1970, 1971, 1993; Parke 1967: 117–19; Eidinow 2007a: 56–71. Dates for the origin of the cult of Dodonaean Zeus range from the Bronze Age between 2600 and 1500 (Dakaris 1993: 7–8) to the eighth century (Parke 1967: 99).

[83] For example, Athens consulted Dodona before embarking on the Sicilian expedition (Paus. 8.11). Demosthenes (19.297; 21.531) urged the Athenians to sacrifice to Zeus at Dodona.

[84] Paus. 5.15.10. These include libation-bearers, a guide, a flautist, and a woodsman.

[85] Plataea (479): Hdt. 9.33; Paus. 3.11.6, 3.12.9. Aegospotami (405): Paus. 3.11.5, 10.9.7. Weniger 1915.

Excavations at Olympia over the twentieth century underscore the relationship between military votive offerings and the military specialization of the oracle. Offerings include weapons, armor, military equipment, and victory monuments, of which the most famous is the statue of Nike erected by the Messenians. Ulrich Sinn argues that the archaeological evidence supports the accounts of Pindar and Strabo, and that we should accept that the sanctuary of Zeus at Olympia was worshipped primarily as an oracular site in early antiquity.[86] Over time, changes in the cult festival shifted the games from periphery to center. The oracle eventually ceded mantic authority to Delphi, but its athletic competitions continued to grow in popularity.

The oracle of Apollo at Delphi

The most important Apolline oracle was the temple of Apollo at Delphi (Figure 4.2). The area was an extensive Mycenaean settlement, and was resettled about 870. Archaeological excavations first show evidence of a sanctuary at Delphi at the end of the ninth century. At that time Greek communities were still small and isolated and Delphi was relatively poor, so the site could only have been of local significance. The shrine of Apollo dates from the eighth century, the establishment of the Pythias from the seventh, and the completion of the temple from the sixth (there is no evidence for a temple before 650).[87]

Little is known of the activities of the priests of Apollo before Plutarch, whose writings provide an important if late account of procedures.[88] By Hellenistic times (323–146), the male staff of Delphi consisted of two priests (*hiereioi*) and five "holy men" (*hosioi*). The priests were selected for life from citizens of elite families. They oversaw sacrifices associated with consultation and were in charge of the yearly cycle of festivals associated with the god, such as the Pythian Games. The *hosioi* were recruited from aristocratic families whose lineage was associated with Deucalion. They assisted the

[86] Sinn 1991. The connection of the cult of Zeus Olympios with warfare is also shown by warrior statuettes and images of Nike, who, in Sinn's view, was not worshipped at Olympia primarily for athletic victory. He argues that a considerable proportion of the memorials and monuments at Olympia were connected to warfare. Sinn also argues that successful colonization in the second half of the eighth century, aided by the oracle of Zeus Olympios, increased the site's reputation to the extent that it was no longer primarily consulted by pilgrims seeking advice. Colonists initially helped by the oracle returned to express gratitude toward the cult site.

[87] The vast literature on the Delphic oracles includes: Parke 1943, 1984, Parke and Wormell 1956, Lloyd-Jones 1976, Fontenrose 1978, Parker 2000a, Dietrich 1965, 1990, 1992, and Roux 1976. Newer perspectives appear in Price 1985, Catherine Morgan 1989, 1990, and Maurizio 1995, 1997.

[88] Personnel: Parke and Wormell 1956, Roux 1976: 54–63, Fontenrose 1978.

Figure 4.2 The temple of Apollo at Delphi.

priests, and their ritual functions were in some sense determined by their uniquely "holy" status.

Central to the operation of the shrine was the Pythia, the priestess of Apollo. Plutarch reports that, at its height, the oracle staffed as many as three Pythias at any time (two regulars and an understudy), but by his own time there was only one. They were selected from the most upright and respectable families of Delphi, and were past childbearing age. Plutarch describes them as personally irreproachable and raised in the houses of poor peasants so as to bring no art (*tekhnē*), experience (*empeiria*), or capability (*dunamis*) with them to their calling.[89]

The prophecies of the Pythia have been a subject of controversy both in antiquity and among modern scholars. Did she speak intelligibly or were her responses put into order by male priests or even professional versifiers? Did she give responses in an altered state of mind, and if so, what kind? Finally, there is the problem of the lacuna between literary accounts of the Pythia's tripod perched over a chasm emitting chthonic vapors and the archaeology of Delphi.

Although Delphic oracles are widely attested from Herodotus on, there is less information about what happened.[90] Literary sources rarely describe procedures at Delphi, perhaps because they were too well known to need

[89] Plut. *Mor.* 414b and *Pyth. Orac.* 405c25–59. He compares them to Xenophon's (*Oec.* 7.5) description of a bride who comes to marriage deliberately sheltered and untaught: the Pythias thus approached the god with virgin souls.

[90] Oracular procedures: Amandry 1950, Parke and Wormell 1956: 1.17–45, Fontenrose 1978: 196–228, Price 1985: 134–140, Bowden 2005: 17–26, Flower 2008: 215–22.

description. A few allude to the delirium or frenzy of the Pythia or other priestesses. A Heraclitean fragment (fr. 92) refers to the "raving mouth" (*mainomenōi stomati*) of the Sibyl; Aeschylus describes the frenzy of Cassandra in the *Agamemnon* (1072–1330); and Plato (discussed above) refers to the madness of the Pythia and the priestesses at Dodona. Later accounts add the chasm, laurel leaves, and chthonic vapors.[91] But fifth- and fourth-century accounts depict her speaking in a self-possessed manner. Aeschylus depicts her as self-possessed as she enters the *adyton* in the prologue to the *Eumenides* (1–61). She runs out in fear because the Erinyes have pursued Orestes into the *adyton* itself, but this is fear, not madness. Herodotus repeatedly describes her as speaking directly. An Attic red figure kylix attributed to the Codrus painter shows King Aigeus of Athens consulting the Pythia in the form of a calm or even pensive Themis, seated on the Delphic tripod and holding a laurel leaf (Figure 2.1).

Ancient sources do make it clear *both* that Apollo spoke through the Pythia *and* that she spoke in her own voice. As Plutarch (who witnessed consultations) puts it:

> For neither the voice, the sound, the diction, or the metre are from the god, but rather from the woman. He sets before her mind only the visions and makes a light in her soul with regard to the future. For inspiration (*enthousiasmos*) is just this. (*Pyth. orac.* 397c4–7)

Plutarch says nothing about frenzy or incoherent speech (with the exception of one oracle he clearly considered abnormal), and ancient sources consistently present the Pythia alone as issuing oracular responses.

An earlier generation of scholars dismissed or rejected the possibility that the Pythias could have given coherent oracles in prose or verse. Yet the archaeology of Delphi completely fails to support traditional accounts of the Pythia's delirium; there is no evidence of a chasm or chthonic vapors, and material remains of its procedures have yet to be found.[92] Nonetheless, a distinguished series of scholars have attempted to rationalize the lacuna. One approach was to provide an alternative material explanation for the Pythia's delirium such as self-hypnosis or self-induced ecstasy; others

[91] Plutarch (*Def. orac.* 432c–438d) describes the *enthousiasmos* of the Pythia as induced by imperceptible currents or emanations, but these are not chthonic vapors. Strabo (9.3.5) refers to a *pneuma enthousiastikon* that induces her to speak oracles while seated on the tripod, but these are second-hand accounts. The chasm is first mentioned by Diodorus Siculus (16.26). See Fontenrose 1978: 197–212.

[92] Archaeology: Catherine Morgan 1990: 148–53. One French archaeologist responsible for the excavations remarked on the systematic destruction of the material remains of the oracle, whether by its last users or by early Christians, hostile to pagan oracles (Flacelière 1965: 43).

simply assumed that the Pythias' pronouncements were incoherent and were made intelligible by temple personnel, or even versified for written preservation.[93] Another approach was to dismiss traditional accounts of the divination methods. The influential French archaeologist Pierre Amandry argued for a lot oracle in which the Pythia spoke in verse or prose, presumably guided by Apollo. Although historical references to oral oracles far outnumber mentions of a lot oracle, Amandry's authority has persuaded many historians, Classicists, and archaeologists to disregard classical accounts of mantic activity.[94]

The most recent and most sophisticated attempt to find a material cause for the Pythia's delirium that is consistent with the literary evidence is a multidisciplinary geological, chemical, and toxicological analysis of the spring waters and travertine deposits at Delphi, which has found traces of methane, ethane, and ethylene at certain times of the year. These studies argue that the effects of inhaling ethylene are consistent with the trances described in classical sources, and that the Pythia's trances may have been induced by inhaling ethylene gas (or a mixture of ethylene and ethane) from naturally occurring geological vents.[95]

All these explanations make the groundless a priori assumption that the Pythia herself could not have composed her responses, or that male priests did.[96] Michael Flower has convincingly argued that the hexameter oracles could have been composed by the Pythias as oral improvisation. Many responses contain epic verse formulae of the kind found in the Homeric poems, and a Pythia with some knowledge of epic hexameter could have improvised them. He argues less persuasively that spontaneous verse forms and ambiguity provided the kind of "randomizing device" that keeps oracles resistant to manipulation, presumably on grounds that the uneducated

[93] Self-hypnosis: Parke and Wormell 1956: 1.39, cf. 17–45. Self-induced ecstasy: Burkert 1985: 116. According to Burkert, her utterances were then "fixed by the priests" into hexameter verse. A more elaborate argument appears in Bowden 2005: 22–24, 33–39. Responses spoken directly by the Pythia: Fontenrose 1978: 212–18, cf. Bloch 1984, Price 1985: esp. 142–45, and Maurizio 1995. From a very different point of view, Ruth Padel (1983) has argued that Apolline inspiration was an invasive, destructive force, akin to madness.

[94] Amandry 1950.

[95] De Boer, Hale, and Chanton 2001; Spiller, Hale, and de Boer 2002; Hale, de Boer, Chanton, and Spiller 2003. They argue that friction along fault planes in bitumen-rich limestone deposits below the site of the oracle could cause vaporization of the lighter constituents of the bituminous layers. The hydrocarbon gases thus formed would dissolve in ground water, rise up through fault lines, and emerge as springs of the kind attested at Delphi. This explanation is consistent with the closure of the Apolline oracle during the winter, when lower ground water temperatures would correspond with diminished gas emissions. (As temperature rose in the spring, more incorporated gas would be released.)

[96] Fontenrose 1978: 197, Maurizio 1995: 72, Flower 2008: 216.

would not have been capable of "faking" a "spontaneous" oracle. That several known attempts were made to bribe the Pythia suggests otherwise.[97]

After Delphi, the shrine of Apollo at Didyma near Miletus may have been the most renowned oracle in the Greek world. It was active at least from the seventh century, and was distinctly Ionian in character. A priestess by a sacred spring gave oracular responses which were interpreted by the temple priests, the Branchidae, a clan descended from Branchus.

Asclepian sanctuaries

Asclepian sanctuaries in the Mediterranean were closely associated with Apollo.[98] The shrine at Epidaurus may date to the late sixth century, and other sanctuaries begin to appear at the end of the fifth. During the fourth century the cult of Asclepius spread throughout the Greek world, and more than 200 new Asclepian temples were established at Athens, Cos, and Pergamum, among many other locales.[99] Epidaurus was claimed as the birthplace of Asclepius, and panhellenic Asclepieia festivals were held there every four years, with poetry and music contests added *c.* 380. The sanctuary was filled with votive offerings and monuments, and remained prosperous throughout the Hellenistic period. It was looted by Sulla in 87 and plundered by pirates in 67.

An inscription at Pergamum confers the priesthood of Asclepius and the other gods in the Asclepion on Asclepiades son of Archias and his descendants. The presiding priest received a portion of all animals sacrificed in the temple and other offerings. (Other benefits included exemption from obligations imposed by the city and a front seat at the games.) The priest was in charge of the temple staff.[100] The main task of the temple priests was the performance of regular sacrifices to Asclepius. They also presided over special sacrifices by individuals or the polis and at festivals of the god Asclepius. They were assisted by one or more sacristans (*neōkoroi*), who had their own subordinates. Moreover, they also interpreted medical advice

[97] Flower 2008: 218–22. Formulae: McLeod 1961, Crahay 1956, Dobson 1979.

[98] Myths of Asclepius also date back to the *Iliad*, where the Greek physicians at Troy, Podalirius and Machaon, are sons of physician-prince Asclepius (*Il.* 2.731–32, 11.518, and 11.833–36; EE, T10, T165, and T136). In Pindar's heroic version, Asclepius is the son of Apollo and the princess Coronis (Pind. *Pyth.* 3 and EE, T1). In this version, Apollo saved the unborn Asclepius, who was reared and taught the medical arts by the centaur Chiron. A great physician, he was slain by Zeus for bringing a dead man back to life. Other accounts take him as a chthonic Epidauran god (EE 2.76 and 90–91).

[99] Herzog 1931; Edelstein and Edelstein 1945.

[100] Inscriptio Permamena 2.251, T491 in EE 1.280–82.

received in dreams by consultors of the temples, and amassed considerable medical expertise.

It is worth asking in what ways Greek oracles were culturally specific. They have no equivalent in China. One obvious reason is a different set of relations between mantic and political authority (discussed in Chapter 6). But another reason may be different attitudes toward mantic potential and place. The prestige of oracles at Delphi, Dodona, and elsewhere derives largely from the presence of the god. (In the case of Delphi, that presence was shared with Dionysus.) But in some cases, particular features of the landscape (or the legendary landscape) are also associated with mantic activity, for example the sacred oak grove at Dodona, and the chasm (if it existed) at Delphi. The idea that a particular place was especially suited to mantic consultation does not seem to have been a Chinese notion. We find no lack of sacred sites (sacred mountains, rivers associated with particular gods, etc.) or the choice of remote locales to practice self-cultivation (especially in its Daoist varieties), but these are not particular to mantic consultation. Instead, mantic potential is linked to notions of auspicious time.

Comparative perspectives

We are now in a position to reassess the three comparative perspectives outlined at the beginning of the chapter.

Divination and authority

Key to the comparison between "official" Chinese and Greek mantic practitioners is the contrast between Chinese mantic officials, who drew authority from the state, and the cultivated independence of the oracle at Delphi. What does this tell us about the relationship between divination and authority?

In both contexts, mantic authority is ultimately religious. It did not arise on its own, even in societies such as early China, where there is debate about the applicability of the category of "religion."[101] Both mantic and political authority are linked through the theological roles of early kings. Even if we cannot trace the details, mantic authority may owe its origins, though not its later development, to these links with kingship. Some form of "official" divination seems to have preceded independent mantic activity in authority if not in origins. In China mantic officials were part of the Shang court.

[101] Applicability of the category of religion to early China: Puett 2002: 5–10.

There is also evidence of Shang mantic activity apart from the court at Anyang, but it lacked the authority of court divination.[102] As Michael Flower points out, we lack the evidence for any account of the early development of Greek mantic authority, and specifically for its diffusion from close links with kingship.[103] This is not to say that divination ultimately depends on royal authority, as some have asserted as an explanation for the so-called "decline" of Delphi.

The independent practitioner

What are the major areas of comparison between Chinese and Greek independent practitioners? First, both have some sense of cosmic or religious authority, but legitimize it in different ways. As Flower aptly characterizes it, the Greek *mantis* legitimizes religious authority through personal charisma, but does not hold political authority.[104] Chinese prognosticators such as Sima Jizhu rely on their reputation for technical expertise, textual knowledge, and moral excellence.

Although Chinese independent practitioners used the same methods as mantic officials, *Shi ji* 127 (which was written by a court astrocalendric official) makes it clear that court officials looked down on independent diviners. And more quotidian arts such as animal physiognomy do not even enter the discussion, though titles in the *Han shu* Bibliographic Treatise indicate the importance of these skills. Finally, since independent diviners may have served a largely illiterate clientele, it is not surprising that writing does not figure prominently in accounts of their activities.

Chinese mantic officials drew their authority and employment from their official roles. The *prophētēs* drew authority from, and was dependent on, a temple that housed a specific cult of a particular god. At Delphi especially, independence from political authority was an element of the oracle's authority. Even primarily local oracles, such as the temple of Apollo at Didyma, were not controlled by a patron polis (in this case Miletus).

Greek independent practitioners enjoyed less prestige than oracular shrines, although some, especially experts in military divination such as Tisamenus of Elis, enjoyed significant rewards and prestige. But *manteis* and chresmologues also became objects of skepticism, ridicule, or accusations of charlatanism.[105]

[102] Flad 2004. [103] Flower 2008: 4, commenting on Halliday 1913. [104] Flower 2008: 30.

[105] Skepticism: Eur. *Hel.* 744ff. Chresmologues are ridiculed in Aristophanes' *Knights*, *Peace*, and *Birds*.

What do we make of these apparently very different understandings of mantic authority? It would be tempting but incorrect to link the authority of Chinese mantic officials with deference to state authority, and the mantic authority of Greek politically independent oracles with regard for political autonomy. There are several objections to this view. Chinese evidence as early as the Zhongba oracle bone inscriptions (discussed in Chapters 2 and 6) suggests the independent, local use of mantic methods, but these records are less reliably preserved than are court records. While oracular divination was privileged by Plato and others, there also is ample Greek evidence of the activity of *manteis* and other independent practitioners from the earliest times. Second, Greek views on mantic authority were not univocal. Aristotle, for example, sought biological explanations for some mantic methods, especially oneiromancy. The authority of Delphi in particular remained consistent for consultation on religious cult, not politics. Finally, the apparent authority of state divination in China may be misleading. The interpretation of anomalies was a focus of political debate, so divination was as much a means to question or intercede with authority as to underscore it (discussed in Chapter 8).

Why did both Chinese and Greek independent practitioners enjoy lower prestige than official divination? One answer is a general tendency to criticize individual practitioners (for incompetence, greed, etc.) while maintaining belief in divination overall.[106] It has been argued that oracles enjoyed higher prestige than *manteis* because their results were less dependent on human agency. African evidence is invoked to contrast the vulnerability of the human element and individual judgment with more "impersonal" methods.[107] For example, the Zande of Sudan were suspicious of the human element in oracles, and put more faith in poison and termite oracles, which worked through natural agencies, than in rubbing-board oracles or witch doctors, who both operated by human agency. Although the Ndembu (Central Africa) used many forms of divination, they considered most reliable a method of divination by shaking up or tossing objects in a basket. This cleromantic method was considered to "sift truth from lies" and uncover hidden malice.[108] In Greece, so the argument goes, the contrast is between the individual judgment of the *mantis* or chresmologue and the impersonal will of the god, expressed through oracular divination.[109] However, oracular divination could only be "impersonal" if the Pythia or

[106] E.g. Parker 2000a: 80–81, Lloyd 2002: 36, Flower 2008: 145.
[107] Flower 2008: 145–46. Impersonal methods: Ahern 1981.
[108] Zande: Evans-Pritchard 1976: 114. Ndembu: Turner 1975: 213–321, esp. 213–15.
[109] Flower 2008: 59–64 and 145–46.

other priestess were a spirit medium, entirely possessed by the god, and beyond the possibility of individual control or manipulation. A few attempts to suborn the Pythia implicitly challenge this assumption.[110] Another possibility is that it is always easier to attack an individual than an institutional system.

The Chinese evidence suggests other possibilities. State-sponsored astrocalendrics would seem impersonal or "natural." It had the status of state patronage, but was not considered inherently more reliable than other methods, since mantic astrolabes (diviner's boards) and turtle and milfoil were used by both official and independent practitioners. The operational contrast may be between individual judgment and institutional authority. The latter included the selection and training of practitioners.

Mantic families

Within a Greek context, descent from a mantic family was important for both types of divination. For the independent *mantis*, a major factor in the ability to attract clientele was the claim of descent from (or adoption into) a mantic lineage, dating back to an eponymous ancestor who had acquired his gifts from a god, usually Apollo. But family lineages also figured in the operation of oracular sites through the priestly clans that managed them, such as the Selloi at Dodona or the Branchidae at Didyma. One inscription from Didyma suggests that the appointment of priestesses was also heredity. It lists the names of several priestesses, including "Tryphōsa, whose grandmother is the prophetess Tryphōsa, whom the god appointed in an oracle."[111] Mantic and oracular lineages combine at Olympia, where Iamid and Clytiad lineages shared management of the shrine, and also gave birth to a significant number of independent *manteis.*

For the independent *mantis*, these descent claims served several purposes. They implied innate gifts (through descent or recognition, in the case of adoption) and competence (through apprenticeship in a system that relied more on oral transmission than texts). From the viewpoint of the lineage, valuable expertise would be retained rather than dispersed. In this sense divination resembled medicine and probably many other occupations.

110 Herodotus describes the famous case of the corruption of the Pythia Perialla by Cleomenes (6.66). A more debatable case involves the Alcmaeonids of Sparta (Hdt. 5.63). Accounts of possible bias: Parker 2000a: 106–8.

111 Τρυπῶσα, μήμης προφήτιδος | Τρυφώσης, ἥν ὁ θεὸς χρησσμῶι | κατέστησε. Fontenrose 1988, H17; Tuchelt 1980: 170; Robinson 1981: 36.

The Hippocratic oath specifies that expertise be retained within the teaching lineage or biological family (one's teacher's sons and one's own).

Lineage was also important for Chinese mantic experts, but for somewhat different reasons. Mantic offices may have been hereditary, the most famous case being Sima Qian's inheritance of the office of *Taishi ling* from his father Sima Tan. Sima Qian's painful choice to complete his father's work on the *Shi ji* also attests to the extent to which that office, from its beginnings, was connected with writing, a potentially independent method for the transmission of mantic knowledge.

The role of family lineages in mantic practice also appears in the collected biographies of *fang* experts in the *Hou Han shu*. The biographies describe official positions gained and refused, and whether particular skills were learned as family arts, from a teacher, from study in youth, or from innate talent. Since this information is not rhetorically charged, and does not seem to conform to a formulaic pattern of biography, the biographies present a valuable source for understanding the transmission of mantic skills.[112] The results may be surprising. Of twenty-four biographies concerned with practitioners of the *fang* arts, only four learned their skills from parents or grandparents, and only five specify a teacher. Most learned their skills through extensive and presumably self-directed study in youth. Over half held office, but not as prognosticators.[113] Although none held specifically mantic office, most used their skills in the furtherance of the offices they did hold. Their reputations (and inclusion in the Collected Biographies) come specifically from their use of their skills to predict or avert famines, floods, fires, and other disasters. Membership in a family or teaching lineage is mentioned only in passing. Similarly, accounts of independent practitioners stress their reputations for skill, rather than claims of descent. Examples include Gongsun Ao consulting Shu Fu and the reputation of Bo Le.

These differences may reflect both the competitiveness of Greek professional life and the overall absence of state patronage of the mantic arts. Reputation was crucial in both contexts, but especially in the imperial Chinese context, patronage and office offered other avenues for it. The *Hou Han shu* biographies emphasize individual merit, not through competition, but through emphasis on individual talent through study, diligence, and innate ability.

[112] Especially the first twenty-four *Hou Han shu* biographies (82AB.2707–42). The remaining nine (82B.2743–52) focus on miracles and practitioners of the arts of longevity and immortality.

[113] See Kalinowski 2010.

Another considerable difference is the relative exclusion of women from the Greek competitive milieu and the Chinese official one. All but one of the mantic experts in the *Hou Han shu* biographies are men; the exception is the daughter of the wind diviner Li Nan, who learned the arts of her family (*jia shu* 家術).[114] Other accounts show women practicing mantic arts, especially oneiromancy and physiognomy, within the context of their families. But there are also a few accounts of female mantic specialists, including officials (the female officials in the *Zhou li*) and independent practitioners such as the horse physiognomist Daughter Li and the female physiognomist Tang Ju of Liang.[115] They also included *wu* specialists, who probably functioned as spirit mediums, and in this sense may be more comparable to the Pythias. By contrast, Greek women clearly functioned as oracular priestesses, but accounts of female *manteis* are harder to establish historically.

Competition, control, and charisma

Michael Flower has argued that independence of employment was a major difference between Greek *manteis* and their Mesopotamian counterparts: when Mesopotamian mantic arts were transferred to Greece, the image of the expert was transformed to accommodate new cultural conditions and circumstances of employment. Divorced from kings, palaces, and archives, the Greek itinerant *manteis* relied on oral rather than written knowledge, and relied on the ability to project charisma as an essential skill for attracting and retaining clientele. Such an individual required quick wits, flexibility, sensitivity, and confidence, a different set of abilities from what would be required for a Mesopotamian mantic official. Personal charisma was distinct from the "official" charisma of an oracle or the authority of office. Clifford Geertz points out that the most flamboyant expressions of charisma often appear at a distance from the center, and it is worth noting that both oracles and *manteis* operated at such distances: oracles through remote locations and *manteis* through itinerant livelihoods.[116]

The transformation Flower describes occurs because of a transition from one cultural context to another: what had been a science to be mastered in

[114] *HHS* 82B.2717.

[115] Daughter Li: *LSCQ*, 1414 ("Guan biao" 觀表 20.8). Tang Ju: *SJ* 79.2418, cf. *Xunzi* 5.72 and *Qianfu lun* 27.3 1 1, discussed in Chapter 7.

[116] Flower 2008: 30–31, 59, 241. Charismatic authority: Weber 1978: 1.215–16 and 241–54. Differences between personal and institutional or official charisma: Shils 1965, Geertz 1983: esp. 144.

Mesopotamia becomes a performance to be staged persuasively in Greece. The Chinese evidence gives a different picture of coexistence and interaction between official and independent mantic experts. It also challenges some distinctions between them that are too easily drawn from the example of Greece and Mesopotamia. Both Chinese and Mesopotamian mantic officials created and used extensive textual records and logically sophisticated methods of interpretation. Both were supported and controlled by court patronage. But Chinese independent practitioners also used mantic astrolabes and other astrocalendric methods. Independent practitioners may also have used daybooks, physiognomy texts, and dream divination.

A Greek penchant for intense political and intellectual competition has been widely noted, and it is tempting to attribute the practices of independent *manteis* to the pervasive competitiveness of Greek society. Vernant, Lloyd, and others have linked the rise of Greek science to the availability of intellectual and political debate and public competition, including the public competition of scientific theories.[117] An analogous competition extended to divination. Diviners and physicians made competing claims to predict the future. Prognosis and divination had similar goals and used similar language, and in some cases similar techniques. Several studies have shown that physicians competed with diviners for clientele and reputation.[118] But these accounts all take the viewpoint of the physician. They, like other broadly naturalistic thinkers, were relative newcomers, and had to compete with established disciplines. There is less evidence that diviners, as the established discipline, felt a strong need to compete with physicians. We find accounts of physicians deliberately distancing themselves from the claims of diviners, but not of diviners deliberately separating themselves from the claims of physicians. More generally, newer naturalistic methods, including Hippocratic medical prognosis and astronomy, competed with older mantic practices. The newer disciplines competed actively with each other, and with their predecessors.

Nonetheless, diviners did not make their reputations or gain a reputation for wisdom by publicly besting rivals. Membership in a mantic lineage was paramount in both Mesopotamia and Greece. Legends of the founders of such lineages also include competition, but it was not central to their

[117] Vernant 1982: esp. 130, 1983: 176–210 and 343–74; Vidal-Naquet 1986: 249–61; Lloyd 1979: 240–67, 1987: 78–83, 1990: 58–67 and 122–26, 1996, 2002: esp. 35–41.

[118] The classic study is Lloyd 1987. A recent study of the Hippocratic corpus by Volker Langholf (1990) contains a chapter on prognosis and divination which provides detailed comparisons of the language of prognostic aphorisms and divinatory formulations.

legitimacy. For example, the status of Mopsus is defined more by his descent claims than by his defeat of Calchas in a mantic contest.

Oracles and independent *manteis* differed in their relations to political authority. Oracles had to come to some accommodation with political power. Local oracles typically were clients of a patron polis, for example the relationship between Didyma and Miletus. An exception was Delphi, which, as a panhellenic oracle (in its heyday), cultivated independence from the influence of any *one* polis.

By contrast, independent, itinerant diviners could move freely from one polis to another, and could optimize their prospects for state clientele. Independent diviners seem to have proliferated in seventh and sixth centuries and were particularly active in the fifth century, in the military context of the Persian and Peloponnesian Wars. Mantic competition took a different form in China.

In summary, competition between diviners, on their own terms, may have been greater in China than in Greece. That competition, however, took the form of ritual rather than public performance, and did not involve debate of the kind associated with the rise of science in Greece. The admittedly very limited evidence of excavated texts does not suggest competition between practitioners, even in situations where multiple practitioners operated concurrently. We do not know, for example, how Chu officials such as Shao Tuo selected the specialists they employed. At times their interpretations and recommendations are contradictory, but we find no comparison or assessment of their relative abilities.

In conclusion, comparison with historical evidence from other societies cannot fill the lacunae in our knowledge of Greek practitioners, especially oracular personnel. Nonetheless, Chinese sources, especially for court-sponsored divination, are much richer than Greek in specifying official roles, duties, and methods. They also provide a stronger contrast than does Mesopotamia between the official and independent divination.

Appendix 4.1: Chinese mantic officials: the *Zhou li*

Offices of Heaven (*Tian guan* 天官). Prime Minister, General Administration.
Offices of Earth (*Di guan* 地官). Public Affairs. Education.
Offices of Spring (*Chun guan* 春官). Ancestral Affairs. Sacrifice and ritual.

Director of Divination (*Taibu* 大卜, *ZL* 17: 12b):
His immediate staff (each with a staff of officials, scribes, assistants, and attendants)
two counselors (*Daifu* 大夫)
Divination Master (*Bushi* 卜師)
high-, middle-, and low-rank officials (*shi* 士)
storekeepers (*fu* 府), scribes (*shi* 史), assistants (*xu* 胥), and attendants (*tu* 徒)
Mantic specialists
Turtle shell prognosticators (*Guiren* 龜人) and their staff of artisans (*gong* 工)
Material supply and preparation staff (*zhuishi* 菙氏)
Prognosticators (*Zhanren* 占人)
Milfoil prognosticators (*Shiren* 筮人)
Dream prognosticators (*Zhanmeng* 占夢)
Director of Incantation (*Taizhu* 大祝, *ZL* 17: 13b–14b):
His immediate staff (each with a staff of officials, scribes, assistants, and attendants)
two counselors (*Daifu* 大夫)
Lesser Incantator (*Xiaozhu* 小祝)
high-, middle-, and low-rank officials (*shi* 士)
storekeepers (*fu* 府), scribes (*shi* 史), assistants (*xu* 胥), and attendants (*tu* 徒)
Incantators
Funerary Incantators (*Sangzhu* 喪祝)
Suburban Incantators (*Dianzhu* 甸祝)
Oath Incantators (*Zuzhu* 詛祝)
Manager of *wu* (*Si wu* 司巫)
Male *wu* (*Nan wu* 男巫)
Female *wu* (*Nü wu* 女巫)
Director of Astronomy (*Taishi* 大史, *ZL* 17: 14b):
His immediate staff (each with a staff of officials, scribes, assistants, and attendants)
two counselors (*Daifu* 大夫)
Lesser Scribe (*Xiaoshi* 小史)
high-, middle-, and low-rank officials (*shi* 士)
storekeepers (*fu* 府), scribes (*shi* 史), assistants (*xu* 胥), and attendants (*tu* 徒)

Offices of Summer (*Xiaguan* 夏官). Military Affairs.

Grand Musician (*Taishi* 大師). Pitch pipe prognostication
Fangxiangshi 方相氏

Offices of Autumn (*Qiu guan* 秋官). Penal Affairs.
Offices of Winter (*Dong guan* 冬官). Records concerning crafts.

Appendix 4.2: Chinese mantic officials: Western Han

Nine Ministers of State (*Jiu Qing* 九卿).

(1) Minister of Ceremonial (*Fengchang* 奉常, after 144 *Taichang* 太常, *HS* 19A.726–27).
 (1) *Taibu ling* 太卜令 (Grand Diviner, *SJ* 127.3215)
 (2) *Taizhu ling* 太祝令 (Grand Incantator)
 (3) *Taishi ling* 太史令 (Grand Scribe or Grand Astronomer)
 The *Taichang* supervised three other officials in charge of:
 (4) *Taiyue ling* 太樂令 (Music)
 (5) *Taizai ling* 太宰令 (Butchery)
 (6) *Taiyi ling* 太醫令 (Medicine)
(2) Minister of the Palace (*Guangluxun* 光祿勳)
(3) Minister of the Guard (*Weiwei* 衛尉)
(4) Minister of Transport (*Taipu* 太僕)
(5) Minister of Justice (*Tingwei* 廷尉)
(6) Minister of State Visits (*Da honglu* 大鴻臚)
(7) Minister of the Imperial Clan (*Zong zheng* 宗正)
(8) Minister of Agriculture (*Da sinong* 大司農)
(9) Minister of the Privy Treasury (*Shao fu* 少傅)

5 | Methods

The last chapter addressed who Chinese and Greek mantic practitioners were and what they did. This chapter takes up how they did it. I present a brief overview of the major techniques, with particular interest in three points: (1) attempts to ensure "objectivity" or randomness; (2) balance between interpreting spontaneous, natural events, and deliberate procedures; and (3) the role of state patronage in the development of mantic methods.

The major Chinese methods were osteomancy and plastromancy, a sortition process of "casting" milfoil stalks, astrocalendrics, weather divination (especially clouds and vapors), oneiromancy, and physiognomy. Greek methods immediately divide into the procedures of oracles and the many methods independent *manteis* used to read signs of divine approval. They all focused on the will of the gods, demonstrated through natural events or responses to deliberate queries. Chinese methods, by contrast, attempted to locate consultors in a cosmic system of temporal cycles of good and ill auspice. Chinese methods, especially hemerology and astrocalendrics, do not fit into conventional classifications of Greek methods.

The comparative focus is on three issues. The first is the explicit or implicit classifications applied to the mantic arts. Greek methods linked divination closely to the gods, while Chinese methods are located within a tacit or explicit cosmic system. Second, apparently similar Chinese and Greek techniques were understood very differently. For example, both Chinese and Greek diviners cast lots, observed the winds, and practiced physiognomy, but they used them in very different ways. A third consideration concerns the cognitive skills or abilities required by mantic procedures.

Chinese methods

The *Shi ji*-collected biographies of diviners make it clear that independent diviners used multiple methods.[1] The oldest were turtle shell and milfoil.

[1] *SJ* 127.3218, quoted and translated in Chapter 4. The oldest account of the relative authority of these methods is the hierarchy of the *Han shu* Bibliographic Treatise, and most contemporary

Turtle and milfoil

Pyroscapulimancy, divination by applying heat to the bones of deer, sheep, cattle, and other animals, has been used in north China since the late fourth millennium. Shang diviners introduced three distinctive innovations. The first was the use of turtle plastrons (plastromancy). Over the course of the Shang, plastrons and scapulae were used in about equal numbers, with no clear principle determining choice of medium. The dominant pyromantic procedure shifted to plastromancy during the Western Zhou, although plastromancy continued in declining use into the Han dynasty.[2]

All these methods involved deliberate procedures of preparing and cracking the bones or shells. The second innovation was to structure the surface by cutting ordered hollows that directed the potential direction of the cracks (see Appendix 5.1). The diviner applied controlled heat to the back of the bone or shell in order to produce a visible crack on the front. The direction of the crack yielded two possible interpretations: auspicious or inauspicious. The hollows made the material thinner and easier to crack, but they also allowed diviners to consistently produce *bu* 卜-shaped cracks in a controlled direction. They were placed with careful attention to symmetry. This innovation modified the objectivity of the procedure by introducing some potential control over the direction of the crack.

The third Shang innovation was the use of written records, dating from about 1400 to 1100. It is widely accepted that the oracle bone inscriptions were created after the divination procedure by incising records of questions, responses, and sometimes verifications into the bone or shell surface (Figure 4.1).[3] However, the vast majority of bones that have been excavated are cracked but not inscribed.[4]

Although pyromancy retained high prestige, it was at least partially replaced by another deliberate procedure sometime during the Western Zhou. Prognostication by counting milfoil stalks (stalk casting) is an elaborate form of cleromancy in which groups of stalks are counted out in complex procedures to generate a sequence of numbers. It is the best-known method of Chinese divination because of subsequent association with the

treatments of Chinese mantic methods follow its hierarchy, e.g. Li Ling 1993, to which all Western scholarship on the subject is indebted. I begin with the two oldest methods known.

2 Aquatic freshwater local (and possibly non-local) turtles were used and possibly reared for that purpose. Most were female, probably because of the smoothness and uniformity of their shells. Differences in techniques: Li Ling 1993: 232–50, Flad 2008: 411–18.

3 Keightley 1978b: 45, cf. Vandermeersch 1977–80: 2.163–64, Allan 1991: 121–22.

4 The finds at Anyang led scholars to concentrate on inscribed bones, but 90 percent of extant oracle bones are uninscribed. See Song Zhenhao 1999: 392 (cited in Flad 2008: 406) and 2000.

Yi jing (see Appendix 5.2). Yarrow or milfoil (*Achillea millifolium*) is a hardy plant originally native to Europe and western Asia; it was widely available and its stalks were easy to prepare.[5]

Milfoil divination is difficult to date because the stalks leave no archaeological profile. We can, however, surmise its use from inscriptions containing sequences of numbers, associated with statements (discussed further in Chapter 9). Numbered statements offer more potential responses than the two outcomes obtainable from pyromancy. Importantly, archaeological evidence suggests that the two methods were used together at a very early period.[6] Milfoil divinations recorded as sequences of numbers also appear in Warring States archaeological sites such as Tianxingguan, Baoshan, and Wangjiatai. Over a long period, milfoil divination evolved into "Yi divination," the association of sequences of six numbers or hexagrams with divination statements in a mantic text such as the *Zhou yi*.[7]

During the Warring States and Western Han, milfoil divination became increasingly prevalent but never replaced pyromancy. On the contrary, turtle and milfoil continued to be used both independently and together. For example, the *Zuo zhuan* contains many accounts of their independent use.[8]

Han sources repeatedly refer to the consultation of "turtle and milfoil" on a variety of subjects. For example, Monthly Ordinance texts (*Yue ling* 月令) specify turtle and milfoil for sacrifices at the winter solstice.[9] The *Li ji* authorizes their combined use for marriage arrangements and funerals.[10] It also specifies that turtle shell and milfoil should not be consulted more than three times, or together on the same question.[11] The *Baihu tong* describes a hierarchy of mantic practitioners from the ruler down to officials of the *shi* rank, with different grades of materials reserved for each rank.[12]

The complementarity of turtle and milfoil introduces two kinds of randomness and corresponding objectivity. Turtle shell divination offers an unambiguous positive or negative recommendation; it has the advantage of two possible outcomes that are in principle equally probable. Stalk casting

[5] Loewe 1981, Zhao Zhenhua 1985, Venture 2002b: 213.

[6] In particular, the Zhouyuan oracle bones are discussed in Chapter 9.

[7] Introduced in Chapter 2. See Appendix 5.2 for methods for generating a hexagram and Chapter 9 for the evolution of the *Zhou yi*.

[8] The *Zuo zhuan* also indicates the early provenance of the hexagram names and the moral status of the *Zhou yi* at least by the fourth century. *Zuo zhuan* descriptions of milfoil procedures suggest that (like oracle bone divination) it had two phases. The "charge" generated a hexagram; the second phase generated a key line within the hexagram.

[9] *LJ* 17.10b (Couvreur 1.392f); *LSCQ* 515–16 ("Meng dong ji" 孟冬紀 10.1); *HNZ* 5.14ab.

[10] Details are discussed in Chapter 6. [11] *LJ* 3.14b–19a (Couvreur 62); *YL* 47.4b.

[12] *BHT* 327–28 ("Shigui" 筮龜 7.3), Som 2.522–23.

Figure 5.1 Divining blocks and *qian* rods (Tian Ho Temple, Lamma Island, Hong Kong, 2003).

offers the possibility of a large number of generic mantic statements. Stalk castings have the objectivity provided by a sortition process, but because they are generic, they also must be interpreted for each situation.

This complementarity is mirrored in Qing and contemporary prognostication by a different combination of two cleromantic procedures. Divining blocks (*jiao* 珓, *jiaobei* 珓杯, *jiaogua* 珓卦) provide "yes–no" responses by the shaking and dropping of two crescent-shaped wood blocks with one rounded and one flat side. Both flat sides landing down indicated a "no," one flat and one round a "yes," and both flat sides landing up was considered unclear. Divination rods (*qian* 籤) provide more detailed commentary. The set of numbered bamboo sticks are shaken together in a bamboo tube until one falls out. Its number corresponds to a written inscription (often a reference to an incident in history or popular drama) and a commentary, interpreted by temple priests (Figure 5.1). Both methods are used today; at times, divining blocks are used to verify the appropriateness of a *qian* divination.[13]

Turtle shell and milfoil divination highlight central features of Chinese mantic methods: the use of writing and written records, and an early preoccupation with number.

[13] R. J. Smith 1991: 234–44, Doolittle 1865: 2.108–10, Eberhard 1970. Smith has argued that divination rods may be based on the structure of the *Yi jing* hexagrams.

The heavens

Star divination and weather divination interpret spontaneous natural phenomena. Both kinds of divination were classed under the category of Celestial Patterns (*Tianwen*). Instruments were used to observe the position of stars and planets. Early astronomical observation focused on the immediate environs of the pole star in the Northern Dipper (*Beidou* 北斗) along a celestial equator always visible in the night sky. An example is provided by a circumpolar star map discovered at Dunhuang. It includes astrological predictions for each region of the sky and the states believed to be influenced by it.[14] By contrast, Greek, Babylonian, and Egyptian astronomy focused on stars that rose and set and were visible only at certain times of the year.

Star divination required mapping the heavens and knowing the position and orientation of the Dipper, and several methods were used to determine the orientation of the Dipper handle and the positions of key celestial bodies. The celestial equator around the pole star was divided into twenty-eight "Lunar Lodges" (*xiu* 宿), grouped into four palaces (*gong* 宫) corresponding to the four seasons, each named for a star or star group within it (Figure 5.2). Each contained seven lodges, corresponding to three signs of the zodiac. As a result the lodges are of widely unequal sizes, ranging (in Chinese reckoning) from two (Turtle) to twenty-six (Southern Dipper) of the 365.25 degrees of the equatorial belt of the sidereal zodiac. Within each palace, the middle sign of the zodiac contains three lodges, while the outer signs each contain two. Thus the three lodges in the middle sign of each palace are smaller than the others. Figure 5.3 shows the center of the circle divided into the four palaces, surrounded by the Twelve Earth Branches, with the Lunar Lodges on the periphery of the circle. The Lunar Lodges were also correlated with the rotation of Jupiter, variously described as Year Star (*Sui xing* 歲星), Grand Year (*Tai sui* 太歲), or Great *Yin* (*Tai yin* 太陰). They form an important ongoing element in Warring States cosmographic imagery. The Lunar Lodges appear in a wide variety of astrocalendric divination methods, including mantic astrolabes (diviner's boards), *liubo* boards, and daybooks. They also were used as a day count.[15]

[14] Celestial equator: Needham 1959: 3.229. The Dunhuang star atlas (British Library S.3326) dates from the early Tang dynasty. It is a spectacular representation of the full Chinese sky observable by eye from the imperial observatory. It is the oldest star atlas known, and consists of thirteen maps, including representations of more than 1,300 stars as well as constellations and their names. See Bonnet-Bidaud, Praderie, and Whitfield 2009.

[15] Relative sizes of the Lunar Lodges: Needham 1959: 3.234–37. They were also used to measure months and times of day. Twelve "monthly lodges" (*yuexiu* 月宿) corresponded to the monthly

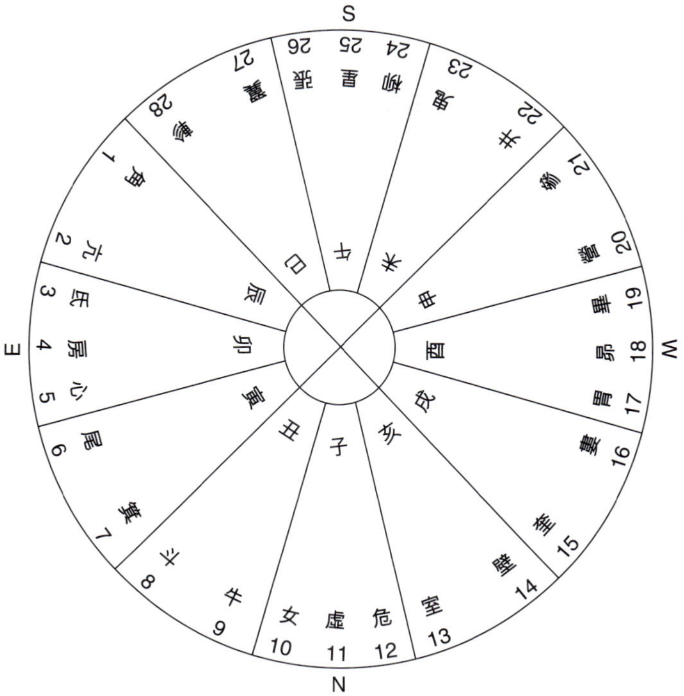

Eastern Palace

1	角	jiao	Horn
2	亢	kang	Neck
3	氐	di	Root
4	房	fang	Room
5	心	xin	Heart
6	尾	wei	Tail
7	箕	ji	Basket

Northern Palace

8	斗	dou	Dipper
9	牽牛	qianniu	Herd Boy
10	女	nü	[Serving] Girl
11	虛	xu	Void
12	危	wei	Roof
13	營室	yingshi	Encampment
14	東壁	dongbi	East Wall

Western Palace

15	奎	kui	Legs
16	婁	lou	Bond
17	胃	wei	Stomach
18	昴	mao	Hair [asterism]
19	畢	bi	Net
20	觜	zui	Turtle
21	參	shen	Three Stars [Asterism]

Southern Palace

22	東井	dongjing	East well
23	輿鬼	yugui	Ghost vehicle
24	柳	liu	Willow
25	七星	qixing	Seven Stars
26	張	zhang	Extended Net
27	翼	yi	Wings
28	軫	zhen	Chariot Platform

Figure 5.2 The Twenty-eight Lunar Lodges.

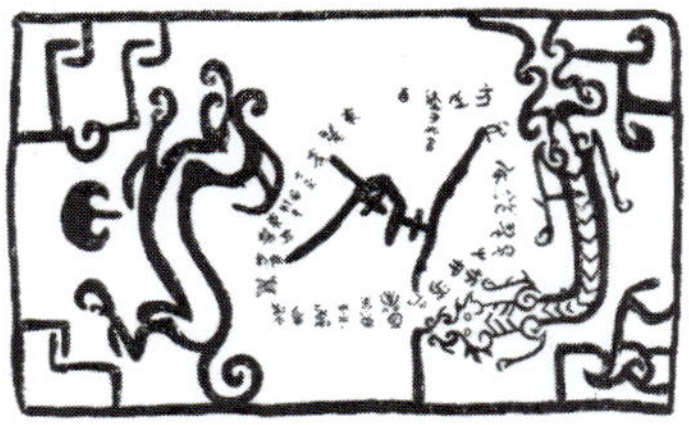

Figure 5.3 Lunar Lodges decoration from the tomb of Marquis Yi of Zeng.

Our oldest evidence for the presence of these astronomical concepts dates from the fifth century BCE. The Lunar Lodges are clearly represented on the lid of a lacquer clothing case from the tomb of Marquis Yi of Zeng (Zeng Hou Yi).[16] It shows the Dipper surrounded by the Twenty-eight Lunar Lodges, and the directional images of the Green Dragon and White Tiger on the right and left (Figure 5.3).[17]

Weather divination focused on clouds, mists, rainbows, and other sub-celestial phenomena, whose shapes were believed to signify future events. References to the observation of clouds and vapors (*yun qi* 雲氣) or the *qi* in the animal shapes in the clouds (*yun wu* 雲物) as predictors of future events first appear in the *Zuo zhuan* and *Mozi*. A *Zuo zhuan* passage dated to 653 calls for the recording of cloud shapes at regular intervals as a method of prediction. A late fifth- or early fourth-century Mohist military chapter describes "observing vapors" (*wang qi* 望氣) to predict the direction of an enemy's arrival, and argues that the technique can be used to predict military victory.[18] Late Warring States texts give a more general account of clouds and mists. The *Lü shi chunqiu* argues that sages recognize signs of things to come by observing the constant flux of the heavens, visible in the motions and changes of the sun, moon, stars, clouds, mists, rain, and dew.[19]

This picture is amplified by a manuscript from Mawangdui, which modern scholars have titled "Miscellaneous Prognostications by Celestial Patterns and Qi Configurations" (*Tianwen qixiang zazhan* 天文氣象雜占, Figure 5.4). It correlates cloud types to at least some of the fourteen states of Warring States China (starting with Chu), to images (such as cloth, ox, carriage, and dragon), and to military prognostications, for example that a city cannot be taken (dog) or that the general of the army will die (pig). Each is illustrated. Another part of the illustration contains the oldest known pictures of comets, which also include prognostications about military and

positions of the sun. Twenty-eight "horary lodges" (*shixiu* 時宿) divided the hours of the day. See Kalinowski 1996.

16 Wang Jianmin and Liang Zhu 1979: 41. Marquis Yi was probably descended from the Ji clan, who brought Zhou rule to northern Hubei in the Western Zhou. By his time, there were close connections between his state of Zeng and the state of Chu. See Thorp 1981, Harper 1999b: 833–36, Falkenhausen 1993b: esp. 50–51 and nn. 55–57.

17 Four of these stars appear in the *Yaodian* chapter of the *Shang shu* (2.9b–10b, Karlgren 3): Niao 鳥 (Bird), Huo 火 (Fire), Xu 虛 (Void), and Mao 昴 (Hair). Most appear in the *Yue ling* (Monthly Ordinances) chapter of the *Lü shi chunqiu*, and all appear in *Shi ji* 27. See Needham with Wang Ling 1956: 2.351–57, Needham 1959: 3.229–59, Chen Zungui 1980–89: 305–84. Rotation of Jupiter: Major 1993: 74, 84–86, 92–94, and 118–26.

18 Zuo, 302–3 (Xi 5.1, Couvreur 1.247–48, Legge 144). *Mozi* 68: 574–75 ("Ying di si" 迎敵祠). The term cloud *qi* also appears in the *Zhuangzi* (1.14, 1.28, 2.96, 11.380, 14.525) and *Guanzi* (39.3a, 49.6a, 64.15b; Rickett 2.105, 2.54, 1.89), but in contexts not related to divination.

19 *LSCQ*, 1412 ("Guan biao" 觀表 20.8), Knoblock and Riegel 2000: 540.

Figure 5.4 Cloud diagram from Mawangdui.

other events.[20] Early accounts of cloud observation focus on military prediction, but by the Eastern Han, there are accounts of emperors themselves ascending to observatories to study the clouds.[21] These images attest to the belief that stars and clouds signified future events.

According to *Shi ji* 127, diviners used both milfoil and mantic astrolabes to make prognostications (127.3218). Mantic astrolabes model the cosmos for purposes of mantic calculation. A movable circular "Heaven" plate was superimposed on a square fixed "Earth" plate (see Figure 9.6). They first appear in the late Warring States period, and become more complex over time.

These round and square plates are presumably what the Han diviner Sima Jizhu refers to when he describes revolving the mantic astrolabe (diviner's board) – the round Heaven plate – and setting the mantic chessboard straight – the square Earth plate (discussed in Chapter 4). Both plates contain bands of information from the sexagenary cycle, whose details vary from instrument to instrument. (The sexagenary cycle refers to the Stems and Branches, *gan zhi* 干支, given in Appendix B.) The Ten Heaven Stems named the days of the ten-day week of the Shang dynasty. The sexagenary

[20] *Zhongguo wenwu* 1 (1979): 26–29 (photographs pp. 1–4) and Fu Juyou and Chen Songchang 1992: 154–60. For discussion see Gu Tiefu 1978 (trans. Harper 1979b) and Loewe 1994: 61–67 and 193.

[21] *HHS* 2.102 (Han Ming Di); 8.353 (Han Zhang Di 漢章帝, r. 75–88 CE); 79A.2545 (Han He Di 漢和帝, r. 88–105 CE). Military cloud observation persisted into the Qing (discussed in Chapter 8).

cycle of sixty days is derived by combining the first stem with the first branch, second with second, etc.[22]

A passage from *Shi ji* 128 gives some indication of how the mantic astrolabe was used. After being awakened by a disturbing dream, King Yuan of Song summoned the diviner Wei Ping to tell him its meaning:

衛平乃援式而起，仰天而視月之光，觀斗所指，定日處鄉。規矩為輔，副以權衡。四維已定，八卦相望，視其吉凶，介蟲先見。

Wei Ping stood up, adjusting the mantic astrolabe [diviner's board] with his hands. Raising his eyes to heaven he gazed at the light of the moon; he looked to see where the Dipper was pointing and determined the position where the sun was situated. As aids he used a compass and square along with a weight and scales. When the four nodal points (*si wei*) were fixed and the eight trigrams were face to face, he looked for the signs of good or ill fortune, and the first to appear was the beetle.[23]

No Han text explains how to use a mantic astrolabe, but the combined evidence of the *Shi ji* and later sources give us some idea. The Earth plate was set so its four sides corresponded to the four cardinal directions. The Heaven plate was revolved in one of several ways, depending on the type of instrument and the method used, possibly with the use of the other instruments as described in *Shi ji* 128. The *Han shu* describes Wang Mang using one during the rebellion of 23 CE, when Han loyalists had invaded the palace:

天文郎桉栻於前，日時加某，莽旋席隨斗柄而坐。

A *tianwen* official placed a mantic astrolabe [diviner's board] before him, adjusting it for the day and hour. The emperor turned his mat so that he sat in conformity with the handle of the Dipper.[24]

Until fairly recently only six actual mantic astrolabes were known and most of our knowledge of them came from Tang and Song dynasty sources. Understanding of these instruments has been greatly increased by the discovery of several pre-Han or Han examples that can be compared to Song accounts.[25] Most extant instruments are of the *Liuren* type, described

22 There are ten stems and twelve branches, so after the first ten, the eleventh branch is combined with the first stem, the twelfth branch with the second stem, the first branch with the third stem, and so on, until all sixty combinations of this sequence have been realized (half the number of possible combinations).

23 *SJ* 128.3229, trans. after Loewe 1979: 77. This section was added to the *Shi ji* by the commentator Chu Shaosun (?104–?30). See Pokora 1987.

24 *HS* 99c:4190; trans. after Needham 1962: 272 and Loewe 1979: 78 and 147 n. 63.

25 The oldest is a bronze mantic astrolabe, probably Han, discovered by the Qing archaeologist Liu Xinyuan 劉心源. Another dates from the Six Dynasties, possibly Sui. First century (CE) Han

in Appendix 5.3. Details vary, but the principle behind their use is to set up the plates to represent the cosmic situation at the time of the consultation. The Earth plate was always oriented to the four directions. The Heaven plate was rotated to key the astrolabe to the correct month and time of day by aligning the month marker on the Heaven plate with the hour marker on the Earth plate. As Li Ling explains it, we can compare the instrument to the face of a clock. The handle of the Northern Dipper (or Taiyi, depending on the type) is the pointer and the Twenty-eight Lunar Lodges are the gradations around the perimeter. All mantic astrolabes are clock-face models but they vary in choice of pointer and layout of the perimeter.[26] Prognostication also requires separate texts or tables with necessary astronomical information such as the position of the stars used as pivots.

There is also evidence that boards used to play the game of *liubo* had a mantic use. There are legendary accounts of individuals playing *liubo* against gods to gain magical power; depictions of such games appear in Han tomb decorations.

These methods all bespeak an early interest in the stars and other asterisms as objects of mantic speculation. That interest combined: (1) systematic empirical observation and record-keeping, (2) early theoretical accounts of the heavens, and (3) hermeneutic correlation with terrestrial geography and events. These attitudes toward the heavens have significant Mesopotamian, and no Greek, parallels.

Hemerology

Hemerological texts include almanacs, daybooks, and Monthly Ordinances (all introduced in Chapter 2). These texts combine astronomic observation and cosmological theory; in particular, they combine knowledge of the heavens with understanding of the calendar, with particular interest in the determination of auspicious days. Such texts had important implications; they systematized the domains of gods and spirits into calendars and made their influence easy to look up for any time period.

Yue ling calendars (Monthly Ordinances) and some sections of the daybooks correlated the months of the year to the Lunar Lodges and the days of the year to the Five Agents (*wuxing*). Some *Yue ling* calendars used *wuxing*

instruments have been found in two Han tombs in present-day Korea excavated in 1925, both in Lelang 樂浪. Since the 1970s, a mantic astrolabe was discovered at Wuwei (1972) and two others (one *Liuren*, one *jiugong*) have been discovered at Wangjiatai (1978). See Needham 1962: 262–69. For a list of six *shi*, see Loewe 1979: 204–5.

[26] Li Ling 1993: 90–99. *Liuren* divination: Appendix 5.3. Types of instrument: Chapter 9.

correlations to specify correct social, ritual, and agricultural activities for each season. Addressed to rulers, they provided political and ritual guidance for regulating state activities over the year. They contained calendric tables listing the days in the year in stem–branch sexagenary order, with annotations on which days were auspicious for particular activities. Similarly, the excavated text titled "Prohibitions" (*Jin* 禁) from Yinqueshan gives seasonal prohibitions, correlated with Four Agents (rather than Five), natural phenomena, and seasonal rules. There are prohibitions against offending Wood in spring (by cutting down trees), Fire in summer, Metal in autumn, and Water in winter. Unlike Monthly Ordinances, which specify actions to take, this text lists activities to avoid at particular times of the year. It also includes what appear to be prohibitions on inappropriate use of convict labor.[27]

Daybooks were used somewhat differently. They were practical guides for action, and had no fixed content. They included two kinds of information. Calendric tables listed the days of the year in stem–branch order and explained different day types (according to several systems). Other parts of the daybooks are organized around types of activity, such as marriage, journeys, construction projects, illness, dreams, and desertion. These sections provided advice on when to undertake (or avoid) them. Daybooks thus correlated the calendar to auspicious action and allowed a user to quickly determine which days to select or avoid for particular activities.[28] The oldest daybooks come from Jiudian (330–270). They are fragmentary, and include astrological, hemerological, and medical materials. For example, entries on illness correlate the day of onset with one of three prognoses: respite, recovery, or death (discussed further in Chapter 6). The most complete daybooks found to date are two texts from Shuihudi of some 425 slips (discussed in detail in Chapters 6 and 9).[29] A recently discovered text from Dunhuang known as the Commands for the Four Seasons (*Si shi ling* 四時令) and dated to 5 CE provides a practical perspective on these documents. It is a decree in the name of the Grand Empress Dowager, but does not appear in the *Han shu*. It lists fifty actions or prohibitions for

[27] Wu Jiulong 1985. Seasonal prohibitions: slip 0260. Convict labor: slips 0365, 1503, 3037. "Prohibitions" is transcribed and translated in Yates 1994: 99–106.

[28] Loewe 1994, Li Ling 1993: 39–43, Poo 1998: 69–101.

[29] Jiudian: *Jiangling Jiudian dong Zhou mu* 1995, *Jiudian Chu mu* 1999, Liu Lexian 1996. Shuihudi: *SHD* (Daybooks), slips 175–255. Kalinowski (2010: Appendix 1) gives an extensive list of excavated daybooks from Fangmatan, Wangjiatai, Zhoujiatai, Wuwei, and elsewhere. Fangmatan: *WW* 1989.2: 1–11; He Shuangquan 1989a, 1989b, 1989c; Li Xueqin 1990. Zhoujiatai: *Guanju Qin Han mu jian du* 2001 (*ZJT*). Wuwei: *Wuwei Han jian* 1964. Dunhuang: transcription in *WW* 2000.5: 34–36. Studies: Rao Zongyi and Zeng Xiantong 1982; Harper 1985; Kalinowski 1986: 175–228; Pu Muzhou 1992; Poo 1993; Liu Lexian 1994.

each month of the year, mostly concerned with agriculture, irrigation, and domestic matters.[30] Its practical tone illustrates the gap between abstract *wuxing* theory and its practical use.

Another approach to selecting auspicious days was Five Agents (*Wuxing*). Titles in the *Wuxing* section of the *Han shu* Bibliographic Treatise indicate methods for selecting auspicious days by means of *yin–yang* and *wuxing* principles. *Wuxing* methods also appear in the Mawangdui manuscripts. For example, a Mawangdui text titled "Sanctions and Virtues" (*Xingde* 刑德) plots calendric cycles on a spatial grid. Another text titled "Book of the Generation of the Fetus" (*Taichan shu* 胎產書) uses a diagram to indicate auspicious directions to bury a newborn child's afterbirth for each month of the year. In the Mawangdui materials, the details of the different systems vary, but they all link mantic formulae to regular spatial representations of time based on the cord and hook pattern (introduced in Chapter 2). These systems may have been developed for private use, but they mirrored the principles of devices used in state ritual.

These calendric methods raise questions about the interrelations between belief in gods and spirits and belief in auspicious days. Was there a contradiction between the threat of a world full of potentially malevolent gods and spirits and the promise of an auspicious day for a particular activity? As with other dangers in life, the choice of an auspicious day could mitigate but not eliminate risk, and could offer some level of security in an uncertain world. In this sense, technically simple daybook "lookup tables" offered some mediation of perceived risk in life. However, the daybooks offered very limited sets of options for day-to-day life, since a large number of days in any given month were inauspicious for particular activities. (These issues are discussed further in Chapters 7 and 8.)

Pitch pipes

Court officials used pitch pipes to calculate the seasons, but they were also used for mantic and military purposes. The *Zhou li* describes one of the duties of the Grand Musician (*Taishi* 大師) as using pitch pipes to listen to the sound of the army and proclaim good and ill auspice. According to the commentary, on the day the army set out, when the general drew his bow, the army shouted, and the Grand Musician used the pipes to prognosticate the impending battle.[31] This method is also briefly mentioned in a Warring

[30] *WW* 2000.5: 34–36, discussed in Loewe 2004: 465.

[31] 大師執同律以聽軍聲。而詔吉凶。*ZL* 23:10a–16a (trans. Biot 2.51n6).

States military text, the *Six Swords of Taigong* (*Taigong liutao* 太公六韜), which describes using pitch pipes to reveal the state of an enemy army on the battlefield. On a still night without clouds, wind, or rain, a mounted rider approaches the enemy and shouts at the enemy forces. He then matches the ensuing clamor to the tones of the pipes to see which gives a sympathetic response.[32]

Another Han method called "watching for *qi*" (*hou qi* 候氣) used sounds generated by *qi* moving through pitch pipes. Like star divination, it was a method of precise measurement of natural phenomena for mantic purposes, in this case of the movements of *qi*. (The invisible energy of *qi* informed all things, and could manifest as vapor, shapes, or perceptible movement, as here.) Accounts of pitch pipe divination also appear in the treatises of the *Shi ji* and standard histories. The Treatise on the Pitch Pipes (*Shi ji* 25) describes the six pipes as fundamental to state decisions (especially military), and attributes their use to the sage kings of antiquity. For example, King Wu supposedly listened to the tones of the pitch pipes for twelve months before his campaign against the Shang.[33] The *Shi ji* also describes their use in prognosticating harvests.[34] These predictions are nuanced by the time of the winds, combinations of cloud, wind, and sun, and the color of the clouds. The chapter concludes with descriptions of the names, tones, and dimensions of the pipes. Further details appear in the *Hou Han shu* Treatise on Pitch Pipes and the Calendar (see Appendix 5.4). The oldest known pitch pipes are from Yutaishan (mid-fourth century). They are made of nodeless bamboo and four have legible inscriptions, but it is not known whether they were used for mantic purposes.[35] Like mantic astrolabes, pitch pipe divination requires precise instruments and record-keeping, both of the calendar and of the measurements themselves. They have no Greek equivalent.

Dream divination

We all dream. Although there are procedures for inducing mantic dreams, most oneiromancy addresses spontaneous dreams, and is thus distinct from

[32] *Liutao* 3.13b, trans. Sawyer 1993: 72; cf. Lewis 1990: 228–29. Another chapter ("Bing zheng" 兵徵 29) associates the color and direction of the *qi* of a besieged city with its prospects for capture.

[33] *SJ* 25.1239–54, esp. 1239, Chavannes 3.293–319, esp. 293.

[34] *SJ* 27.1340 (Chavannes 3.396–97), cf. Loewe 1994: 202–3. See also *HSBZ* 26.46a, Bodde 1975: 45. The winds are described more briefly in the *Tianwen* treatise of the *Han shu* (26.1299) and in *BHT*, 341 ("*Ba feng*" 八風 7.32, Som 2.534).

[35] *WW* 1988.5: 35–38; Chen Cheng-Yih 1996: 46–47.

methods used in deliberately induced mantic encounters. The *Han shu* Bibliographic Treatise is explicit on the importance of oneiromancy, but gives little indication on how dreams were interpreted.

衆占非一，而夢為大，故周有其官。而詩載熊羆虺蛇衆魚旐旟之夢，著明大人之占，以考吉凶，蓋參卜筮。

Of the various prognostications there is no one [preeminent], but dreams are of great [importance]. Therefore the Zhou had an office for it. The *Shi jing* records dreams of black and brown bears, cobras, serpents, fish, flags, and banners, illuminated by the chief of diviners to elucidate good and bad fortune. They surpass the consultation of turtle shell and milfoil.[36]

In the *Zhou li* dream prognosticators were under the office of the Director of Divination. We know nothing of their methods beyond the mention of six kinds of dream:

占夢掌其歲時。觀天地之會。辨陰陽之氣。以日月星辰占六夢之吉凶。一曰正夢。二曰噩夢。三曰思夢。四曰寤夢。五曰喜夢。六曰懼夢。

The dream interpreter links [dreams] to the seasons of the year. He observes the conjunctions of heaven and earth, distinguishes the *qi* of *yin* and *yang*, and uses the sun, moon, and stars to interpret good and ill auspice from the six types of dreams: regular, terrible, longing, wakeful, happy, and fearful.[37]

There are many references to oneiromancy in the *Zuo zhuan*. Milfoil was used to clarify the meaning of dreams. *Zuo zhuan* accounts of predictive dreams may be interpolations for rhetorical purposes, but they still provide valuable information about method. The *Shi ji* also mentions dream divination, including accounts of the Qin emperor Qin Shihuang consulting dream diviners, two cases of oneiromancy in the collective biographies of the Zhao clan.[38] It gives a fuller account of the dream divination for King Yuan of Song, discussed above. The anecdote is not primarily concerned with oneiromancy, but it does indicate that other divination methods (such as the mantic astrolabe) were used to interpret dreams.[39] Dream

36 *HS* 30.1772–73, cf. *Shi jing*, Mao 189.8 ("*Si gan*" 斯干 [Sweeping Banks]).

37 *ZL* 25:1a–2b, trans. after Biot 2.82.

38 Qin Shihuang: *SJ* 6.263, 273–74. Zhao Shun 趙盾: *SJ* 43.1783, cf. 43.1824–25.

39 *SJ* 128.3229–35. King Yuan had dreamed of a man with a long neck and black embroidered clothing who rode a covered chariot. He explained that he was an emissary of the river but had been caught by a fisherman, and asked the king's help in freeing him. Wei Ping explained that the man was named Gui ("Turtle"), and urged the king to find and help him. The king discovered that a fisherman had caught a turtle in the river the previous day, and the turtle was presented to him. He wanted to let it go but Wei Ping persuaded him to kill it for

divination does not figure in the *Han shu* beyond lists of titles in the Bibliographic Treatise. (*Hou Han shu* accounts of dream divination are discussed in Chapter 8.)

The Shuihudi daybooks also attest to the importance of oneiromancy. Daybook A gives a prayer to relieve bad dreams by making them return to their source; it has a close counterpart in Tang dynasty materials excavated from Dunhuang.[40] Daybook B correlates auspicious dreams with the Five Agents, based on colors in the dream and day type (discussed in Chapters 6 and 9).

Physiognomy

In the strict sense, physiognomy is: (1) the belief that physical characteristics could be used to foretell the fortune of an individual. These include accounts of divine destinies revealed through physiognomy (several are discussed in Chapter 8) and (2) practical techniques for physiognomizing people and objects. But in a broader sense physiognomy also includes: (3) accounts of self-cultivation visible through the body.

In the first sense, physiognomists use several aspects of the body. First, parts of the face are identified with periods in one's life (for example, a large chin indicating many descendants). Second, individual features can be compared to the features of animals and the qualities associated with them (for example, features associated with the dragon and phoenix are best; the features of a wolf or tiger are dangerous). Third is the question of one's general "aura" (*feng* 風). Finally, a physiognomist can describe a person's *qi* or color (*se* 色), as in the case of Mencius. As Wang Fu 王符 (*c.* 90–165 CE) describes it:

人之相法，或在面部，或在手足，或在行步，或在聲響。面部欲溥平潤澤，手足欲深細明直，行步欲安穩覆載，音聲欲溫和中宮。頭面手足，身形骨節，皆欲相副稱。此其略要也。

As to methods of physiognomizing people, some of it is in the face, some in the hands and feet, some in the gait, some in the sound. The face should be broad, level, smooth and glossy. The hands and feet should be long, thin, clear and straight. The

divination instead. The point of the anecdote is the power of the turtle, not the nature of oneiromancy.

40 *SHD* (Daybooks): 210, slips 13–14, cf. *Xinji Zhougong jiemeng shu* 新集周公解夢書 [The Duke of Zhou's Explanation of Dreams] (伯 3908) in Liu Lexian 1994: 212–17. This Tang dynasty work on dream interpretation offers interpretations of common dreams, described in seven-character phrases. For translation see Liu Wenying 1995: 515–33. Dunhuang hemerological manuscripts: Harper 2001: 107–9, Kalinowski 2003: 213–99.

gait should be smooth and steady between heaven and earth. The sound should be moderate at the polar regions. The appearance of the face, hands and feet, the figure, and the bones and joints should all be complementary and symmetrical.[41]

Wang Fu held that a good physiognomist could discern how to employ people the same way a skilled carpenter assesses the best use for a piece of timber:

人之有骨法也，猶萬物之有種類，材木之有常宜。巧匠因象，各有所授，曲者宜為輪，直者宜為輿。

For humans, there is the bone-method, just as there are categories and types for the myriad things. With wood, for instance, there is always suitability, so that the skillful carpenter need only base himself on its shape and in each case it will provide something. The twisted will be suitable for wheels; the straight for a carriage chassis.[42]

These accounts include both fanciful or rhetorical descriptions and verifiable accounts of physical features or characteristics. Most animal comparisons are probably fanciful or rhetorical. Facial features, by contrast, are empirically verifiable, as, arguably, are aura and color, which are used in medical diagnosis.

Accounts of physiognomy in the second sense appear in only fragmentary form in the transmitted tradition. Titles of texts on physiognomy appear in the "Numbers and Techniques" section of the *Han shu* Bibliographic Treatise. All these texts are lost, but their titles give an indication of their concerns, which are not limited to human physiognomy. They include titles on physiognomizing clothing and equipment, the earth (for agriculture), silkworms, swords and knives, and domestic animals. These titles suggest the practical and technical uses to which these skills were put. The ability to physiognomize persons and things allowed a skilled reader to assess the future or merit of individuals and also the qualities of other living things or even inanimate objects. It could be used to assess the economic worth of objects (clothing, equipment, swords), animals (domestic animals, silkworms), and people. Excavated texts on physiognomy emphasize these practical contexts, for example a text on physiognomizing dogs from Yinqueshan, a Han sword physiognomy text from Juyan, and a text on the physiognomy of horses from Mawangdui.[43] These

41 *Qianfu lun*, 310 ("Xiang lie" 相列 27).

42 *Qianfu lun*, 312 ("Xiang lie" 27), trans. Bokenkamp in Lupke 2005. The Eastern Han scholar Liu Shao's 劉劭 (*c.* 250 CE) *Renwuzhi* 人物志 or *Essay on Human Abilities* also uses physiognomy to assess men for different kinds of office and employment, based on body shape, coloring, voice, etc.

43 Li Ling 1993: 84–87. The Yinqueshan texts contain fourteen slips of a text titled Recipes for Physiognomizing Dogs (*Xiang gou fang* 相狗方). See Wu Jiulong 1985: 243 and slips 208, 213, 221, 242, 261, 271, 302, 315, 374, 889, 899, 1937, 2570, 3788, and 4047. For transcription of the

included animals and plants used in agriculture and even military materiel. It is not easy to reconstruct the methods used, because many of the passages that mention these arts do so for rhetorical purposes that have no interest in the techniques themselves (discussed in Chapter 9).

Although the *Lü shi chunqiu* sometimes discusses physiognomy for rhetorical purposes, one passage describes the actual techniques of horse physiognomists:

古之善相馬者：寒風是相口齒，麻朝相頰，子女厲相目，衂忌相髭，許鄙相尻，投伐褐相胸脅，管青相膹吻，陳悲相股腳，秦牙相前，贊君相後。凡此十人者，皆天下之良工也，其所以相者不同，見馬之一徵也，而知節之高卑，足之滑易，材之堅脆，能之長短。非獨相馬然也，人亦有徵，事與國皆有徵。

Of those in antiquity who were expert at horse physiognomy, Hanfeng Shi physiognomized by the mouth and teeth, Ma Chao the forehead, Zinü Li the eyes, Wei Ji the whiskers, Xu Bi the rump, Toufa He the chest and ribs, Guan Qing the lips and spittle, Chen Bei the legs and hooves, Qin Ya the front, and Zan Jun the rear. All ten were the most skilled in the empire. They differed in how they physiognomized horses but in observing one key point about a horse they all knew whether its joints were high or base, whether it could run or would stumble, whether it was strong or brittle, and whether it would last for a long or short time. It is not thus only for physiognomizing horses: people also have key points; situations and countries all have key points.[44]

Early accounts of horse physiognomy are not systematic and say little about method. There may be a continuum between assessments described as physiognomy and straightforward physical inspection. A fragmentary text of some 5,000 characters from Mawangdui, which scholars have called the Classic of Horse Physiognomy (*Xiang ma jing* 相馬經), gives some idea of its principles.[45] It contains passages almost identical to brief descriptions of horse physiognomy in the *Zhuangzi* and *Liezi*, and may incorporate even earlier material.[46] Many passages are illegible or very difficult to interpret. The first and third chapters concern the techniques of the legendary horse physiognomist Bo Le 伯樂. The second chapter describes the physiognomy of horses' eyes and heads and methods for predicting a horse's strength and speed by observing the size, fullness, luster, and movements of the eyes,

Juyan slips see *Juyan xin jian* (1990: 98). Mawangdui: *WW* 1977.8: 17–22. For other physiognomy titles in the Treatise see Chapter 2.

44 *LSCQ*, 1414 ("Guan biao" 觀表 20.8), trans. after Knoblock and Riegel 542–43.

45 *WW* 1977.8: 17–22. A silk painting of horses and human figures also discovered at Mawangdui is unrelated. See Jin Weinuo 1974.

46 Xie Chengxia 1977: 23–24, cf. Zhao Kuifu 1989.

eyelashes, and eye muscles. There is also some discussion of the overall proportions of a horse's body. The four areas of the body should be proportionate, and square and round bones should conform to compass and square. As in human physiognomy, forms of the body should also conform to shapes derived from Heaven and Earth; for example, the eye should resemble the moon and the upper part of the eye a crescent moon.[47] Some of these principles appear in later texts on horse physiognomy such as the sixth chapter of the Essential Arts of the Common People (*Qimin yaoshu* 齊民要術, 544 CE). This text and later texts based on it are concrete and specific; they discuss the various parts of horses' bodies from head to hooves.[48] All these texts share the view that internal *qi* is reflected in appearance and makes it possible to judge character or potential.

Under the third group are several Warring States texts that associate virtue with the accumulation or concentration of *qi*. At 2A2 Mencius famously describes *qi* as filling the body and moved by the will, and mentions that he himself is "good at nurturing his radiant (or "flood-like") *qi*" (*haoran zhi qi* 浩然之氣). Here, physical practices for cultivating *qi* seem to be an important element of self-cultivation. Mencius suggests (7A21) that self-cultivation transforms the body in visible ways, producing a glossy jade-like color visible in the face and limbs.[49] He emphasizes that the results of self-cultivation are visible in the body:

存乎人者，莫良於眸子。眸子不能掩其惡。胸中正，則眸子瞭焉；胸中不正，則眸子眊焉。聽其言也，觀其眸子，人焉廋哉？

In examining others, nothing is more effective than the pupils. The pupils cannot conceal evil. If that within the chest is upright, the pupils are clear and bright; if it is not, they are clouded. If you listen to their words and examine their pupils, how can people hide anything?[50]

Here Mencius defends the practice of eye physiognomy. By contrast, Xunzi attacks physiognomy on ethical grounds, and several other early Han texts discuss the issue.[51]

47 *WW* 1977.8: 17–22, cf. Hu Pingsheng 1989, Harrist 1997.

48 An example is the illustration of the traits of a superior horse in the Southern Song text *Simu anji ji* 司牧安驥集 (*Collected Herdsmen's Methods for Pacifying Horses*) by Jia Sixie 賈思勰 between 534 and 549 CE. This chapter was the main source for horse physiognomy in later texts for some 1400 years. The Nanjing Library edition (1504) is reprinted in an edition edited by Li Shi 李石 and Xie Chengxia 謝成俠 (Beijing, 1957).

49 *Mengzi zhengyi* 6.194–99 and 26.906; 2A2 and 7A21 in Lau 1970.

50 *Mengzi zhengyi* 15.518, trans. Csikszentmihalyi 2004: 101, cf. 4A15 in Lau 1970.

51 Xunzi 5 ("Fei xiang" 非相). Needham with Wang Ling 1956: 2.363–64, R. J. Smith 1991: 188–201, Csikszentmihalyi 2004: esp. 127–43.

Mencius' views about *qi* conform to and probably draw on a culture of embodied (bodily based) self-cultivation practices. Such "material virtue" traditions held that the body-mind was constructed of *qi* and that embodied self-cultivation practices could transform *qi*. Such views informed Warring States accounts of dietary practices, exercise regimens, breath meditation, sexual cultivation techniques, and other technical traditions associated with *fangshi*.[52]

Dream divination and physiognomy differ from the other methods discussed above in their relative lack of "controls" to offset bias by the diviner. They lack either the chance procedures of turtle shell and milfoil or the inevitability of natural phenomena (whether regular or anomalous). Dreams are by their nature unverifiable; physiognomy was less systematic than other techniques. These characteristics may account for their relative de-emphasis in the Bibliographic Treatise (which was in any event written by an astronomical official). It may also have made them especially attractive for the rhetorical purposes of the quasi-fictional narratives discussed in Chapter 8.

Fang techniques

All these methods were associated with the "recipe masters" or *fangshi*. Their expertise included turtle and milfoil, *Yi* divination, astrocalendric techniques, omenology, medicine, and physiognomy. Some were credited with magical powers and the ability to predict the future, including anomalies such as eclipses and the time of their own deaths. Many were officials, versed in classical texts or in Huang-Lao and Daoist lore.[53] The *Hou Han shu* chapter "Fang Techniques" (*Fang shu* 方術) describes their arts as:

風角、遁甲、七政、元氣、六日七分、逢占、日者、挺專、須臾、孤虛之術，及望雲省氣。

Wind Horns, Hidden Stems, Seven Governors, Original Qi, Six Days and Seven Parts, Meetings and Greetings, Auspicious Days, Bamboo Twisters, Reading Changes, and Orphans and Voids, as well as examining *qi* by observing clouds.[54] (These methods are discussed in Appendix 5.5.)

In summary, most Chinese methods, especially milfoil and astrocalendrics, attempt some systematic (if not comprehensive) account of the workings of the cosmos. It includes gods, but they do not control the cosmos directly and

[52] Csikszentmihalyi 2004, V. Lo 2005. [53] Li Ling 1995, Kalinowski 2010, esp. app. 2.
[54] *HHS* 82A.2703, trans. substantially modified from DeWoskin 1983: 44–45, cf. Ngo Van Xuyet 1976: 74, 161–95 and DeWoskin 1983: 22–29.

cosmic behavior is not arbitrary. Greek techniques, by contrast, focus on the mutable will of very anthropomorphic gods.

Greek methods

The major distinction in Greek divination is between the methods of the *mantis* and the methods of oracles. Oracles used spirit mediumship (Apollo and Zeus) or oneiromancy (Asclepius), and possibly lot oracles. *Manteis* used a wide range of methods to interpret the significance of spontaneous events and also to interpret the answers to mantic questions posed during sacrificial rituals.

It is striking that most forms of Greek divination appear in the Homeric poems (see Appendix 5.6). These elements may reflect the legacy of the Epic Cycle, which abounds with oracles, prophecies, and supernatural interventions. The Homeric poems suppress the Cycle's fantastic and supernatural elements, and insist on a realistic world in which old age and death separate mortals from gods, but they prominently feature accounts of divination.[55] Homeric divination is focused on the activities of the *mantis*; oracles are mentioned only in passing.

Homeric *manteis* interpret omens in animal and human movement, spontaneous speech, and dreams, including ornithomancy, weather omens, lots, and divination by the entrails of sacrificial animals (hieroscopy). There is one account of divination by the invocation of the dead (necromancy). Despite later claims for the antiquity of inspired divination, the Homeric *mantis* is either a technical specialist or a ruler endowed with mantic abilities by royal birth or particular virtue and wisdom. Odysseus and Penelope have mantic gifts; Agamemnon and Clytemnestra do not (a moral contrast made explicit by Agamemnon's ghost at *Od.* 11.440–60).

The Mediterranean context

These Homeric methods are part of a broader Mediterranean context. Babylonian and Assyrian omenology and Greek divination interpreted some of the same phenomena: birds, animals, dreams, the movements of the heavenly bodies, and the entrails of sacrificial victims. However, there are important differences, and several important aspects of Mesopotamian divination had no Greek counterparts. Babylonian diviners used

[55] Griffin 1977, Monro 1884.

physiognomy and worked closely with incantators, who attempted to avert or mitigate undesirable circumstances.[56] The early appearance of conditional statements in omens and the keeping of systematic records also have no Greek counterpart. Akkadian texts such as the Venus tablet (*c.* 1600) and the Enūma Anu Enlil (*c.* 1500–1200) include conditional divination statements. Mesopotamian diviners created large omen collections such as those in the library of Ashurbanipal at Nineveh in seventh-century Assyria.[57] It is of course speculative to ask why similar methods were used in different ways in two neighboring cultures, possibly with extensive contact. One possibility is that Greek *manteis* were independent, while Mesopotamian diviners operated under royal sponsorship and control. Assyrian seers (*bārû*) operated in the service of kings, and were supported and constrained by ties to the state.

Some scholars consider virtually all Greek mantic techniques to be of Mesopotamian origin. Probably most influential is M. L. West's *The East Face of Helicon*. West argues that a wide range of important resemblances between Greek and Near Eastern cultures suggest either a common origin or direct transmission, rather than parallel evolution; and that this cultural transmission occurred from the Early Mycenaean period to the sixth century.[58] It has been speculated that Greek and Assyrian hepatoscopy share similar terminology and even that the Greek terms for the parts of the liver were translated from Akkadian.[59]

These accounts portray Greek divination as a vastly simplified version of Assyrian and Babylonian practices, in which Greek *manteis* borrowed and adapted what was useful to them. Unlike highly specialized Mesopotamian court personnel, Greek *manteis* were generalists in two senses. One was the relative diversity and simplicity of their methods, compared to the sophistication of Mesopotamian omenology, omen classification, archives, and literacy. The other was their use of other kinds of technical expertise, especially healing and purification. However, Greek independent *manteis* did not need royal patronage or archival competence. In their situation, success at the mantic art required confidence, claims to authority, and

[56] Gadd 1966.

[57] Signs were logically correlated to their signifieds in statements of the form: If X then Y. The library of Ashurbanipal contained over 300 divination records on clay tablets. Omens were organized by types and categories, including anomalies in the heavens or on earth and signs from hepatoscopy. See Bottéro 1992: 125–37 and 2001: 170–202, Sweek 2002: 48–50, Lloyd 2002: 24–25, Rochberg 2004: 1–43, 287–99, cf. Oppenheim 1977: 206–27.

[58] West 1997: esp. 46–51 and 610–11, cf. Rochberg 2004: 14–43, Dillery 2005: 177–79.

[59] Assyrian terms: Jeyes 1978. Translation argument: Burkert 1992: 49–50.

charisma. The new Greek mantic specialist was itinerant rather than court-based, and relied on oral, rather than written, knowledge.[60]

Several problems with this view of Greek *manteis* must be mentioned. Homeric *manteis* relied on bird and weather divination, not extispicy. Accounts of historical *manteis* from the late sixth century on show the use of extispicy, with little reference to the earlier methods. Greek textual sources give no indication of Mesopotamian influence, and similarity of techniques, names, or practices is not evidence of influence.

The methods of the *mantis*

Drawing on Plato and Cicero's categories of natural and technical divination, Bouché-Leclercq distinguished eight kinds of "inductive" methods (technical, and associated with *manteis*), as well as three "intuitive" techniques (inspired, mostly associated with oracles). His schema forms the basis for most subsequent treatments.[61] All were based on the assumption that the gods knew the future and sometimes sent signs to humans about future events and divine good or ill will. The interpretation of some signs depended on the correct interpretation of natural events. "Natural events" spanned a wide range, including weather omens, the structure and spontaneous movements of animate and inanimate objects (including people), and deliberate human action.

Some techniques used the instinctive acts of animals (birds, small mammals, reptiles, fish, and insects). Most important was ornithomancy: divination based on the flight, cries, attitudes, and actions of birds, considered to be messengers of the gods because of their speed and precision of movement. Flight linked them to the sky and to Zeus and Apollo. Ornithomancy also took account of where and when they were seen. A bird in the east was a good sign but "sinister" in the west. Specific gods were linked to particular birds: Zeus the eagle and vulture, Apollo the raven, Athena the owl and heron, and Hera the crow.[62] Other animals had mantic associations with particular gods: bears with Artemis, wolves with Apollo, serpents with Apollo and Asclepius. In *On the Intelligence of Animals*, Plutarch remarks that he has heard of people who observe fish as a kind of *tekhnē*, as the Greeks do birds (*Mor.* 976c–d). Human language was also a source of signs or omens. Cledonomancy was the interpretation of involuntarily or

[60] For this view see Flower 2008: 33–35. [61] Bouché-Leclercq 1879: 1.124–245.

[62] Birds were particularly important for divination in Indo-European societies, for example the importance of augury or bird divination in Rome. See Bloch 1984: 14–15, 34–35.

unconscious speech, such as remarks by children or speech out of context. Tremors and other body movements could also signify.

Bouché-Leclercq's second category is divination based on signs derived from the structure of animate beings, especially the entrails or liver of sacrificial animals (hieroscopy or extispicy). This category also included reading human destiny in the configurations of the body (the forehead, hands, skin, or overall shape) and its temperament (*phusiognōmonia*).[63]

His third category, "inanimate objects," interprets animate and inanimate objects without power of voluntary locomotion, including plants, stones, fire, water, and the movement of objects by magic. For example, in hydromancy objects were thrown into water to interpret their behavior: whether they sank, floated, dissolved rapidly, etc. Pyromancy interpreted the behavior of burning objects, especially sacrificial offerings (usually thigh pieces of animal victims wrapped in fat): the brightness of the flame, the appearance of the smoke, and the length of time it took for the offering to burn. Pythagoreans practiced a form of "vegetable" pyromancy by interpreting the smoke of the incense and the crackling of the laurel wood and barley.

Four sections on divination by the heavens describe the interpretation of winds, clouds, rain, and astrology. Bouché-Leclercq considered meteorological divination a decadent devolution of earlier techniques for the interpretation of the will of Zeus, the god of thunder and lightning. Meteorological divination was relatively simple until the introduction of astrology, which probably was not native to Greece.

Military methods: *hiera* and *sphagia*

Military *manteis* have a significant presence in the *Iliad* especially, but we find fuller and sometimes more reliable accounts of their activities in histories, especially in the works of Herodotus and Xenophon. The major activity of military *manteis* was two kinds of sacrifice. *Hiera* or "normal sacrifice" included animal sacrifice (usually a sheep), offering cooked meat to the gods, a sacrificial feast, and the *mantis* examining the victim's liver. It involved burnt offerings, an altar, and human consumption of sacrificial meats. *Manteis* obtained signs from *hiera* by examining the liver and *splanchna* (the kidneys, gall bladder, urinary bladder, heart) of the victim

63 Bouché-Leclercq 1879: 1.174–75. These terms have relatively few and late attestations. *Metōposkopos*: Clem. *Al.* 261, cf. LS 957; *kheiroskopia*: Joseph. *Hypomn.*, cf. LS 1721; *morphoskopos*: Artem. 2.69, cf. LS 979; *phusiognōmonia*: Arist. *Physiogn.* 2.2, cf. LS 1701.

and also the smoke when they were put on the fire. *Hiera* usually took place before setting out, in a town or camp, and unfavorable results could delay departure or military action.[64]

Sphagia or "blood sacrifice" were prayers of supplication or propitiation performed immediately before battle, sometimes after troops were already committed. The term referred to piercing the throat of a sacrificial victim, bloodletting, and the act of killing. *Sphagia* did not require sacrificial fire, an altar, or human consumption of sacrificial meat. It is unclear what mantic techniques were used in *sphagia* sacrifice on the line of battle.[65]

The two types of sacrifice seem to have been used at different ritual moments in the movement toward battle. Crossing borders required *hiera*; crossing water required *sphagia*.[66] Polis borders were not under the control or protection of tutelary deities, whereas water involved the many river and sea gods of ancient Greece. The Spartan sequence (for which there is the most evidence) seems to be (1) *hiera* at home, (2) *hiera* at (polis) borders, (3) *sphagia* at rivers or the sea, (4) *hiera* in camp ground sacrifice, and finally (5) *sphagia* at the final battle-line sacrifice.[67] In practice, the distinction is more difficult to draw. Both methods were used for divination, and negative results could stop an expedition. Mantic aspects of battle-line *sphagia* blur any simple distinction between *hiera* as divinatory and *sphagia* as propitiatory.[68] There are also differences of language between accounts of the same event by earlier and later writers, for example the accounts of divination before the battle of Plataea by Herodotus and Plutarch.[69]

The subject of Roman divination and its Etruscan antecedents are beyond the scope of the present study, but in Rome, as in Greece, significant public undertakings required consulting the will of the gods. Roman divination used

[64] E.g. Xen. *An.* 6.4.13; Thuc. 5.54.2, 5.55.3, and 5.116.

[65] Pritchett 1974: 109–13. They also were used with different verbs: *thuein* or *thuesthai* for *hiera* and *sphazein*, *sphattein*, and *sphagiazesthai* for *sphagia*. *Sphagia* were also used for oaths, certain kinds of purification, some rites for the dead and heroes, and to assuage the winds. See Durand 1989a and 1989b.

[66] Borders: Xen. *Hell.* 3.5.7, 4.7.2, 5.4.47. Water: Aesch. *Sept.* 377–79, Hdt. 6.76, Xen. *An.* 4.3.17. By contrast, Arrian (1.11.6) describes *hiera* before Alexander's three water crossings.

[67] Jameson 1991: 200–12.

[68] Pritchett 1974: 110, 1979: 86 and 212–13; Harrison 1903: 65. For example, before the battle of Cunaxa, Cyrus requested Xenophon to tell the Greek troops that both the *hiera* and *sphagia* were good (Xen. *An.* 1.8.15–16). Later passages clarify that the *hiera* were the results of Xenophon's initial sacrifice to verify departure for battle: the sighting of a lucky eagle (6.5.2). Later that day, *sphagia* was performed in sight of the enemy, with the best possible results, after which they successfully engaged the enemy (6.5.21). Herodotus (6.76 and 7.113–14) uses the verb *kallierein* (associated with *hiera*) for signs obtained from *sphagia* sacrifice at rivers. *Manteis* performing *sphagia*: Xen. *An.* 4.3.7, 4.3.17–19, 6.5.7–8, Thuc. 6.69.1–2.

[69] E.g. Hdt. 9.61.3–62.1 and Plut. *Arist.* 17–18, cf. Jameson 1991: 207–8.

techniques similar to Greek military divination. It was overseen by two special priests: the augur and the *haruspex*. Augurs interpreted bird signs; the *haruspex* observed how the victim approached the altar, the condition of the viscera, and the behavior of the flames and smoke as the sacrifice burned.[70]

In summary, whether or not we adopt Bouché-Leclercq's classification, the methods of the *mantis* all sought to ascertain the goodwill of the gods, expressed as signs of two kinds. One was encoded in spontaneous and humanly uncontrollable events – ornithomancy, cledonomancy, etc. The other was responses to deliberate questions posed during sacrifice, through hieroscopy or spontaneous signs during sacrificial rituals.

Oracular methods

In a Greek (as distinct from a Mesopotamian) context, *manteis* were individual practitioners par excellence. By contrast, oracles were institutions: temples of a particular god, typically managed by priests (often organized into lineages), and in some cases staffed by priestesses who made oracular pronouncements. Despite the relatively higher prestige of oracular divination, its methods are difficult to establish, because of either too little information or too much, the latter in the form of legends of uncertain historical provenance.

Oracles used multiple methods. The first is direct pronouncements by priestesses, possibly through spirit mediumship (discussed in detail in Chapter 4), and possibly through use of the same methods as the *mantis*. The second is lot oracle or cleromancy: the casting of lots, stones, or dice. Cleromancy is another case of the movement of inanimate objects. Here, movement guided by chance revealed and expressed divine will. Objects used as lots included pebbles, black and white beans, rods, arrows, and dice; they could be shaken in an urn, thrown on a table, or thrown into water. Cleromancy was practiced at many Greek oracles, including Dodona and Delphi. Bouché-Leclercq argued that cleromancy was originally a mantic technique and only later used for other purposes. Sortition was also important for other purposes. In *Iliad* 7 the Greek kings draw lots to determine who would accept Hector's challenge, and the Achaeans pray to the gods to choose the best champion. Magistrates and judges were chosen by lot, and machines existed for this purpose (*klēroteria*). Oracular responses of the Pythia were described by the verb *anairein*, "to draw a lot." A third is dream oracles, which used ritual and purification to attempt to induce revelatory dreams. All three methods could be assisted by the interpretation, rewriting,

[70] Roman divination: Barton 1994b.

or additional advice by male priestly clans or temple personnel. Most oracles used multiple methods.

The oracle of Zeus at Dodona offered consultation to priestesses and a lot oracle. There are varied accounts of the nature of prophecies from Dodona. The *Iliad* (16.220) describes a male priesthood called the Selloi, but the *Odyssey* (14.327) describes direct prophecy arising from a great oak. A Hesiodic fragment also describes something dwelling in the oak and mortals fetching prophecies from it.[71] By contrast, Herodotus (2.55–57) describes divination by priestesses who were not possessed or in trance, through the careful interpretation of signs coming from the oaks, the spring, bronze cauldrons, and thunder: skills like those of the *mantis*, described above. Accounts of responses from the sound of the oak or doves speaking with human voices are all from late sources.[72] Parke has suggested that procedures at Dodona followed the model of a local temple of Apollo at Corope in Thessaly. Each consultor submitted a written tablet, which was placed in a sealed jar overnight and returned the next day, presumably with a response. This explanation accounts for the lead tablets from Dodona, but also is consistent with descriptions of priestesses as being skilled, austere, and incorruptible.

The fourth-century historian Callisthenes describes a Spartan military consultation at Dodona using a vessel and written lots, but it is unclear whether they specified a simple "yes–no" choice or more complex options. Several tablets from Dodona contain the phrase *peri klētrou* ("concerning the lot"), suggesting some kind of lot oracle.[73]

We can learn little from the oracle of Zeus at Olympia, even though Pindar describes the oracle as equal to the Olympic Games in the cult of Zeus there.[74] Herodotus (8.135) describes it as known throughout Greece, although it is not one of the oracles tested by Croesus.[75] According to

[71] Schol. in Sophoclem *Trach.* 1167.12 = Hes. fr. 240.9, trans. Parke 1967: 46.

[72] E.g. Philostr. 1.c., Ap. Rhod. 1.527, 4.580, Strab. *Geog.* 7.7.9.

[73] Callisthenes: FGr fr.22a and b (Cic. *Div.* 1.34.76 and 2.32.69), cf. Eidinow 2007a: 95–96 ("Farmwork," no. 3). Lot oracles at Dodona: Nicol 1958: esp. 140–42, Parke 1967: 109–12, Eidinow 2007a: 68–71. Counters and lots: Halliday 1913: 205–17, Netz 2002.

[74] *Ol.* 8.1–17.

[75] The one historically attested query at Olympia is from Xenophon (*Hell.* 4.7.2), who reports that a Spartan delegation petitioned the oracle about the legitimacy of a planned assault against Argos. Elsewhere he reports that the Spartans undertook a "double" consultation, and verified a positive response from Olympia against the Delphic oracle (*Hell.* 3.2.21–22). This contradicts another account that Agis of Sparta wanted to consult Olympia about victory, but was prevented by the Eleans because tradition forbade Hellenes to petition the oracle about war on other Hellenes (*Hell.* 3.2.21–22). The double consultation does fit the dedication practice of the general Phormis, who made equal dedications at Olympia and Delphi (Paus. 5.27.1–2).

Strabo, Olympia's fame originally came from the oracle, but when its importance waned, the sanctuary increased its reputation by means of its cult festival and games.[76] Little is known of its methods and procedures.

The oracle of Apollo at Delphi also may have combined consultation of the Pythia with a lot oracle. At Delphi the lot oracle may have served to augment the considerable constraints on access to consultation of the Pythia.

One constraint was time. According to Plutarch and incidental descriptions in tragedies, the oracle only functioned part of the year. Initially the Pythia offered oracles only one day a year: the seventh day of the month of Bysios in March. According to Plutarch, this was expanded (exactly when is a matter of controversy) to nine days: one day each of the nine months Apollo was believed to be in residence, in spring, summer, and fall. These time constraints applied to both public and private consultors.[77] The Pythia offered consultation on the seventh day of consultation months. Even these days were not entirely predictable. An initial ritual was the sacrifice of a goat by the temple priests. They sprinkled it with cold water and observed whether it trembled throughout its limbs, signifying its "willingness" to be sacrificed, and the god's willingness to respond to an inquiry. Only then could matters proceed; the Pythia was admitted to the temple, entered the *adyton* (the subterranean chamber where consultations took place), and took her seat on the tripod.[78]

Consultors were required to offer the *pelanos*, a sacred cake, at the main altar before the temple. Its price for non-Delphians was fixed by covenants between Delphi and other *poleis*. For example, a fourth-century inscription containing a covenant between Delphi and Sciathus awards *promanteia* and other privileges, and waives all charges except the *pelanos*. It specifies the *pelanos* as one Aeginetan stater (12 obols) for a state query and two obols for a private query.[79] This covenant also specifies other procedures. The consultor was to sacrifice a choice buck and other consecrated objects. Delphi would supply a banqueting room, wood, vinegar, and salt. An agreement between Delphi and Phaselis sets the *pelanos* at seven Delphian drachmas and two obols (44 obols) for public and four obols for private queries.[80]

76 Strab. *Geog.* 8.3.30. This account belies the silence of Pausanias (5.14.10), who barely mentions this oracle but does mention a defunct oracle of Gaia.

77 Plut. *Mor.* 292e–f, 398a; Parke 1943.

78 Purifications: Plut. *Pyth. Orac.* 3.397a; goat sacrifice: Eur. *Ion* 415, Plut. *Def. or.* 435b. Procedures: Rosenberger 1999 and 2001.

79 τὸν μ[ὲν] δαμόσιον στατῆ[ρ]α αἰγιναῖ-ον,τὸν [δ]ὲ ἴδιον δύ-ο ὀδελώ, Amandry 1939: 184, lines 9–12.

80 ἅδε Δελφοῖς· Φασελίτας τὸν πελανὸν διδόμεν, τόδαμόσι-ον ἑπτὰ δραχμὰς δελφίδες δ-ύ' ὀ<δ>ελός, τὸν δὲ ἴδιον τέτορε-ς ὀδελός· FD III Delphi 4:369.1, cf. Amandry 1939: 216.

There were also procedures for determining access to the Pythia. Delphi and its citizens had first right of access, followed by other Greeks, and finally by non-Greeks. A polis took precedence over individuals. Delphi could confer *promanteia*, the privilege of consulting the oracle on the same terms as citizens of Delphi, to a polis or an individual, for example a grant of *promanteia* to Synensis the Archon of Pella, his brothers, and their descendants.[81] There is some inconsistency on whether women were permitted to consult the oracle. Plutarch states that no woman other than the Pythia was allowed to enter the temple, but other accounts suggest otherwise.[82] Non-citizens of Delphi were accompanied by a *proxenos* or other citizen sponsor, sometimes a temple *prophētēs*.[83] If a foreign consultor was a *theōros* (an authorized ambassador from a polis or other group), he was strictly enjoined against altering the response in any way.[84]

Only after these procedures could the consultor enter the *adyton* and question the Pythia, having been enjoined to think pure thoughts and speak auspicious words. It is not clear what happened in the *adyton*, since no ancient source describes it directly. Ancient accounts consistently state that the Pythia gave oracles, and no source suggests that anyone else did. One possibility is that she gave straightforward responses that were carefully written down and taken away by local or foreign consultors or *theōroi*. This view is supported by the evidence of inscriptions and law court speeches, which suggest that the most common question form was "would it be more profitable and better for us to do X?" This type of question invited straightforward affirmation or denial. According to some sources, the question

[81] *Promanteia*: Legrand 1900, cf. Amandry 1950: 113–14. Decree to Synensis: *BCH* 83 (1959) 157, figs. 12–14, reproduced in RO, 466–70, no. 92. According to the Packard Inscriptions database (www.epigraphy.packhum.org/inscriptions/main), there are some 659 inscriptions on *promanteia* in the third volume of *Feuilles de Delphes* alone! "Greeks": Hall 1997, 2002, Konstan 2001, Catherine Morgan 2001. Didyma: Fontenrose 1988: 105.

[82] Plut. *E apud Delph.* 385a. Other evidence is discussed in Chapter 6.

[83] A *proxenos* was a citizen of one polis who served as a representative of the interests of another (of which he was not a citizen). Grants of *proxenia* were much sought after because *proxenoi* were typically rewarded with honors and privileges. See Eur. *Ion* 228 and 335.

[84] Sacrifices: Plut. *De Is et Os.* 378d. According to Theognis (805–10), a *theōros* must be straighter than a carpenter's rule or square, and must neither add nor subtract words from the oracle. *Theōroi*: Nagy 1990: 164–66, Maurizio 1997: 315. *Theōros* is also the origin of Greek *theōria*, Latin *theoria*, and English "theory." Meanings of Greek *theōria* included the dispatch of *theōroi*, an embassy or mission, a sight or spectacle, and a speculation or theory. Latin *theoria*, by contrast, was the perception of divinity or beauty, regarded as a moral faculty. In English a theory, like a *theōros*, promises to observe with detachment and impartiality. Some oracular resonances may still cling to the term; the theory of a scientist or detached observer promises order, truth, and accurate prediction. See Sourvinou-Inwood 1990.

could be asked by the *prophētēs*, who could also interpret or write down the answer.[85]

The convenant between Delphi and Sciathus also indicates the use of a lot oracle. It specifies the fee for a consultation "by two beans" (presumably a lot) as an Aeginetan stater for a public matter (there is a lacuna in the text where the fee for a private matter might have been expected).[86] This suggests that a lot oracle was an alternative mode of consultation. Presumably, a white bean and a black bean stood for positive and negative responses to a yes–no question. Literary sources mention no such procedure, but a lot oracle is not inconsistent with their accounts.[87] A more complex bean oracle might have been used for a selection among a greater variety of choices. Plutarch (*Mor.* 492a) describes the Pythia selecting the king of Thessaly among several prospects by drawing a bean with his name on it.

The first record of the cult of Apollo Didymaos is in the Homeric Hymn to Apollo (3.180). Herodotus claims that both the shrine and the Branchidae predated the arrival of the Ionian Greeks.[88] The shrine became famous in the sixth century; its wealth included offerings by Croesus of Lydia (Hdt. 5.36.34). Although it was within the territory of Miletus, the oracle was independent until its destruction when Xerxes conquered Miletus in 494 (Hdt. 1.46.2, 1.92.2). It resumed operations after the liberation of Miletus from the Persians by Alexander in 334, but thereafter was controlled by Miletus, which appointed its priests. Didyma is a case of an oracle whose major relations were with its patron city, and this affected its procedures. For example, it rarely awarded *promanteia*. After its revival, the oracle was always under the control of Miletus, and its demise underscores the importance of political independence for divination at the state level.[89]

After the revival of the oracle, new cults of Alexander were established in Miletus and elsewhere in Asia Minor. They were located in city centers, not marginal sanctuaries. The inscriptional evidence of consultation at Hellenistic Didyma suggests that most queries were from Milesian citizens and government representatives, primarily about civic matters, for example a complex situation arising out of a request for citizenship by a group of

[85] Roux 1976: 63–64, Fontenrose 1978: 224, Maurizio 1995: 69, Bowden 2005: 21. Form of questions: Fontenrose 1978: 11–57, PW 1.33. Role of *prophētēs*: Eur. *Ion* 100, 369–71, 413. Written response: Hdt. 1.48 and 7.142. Verbal response: Plut. *Pyth. Orac.* 397c.

[86] Amandry 1939: 184, lines 15–19.

[87] Amandry has argued that Herodotus and later writers used the verb *anairein* for oracular speech. One of its meanings is to cast a lot. See Amandry 1939: 184–85, 1950: 245 (no. 16), 29–36, 84–85, 232–33; PW 1.18–19 and nos. 219–23.

[88] Hdt. 1.157.3; Paus. 7.2.6. See also Hdt. 1.46 and 92 and 2.159.

[89] Hammond 1998, Catherine Morgan 1989: 18–26.

Cretan mercenaries. There is also evidence of consultation about religious matters. In the revived oracle, prophets in charge of the sanctuary were chosen by lot, and anonymous priestesses delivered oracular responses. Didyma had become part of the civil bureaucracy of Miletus.[90]

The oracle at Didyma also reflects differences between conditions in Asia Minor and on the Greek mainland. Didyma's fortunes rose and fell with those of its patron city. The oracle was most active during the period of Milesian power, cosmopolitanism, and independence, with corresponding pressures to balance the desiderata of competing local interests.

In summary, oracles of Zeus and Apollo offered both direct access to priestesses and consultation by lot. Each had advantages. Lot oracles offered the impartiality of sortition, and at Delphi they may have been available when the Pythia was not. (If the treaty with Sciathus is an indication, lot oracles were no less expensive than direct consultation; the same fee applied to both.) But direct consultation offered the promise of the voice of Apollo or the probity of the priestesses of Zeus.

In contrast to both oracles, Asclepian temples practiced a specialized form of dream divination (oneiromancy). Oneiromancy was a special case for several reasons. They could be either direct communications from a god or signs that required interpretation. They could be spontaneous or induced. Because dreams can simulate any human experience, they could include any other mantic method. Finally, dreams are not amenable to ritual performance. Ritual could be an element of attempts to induce revelatory dreams, but its results could not be guaranteed.

The method of consultation at Asclepian temples was *enkoimēsis* (Latin *incubatio*): a ritual practice of sleeping in the temple after purifications, baths, fasting, and sacrifices. The hope was that Asclepius would appear to the patient in a dream and provide either an instant cure or medical advice, interpreted by the temple priests. Asclepian divination was thus therapeutic rather than diagnostic. Asclepiad practitioners stressed the role of divine intervention in both disease and cure, and were less interested in diagnostics. (Examples are discussed in Chapters 7 and 9.)

Magical oracles

We find an overlapping set of divinatory methods in the Greek magical papyri, a group of papyri from Greco-Roman Egypt dating from the second century BCE to the fifth century CE. Literary sources indicate the existence of many

[90] Price 1985, Catherine Morgan 1989: 29–31.

collections of magical spells in late antiquity, but systematic destruction and suppression have destroyed most. Extant texts include divinatory spells, procedures for revealing the future, and memory spells to recall what is said during the ritual. Some are connected with a specific figure, such as Kronos, Sarapis, or even Homer.[91] The papyri include methods for oneiromancy, including procedures attributed to Pythagoras and Democritus and magical methods to induce revelatory dreams. There are also techniques for saucer and lamp divination and astrocalendric information, such as listings of days and hours for divination, an astrological calendar, and horoscopes.

In these methods magic was used to establish control over the mantic process. An invocation of Apollo provides an example. After purification from "all unclean things," the officiant creates a protective charm by inscribing special characters on laurel leaves. He next prepares a lamp, a cloth, prophetic attire, an altar, and the necessaries for sacrifice. When the spirit enters, he sacrifices burnt offerings, libations, and special cakes. He writes magical names on the cloth, puts it into the lamp as a wick, and calls Apollo with an invocation. The spell continues:

> And when he comes, ask him about what you wish, about the art of prophecy, about divination with epic verses, about the sending of dreams, about obtaining revelations in dreams, about interpretations of dreams, about causing disease, about everything that is a part of magical knowledge.[92]

The officiant releases the god by shifting the staff and laurel from one hand to the other, extinguishing the lamp, and reciting a spell to dismiss the spirit. Other divination spells are invocations to Apollo and Helios.[93]

Several use a child as a spirit medium.[94] Here, the practitioner uses incantations to call down a god or spirit into a child, who would be told to gaze into a flame or a bowl of some liquid. The god or spirit would appear in it and speak to the child, who would relay the information to the practitioner, who remained self-possessed and in control of communication with the god.[95]

[91] Preisendanz and Henrichs 1973–74: nos. 4.3086–3124 (Kronos); 5.1–53 (Sarapis); 4.471–73, 474, 830 (Homeric verses); 4.2145–2240 (a spell for divine assistance from Homer).

[92] Preisendanz and Henrichs 1973–74: no. 1.262–347, trans. Betz 1986: 10–11.

[93] Preisendanz and Henrichs 1973–74: nos. 2.1–64, 64–183; 3.187–262, 263–75, 282–409, 479–83; 5.370–446 (also to Selene and Hermes), 5a 1–3. There are also spells for a direct vision of Apollo (7.727–39), two spells to establish a relationship with Helios (3.494–611 and 4.88–93), and a prayer for an encounter with Helios (6.1–47).

[94] Preisendanz and Henrichs 1973–74: no. 4.88–93, cf. nos. 7.348–58 and 7.540–78, cf. Johnston 2001.

[95] Johnston 2001: 103, 112–15. Some spells included warnings to ensure the virginity of the spirit medium.

Accounts of child mediums only become prominent in the magical papyri, and children would have been attractive subjects for several reasons. They combined apparent integrity with openness to manipulation, and ancient sources preferred children for their combination of purity, youth, straightforwardness, and lack of art. Contemporary psychological studies indicate that children tend to try to comply with what they think a questioner wants, but are perceived as reliable witnesses who do not lie or invent details.[96]

But the use of child spirit mediums may have been a deliberate adaptation and imitation of procedures from Delphi or Claros. The magical papyri are the earliest known Greek "recipe books" for private rituals, as distinct from established cult sites such as Dodona or Delphi. Oracular sanctuaries had the resources to recruit employees whose integrity could be guaranteed. Private freelance diviners, like itinerant *manteis*, had to acquire and maintain clientele.

Physiognomy

Physiognomy was distinct from the methods of *manteis* and oracles because physiognomists represented their art as a *tekhnē*, with close links to medicine and rhetoric. Its origins probably were not Greek; Mesopotamian texts from the second millennium use physical characteristics to foretell their possessor's future. For example:

If the hair of a man's chest is curled facing up he will become a slave.
If a man with a contorted face has a prominent right eye, dogs will devour him far from home.
If on the skin of his face, on the right side, he has [a birthmark of the type] *umṣatu*, he will be lucky; (or) the man will become poor.[97]

These statements are predictive. By contrast, the focus of much Greek (and later Roman) physiognomy was on analogies between particular physical characteristics and personality; it was thus used to assess others, rather than oneself. Expertise in physiognomy was attributed to several philosophers, including Socrates, Pythagoras, and the Stoic philosopher Cleanthes.[98]

96 Iambl. *Myst.* 3.24 (157.16–20); Olympiodorus in *Alc.* 8.12. Children: Ceci and Bruck 1993.

97 Bottéro 1974: 82 and 84, cf. Lloyd 1983: 22–25 and Barton 1994a.

98 Apuleius (*De Dog. Plat.* 1.1) claims that Socrates used it to select disciples. Xenophon (*Mem.* 3.10.5) more plausibly attributes to him the view that nobility, dignity, and other traits of character are reflected in the face and attitudes of the body. Pythagoras and Cleanthes: Barton 1994a: 207.

Aristotle correlated human physiognomic elements with character traits, based on resemblances to animals with those characteristics: for example, a person with a large (ox-like) forehead is sluggish.[99]

Surviving Greek and Roman treatises on physiognomy also stress character traits. The two most important such treatises are the pseudo-Aristotelian *Physiognomica* (On Physiognomy) and the *De Physiognomonia* of the Sophist Polemo of Laodicea (*c.* 90–144 CE). *Physiognomica* describes which parts of the body reveal character and the physical manifestations of such attributes as bravery, cowardice, prudence, etc. It also compares male and female physique and behavior to that of animals, arguing that female animals are tamer, gentler, weaker, and more tractable than males: with smaller heads, narrower faces, thinner necks, weaker chests, and more delicate builds. Finally, it systematically correlates aspects of character to parts of the body. It describes the significance of the eyes and face, movements and gestures, color, facial expressions, the hair and skin, the voice, and the condition of the flesh, the parts of the body, and its overall build.[100]

Polemo's *De Physiognomonia* gives twenty-two character types and their physical signs. The typologies are based on analogies to the characteristics of animals, to gender, and to contrasts between Greeks and barbarians.[101] These two texts had very different purposes and audiences. The Aristotelian text (*Physiognomica*) is theoretical in tone, although it clearly has practical applications. Polemo viewed physiognomy as a powerful aid to rhetoric; a skilled rhetor used it both to assess his audience and to control the physical persona he projected (that could be "read" by others).

Both approaches contrast to that of Galen, who took a purely medical and empirical view of the same subject. Galen credited the invention of physiognomy to Hippocrates, and attempted to combine physiognomic principles and humoral theory in the context of medical diagnosis, titling one treatise "That the Faculties of the Mind Follow the Temperaments of the Body." He draws on Plato for the importance of the humors in the equilibrium of the body and on Aristotle for the view that the faculties of the soul depend on the mixture and balance (*krasis*) of humors in the mother's blood, as well as for his doctrine that the forms of animals' bodies correspond to different characters and faculties of the soul. To this Galen adds the physiognomists' view that some characteristics represent a mixture (*krasis*) of soul and body: the

[99] Arist. HA 1.8491b, cf. *An. Pr.* 70b7, 70b11, where it is discussed in hypothetical terms.
[100] Detailed description: Evans 1969: 7–10. [101] Foerster 1893, discussed in Barton 1994a: 101.

eyes, coloring, hair, voice, and bodily actions.[102] He also follows Aristotle in holding that the best blend is to be exactly midway between extremes.[103] His reverence for Hippocrates in particular is closely linked to the ethnological physiognomy of *Airs, Waters, and Places.*[104]

In summary, with the exception of physiognomy, most Greek divination focuses on sacrificial exchange between mortals and gods that are noticeably anthropocentric. Both *manteis* and oracles were centrally concerned with interpreting their will and maintaining their goodwill. In comparison, Chinese methods show that, pace Cicero, an active engagement between humans and gods is not inherent in divination as a cross-cultural phenomenon.

Comparisons

There is little immediate commensurability between Chinese and Greek mantic techniques, or the schemata used to describe them. Greek methods reflect the primacy of the will of the gods, mediated through different kinds of natural event. Some Chinese methods address gods and spirits, but most are better described as attempts to locate the consultor within a tacit or explicit system.

Mantic methods

Bouché-Leclercq attempted to distinguish different kinds of divinatory sign within what he called inductive divination, moving from animate to inanimate nature. Most of his categories have equivalents in China, but some Chinese methods, especially hemerology and astrocalendrics, do not fit into his system (Appendix 5.7). This is not surprising when we consider two characteristics of most methods he discusses. First, most are understood as directly or indirectly motivated by the gods. Second, with few and mostly late exceptions (such as physiognomy), most do not belong to any comprehensive system of signs and have no cosmological significance. By contrast, most Chinese methods, with few and mostly very early exceptions, draw on worldviews that are, to varying extents, systematic, abstract, and eventually cosmological. (This issue is pursued in detail in Chapter 9.) Although many Chinese and Greek procedures seem similar, they had different foci and

[102] Galen, *Quod Animi Mores Corporis Temperamenta Sequantur* (K4.767–822). Plato and balance of humors: 4.791 (cf. *Tim.* 86a–87a). Aristotle on *krasis* and analogy to animals: 4.796 (cf. PA 2.2, 648a and HA 1.8, 491b). See Evans 1945: esp. 294–98.

[103] Galen, *De Temperamentis* 2.1 (K1.576).

[104] Galen, *Quod animi mores*, K4.798, cf. Hippoc. *Aer.* 12 (cf. 5 and 16).

assigned different significance to the same phenomena. (These procedures are summarized in Appendix 5.7.)

Greek procedures were closely connected to the gods. Birds and the weather came from the heavens and thence the gods. By contrast, Chinese references to ornithomancy are rare.[105] Weather divination was important in China, but in different contexts and for different reasons. The technical methods of the *mantis* had no Chinese counterpart since they understood events such as thunder, lightning, and spontaneous animal and human behavior as indicators of the will of the gods. By contrast the Chinese methods of turtle shell, milfoil, astrocalendrics, and hemerology sought to determine auspicious times for intended activities. They drew on systematic views of the world, especially theories of *yin–yang*, *qi*, the four seasons, four directions, etc. By contrast, before the late introduction of horoscopy, the use of Greek almanacs was limited to agricultural prediction.

Even Greek dream divination was linked to the gods, who appear to dreamers in examples from Homer to Xenophon. Producing divine dream epiphanies was the explicit goal of Asclepian incubation methods. By contrast, many Chinese accounts of dream interpretation present dreams as codes whose successful interpretation hinges on the interpreter's ability to understand the code and to interpret its significance to the consultor.

Given these differences, it is no surprise that apparently similar techniques were understood very differently. Wind divination is a case in point. In both China and Greece, winds were linked to change, and wind oracles appear in both traditions, but with different significance. In Chinese accounts, directional winds could presage shifts in dynastic cycles, harvests, wars, famines, floods, and epidemics, as well as individual fortunes. Wind and breath were important concepts in early Greek thought, but not primarily for mantic purposes. Wind could carry the voice of a god, for example the voice of Zeus in the oaks at Dodona, but it was not part of weather divination. In tragedy, winds carried luck and fate, but were not interpreted by divination.[106] Winds

[105] The Mohist canon refers to the omen of a red bird alighting on Mt. Qi and proclaiming Heaven's mandate that King Wen of Zhou conquer the Shang (*Mozi* 19: 151–52 ("Fei gong xia" 非攻下)). The poem "Heavenly Questions" in the *Chu ci* asks: "A flock of *cang* 蒼 birds flying, who summoned them to gather?" (蒼鳥群飛，熟使萃之。 *Chu ci bu zhu*, 107 ("Tian wen" 3)). But in these passages, birds are omens. These are not examples of ornithomancy in that the details of the birds' species, direction of flight, cries, etc., do not have mantic significance. Similarly, accounts of the appearance of phoenixes when sages appear in the world are also not ornithomancy. I am grateful to Stephen Field for bringing this issue to my attention.

[106] Aeschylus describes changes of wind as turning good fortune to bad (*Sept.* 707–8). Euripides speaks of fear of losing the wind (*Suppl.* 549–54). Sophocles speaks of "imperceptible shifts in wind" undermining relations between friends and allies (*OC* 607–15). See Kuriyama 1999: 239–51.

are only linked to a systematic theory of nature in the Hippocratic corpus. In *Airs, Waters, and Places* they are a major determinant of the effects of geography upon health and predisposition to certain diseases.

Physiognomy is another case in point. Chinese physiognomy indicated the potential of a person, animal, or object, including for immediately practical purposes. Greek physiognomy drew on the body structures of humans and animals, but despite some Greek interest in the notion that human character could be read in configurations of the body, the major Greek "structural" divination method was hieroscopy.

There are also differences between Chinese and Greek uses of cleromancy (lots). Bean oracles were used at Dodona and Delphi, but were not the main consultation method. Sortition was used in other contexts, notably in selecting officials. For example, lots were used to determine membership on the Council (*Boulē*) and to select the *Prytaneis*, an office Socrates himself held. Socrates opposed the use of lots for public office, and advocated selection based on expertise.[107] By contrast, Chinese officials were selected by merit or by heredity, but never by lot.

The randomness offered by cleromantic procedures did not seem to be an important signifier of mantic "objectivity" in Greece, despite the presence of bean oracles at temples of Zeus and Apollo. Nor is there evidence of the use of bean oracles by *manteis* or private individuals. By contrast, Chinese milfoil divination, even in the early forms suggested in oracle bone inscriptions and Warring States archaeological sites, involved multiple sortition procedures that generated multiple sequences of numbers. For example, casting two hexagrams (as at Baoshan) requires twelve cleromantic procedures, understood as nuanced shifts of *yin* and *yang* (represented by four numbers). The *Yi jing* was also widely used for private divination.

Cognitive skills

We can also compare the cognitive skills or abilities required by different mantic procedures. Literacy was central for Chinese and Mesopotamian mantic techniques. Extant Chinese astrocalendric records are more extensive than the Mesopotamian omen literature. Both official and independent Chinese mantic experts used texts and instruments that required at least partial literacy. Thus the ability to work with written materials – knowledge of textual

[107] Use of lots to select officials: Arist. *Ath. Pol.* 43.2–44.3. Socrates served as a member of the Council for a one-year term in 406 (Pl. *Ap.* 32a9–c3) and on another occasion held the office of *prytanis* as a member of the Council's standing committee, the Council of Five Hundred (Pl. *Grg.* 473e6–474e1). His opposition to use of lots: Xen. *Mem.* 1.2.9–10, Arist. *Rh.* 1393b5–9.

traditions and competence at recording and managing written records – was a key skill for Chinese and Mesopotamian mantic officials. Writing was not central to Greek divination, although written queries were submitted to some oracles, and there are passing references to books of mantic knowledge.

This difference in the role of texts and writing is consistent with the kind and complexity of technical knowledge expected of diviners and the kind of abilities ascribed to them. Both Chinese mantic officials and independent practitioners required considerable technical expertise, including knowledge of rituals, texts, calculations, the ability to work with charts and tables, and in some cases medical expertise.

These mantic skills also had extended practical applications to many non-ritual technical contexts. The *Hou Han shu* biographies show some of them, and Richard J. Smith has pointed to others in a Qing context.[108] Specialists in the configurations of winds, clouds, and rain could predict weather; and both Eastern Han and Qing diviners predicted weather, droughts, and famines. Diviners performed official tasks, handled legal cases, solved crimes, and advised officials on water management, public works, and the construction or repair of city walls, temples, and government buildings. Even the skills of physiognomists were applied to negotiation, interrogation, and personnel decisions.

Conclusions

Anthropological fieldwork has provided detailed information on how consultors judged the value and authority of various mantic procedures. Mesopotamian and Chinese mantic practices present a different kind of comparandum. In both cases, astronomical and astrocalendric methods were sponsored – and to some extent controlled – by states. Both required literacy and the accumulation of continuous written records. The Chinese evidence is quantitatively and qualitatively richer. Quantitatively it is unparalleled. Qualitatively it is of interest for the variety of methods and descriptions of their use, in both official and independent contexts.

Compared to both, Greek divination is arbitrary. Greek *manteis* tried to determine the will of the gods through signs manifested in a wide variety of phenomena. But with limited use of writing and no observation records, Greek practitioners depended on skills presumably

[108] *HHS* 112 (72A and 72B of the collected biographies), summarized in Kalinowski 2010 (Appendix 2), R. J. Smith 1991: 212–16.

gained through experience and apprenticeship within a mantic lineage. The pedigree of that lineage, probably combined with personal charisma, also allowed a *mantis* to gain and retain clientele. By contrast, Mesopotamian divination was systematic in both logic and record-keeping, but provides far less evidence for the activities of independent practitioners. Chinese practices contrast to the Mediterranean context in several ways. Chinese divination was systematic in that mantic signs were organized on comprehensive accounts of the world such as cycles of time, the arrangement of space, and the comprehensive schemata of *qi* and *yin–yang*. At some point *wuxing* was added to earlier cosmologies in what has come to be called correlative cosmology (discussed in Chapter 9). Chinese mantic practices challenge the centrality accorded to Greek methods in the history of divination in ways that Mesopotamian and African divination systems do not.

For example, Greek and Chinese divination methods also present very different relations to naturalistic thinking. Cicero stressed that for there to be divination, there must be gods. Chinese practices challenge this view. Although the earliest records were addressed directly to gods and ancestors, Chinese methods became increasingly independent of direct human–divine interactions. The systematic outlook that informed most Chinese divination methods by the late Warring States was entirely compatible with naturalistic inquiry. In Greece, by contrast, naturalistic thinking and divination went in different directions and became pointed competitors, especially in medicine. Their opposition, claimed and occasionally refuted, is fundamental to the positivist historiography of Greek science. The Chinese evidence presents the very different possibility that there is no inherent contradiction between the two modes of activity. Comparison to the Mediterranean context also foregrounds the Chinese cultural peculiarity of the very early development of abstract, mathematical, and systematic mantic techniques. The wide range of such methods in turn expanded opportunities for empirical observation, as well as interaction and competition between technical specialists.

Appendix 5.1: On oracle bone preparation

Shang diviners structured the surface of bones and shells by cutting ordered hollows that directed the potential direction of the cracks. The earliest excavated bones (5300–3500) were not bored or drilled. Later pre-Shang bones (4300–3500) show evidence of drilling but not chiseling. By the late Shang bones and shells were pretreated in elaborate and standardized ways and were drilled and hollowed with round hollows. Bones were initially cleaned, smoothed, and cut, removing cavities, spinal material, etc., to leave a leveled surface. In the case of shells, the dorsal portion (the carapace) was removed and the ventral portion (the plastron) was trimmed and smoothed, leaving the nine plates of the plastron in an even and symmetrical surface. Hollows were bored or chiseled into the back (inner) surface of the bone or shell, and occasionally on the front or outer surface, probably with bronze or stone drills and jade, bronze, or stone knives. The shape and number (single, double, etc.) of the hollow varied with the thickness of the bone or shell surface. The hollows were placed with careful attention to symmetry. For shells, this was exact and rigorous; for bones it was less regular. The creation of double hollows by combining bored round pits with chiseled oval pits allowed the diviners to consistently produce T-shaped cracks in a controlled direction. In the late Shang this technique was used for divinations on a wide variety of subjects. By contrast Western Zhou oracle bones had square hollows and were prepared by somewhat different drilling and hollowing techniques. At the time of divination, controlled heat was applied to the back of the bone or shell, possibly with a hardwood or thorn brand, in order to make a crack visible on the front. Its direction was interpreted as auspicious or inauspicious.[109]

After cracking, bones and shells were polished to emphasize the cracks and facilitate inscription. Numbers engraved by the cracks sometimes indicated the order in which they were made. Marginal administrative notations recorded the source of the material, names of officials who had prepared them, and the date of preparation. These were carved on the back of the bridge (for turtles) or near the socket or lower portion of the bone (for scapulae). The officials sometimes (but not always) had the same names as the court diviners named in the inscriptions.

Appendix 5.2: How to generate a hexagram

How was a hexagram generated? The *Yi jing* is the subject of a huge exegetical tradition, both canonical and popular, initially in China, but now on a global level. The oldest known account comes from one of the *Yi jing* commentaries, the Great Treatise or *Xi ci zhuan*. It describes a procedure of counting up stalks to generate a sequence of six numbers, which corresponded to one of the sixty-four hexagrams that form the organizing principle of the *Yi jing*. The text associated with that hexagram was then interpreted and applied to the question at hand. According to the *Xi ci*:

大衍之數五十。其用四十有九。分而為二以象兩。掛一以象三。揲之以四以象四時。歸奇於扐以象閏。五歲再閏。故再扐而後掛。

[109] Scapulae and plastron preparation and use: Keightley 1978b: 3–27, esp. 10.

The number of the Great Expansion is 50, of which 49 [stalks] are used. They are divided into two as an image of the two [Heaven and Earth]. Place one [more] for an image of the three [Heaven, Earth, humanity]. Manipulate them by fours for an image of the four seasons. Return the remainder between the fingers as an image of the intercalary month. In five years there are two intercalary months; therefore there are two operations; so the process is repeated two more times.[110]

Modern commentators describe this procedure as follows. One stalk of the initial fifty is removed and not used further. Then a sequence of counts is used to generate each of the six lines of the hexagram: (1) The remaining 49 stalks are divided into two groups at random. (2) One stalk is taken from the right-hand group and placed between the last two fingers of the left hand. (3) The left-hand group is counted off by fours until four or fewer remain. These remaining stalks are placed between the next two fingers of the left hand. (4) The right-hand group is counted off in the same manner. The stalks left over are added to the stalks in the left hand and counted to tally the first number, which is either 5 or 9. They are then put aside.

The groups of four are reassembled and this procedure is repeated to generate a second number, which is either 4 or 8. The groups of four are again reassembled and the process is repeated a third time to generate a third number, again either 4 or 8. The sum of these three numbers is the first "change." These numbers are then converted: 8 or 9 to 2 and 4 or 5 to 3. The sum of the three converted numbers is either 9 (old *yang*), 6 (old *yin*), 7 (young *yang*), or 8 (young *yin*). This entire sequence is repeated five more times to generate the six lines of the hexagram.[111] Recent studies on *Yi jing* probabilities indicate that the four numbers have different probabilities.[112] These four possible numbers correspond to four types of *yin* or *yang* line. Similar procedures are described in the *Huainanzi* and *Lun heng*.[113]

Appendix 5.3: *Liuren* divination

The Song Astronomical Bureau preserved methods of "Three Mantic Astrolabes" (*Sanshi* 三式): *Taiyi* 太乙, *Dunjia* 遁甲 (Hidden Stems), and *Liuren* 六壬 (Six Ren Days). They were partially secret and little studied.[114] The oldest known account of

110 *ZY* 7.20ff ("Xi ci shang" 繫辭上), trans. substantially modified from Legge 365. Milfoil methods were probably standardized by the time of the composition of this commentary. See Shaughnessy 1996: 7–13.

111 Gao Heng 1958: 113, discussed in Shaughnessy 1983: 88.

112 Diaconis 1985. I am indebted to unpublished papers by Parsi Diaconis and Mark Elvin on probabilities associated with the lines.

113 *Xi ci*: Nylan and Sivin 1987: 43; R. J. Smith 1991: 19. *HNZ* 8.lb, note and 117.3a; *LH*, 997 ("Bu shi" 卜筮 24.71), Forke 1.184. See Loewe 1994: 181.

114 The Song Emperor Renzong 宋仁宗 (r. 1023–63 CE) ordered the compilation of three texts on them: the Jingyou [reign] Classic of Auspicious Taiyi Responses (*Jingyou Taiyi fuying jing* 景祐太乙符應經), Dunjia Responses (*Jingyou Dunjia fuying jing* 景祐遁甲符應經), and Liuren

Liuren divination is in a Six Dynasties mantic text preserved in the Ming Daoist canon.[115] The Song polymath Shen Gua 沈括 (1031–95), himself a master of one method, mentions *Liuren* divination, but the layout of *Liuren* mantic astrolabes in his time was different from that of Han *Liuren* devices.[116] Nonetheless, his account can help us get an idea of the procedure. The first step is to key the marker for the monthly spirit who governs the month of interest on the Heaven plate to a marker on the Earth plate. It is selected, either according to the double hour of interest (from the twelve double hours of the day) or by a chance procedure, such as rotating the Heaven plate spontaneously, selecting numbered sticks from a tube, or other chance operations.

The second step is to determine the placement of Eleven Spirit Generals, led by "the Honorable One" (*Gui ren* 貴人). His position is determined by the Earth plate marker that corresponds to the double-hour marker on the Heaven plate. Reference tables are used to determine the position of his ten generals: according to a Day or Night order and a clockwise or counterclockwise direction. The resulting Heaven plate shows the heavenly influences.

The third step is to determine "Four Prognostications" (*Si ke* 四課), the *yin-yang* characteristics of the day of interest. The procedure is to locate the stem of the day of interest in its corresponding branch on the Earth plate and identify its correlate on the Heaven plate. That correlate is used to generate the second prognostication. The same procedure is applied to the branch of the day of interest to generate the third and fourth prognostications. The result is a chart of eight branches. The fourth step is to apply the *wuxing* "Conquest" cycle to the chart to select the first of three monthly spirits responsible for Three Messages (*san chuan* 三傳). The *wuxing* correlations of the eight branches in the chart are used to identify the best pair in which the Earth plate branch "conquers" its corresponding Heaven plate branch.[117] Once the First Message is selected, its correlate on the Heaven plate generates the Second Transmission, which in turn is used to generate the Third. The Three Transmissions are identified with their three corresponding Monthly Spirits from

Responses (*Jingyou Liuren fuying jing* 景祐六壬符應經). They no longer exist in complete form. See Ho Peng Yoke 2003: 5–6.

115 *Huangdi longshou jing* 皇帝龍首經 [The Dragon's First Manual of Huang Di] (*Daozang*, ce 135), discussed in Kalinowski 1983: 396–401 and 1989–90.

116 In Song dynasty *Liuren* instruments, both the Heaven plate and the Earth plate contained the Twelve Earth Branches, which could be rotated against one another (*Mengxi bitan* 7.281–90, trans. Ho Peng Yoke 2003: 113–23). Shen Gua 沈括 (1031–95) also associates the twelve months with Twelve Heavenly Spirits and Eleven Spirit Generals (*Liuren daquan* bks. 1 and 2). Other manuals: Kalinowski 1983: 394–408.

117 According to what came to be known as the Mutual Conquest Order of the Five Phases (*xiang sheng* 相勝): Water conquers Fire; Fire conquers Metal; Metal conquers Wood; Wood conquers Earth; and Earth conquers Water. This stage can be complex because many rules govern the possibilities for mutual control.

tables of the spirits governing the twelve months. At this point, the prognosticator must go beyond the instrument and use art and expertise.

Tang military encyclopedias such as the *Taibo yinjing* and *Wubeizhi* give modifications of the system for use in military situations where divination using a mantic device was impracticable. The method was to use the left hand as the Earth plate and the right hand as the Heaven plate by visualizing the Twelve Earth Branches on the fingers of the left hand and the Ten Heaven Stems on the fingers of the right hand.[118]

An example appears in the *Sanguo yanyi* (*Romance of the Three Kingdoms*), when Liu Bei and Zhuge Liang are on their way to Changsha to support Guan Yu. They observe omens: a banner furled down and a crow cawing three times as it flew from north to south. Liu Bei asks the meaning of these signs and:

孔明就在馬上袖占一課曰：長沙郡已得，又主得大將。午時後定見分曉。

On horseback, Kong Ming immediately calculated the prognostication [on his fingers, with his hands hidden] in his sleeves and said: Changsha is taken and my lord has taken a great general. The news will come after noon.[119]

Several things are noteworthy about the *Liuren* procedure. It uses the results of observation, the regular behavior of the Heavens (the initial marker for the Heaven plate), and a very specific, or even chance, component (the initial marker for the Earth plate). It also involves constant interactions of Heaven and Earth, through the constant method of transposing the Heaven plate marker of one operation to the Earth plate for the next. Finally, its actual interpretation depends on the skills of the diviner.

Liuren divination could also be used for the prediction of mundane affairs. Ho Peng Yoke illustrates this point with a historical example of a weather prediction by the Ming dynasty *Liuren* diviner Chen Liangmo 陳良謨 on the eve of the lunar new year of 1645 (that there would be snow on New Year's Day).[120] Ho Peng Yoke applies the detailed account of the readings to an imaginary problem: a theft by a servant on the same night. He interprets the same data to predict that the imaginary thief is a man in his prime, with big eyes, thick eyebrows, and a long beard, who wears yellow and enjoys hunting or fishing. He also uses the data to predict the location of the stolen object and other information.[121]

Different types of mantic astrolabe vary in their clock-face arrangements as follows:

[118] Ho Peng Yoke 2003: 136–37. Broader context of hand mnemonics: Hanson 2008.

[119] *Sanguo yanyi* 53.671, trans. Brewitt-Taylor 1925: 53.552. The news came as predicted. *Liuren* divination was also used for weather forecasting in the Song and Yuan periods.

[120] This prediction appears in his *Liuren zhanyan zhinan* 六壬占驗指南 (Guide to the Verification of *Liuren* Prognostications, preface dated 1810), discussed in Yan Dunjie 1978.

[121] Ho Peng Yoke 2003: 133–35.

Type	Pivot star(s)	Pointer star(s)	Perimeter
Liuren	Northern Dipper	Dipper handle	Nine Palaces
Nine Palaces, Taiyi, Dunjia	(Jade Transverse, yuheng 玉衡) Taiyi	Tianyi	
Fuyang Nine Palaces[a]	Zhaoyao 招搖 (in Bootes)		Nine Palaces

[a] This is also the arrangement in the "Jiugong bafeng" chapter of the *Huangdi Lingshu* (Harper 1995–96: 20–21).

Appendix 5.4: Pitch pipe divination

The *Hou Han shu* Treatise on Pitch Pipes and the Calendar describes their use in detail:

候氣之法，為室三重，戶閉，塗釁必周，密布緹縵。室中以木為案，每律各一，內庳外高，從其方位，加律其上，以葭莩灰抑其內端，案曆而候之。氣至者灰(去)[動]。其為氣所動者其灰散，人及風所動者其灰聚。殿中候，用玉律十二。惟二至乃候靈臺，用竹律六十。候日如其曆。

For the method of watching for *qi*: a triple-walled chamber is prepared, the doors of which bar it off [from the outside world] and [the walls of which] must everywhere be closely covered with plaster. Within the chamber a covering of reddish silk is spread. Stands are made of wood, one for each pitch pipe, which extend deep down within [the ground] and high up outside [the ground]. The pitch pipes, each in accordance with its compass point, are mounted upon these. Ashes made from reed pith are stuffed into the inside [of each pipe], and watch is kept on them in accordance with the calendar. Whenever one [of the pitch pipes] is reached by the *qi* [of its corresponding month], its ashes move. The ashes thus caused to move by the *qi* are scattered, whereas those [accidentally] moved by people or wind remain together. In the palace when thus watching [for the arrival of the *qi*], twelve jade pitch pipes are used and only at the two solstices does the watching take place. At the Spirit Terrace, however, sixty bamboo pitch pipes are used, and the days for watching are those corresponding to these pitch pipes.[122]

The twelve pipes were of graduated lengths, covering one octave in twelve half-notes of the chromatic scale. The pipes were arranged in a circle according to their corresponding months and compass directions. Imperceptible shifts in seasonal *yin* and *yang* could be "magnified" through subtle movements of the ash in the pipes, as each month's *yin* or *yang qi* would stir the ash in "its" pipe as the *qi* moved up from below the ground toward the surface. The movement would only register in the pipe correlated to that month. The upward movement would force ash out of the tube in a coherent pattern that could be distinguished from random wind or human interference.

[122] *HHS* 11.3016 (treatise 1), trans. after Bodde 1959: 356–57, cf. Huang and Chang 1996.

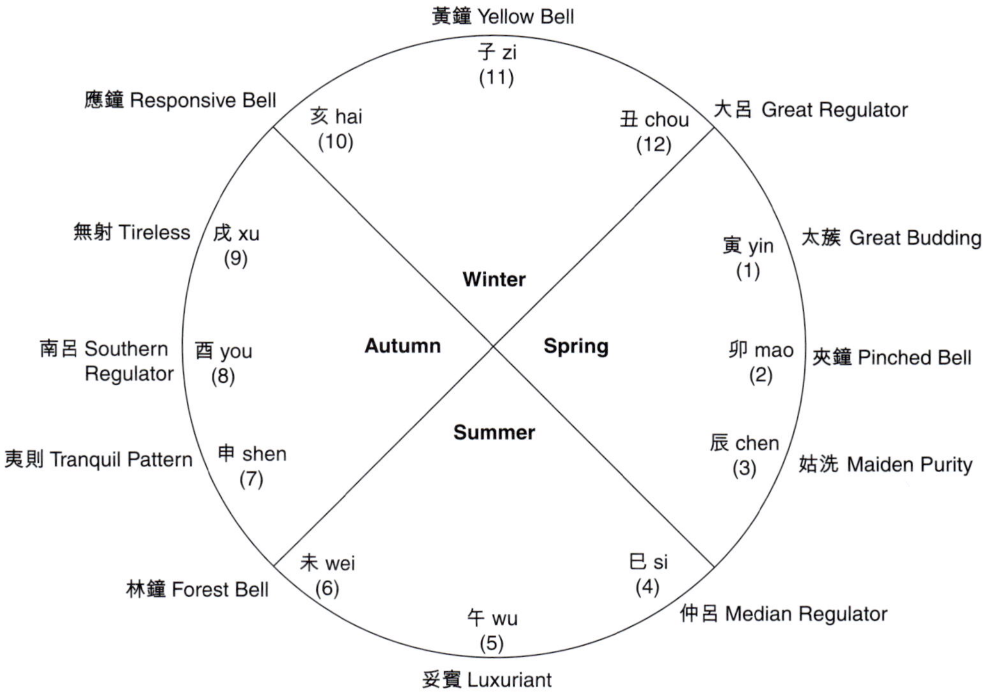

Pipe	Note	Branch	Number	Month	Path-next
Yellow Bell Huang zong 黃鐘	geng	zi	81	11	↓ Forest Bell ↑ Great Budding
Great Budding Tai cou 太蔟	shang	yin	72 (54 x 4/3)	1	↓ Southern Regulator ↑ Maiden Purity
Maiden Purity Gu xian 姑洗	jue	chen	64 (48 x 4/3)	3	↓ Responsive Bell ↑ Luxuriant
Forest Bell Lin zhong 林鐘	zhi	wei	54 (81 x 2/3)	6	
Southern Regulator Nan lü 南呂	yu	you	48 (72 x 2/3)	8	
Responsive Bell Ying zhong 應鐘	[geng]	hai	42 (64 x 2/3)	10	
Luxuriant Sui bin 蕤賓		wu	57 (42 x 4/3+1)	5	↑ Great Regulator ↓ Tranquil Pattern
Great Regulator Da lü 大呂		chou	76 (57 x 4/3)	12	↑ Pinched Bell ↓ Tireless
Tranquil Pattern Yi ze 夷則		shen	51 (~76 x 2/3)	7	
Pinched Bell Jia zhong 夾鐘		mao		2	
Tireless Wu yi 無射		xu		9	↑ Median Regulator
Median Regulator Zhong lü 仲呂		si	60 (45 x 4/3)	4	

Figure 5.5 The twelve pitch pipes.

Descending pipes are created by multiplying the previous number by 2/3. Ascending pipes are created by multiplying the previous number by 4/3 (Figure 5.5).[123]

Appendix 5.5: *Fang* methods

Wind Horns (*fengjiao* 風角) was used to predict military victory or political prosperity based on the direction and quality of the winds. Although wind divination dates to the oracle bone inscriptions, systematic accounts of the winds only appear in Qin and Han texts. Fragmentary texts on wind divination also appear in the bamboo slips from Yinqueshan.[124]

Hidden Stems (*Dunjia* 遁甲, also known as Hidden Cycles) was a mantic astrolabe (diviner's board) technique for avoiding inauspicious days by linking the calendar to the sexagenary cycle. Because there are more Earth Branches than Heaven Stems, each stem has six "hidden" branches that are not matched with it in the sexagenary cycle.[125]

Seven Governors (*qi zheng* 七政) was a *wuxing*-based astronocalendric method for determining auspicious days. The "Seven Governors" probably referred to the sun, moon, and five planets. Alternatively, they may have referred to the seven stars surrounding the Dipper or to the Twenty-eight Lunar Lodges.[126]

Original Qi (*yuan qi* 元氣) was another method for predicting military victory or political prosperity based on *yin–yang* and *qi* configurations.

Six Days and Seven Parts (*liu ri qi fen* 六日七分) was derived from the *Yi jing* and attributed to Meng Xi 孟喜 (*c.* 90–40) and Jing Fang 京房 the Younger (77–37). It divided the sixty-four hexagrams into periods of six days and seven parts, with a hexagram presiding over each period. The method consisted of observing wind, rain, and heat and cold in relation to the character of the hexagrams in order to determine which days are auspicious.[127]

[123] Figure follows *HNZ* 3:21b–24a; Major 1993: 112–14.

[124] One, titled "*Yin–yang* Seasonal Orders and Prognostication" (*Yinyang shiling zhanhou* 陰陽時令占候), includes twelve *yin–yang* texts, one of which may have included a chart or diagram, possibly for military divination. See Wu Jiulong 1985, slip 0860; Yates 1994: esp. 140–41; Luo Fuyi 1974: 32 and 35; and Rao Zongyi 1993.

[125] *HHS* 72A.2703. For example, the first stem *jia* is matched with the stems: (1) *zi*, (11) *xu*, (21) *shen*, (31) *wu*, (41) *chen*, and (51) *yin*. The six "hidden" branches for *jia* are thus *chou*, *mao*, *si*, *wei*, *you*, and *hai*. They are then used to identify inauspicious time periods. See Ngo Van Xuyet 1976: 192–93, DeWoskin 1983: 25, Li Ling 1993: 23–27, Ho Peng Yoke 2003: 83–112.

[126] They are the subject of chapter 39 of Xiao Ji's 蕭吉 *Wuxing dayi* 五行大義 (Compendium on the Five Phases), trans. Kalinowski 1991: 331–50.

[127] Ngo Van Xuyet 1976: 171–77. Jing Fang the Younger applied the *Yi jing* to natural, human, and dynastic history. Jing Fang the Elder (*c.* 140–*c.* 80) was also a student of the *Yi jing*. For both see Loewe 2000: 199.

Orphans and Voids (*guxu* 孤虛) was another mantic astrolabe method that used the qualities of time within the sexagenary cycle to avoid inauspicious times. The "orphans" are the last two Earth Branches (*xu* and *hai*), the two that remain after the Ten Stems are combined with the first ten branches. The "voids" are their two opposites, plotted on a circle: the stems *chen* and *si*. Thus any ten-day period will have two orphans and two voids.[128]

Several other methods are obscure. There is debate about the meaning of Meetings and Greetings (*feng zhan* 逢占, also interpreted as "contrary divination"). It may refer to the analysis of spontaneous words uttered during chance meetings. Diviners of auspicious days (*ri zhe* 日者) used the arts of the marketplace diviners described in *Shi ji* 128. Bamboo Twisters (*ting zhuan* 挺專) was a Chu divination method based on "cracking" bamboo. The Warring States poem "Encountering Sorrow" (*Li sao* 離騷) mentions its use on behalf of the narrator of the poem.[129] Reading Changes (*xu yu* 須臾) was another *yin–yang* method. The daybooks from Fangmatan and Shuihudi have sections on "Yu Reading the Changes" (*Yu xu yu* 禹須臾).[130]

Appendix 5.6: Homeric examples of mantic methods

Most major forms of Greek divination appear in the Homeric poems. These accounts may reflect the priorities of an earlier literary past, reflected in the Epic Cycle, which feature a large number of oracles and prophecies. It is striking that, although the Homeric poems suppress fantastic and supernatural elements, they prominently feature accounts of divination.[131] These included divination by birds and other animals, the weather, "speech signs" (cledonomancy), dreams (oneiromancy), lots (cleromancy), and the behavior of inanimate objects (especially fire during sacrifice), including divination by the appearance of the entrails of sacrificial animals (hieroscopy). The Homeric poems also contain one instance of divination by the invocation of the dead (necromancy).

128 *HHS* 82A.2704.

129 *Chu ci bu zhu*, 35 ("*Li sao*" 1), cf. Li Ling 1993: 24. The name refers to a method of knotting grass and breaking bamboo to determine good and ill auspice. The diviner grasps a handful of an unknown number of bamboo joints, grass stalks, or twigs. The stalks are counted between the fingers in the manner of milfoil divination. The number of stalks retained between the fingers are used to calculate good and ill auspice. See Field 2008: 91.

130 Reading Changes: Fangmatan: *Tianshui Fangmatan Qin jian* 2009: slips 42–73; Shuihudi: *SHD* (Daybooks): p. 222, slips 97v–101v; Li Ling 1993: 198 (Fangmatan) and 210 (Shuihudi).

131 Griffin 1977. The Homeric poems, especially the *Iliad*, consistently suppress the fantastic, miraculous, and romantic. They insist on a realistic world in which the inevitability of old age and death separate mortals from the gods. By contrast, the Cycle abounds with supernatural abilities, interactions, and interventions, including "deterministic" accounts of prophecy and divination. Epic Cycle: Monro 1884.

Most Homeric divinations are direct communications from gods in which the form of the message often indicates its source. For example, when an eagle with a fawn in its talons drops it on the altar of Zeus, the army recognizes it as an omen from Zeus and renew their efforts (*Il.* 8.245–50). When Athena sends a heron flying on the right to encourage Odysseus, he recognizes the omen as hers (*Il.* 10.275–80). Some omens work by analogy: when Telemachus sees an eagle flying on his right, Helen interprets it as an omen of Odysseus' return; his revenge on the suitors is like the eagle flying from its home in the mountains (*Od.* 15.160–78). Helen's prediction is repeated by the seer Theoclymenus, who interprets a bird appearing on shipboard as a sign that Odysseus has arrived in Ithaca (*Od.* 17.150–60).

Positive omens are typically straightforward, but negative omens occasion debates. For example, when an eagle carrying a live snake soars on the left and drops it on the Trojan host, Polydamas interprets it as a warning, but his interpretation is belittled by Hector (*Il.* 12.200–25). The Ithacan seer Halitherses interprets two eagles as a sign of Odysseus' return, but is disregarded by the suitors under the influence of Eurymachus (*Od.* 2.140–207).

Weather omens were associated with Zeus and sometimes linked to sacrifice, prayer, and battle. For example, Nestor interpreted thunder on the right as the Greeks sailed from Aulis for Troy as a sign of victory (*Il.* 2.353); Hector also reads thunder on the right as promise of victory (*Il.* 9.236–40).

The Homeric poems also describe cledonomancy, the spontaneous utterance of a word of good omen (*phēmē*). When Penelope sends for the beggar Odysseus, Telemachus sneezes so loudly that the house resounds, and Penelope recognizes it as a portent of Odysseus' return and the death of the suitors (*Od.* 17.541–51). When the beggar Odysseus prays to Zeus for an omen through the speech of someone in the household, there is a "word of good omen" (*phēmē*) from a woman grinding at the mill, who "spoke a word as a sign for her lord" (*epos phato, sēma anakti*), praying that the suitors feast their last feast in the halls of Odysseus (*Od.* 20.103–20). There is one possible example of cleromancy when the Greeks cast lots to determine who should fight Hector (*Il.* 7.175–85).

The Homeric poems give several accounts of the origin of dreams, but most Homeric dreams are sent by gods in the guise of mortals. Zeus takes the form of Nestor to bid Agamemnon arm his troops (*Il.* 2.5–30). Athena takes the form of Penelope's friend Iphthime to reassure her that Telemachus will not be killed (*Od.* 4.796), and of Nausicaa's friend to urge her to do laundry on the seashore (6.48).[132] An omen is central to what is perhaps the most famous dream recital

[132] The *Odyssey* describes revelatory and false dreams as rising from the gates of Horn and Ivory (19.561–64), but Achilles (*Il.* 1.62–65) describes dreams as coming from Zeus. By contrast, Hesiod describes dreams as the sons of Night and the brothers of Sleep (*Theog.* 211); Euripides describes them as children of Gaia, sent in revenge for Apollo's acquisition of Delphi (*Hec.* 70ff.).

in the history of literature. In *Odyssey* 19 Penelope asks Odysseus to interpret a dream in which a great eagle swooped down from the mountain and killed the twenty geese that fed at the trough. As she grieved for her dead birds, it spoke in human voice and urged her not to mourn because: "This is no dream but a waking vision of good that surely shall come to pass. The geese are the suitors, and I am an eagle no longer but now am your own husband returned" (19.546–48). The dream thus announces itself as an omen, and Odysseus replies that it can have only one interpretation since "Odysseus himself has told you how it will come to pass" (19.535–50).[133]

Another famous Homeric divination is Odysseus' journey to Hades to consult the ghost of Tiresias. Bouché-Leclercq and others treat necromancy as inspired divination, but several details of this account show its technical and ritual aspects. Odysseus has precise instructions from Circe, not only for the journey, but for the necessary sacrifices to Hades and Persephone and the blood offering that would revive the shade of Tiresias (*Od.* 11.500–45). An important part of his homecoming is that he follows these necromantic rituals to the letter.

Hepatoscopy also first appears in the Homeric poems, which mention a *thuoskoos* ("sacrifice diviner," Latin *haruspex*), literally someone who looks (*skoos*) at the sacrificial offering (*thuos*). This official is comparable to a priest or *mantis*. When Hecuba tries to dissuade Priam from retrieving the body of Hector he tells her that he would disregard such advice from a *mantis*, *thuoskoos*, or priest (*hiereus*), but would obey it from Iris, the messenger of Zeus (24.220–21). The *thuoskoos* Leiodes disapproves of the suitors' conduct, but performs sacrifice for them nonetheless (21.145). He pleads with Odysseus that he sought to check the suitors' excesses, and that a diviner should not share their fate. But Odysseus is not moved; the *thuoskoos* must have prayed on the suitors' behalf for Odysseus' death and the hand of Penelope (22.318–25). These passages attest to the status of hieroscopy as a recognized mantic function in the Homeric poems.

Three Homeric figures prophecy directly without recourse to technical methods. One is Tiresias. A second is the Trojan prince Helenus, "far the best of the bird diviners" (*Il.* 6.72), who "knows in his heart what the gods are planning" (7.43). Third is the Ithacan *mantis* Theoclymenus, who, on entering the house of Odysseus, sees a vision of walls splashed with blood and the porch filled with ghosts (*Od.* 20.350–58).

Finally, although certain stars were connected with good and ill auspice, astrology does not figure in the Homeric poems. The *Iliad* describes Orion as "brightest of all, but a sign [*sēma*] of evils laid away" (22.25–35). In *Works and Days* (743 and 768), Hesiod refers to auspicious days, and considers the seventh day of each month a day of good auspice.

[133] John Winkler (1990) has argued that Penelope used the dream (real or fabricated) as a code to exchange information with Odysseus before the hostile audience of her maids.

There are also brief references to oracles. The *Iliad* also mentions the oracle of Zeus at Dodona (16.232–34) and Apollo at Delphi (9.404–5). The *Odyssey* mentions consultation of Delphi about the Trojan War (8.75–81).

Appendix 5.7: Greek and Chinese divination methods

Bouché-Leclercq's category	Greek methods	Chinese methods
1 spontaneous movement	birds (from gods)	–
(animate beings)	animals (from gods)	omens
	human speech (from gods)	–
2 structure (animate beings)	hieroscopy	–
	physiognomy	physiognomy
3 movement (inanimate)	pyromancy (sacrificial)	pyromancy (bones, shells)
	hydromancy	–
	sound of winds (Dodona)	direction of winds
4 cleromancy (lots)	bean oracles	yarrow divination
5 weather	winds (from gods)	–
6 clouds	clouds (from gods)	clouds
7 rain	from gods	rain
8 astrology	–	tianwen
9 dreams	from gods	turtle and milfoil
–	–	hemerology
Han shu Yiwenzhi (shushu)	Chinese methods	Greek methods
1 *tianwen*	star divination	–
	clouds and rain	clouds and rain
	mantic astrolabes	–
2 *lipu*	almanac texts	–
	daybooks	–
	yue ling calendars	–
3 *wuxing*	directional winds	winds (in trees, Zeus)
	pitch pipes	sounds of bells (Zeus)
	xingde	–
4 shells and stalks	pyromancy	pyromancy (sacrificial)
	milfoil	lots (bean oracle)
5 miscellaneous	dreams	dreams
	omens	birds, animals, speech
	exorcisms	–
6 topomancy	physiognomy	physiognomy
	topomancy	hieroscopy

6 | The questions

What questions were considered appropriate topics for mantic query in early China and Greece and how did they change? The *Zhou li* specifies eight topics considered appropriate for divination, but in other periods, and for the Greek materials, we must infer answers from extant questions. Several other problems must be taken into account. One is the context and motivation for accounts of mantic consultation. Comparison creates its own difficulties because the same topic may be categorized differently in different periods or in different cultural contexts. For example, Chinese questions about harvests, rainfall, illness, and military defeat may correspond closely to the Greek category of *lusis kakōn* – release from evils, but in other cases, the same category, for example questions about marriage or children, may include very different questions. No one elegant framework can address all these issues.

I begin by identifying four types of mantic question: (1) requests for predictions of fact or probability, (2) requests for advice or recommendations for action, (3) theological and cosmological questions, and (4) hermeneutic questions about the meaning of past events.

The most straightforward type of mantic query seeks a prediction: "Will it rain within the next ten days?" "Will X bear a son?" "Will we be victorious?" They ask what will happen, rather than what should happen. Requests for predictions may seek facts (it will rain on Tuesday) or more complex and equivocal judgments of outcome (success, benefit, etc.). Both are verifiable, although judgments such as "success" are subject to interpretation and equivocation. Although queries of this type can be verified or falsified, accurate prediction may or may not be their primary motivation. Factual predictions may address practical matters, but may also reflect scientific, philosophical, or cosmological interests.

Predictions could be sought about any event of interest, private or state. In the Chinese materials, they appear in the oracle bone inscriptions, in omen texts such as the Fuyang *Zhou yi*, and in standard histories and technical treatises. But predictions can also be inserted into narratives for didactic or ideological or literary reasons. For example, many predictions in the *Zuo zhuan* are probably interpolations that reflect the moral judgments of the *Zuo* authors, rather than predictions made at the time of the events described. Some Delphic oracle stories turn on obscurity of language and problems of interpretation.

A second type of query is a request for a recommendation about something the consultor considers problematic, dangerous, or risky. These include questions about the success and appropriateness of a contemplated action, broad questions about securing wellbeing, questions on release from particular evils, and specific requests to select an individual, group, or location from a choice from a group of alternatives. Should I take citizenship in Argos? Should I marry so-and-so? Should we invade? What is requested here is advice on the practical advantage or disadvantage of a course of action, from a limited and predetermined list of choices.

Questions about the success and appropriateness ask what one *should* do. They appear in both state consultations (military actions, personnel, alliances, etc.) and private queries (marriages, journeys, seeking office, etc.). They are partially normative; outcomes can be verified, but there is also a moral element. Whether the war was won or lost is a matter of fact, but it is also a reflection on the appropriateness of the action or the moral status of the consultor. The same could be said of the selection of the right heir to the throne, or of success in a bid for office or the year's service to the king.

A third type of query can be framed in theological or cosmological terms. These questions seek particulars about religious cult or advice on obtaining divine aid. They are constrained by beliefs about what kinds of question are appropriate for mantic query, and both Chinese and Greek sources address this issue explicitly. A common question in both traditions seeks to identify the right divine power to supplicate or propitiate for a desired result: wellbeing, victory, relief from difficulty. Such questions seek religious commands or prohibitions, ask the will of the gods, or seek the best alignment with impersonal cosmic forces. They may seek very specific ritual advice, including the confirmation of personnel or other decisions considered potentially (dis)pleasing to the gods. Cosmologically framed questions ask about good or ill auspice, often for a specified period of time, based on astrocalendric and cosmological notions of auspiciousness. What day is best for a wedding or funeral? For a particular sacrifice? To start a military campaign? Are the signs auspicious for victory? These questions do not address gods or divine powers directly, even if they are believed to govern the time or place in question.

All three of these question types address future action. A fourth type of question seeks the significance of events in the present or past. All four types of question could be posed by either official or private consultors. (The distinction breaks down in the case of nominally personal queries by rulers, whose personal decisions are also matters of state.)

Three points must be emphasized. The first is the distinction between predictions of fact, which can be verified or falsified, and requests for cult advice or good fortune, which cannot. We may also ask whether consultors or diviners themselves were interested in accuracy or verifiability. Second, it is important to note that mantic questions are not open-ended. There is only one heir or one general to be named, one ritual to be performed, and one house or tomb to be constructed at a time. Mantic queries typically request either a yes–no answer or a choice from a limited list, drawn up in advance. The scope of the advice given is limited by the alternatives posed. Third, mantic narratives also function as a form of literary production and historical reflection in their own right. This issue is reserved for Chapter 8.

We can also consider mantic queries as indicators of what consultors considered dangerous or risky. From this viewpoint, mantic consultation becomes a method of managing risk and uncertainty. This approach draws on the anthropological view that risk is socially constructed (sometimes called Culture Theory). As Mary Douglas puts it, "dangers are culturally selected for recognition"; the question of what areas of life are viewed as "risky" is part of culturally specific views of agency and the nature of luck and misfortune.[1] The latter are expressed by the Greek term *kindunos* ("risk," "threat," "danger") and the Chinese terms *wei* 危 and *xian* 險 (contemporary *wei xian* 危險).

Several problems complicate the study of notions of risk in antiquity. The subject of uncertainty is widely discussed in Chinese and Greek philosophical literature, but the management of uncertainty in daily life is less studied. A second difficulty is the tendency to focus on situations considered risky from a modern viewpoint. Some situations are probably perceived as sources of risk or danger by most societies, including interruptions of food supply, disease, warfare and its consequences, and reversals of individual or family fortune, but even here nuances differ according to local factors such as climate and political and social institutions. Other perceptions of risk may be quite socioculturally specific. Anthropologists and sociologists have developed several theories of risk and culture.[2] What a

[1] Douglas 1985: 54. The term risk itself has a complex history. In a European context, before the nineteenth century the term was neutral and referred to both positive and negative situations; only later was it restricted to negative or dangerous situations. See Hacking 1975, 1990.

[2] Risk-society theory and governmentality theory derive from considerations of the modern nation-state. Mary Douglas (1985: esp. 38–41, 1992) also is primarily concerned with perceptions of risk in Western societies, but her cultural-symbolic approach can be applied to premodern societies.

society perceives as *particularly* dangerous and what steps it takes to manage that risk vary according to ideas of time, space, values, and beliefs, especially notions of choice, blame, and responsibility.

One can look at, for example, Greek accounts of agriculture, famine, and floods, and at maritime and other loans. Similarly Chinese accounts of family regulations, the management of family property, and even military strategy provide different accounts of risk. In addition, for different reasons, in both early China and Greece, the line between what moderns would call natural and supernatural was not firmly drawn. For example, Greek perceptions of risk might include the arbitrariness of the gods, the inheritance of responsibilities for ancestors' crimes, and the working out of that responsibility in "fate." Chinese notions about risk might include angry ghosts or ancestors and the influence of inauspicious times in matters ranging from the time of one's birth to the planning of almost any action.

Much of the study of Greek oracles has focused on the role of Delphi as a panhellenic oracle, potentially including the question of what uses state consultors considered especially dangerous or risk-laden. Focus on states and elites fails to consider the roles of divination in the lives of ordinary individuals or the kinds of concerns that motivated them to consult mantic expertise. Esther Eidinow addresses the latter issue by considering oracular consultations by private individuals as strategies for managing risk and uncertainty. She juxtaposes private oracular consultation and curse tablets (*katadesmoi*) to argue that both were strategies for managing risk in everyday life and, taken together, provide an index of aspects of risk and uncertainty in ancient Greek culture.[3] Consultors of oracles were uncertain about a course of action, and sought assurances that their choices were the best ones.

This chapter is divided into three parts. The first takes up the kinds of questions posed by Chinese and Greek official divination, with particular interest in the problem of Delphic oracles. The second turns to the problem of individual consultors and how they handled issues of danger and risk. The third compares Chinese and Greek perceptions of risk, based on mantic queries.

[3] Eidinow 2007a: 3–5. She focuses on the lead question tablets from Dodona and on curse tablets from the sixth to the first centuries. People in situations already perceived to be dangerous used curses to limit vulnerability at the hands of a competitor or enemy. They were typically used in agonistic relationships – by athletes, litigants, lovers, rival tradesmen, etc.; they allowed an otherwise weaker party to avoid defeat. Eidinow speculates that a historiographical legacy has partially legitimated oracular consultation, but has tended to ignore curses until a recent upsurge of interest in magical studies.

State and official questions

The Chinese questions

Were the same questions always considered appropriate for mantic query? Texts from four historical periods help answer this question: Shang oracle bone inscriptions, fourth-century records from Chu sites and the *Zuo zhuan*, late Warring States or Qin (late third-century) divination questions in the *Zhou li*, and first-century (BCE) evidence from the Western Han.

Shang prognostications follow a consistent structure and include both predictions about future events and queries about the causes of past ones. Prognostications about the future sought assurances of fertility (of childbirth, rainfall, and harvests) and auspicious times for planned actions, especially hunting, warfare, receiving tribute, and performing sacrifice. There has been considerable debate over whether its purpose was to predict the future or to influence and control it through ritual sacrifice: there is a fine line between inquiry and propitiation or pleas for aid or good fortune. However, even within the Shang, there may have been changes in question topics. The archaeological record shows queries becoming increasingly streamlined over time. By the late Shang, they focused on ancestral cult, especially inquiries to royal ancestors about regular royal hunts and requests for "no harm" for the ten-day ritual week.[4]

Three points are particularly noteworthy about the evidence of the oracle bone inscriptions. First, they attest to the antiquity of topics such as rainfall, warfare, and queries about auspicious times as topics of mantic query. Second, they reflect the major categories of mantic practice described in the *Han shu* Bibliographic Treatise, especially astrocalendrics, pyromancy, and oneiromancy. Third, the evidence of (uninscribed) bones and turtle plastrons excavated from the salt production site at Zhongba, Zhongxian, suggests that similar practices may have been used outside the Shang court. This evidence suggests (1) the early use of oracle bone divination for non-official queries and (2) that mantic activity correlated to social uncertainty.[5] The early development of these techniques suggests continuity between

[4] Keightley 1978b: 28–44, 1998: 790–804, 1999b: 247, Allan 1991: 113–20, Nivison 1982.

[5] Flad 2004: esp. 235, 259–62, 527–47. The Zhongba managerial elite employed ritual specialists to prognosticate about salt production. The frequency of marks on the bones and plastrons indicates how often pyroscapulimancy was used. This evidence indicates two pyromantic peaks at Zhongba, which coincided with two periods of social uncertainty: one between 1100 and 700 and the other between 380 and 310, when the rise of Qin brought the Sichuan basin into Chinese geopolitics. Archaeological report: "Zhongxian Zhongba yizhi fajue baogao" 2001.

Shang and Western Zhou practices. This point is not to argue for a timeless, eternal China, but to argue against claims for a complete breach between the Shang and Western Zhou.

Records of turtle and milfoil queries from late fourth-century Chu sites at Tianxingguan, Baoshan, and Wangshan reveal prognostications performed for officials (rather than rulers) about private concerns, especially official prospects over the upcoming year. There are many unanswered questions about these records, including their sources and why they were placed in the tombs. They clearly show such queries moving from a court context to the more private sphere of officials who possessed the means to employ mantic experts. The *Zuo zhuan* gives additional evidence on fourth-century mantic queries. It shows the use of turtle and milfoil to resolve questions about marriages (to whom to give a daughter in marriage), progeny (the fortunes of a newborn son), whether a state should form a particular alliance, military decisions (whether to attack another state), and resolving problems in royal succession (see Appendix D).

The *Zhou li* specifies eight types of state question that could be addressed by turtle shell divination: (1) military campaigns, (2) anomalies and strange phenomena, (3) conferring gifts, (4) major plans and policies, (5) the success of planned ventures, (6) the arrival of (expected) individuals, (7) rainfall, and (8) illness.[6] The addendum of Chu Shaosun (? 104–? 30) to *Shi ji* 128 gives a detailed account of questions considered appropriate for prognostication in the Western Han. Michael Loewe has summarized these into five types of question or request: (1) predictions of fact or probability, (2) the success and appropriateness of contemplated actions, (3) whether a particular time was auspicious for a contemplated action, (4) the best location for a residence or tomb, and (5) selection of an heir, general, etc. from a group of alternatives.[7]

These four "snapshots" indicate nine topics of ongoing Chinese official interest that may serve as grounds for comparison: (1) predictions about weather, harvests, and rainfall; (2) questions on the success of planned ventures, especially warfare and alliances; (3) advice on selecting personnel, including military commanders and allies; (4) political questions, specifically on resolving doubts and disagreements between rulers, ministers, and other members of the decision-making elite; (5) questions about marriage and progeny, including whom the king should marry, whether to rear a child, and royal succession; (6) determining auspicious days, times for

6 *ZL* 24:10a–18a; Biot 2.72; Loewe 1994: 175.

7 *SJ* 128.3241ff., cf. Loewe in Twitchett and Loewe 1986: 678.

planned activities, and other questions about sacrifice and ritual; (7) questions about illness; (8) questions on the meaning of anomalies; and (9) questions on the meaning of dreams. Some (2, 5, 6, 7, and 9) have equivalents in private queries. Of these, only two (1 and 7) involve predictions of fact or probability. Most (2, 3, 4, 5, and 7) are requests for advice or recommendations for action. Two (6 and 8) involve cosmological and theological questions. One (9, but to some extent 5) is concerned with questions of hermeneutics or ideology.

Weather divination first appears in the oracle bone inscriptions, and continues as a topic of interest in Warring States and Han records (Loewe's first category). Rain and wind were considered to be under the command of the high god Di 帝, the main god of the Shang pantheon; and inscriptions ask whether rain, thunder, or wind will occur in a given time period and their directional source. Other inscriptions describe propitiatory sacrifices and prayers for harvest offered to the four regions (*fang* 方), which were associated with named directional winds under Di's authority.[8] Some of these predictions contain verifications. For example, one inscription predicts that Di will not order wind. A verification follows: that on the evening in question, it was overcast (not windy).[9] Other divinations concern propitiatory sacrifices and prayers for harvest offered to the four regions.[10]

Warring States and Western Han sources also include prognostications about rain and winds. For example, rain appears as a topic in the Fuyang *Zhou yi*:

大有元亨卜雨不雨

Great Possession: Prime receipt. In divining about rain, it will not rain.[11]

[8] For example, inscriptions ask whether Di will order rain in the next eleventh month (*Heji* 5658r), whether Di will order thunder (*Heji* 14127r), and about offerings to Di's clouds (*Heji* 14227, cf. Keightley 2000: 5–6). Another inscription states that it will rain, and that the rain may come from the east, west, north, or south (*Heji* 12870AB, Keightley 2000: 91). Clouds and thunder were linked to rain. Names of directions and winds: Hu Houxuan 1944 and 1956, Feng Shi 1994, Wang Aihe 2000b: 29, 35–36. In particular, rainbows with a directional source were considered to presage disaster. See *Heji* 10405B, Keightley 2000: 91, cf. Hu Houxuan 1944: 19b–20b.

[9] *Heji* 672r, Keightley 2000: 4.

[10] *Heji* 14294 and 14295, Keightley 2000: 70–71. Two inscriptions describe sacrifices to "Di's emissary, Wind" (*Di shi feng* 帝史風, *Heji* 14225 and 14226, cf. Keightley 2000: 4–5). Other sacrifices sought to pacify damaging winds, possibly understood as sources of illness. See *Heji* 30260 (trans. Wang Aihe 2000b: 36) and *Heji* 34137 (trans. Keightley 2000: 4).

[11] Han Ziqiang 2000a: 53, slip 64, trans. Shaughnessy 2001: 9. By contrast, in the received *Zhou yi* text, the statement for Hexagram 14 (*Da You* 大有, "Great Possession") is simply Great Possession: Prime Receipt 大有元亨.

The association of the winds with *qi* and with directionality becomes more explicit in the Warring States and Western Han wind divination methods discussed in Chapter 5.

Questions about the success of planned ventures take many forms. For state consultors, perhaps the most important was warfare. Predictions about warfare were both descriptive (will there be victory?) and normative (is military activity auspicious or pleasing to the gods?). Oracle bone inscriptions on warfare ask whether an opponent will be captured and whether to enter into an alliance. *Zuo zhuan* prognostications ask about plans to form alliances or attack neighboring states; one attempts to resolve a disagreement on the meaning of a turtle shell divination (discussed in Chapter 8). These examples suggest that turtle and milfoil were used together to resolve uncertain or disputed military situations. Crucial to both military and political success was the selection of personnel (Loewe's fifth category), and several passages in the *Shu jing*, *Li ji*, and *Zuo zhuan* discuss the use of mantic procedures to select ministers of state and royal heirs. Another passage from the *Shu jing* discusses how to use divination as a tool for political consensus, in resolving disagreements between rulers, ministers, and the people. (Details are discussed in Chapter 7.)

Marriage, children, and family welfare were topics of both state and private concern, but most accounts concern the marriages of the elite. For example, the *Zuo zhuan* describes prognostications about marriages and the future of newborn sons (see Chapter 8 and Appendix D). These passages are probably late interpolations, but they still indicate the appropriateness of these question topics for divination. The *Li ji* authorizes the use of turtle shell and *Yi* divination to select a bride for a son and to finalize marriage arrangements.[12] In a narrative that reads more like a "test oracle" than an actual query, Han Wu Di consults a full range of mantic specialists on an auspicious day for marriage.[13]

Another approach to ensuring the success of planned actions was to ascertain that there would be no disasters or calamities over a given period of time. Such questions first appear in the oracle bone inscriptions, either about the day of the divination or about the ensuing ten-day week.[14] Similar questions appear in the Year divinations from Baoshan, which concern an entire year for the consultor official (translated and discussed in Appendix E).

[12] *YL* 6.9ab (Steele 1.21); *LJ* 2.14a and 51.25a (Couvreur 1.31 and 2.423).

[13] *SJ* 127.3222–23. They cannot agree, and he arbitrarily chooses one recommendation.

[14] E.g. *Heji* 28509 (today) and 21016, 21021 (ten-day week). See Keightley 2000, nos. 17 and 42.

The positive equivalent of disasters is good auspice, and auspicious days are the major focus of the astrocalendric texts already described in the "Hemerology" section of Chapter 5. Queries about auspicious days also appear in precursors of the *Zhou yi* excavated from Wangjiatai. A chance procedure was used to retrieve an omen statement in order to determine whether a contemplated action was auspicious.[15] Each entry associates the diagram and name of a hexagram with a statement, of the form:

[Diagram] Hexagram A says: "In the past, X requested a prognostication about Y from Z; Z prognosticated and said: (in)Auspicious."

For example:

 節曰，昔者武王卜伐殷而支占老考，老考 占曰吉。

1–1–6–6–1–6 Jie says: In ancient times King Wu prognosticated about attacking the Yin [Shang] and requested a divination from Lao Kao. Lao Kao prognosticated and said: Auspicious.[16]

These hexagram statements refer to legendary and historical events, and are completely unlike the corresponding hexagram statements of the *Zhou yi*.[17] Queries about auspicious times were sometimes combined with other questions about sacrifice and ritual (Loewe's fourth category). Particularly important was the location of the residences of the living and tombs (residences of the dead). The *Li ji* and *Yi li* specify the use of turtle and milfoil for various details of funeral rites.[18] Questions about illness first

[15] The Wangjiatai texts include two copies of the *Guicang* (discussed in Chapter 9). These fifty-three hexagram texts are written on slips of different sizes and in different hands. Archaeological report: *WW* 1995.1: 37–43, esp. 39–42. Detailed summary: Wang Mingqin 2004: esp. 439–45. Several other papers in that volume are also devoted to the *Guicang*.

[16] Slip 198 as transcribed in *WW* 1995.1.41. This hexagram corresponds to Hexagram 60 (Jie 節, "Articulation"), in the transmitted tradition.

[17] The hexagram names resemble those of the received *Zhou yi*, the transmitted *Guicang* (which they partially correct), and the Mawangdui *Zhou yi*. Xing Wen (2002, 2003, 2004) argues that the structure of the text is different from the reconstructed versions. There are also daybooks from Wangjiatai, which include sections on auspicious days for sacrifice and choices of days for various activities. There are also sections on *jianchu* oracles and auspicious days (*riji*), which describe activities for each day of a thirty-day cycle. Other mantic implements found in the tomb include a divining stick and twenty-three lacquered six-sided wood dice, possibly used to cast hexagrams. See "Jiangling Wangjiatai 15 hao Qin mu" in *WW* 1995.1: 37–43.

[18] They specify turtle shell to determine an auspicious time for funeral rites and milfoil to determine the place of burial and choose an impersonator of the dead. Burial: *LJ* 3.14a (Couvreur 1.60–61); *YL* 47.3b (Steele 2.159); *LJ* 40.11a (Couvreur 2.122f); *YL* 37.15b and 17a (Steele 2.73 and 75); *YL* 41.8b (Steele 2.101); *YL* 44.2a (Steele 2.127). Impersonator of the dead: *YL* 47.5a and 24.14b (Steele 2.128 and 159); *LJ* 33.9b (Couvreur 1.764). The *Yi li* also gives a detailed

appear in the oracle bones. They are the subject of most of the Baoshan divinations (discussed in detail in Chapter 9), and appear frequently in the *Zuo zhuan* and other historical narratives.

Anomalies (*zaiyi*) were portents from the physical world that were so singular or so awe-inspiring that they required explanation. Questions about anomalies appear in the oracle bone inscriptions, the received tradition, and excavated texts. In the oracle bone inscriptions, the most important were solar and lunar eclipses and "blemishes" on the sun (sunspots), of which several have been verified independently.[19] Texts excavated from Shuihudi and Wangjiatai include sections on misfortunes and anomalies. For example, a Qin statute from Shuihudi requires reports of harvests affected by weather anomalies and plagues of insects.[20] In the received tradition, the *Li ji* specifies the use of turtle and milfoil to interpret anomalies involving the royal house.[21] Interpreting anomalies was an activity of both mantic specialists and Ru. The latter used omens and anomaly interpretation as foci for their ideas about heaven, and argued that anomalies and natural catastrophes revealed heaven's intentions and judgments on human, and especially imperial, misconduct.[22]

Oneiromancy differs from other types of mantic activity because any topic of mantic interest, or even method of mantic inquiry, can appear in a dream. It also presents particular problems, because most accounts come from narratives that cannot be taken at face value, the *Zuo zhuan* especially. (This issue is discussed further in Chapter 8.) Nonetheless, we cannot dismiss dream divination as a purely literary or rhetorical mode of expression, since a variety of evidence attests to its use.

Dream divinations first appear in the oracle bone inscriptions, including questions about the meaning of dreams about military victory and dreams about animals.[23] Dreams are also a category in the daybooks from Shuihudi,

account of the mantic procedures for the selection of a tomb (*YL* 37.15b, Steele 2.73, Couvreur 1916: 474). For discussion see Loewe 1994: 177–78.

19 Solar eclipses: *Heji* 11480, 33694, 33695. Lunar eclipses: *Heji* 11482v, 11483r and v, 11484, 11485, 40204, 40610. Sunspots: *Heji* 33696, 33697, 33698, 33699, 33700, 33703, 33704, 33710. See Xu Zhentao et al. 2000: 18–21.

20 *SHD* (Statutes): 19, slips 1–3, Hulsewé 1985: 21. A text from Wangjiatai is titled "Prognostication by Portents" (*Zaiyi zhan* 災異占). See Wang Mingqin 2004: 47–48.

21 For example, the apparition of the ghost of the recently suicided Liu Xin in 23 CE (*HSBZ* 99C.23b), the birth of Liu Xiu 劉秀 (Guangwu Di 光武帝, r. 5–57 CE), the first emperor of the Eastern Han (*HHS* 10B.438–39), and the accession of Han Shun Di 漢順帝 (r. 125–44 CE) about 126 CE (*HHS* 54.1767). See Loewe 1994: 185–97.

22 Han omenology: Wu Hong 1989: 73–107, Lippiello 2001, Mansvelt-Beck 1990: 131–74, Wang Aihe 2000b: 155–67, Loewe 2004: 487–90.

23 Dreams about military victory: Qinbian 8.13.2, cf. Fan Yuzhou 1989: 532. Dreams about animals: *Heji* 17393r, 376r, 17391, 17392r, cf. Keightley 2000: 113 n. 53.

but the entry in Daybook A consists of one item, an incantation to stop nightmares.[24] The "Dreams" (*Meng* 夢) section of Daybook B includes a description of five kinds of dream (associated with the Five Colors) correlating the day of the dream to the Heaven Stems of the sexagenary cycle. The emphasis is shifted from magical techniques for stopping nightmares to predicting them by means of the sexagenary cycle.[25]

Was there a systematic account of the meaning of dreams? The predictive limits of dream divination become a topic of discussion in Eastern Han texts within the genre of discourse (*lun* 論): critiques directed at what their authors considered the misguided ideas of their own times. Both Wang Chong (27–97 CE) and Wang Fu (*c.* 90–165 CE) discussed dreams in texts written as private individuals, rather than as officials. Wang Chong was an original and iconoclastic thinker, with a broadly skeptical and rationalist approach to classical texts. He attacked their uncritical treatment of dreams, arguing that even if a dream offers accurate signs, the limits of human skill may prevent their correct interpretation:

夫占夢與占龜同。晉占夢者不見象指，猶周占龜者不見兆者為也。象無不然，兆無不審， 人之知闇, 論之失實也。

Dream divination is like turtle shell divination. The Jin dream diviners did not see where the images pointed, just as the Zhou turtle diviners did not understand what the omens meant. The signs were true and the omens correct, but since human knowledge was insufficient, exegesis was not to the point.[26]

In his preface to the *Qianfu lun*, Wang Fu explains that he wrote the text out of frustration at contemporary affairs and being unable to hold office. He attempted a systematic typology, with an implicit criticism of dream divination in a chapter titled "Dreams Expounded" (*Meng lie* 夢列). He classed dreams as: straightforward (*zhi* 直), symbolic (*xiang* 象), produced by concentration (*jing* 精), longing (*xiang* 想), personal (*ren* 人), stimulating (*gan* 感), seasonal (*shi* 時), oppositional (*fan* 反), pathological (*bing* 病), and affective (*xing* 性). This detailed typology is an aid to the correct understanding of dreams, but Wang Fu argues that even apparently clear dreams do not form a good basis for advising action.[27] Other dream

[24] *SHD* (Daybooks): 210, slips 13–14v, trans. Harper 2010: 52.

[25] For example, the spirit overseer in Daybook B is named Wanqi 宛奇. *SHD* (Daybooks): 247, slips 189–95, trans. Harper 2010: 54.

[26] *LH* 1006–7 ("Bu shi" 24.71), trans. after Forke 1.189. For Wang Chong see Kinney 1991 (esp. 23–30) and Kalinowski 2011.

[27] *Qianfu lun*, 315 and 320 ("Meng lie" 夢列 28). See Kinney 1991: 119–24 (translation) and R. J. Smith 1991: 247–57.

typologies appear in medical and military texts, and are not posed in opposition to divination.[28]

In summary, we can use the evidence of other periods to contextualize the questions specified in the *Zhou li* as appropriate for divination. Most are of ongoing provenance, but a few may be particular to certain historical periods. (We cannot know this with any certainty, since absence of evidence is not evidence of absence.) Queries about the cause of illness and the meaning of dreams appear in the oracle bone inscriptions, fourth-century sources, and excavated texts, but are not mentioned in the *Zhou li* and are not common in Han sources. Queries about anomalies appear in the *Zhou li* list, and are frequent in Han accounts, but less so in pre-Han accounts. Questions about conferring gifts and the arrival of expected persons appear in the *Zhou li* list, but are not common in Han or pre-Han sources. Differences in question topic or the prevalence of certain questions may suggest changing state concerns and notions of danger and uncertainty.

The Greek questions

Recent scholarship has addressed controversies over the influence of *manteis* and oracles on Greek politics: why the oracle was consulted and how the results were used. A preliminary question is what topics were considered appropriate for state consultation, and how or whether they changed over time. States clearly employed independent *manteis*, especially on military matters, but there is no consistent record. Questions asked of independent *manteis* are preserved, if at all, in anecdotal form in historical narratives.

The richest source for state queries is clearly the oracle of Apollo at Delphi, because of its status as a panhellenic oracle. However, several problems complicate a clear account of state questions posed at Delphi. Although there are extant records of oracular consultations, many provide only the answer, leaving question and context to be surmised. And responses, especially from the archaic period, are of questionable authenticity. Thus our understanding of changing consultation topics depends on our selection of oracles, and specifically on vexed questions of historicity and authenticity (discussed in Chapter 2).

The compendia of Parke and Wormell and Fontenrose take different approaches to this question.[29] Both distinguish quasi-historical oracles from

[28] For further discussion see Drège and Drettas 2003 and Drettas 2007.

[29] Fontenrose (1978: esp. 7–10) grouped oracles as historical, quasi-historical, legendary, or fictional. Parke and Wormell grouped them into eight chronological periods and a ninth for

legendary or fictional responses; the problem comes in distinguishing quasi-historical from genuinely historical responses. According to the stringent criteria advocated by Fontenrose, about half the known Delphic oracles are merely quasi-historical, mostly from the works of Herodotus, Plutarch, and Pausanias. Yet it is precisely these authors who are our major sources for a literary topos or genre of Delphic oracle stories. Rather than attempting to resolve the authenticity question, my approach is to compare two overlapping groups of divination questions, as a broad and a narrow sample of Delphic responses. The broad sample consisted of the responses Fontenrose considered historical (75) or quasi-historical (268), eliminating responses with no clear question topic. Several influential discussions of the history of the oracle seem to use this group of questions.[30] The narrow sample eliminates the quasi-historical oracles Fontenrose considers not genuine, leaving 100 responses (Appendix C).[31] The major difference between the two is that the narrow sample does not include most quasi-historical responses from the Archaic period or a number of responses reported by Herodotus, Pausanias, and Plutarch. Details of the evidence for both samples appear in Appendices 6.1 and C (narrow sample) and 6.2 (broad sample).

I consider state queries from the narrow sample under four broad headings: (1) Government queries on planned ventures, including colonization, political and diplomatic questions on rulership, tyranny, legislation, civil welfare, and interstate relations. (2) Warfare. (3) Release from evils (*lusis kakōn*), including famine, plague, religious remedies for military defeat, and purification. This category also includes the opposite of *lusis*, wellbeing: how to prevent evils and maintain present prosperity.[32] (4) Cult, including cult foundation, how to please the gods, and questions on sacrifices and other matters. Religious queries in particular were posed by both state and private consultors to Delphi. The most common topics (for both private and state

oracles of uncertain date. Within each period, they distinguished responses they considered genuine, legendary, fictional, dubious, or spurious. Legendary responses were either timeless or from clearly legendary narratives (before the eighth century). Fictional responses were deliberate literary inventions of poets, dramatists, etc.

[30] In particular Price 1985, 1999, Parker 2000a, and Catherine Morgan 1990.

[31] Responses are cited by Fontenrose's letter prefix (e.g. H10 or Q219), the numbering of Park and Wormell (PW no.), and original sources. The broad sample consists of all the H and Q oracles with the exceptions of H55, H61, H70, H72, Q108, Q195, Q197, Q199, Q227, Q238, Q244, Q261, and Q264. The narrow sample consists of the above H oracles and 29 Q oracles: 8, 11, 12, 22, 65, 69, 111, 124, 125, 137, 142, 148, 154, 156, 157, 167, 169, 178, 187, 189, 190, 205, 222, 236, 237, 241, 266, and 267.

[32] On this point see Parker 2000a: 83. Fontenrose (1978, Appendix BII) distinguished three broad areas of consultation: religion, government, and private, each with five to ten subcategories. Most extant Delphic consultations fall within the first two. State and private consultation: Arnush 2005.

consultors) were requests for good fortune, prosperity, and wellbeing, including the question of which god or hero to sacrifice to in order to obtain a desired result. I consider private consultations on these and other topics in the second part of the chapter, in conjunction with the more extensive records from Dodona and Didyma. Queries from the broad sample on these topics are taken up in Chapter 8.

These categories overlap with, but do not correspond exactly to, the Chinese categories. Chinese questions about weather, harvest, rainfall, or famine and plague often appear as requests for predictions. By contrast, Greek queries on these topics fall under the broad rubric of *lusis kakōn*, which has no Chinese counterpart. *Lusis* questions seek a recommendation, not a prediction, and cannot be verified. The difference is suggestive, and may reflect a contrast between a broadly theological orientation of Greek divination and a broadly cosmological orientation of Chinese divination. Similarly, Chinese questions on auspicious times and anomalies and Greek questions on religious cult both fall under the broad rubric of theological and cosmological inquiries, but they are very differently phrased.

The broad sample shows *poleis* consulting Delphi about colonization, tyrants, internal politics, legislation, and inter-state matters. Political questions in the narrow sample are limited responses to very specific questions. By contrast, the three colonization questions in the narrow sample address two very specific topics: whether to found a colony and who should be *oikist* (*oikistēs*).[33] Colonization oracles seem to disappear after the fifth century. (A wave of Greek colonization from the mid-sixth to the mid-fifth century was not reflected in extant Delphic consultations.) Foundation decrees of eighth-century colonies are especially doubtful.[34] There are no oracles on tyranny in the narrow sample.

The broad sample also contains two problematic queries attributed to the Delians on questions of pollution and purification. In one (which

[33] Most colonies were state ventures; the Chalcidians founded colonies at Messene and later Rhegium; Sparta founded colonies at Tarentum; Corinth colonized Syracuse; Thera colonized Cyrene in North Africa. The Ionians colonized Megara and Miletus and the Black Sea area. A few colonies were private ventures, founded by individuals exiled or defeated in civil strife.
Most narrow-sample colonization oracles are fifth century (Appendix C, H6, H14). One (Appendix C, Q111) is sixth century. The *oikist* (from *oikos*, household) was the founder of a colony, designated by the founding polis. Foundation decrees for colonies included accounts of the decision, the choice of *oikist*, and legal provisions, including a formal oath by colonists and the mother polis. See Malkin 1987.

[34] Both Fontenrose (1978: 137–44) and Parker (2000a: 85–92) express doubts whether any recorded colonization oracles are genuine. By contrast, Catherine Morgan (1990: 9–16) uses broad sample oracles to argue that Archaic patterns of consultation reflect patterns of community tension and Delphi's particular relations with Corinth, Sparta, Argos, and Athens.

Fontenrose explicitly considers not genuine), the Delians ask about their expulsion, and are advised to find the birthplace of Apollo and to sacrifice there.[35] In the other, the Delians ask about release from the plague and are told to double the altar and sacrifice on it. This oracle is the source for one of three classical mathematical problems that the ancient Greeks were unable to solve with compass and straight edge.[36] Other broad sample queries on religious cult request divine approval for contemplated actions or seek other advice. Three topics appear only in the broad sample: requests for divine approval for moving or removing a tomb, requests for divine sanction for punishments, and questions about someone who has disappeared. Both samples include questions on the meaning of spontaneous events (apparitions, omens, dreams, and prodigies), requests for direction on sacrifices to the gods, and queries on cult and administration.

The narrow sample does contain questions on legislation, internal politics, or inter-state matters. These oracles either request a yes–no response or a choice between a limited number of alternatives. One such response advises the Spartans that they should obey the laws of Lycurgus.[37] Another affirms that Athens should provide public maintenance in the Prytaneion.[38] A third advises that Philip of Macedon and Chalcidice should become allies (and perform particular sacrifices).[39] An Athenian request to name the ten tribes of Athens from a list of some hundred names required selection from a list.[40]

In summary, political topics in the narrow sample are limited responses to very specific questions: whether to found a colony, who should lead it, whether to adopt a specific law code, and whether to enter into an alliance with another polis. State queries from Dodona are similarly specific, for example by a group from Epirus considering a military alliance with the Molossians (Appendix 6.4), as are state queries to Didyma. They concern government and diplomacy, and seek recommendations on such matters as the recruitment of new citizens, alliances, religious festivals, and grants of *asylia*.[41] These topics

[35] Q191, PW no. 161, Thuc. 5.32.

[36] Q191, PW no. 161, Thuc. 5.32 and Q200, PW no. 179, Plut. *Mor*. 386e–f, cf. 579bd. According to Plutarch, the oracle was ambiguous whether the doubling referred to linear or cubical dimensions. The latter required skill in geometry, and Plato took the response as an injunction to study geometry. The other two were squaring the circle and trisecting any angle. Modern mathematics has shown that none of these problems can be solved this way. Most relevant are the algebraic theories of Évariste Galois (1811–32) and a proof by Pierre Wantzel, published in 1837.

[37] Q8, PW no. 21, 217, 219–21, Plut. *Lyk*. 29. [38] H1, PW no. 123, *IG* I^2.77.

[39] H19, PW no. 260, TAPA 65 (1934), 103–22, esp. 103, lines 12–16; RO no. 50. The unstated question can be inferred from the response.

[40] Q125, PW no. 80, Hdt. 5.66–69 and 6.131. See Appendix 6.1 for further discussion.

[41] *Asylia* (cf. modern "asylum") was a decree that persons or places were "sacred and inviolable" to the tutelary god of the polis. Grants of *asylia* to individuals meant that their property was safe

diminish during the late second century, after which public inquiries are confined to questions of health, crops, and changes in religious ritual.[42]

Plutarch (*Mor*. 386g) heads his list of the most typical subjects for queries of Delphi with "whether they will be victorious" (*ei nikēsousin*). Military queries from both samples ask how to gain victory or avoid defeat, whether to form or refuse alliances, and questions on dependencies and truces. Some also ask the meaning of spontaneous anomalies observed on the battlefield. Both samples suggest that divination was an important factor in the decision to go to war (or how to prepare for one, for a polis facing invasion). Both samples suggest that such decisions were referred to Delphi and that Delphi had the authority to sanction war.

During much of the period of the Athenian democracy (roughly 508–300), Athens was at war, including the Persian Wars (490 and 480 or 479), the Peloponnesian Wars (462–446 and 431–404), and other conflicts. Much of the broad sample comes from Herodotus and Pausanias. These include oracles reported by Pausanias on the Messenian Wars (740–680), the so-called "First Sacred War" and oracles reported by Herodotus on the Persian Wars. (See Appendix 6.2. These oracles are discussed in Chapter 8.) The narrow sample is far more modest. It includes only one response from the Archaic period: Cleisthenes' alleged attempt to bribe the Pythia.[43] Narrow sample military oracles begin late in the Classical period, and typically advise or reject a stated course of action: for example, whether the Epidamnians should return their city to Corinth (its founder) or whether Sparta should attack Athens.[44] There is also one Macedonian response (on anomalies) and three queries from Rome. In summary, many Greek state divinations about planned ventures seem to have a range of literary or ideological motivations, and most cannot be read as actual records of mantic inquiries.

In both samples, questions on release from evils (*lusis kakōn*) and its opposite, wellbeing, are religious in form, but may be motivated by political, military, or personal "evils."[45] *Lusis* questions about military defeat ask for

from seizure through the claims of another polis. Decreed of places, it granted inviolability to a sanctuary or even an entire polis (*OCD*[3] 136).

42 Parker 2000a: 101–5.

43 Q124, PW no. 79, Hdt. 5.63.1 and 6.123.2. In an attempt to end the Pisistratid tyranny, he bribed her to respond "free Athens!" to any Spartan query.

44 Epidamnians: H4, PW no. 136, Thuc. 1.25.1. Spartans: H5, PW no. 137 and Q245, PW no. 431, Thuc. 1.118.3, 123.1, 2.54.4; Plut. *Mor*. 403b.

45 The prophylactic versions of *lusis* queries ask how to ensure wellbeing and continued prosperity. The broad sample contains some fifteen state queries on wellbeing, starting in the Archaic period. For example, a query from Cyrene *c*. 550 asks the broad question of how best to organize the state; they are advised to bring in a lawgiver from Mantinea (Q118, PW no. 69, Hdt. 4.161.2).

cult advice, the causes of anomalies on the battlefield, and whether dedications of victory offerings are sufficient. The two samples also differ considerably in their treatment of these topics. The narrow sample *lusis* queries are restricted to questions on military defeat, plague, and wellbeing. Broad sample *lusis* queries also address civil strife, famine (from crop failure, drought, or sterility), pollution (*miasma*) in its civic or medical senses, and purification (*katharsis*).

The ten *lusis* queries in the narrow sample address military defeat, plague, and wellbeing, but without reference to pollution, civil strife, famine, or anomalies. Military *lusis* queries ask to which god to pray to for victory. For example, in 479 Athens sought relief from Mardonius during the campaign that ended with the battle of Plataea, and was advised to sacrifice to Zeus, Hera, and several heroes.[46] Other questions ask about first fruit offerings; for example, the Hellenes asked whether offerings after the Greek victories at Salamis and Plataea were sufficient and pleasing.[47]

Queries on plague are also closely focused. For example, one (the only *lusis* query from the Archaic period) addresses a plague in Athens in 596. According to Plato, ten years before the Persian War, Epimenides went to Athens in obedience to the oracle and offered sacrifices ordained by the god.[48] This account suggests a response to epidemics: the diagnostic procedure of oracular consultation followed by ritual purification according to oracular instructions. It is striking that all extant queries on pollution (*miasma*) come from the broad sample.[49] This point is important because it has been argued that the rise of Delphi was connected with changing views of pollution and purification, the rise of purification rituals, and the perceived need to institutionalize vengeance, expiation, and purification.[50] One oracle to Athens in 421 advises the Athenians to restore the Delians, who had been exiled for blood pollution, but the Athenians' question was about a military problem, not about pollution or purification.[51]

46 Q154, PW no. 102, Plut. *Arist.* 11.3.

47 Salamis: Q157, PW no. 105, Hdt. 8.122. Plataea: Q156, PW no. 104, Plut. *Arist.* 20.4.

48 Q65, PW no. 13, Pl. *Leg.* 642d. In Diogenes Laertius' version (1.110), the Pythia required Athens to purify the city (*kathērai tēn polin*), but his account is further removed from the event.

49 Several queries from Dodona concern pollution. For example (Appendix 6.4, Parke 1.7), a question whether the god sends the storm on account of the impurity of some human being.

50 Dodds 1951: esp. 35–45. However, as Parker argues (1983: 138–43), Zeus was the god of suppliants, at whose altars murderers sought purification, and Delphi did not perform blood purification rituals.

51 H8, PW no. 162, Thuc. 5.32.1. The Athenians had performed purification rituals throughout Delos in 426 or 425. In 422 they expelled the Delians on grounds that they were tainted by blood pollution and resettled them in Adramyttium (modern Edremit on the west coast of Turkey).

The narrow sample also includes four state queries on wellbeing. Most detailed is an account by Demosthenes, who describes oracular instructions for traditional worship of the gods. He enjoins his audience to read the oracles aloud and quotes them at length: to honor all the Olympian gods and goddesses; to sacrifice and pray to Zeus, Heracles, and Apollo for health; and to pray to Apollo, Leto, and Artemis for good fortune. He clearly assumes his audience is familiar with the details of these procedures.[52] Another speech by Demosthenes (delivered in 340) records details of an Athenian query on sacrifices after a portent.[53]

Narrow sample queries about religious cult address requests for direction on sacrifices to the gods and other queries on cult and administration. Because these questions come from inscriptions, they offer little context. Other queries on sacrifices concern agriculture and offerings of first fruits to Demeter and Kore.[54] There are also questions about granting honors, for example a question from Delphi on honors to Pindar.[55] Several fifth-century Athenian queries ask about honors to the gods or particular sacrifices, for example a request for approval for dedicating a house to Asclepius.[56] Other cult queries involved the Olympian and Pythian games. The Achaeans ask why they have failed to triumph at the Olympic games for two centuries.[57] Another oracle approved an Elean decision to fine Athens after misconduct by an Athenian athlete at the 112th Olympiad in 332.[58]

Private queries

The overwhelming majority of extant mantic queries are official questions, especially in the Chinese and Greek received textual traditions. Chinese evidence of private queries comes from excavated texts, especially queries about the success of planned ventures and the prognosis of illness.

[52] H28, PW no. 282, Dem. 21.51–52.

[53] H29, PW no. 283, Dem. 43.66. The speech is part of an argument about familial duties, and may have been a formulaic request for guidance after anomalies such as the appearance of a comet. See Bowden 2005: 118–19.

[54] H9, PW no. 164, *IG* 1^2.76 (*SIG* 83, lines 4–8, 25–26, 32–34).

[55] Q178, PW no. 119, Paus. 9.23.3.

[56] H24, PW no. 278, *IG* 2^2.4969.1–3, trans. Bowden 2005: 123 (no. 21).

[57] Q169, PW no. 118, Paus. 6.3.8 and 7.17.6.

[58] H35, PW no. 274, Paus. 5.21.5–7. Delphi refused to deliver any oracle to the Athenians until they paid fines imposed by the Eleans. After the oracle approving the Elean decision, Athens paid the fines and dedicated six statues to Zeus.

One type of private query seeks confirmation of overall success over a given time period. Modern scholars have termed these types of query "Year" (*sui* 歲) and "Illness" (*jibing* 疾病) divination. Year divination sought confirmation of overall success over a given time period. It seems to have been a standard sequence, performed to ascertain (or establish) success in official service to the king. Illness divinations punctuate a normal sequence of Year divinations after the appearance of a health problem.[59] The most complete Year and Illness divinations occur in records excavated from Baoshan, which record a series of prognostications on behalf of the tomb's occupant (Appendix E). Other more fragmentary Illness divinations have been excavated from Warring States tombs at Tianxingguan and Wangshan.[60] Much remains to be learned about these texts, but we can say that they reflect a prevailing view of disease before the second century, in which disease was seen as the result of invasive influences: animal-inflicted injuries, natural forces (wind, heat, cold), and demonic entities and magic. The oracle bone inscriptions and Warring States excavated texts describe types of sacrifice to mollify these entities.

Private consultations at Delphi included questions about marriage, progeny, and wellbeing, since private questions about wellbeing frequently involve the welfare of family or children. Other personal questions asked advice on actions or occupations, including choice of profession, money, place of residence or citizenship, whether or how to undertake a contemplated action, and whether it will be successful. This rubric also includes broadly ontological queries: questions about truth, gnomic utterances, etc.

The broad sample from Delphi includes personal queries by legendary and historical individuals. Topics include how to have children, advice on contemplated actions such as changes of residence, choice of career, or financial decisions, questions on illness and wellbeing, and gnomic questions or requests for truth (Appendix 6.3). These topics all have counterparts in the private questions from Dodona, discussed below.

59 For this distinction see Chen Wei 1996: 152–54. Of the twenty-seven entries, eleven are Year divinations; twelve concern illness; and the others do not involve divination. Although the ritualists specialized in methods and instruments, they did not specialize in Year or Illness divination. Eight perform Year divination, three exclusively; four perform Illness divination exclusively; and four perform both Year and Illness divination. See Raphals 2005.

60 "Jiangling Tianxingguan yihao Chu mu" in *Kaogu xuebao* 1982.1: 71–116, esp. 109–10. There are significant differences between two published transcriptions of the Wangshan text: Shang Chengzuo 1995 and *Jiangling Wangshan Sha zhong Chu mu* 1996. Cook 2006 translates Shang Chengzuo 1995. The Wangshan tomb's occupant Shao Gu 卲固 seems to have suffered from an ailment of the chest or abdomen, with inability to eat, abscesses, nausea, and intestinal problems. Ailments of the feet, bones, and head are also mentioned. See Shang Chengzuo 1995: slips 10–14, 58–59, and 106–7; *Wangshan* slips 36–39 and 41–42.

By contrast, the narrow sample from Delphi contains only one personal query on domestic matters, by an unknown man about 360 on having children.[61] It also includes five queries on contemplated actions. Best known is a question by Xenophon in 401, after being invited to join the expedition of Cyrus. Xenophon asked to which god to offer sacrifice and prayers to make his intended journey successful and to return safely. (He is advised to sacrifice to Zeus Basileus.)[62] In 356, the exiled Athenian Callistratus asked whether he would be treated according to law if he returned to Athens after fleeing a death sentence for pro-Spartan sympathies. (He was advised that he would; he returned and was put to death.)[63] The narrow sample has one personal query on *lusis* and one on wellbeing. A priest seeks absolution for some violation of his vows.[64] About 250, Poseidonius of Halicarnassus asks what is better for himself and his children to do.[65] Individuals also consulted Delphi on private questions of interest to themselves. Heading the narrow sample is Chaerophon of Athens, who about 430 asks whether anyone is wiser than Socrates.[66] The narrow sample contains two other personal queries.[67]

In summary, our information about personal inquiries at Delphi is limited, and mostly restricted to the broad sample. Its usefulness for the present discussion is to demonstrate the consistency of consultors' question topics: progeny, travel, livelihood, financial matters, *lusis*, wellbeing, and religious cult.

The same topics appear in the lead tablets from Dodona, which record mantic queries by ordinary individuals. They also include queries on topics that do not appear at Delphi: crime, questions about military matters by private individuals, slavery, freedom, and judicial and legal activity. The overall effect of the queries from Dodona is to reaffirm the plausibility of questions that at Delphi only appear in the broad sample.

Dodona

The lead tablets from Dodona (Figure 6.1) present an extensive sample of personal queries, and indicate which topics were considered areas of risk

61 H34, PW no. 334, FD 3.1.560 (*BCH* 80 (1956): 550, line 3). He is told that he will have a child, and should make an offering of hair.

62 H11, PW no. 172, Xen. *An.* 3.1.5–8, 6.1.22, Cic. *Div.* 1.54.122.

63 H18, PW no. 259, Lycurg. *Leoc.* 93.

64 H63, PW no. 464, Plut. *Mor.* 404a.

65 H36, PW no. 355, *AGIBM* 896. He is advised to follow the example of his ancestors and told which gods to worship.

66 H3, PW no. 134, Pl. *Ap.* 21a–c, Xen. *Ap.* 14.

67 The Roman emperor Hadrian (r. 117–38 CE) on the birthplace and parentage of Homer: H65, PW no. 465, *IG* 2^2.5006. The Neoplatonist Amelius on where the soul of Plotinus had gone: H69, PW no. 473, Porph. *Plot.* 22.

Figure 6.1 Inscription from Dodona.

and uncertainty by private consultors.[68] At Dodona as at Delphi, a common topic for both private and state consultors was requests for good fortune, prosperity, and wellbeing, including the question to which god or hero to sacrifice to in order to obtain a desired result.[69]

Most questions are asked by men. Sometimes consultors' names establish their gender. In other cases grammatical structures tell us whether a man or woman is speaking. Some are unclear. I group the Dodona inquiries into ten categories, modified from Eidinow's and based in part on comparative considerations: (1) Travel and Migration; (2) Women; (3) Children; (4) Illness; (5) Occupation, Property, and Good Fortune; (6) Construction; (7) Ritual Activity, Military Campaigns, Judicial Activity; (8) Crime and Lost, Stolen, or Hidden Objects; (9) Slavery; and (10) Other Matters. (See Appendix 6.4, which summarizes the Dodona inscriptions in Parke's Appendix (Parke 1967) and Eidinow's Catalogue of the Dodona Oracle (Eidinow 2007a: 72–124).) Eidinow's material includes both published and unpublished material. Her question topics and subdivisions rely in part on the very consistent phrasing of many of the questions themselves as "*peri X*," where X may be descendants, wives, property, work, or travel (followed by its purpose).[70]

Many private queries concern travel, for purposes of either livelihood or migration. Some questions concern whether it would be better to go to a certain place, for example Epidamnus (T1), Sybaris (T2), Hipponion (T3), the Ionian Gulf (T4), Sicily (T5), Apollonia (T8), and other locations. Other questions specifically refer to migration. One consultor asks whether he would fare better in Oricus in the countryside, or as he is living now (R1).

68 Eidinow's (2007a) catalog and analysis is more complete than Parke (1967) and different from L'Hôte 2006. It includes unpublished material made available to her by the late Professor Anastasios-Phoivos Christidis of Thessaloniki University.

69 For example, the Corcyraeans ask to what god or hero to sacrifice and pray for wellbeing, prosperity, and the common good (1.2, 1.3, 1.6). Tarentum asks about good fortune (1.1).

70 Eidinow 2007a: 126. She divides her inquiries into concerns about the future and questions about the present or past, and then divides them into categories by number of consultations.

Another asks a more complex question about both possessions and a place to live, specifically whether he should take his family to Croton (R2). The opposite side of the tablet contains what is probably a response: "Croton." Other queries ask about going to Alyzea (R3) or living in Chemara (R4). A related topic is the bureaucracy of residence: whether to change registration (R5) or whether to take citizenship this year or next (R7). These questions speak to the dangers of travel and to the particular uncertainties of migration. In all these questions, the consultor has the choice of making the contemplated move. There is also no clear way to assess its outcome and chances of success.

Questions about women (*peri gunaikos*) typically ask whether the consultor will do better if he marries a particular woman, named or unnamed; for example:

> About a woman, whether I will be fortunate taking Cleolais as a wife. (W1)[71]

Sometimes the woman is unnamed, and the question is whether the consultor will do better or gain profit if he marries (W4, W7) or whether to marry another woman (W6). The decision may involve profit:

> If the guardianship will be fortunate to me which I Lyccidas gain by marrying. (W2)[72]

Or it may involve multiple factors. One man asks if he will do better by taking a wife, whether there will be children for Isodemus, who will take care of him, and if he should live in Athens and become a citizen there (W3). In some cases fathers ask whether to marry off their daughters, or to whom. One man asks Zeus whether it is more serviceable to give his daughter in marriage to Theodorus or to Tessias (W5). These questions highlight the role of women as possessions (*ktēmata*): assets who may bring children and other profit. The question is typically which woman will bring the greatest advantage, and the clear recognition that women differ, not only in fertility, but possibly also in abilities and resourcefulness. Although these questions suggest that marriage was considered subject to divine guidance, the questions are not open-ended and typically ask about a specific woman, either by name or the woman the consultor has in mind.

Most questions about children (*peri genea*) address the future: how to get them or how to ensure their prosperity. Most come from men. Some concern

[71] περὶ γυναικὸς / πότερον κα τύγ- / χάνοιμι λαμβάνων / Κλέολαΐν. *Ep. Chron.* 10 (1935): 257, no. 18; side b, ii, trans. Eidinow 2007a: 83–84, no. 1.

[72] αἰ τύχαια μοι ά ἐπι- / τροπεία τὰν ἔχω / γαμῶν Λυκκίδας. Evangelidis 1935: 252, no. 36, trans. Parke 1967: 266, no. 10, cf. Eidinow 2007a: 84, no. 3.

the likelihood of having children from a particular woman, usually named (C1, C2, C3, CR). For example, Heracleidas asks whether he will have a child by Aiglē, his present wife (C4). Other questions ask to which gods to pray for progeny (C1, C5, cf. C11). One asks specifically about male children (C6) and a certain Lysanius asks whether the child Annyla bears is not his (C12). One question may be made by a woman (C8, as indicated by the participle of the verb for consulting) and another in the unpublished material definitely is.[73] In another unpublished question a husband and wife ask what they should do for health and for a male child who will be safe and prosper.[74]

The most frequent form of questions about health is to ask to which gods to sacrifice and pray to either to be released from sickness or to retain health or both (I4, I7). Two are inquiries by women asking to which god to sacrifice and pray for relief from an unnamed disease (I1 and I2); one is named (Nicocrateia, I2). Several are queries on behalf of others. Leontius seeks a cure for his son (I3); a man named Antiochus asks about the health of himself and his father and brother (I6). Amyntas asks about his child's foot (I9). One question (I1) is by a woman. Two (I5 and I8) give no indications of the gender of the consultor; the rest of the questions are by men. There are also queries about specific parts of the body, such as the eyes (I8, I10) and the foot (I9). Eidinow reports that in the unpublished material there are more questions about the eyes, hearing, skin disease, tumors, jaundice, and paralysis, as well as a question about a mental or emotional state.

Many questions about travel are closely related to concerns about work and livelihood. All consultors are male and most are named. Most questions deal with very specific courses of action, starting with choice of livelihood. Several men ask if they will gain profit or good fortune through a specific choice of livelihood: herding (O1), agriculture (O2, O3), working bronze (O4), fishing (O5, in this case specified as a family livelihood), working on the sea (O12, O13), or becoming a shipowner (O10). Only one question is open-ended:

> Gods. Good fortune. Arizelus asks the god by making or doing what thing it will be better and more good for him and he will have a good possession of property. (O14)[75]

Other questions ask how to do better at a trade or craft, or whether to practice it abroad (O6, O7, O8). Some ask about specific tasks or expenditures (O9).

[73] Eidinow 2007a: 92, no. 15 (from the gender of the participle of dedication).

[74] Christidis, trans. Eidinow 2007a: 92, no. 13.

[75] Θεοί. τύχη ἀγαθή. / Ἀρίζηλος ἐπανερωτᾷ τὸν θεὸν / ὅ τι δρῶν ἢ ποιῶν λῷον και ἄμεινον / ἔσται αὐτῷ καὶ χρημάτων κτῆσις ἀγαθὴ ἔσται. Evangelidis 1952: 305, no. 21; *SEG* 15 (1958): 105, no. 405a, trans. Parke 1967: 271, no. 25, cf. Eidinow 2007a: 99, no. 14.

These questions all concern proactive choices, including choice of career itself, which clearly is not determined by birth or family occupation. Here the major perceived risk is profit and general prosperity within an occupation. It is possible that questions about career may also involve a change from one occupation to another.

Most questions about property are demonstrably written by men. For example, a man asks about his, his wife's, and his children's property, and to which god to pray to in order to fare well (P1). One asks whether it will be better for him to return the rope he gave to Aristophantus later or never (P4).

Questions about general good fortune overlap with questions about health and property. At times they specifically seek an improvement, for example a man who asks to which god to pray and sacrifice for his fortunes to improve (F1) or another who asks the predictive question of whether he would do better now and in the future (F2). A more standard question is by a couple. Eubandrus and his wife ask to which gods, heroes, or daimons to pray and sacrifice in order for them and their household to do better both now and for all time (F4). Finally, questions about wellbeing also overlap with safety. For example, one Archephon asks whether there will be safety for him and his ship, built according to Apollo's orders, and whether he will pay back what is needed (F3).

Related questions involve dwellings and construction, for example whether to use a new house or another (CD1), whether to build a workshop (CD2), whether it would be better and more profitable to acquire a house in the city and a piece of land (CD3), or whether it will be a good thing to buy a marsh by the temple of Demeter (CD4).

Two questions concern military activity from the viewpoint of a man going on campaign. The first is a variant of a travel question, asking whether to campaign by land. Here the consultor could be asking whether a land expedition should take place, whether he should join it, or what route to take. The response "Stay on land" on the other side of the tablet suggests the third possibility (MC1). Another question asks whether it is advantageous to set off on campaign against Antiochus (MC2).

Most questions about past events ask about crimes, especially stolen property, and seek confirmation of a suspect's guilt. Stolen objects include: silver, wool, blankets and pillows, clothing, and possibly a horse. Several questions attempt to establish whether a missing object is simply lost or has been stolen. One asks about the silver Dion lost (L1), another whether Thopion stole the silver (L2), whether Doriclus stole the cloth (L5), and in a fourth:

Agis asks Zeus Naios [and Dione] about the covers and pillows he lost, whether someone outside the household stole them. (L3)[76]

Another question (L6) asks about the whereabouts of hidden treasure.

Two questions concern murder, a crime of a different order. One man asks whether someone (a man or a woman) tried to poison his children, his wife, or himself (M1). The other asks whether Timō bewitched/poisoned (*katepharmaxe*) Aristoboula (M2).

Several questions involve slavery, most from unpublished material. Questions by slaves ask about freedom (*peri eleutherias*), either through manumission (*paramonē*) and its obligations or through flight. It is not clear what kinds of slaves were present at Dodona: whether they were public slaves who were locally employed or domestic slaves who had arrived at the sanctuary with their owners.

Some questions are about freedom, for example "Anthropus, about freedom" (S1). One method of obtaining freedom is manumission, and several queries ask about this:

(a slave) asks what he should do about his freedom and whether his master will give him manumission (S5).[77]

Razia asks whether she will attain an agreement from Teitucus while he lives and a place of safety (S2).[78]

For Cittus, whether he will obtain the freedom that Dionysius promised him (S6).[79]

In this case, a third party may be making the inquiry for the slave Cittus. Other questions clearly concern the second alternative, flight, and consultors with this on their minds do not hide it from the oracle:

Leuca, whether she would do better if she remains (S3).[80]

whether, by leaving, there will be something else that is good for me (S7).[81]

[76] Ἐρωτεῖ Ἄγις Δία Νάον [καὶ Διώναν] / ὑπὲρ τῶν στρωμάτων κ[αὶ τῶν προσ-] / κεφαλαίων, τὰ ἀπώκικ[ε . . . . ,] / ἤ τῶν ἔχωθέν τις ἀνέκ[λεψεν]. Carapanos 1878: pl. 36.1, *SGDI* 1586, trans. after Parke 1967: 272, no. 27 and Eidinow 2007a: 117, no. 4.

[77] [- - -]ν ἐπερωτῇ τὸν θεὸν τί κα ποι / [έων] περὶ ἐλευθερίας ἔστι αὐτῶι / [παραμο]νὰ πὰρ τὸν δεσπότα. Christidis, trans. Eidinow 2007a: 102, no. 5.

[78] θεὸς τύχα ἀγαθά / Ραζία ἐπέθετο / αἰ διαλλαγὰ μέλλει / γενέσθαι ἀπο Τει / τύκō ζόοντος / καὶ ἀποχώρησ<ις>. Christidis, trans. after Eidinow 2007a: 102, no. 2.

[79] Κίττωι εἰ ἐστὶ ἡ ἐλεθ / [θ]ερία ἡ παρὰ Διονθσίου / ἥν οὖν ἔθετ' αὐτῶι / Διονύσιος. Christidis, trans. after Eidinow 2007a: 102, no. 6.

[80] Λε / ύκα πότερα με[ί] / [ν]ασα ἢ βέντιον εἴη. Christidis, trans. after Eidinow 2007a: 102, no. 3.

[81] Ἡ απιοῦσα ἄλλ[ο] τι μοι αγαθον / έσσειται / Διοι . . . τ .τκ . Christidis, trans. Eidinow 2007a: 103, no. 7.

(a woman), what will happen to me if I leave? | Shall I make it happen? (S4)[82]

These questions ask an established oracle whether to flee, with the implication that the gods might sanction illegal actions. We do not know what circumstances might have prompted the questions, or whether there were situations in which it was legitimate for a slave to escape in this way. Would divine sanction itself legitimate the escape? We do not know.

There are also questions by masters about their slaves: about a servant (S9), and about the price of a slave (S10). Several involve what appear to be attempts to enslave individuals who had been freed or had been illegally enslaved:

whether I should re-enslave PA . . . (S8)[83]

Scidarcas, whether to proceed quickly with the private legal case of the enslaved captive (S11).[84]

The risks and uncertainties for a slave in obtaining freedom, legally or illegally, were surely as great as any other decision about livelihood. In this sense the slaves' questions are proactive, but their questions, in contrast to those of free consultors, tend to ask whether something will happen or not, not what action of their own will be most advantageous.

The topic of ritual activity pervades most of the questions from Dodona, since so many ask to which gods to pray and sacrifice for a desired result. However, a few are more specific. One asks whether to make the triple sacrifice (RA3); another whether or not to hire the spirit-raiser Dorius (RA2). Another question (RA5) involves something about a body and burial. Finally, one seems to involve improper treatment of an oracular response. A certain Socrates asks about the response of the god and the omens, which one Aristolaus did not seal and did not set down (RA4).

There are two inquiries about judicial activity. One, a request for victory in a court case (J1), specifically mentions victory, a topic that is rare in the published questions. A second question:

Sosandrus asks about the curse of Ale . . . whether I would do well if I went to court (J2).[85]

82 Side A: ἦ ἰFῶν τυνχάνω. Side B: ἁ γυνὰ / μένε. (The woman remains. Or: Oh woman remain!) Christidis, trans. Eidinow 2007a: 102, no. 4.

83 Ἔ ἀμδό̄λό̄ / μα μὲ̄ ἄγσō / ΠΑ [- - -]. Christidis, trans. Eidinow 2007a: 103, no. 8.

84 Τοῦ ἀωδραπόδου {ου} τὰν δίκαν δικα / ξοῦμαι Σκιδάρκας ὦκα τού[τ]αν. Christidis, trans. after Eidinow 2007a: 103, no. 11.

85 Ἐπικοινῆται Σώσανδρος [πὲρ] / τᾶς ἐπαράσιος τᾶς Ἀλε [max 4] / ἦ τυγχάνοι "μι" κα δικαζομ[ενος]. *Ep. Chron.* 10 (1935): 259.32, trans. Eidinow 2007a: 114–15, no. 2.

This suggests that the decision to launch legal action was also viewed as a matter of divine guidance.

Finally two questions seem to be requests for truth. One (RT1) refers to "we know the truth" (RT1), the other refers to believing something true (RT2).

The Shuihudi daybooks

The daybooks from Shuihudi do not have a set form, but they give substantial information about the concerns of their presumptive users. Parts of the daybooks consist of calendric tables (introduced in Chapter 5). The calendric sections combine different types of information. A few examples from the section titled "Stars and Constellations" (*Xing*) illustrate this variety ("Stars and Constellations" refers to the Twenty-eight Lunar Lodges, discussed in detail in Chapter 5):

75 斗，利祠及行賈、賈市，吉。取妻，妻為巫。生子，不盈三歲死。可以攻伐。

Dipper: beneficial for sacrifice, also for business travel, markets: auspicious. For marriage, the wife will become a *wu*. Children: within three years they will die. Invasions are permitted.

94 翼，利行。不可藏。以祠，必有火起。取妻，必棄。生子，男為覡，女為巫。

Wings: beneficial for travel, storing away is not permitted. For sacrifice, the fire will flare up. Marriage: she is sure to be abandoned. Children: a boy will become a *xi* [spirit medium], a girl will become a *wu*.[86]

Other sections give additional information about particular activities, including marriage, children, making clothes, building projects, travel, and illness. The names of these activities appear at the top of the bamboo slip or in the upper margin of the transcriptions, and they provide a comparandum for the Dodona categories.

Both types of entry show the possibilities for different day types and mention different kinds of activity. As the above examples show, a wide variety of activities were considered appropriate for daybook

[86] *SHD* (Daybooks), slips 75 and 94; trans. after Poo 2009, cf. Liu Lexian 1994: 109–16. For additional examples from the section see Appendix F.

prognostication, including leisure pastimes such as eating and drinking and singing.

The daybooks present many difficulties, and a full consideration is beyond the scope of the present discussion. The texts are often difficult to understand, and all translations are provisional. In addition, they are not internally consistent, and probably represent an amalgam of different systems.[87] Here I briefly consider examples within several categories that suggest comparison to the concerns of the Dodona tablets: (1) Travel (*xing* 行, 歸行 *gui xing*), (2) Marriage (*qu qi* 娶妻), (3) Children (*sheng zi* 生子), (4) Illness (*bing* 病), (5) Occupation (*zuo shi* 作事), Official Position (*li* 吏), Entering Office (*ru guan* 入官), Audiences (*jian ren* 見人), (6) Construction and Gates (*men* 門), (7) Ritual Activity (*li* 禮), (8) Fighting (*bing* 兵), Thieves (*dao* 盜), (9) Desertion (*wang* 亡), and (10) Other Categories. The most extensive discussion is given to the first four.

Travel receives extensive treatment in the daybooks, which indicate auspicious days for commencing travel and for returning home. Daybook A lists days which are inauspicious for travel, feasting and singing, acquiring domestic animals, or the cohabitation of husband and wife:

凡是日赤帝恒以開臨下民而降其殃，不可具為百事，皆無所利。即有為也，其殃不出歲中，小大必至。有為而遇雨，命曰殃早至，不出三月，必有死亡之志至。凡是有為也，必先計月中閒日，苟無直赤帝臨日，它日雖有不吉之名，無所大害。

On these days the Red Emperor is in descent and brings disasters to the people. You must not do any of these things, since nothing will be beneficial. If you do, there will be disaster within the year; whether large or small it will surely arrive. If you act and you meet with rain, this is named "disaster comes early." Within three months there is certain to be news of death and doom. If you are going to do something you must first calculate the leisure days of that month. So long as it is not the day when the Red Emperor is in descent, all the other days will not produce great harm, even if they have inauspicious names.[88]

The passage then turns specifically to travel:

87 Mu-chou Poo (1998: 69–101) presents a particularly useful discussion of how the daybooks reflect concerns of ordinary life and personal welfare. I am indebted to him for access to unpublished translations and ongoing discussion of the daybooks. For additional information on the context of the daybook see Pu Muzhou [Poo Mu-chou] 1992.

88 *SHD* (Daybooks), slips 127–29, trans. after Poo 2009, cf. Liu Lexian 1994: 153–56. For example, a *wu* day in the first decad [10-day period] of month 1, a *hai* day in month 2, etc.

凡民將行，出其門，無敢顧，毋止。直術吉，從道右吉，從左吝。小顧是謂小楮，吝；大顧是謂大楮，凶。

Whenever you are about to travel, as you go out of the gate, do not dare look back, do not stop. To keep to the middle of the road or to the right is auspicious; the left is somewhat inauspicious. If you look back a little it is called a small stop, it is somewhat inauspicious. If you look back for long it is called a long stop, it is truly inauspicious.[89]

Daybook A also has a named section for returning home from a journey.

歸行：凡春三月己丑不可東，夏三月戊辰不可南，秋三月己未不可西，冬三月戊戌不可北。百中大凶，二百里外必死。

Returning Home: In all cases in the third month of spring on a *ji* or a *chou* day you cannot go east. In the third month of summer on a *wu* or a *chen* day you cannot go south. In the third month of autumn on a *ji* or a *wei* day you cannot go west. In the third month of winter on a *wu* or a *xu* day you cannot go north. [Travel] within a hundred [*li*] is severely inauspicious. Travel beyond two hundred *li* is fatal.[90]

The passage continues with day types that are prohibited for travel in particular directions: southeast on a *xin* or a *ren* day, southwest on a *gui* or a *jia* day, northwest on a *yi* or a *bing* day, and northeast on a *ding* or a *geng* day. Finally, it gives prohibited days for arrival: for the first three months, these are days seven, fourteen, and twenty-one. Each quarter the pattern of doubling and trebling continues, adding a day. In the second quarter of the year the prohibited arrival days are days eight, sixteen, and twenty-four; in the third quarter days nine, eighteen, and twenty-seven; and finally in the fourth quarter days ten, twenty, and thirty. The section ends: "for all these days, if you return home, there will be death, if you travel, destruction."[91] The initial table for Daybook A also specifies that "outside harm" (*wai hai* 外害) days are bad for travel. Traveling to the countryside at these times is sure to result in encountering thieves or fighting (both discussed below).[92]

The dangers outlined in these travel warnings would present a truly complicated set of heuristics for any traveler attempting to implement all these recommendations.

Both the daybooks and the received tradition attest that prognostication was used to determine an auspicious day for marriage (rather than to determine *who* to marry). An analogous query from the received tradition

89 *SHD* (Daybooks): slips 129–30, trans. after Poo 2009.

90 *SHD* (Daybooks): slip 131, trans. after Poo 2009, cf. Liu Lexian 1994: 157–61.

91 凡此日以歸，死；行，亡。*SHD* (Daybooks), slips 132–33.

92 *SHD* (Daybooks): slip 9.

is attributed to Han Wudi.[93] The two sections on marriage begin by specifying seasonal days that were good or bad for marriage, described from the viewpoint of a prospective husband taking a wife or a father giving a daughter in marriage. They take up particular aspects of marriage to be desired or avoided by a prospective husband (and his family), a prospective wife (and hers), or both. These include: death in childbirth, abandonment, no home or a depleted dwelling, childlessness, child mortality or lack of sons, and calamities for the parents. (See Appendix F for examples.) Additional information comes from the calendric tables for the Lunar Lodges. Not all mention marriage, but most astral influences are negative. If a marriage occurs under the influence of the wrong Lunar Lodge, the wife will be jealous (Horn), poor (Root), ferocious (Heart), talkative (Basket), a *wu* (Dipper), not present (Void), restless (Encampment), or abandoned (Wings). Not many Lodges bode well for marriage. Of the twenty-eight, only six are specified as auspicious (Room, Servant Girl, Three Stars, Willow, Extended Net, and Chariot Platform). In addition, East Wall specifies many children, and three Lodges bode a loving relationship (under Legs and Stomach the woman will be loved; under Bond, the man).

All these difficulties bespeak the uncertainty of a wife's temperament or a husband's loyalty, in a society of arranged marriage, where the betrothed couple never meet and surviving children are the priority for both families. In the daybooks, these considerations seem more important than a wife's dowry or beauty. The Lodge prognostications also attest to the value placed on love between husband and wife.

The Shuihudi daybooks deal extensively with the predictions for children's futures in several ways. The marriage predictions are followed by predictions about children. The two are not linked, and in several cases a positive prediction about children follows a negative prediction about marriage. For example, the lodge Root specifies a wife who is poor, but children who are skilled (artisans).

A separate section titled "Bearing Children" gives extensive additional information. First there is a prognostication for each stem–branch combination. For example, a child born on the day *dinghai* will be a skillful artisan and filial. A child born on the day *bingzi* will be inauspicious. (See Appendix F.) The child's fortune is further determined by locating the branch sign of the child's birth in two diagrams for fall and winter or spring and summer (Figure 6.2).

93 See *SJ* 127, discussed in Chapter 4. For Han Wudi see Chapter 7 and Loewe 1994: 221.

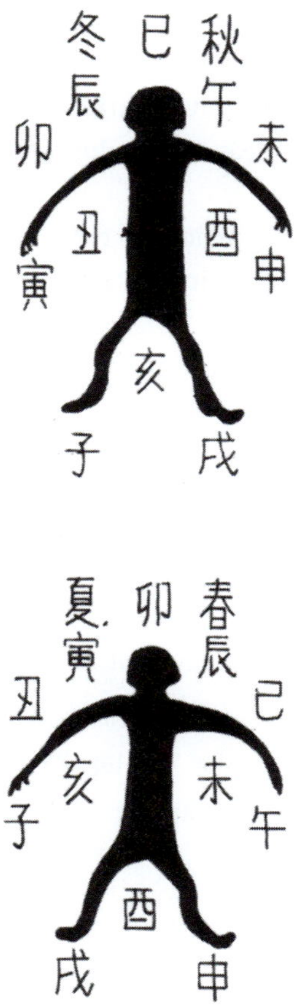

Figure 6.2 The birth prognostication diagram from Shuihudi.

The child will be extremely wealthy if the natal branch sign appears at the head (*si* for fall or winter, *mao* for spring or summer), but noble if it appears by the neck (*wu* or *chen* for fall and winter, *si* or *chou* for spring and summer). If the character is in the figure's crotch, the child will be wealthy; under the arms, loved; in the hands, a skillful thief; under the feet, humble; on the "outside" (above the arms), a vagabond.[94] The skillful and filial *dinghai* child will turn out well in any season: wealthy if born in the fall or winter and loved if born in spring or summer. The inauspicious *bingzi* child will be equally unlucky: humble if born in fall or winter and a thief if born in spring or summer.

[94] *SHD* (Daybooks): slips 140–54.

The childbirth predictions, like predictions about illness, suggest no method of altering the child's future beyond the choice of the time of marriage. Nor, aside from the possibility of infanticide in a particularly bad configuration, do they offer any formula for improving the fortunes of a child.

The "Illness" section of the daybook correlates particular types of illnesses with the Ten Heaven Stems in pairs, as well as invasive source, foods, direction, and the (facial) color that bodes death. The sequence begins:

甲乙有疾，父母為祟，得之於肉，從東方來，裹以桼（漆）器。戊己病，庚有閒，辛酢。若不酢，煩居東方，歲在東方，青色死。

If there is illness on a *jia* or *yi* [stems 1–2] day, [the ghosts of] parents are the calamity; it is obtained from meat, from the east, placed in a lacquer container. It will manifest on a *wu* or *ji* day, with respite on a *geng* day and recovery on a *xin* day. If there is no recovery, Fever will be in the east, Year will be in the east, and the color azure means death.[95]

Daybook B contains a section on prognostication by the Twelve Earth Branches, which includes prognostications on illness; for example:

子以東吉，北得，西聞言兇（凶），... 以有疾，〈辰〉少翏（瘳），午大翏（瘳），死生在申，黑肉從北方來，把者黑色，外鬼父葉（世）為姓（眚），高王父譴適（謫）。

On a *zi* day [branch 1], east is auspicious, north is successful, hearing words is in the west, south is inauspicious . . . if there is illness, there will be respite on a *chen* day [branch 5], recovery on a *wu* day [branch 7], and death on a *shen* day [branch 9]. Black meat comes from the east; the bearer is black. External demons and great-grandfather are the calamity.[96]

The rest of the sequence (discussed further in Chapter 9) correlates the manifestation of illness, respite, recovery, and death signs for all Twelve Earth Branches. In addition to telling us that illness was perceived as a source of danger and uncertainty, these tables indicate that it was associated with invasive activities by the ghosts of ancestors, demons, the premature dead, and the magical activities of *wu*. It was also associated with food, especially meat and fish, foods that are subject to spoilage or parasites. In

[95] *SHD* (Daybooks): slips 68–69r, trans. after Poo 2009, cf. Liu Lexian 1994: 116–22. Transcription follows *SHD* and Liu Lexian 1994.

[96] *SHD* (Daybooks): slip 158, trans. after Poo 2009, cf. Liu Lexian 1994: 368.

these tables, nothing can be done about the day of onset of an illness, but they outline its normal course and prospects.

Other sections of the daybooks indicate what days to use and avoid for matters of business, success in government office, entering office, and seeking an audience. For example:

陰日，利以家室。祭祀、嫁子、娶婦、入材，大吉。以見君上，數達，無咎。

Yin-day: beneficial for the family. Ancestral sacrifice, giving a daughter in marriage, taking a wife, receiving goods: very auspicious. For seeking audience with a superior, often it will be successful, there will be no blame.[97]

Other sections link the construction of the parts of a house to the fortunes of its occupants. A house's orientation, size, and relation to other structures also affected its owner's fortunes. For example, on an inauspicious day for building houses:

築大內，大人死。 筑(築)右，長子婦死。 築左，中子婦死。 築外垣，孫子死。築北垣，牛羊死。

If you build the great inner [chamber] the parents will die; if you build the right, the oldest son's wife will die; if you build the left, the middle son's wife will die; if you build the outside wall, the grandson's son will die; if you build the north wall, cattle and sheep will die.[98]

Fighting appears at several points in the daybooks. The *jichen* calendric section gives days on which there will or will not be war. Other sections on warfare seem to be written from the viewpoint of lower-rank officers. They specify days that are beneficial for fighting in the fields and for sacking cities in aggressive warfare.[99]

The section on robbers describes the kind of thief that is likely to manifest on a particular day type: the animal he resembles, his height, facial features, possible name, and where he is likely to be in hiding. It is not clear whether this information referred to a past theft for purposes of catching the thief, or to guard against robbery on a particular day type:

未，馬也。盜者長鬚耳，為人我我然好歌舞，疵在肩，藏於芻中，阪險，必得。名建章丑吉。

97 *SHD* (Daybooks): slip 6, trans. after Poo 2009.
98 *SHD* (Daybooks): slip 101r and v, trans. after Poo 1998: 74 and 2009.
99 *SHD* (Daybooks): slips 32, 40, and 44.

Wei is the horse. The thief has a long beard and long ears. He is effeminate and loves to sing and dance. He has a scar on his shoulder and he hides in fodder. On a wild slope, he is sure to be taken. His name is Jian, Zhang, Chou, or Ji.[100]

Other entries specify that the thief can be taken (or not) early in the morning or after dusk.

Desertion is not an explicit category in Daybook A but it occurs in several of the calendric tables. The beneficiary of these entries is probably a military, village, or family head charged with the capture of absconders, rather than a soldier, servant, or concubine contemplating flight.[101] For example:

8 外陽日，利以建野外，可以田獵。以亡，不得，□門。

Waiyang-day: Beneficial for going out to the fields, hunting is permissible. If there is a desertion, they will not be caught, [] the gate.

15 除日，臣妾亡，不得。

Chu day: if a servant or concubine runs away (s)he will not be caught.

36 危陽 . . . 亡人，自歸。有疾，不死。

Wei day: . . . If there is a desertion, he will return of himself. If there is illness it will not be fatal.

40 . . . 亡者，得。利弋獵、報讎、攻軍、圍城、始殺。

A deserter will be caught; beneficial for hunting birds with bow and arrow, revenging feuds, military attack, surrounding walled cities, initiating slaughter.[102]

Daybook B has an explicit topic on desertion (*wang ri* 亡日), including days for desertion, and a section on deserters (*wang zhe* 亡者) also gives a list of days and ends with the statement that:

凡是往亡必得，不得必死。

On all these days deserters will surely be caught; if they are not caught, they will surely die.[103]

In summary, flight from military service, slavery, or concubinage was clearly a preoccupation addressed in the daybooks. It is not entirely clear whose

[100] *SHD* (Daybooks): slip 76v, trans. after Poo 2009. "Effeminate" (我我): Liu Lexian 1994: 272 n. 14.

[101] Marc Kalinowski (personal communication), cf. Li Xueqin 1985b.

[102] *SHD* (Daybooks): slips 8, 15, 36, 40, trans. after Poo 2009.

[103] *SHD* (Daybook B): slips 149–52, trans. after Poo 2009.

viewpoint is represented, but the daybooks probably reflect the perspective of officials, rather than those contemplating flight.

References in the "Stars and Constellations" section to days for sacrifice confirm that ritual activity was an ongoing concern in the daybooks. Days are specified as auspicious (or not) for capping ceremonies and also for making clothes, possibly connected with ritual activity. The emphasis on the roles of ancestors in causing illness also suggests interest in apotropaic prayer and sacrifice.

In addition, a named section titled "Inquiry" or "Interrogation" (*Jie* 詰) gives instructions for handling ghosts, demons, and gods; and offers methods for identifying and expelling invasive entities.[104]

The daybook sections on dreams correlate auspicious dreams of different colors on specified days (in the stem–branch cycle) with the Five Agents:

甲乙夢被黑裘衣寇〈冠〉，喜，人〈入〉水中及谷，得也。

On a *jia* or *yi* day, dreaming of a black fur coat, robe, and cap is fortunate; entering water and reaching the valley produces results.

丙丁夢被 □，喜也，木金得也。

On a *bing* or *ding* day, dreaming of [] is fortunate; powers are wood and metal.

戊己夢黑，吉，得喜也。

On a *wu* or *ji* day, dreaming of black is auspicious; the results are fortunate.

庚辛夢青黑，喜也，木水得也。

On a *geng* or *xin* day, dreaming of azure or black is fortunate; powers are wood and water.[105]

In summary, the daybooks suggest multiple viewpoints on which activities were considered risky or desirable. Most advice is on avoiding adverse situations, primarily by avoiding an activity on days prohibited or inauspicious for it. This approach was especially directed at activities that can be planned and scheduled: travel, marriage, ritual, leisure activities, entertainment, even initiating military action or slaughtering farm animals. Other situations, childbirth and illness especially, are not subject to human scheduling, but even here, the information could be used for diagnosis and prognosis or for planning for a child's future.

104 For translation and discussion see Harper 1985.

105 *SHD* (Daybooks): slips 189–93, trans. after Poo 2009.

As Mu-chou Poo observes, the content of the daybooks also suggests that they were used by both men and women (or their families), since the predictions reflected the interests and expectations of both. Some clearly reflected the interest of only one party, for example the wealth and character of a prospective wife. Others addressed the interests of both, for example the number of births and surviving children, their prospects, or the abiding love of a spouse. The daybooks clearly reflect the interests of private individuals, acting outside court and ritual contexts, rather than the behavior of rulers. It is not clear who used the daybooks. Some prognostications seem to reflect the interests and concerns of those outside of the elites. However, a recent survey of the contents of tombs from the state of Chu (the state having the largest number of excavations) suggests that daybooks and other bamboo texts were primarily buried in the tombs of officials of the highest rank, rather than in tombs of the lower-level *shi* 士 rank with which they have been associated.[106]

Questions and risks compared

We are now in a position to compare Chinese and Greek mantic queries and perceptions of risk. Both Chinese and Greek consultors, official and private, sought predictions, advice on contemplated actions, and theological and cosmological guidance. Within each cultural context, questions considered appropriate or useful for mantic guidance changed over time. Chinese and Greek consultors also differed in the topics and kinds of advice they sought.

In some cases, Chinese and Greek consultors are interested in different topics. Chinese requests for predictions on weather, harvests, and rainfall have no immediate Greek equivalent. They might seem to resemble Greek *lusis* queries, but do not, since *lusis* questions do not request predictions. Chinese official questions on illness, anomalies, and dreams have little Greek equivalent, especially in the narrow sample. (Most queries on anomalies from Delphi come from the broad sample.) Finally, Chinese queries on auspicious times for the performance of state rituals have no Greek equivalent.

Similarly, Greek *lusis* queries have no exact Chinese equivalent, although their concerns overlap Chinese questions on auspicious days, illness, anomalies, and ritual. There is greater overlap in political requests for

[106] Poo 1998: 74, Falkenhausen 2003.

confirmation of planned ventures, including warfare, alliances, choice of personnel, and the resolution of disagreements.

Official consultors

Both Chinese and Greek official consultors sought mantic advice about alliances, truces, or tribute. Both posed questions about military action, especially the decision to go to war. Both sought advice on law and administration, including the selection of personnel (including royal succession) and in general major plans and policies and planned ventures. Both sought to prevent plague and famine, and to explain eclipses and other visible natural anomalies. Finally, both posed questions about religious cult, including what sacrifices to make and to whom.

It is immediately striking that many of these questions, especially the Greek ones, did not seek predictions. Questions about wellbeing and choices of action ask, not what *will* happen, but rather what will be advantageous; such questions are slippery when it comes to verification. *Lusis* questions are more easily verifiable; the "evil" either does or does not improve after the recommended steps are taken. In China (and Mesopotamia) some of the *methods* used to answer these questions were predictive, especially techniques that involved astronomical prediction. Most Greek methods were not.

Chinese questions pervasively map good and ill auspice onto calendric and cosmic cycles. Negatively they attempt to predict (or ensure that there would be no) disasters within a fixed period. (This formulation appears in the oracle bone inscriptions but is not an explicit topic in the *Zhou li* or *Shi ji*.) Positively, they seek to determine auspicious times for particular events. And, as has been discussed in Chapter 5, they use complex methods to do so, for example milfoil and *Liuren* divination.

Personal queries

At first glance, many areas of perceived risk seem to be common to Chinese and Greek consultors. But within each apparently similar category there were important differences in perception of what the risk or danger was. There are also differences inherent in the different contexts of consultation. The queries at Dodona frequently specify individual persons, places, and circumstances. While the user of a calendric text may have had a specific journey, wife, or business in mind, the daybook recommendations are generic in form. The presupposition of the daybooks, that certain days of the calendric cycle are inherently auspicious or inauspicious for particular activities, has no Greek equivalent.

Greek questions about travel tend to ask whether it is profitable, either for livelihood or whether migration is in an individual or family's interest. Questions about changes of residence are specific, and many name particular destinations. These questions reflect a society on the move, in which trade, pilgrimage, and migration are commonplace. Some questions bespeak concerns about how to make a journey; others are linked to other concerns about marriage and future prosperity. Travel is also extensively treated in the daybooks, but it is differently categorized. Although some childbirth predictions state that a son or a daughter will leave the country (a bad thing), recommendations for travel distinguish embarkation from return and local from distant travel. Migration is not a theme. The positive concern is to travel on an auspicious day in an auspicious direction, expressed in terms of *wuxing* correlates. The negative concern is to avoid travel's many dangers, such as encountering fighting or thieves. These entries reflect a late Warring States milieu in which both thieves and local governments were potential sources of violence and danger.

It is no surprise that both Chinese and Greek consultors would want to make the right marriage and bear children who would survive and prosper. Yet again, their questions differ in kind. Men ask most of the questions: either potential husbands or fathers contemplating their daughters' marriages. As with travel, Greek questions about marriage are often quite specific: will marriage to so-and-so bring good fortune, children, profit? Is it better to give my daughter to this man or that? The question of whom to choose as a wife or son-in-law is categorized in the daybooks in two ways. The first way concerns (usually) negative traits in a prospective wife. While a few address wealth, most of the questions concern her temperament. Will she be talkative, restless, ferocious, jealous? In positive terms, the daybooks also try to identify prospects for a loving relationship. Some entries specify that the wife will love the husband, the husband the wife, or that the children will be loved by others. This concern with the day-to-day fabric of married life does not appear in the Greek questions.

Both Chinese and Greek questions on marriage seek many children, and sons, but several of the Chinese questions concern the welfare of the prospective wife. Will she die in childbirth? Will she be abandoned? These questions have no equivalent in the inquiries from Dodona. The marriage section of the daybooks specifies both taking a wife and giving a daughter in marriage as topics. Despite the conventional Chinese view that after marriage a daughter leaves her natal family and joins the family of her husband, the daybooks show a consistent concern for the welfare of daughters after marriage.

The overwhelming concern of questions about children in the Dodona tablets is how to beget them. Almost all questions are asked by men. (By contrast, there are questions by women seeking children at temples of Asclepius.) The questions take several forms. How can I have children by so-and-so? Will so-and-so bear children? To which god shall I sacrifice for children? In some cases the consultor specifically seeks sons; one tablet questions the legitimacy of an unborn child.

The focus of the daybooks is less on how to have children than on the prospects for children born on particular days. Unlike many other entries, the information on children is extensive and systematic, including two diagrams and an entry for all sixty of the stem–branch combinations. These entries bespeak both risks and advantages, often from the viewpoint of the parents. The daybooks seem to class child mortality under the heading of marriage, so the entries for children all concern children who survive to adulthood. In addition to days that are simply inauspicious, risks to a family include children leaving their parents' home region, that they will be poor, sickly, orphaned young (in other words, that the parents will die), or that a son will grow up into a drunkard, womanizer, that he will end up in prison, become a servant, or wear filthy clothes.[107] Desirable prospects for children include temperament, prosperity, happiness, wealth, martiality, strength, bravery, filiality, goodness, sagacity, success, honor or fame, skill, and career or occupation. Also important are physical beauty or that the child be loved. Some predict the career of a son (as a scribe) or a daughter (as a merchant or physician).[108] It is noteworthy that while the undesirable futures for children also affect their families, several of the desirable predictions seem to concern the child's personal welfare. The single largest number of entries is for happiness. By contrast, the treatment of progeny in the Dodona tablets only reflects the welfare of the parents.

Illness is not a major topic of questions at Dodona, or of the personal queries extant at Delphi. Several questions mention relief from a particular malady, but the main focus of the questions is ritual: to which god to

[107] See the childbirth prognostications in Appendix F. Leaving home: days 5, 6, 15; poverty: days 16, 37; illness: days 16, 22, 40; death of parents: days 21, 22, 27, 34, 51; drunkenness: days 24, 33; womanizer: day 7; imprisonment: day 34; servitude: day 56; filthy clothes: day 51.

[108] Happiness: days 2, 9, 12, 18, 20, 26, 31, 36; wealth: days 2, 8, 22, 33; martiality: days 9, 19, 37, 53; strength: days 21, 57; bravery: days 39, 43; filiality: days 14, 23, 31, 49; goodness: day 47; sagacity: day 53; success: day 10; honor or fame: days 17, 59; skill: days 11, 14; occupation: days 11, 13, 36; physical beauty: day 44; being loved: day 55; scribe: days 40, 41; daughter a merchant; day 17; a physician: day 29.

sacrifice for relief. By contrast the daybooks offer extensive and systematic treatments of illness, based on *wuxing* correlations to color and direction. Their emphasis is diagnostic, linking illnesses to three factors: day of onset, ancestral or demonic influences, and food. They also offer prognoses for respite, recovery and, in the case of a fatal illness, signs of impending death.

Occupation, livelihood, and business are areas of concern in both the Dodona tablets and the daybooks, but the concerns are framed very differently. Both seek to optimize business ventures but in different ways. The Greek questions seek improved prosperity through choice of occupation, change of location, and business ventures, including loans of money and leases of property. They clearly presume free choice of occupation and freedom of movement. Questions of construction are also framed in terms of profit. Should one build a new house, a workshop, or acquire land or a house in the city?

The daybook entries focus on different aspects of welfare. Change of career seems not to be an option; Greek questions on whether to take up a particular livelihood have no Chinese equivalent. The daybooks focus on the correct timing of business travel, commerce, and markets, and specific occupational activities such as slaughtering farm animals. Several of their concerns involve government office and relations with superiors. Seeking an audience is a specific topic in the daybooks that has no Greek equivalent. Questions about leisure and entertainment in the daybooks also have no equivalent in the Dodona tablets or queries to Delphi. The idea that even leisure and pleasure can be managed in such a way as to avoid disaster or ill auspice seems to have no Greek equivalent.

Construction is an important topic in the daybooks, but its focus is not on profitability. Rather the concern is that a building be correctly oriented and built on an auspicious day in order to ensure the prosperity, or even survival, of its occupants.

Both the Dodona tablets and the daybooks indicate concerns about military activity and crime, but the concerns are very different. The two individual questions about military activity from Dodona ask whether to participate in a military campaign and what means to use. The first question – should I join such-and-such a campaign? – is also the question Socrates instructed Xenophon to ask at Delphi. These questions are from the viewpoint of an individual contemplating military activity as a career choice. Some daybook entries also reflect what are clearly concerns of military personnel – whether a given day is good for initiating military activity and what kind: sacking a walled city, fighting in the countryside, initiating a military offensive. Other responses about warfare are from the viewpoint of a traveler who is concerned to avoid battle areas on his route, for example entries in the calendric sections on whether there will be war on a certain day.

Crime is a concern in both the Dodona tablets and the daybooks, but in very different ways. In the Dodona tablets questions about lost or stolen objects seek the cause of past events. Who stole the silver? Who stole the pillows? Although two consultors ask about murder, most address non-violent thefts of household items, presumably to recover them or to establish guilt. There are broad questions about safety (*sōtēria*) and security (*asphaleia*), but they are not concerned with immediate danger or violence. By contrast, Chinese questions about thieves are future-oriented. Their problem is to avoid thieves or possibly to capture them. These entries seem particularly mechanical in nature. Each correlates that day's thief type with an animal and describes his height, facial hair, scars, deportment, and hiding place. A traveler could use this information to protect himself from theft or violence. Information on the thief's name and when he can be caught seems intended for the pursuer of thieves, rather than their potential victims. The Dodona tablets do not address theft from a judicial viewpoint, but two tablets do concern judicial activity from the perspective of potential litigants.

Both the Dodona tablets and the daybooks include questions about flight from slavery or servitude. These are of particular interest for several reasons. First, insofar as they reflect the interest of the slave or servant, they suggest that mantic access was available in some form even to slaves, servants, and concubines, whose mobility was presumably highly restricted. Some responses do reflect the viewpoint of the runaway. Several of the Dodona tablets (mostly from unpublished Christidis material) are queries about freedom or manumission, presumably by slaves. Some questions address legal freedom through manumission, but others clearly concern flight. As Eidinow points out, the queries by slaves seeking divine sanction for flight raise questions about the legitimacy of slavery, as do questions about possibly illegal enslavement. The Shuihudi daybook sections on desertion probably reflect the viewpoint of officials or family heads charged with the management of conscripts, servants, or concubines, since they repeatedly address prospects for their return or capture. They indicate no institutional way of buying or otherwise obtaining freedom.

A few other areas of difference are noteworthy. Dreams receive extensive treatment in the daybooks, but are not consistent topics in extant oracular inquiries. When Xenophon reports troubling dreams he does not take them to a *mantis*. Dreams are central to the operations of Asclepian temples and appear in the magical papyri, but not as a risk or concern to be consistently addressed by divination.

Several types of question about past events from Dodona and Delphi have no clear equivalent in the daybooks. The daybooks focus on prediction, and do not address gnomic questions or questions about truth. Finally, both the Dodona tablets and the daybooks suggest that mantic guidance was necessary and possible to mitigate the perceived risks of daily life and important decisions. Do the gods take care of us? But this question needs to be nuanced: what gods and what kind of care?

Xenophon raises this question at the beginning of the *Memorabilia*. He has a rhetorical aim: to refute the charge of impiety leveled against Socrates. Divination is also an issue in the *Apology*, but it is differently handled. Socrates repeatedly reaffirms his belief in the predictive guidance of his divine guide or *daimonion*, and an important argument for Socrates' piety is his regard for divination.[109] Xenophon's claim, both about Socrates and about divination, is that the gods use signs to give guidance to mortals. In clear cases, Xenophon's Socrates advises his friends to make their own decisions, but where the outcome was unclear he sent them to seek mantic counsel (1.1.7). Socrates argues that this guidance was necessary. Technical mastery is sufficient for the management of a household or polis, but the gods reserve the deepest secrets for themselves. One may know how to plant a field but not who will harvest it; we can know how to build a good house but not who will live in it. A general may know how to lead troops, or a master of statecraft how to lead the state, but neither can know whether it will benefit him to use his art. Marrying a pretty wife may bring sorrow; securing influential connections may lead to exile (1.1.7–8).

Similarly Plutarch remarks that, in his own time, questions to the oracle were limited to everyday concerns: people ask if they will gain victory, if they will marry, or whether it is profitable for them to lend money, to sail, to farm, or to travel.[110] In all these cases, the consultor has taken his abilities and judgment as far as they will go. There is also an awareness that good fortune may turn to its reverse. These are all activities that offer both opportunities and dangers. Xenophon remarks that divination was used extensively for decisions about warfare because it was so unpredictable and dangerous.[111] He adds:

[109] This issue is discussed in Chapter 9. [110] Plut. *Pyth. orac.* 26.408c, cf. *E apud Delph.* 386c.

[111] Xen. *Hipparch.* 9.8–9. Xenophon also relates that divinatory sacrifice was used at every stage of military campaigns (*Lac.* 13). The many examples in the *Anabasis* include 2.2, 4.3.9, 4.3.19, 5.4.2, 5.5.3, 5.6.17, and 6.5.8. See Parker 2000a: 87–88 and Chapter 4 n. 66.

what the gods have granted us to do by help of learning we must learn; what is hidden from mortals we should try to find out from the gods by divination for to him that is in their grace the gods grant a sign.[112]

In these passages we see the view that the gods are interested in human affairs at some level. Both the Dodona tablets and queries from Delphi support this view of divination. Many questions ask to which god to sacrifice and pray in order to obtain some desired result. We see a picture that could be described as a very finely tuned version of *do ut des* ("I give that you may give"): the creation of networks of reciprocity through sacrifice.

The situation is more complex in the case of the daybooks. Various scholars have attributed "*do ut des*" attitudes to the Eastern Zhou and Warring States, and even to the Han. Although most of the hegemonic texts of Chinese philosophy keep a respectful distance from ghosts and spirits, this distance contrasts with the attitude of the daybooks. They attribute illness to the influence of ancestors and spirits and give detailed instructions for their exorcism and management. As Mu-chou Poo points out in his landmark study of early Chinese religion, the daybooks present a double view of the cosmos. On the one hand, it operates through predictable cycles of time; on the other, it is full of extra-human powers, including ancestors, ghosts, and demons.[113] Thus risk enters human life both through human decisions, which are readily subject to analysis and prediction, and through the operations of extra-human powers. In both cases, the daybooks seek to mitigate risk by a system of correlations between particular actions and auspicious times. But there is no interaction with the cosmic powers that control good and ill auspice; in this sense the system is mechanical and amoral.

Finally, the Shuihudi daybooks and the Dodona lead tablets are useful "comparables" because each presents a taxonomy of risks that spoke to the needs of ordinary people. Here too it must be remembered that the contexts of consultation were very different. The daybooks are generic, mechanical, and mostly address things to avoid. The Dodona tablets purport to be individual, divine responses to individual queries. Nonetheless, these two corpora tell us something about how their consultors perceived risk in everyday life. In both cases, inquiries were not open-ended; consultors sought advice in choosing between alternatives. Many of the questions to Dodona ask "will I fare better?" (*lōion prattein*) or whether a choice will be "better and more good" (*lōion kai ameinon*). Many of the daybook responses are that a choice is auspicious (*ji* 吉). Questions of this kind

[112] Xen. *Mem.* 1.1.9, trans. Marchant.

[113] Eastern Zhou: Poo 1998: esp. 61–62 and 79–88; Han: Nylan 2001b: 86.

seek to optimize alternatives; they do not seek certainty or prediction. If we limit ourselves to these questions, we may be tempted to agree with functionalist theories of divination that stress its roles in social equilibrium and individual reassurance.

What does comparative study tell us about the questions that are referred to mantic inquiry? For all their limitations, Greek oracle collections provide a means to examine how prognostication was used over a broad range of time and of consultors; Delphi effectively channeled a large number of mantic queries to one location. Evidence about non-oracular divination is more limited.

Do common Chinese and Greek consultation topics suggest features of divination as a cross-cultural phenomenon? The Greek questions are universally addressed to gods: especially Zeus, Apollo, and Asclepius. Some Chinese questions, such as the queries excavated from Baoshan and Wangshan, include responses that name particular gods and detailed instructions for sacrifices to them. But daybooks and astrocalendric texts present a different, more mechanical, and arguably more naturalistic picture. In systems such as *Liuren*, different gods are in charge of different segments of the sexagenary cycle, but the mantic procedures do not attempt to intercede with them. Rather the point is to map good and ill auspice onto cycles of time and schematic representations of space. It could be claimed that Chinese mantic practices evolved in ways that, at least according to the available evidence, Greek practices did not. (The situation might have been very different had Babylonian astrology and horoscopy made earlier entrances into Greece. This issue is discussed briefly in Chapter 9.)

To date, the major cross-cultural reflection on Greek divination has come from African divination systems, accessed through anthropological fieldwork. They have been a rich source of both theory and information on the kinds of questions posed to mantic specialists. The limitations of the African evidence are lack of historical depth and an orientation toward oral traditions and procedures. This type of evidence is richest for the social context of divination, and for interactions between consultor and specialist. It is less illuminating for practices that focus on predictions and archival and textual knowledge, as do the mantic traditions of China and Mesopotamia.

What does comparison add to our knowledge of early Chinese divination, for which there exist rich textual and material sources? The Greek material is suggestive of what kinds of problem may be universally referred to the mantic arts: which problems were considered risky or unknowable by normal human agency. For example, despite the many commonalities,

Chinese mantic questions are particularly focused on the selection of auspicious times in a way that has no Greek counterpart.[114]

This chapter has not pursued the fourth type of question introduced at the beginning of the chapter, namely the problems of interpretation and ambiguity raised by some mantic responses. The problems raised by mantic literature as a distinct topos or genre warrant separate consideration, and are taken up in Chapter 8.

Appendix 6.1: State questions from Delphi: narrow sample

State queries on colonization, laws, and alliances

Colonization (3 queries)

1. 426. Sparta asked whether to found the colony of Heracleia in Trachinia. They were advised to do so (H6, PW no. 159, Thuc. 3.92.5).
2. After 385. The Parians asked Delphi for authority to found a colony (H14, PW no. 177, Diod. 15.13.4). They were advised to found a colony on the island of Pharos in the Adriatic.
3. About 560. The Athenians asked who should lead a planned colony in the Thracian Chersonese. They were told to appoint Miltiades and that the colony would succeed if they did so (Q111, PW no. 62, Nepos 1.3).

Internal politics (3 queries)

1. Early seventh century. The Spartans ask whether to obey the laws of Lycurgus; they are told that it is better in every respect to obey them (Q8, PW no. 217, Xen. *Lac.* 8.5).
2. 508 or 507. Cleisthenes requested the Pythia to choose the names of ten heroes, to name the ten tribes of Athens (Q125, PW no. 80, Hdt. 5.66–69 and 6.131).
3. About 491 the Spartans asked about the legitimacy of King Demaratus; they are told he is not the son of Ariston (Q137, PW no. 87, Hdt. 6.66.3 and 75.3).

Kingship or royal succession (7 queries)

1. Arcesilaus of Cyrene asks about gathering an army to restore his rule (Q119, PW no. 70).
2. An unspecified question (Q163, PW no. 112).

[114] This concern is not unique to China. Several African divination systems focus on auspicious times. For example, Malagash Antemoro diviners use an astrological system to select auspicious days and a geomantic system to diagnose disorders and evils. Both are probably of Arabian origin. See Peek 1991: 53–68.

3. Tarquin's sons ask who will be king of Rome (Q139, PW no. 439).
4. Deinomenes of Syracuse asks about his sons' futures as tyrants (Q140, PW no. 484).
5. Thucydides reports a Spartan query on an unstated topic (H7, PW no. 160, Thuc. 5.16.2).
6. Late fifth century. Athens asks about the public maintenance of the Prytaneion (H1, PW no. 123, *IG* I^2.77).
7. 300–290. The Eretrians request approval of legislation voted by the demos. They are told that it is good and to the city's advantage to adopt these measures (H47, PW no. 351, *IG* 12.9.213.3–4).

Inter-state matters (1 query)

1. 356. Philip of Macedon and Chalcidice ask about a treaty of alliance. They are advised to become allies and instructed on particular sacrifices to make (H19, PW no. 260, TAPA 65 (1934): 103–22, esp. 103, lines 12–16; RO no. 50).

Warfare (12 queries)

1. The one Archaic military response is Cleisthenes' alleged attempt to bribe the Pythia to respond "free Athens!" to any Spartan query, in an attempt to end the Pisistratid tyranny (Q124, PW no. 79, Hdt. 5.63.1 and 6.123.2).
2. 433. When Corcyra refused to help the Epidamnians, they asked whether to hand the city over to its founder Corinth (H4, PW no. 136, Thuc. 1.25.1). They were advised to do so.
3. 432 or 431. The Spartans asked whether it was better to attack Athens (in response to breaches of truce). They were told that if they fought with all their strength they would be victorious and Apollo himself would aid them (H5, PW no. 137 and Q245, PW no. 431, Thuc. 1.118.3, 123.1, 2.54.4; Plut. *Mor.* 403b).
4. 404. The victorious Spartans asked whether to destroy Athens and were warned not to disturb the common hearth of Greece (Q198, PW no. 171, Ath. 5.187d, 6.2546).
5. 387. The Spartans asked Delphi and Olympia about a suspicious truce with Argos. Both responded that Sparta could refuse an unjust truce, whereupon Sparta invaded Argive territory (Q198, PW no. 171, Ath. 5.187d, 6.254b. H13, PW no. 175, Xen. *Hell.* 4.7.2).
6. On a contemplated revolt after 385 by Tiribazos against Artaxerxes II (H73, PW 176, Diod. 15.8.4). No response is recorded.
7. The impending battle at Leuctra, by the Thebans in 371 (Q205, PW no. 253, Paus. 4.32.5).
8. The conduct of the Third Sacred War, by the Phocian chief Philomelus after 355 (H20, PW no. 261, Diod. 16.27.1 (25.3)). Before he could pose his question the Pythia told him that "he may do as he wishes."

9. The narrow sample contains only one Delphic response on the Macedonian military campaigns: a query from an unknown source about prodigies that accompanied Philip's entry into war against Amphissa about 340. No question is stated, but there are "dire responses" (*deina manteumata*) favorable to Philip (H22, PW no. 265, Cic. *Div.* 2.57.118, Plut. *Dem.* 19.1 and 20.1).
10. 216. The first of three Roman military queries: To which god to pray after defeats in the Second Punic War (H48, PW no. 354, Fabius Pictor in Liv. 23.11.1–3). They were advised to pray to Zeus and the other gods, to send a gift to Apollo Pythios, and to avoid licentiousness.
11. 207. With the dedication of spoils from Hasdrubal. The exact query is not stated, but the response predicts a great victory for Rome (Q236, PW no. 355, Livy 29.10.6).
12. 205. On Rome's prospects for driving the Carthaginians from Italy in accordance with a Sybilline oracle. The query is a ritual question of how to follow its instructions (Q237, PW no. 356, Livy 29.11.6).

State queries on *lusis* and wellbeing (10 queries)

Military defeats in the Persian Wars

1. 480. Delphi sought relief from the Persian threat and was advised to pray to the Winds, which would be great allies for Hellas (Q148, PW no. 96, Clem. Alex. *Strom.* 6.3, 753P).
2. 479. Athens sought relief from Mardonius during the campaign that ended with the Battle of Plataea. They were advised to sacrifice to Zeus, Hera, and several heroes (Q154, PW no. 102, Plut. *Arist.* 11.3).
3. 216. Rome asked for help after early defeats in the Second Punic War, and what the outcome would be. They were told to sacrifice to Zeus and other gods and to send gifts and victory spoils to Delphi. The result would be military victory and prosperity for the republic and the Roman people (H48, PW no. 354, Liv. 23.11.1–3 (22.57.5)).

Plague

4. 596. Athens, on plague, no question stated. The response is that they must cleanse the city (Q65, PW no. 13, Pl. *Leg.* 642d).
5. 430. Athens, on plague, following the outbreak of the Peloponnesian War, no question stated. The response is that they should set up an image of Apollo (Q189, PW no. 125, Paus. 1.3.4). The plague lasted four years and killed a third of the population, in part because of overcrowding caused by the decision to evacuate the countryside.
6. About 430. The Cleonaeans, on plague. They were instructed to sacrifice a goat to Helios (Q190, PW no. 158, Paus. 10.11.5).

Wellbeing

7. Late fourth century. The Acharnians or Athenians ask about constructing altars of Athena and Ares (H27, PW no. 281, Robert 1938: 294, lines 5–10).
8. The Athenians ask what to do or to which god to pray for better consequences from a portent seen in the sky (H29, PW no. 283, Dem. 43.66). They are told to sacrifice to Zeus, Athena, Heracles, and Apollo.
9. About 180. Emissaries from the Parian colony of Pharaos ask to whom to sacrifice to save Paros from harm and make it prosper in other places (H56, PW no. 429, *IG* 12 suppl 200, *BCH* 59 (1935): 490, lines 24–26).
10. Before 348. On the wellbeing of the Athenians (H28, PW no. 282, Dem. 21.51–52).

State queries on cult and the gods (16 queries)

1. 340. A speech of Demosthenes. He states that, to gain the best from the sign, the Athenians should sacrifice to Zeus, Athena, Heracles, and Apollo and for good fortune to sacrifice to Apollo Leto and Artemis (H29, PW no. 283, Dem. 43.66).

On sacrifices

2. 480 or 479. The Hellenes ask whether offerings after the Greek victory at Salamis were sufficient and pleasing (Q157, PW no. 105, Hdt. 8.122).
3. 479. The Hellenes ask about offerings after the battle of Plataea (Q156, PW no. 104, Plut. *Arist.* 20.4).
4. 421–415. The Athenians offer first fruits of the harvest to the goddesses Demeter and Kore (H9, PW no. 164, *IG* 1^2.76, *SIG* 83, lines 4–8, 25–26, 32–34, discussed above).

Cult and administration

5. About 500. A Spartan query, possibly a proposal to swear certain oaths by Heracles (Q11, PW no. 561, Plut. *Mor.* 271c).
6. About 400. A Delphic query on honors to Pindar (Q178, PW no. 119, Paus. 9.23.3).
7. 433. A Thurian query on whom to recognize as the founder of their city (Apollo himself, Q187, PW no. 132, Diod. 12.35.3).
8. About 373. The Ionian league ask permission to transfer Panionia to the area of Ephesus (H16, PW no. 182, Diod. 15.49.1).

Fifth-century Athenian queries on honors to gods or particular sacrifices

9. About 430. Instructions for honors to the Moirai, Zeus, and Ge (H2, PW no. 124, *IG* 1^2.80.10–12).

10. 420. Response to an unknown question, that Apollo is the exegete to the Athenians (H10, PW no. 165, *IG* 1^2.78.4–5). The inscription also contains a decree about the adornment of Apollo's chair in the *prytaneion*, the sacrifice of an ox, and the distribution of the sacrificial meats.

Mid-fourth century

11. On the erection of altars to Athena and Ares (H27, PW no. 281, *SEG* 21 519.4–10).
12. On improving the temple of Artemis (H33, PW no. 283, *IG* 2^2.333.24–29).
13. On dedicating a house to Asclepius (H24, PW no. 278, *IG* 2^2.4969.1–3).

On the Olympian and Pythian games

14. The Achaeans ask about ongoing defeat (Q169, PW no. 118, Paus. 6.3.8 and 7.17.6).
15. Delphi seeks approval for one Jason to preside at the Pythian Games (H17, PW no. 256, Xen. *Hell.* 6.4.30).
16. On a case of athletic misconduct at the 112th Olympiad (332). An Athenian athlete bribed his fellow-competitors in the pentathlon. The Eleans imposed fines which the Athenians refused to pay and boycotted the Olympic Games. Delphi refused to deliver any oracle to the Athenians until they paid. They did so, and offered six statues to Zeus, with epigrams explaining that the dedications were offered in response to an oracle approving the original Elean decision to fine the offending pentathletes. One source records the oracle given to the Athenians, but Pausanias does not repeat it (H35, PW no. 274, Paus. 5.21.5–7).

Private queries

One personal query on domestic matters

1. By an unknown man about 360 on having children. He is told that he will have a child, and should make an offering of hair (H34, PW no. 334; *FD* 3.1.560, *BCH* 80 (1956): 550, line 3).

Five queries on contemplated actions

1. Best known is a question by Xenophon in 401 about joining the expedition of Cyrus (H11, PW no. 172, Xen. *An.* 3.1.5–8, 6.1.22, Cic. *Div.* 1.54.122).
2. In 356, the exiled Athenian Callistratus asks whether he would be treated according to law if he returned to Athens after fleeing a death sentence for pro-Spartan sympathies (H18, PW no. 259, Lycurg. *Leoc.* 93).
3. The other three queries date from the first century CE. The philosopher Dio Chrysostomus (85 CE) asked about the course of life after the Emperor Domitian banished him from Rome and Italy (H62, PW no. 462, Dio Chrys. 13.9). He was advised to continue with his occupation.

4. The other two address personal activities within the broader context of religious cult. About 240 King Dropion of Paines asks about dedicating a statue (H53, PW no. 340, *BCH* 76 (1952): 136).
5. During the reign of Augustus (27 BCE–14 CE), a priest of Zeus at Palladion asks a question about preparing a seat for Pallas at his own expense (H59, PW no. 457, *IG* 2^2.3177, 3178).

One personal query on lusis

1. Poseidonius of Halicarnassus (250) asks what is better for himself and his sons and daughters to do (H36, PW no. 355, *AGIBM* 896). He is advised to follow the example of his ancestors and told which gods to worship.

One personal query on wellbeing

1. A Phocian priest of Heracles Misogynus seeks absolution for some violation of his priestly vows (H63, PW no. 464, Plut. *Mor.* 404A, 50–100 CE).

Consultations on private matters

1. Chaerophon (430) asks whether anyone is wiser than Socrates (H3, PW no. 134, Pl. *Ap.* 21a–c, Xen. *Ap.* 14).
2. Hadrian of Rome (r. 117–38 CE) asks about the birthplace and parentage of Homer (H65, PW no. 465, *IG* 2^2.5006).
3. The Neoplatonist Amelius (262 CE) asked where the soul of Plotinus had gone (H69, PW no. 473, Porph. *Plot.* 22).

Appendix 6.2: State questions from Delphi: broad sample

State queries on colonization, laws, and alliances

Colonization

- Colonization questions come from *poleis*, dispossessed factions, individuals, and colonists. Most are from the Archaic period and very questionable.[115] State consultors included Corinth (on Syracuse), the Chalcidians (on Messene and Rhegium), Sparta (on Tarentum), and Rhodes (on Gela).

[115] Rhegium was established by force when colonists were effectively exiled as scapegoats. Tarentum was founded because of the circumstances of a dispossessed group. Other examples include colonies at Croton and Abdera. It is debated whether eighth-century colonization was primarily motivated by trade, overpopulation, or the prospect of more arable land. See A. J. Graham 1982: 143–45, 157–58, Gwynn 1918, and Snodgrass 1980: 10. Overpopulation: Pl. *Leg.* 740c, 708b; Thuc. 1.15.1.

Kingship, royal succession, tyranny

- Oracles on the rise of tyrants typically justify the tyrant's rise to power. Unlike the narrow sample and private queries from Dodona, they do not specify what god to please or what prayers or sacrifices to make. Instead, they offer unsolicited, broad predictions that justify the tyrant's seizure of power.
- Eetion of Corinth, about his lack of children: "Eetion, nobody honors you, though you deserve much honor. Labda conceives and will bear a rolling stone, which will fall among monarchs and will set Corinth right" (Q59, PW no. 6, Hdt. 5.92, trans. Fontenrose).
- His son, the tyrant Cypselus: "Blessed is this man who enters my house, Cypselus, Eetion's son, king of Corinth: his sons will be kings too, but not his grandsons" (Q61, PW no. 8, Hdt. 5.92, trans. Fontenrose).

Warfare

Legendary

- To Agamemnon: Troy will fall when the best of the Achaeans quarrel (L1, PW no. 19, *Od.* 8.75–8).
- To the Epigoni, about war on Thebes (L38, PW no. 203, Diod. 4.66.1, Apollod. *Bibl.* 3.7.2).
- To the Heraclids, about war on the Peloponnese (L15, L62, and L67, PW nos. 146, 289, and 295, Apollod. *Bibl.* 2.8.2).

Archaic oracles on the Messenian Wars (740–680)

- 725. The Messenians, on how to overcome the Spartan siege of Mount Ithome: (1) Sacrifice a maiden chosen by lot from a willing family to the gods of the underworld (Q14, PW nos. 361–62, Diod. 8.8.2, Paus. 4.9.4). (2) Beware a Spartan victory through trickery (Q16, PW no. 364, Paus. 4.12.4).
- Delphi told the Spartans that the Messenians had acquired their land by trickery and it would be taken by trickery (Q15, PW no. 363, Diod 8.13.2, Paus. 4.12.1).
- Pausanias reports two oracles on the "First Sacred War." One instructs the Delphic Amphictyony to go to war, enslave the offenders against Delphi, and dedicate their land to Apollo Pythios and other gods. The other asks about prospects for victory in the siege of Crisa (Q71, PW nos. 17 and 18, Plut. *Mor.* 76e, Paus. 10.37.6). Both the oracles and the conflict itself are highly doubtful.[116]

[116] The "First Sacred War" first appears in Greek literature in the fourth century. See PW 1.99–108 and Robertson 1978.

Military oracles reported by Herodotus

- 560. Sparta, on conquering Arcadia (Q88, PW no. 31, Hdt. 1.66.2).
- Sparta, on which gods to propitiate to attain victory in the Tegean war. They were told to bring the bones of Orestes to Sparta. They did, and defeated Tegea (Q89–90, PW nos. 32–33, Hdt. 1.67–68).
- Queries on the Persian Wars by the Argives: Q144, PW no. 92, Hdt. 7.148.
- Queries on the Persian Wars by the Cretans: Q145, PW no. 93, Hdt. 7.169, cf. Fontenrose 1978: 316, Crahay 1956: 324–25.
- 505. The Athenians, on attacking Aegina after ongoing hostilities. They were advised to desist. Thirty years after Aegina had first begun hostilities, Athens should consecrate land to the hero Aeacus and only then declare war. They would be victorious but at a high cost (Q131, PW no. 82, Hdt. 5.89.2).
- 481. Athens, on the Persian Wars (the "Wooden Wall" oracle).[117]
- 494. Argos, on threat of invasion by Sparta (Q134, PW no. 84, Hdt. 6.18 and 19.2, cf. Paus. 2.20.9).
- 494. Cleomenes of Sparta, on invading Argos: Q136, PW no. 86 and Q86, PW no. 495, Hdt. 6.76.1, 80 (82.1).

Oracles on the military campaigns of Philip II and Alexander III

- 335. The Thebans, on portents before Alexander's attack (Q220, PW no. 273, Diod. 17.10.3).
- 335. The Thebans, on whether Thebes would ever be rebuilt (Q221, PW no. 508, Tzetzes, *Chil.* 7.421–22).
- 334. The Delphic Amphictyony (or Hellenes). They were told to honor Zeus, Athena, and Alexander, a son of Zeus concealed in a mortal body (Q218, PW no. 509, Socr. *Hist. eccl.* 3.23, Migne p. 448).

State queries on *lusis* and wellbeing

Remedies for military defeat

- 415. Athens, what sacrifices to make for victory against Syracuse in the Sicilian Expedition (Q193, PW no. 166, Plut. *Mor.* 403b and *Nic.* 13.6).
- 490. Athens, after the appearance of an apparition at the battle of Marathon (Q142, PW no. 90, Paus. 1.32.5).

Requests for directions on dedications at Delphi

- 480. The Delphians, on whether to bury or remove their sacred treasures for fear of a Persian attack (Q149, PW no. 97, Hdt. 8.36.1).

[117] PW 1.169–71, Fontenrose 1978: 124–28, Maurizio 1997: 329–32, Osborne 1997: 353–54, Bowden 2005: 100–7.

- 278. The Delphians, on whether to remove their treasures, women, and children to save them from the approaching Gauls (Q231, PW no. 329, Diod. 22.9.5, Paus. 10.22.12, Cic. *Div.* 1.81).
- 325. Rome, on the dedication of images during the war with the Samnites (Q228, PW no. 352, Pliny, *NH* 34.12.26).

Plague, famine, civil strife

- 776 or earlier. King Iphitus of Elis requests relief from civil strife and plague (Q1, PW no. 485, Paus. 5.4.6).
- 884–776. Lycurgus of Sparta requests divine approval for restoration of the Olympic Festival (Q2, PW no. 486; Phlegon, *Ol.* 1.3).
- 776 or earlier. The Peloponnesians, on Lycurgus' request for relief from plague and famine on their behalf (Q3 and Q4, PW nos. 487 and 488; Phlegon, *Ol.* 1.6 and 1.7).
- About 675. Sparta, on relief from civil strife. They are advised to summon the Lesbian bards Terpander and Thaletas (Q53–54, PW nos. 485–86, Schol. on *Od.* 3.267 and Phld. *Mus.* 4.18.37–38).
- About 545. The Cnidians, on eye injuries to workmen cutting through the isthmus of Cnidus. They were told to abandon the project; Zeus would have made Cnidus an island had he so chosen (Q112, PW no. 63, Hdt. 1.174.5).
- About 476. Athens after an outbreak of plague. They were instructed to bring the bones of Theseus from Syracuse to Athens (Q164, PW no. 113, Plut. *Thes.* 36.1, *Cim.* 8.6).
- 390. The Delians, on release from plague (Q200, PW no. 179, Plut. *Mor.* 386e–f, cf. 579b–d).
- Syracuse, on plague (Q84, PW no. 552, Plut. *Mor.* 310b).
- The Delphic Amphictyony, on plague (Q72, PW no. 237, Hippoc. *Ep.* 27.13, L 9.410).

Famine or crop failure (only in the broad sample):

- Epidaurus (Q63, PW nos. 10–11, Hdt. 5.82.1–2).
- Sicyon (Q83, PW no. 28, Pliny, *NH* 36.4.10).
- Ephesus (Q82, PW no. 27, Ael. frag. 48 (Sud. P3122)).
- The Pelasgians of Lemnos (Q132, PW no. 83, Hdt. 6.139.2).
- Delphi (Q107, PW no. 58, Hdt. 2.134.4).

Plague or famine as punishment for religious infractions or violence against individuals:

- Early in the fifth century the Spartans sought relief from plague after the death of the regent Pausanias. They were told to move his bones to the place where he died (Q174, PW no. 114, Thuc. 1.134.4, Diod. 11.45.8).

- Sparta (about 464) also requested healing after omens or portents of divine wrath (Q177, PW no. 314, Paus. 2.33.2).
- After the Etrurians of Agylla (Caere) stoned their Phocaean prisoners, people and animals who passed their grave developed a strange affliction. The Etrurians asked how to expiate this guilt (*c.* 535–530) and were told to hold games and sacrifice to the dead (Q113, PW no. 64, Hdt. 1.167.2, cf. Fontenrose 1968: 97–98).
- Two incidents involve mistreatment or exile of athletes: by the Epizephyrian Locrians, for abusing Euthykles (Q168, PW no. 388), and by the Thasians after the exile of Theagenes (Q170 and 171, PW nos. 389 and 390/391).
- About 530. The Crotonians, after pestilence and civil strife. They were told to placate Athena and the souls suppliants, murdered at the altar of Athena (Q126, PW no. 75, Just. *Epit.* 20.2.6).
- About 510. Rome, on healing, after omens or portents of divine wrath (Q138, PW no. 438, Zon. *Hist.* 7.11, p. 332b).
- About 500. Athens, on plague (or crop failure) after the murder of a Metragyrtes (Q133, PW no. 572, Jul. *Or.* 5.159b).[118]

Wellbeing

- About 550. Cyrene, on how best to organize the state. The Cyrenians are advised to bring in a lawgiver from Mantinea (Q118, PW no. 69, Hdt. 4.161.2).
- The Siphnians, whether their present prosperity can endure (Q114 and Q115, PW nos. 65–66, Hdt. 3.57.4).
- About 450. Athens, on how to ensure wellbeing and continued prosperity (Q194, PW no. 578, Stob. *Ecl.* citing Dio Chrys. *Or.* 32.3).
- Before 400. Athens, on the welfare of the polis (Q180, PW no. 121, Schol. on Aristeides 13.196, Dind. p. 341).

Cult and the gods

Three topics appear in the broad sample only:

(1) Requests for divine approval for moving or removing a tomb:
  - Mantinea, on moving the bones of Arcas (Q192, PW no. 163, Paus. 8.9.4).
  - Messene, on bringing the bones of Aristomenes to Ithome (Q22, PW no. 269, Paus. 4.32.3).
  - Athens, on bringing the bones of Theseus to Athens after the Persian War (Q164, PW no. 113, Plut. *Thes.* 36.1, *Cim.* 8.6).
  - Sparta, on bringing the body of Tisamenus to Sparta (Q91, PW no. 34, Paus. 7.1.8).

(2) Requests for divine sanction for acts of punishment:

[118] Metragyrtai were itinerant mendicant priests of Cybele (*OCD*^{3} 679).

- Paros, whether to kill a priestess who had helped Miltiades (Q143, PW no. 91, Hdt. 6.135.2).
- Sparta, whether to free the revolting Messenians who had sought sanctuary as suppliants (Q175, PW no. 115, Thuc. 1.103.2).

(3) Questions about the disappearance of an individual.

- The Astypalaeans, on the disappearance of Cleomedes (Q166, PW no. 88, Paus. 6.9.8).

On the meaning of omens, dreams, and prodigies:

- The Metapontines, on a vision at the altar of Apollo (Q165, PW no. 116, Hdt. 4.15.3).
- Sybaris, on omens in the temple of Hera (Q123, PW no. 74, Ael. *VH* 3.43).
- The Epizephyrian Locrians, on lightning striking statues (Q167, PW no. 117, Pliny, *NH* 7.47.152).
- Rome, on unspecified prodigies (Q202, PW no. 440, Liv. 5.16.9–11).

On sacrifices

- Themistocles, on whether to place Persian spoils in the temple (Q158, PW no. 106, Paus. 10.14.4).

Cult and administration

- Polycrates of Samos, on whether sacrifices were timely and whether games should be called Pythian or Delian (Q116, PW no. 67, Epicurus in Phot. *Lex.* 2.121 Naber).
- Sicilians, on authorization to drain a marsh (Q183, PW no. 127, Serv. *Aen.* 3.701).
- Athens, on approval to reconstruct the approach to the Acropolis (Q181, PW no. 122, Thuc. 2.17.1).

Appendix 6.3: Private queries from the broad sample

On children

- Croesus: Q104, PW no. 249, Xen. *Cyr.* 7.2.19.
- Tisamenus of Elis: Q160, PW no. 107, Hdt. 9.33.2, Paus. 3.11.6.
- Aigeus: L4, PW no. 110, Plut. *Thes.* 3.5, Apollod. *Bibl.* 3.15.6.
- Erginus of Orchomenus (the father of Trophonius): L5, PW no. 11, Paus. 9.37.4.
- The father of Pythagoras (a famous son): Q78, PW no. 494, Iambl. *Pyth.* 5.
- The father of Euripides (a famous son): Q159, PW no. 418, *Vit. Eur.* 1.

On illness

- King Grinnos of Thera (about his son's illness): Hdt. 4.150.3, Q45, PW no. 412.
- Battus I of Thera (on a speech impediment): Hdt. 4.153.3, Q47, PW no. 71.
- Alyattes (on an illness): Hdt. 1.19.3, Q98, PW no. 50.
- Croesus (on his son's dumbness): Hdt. 1.85.2, Q102, PW no. 55.

On travel

- Manto (daughter of Tiresias), on herself and other Theban captives brought to Delphi by the Epigoni: L2, PW no. 20, Paus. 7.3.1–2 and 9.33.2.
- An unknown Asian, whether to move to Corinth: Q242, PW no. 424, Strabo 8.6.22.
- Hegesistratus of Ephesus, where to settle after exile from Ephesus after a murder: Q25, PW no. 412, Plut. *Mor.* 315.

Financial matters

- A man, whether he might seize a deposit left with his father by taking an oath: Q92, PW nos. 35 and 36, Hdt. 6.86c.2.
- Diogenes of Synope (head of the Synope mint): whether to falsify coins, as urged by his workmen (a positive response): Q201, PW no. 180, Jul. *Or.* 6.188ab.
- Polycrates of Thebes, how to find treasure buried by Mardonius at Plataea (turn over every stone): Q162, PW no. 109, Zen. 5.63, Suda Π222.

Career choice

- By Zeno of Citium: Q224, PW no. 421, Schol. Ven., Aristoph. *Nub.* 144.
- By Cicero: Q248, PW no. 435, Plut. *Cic.* 5.1.
- By Galen: Q252, PW no. 463, Sopater *Prol.* in Aristid. *Panath.* Dind. 740.

On wellbeing

- Gyges of Lydia (about 680) asks whether anyone is happier than himself (he is told that Aglaus of Psophis is happier): Q97, PW no. 244, Pliny, *NH* 7.46.151.
- Nero (67 CE) is told to beware his seventy-third year: Q251, PW no. 461, Suet. *Nero* 40.3.

Gnomic questions

- "What is best for humanity?" ("Know thyself"): Q77, PW no. 423, Aristotle frag. 3, Clem. Alex. *Strom.* 1.351p.

Appendix 6.4: Selected queries from Dodona

State queries from Dodona (after Parke 1967, Appendix)

1.1 (C 34.1) a question by the city of Tarentum about good fortune.
1.2 (C 34.4) the Corcyraeans ask to what god or hero to sacrifice and pray to live in the best way in both the present and the future.
1.3 (C 34.5) the Corcyraeans ask to what god or hero to sacrifice and pray in order to be of one mind for the common good.
1.4 (C 34.3v), the Mondaeans, on whether to loan out the money of Themis.
1.5 (not in C) city of Chaones, for good fortune, transfer of building of temple of Athena.
1.6 the Corcyraeans and Oricians ask to which god or hero to sacrifice for prosperity.
1.7 the Dodonaeans, asking whether the god sends the storm on account of the impurity of some human being.
1.8 (C 34.2) [an unknown city or a state of Epirus] ask Zeus Naios and Dion[ysus] how they can guarantee their safety if they make a war alliance with the Molossians.
1.9 the arbitrators, on whether to spend the money on the council chamber.

Concordance to Eidinow 2007a

For each pair of columns the left column gives my numbering and the right column gives the corresponding page range and numbering in Eidinow's Catalogue of the Dodona Oracle (Eidinow 2007a: 72–124).

	75–80		83–87		95–100		101–3		108–9		113–14
T1	1	W1	1	O1	1	S5	5	P1	1	MC1	1
2	2	2	6	2	2	6	6	2	2	2	2
3	3	3	2	3	4	7	7	3	3		**114–15**
4	8	4	9	4	5	8	8	4	7	J1	1
5	9	5	12	5	6	9	9			J2	2
6	12	6	14	6	7	10	10		**109**		**117–18**
7	13	7	15	7	8	11	11	CD1	1	L1	2
8	16		**89–93**	8	9	12	12	2	2	2	3
9	17	C1	1	9	10		**104–7**	3	3	3	4
10	18	2	2	10	11	I1	1	4	8	4	5
11	27	3	3	11	p. 78 no. 15	2	2		**110–11**	5	6
12	20	4	5	12	12	3	3	F1	1	6	[p. 120]
13	21	5	6	13	13	4	4	2	2	M1	8
14	19	6	7	14	14	5	5	3	4	M2	9
R1	4	7	8	15	15	6	6	4	6		**119**

75–80		83–87		95–100		101–3		108–9		113–14	
R2	5	C8	9	W16	16	I7	7		**112–13**	RT1	1
3	6	9	10		**101–7**	8	8	RA1	1	2	2
4	10	10	11	S1	1	9	9	2	2		
5	11	11	16	2	2	10	10	3	3		
6	14	12	p. 120	3	3			4	119 no. 1		
7	p. 115 no. 1			4	4			5	[p. 121]		

Travel (T)

T1 about a journey for trade to Epidamnus (*SEG* 43.335).

T2 whether to go to Sybaris to do certain things (*SEG* 43.323; C 157/8, V no. 6).

T3 whether to go or sail to Hipponion (*SEG* 43.321).

T4 a man, whether it will be advantageous for him when he arrives in the Ionian Gulf at Pharos with those from Pharos (*SEG* 43.328).

T5 whether to sail into Sicily (*SEG* 43.329).

T6 about Heracleia and conveying something safely, with guards (?) (*SEG* 43.328).

T7 about a group traveling to Messene or Ambracia (*PAAH* 1973: 94–96.2a).

T8 about having sailed to Apollonia (*SEG* 43.333).

T9 Ariston, whether to sail to the colony at Syracuse (*SEG* 43.330).

T10 whether to go to Elis or Anactorion (C p. 35r).

T11 Parmenides, whether he will fare better if he stays home (Parke 22).

T12 on making a voyage to Epilomichus (*SEG* 15.387).

T13 whether it is better to journey into Caria (*PAAH* 1958: 105).

T14 Aischylinus, whether to sail the Adriatic to Tisates (Parke 24).

Change of residence (R)

R1 a man, whether he would fare better in Oricus and its environs or in his present mode of life (DCV 60; M-526).

R2 a man, whether he and his family would fare better in Croton (*SEG* 43.325). The opposite side says "Croton," probably the response.

R3 a man, whether to depart to Alyzea (Parke 23, *SEG* 15.393).

R4 a man, whether to live in Chemara (*SEG* 43.338).

R5 Nicomachus, whether to move his registration from Heracleia to Taras (*SEG* 43.326).

R6 Hexakon, whether it will be better for him to live in Pharos (*BE* 1969: 348.6, *PAAH* 1967: 33–54.6).

R7 whether to request citizenship this year or next (*SGDI* 1589; C, pl. 35.3).

Women (W)

W1 about a woman, whether he will be fortunate in taking Cleolais as a wife (*Ep. Chron.* 1935: 257.18; side b.ii).
W2 Lyccidas, whether a guardianship through marriage will bring fortune (Parke 10).
W3 a man, whether he will do better by taking a wife, whether there will be children for Isodemus, who will care for him, and whether he should live in Athens and become a citizen there (*SEG* 24.454a; Parke 1967: 133(1)).
W4 Gerioton, whether it is better for him to take a wife (Parke 1967).
W5 whether to give his daughter in marriage to Theodorus or to Tessias (KW 41).
W6 whether to marry another woman (*Ep. Chron.* 1935: 260.39).
W7 Polemarchus, on whether he will have a share in something good and trustworthy from this woman (*SGDI* 1568b).

Children (C)

C1 Hermon, to which god to align for advantageous progeny from his wife Cretaia (Parke 5; *PAAH* 1931: 89–91).
C2 for Cleanor, about offspring to inherit, from his present wife Gonthe (*Ep. Chron.* 1935: 255.15).
C3 about Mydra, will there be children? (*Ep. Chron.* 1935: 259.34).
C4 Heracleidas, about whether he will have a child by Aiglē, his present wife (C, pl. 38.4 and 35.1, Parke 7).
C5 Callicrates, whether he will have offspring from his wife Nike by remaining with her and praying to which god for wellbeing (Parke 8, *SEG* 19.426).
C6 Anaxippus, whether he will have sons from his wife Philista, to which god to pray for wellbeing (Parke 9; *BE* 1959: 231; *BCH* 1957: 584).
C7 for the sake of the birth of a child (*Ep. Chron.* 1935: 257.19).
C8 possibly a woman, whether there will be children if (s)he consults the oracle (*Ep. Chron.* 1935: 258.27).
C9 about Philotas and offspring (C, pl. 35.3).
C10 Menon, about offspring, whether he would fare better by living with . . . (*SGDI* 1572b).
C11 Deinocles of Apollonia, about offspring, to which gods to sacrifice and pray to have children (*SEG* 43.332).
C12 Lysanius, whether the child Annyla bears is not his (Parke 11; *SGDI* 1565a; C, pl. 36.2).

Occupation and profit (O)

O1 Cleouts, whether it will be better and more profitable for him to keep cattle (Parke 17; *SGDI* 1559; C 37.1).

O2 a man, whether he have good fortune as he works the land (*Ep. Chron.* 1935: 258.24).
O3 whether it will be better for Agelochus of Ergetion to be a farmer (*SEG* 43.331; V no. 14).
O4 a man, whether it will be useful to work bronze (*SEG* 15.403; *BE* 1956: 143).
O5 Phainylus, whether he should work at his ancestral trade as a fisherman (Parke 18).
O6 a man, whether he would do better at his trade by going abroad (*Ep. Chron.* 1935: 254.12).
O7 a man, whether he will do better at this craft (*PAAH* 1973: 94–9.3).
O8 a man, whether he would do better to travel to where it seems good to him, do business there and practice this craft (Parke 19; *SGDI* 1568a; C, pl. 37.4).
O9 Timodamus, whether it is best to do business by land and by sea, using money (his silver mine) for as long as he chooses (*SEG* 43.341; *BE* 1993: 346). Side B contains a possible response: to live in the city, work as a trader, do business, and give up the share in the boat.
O10 Hippostratis, whether he would do better to become a shipowner (*SGDI* 1583; C, pl. 37.3).
O11 whether it would be better to work with Diotimus in Megara (*SEG* 24.454b; *BE* 1968: 318; Parke 1967c: 133(2)).
O12 Lochiscus, about work, whether by sea he would have good fortune and fare better (*SEG* 15.398; *BE* 1956: 143; *PAAH* 1952: 301.5).
O13 Lysias, whether to stick to the sea and take a share of a ship (*SEG* 23.475; *PAAH* 1958: 104.2). Side B seems to contain a response: Do nothing by land.
O14 Arizelus, what occupation or activity would be better and provide good possession of property (Parke 25; *SEG* 15.405a).
O15 Cratylus, about something useful and profitable for him in the near future and for all time (*SGDI* 1560a; C, pl. 37.9).
O16 Socrates, whether by working he and his descendants will fare better now and in the future (Parke 1967: 16; *SGDI* 1575; C, pl. 35.2a).

Slavery (S)

S1 Anthropus, about freedom (Christidis).
S2 Razia, whether she will attain a place of safety and an agreement from Teitucus while he lives (Christidis 2).
S3 whether Leuca will fare better if she stays put (Christidis).
S4 a woman, What will happen to me if I leave? | Should I make it happen? (*SEG* 15.389; *PAAH* 1952: 303.10). Side B contains a response: The woman remains | O woman stay!
S5 a slave, what he should do about his freedom and whether he will gain manumission from his master (Christidis).

S6 for Cittus, whether he will obtain the freedom that Dionysius promised him (Christidis).
S7 a slave, whether by leaving there will be something else good for me (*PAAH* 1931: 89–91.3).
S8 a master, whether to re-enslave (Christidis).
S9 of a servant (Christidis).
S10 about the price of a slave (Christidis).
S11 Scidarcas, whether to proceed quickly with the private legal case of the enslaved captive (Christidis). This inscription seems to concern someone who may have been illegally enslaved.
S12 a slave owner or kidnapper, whether Archondas enslaved the son of Aristocles and Archebius, the son of Archondas or Sosandrus, who was then the slave of Archondas or his wife (Parke 26; *SEG* 15.385).

Illness (I)

I1 a woman, by sacrificing and praying to which god will she do better and be released from this disease? (C, pl. 35b).
I2 Nicocrateia asks to which of the gods she had better or more advantageously offer sacrifice and have the illness cease (Parke 15; *SGDI* 1561b; C38.4v, 35.1v).
I3 Leontius, whether his son Leon will be healthy and cured of the disease which has gripped him and recover from a disease (breast) (Parke 13).
I4 he asks . . . by praying and sacrificing to Zeus and Dione and to which of the gods or daimons or heroes might he be healthy? (*SGDI* 1566a).
I5 about health (*SGDI* 1577).
I6 Antiochus, about his health and that of his father and brother. By honoring which of the gods or heroes will he be better? (*SGDI* 1587).
I7 Socrates, of Ambracia, asks Zeus Naios and Dione about his present and future health and which of the gods to appease in order to fare better? (Parke 12; *SGDI* 1564; C, pl. 36.5).
I8 about the eyes (*PAAH* 1973: 96.4).
I9 Amyntas, about his child's foot (*SGDI* 1588; C, pl. 37.5).
I10 Thrasyboulus, to which god to sacrifice for relief of an eye illness (Parke 14).

Property (P)

P1 a man, about his, his wife's, and his children's property, to which god to pray to in order to fare well (Parke 3; *Ep. Chron.* 1935: 253.10).
P2 Damys, about all his property (*SEG* 15.391).
P3 Glaucias, about possessions (8.3 *Ep. Chron.* 1935: 254.11).
P4 Themis, whether to return the rope he gave to Aristophantus later or never (*SGDI* 1581; C, pl. 37.7).

Construction and dwellings (CD)

CD1 a man, it will be advantageous for him to having the dwelling recently built or to have another (*SGDI* 1569a).

CD2 Alcinous, whether it will be advantageous for Niceas to build the workshop (Parke 21).

CD3 whether to acquire the house in the city and the piece of land (Parke 20; *SGDI* 1573; C, pl. 37.1).

CD4 whether to buy the marsh by the temple of Demeter (*SEG* 19.432; *PAAH* 1955: 172.b).

Good fortune (F)

F1 a man, to which god to pray and sacrifice for his fortunes to improve (*SEG* 15.395; *BE* 1956: 143; *PAAH* 1952: 303.13).

F2 a man, would he do better now and in the future (*SEG* 15.402; *PAAH* 1952: 303.14).

F3 Archephon, whether there will be safety for him and his ship, built according to Apollo's orders, and whether he will pay back what is needed (*PAAH* 1967: 49.5; *BE* 1969: 348.5).

F4 Eubandrus and his wife ask what sacrifices and vows will ensure them the protection of gods, daimons, and heroes in the present and future (Parke 1; *SGDI* 1582a; C, pl. 34.3).

Ritual activity (RA)

RA1 praying to which gods (CDV no. 2; M-269).

RA2 whether to hire Dorius the spirit-raiser (CDV no. 5; *BE* 1938: 153).

RA3 whether to make the triple sacrifice (*BE* 1998: 202; *SEG* 1997.819).

RA4 Socrates, about the response of the god and the omens, which Aristolaus did not seal and did not set down (*SGDI* 1578; C 38.2).

RA5 Lysias (?), a question about a body and burial (*SGDI* 1569b; C, pl. 36.4).

Military campaigns (MC)

MC1 whether to go on campaign by land (*BE* 1998: 202; *SEG* 47.820). Side B has the response: "Stay on land."

MC2 whether it is advantageous to set off on campaign against Antiochus (*SEG* 15.407; *BE* 1956: 143).

Judicial activity (J)

J1 a request for victory, with a reference to judicial opponents and households (*SEG* 15.391a; *BE* 1956: 143.22).

J2 Sosandrus, about the curse of Ale and whether he would do well in court (CDV no. 3; M-186).

Lost, stolen, or hidden objects (L)

L1 about Bostrycha of Dorcus and the silver Dion lost (*SEG* 15.400; *BE* 1956: 143).
L2 whether Thopion stole the silver (*Ep. Chron.* 1935: 259.32).
L3 Agis asks about the covers and pillows he lost, whether someone outside the household stole them (Parke 27; *SGDI* 1586; C, pl. 36.1).
L4 Satyrus, whether if his Scythian horse was not packed up in Elea he would have plucked the hair off the horse of Dorilaus (Parke 28; *SEG* 19.428).
L5 a man, whether Doriclus stole the cloth (Parke 29; *SEG* 19.429).
L6 about the location of hidden treasure (*SEG* 15.408a; *BE* 1956: 143; *PAAH* 1952: 304.16).

Murder (M)

M1 a man, whether someone (man or woman) tried to poison his children, his wife, or himself (CDV no. 1; M-257).
M2 whether Timō bewitched/poisoned Aristoboula (CDV no. 4; M-433).

Requests for truth (RT)

RT1 "we know the truth" (*SGDI* 1575b; C, pl. 35.2).
RT2 about believing something true (C, pl. 35.6).

7 | Consultors

Who consulted mantic experts in China and Greece, and why? This chapter takes up the mantic encounter from the viewpoint of the consultor. What were the dynamics of consultation for states and individuals? Detailed information is in short supply, and often the context of consultations is unknown. Yet even fragmentary accounts show tensions between diviners and officials, and suggest complex relations between client and practitioner. In this chapter I turn to Greek and Chinese accounts of the mantic session and questions of who had access to mantic expertise. The methods and questions surveyed in Chapters 5 and 6 make it clear that neither Chinese nor Greek divination was open-ended. Most questions were asked in forms that limited the possible responses, but left much to interpretation.

There are also important differences between official and private consultation. They shared many concerns, but their different relations to political power affected the process of mantic consultation. At one extreme are court officials charged with mantic activity, such as Babylonian court astronomers or Chinese astrocalendric or ritual officials. Here we have an interaction (and possible conflict) between two kinds of authority. Political power gives the consultor some control of the mantic encounter, but practitioners had ways to make their views known. At the other extreme are private individuals consulting independent mantic experts. Here consultors may exercise power in their freedom to take their business elsewhere. Other situations fall between these two extremes. The "dependent" Greek oracular diviner did not actively seek clientele, but the shrines were nonetheless indirectly dependent on patronage. Delphi, Dodona, and Didyma over time became wealthy through dedications and offerings.

It is difficult to reconstruct the purposes or dynamics of mantic consultations in the ancient past, a problem we have already seen in accounts of the methods of the Pythia in Chapters 4 and 5. This problem becomes especially difficult in considering consultations by women and other private individuals of limited mobility or resources. On the Chinese side, because mantic consultation is still widely practiced, we can make careful use of contemporary accounts.

Chinese and Greek evidence presents different aspects of the spectrum of state and private mantic consultation. Much of the Chinese evidence focuses on court divination, and many accounts of private consultation, especially in the *Zuo zhuan*, have a clear rhetorical purpose. The Greek evidence, by contrast, is fullest for the consultation of independent *manteis*, with their need to establish authority and legitimacy. In this chapter I survey several extant accounts of both official and private consultation, based on the very uneven testimony of available evidence, with a view to the following issues.

First, how did rulers and officials use mantic consultation to resolve disagreements on matters of state? In both China and Greece, warfare in particular was a focus of state mantic activity, and distinct modes of divination were used for the decision to go to war, battlefield divination *in situ*, and for administrative matters. Second, how did private consultors and practitioners interact during mantic consultation? How did practitioners deliver unwelcome responses? Could they change an unwelcome result? Third, how did gender in particular affect mantic access and mantic interactions? I conclude with a few Chinese examples of contemporary mantic consultation.

Immediate grounds for comparison suggest themselves. How did mantic consultation mediate relations between individuals and groups? How were conflicts of interest addressed? How did mantic experts couch unwelcome advice to powerful superiors, or diagnose the needs of private clients? Finally, how did gender affect problems of mantic access?

Official consultors

Chapter 6 surveyed a range of state or official questions posed to mantic authority. These included warfare, government decisions, and religious and ritual matters. How were these responses used? It has been argued, on the model of African divination, that Greek states used divination as a source of legitimation, authority, and consensus, and that oracles provided new ways to resolve doubts and validate decisions. In this view, their primary function was political; they created social order by sanctioning decisions already made and creating social consensus. Others have challenged this sociological view.[1] What does Chinese evidence offer to this debate?

Warring States texts are clear on the appropriateness of mantic queries about warfare and government projects, as well as the view that both omens and prognostication can predict the rise and fall of states:

[1] For these arguments see Chapter 3, esp. nn. 32–36.

國家將興。必有禎祥。國家將亡。必有妖孽。見乎蓍龜。動乎四體。

When a state or family is about to flourish, there are sure to be lucky omens, and when it is about to perish, there are sure to be unlucky omens. They are made visible by turtle and milfoil; and they affect the movements of the four limbs.[2]

Warfare

How did military consultors use the results of military divination? A first point is that the religious and ritual character of both early Chinese and Greek warfare was often understated or overlooked.

The *Zuo zhuan* explicitly defines warfare as a ritual activity of the state:

國之大事。在祀與戎。祀有執膰。戎有受脤。神之大節也。

The great concerns of the state are sacrifice and warfare. In sacrifice we offer cooked meat; in warfare [before setting out] we give raw meat. These are the great ceremonies of the spirits.[3]

Chinese military historians have tended to ignore prognostication, but a recent study by Robin Yates argues that military divination (*bing zhan* 兵占) was a fundamental feature of warfare in premodern China.[4] It was used to decide whether to go to war, and also on the battlefield, for immediate decisions. This history begins with oracle bone inscriptions attempting to predict military victory and to select alliances and personnel:

貞: 王[勿]惟沚馘比伐巴方帝受我祐。王惟沚馘比伐巴方帝不我其受祐。

Divined: The king should join with Zhi Guo to attack the Bafang and Di will confer assistance on us.[5]

The *Zuo zhuan* contains many accounts of military prognostication on whether to go to war. For example, in a series of military encounters between Jin, Qin, and Chu, all sides prognosticate to predict victory and

[2] *LJ* 53.4a (*Zhong yong* 中庸), cf. Legge 1885: 2.320. The *Zhou li* (see Chapter 6, n. 6) specifies warfare, policy decisions, queries on planned ventures, and anomalies as appropriate topics for mantic consultation. The meaning of the phrase "four limbs" (*si ti* 四體) is not entirely clear. Commentators gloss the phrase as the four feet of the turtle, the limbs of the human body, and the entire body. The Morohashi dictionary (4682:528, no. 2) glosses the phrase to mean the four limbs of the turtle, but this is not convincing, since mantic consultation uses the plastron of a dead turtle, whose limbs are not present. The phrase also appears at *Analects* 18.7 and *Mencius* 4A3 and 7A21, where it seems to mean the four limbs of the body. See Ames and Hall 2001: 127 n. 71.

[3] Zuo, 861 (Cheng 13.2), cf. Lewis 1990: 17 and Legge 382, reading *shou* 授 for *shou* 受.

[4] Yates 2005. [5] *Heji* 6473, trans. after Keightley 1997: 32.

defeat.[6] Some prognostications sought concrete battlefield advice: whether it is auspicious to engage the enemy, on immediate preparations, and whether the impending battle will result in victory. Some feature debates about interpretation or arguments over strategic decisions.[7]

These prognostications may have been added to dramatize or moralize the events chronicled, so we cannot assume that their recommendations were followed or that they even took place. Nonetheless, they indicate attitudes toward military and battlefield divination. Taken together with the detailed descriptions of the military divination in technical treatises and excavated texts discussed in Chapters 5 and 6, these narratives suggest that consultors made genuine use of prognostication in warfare, and did not simply use mantic results to affirm decisions they had already taken. Examples include the military significance of cloud formations in the *Shi ji* and *Han shu* astronomical treatises, and military prognostication by clouds, observing *qi*, "Sanctions and Virtues" (*Xingde*), and wind horns described in excavated texts. These methods persist into the Ming and Qing dynasties.[8]

Did military oracles or battlefield divination affect actual military decisions? Many discussions of Greek military divination also tend to underestimate specifically religious and ritual aspects of early Greek warfare.[9] For example, an older view simply rationalized battlefield divination as deliberately manipulated by generals.[10] Yet there is evidence that mantic consultation played an important role in Greek warfare. Xenophon remarks that divination was used extensively for decisions about warfare because it was so unpredictable and dangerous (*Hipparch.* 9.8–9). As Socrates remarks: "In warfare, you see men propitiating the gods before they engage in battle and questioning them by means of sacrifices and bird divination as

6 In 645 Duke Mu of Jin uses milfoil to decide whether to launch a retributive invasion against Duke Hui for denying Qin grain relief in a famine (Xi 15.4). In 635 Duke Wen of Jin prognosticates on whether to ally with Qin to restore the king of Zhou (Xi 25.4) and comes into conflict with Chu. These incidents are discussed in Chapter 8.

7 Military prognostication does not end with the transformation of warfare in the late Warring States. For example, the *Hou Han shu* records that in 28 CE the rebel leader Tian Rong 田戎 prognosticated to decide whether to surrender to Cen Peng 岑彭 (*HHS* 17.6580). Transformation of warfare: Lewis 1999.

8 E.g. Fan Jingwen, *Zhan shou quan shu* 18: 37ab, cf. Yates 2005: 22–24.

9 Nineteenth-century historians such as Wilamowitz stressed the role of religion in warfare (Wilamowitz-Moellendorff 1893: esp. 85), but this approach came under attack by the German military historian Hans Delbrück (1904), who advocated *Sachkritik* ("objective analysis"), the attempt to reconstruct ancient battles by applying knowledge of modern warfare to ancient texts. See Pritchett 1974–79 and Jameson 1991.

10 E.g. Nilsson 1940: 126, Delbrück [1920] 1975: 116, Hignett 1963: 336, cf. Pritchett 1974–79: 3.78–80.

to what they should do and not do."[11] His point was that Greek military rituals had the double purpose of predicting outcomes and propitiating the gods.[12]

Did military oracles affect the decision to go to war? Several types of military query can be discounted. Requests for sanction for aggressive warfare are all historically problematic. Many oracular queries are *lusis* queries, which address religious cult rather than military decisions. The narrow sample of Delphic military oracles discussed in Chapter 6 asked about prospects for victory (for consultors presumably intending to fight) and about particular decisions, such as truces and alliances. In short, there is little reason to believe that a response from Delphi could entirely prevent a prior decision to go to war, but it could affect how military action was conducted.

Military ritual continued with *hiera* sacrifices throughout the army's march to battle and *sphagia* sacrifices before the battle itself.[13] Spontaneous events such as omens, portents, and epiphanies (the appearance of gods on the battlefield) also required sacrifice and interpretation.[14] Both Herodotus and Xenophon extensively describe battlefield divination, a role that dates from Archaic times. Inscriptional evidence and epitaphs place military *manteis* at important historical battles. Most famous is Megistias, the *mantis* who predicted defeat at Thermopylae.[15] A fourth-century stele mentions the grant of Athenian citizenship to the Tasian

[11] Xen. *Oec.* 5.19–20, trans. after Marchant.

[12] Lonis 1979: 109, Pritchett 1974–79: 3.87–88, Jameson 1991: 199.

[13] The most complete accounts are from Spartan sources, but they may differ from other Greek practices. Once war was decided, the Spartan king sacrificed to Zeus Agetor before leaving his home and to Zeus and Athena at the border. Only if all sacrifices produced favorable signs did the army proceed. Armies took entire flocks of sheep for sacrificial purposes (Paus. 9.13.4). Sacrifices were performed on the march and before any major action (building a fort, attacking a town) to the limit of three victims a day (e.g. Xen. *Hell.* 3.1.17, 4.7.7, 6.4.16). Xenophon also relates that divinatory sacrifice was used at every stage of military campaigns (*Lac.* 13). See Jameson 1991: 197–99, Parker 2000a: 87–88.

[14] Homeric military dreams and epiphanies: Dodds 1951: 102–21, Nock 1972: 1.46. Historical military epiphanies: Pritchett 1974–79: 3.14–39. Pritchett argues that epiphany legends cannot be dismissed as later embellishments; they occur throughout the Greek world and are recorded in all but two major histories (Thucydides and Polybius). Pausanias records the greatest number, which is consistent with his belief in the active intervention of the gods in human affairs. Pritchett also points out (1974–79: 3.39–45) that generals clearly exploited widespread belief in battle epiphanies, and used (or manufactured) them strategically, to exhort or inspire their troops.

[15] Hdt. 7.219 and 7.221. When the pass was surrounded, Megistias sacrificed, inspected the victim, and foretold that death would come with the dawn. Leonidas sent his troops to safety, including Megistias, but he sent his only son away and remained. Inscriptions for the dead at Thermopylae include an epigram by Semonides, who described Megistias as "a *mantis*, who at the time clearly saw the fates drawing near, but could not bear to flee and leave the leaders of Sparta" (Hdt. 7.228).

mantis Sthorys for his role in a sea battle.[16] Military *manteis* figure prominently in Xenophon's *Anabasis*, and in Plutarch's biographies of Cimon, Nicias, Dion, Timoleon, and Alexander.[17]

Recent studies have addressed the complex and often symbiotic relationship between general and *mantis*.[18] The general was subordinate to the *mantis* in expertise but superior in power of decision. Did generals use prebattle sacrifice to legitimate decisions and encourage the troops, or did the recommendations of *manteis* actually influence military action?

It is important that many *manteis* were also military specialists. This double role begins with the Homeric Calchas, both a priest of Apollo and the head of the Greek naval forces. His advice is often unwelcome, but not even Agamemnon ventures to question his authority.[19] Historic military *manteis* were also trained in warfare and strategy. Examples include the Spartan *mantis* Hekas (who used a plan of resting and fighting against the Messenians), the Elean *mantis* Tellias (who enabled the Phocians to defeat the Thessalians), the Plataean *mantis* Theaenetus (who used ladders to escape the siege of the Peloponnesians and Boeotians), and possibly Alexander's *mantis* Aristander of Telmessus.[20] Military *manteis* could also change allegiance if their advice was not followed, for example the departure of Callias of Elis from Sybaris to Croton (discussed in Chapter 4).

W. K. Pritchett has argued the strong case for the independence and professionalism of military *manteis*, citing examples of unfavorable sacrifices that delayed or halted military advances. Most famous is the delay before the battle of Plataea in 479, when the *manteis* of Pausanias,

[16] Xen. *Hell.* 2.4.19. Presumably the battle of Cnidus in 394. See M. J. Osborne 1981–82: 1.43–51, 2.45–48; cf. Bremmer 1996: 108 n. 58.

[17] The *mantis* Astyphilus of Poseidonia interprets Cimon's dream before Cyrus (*Cim.* 18). The *mantis* Orthagoras, an intimate of Timoleon of Corinth, remonstrated with, and eventually killed, Timoleon's brother Timophanes (*Tim.* 4). Alexander always heeded his *mantis* Aristander when he would not listen to others (*Alex.* 52.1), and spent the night in sacrifice with him before the battle of Gaugamela (*Alex.* 31.9). The *manteis* of Nicias and Dion are discussed below.

[18] E.g. Pritchett 1974–79, Jameson 1991, Parker 2000b, Flower 2008.

[19] Michel Woronoff (1999) has argued that the presence of Calchas on the Greek side was of considerable importance. Although he created a conflict between political power and divinatory expertise, his status as a *mantis* lent authority to his interventions. By contrast, the Trojans had no comparable figure to oppose the authority of Hector. Because the Trojan *mantis* Helenus was a fighting prince of the ruling Priamid family, he was directly under Hector's authority. Polydamas, a close companion of Hector, had the independence Helenus lacked, but his membership in the rival Panthoides family undermined his authority in the eyes of the Priamids.

[20] Paus. 4.21.7–8 and 4.16.1 (Hekas), 10.1.8 (Tellias); Thuc. 3.20.1 (Theaenetus). For these and other examples see Pritchett 1974–79: 1.56–57. While these stories may have been created or exaggerated for rhetorical effect, they suggest that Alexander consulted Aristander and other *manteis* on matters of strategy (discussed below under rhetoric).

Mardonius, and the Greeks in the Persian army all reported results favorable for resistance but unfavorable for initiating battle, delaying battle for ten days.[21] In a more extreme case, the Spartan army waited until King Aegispolis consulted first Olympia and then Delphi in 387 for permission to break a truce with Argos.[22] Xenophon reports several instances of delay because of adverse omens. The Ten Thousand were detained at Calpe for three days without provisions. On another occasion, a planned attack on the Tinarenians was abandoned because the omens forbade war.[23]

Oracular advice could also conflict with prebattle divination, and the result was typically delay. For example, Delphi had encouraged Cleomenes to attack Argos in 494, but unfavorable omens held him at the Argive border by the Erasinus River. Eventually he redeployed his troops and fought the Argives at Sepeia near Tiryns (Hdt. 6.76).

Another factor was the subjective nature of prebattle mantic techniques. Hieroscopy was a subtle and subjective art. Except in the most dire cases, there was considerable room for interpretation and negotiation. There could be disagreement between *mantis* and general, as well as conflicts between the *mantis*'s dual roles as both religious and military specialist.

Military divination could present conflicts of authority between ruler, general, and military mantic specialist. These took a different form in Warring States China, where an emergent class of military strategists, typified by the strategist-general of *Sunzi's Art of War*, positioned themselves against diviners in arguing for their own rationalized techniques for predicting victory and defeat. In an atmosphere of decreased competition, with only one Chinese state employing generals, there was less place, or need, for such polemics.

In summary, both ancient sources and modern scholarship emphasize the uncertainty and unpredictability of warfare. Of all situations considered full of danger, and requiring the best possible alignment, warfare was the most grave. But military divination presents a particularly strong counterexample to the functionalist arguments mentioned at the beginning of this chapter. Three points are especially relevant.

First, Chinese and Greek accounts describe warfare as a ritual activity, closely linked to religious considerations. This aspect of warfare may explain *why* mantic results received such deference. In the Chinese case, warfare was explicitly considered a ritual activity of the state; military

[21] Hdt. 9.37, 9.42. Other battle delays were caused by the Greek *mantis* Teisamenus (Hdt. 9.61–62) and by unfavorable omens to Cleomenes in 494 (Hdt. 6.76). See Pritchett 1974–79: 1.77–82. For discussion see Flower 2008: 154–56.

[22] Pritchett 1974–79: 3.315, cf. H13, PW no. 175, Xen. *Hell.* 4.7.2.

[23] Xen. *An.* 6.4.13–27 and 5.5.1–4.

divination was thus an aspect of state ritual.[24] Pritchett, Bowden, and others have argued persuasively that piety was an important consideration in both Athenian politics and the practice of warfare. Their arguments, and the overwhelmingly theological orientation of mantic queries at Delphi and elsewhere, suggest that Greek military divination was far more than a means to legitimate decisions or provide consensus.

The understanding of military divination as a ritual activity did change with the rise of large armies and extensive campaigns, in China during the late Warring States and in Greece under the Macedonian kings. But even here, as Angelos Chaniotis points out, Hellenistic responses to military rituals were ambivalent. Prebattle divination and other military rituals were criticized, but this criticism shows that they were still practiced, and belief in military epiphanies persisted.[25]

The second point is evidence in both traditions of ongoing efforts by military leaders to reaffirm divine mandates for military activity. If the primary function of divination were to ensure consensus or military morale, there would be every incentive not to repeat divinatory procedures, at least once a desired response had been obtained. This is exactly the opposite of what we see in Greek military practice. Armies repeatedly performed *hiera* and *sphagia* sacrifices. Similarly in China, even when a military decision had been made at the state level, battlefield divination was repeated continually to determine personnel, to choose auspicious times, and to prognosticate immediate prospects for victory.

The third point is evidence in both traditions of ongoing disagreement about how mantic responses should affect military decisions. We find this in *Zuo zhuan* debates about the meaning of prognostication results, and also in later critiques of military prognostication by *bingfa* authors. We also find it in disagreements between generals and *manteis*, especially on whether to fight when the omens were bad. These debates also underscored the potential for conflict of authority between general and *mantis*.

Administration

How did consultors use mantic procedures to select personnel and make political decisions? Chinese and Greek prescriptive statements do not indicate how consultors used the results, but they do emphasize the role of mantic consultation in selecting personnel from shortlists of candidates,

24 This ritual aspect of warfare is also attested by the ritual purifications necessary before commencing a military expedition. See Yates 2005: 17–20.

25 Lewis 1990, Chaniotis 2005: esp. 160–63.

and for other matters of administration. A passage from the *Zuo zhuan* on royal succession specifies prognostication to resolve questions that fall outside of conventional criteria for judgment:

昔先王之命曰，王后無適，則擇立長，年鈞以德，德鈞以卜。

The mandate of the former kings says: If the queen has no son, then select the eldest son of the king. If their years are equal, select according to virtue. If their virtue is equal, select according to prognostication.[26]

The *Li ji* prescribes the use of turtle shell divination for matters of state: to choose an heir or an interim ruler, to select the bearers and nurses of a king's newborn son, to select women to supervise sericulture, and for building a city.[27] A *Shu jing* passage in the "Council of Yu the Great" advises that in selecting ministers one should first determine one's own intentions and only then consult turtle and milfoil. Their agreement signifies the assent of ghosts and spirits; after this auspicious result a query should not be repeated.[28] This (probably late) passage also emphasizes the need to formulate one's own intentions before engaging in prognostication.

Some such choices may have been routine, but the choice of royal heirs and high ministers, in particular, invited disagreement. Several texts recommend mantic consultation to resolve disagreements. As the *Zuo zhuan* authors put it, divination should be reserved for doubtful cases: "We divine to resolve doubts. Where we have no doubts, why divine?"[29] The "Hongfan" chapter of the *Shu jing* provides more detail:

立時人作卜筮。三人占。則從二人之言。汝則有大疑。謀及乃心。謀及卿士。謀及庶人。謀及卜筮。

Set the time and have them prognosticate by milfoil and turtle shell. Let three people prognosticate; follow the words of two of them. If there is great divergence, take counsel with your own heart, with ministers and officers, with the people, and with turtle shell and milfoil.[30]

[26] Zuo, 1478 (Zhao 26.9), trans. after Legge 718. *Yi* divination to determine a child's future prospects: Zuo, 1263–65 (Zhao 5.1, Legge 604) and 1520, cf. Zhao 32.4, Legge 693. This principle is also invoked in Eastern Han debates about succession. See *HHS* 64.2114, during the reign of Ling Di (r. 168–89 CE), cf. Loewe 1994: 187.

[27] Use of turtle shell to choose an heir: *LJ* 10.1b (Couvreur 1.225); *LH*, 999 ("Bu shi" 24.71); Forke 1.186. Choice of interim ruler: *LJ* 51.21a (Couvreur 2.419). Choice of bearer and nurse of a ruler's newborn son: *LJ* 28.12a (Couvreur 1.663). Women to supervise sericulture: *LJ* 48.2a (Couvreur 2.294). Building a city: *LJ* 54.28a (Couvreur 2.512); *Shi jing*, Mao 16.5 ("Wen wang you sheng"); Karlgren 199.

[28] SS 4.11a ("Da Yu Mo" 大禹謨), Legge 63.

[29] Zuo, 131 (Xuan 11.1, cf. Legge 56–57).

[30] SS 12.16b–17a ("Hongfan" 洪範). For a different translation see Legge 334–35.

It then describes each possibility, ranging from complete consensus to several kinds of disagreement. Disagreement is auspicious if there is agreement between mantic methods and any one human viewpoint. But it is inauspicious if mantic results disagree, or if mantic results oppose human judgment. The implication is to place the authority of prognostication over human judgment; agreement between turtle shell and milfoil is more important than agreement between groups of consultors.

Other accounts of disagreement suggest the use of prognostication by rulers to test their officials. In a *Shi ji* account of a mantic consultation, Han Wu Di summoned his officials and questioned experts from several schools on an auspicious day for marriage:

孝武帝時，聚會占家問之，某日可取婦乎？五行家曰可，堪輿家曰不可，建除家曰不吉，叢辰家曰大凶，曆家曰小凶，天人家曰小吉，太一家曰大吉。

During the time of Emperor Wu, he gathered together all the prognosticators and asked them: is a certain day appropriate for taking a wife? The *Wuxing* master said it was; the master of siting [*kanyu*] said it wasn't. The *Jianchu* master called it not auspicious, the *Congchen* master very inauspicious, the Calendrics master somewhat inauspicious, the *Tianren* master somewhat auspicious, the *Taiyi* master very auspicious.[31]

They could not agree and petitioned the emperor, who chose the principles of *Wuxing*. In this case the ruler clearly has the upper hand. This passage reads more like an account of factionalism than a real consultation about an actual marriage.

In summary, these various accounts also suggest how rulers could or should use mantic advice. First, the ruler is advised to determine his own intentions beforehand. Mantic consultation is not open-ended, and should be used to confirm intentions, rather than to determine them. Second, they recommend mantic consultation for genuine cases of indecision or disagreement, and provide frameworks for resolving differences of opinion. When mantic procedures themselves yielded mixed or contradictory results, the ruler must use independent judgment and exercise authority, as in the case of Wu Di's consultation on marriage. But does this mean that divination is nothing more than an authorization of what the ruler intended all along? The *Zuo zhuan* passage on imperial succession makes it clear that

[31] *SJ* 127.3222, trans. after Pokora 1987: 227–28. *Kanyu* 堪輿 or "siting" (literally canopy of heaven and chariot of earth) differs in important ways from the contemporary geomantic practices of *feng shui* 風水. See Chapter 2 and Loewe 1994: 112–13.

divination is most useful when the merits of the situation are equal or undecidable.

Turning to Greek evidence, treaties between Delphi and consultors make explicit distinctions between state and private consultors, charging separate fees for public (*dēmosion*) and private (*idion*) queries.[32] There is clear evidence that public queries were used to narrow down potential choices. In an account from 508 or 507 Cleisthenes requested the Pythia to choose the names of ten heroes from Athenian history (from a list of a hundred names) to name the ten tribes of Athens. Cleisthenes had reorganized the Athenian citizenry into ten military units, each under the leadership of a general. The general was chosen by election each year, but the names of the tribes were referred to Delphi.[33]

Consultor states also had their own procedures to ensure the accurate transmission and reperformance of responses. An example is the Sacred Orgas decree of 352, the one extant document to specify official procedures for state consultation. It concerned a dispute about the boundaries of the Sacred Orgas, a parcel of consecrated land owned by the sanctuary of Demeter and Kore at Eleusis. One group wanted to leave the land untilled for the goddesses, the other to lease out parts of it to finance building the portico and repairing the sanctuary. The decree specifies a detailed sequence to ensure impartiality. Before consultation, two identical tin sheets were inscribed with the two proposed resolutions to the dispute. Both were to be wrapped identically and placed in a bronze jug in public view. The jug was shaken and the two wrapped sheets were removed and placed, respectively, in a gold jug and a silver jug from the temple of Athena. The jugs were sealed and stored in the Acropolis. Three elected representatives were then sent to Delphi. Their question was whether to follow the inscription in the gold or the silver jug. On their return, the oracular response and both inscriptions were to be read in public, and Athens would follow the resolution selected by the oracle. The decree also mandated that both it and a previous decree concerning holy places be inscribed on stone pillars at Eleusis and in the Eleusinion at Athens. It also specified the composition, manner of election, and duties of the Athenians in charge of administering the matter, and the outlay of funds.[34]

This method of consultation reduces the question to Delphi from a substantive one – how should we use the Sacred Orgas land? – to a

[32] E.g. in the treaties with Sciathus and Phaselis, discussed in Chapter 5.

[33] Fontenrose Q125, PW no. 80, Hdt. 5.66–69 and 6.131. See Bowden 2005: 95–100.

[34] Fontenrose H21, PW no. 262, *IG* 2^2.204 (SIG^3 204), RO no. 58, trans. in Bowden 2005: 88–90.

sortition procedure: should we use the gold or the silver jug? Additional procedures such as the public reading, the inscription of the decree, and the selection of administrators further ensure the integrity of the procedure by removing opportunities to intervene. No particular mantic skill or judgment is involved. The authority of the consultation comes precisely from its mechanical nature.

As this point we can suggest several conclusions about how official consultors used mantic results. First, cross-cultural evidence emphasizes that mantic consultation, official or private, was a limited process in which consultors exercised the power of decision beforehand in the phrasing of their questions, but were then bound by the results. Second, official divination did mediate disagreements and resolve conflicts. But its effectiveness required confidence in the mantic procedure, hence the preoccupation with ensuring the integrity and objectivity of the process. Private consultors, by contrast, typically sought mantic advice either in person or on behalf of a family member. Third, in cases where the results were wholly unsatisfactory, attempts could be made to invalidate or repeat the consultation (discussed below and in Chapter 8). In summary, official consultors did not primarily seek either predictions or confirmation of decisions already taken. In dangerous or irresolvable situations, both Chinese and Greek consultors sought some kind of theological or cosmological affirmation of a course of action.

Private consultors

The very notion of private consultation is problematic. Did any Chinese or Greek consultor represent purely private interests in a modern, Western sense of the term? Many "private" Chinese mantic questions address family or group concerns, not the welfare of isolated, autonomous individuals. As the Chinese marketplace diviner Yan Junping makes very clear, his clients sought advice about families and groups, not isolated individual welfare. Other accounts show consultors bringing their children to physiognomists, to ensure that any report will apply to the next generation. Predictions in the Shuihudi daybooks also tend to refer to the interests of groups: families sacrificing to ancestors, husbands, wives, soldiers, etc. Even marriage is described in terms of group, rather than individual, benefit.

The same reservations apply to "private" Greek divinations. Personal questions about wellbeing at Delphi, Dodona, and Didyma frequently ask about the wellbeing of the consultor's family, rather than himself individually.[35] Most Greek "private" consultations to Delphi are by rulers, whose queries on health, marriage, or progeny had political ramifications. But there are also consultations by individuals, such as Socrates' friends Xenophon and Chaerophon.

Xenophon on consulting a *mantis*

Xenophon's *Anabasis* relates many instances of private mantic consultation. He describes his own experiences and suggests how *manteis* adapted to different circumstances. When first invited to join the expedition of Cyrus, Xenophon consulted Socrates, who sent him to Delphi. As Xenophon tells it, Socrates was concerned at the consequences of Xenophon attaching himself to a man who had sided with Sparta against Athens. With a positive response from Delphi, Athens would have no grounds to act against him. Xenophon, however, got his instructions wrong and asked the standard question: to which god to sacrifice for a good result and safe return:

> When he heard, Socrates reproached Xenophon that he had not, at the outset, asked the god whether it were better for him to go or to stay. He had himself made the judgment to go, by first asking how to best perform the journey. "However, since you asked it in this way," he said, "you must do as the god bids." (Xen. *An.* 3.1.6)

Socrates' response makes clear that simply putting aside an unwelcome oracle was not an option. Xenophon joined the expedition, and continued to follow the oracle's instructions. At first opportunity, he dedicated an offering to Apollo in the Treasury of the Athenians (5.3.4). When undecided whether to accept generalship of the army, he sacrificed to Zeus Basileus as instructed by Delphi: the god gave a clear sign (*diaphanōs ho theos sēmainei*) neither to seek nor to refuse the office (6.1.22–24).

The many accounts of Xenophon consulting *manteis* or even acting as one himself suggest Xenophon's own attitudes toward mantic consultation. One ongoing topic of concern to him was troubling dreams. The first occurred just after his departure from Athens: a storm and a lightning bolt striking his father's house and setting it afire. The next day, he initiated a debate on how to proceed. Generals were chosen (including himself) and oaths were taken to sacrifice thank offerings (3.1–2). Several days later, overtaken by Tissaphernes and in retreat toward Babylon, he dreamed of

[35] For example, in a query from Delphi, Poseidonus of Halicarnassus asks what is better for his sons and daughters to do (Fontenrose H36, PW no. 335). At Dodona, one man asks whether he and his family would be better off in Croton (Appendix 6.4, R2). Another asks to which god to pray to in order to fare well concerning possessions, offspring, and his wife (Appendix 6.4, P1).

being bound in fetters which fell away of themselves. The next morning he offered *hiera* sacrifice and the omens were good (4.3.9). Xenophon clearly took the first dream as a sign that spurred him to initiate a discussion on the army's course of action. It is not clear whether the *hiera* sacrifices were a response to the dream or a normal procedure. There follows an account of *sphagia* before battle:

> the *manteis* were performing *sphagia* into the river. The enemy were shooting arrows and slings but they were still out of range. But as soon as the *sphagia* were favorable all the soldiers began singing the paean and raising the war cry, and all the women joined their ululations with the men's shouting, for there were many women in the camp. (*An.* 4.3.17–19)

In other words, the battle had already begun while the *manteis* were still making sacrifice. Xenophon does not say how much time passed before the favorable sign appeared, or what would have happened if it had not.

Immediate natural adversity could also prompt *sphagia*. For example, after crossing the Euphrates in waist-deep water, Xenophon and his companions marched over a plain through deep snow, against a north wind, and numb with cold. At this point one of the *manteis* suggested they perform *sphagia* sacrifice (*sphagiasasthai*) to the wind. They did so and its violence abated.[36]

Xenophon also describes several conflicts of interest either between generals and *manteis* or among generals. When they came to the country of the Tibarenians the generals wanted to attack in order to gain spoils for the army, and refused hospitality gifts from the Tibarenians:

> After repeated sacrifices, the *manteis* were of the opinion that the gods in no way would permit war. So the generals accepted the hospitality gifts and proceeded through a friendly country. (*An.* 5.5.2–3)

This instance shows that, despite their power of decision, the generals were unwilling to disregard unambiguous omens against military action.

A second conflict occurred in Sinope, where Xenophon wanted to found a colony. Before discussing it with the army, he summoned the Ambraciot *mantis* Silanus to offer sacrifices (5.6.16–17). Silanus, however, wanted to return to Greece as quickly as possible, so he told the troops that Xenophon planned to found a city and delay their return for his own purposes (5.6.27–30). A debate ensued and Xenophon was accused of sacrificing privately without prior discussion. Xenophon defends himself thus:

[36] Xen. *An.* 4.5.2–4. *Hiera* sacrifices occur at many points in the narrative, e.g. 5.4.22.

As you see, I sacrifice as many times as I am able, both on your behalf and on my own, in order that I should happen to say, think, and do such things as will be best and fairest both for you and for me. In the present matter, I was sacrificing with regard to this only: whether it would be better to begin to speak to you and to take action on this matter, or not to touch it at all. Now the *mantis* Silanus gave me a judgment on the major point, that the *hiera* were good. For he well knew that I am not unexperienced on account of always being present at the sacrifices. But he said that the *hiera* revealed some kind of trick and a plot against me, because he knew that he himself was planning to slander me to you.[37]

In other words, Silanus is willing to scheme against Xenophon, but not to misrepresent the *hiera*. Silanus does manage to scheme against Xenophon, but not at the expense of his professionalism. On another occasion, divination was used to confirm a decision to purify the army. Some of the men had stoned three Cerasuntian ambassadors to death, and the generals put the men responsible on trial. Xenophon recommended purification rites (*katharmoi*) for the army, with the support of the *manteis*.[38]

These incidents show a wide range of interactions between client and *mantis*. Sometimes Xenophon is asking about his individual welfare; at other times he acts as a general charged with bringing his men safely home. All these accounts show consistent regard for mantic results. In several cases, individuals with strong motives to disregard unwelcome responses do not do so. Xenophon obeys the oracle from Delphi; the retreating soldiers delay their attack until the *sphagia* are favorable; the generals spare the Tibarenians because of adverse *hiera*; and Silenus does not misrepresent the *hiera*.

The most detailed account of mantic consultation takes place toward the end of the *Anabasis*. It illustrates the ability of a good *mantis* to diagnose a consultor's broader needs. At Lampsacus, Xenophon meets the *mantis* Eucleides, who asks about his circumstances. Xenophon replies on oath that he had to sell his horse and possessions in order to get home, but Eucleides did not believe him:

When the Lampsacenes sent hospitality gifts to Xenophon and he was sacrificing to Apollo, he had Eucleides stand by him. Looking at the *hiera*, Eucleides said that now he believed him about having no money. "But I know," he said, "that even if it is about to arrive, some obstacle appears, and that obstacle is nothing other than you yourself." Xenophon agreed to this. Eucleides then said: "Now the obstacle to you is Zeus Melichios [the Merciful]." And he asked Xenophon whether he had already offered that sacrifice, "just as at home, he said, I used to sacrifice for you and offer up

[37] Xen. *An.* 5.6.28–30, trans. Brownson. [38] Xen. *An.* 5.7.13–35, esp. 19 and 34–35.

whole victims." And he replied that he had not sacrificed to that god since he left home. Eucleides accordingly advised him to sacrifice in his customary way, and that it would be more profitable for him. The next day, Xenophon went to Ophrynium and sacrificed, offering up whole pigs according to his family custom, and obtained favorable signs.[39]

The passage continues that, the same day, two of his friends arrived with gifts for the army. They had bought back his horse because they suspected that he had sold it out of need, and had heard that he was fond of it. This incident illustrates Eucleides' competence in using contextual knowledge to diagnose Xenophon's broader needs and situation. Eucleides had acted as *mantis* for Xenophon in the past, and knew his family and its customs. At first he did not believe Xenophon's account of his poverty and could not advise him. But Eucleides used his knowledge of Xenophon's family history to diagnose the problem as a ritual failure: that Xenophon had neglected the familial custom of sacrifice to Zeus the Merciful. This recommendation was successful in several ways. It gave Xenophon immediate satisfaction. It also resulted in favorable signs and the return of Xenophon's horse.

Chinese accounts of private consultation

The oldest accounts of private mantic consultation in Chinese literature occur in the *Shi jing*, which refers to oneiromancy across the social hierarchy. Two poems describe a consultation in which a headman or head official prognosticates a dream (*da ren zhan zhi* 大人占之). In one, the consultor is clearly a ruler. Animals in his dreams predict the gender of his children; bears signify sons, snakes signify daughters.[40] In another, the headman prognosticates the dreams of herdsmen. Their dreams of crowds turning into fishes portend a plentiful harvest; dreams of snakes turning into banners means the population will increase (in this context, a good thing). The headman seems to enjoy the confidence of the local population. A third poem laments the incompetence of court dream diviners who "cannot tell male from female crows." Male and female crows share the same coloring; the point is that the dream interpreters cannot read beyond the surface of things.[41]

[39] Xen. *An.* 7.8.3–6, trans. slightly after Brownson.

[40] *Shi jing*, Mao 189.8 ("Sigan" 斯干 [Sweeping Banks]). The remainder of the poem is widely cited to authorize the relegation of women to subordinate status. It describes the sons as princes who sleep on couches, wear robes, and play with scepters. Daughters sleep on the ground, wear wrappers, play with tiles, and prepare food and drink. See Raphals 1998a: 199–200.

[41] *Shi jing*, Mao 190 ("Wuyang" 無羊 [No Sheep]) and 192 ("Zheng yue" 正月 [First Month]).

Extended accounts of mantic consultation appear in *Shi ji* 127 and in the *Hou Han shu* collected biographies of *fang* experts. The problem here is that the biographies feature individuals who impressed rulers or local elites: by erudition, public service, or moral rectitude. They concentrate on the skills of the practitioner or on explanations of his art. We do learn that freelance diviners did not make much money; for example, the Chengdu diviner Yan Junping saw only a few customers a day and earned one hundred cash.[42] We learn that they used multiple methods, that most were men, and that many were itinerant.

A detailed account of a mantic session from the *Shi ji* describes an encounter between the fifth-century physiognomist Gubu Ziqing 姑布子卿 and King Jianzi of Zhao, who had requested an assessment of his sons in order to choose an heir:

姑布子卿見簡子，簡子徧召諸子相之。子卿曰：「無為將軍者。」簡子曰：「趙氏其滅乎？」子卿 曰：「吾嘗見一子於路， 殆君之子也。」簡子召子毋卹。毋卹至，則子卿起曰：「此真將軍矣！」簡子曰：「此其母賤，翟婢也，奚道貴哉？」子卿曰：「天所授，雖賤必貴。」自是之後，簡子盡召諸子與語，毋卹最賢。簡子乃告諸子曰：「吾藏寶符於常山上，先得者賞。」諸子馳之常山上，求，無所得。毋卹還，曰：「已得符矣。」簡子曰：「奏之。」毋卹曰：「從常山上臨代，代可取也。」簡子於是知毋卹果賢，乃廢太子伯魯，而以毋卹為太子。

Gubu Ziqing went to see Jianzi of Zhao, who had made all his sons come so that he [Ziqing] could physiognomize them. Ziqing said: "None of them will be a general." Zhao Jianzi asked: "Must the Zhao family then be wiped out?" Ziqing said: "I saw a boy on the road; he is without doubt your son." Zhao Jianzi then summoned the boy Wu Xu. As soon as Wu Xu arrived Ziqing got up and said: "This is the true general." Jianzi said: "This boy's mother is of low birth, she is a servant from the Di [tribe]. How do you explain a destiny of such high honor?" Ziqing replied: "It is what Heaven has bestowed. Although of low birth, he is certain to attain honor." After this, Zhao Jianzi summoned all his sons and spoke with them, and Wu Xu was the most worthy. Jianzi then told his sons: "I have hidden a precious tally on the peak of Mount Chang. I will give it to whichever of you finds it first." All his sons galloped off to the peak of Mount Chang, and looked but could not find it. Wu Xu returned and said: "I have found the tally." "Give it to me," said Jianzi. Wu Xu replied: "On the peak of Mount Chang I looked down on the land of Dai, and it is possible to conquer it." Jianzi recognized that Wu Xu was truly worthy. He demoted the heir apparent Lu and named Wu Xu heir apparent.[43]

[42] *HS* 72.3056. Yan Junping is introduced in Chapter 4.

[43] *SJ* 43.1789–90, trans. after Chavannes 5.31–33. Zhao Jianzi 趙簡子 (Ying Yang 嬴鞅) ruled the state of Zhao from 517 to 458. Cf. Despeux 2003: 513–14.

The physiognomist is not part of King Jianzi's court. The *Shi ji* tentatively confirms Gubu Ziqing's prognostication, but does not say how he reached his conclusions. Several other features of this narrative are of interest. First, Gubu goes to King Jianzi, but King Jianzi has arranged in advance for his sons to be present for the consultation.[44] The immediate question concerns the family fortunes. No question is stated but the response is that "None of them will be a general."

King Jianzi's immediate response is "must my family be wiped out?" This is a potentially devastating prognostication. But Gubu adroitly diverts the conversation, and does not address King Jianzi's question directly. The true general, he responds, is a commoner he has seen on the road, whom he identifies as another son of the king. The boy is of course not present, because, as the son of a commoner, he is not a potential heir. Is the boy really his son? The narrative does not tell us, but the astute physiognomist has given the king a solution to his real problem: the problem of succession, if he chooses to take it.

But is the word of a physiognomist sufficient to justify bypassing his own sons in favor of a commoner? Here the astute consultor takes the physiognomist's advice, but devises an independent verification. King Jianzi creates an impartial test that will determine which young man is most worthy to succeed him by promising the heirship to whichever youth first finds a tally he has secreted on Mount Chang. Only the commoner Wu Xu is able to do so. The test enables King Jianzi to verify the physiognomist's assessment, but also to justify and legitimate his own decision in demoting an already recognized heir apparent.

Another account of a mantic interaction appears in the *Lun heng*. It describes an interaction between Lü Zhi 呂雉 – the future Empress Lü (241–180) – and a wandering physiognomist. Accounts of physiognomy typically appear in biographies of rulers, and serve to prefigure the noble destiny of a commoner. Nonetheless, they can suggest what a mantic consultation was like:

有一老公過，請飲，因相呂后曰：「夫人，天下貴人也。」令相兩子。見孝惠，曰：「夫人所以貴者，乃此男也。」相魯元，曰：「皆貴。」老公去，高祖從外來，呂后言於高祖。高祖追及老公，止使自相。老公曰：「鄉者夫人嬰兒相皆似君，君相貴不可言也。」後高祖得天下，如老公言。

There was an old man who passed by and asked for a drink, and in return he physiognomized Lü Hou and said, "Madam, you are a noble of the empire." She asked him to physiognomize her two sons. He looked at [the future emperor] Xiao

[44] *SJ* 43.1789–90 (Chavannes 5.31–33), quoted in full in Chapter 4.

Hui and said: "What ennobles you, Madam, is this boy." He looked at Lü Yuan and said: "All noble." After the old man had gone, Gaozu returned from abroad and Lü Hou told him what had happened. Gaozu went after the old man and stopped him and requested that he physiognomize him too. The old man replied: "The earlier physiognomies of the lady and her children all resembled you, Sir, but your physiognomy is so high that words cannot describe it." Later, Gaozu attained the empire, as the old man had foretold.[45]

What is interesting for present purposes is the interaction described in the story. (Its rhetorical elements are discussed in Chapter 8.) First, the old man does not seem to be local. There is no mention of his name, or any prior or local acquaintance with Lü Zhi. Second, there is no suggestion of impropriety in his physiognomizing her, even in her husband's absence. Third, as soon as she receives a good response, she immediately asks him to physiognomize her sons, to ascertain that they too share her inborn qualities. When Gaozu returns, he is not angry, but rather seeks out the physiognomist himself. That he goes after the old man indicates that he knows where to find him.

Contemporary accounts

We find many elements of the mantic session in late imperial and contemporary China. Richard J. Smith notes the prevalence of blind fortune-tellers in cities, where some had street stalls. These were public performances, typically in the diviner's stall near a temple, in the marketplace, or even on the street. (Other diviners called on clients in their homes, especially women.) Several Qing accounts note that a great deal of banter accompanied these consultations. Several accounts describe street fortune-tellers as extremely self-confident, clever speakers, shrewd psychologists, and astute observers of character. They used observations of their clients' manner, clothing, possessions, facial expressions and responses, body language, and speech patterns. Blind fortune-tellers were particularly skilled at using indirect questions to get information about their clients.[46]

Smith's own fieldwork in Hong Kong and Taiwan in the 1980s suggests patterns that probably applied to Qing and possibly much earlier divination interactions. First, fortune-tellers made a point of giving clients information about the past in order to establish credibility, using their expertise to establish a consistent biography of the client's past, present, and future. This was done through a mixture of fate calculation techniques,

[45] *LH*, 113–15 ("Gu xiang" 3.11), trans. after Forke 1.305.

[46] R. J. Smith 1991: 205–6, esp. nn. 144–45, cf. Doolittle 1865, Nevius 1869.

observation, and direct and indirect questioning of the client. Smith notes that futures were negotiated. In these discussions the mantic specialist took pains to establish trust and respect, but also to maintain the distance and superiority of the expert. This process entailed both seeking and giving information. The more information the diviner could elicit, the more accurate his predictions were likely to be; the more accurate the predictions, the more likely that the client would return. Sensitivity to the client's reactions also told the fortune-teller when to pursue additional clues or even reinterpret earlier information or statements. Finally, the fortune-teller also established moral bona fides by the quotation of moral maxims, especially to the wider audience of the consultation. Like Sima Jizhu and Yan Junping, these diviners genuinely sought to benefit their clients by helping them solve problems and realize their human potential.[47]

My own less systematic observations in Hong Kong, the People's Republic of China, and Taiwan from 2002 to 2008 are consistent with Smith's findings. I also noted the ability of diviners to deflect negative results. For example, on one occasion I visited a temple in Hong Kong with a friend who had performed a *qian* rod divination that had come out so badly that the temple attendant refused even to discuss it.[48] Instead, he advised her that she had begun with too specific a question, and needed to repeat the procedure. She did so, and the attendant was able to interpret a better result.

Mantic sessions are also affected by official attitudes. In Hong Kong and Taiwan, diviners practice openly in stalls either inside the temple grounds or in markets near major temples. For example, extensive diviners' stalls are adjacent to the metro station adjacent to the Longshan temple in Taipei (Figures 7.1 and 7.2) and courtyards full of people casting *qian* rods in Hong Kong (Figure 7.3).

By contrast, in the People's Republic of China "superstition" is officially discouraged. For example, there are no temple stalls near the temple of the City God in Shanghai, but I have observed several diviners practicing on the street in smaller streets of the same neighborhood, surrounded by locals and passers-by (Figure 1.2). They had no fixed spot, but were easily reachable through the cell phone numbers on their name cards. In other locations diviners practiced inside the temples. A woman diviner I met at the Changchunguan temple in Wuhan in 2006 was self-employed, but practiced in the temple with the permission of its management. At the Baochu temple in Hangzhou I was told that no "fate calculators" (*suan ming xiansheng*

[47] R. J. Smith 1991: 206–9. [48] *Qian* divination is introduced in Chapter 5.

Figure 7.1 Diviners' stalls, Longshan Temple, Taipei, 2008.

算命先生) practiced there, but encountered a fate calculation specialist in the Year God hall.

In an officially hostile environment, anti-divinatory press articles make use of the skills of mantic consultation in order to "expose" the methods of fraudulent diviners who "cheat" people by learning enough about them to prognosticate accurately. Examples include *wu* who use accomplices to gather information about clients in advance and blind diviners who use non-visual sensory impressions or rely on assistants for information such as the wealth of prospective clients or mourning for a recent death.[49]

[49] Anagnost 1987: esp. 47–49.

Figure 7.2 Diviners' stalls, Longshan Temple, Taipei, 2008.

Recent studies by Michel Strickmann, Hsu Jin, and Arthur Kleinman have pointed to some of the psychiatric implications of contemporary practices such as consultation of *qian* rods. Kleinman describes temple oracle consultation in Taiwan as "probably the most widely resorted to form of talk therapy."[50] Despite the popular ideology that efficacy lies in the written oracle texts, these studies point to the importance of effective communication between *qian* rod interpreter and consultor.[51]

These ancient and modern examples contrast with methods that were largely mechanical, and did not rely on or provide the benefits of extended mantic consultation. For example, daybooks and almanac-type calendric techniques do not necessarily involve consultation, and require no expertise beyond the ability to read a table. Without other context or interpretation, they provide correspondingly little in return. Daybook accounts of the meaning and significance of human events are very restrictive. Daybooks are organized not in linear time but according to a repetitive structure, and meaning and significance operates only through the patterns of the sexagenary cycle. They thus restrict the options for human action to choices that could recur every ten to sixty days. The quality of prediction they offered was limited and inferior to the nuanced and interpretive modes of divination available to both elites and commoners.[52]

[50] Kleinman 1980: 254.

[51] Eberhard 1970: 191–99, Strickmann 2005: 41–46, Kleinman 1980: 243–58.

[52] Possible users of the daybooks are discussed in Chapter 5. Possible ritual dimension: Giele 2003 and Falkenhausen 2004.

Figure 7.3 Wong Tai Sin Temple, Hong Kong, 2003.

Gender and mantic access

Finally, the emerging body of scholarship on divination has paid little attention to women as consultors of mantic expertise. Historical sources tend to neglect the activities of women, and accounts of divination are no exception. There is every reason to believe that most mantic experts and their clientele were men. Given the overall lack of historical sources on women in both China and Greece, such accounts as do appear become all the more significant. For this reason it is useful to distinguish two very different roles of mantic object and mantic subject or agent. A mantic object is the individual about whom a question is asked, but that person may derive no benefit from the consultation. Mantic subjects, by contrast, had access to divinatory expertise as direct or indirect consultors or even as practitioners. Some mantic subjects were able to consult diviners on questions of their own choice, on behalf of themselves or others. Others possessed the expertise and liberty to act as both consultor and practitioner; such individuals could use mantic expertise in their own interests. They are thus distinct from practitioners (such as the Pythias and possibly priestesses elsewhere) who used their gifts on behalf of others.

Greek women as mantic objects and subjects

Greek accounts of women as subjects or practitioners of divination are far sparser than in China. Evidence for women as mantic objects is more plentiful. In the lead inscriptions from Dodona questions "about woman" (*peri gunaikos*) were a set topic of consultation. Most of the extant queries about women as mantic objects are from the viewpoint of a prospective husband asking whether he will "do better" by marrying a particular woman or by marriage. A few are from the viewpoint of fathers who ask the oracle to choose between prospective husbands (both discussed in Chapter 6). These questions emphasize the roles of women as a possession (*ktēma*), and typically ask about a particular woman.

A few questions about women concern their appointments as temple priestesses. One response from Didyma confirms the appointment of Tryphōsa, the granddaughter of another *prophētis* named Tryphōsa. This inscription suggests that both male and female priesthoods had a hereditary element. The response to another Milesian query at Didyma directs the appointment of a woman named Satorneila as priestess of Athena, despite her being married, because of the nobility of her family.[53]

Could women consult oracles? It has been asserted that women could not consult oracles directly, largely on the strength of Plutarch's statement that no woman could approach the *khrēstērion* at Delphi.[54] There are legendary accounts of consultation by Manto, the daughter of Tiresias and herself a priestess of Apollo.[55] Several inscriptions from Didyma show women as consultors in the specific connection of their duties as priestesses. For example, Alexandra, a priestess of Demeter, asks why the gods have not manifested during her tenure as priestess, and whether their absence is auspicious. A subsequent query, possibly by the same priestess on what deity to honor, instructs her to honor Deo (Demeter).[56]

[53] Tryphōsa: Fontenrose 1988: H17, discussed in Chapter 4. Satorneila: Fontenrose 1988: H25, *Chiron* 1 1971: 292, Robinson 1981: 57.

[54] Plut. *E apud Delph.* 385c–d.

[55] *Epigoni* fr. 4 (PW no. 20) and Paus. 7.3.1 (PW no. 523). For Manto see Chapter 4.

[56] *DI* 496A.8–10 and 496B, Robinson 1981: 48 and 49, Fontenrose 1988: H22 and H23. Access to the oracle by women was not limited to priestesses. Another response instructs an unknown woman to appease Hera. Fontenrose 1988: H24, *DI* 501, Robinson 1981: 56.

As mantic practitioners, the roles of Greek women were central but restricted. As "channels" for divination they were more likely to practice it than to be consultors. There may be some correspondence between the roles of Greek women as "possessions" in the transmission of both oracles and property. Women were central to the social system as transmitters of property, but could not themselves control it. As priestesses of Zeus at Dodona and of Apollo at Delphi and Didyma, women were transmitters of oracles.[57]

To what extent did women have mantic access as consultors? Even if we discount Plutarch, there are reasons to believe that women's access to Delphi was limited for practical reasons. Non-local women would lack means of travel and would lack *promanteia* once they got there. Nor is there extant testimony of consultation by women.

Outside of Delphi, there is ample evidence of women consulting oracles directly. The Dodona inscriptions include several consultations by women. One questions the oracle about children (Appendix 6.4, C8). Queries by female slaves contemplate flight or ask about manumission (S2, S3, S4). At least two women ask about relief from an illness, or to what god to pray for such relief (I1, I2). A husband and wife (F4) ask how to gain and keep divine protection. But women do not ask other questions: about travel, change of residence, occupation, profit, property, construction, prosperity, ritual, judicial activity, or lost or stolen objects.

Women were also visible consultors of temples of Asclepius. The stelae at Epidaurus contain accounts of forty-two consultations of which twelve are by women, most non-local (Appendix 7.1). Most were seeking children or relief from extended pregnancy. Some are straightforward accounts in which the consultor sleeps in the temple and dreams of Asclepius, who promises her children. For example, a certain Ithmonice of Pellene (no. 2) wishes for a daughter; in a dream Asclepius agrees to make her pregnant with a girl. Andromache of Epirus (no. 31) dreams that Asclepius touched her with his hand and she bore a son. A woman of Troezen (no. 34) dreamed that Asclepius asked her whether she wished for a son or daughter; she specified a son and he was born within the year. Others are more dramatic. Agameda of Cos (no. 39) slept in the sanctuary to have children and dreamed that a snake lay on her stomach as she slept; later she had five children. A Messenian woman named Nicasibula (no. 42) dreamed she had intercourse with a snake borne by Asclepius and had two sons within the

57 Recent studies consider the position of the Pythias as a rare example of female power in the Greek world. See Maurizio 2001.

year. Other quasi-miraculous accounts describe extended pregnancies. A woman (no. 1) who had been pregnant for five years slept in the temple and then gave birth to a son old enough to wash himself and walk. A woman with a three-year pregnancy dreamed of Asclepius and gave birth to a daughter (no. 2).

The other five women requested cures from various illnesses, including blindness, dropsy, worms, and an unspecified abdominal ailment. A woman with a swollen abdomen, fever, and vomiting (no. 41) dreamed that Asclepius massaged and kissed her, gave her a drug, and ordered her to vomit the contents of her stomach. Several inscriptions describe surgeries of varying plausibility. A certain Sostrata of Pherae (no. 25), who had a false pregnancy of worms, failed to dream, but Asclepius appeared to her on her homeward journey and cut the worms out of her abdomen. Ambrosia of Athens (no. 4) was blind in one eye; Asclepius cut out the sick eyeball and poured in a drug. In other accounts Asclepius cuts off and refits the sufferer's head. Arata of Lacedaemon (no. 21) suffered from dropsy. Her mother slept in the temple and dreamed that Asclepius cut off her daughter's head, emptied it of fluid, and refit it. Aristagora of Troezen (no. 23) suffered from a tapeworm. She dreamed that Asclepius' sons cut off her head but were unable to refit it; Asclepius himself came and reattached her head.

These accounts are consistent with the rhetorical nature of the stelae: they record successful and miraculous outcomes. They advertise the powers of a god who in the fourth century threatened to eclipse Apollo himself in the popularity of his shrines.[58]

Women in early China as mantic objects and subjects

Evidence of mantic consultation by men about women begins with the oracle bone inscriptions, where Shang royal women appear in divinations about childbirth, illness, dreams, and ancestral cult. The inscriptions indicate that women's political and economic status was consistently lower than that of men of corresponding rank. Shang royal women appear as objects of queries about prospective marriages and prognostications about auspicious times for childbirth.[59] Yet other queries treat royal men and women much the same. For example, one inscription asks whether the king's dream was due to Ancestor Yi; another asks whether Queen Fu Hao's dream was due to Ancestor Yi.[60]

58 Popularity of cult: EE, Lloyd 2003: 53. 59 *Heji* 14002r. Keightley 1997: 38.
60 *Heji* 776r and 201r, respectively.

The *Zuo zhuan* also describes women as mantic objects in prognostications about marriage and childbirth and in accounts of dreams about progeny and the choice of succession. There are also dream narratives, in which the woman is the dreamer, but not the agent, consultor, or beneficiary of prognostication. The dreams are presented as mantic objects for the benefit of others, usually as predictions of the birth of a future ruler (discussed further in Chapter 8).

In his account of the physiognomy of Han Gaozu (discussed above), Wang Chong describes Lü Zhi's father as a skilled physiognomist, who married her to Liu Bang 劉 邦 (the future Han Gaozu) because of his extraordinary appearance.[61] This choice furthered the interests of the Lü family, and placed her in the role of mantic object. By contrast, in her own encounter with the physiognomist, she is the consultor and immediate beneficiary of the consultation.

Chinese sources also portray women as mantic subjects, either as self-interested consultors or as practitioners of mantic arts. There is evidence that, as early as the Shang, some women had sufficient ritual status to prepare and consecrate divination materials.[62] The *Zuo zhuan* portrays women reading cracks, casting milfoil stalks, physiognomizing people and animals, and interpreting dreams. In one account of questionable authenticity dated to 563, Mu Jiang uses milfoil to determine whether she would ever be released from house arrest.[63] Another account, also dated to 563, describes a woman being requested to read the cracks for a military divination. The Wei official Sun Wenzi prognosticated on whether to counterattack, but referred the interpretation to the king's stepmother Ding Jiang:

孫文子卜追之獻兆於定姜。姜氏問繇。曰: 兆如山陵，有夫出征而喪其雄。姜氏曰: 征者，喪雄禦寇之利也。

Sun Wenzi cracked a turtle on whether to pursue them and presented the crack to Ding Jiang. Lady Jiang asked for the omen verse. He said: "The crack is like a hill; a party go forth on an expedition, and lose their leader." Lady Jiang said: "The invaders losing their leader is beneficial for those who resist them."[64]

[61] *LH*, 113–15 ("Gu xiang" 3.11), Forke 1.305.

[62] Several inscriptions (*Heji* 390, 527, 6040, 17517) indicate that a Lady Xi prepared scapulae and plastrons for mantic use during the reign of Wu Ding. *Heji* 12336v indicates that a Lady Jing had ritually prepared a turtle plastron. See Keightley 1978b: 16–17, 1999a: 33 n. 106.

[63] Zuo, 964–66 (Xiang 9.3, Legge 439–40). For problems connected with this and other *Yi* divinations in the *Zuo zhuan* see K. Smith 1989: esp. 435–38 and Schaberg 2001: 65–70.

[64] Zuo, 978–79 (Xiang 10.5), after Legge 447.

The passage ends with a verification that Wei did counterattack and captured Huang Er of Zheng.

What do we make of Sun Wenzi asking Ding Jiang to interpret the crack? In the oracle bone inscriptions, a named diviner makes the cracks and the king interprets them. Here, Ding Jiang takes the latter role. Is she a substitute for her absent stepson? The *Zuo zhuan* suggests otherwise; other narratives describe her marriage, her husband's death, her observations of the unsuitability of his heir, and her prediction of the impending ruin of the state of Wei.[65] According to the *Zuo zhuan*, Sun Wenzi took her opinion so seriously that he deposited all his valuables in Qi and cultivated political relations in Jin. Another *Zuo zhuan* narrative describes her interpretation of a prognostication about the invasion of Wei by Huang Er of Zheng. It confirms the accuracy of her earlier prediction, including a detailed account of Duke Xian's loss of Wei.[66] This confirmation validates both her interpretation and, more generally, her ability to prognosticate state affairs. But in this incident, Ding Jiang is not the consultor. The question is Sun Wenzi's, and he calls upon her expertise.

In another *Zuo zhuan* narrative, a female *wu* and a physician from Qin use oneiromancy to predict the death of the Duke of Jin.[67] Both reach the same conclusion, interpreting different dreams and without mutual consultation, but they are treated very differently. The physician is rewarded for his skill and sent home; the *wu* is executed for a "false" prediction shortly before the duke's actual death. Both were skilled practitioners, but the foreign Qin physician had higher status than the local female *wu*. (The rhetoric of the anecdote is to show the duke as unjust.)

Other accounts in the *Zuo zhuan* and *Guo yu* depict the activities of male and female *wu* as exorcists, in rituals to bring rain or ward off calamity, and as healers.[68] The *Guo yu* clearly states that male and female *wu* were the same kind of person:

古者民神不雜。民之精爽不攜貳者，而又能齊肅衷正，其智能上上下比義，其聖能光遠宣朗，其明能光照之，其聰能聽徹之，如是則明神降之，在男曰覡，在女曰巫。

65 *LNZ* 1.5a–b, cf. Zuo, 868–71 (Cheng 14.5, cf. Legge 385).

66 Zuo, 1013 (Xiang 14.4), *LNZ* 1.5b.

67 Zuo, 849 (Cheng 10.4, cf. Legge 372–74). There is a textual problem here: it is presumably the duke who has the dream, not the marquis.

68 Rain: Zuo, 1382 (Zhao 16.6, Legge 665); *LSCQ*, 478–80 ("Shun min" 9.2). Calamity: Zuo, 1394 (Zhao 18.1, Legge 671). Healing: Zuo, 849 (Cheng 10.4, cf. Legge 372–74). Accounts of *wu* in the *Zhou li* are described in Chapter 4.

In ancient times people and spirits did not intermingle. There were people whose essence was keen, who were without discord and who were able to be single-minded, reverent, correct, and upright. Their wisdom could compare what was appropriate with regard to above and below, their sagacity could glorify what was distant and announce what was bright. Their clear sight could glorify and illuminate it; their keen hearing could hear it pervasively. If they were like this, the spirits would descend to them [or descend and arrive]. If to a man, he was called a *xi*; if to a woman, she was called a *wu*.[69]

There is considerable debate about this passage.[70] For the limited purposes of the present discussion, the important point is that in this passage men and women are equivalent. Spirits choose to interact with both, but they are known by different names. The passage also suggests that both male and female *wu* met important social needs by functioning as diviners or healers.[71]

The *Lienü zhuan* mentions women with astronomical expertise. Jian Di 簡狄, the mother of Xie, Minister of Instruction to Shun, is credited with knowledge of *tianwen*:

簡狄性好人事之治， 上知天文， 樂於施惠。

Jian Di was good at management by nature. She was especially knowledgeable about astronomy, and she took pleasure in giving gifts.[72]

Jian Di is a character out of legend. A historical case of possible astronomical expertise is Ban Zhao 班昭 (*c.* 35–100 CE), daughter of Ban Biao 班彪 (3–54 CE) and sister of Ban Gu 班固 (32–92 CE), the authors of the *Han shu*. After Ban Gu's death in prison, the Eastern Han Emperor He commanded her to complete several unfinished chapters of the *Han shu*, including the Treatise on Astronomy (*Tianwen zhi*). He also brought her to court to

69 GY, 559 (Chu 2 18.1), cf. Bodde's very different paraphrase (1981: 66).

70 Some scholars have read it as a description of shamanism, in which the spirits "descend into them" or "descend and arrive" (*jiang zhi* 降之). K. C. Chang (1994: 18–21) argues that *jiang* 降 had two meanings in the oracle bone inscriptions, transitively to bring down a disaster on its object, and intransitively to descend. He argues that, in the latter sense, its opposite is *zhi* 陟, to ascend (to heaven to meet with deities); and that the compound *jiang zhi* 降陟 refers to ascending and descending within the context of communication between heaven and earth, either by the shaman's ascending to heaven or by causing the spirits to descend to earth. David Keightley (1998: 821–24) and Michael Puett (2002: 104–9) have argued that this passage does not refer to shamanism, and that the *wu* and *xi* were ritual specialists who maintained proper boundaries between gods and humans, a view that is hard to reconcile with traditional accounts of the activities of *wu*.

71 See Loewe 1982: 104–13.

72 *LNZ* 1.3ab. It is interesting that *Lienü zhuan* 6, the biographies of women skilled in argument, does not include women with mantic expertise.

instruct the empress and court ladies (probably not on astronomy), a role she continued both during his reign and during the regency of Empress Deng.[73]

An area of mantic expertise that is repeatedly attributed to women is physiognomy. One case is Shu Ji 叔姬 of Jin, the mother of the Jin statesman Shu Xiang 叔向. The *Guo yu* and *Zuo zhuan* describe her physiognomizing her children and grandchildren to predict the fortunes of the family. The first is Shu Xiang's younger brother Shu Yu:

叔魚生，其母視之，曰：是虎目而豕喙，鳶肩而牛腹，谿壑可盈，是不可饜也，必以賄死。遂不視。

When Shu Yu was born, his mother looked at him and said: "He has the eyes of a tiger, the snout of a pig, the shoulders of a kite, and the belly of an ox. A river valley can be filled but he will be insatiable; he is sure to be executed for taking bribes." Thereafter she never looked at him again.[74]

The second is her grandson, the son of Shu Xiang and a great beauty:

楊食我生，叔向之母聞之，往，及堂，聞其號也，乃還，曰：「其聲，豺狼之聲，終滅羊舌氏之宗者，必是子也。」

When Yang Shiwo was born, the mother of Shu Xiang heard about it and was going [to see him], but when she reached the hall, she heard his voice and turned back, saying, "His cry is the sound of a wolf. The one who brings down the Yang She clan will surely be this child."[75]

The second prediction clarifies the rhetorical purpose of these incidents: to illustrate the principle that beautiful women give birth to dissolute sons. Physiognomy is used here to predict disaster. There is no account of Shu Ji using her skills to predict the illustrious career of her virtuous son Shu Xiang, though according to her eulogy in the *Lienü zhuan*: "She investigated into people's essential dispositions and calculated their life spans to elucidate their destinies."[76]

But should the obviously rhetorical nature of these narratives make us dismiss the possibility that women practiced physiognomy? Several

[73] Han He Di 漢和帝 (r. 88–105 CE). *Tianwen zhi*: *HS* 26.1273–1312. We cannot be sure whether Ban Zhao herself had astronomical expertise or simply recorded the results of court astronomers. Even the latter role would have required some familiarity with the subject.

[74] GY 14.453 (Jin 14.3), cf. *LNZ* 3.7a. Wang Chong cites these incidents as evidence against Mencius' claim that original nature is good (*LH*, 133–35 ("Ben xing" 3.13), Forke 1.385).

[75] Zuo, 1491–93 (Zhao 28.2), trans. after Legge 726. She was the wife of Yangshe Zi 羊舌子 of the Yangshe clan of Jin, and the mother of the great Jin minister Shu Xiang 叔向. Yang Shiwo was put to death as she had predicted and the Yangshe clan was extinguished.

[76] 察於情性，推人之生以窮其命. *LNZ* 3.7b.

accounts indicate otherwise. According to the *Shi ji*, a female physiognomist named Tang Ju 唐舉 of Liang prognosticated that Li Si 李斯 (280–208), the minister of Qin Shi Huangdi 秦始皇帝, would obtain the power of the empire within a hundred days.[77] No works attributed to her appear in Han sources, but a Ming dynasty textbook on physiognomy attributes two titles to her.[78] There is other evidence that women mastered horse physiognomy. The *Lü shi chunqiu* account of the ten most famous horse physiognomists in the empire includes one woman, a "Daughter Li" (*Zi nü Li* 子女厲), whose particular expertise was physiognomizing horses by their eyes.[79] Finally, the biography of Empress Deng Sui also portrays her as a physiognomist. As regent, she used physiognomy to determine the innocence of some of her attendants after an incidence of theft in the palace. It is not surprising that women should practice physiognomy. It was not overly appropriated by state ritual, and did not require specialized equipment or texts.[80]

Shi ji 127 mentions no women diviners. This is not surprising, since the rhetorical framework is a visit to the diviners of the marketplace, which presumably would not have included women. Its force is to favorably compare the rectitude of marketplace diviners with those of court officials. But accounts of *fangshi* also briefly mention women experts. The *Shi ji* biography of the Han physician Chunyu Yi mentions a female slave skilled in *fang* techniques for health and longevity.[81] Another account of a woman expert in *fang* arts appears in the *Hou Han shu* biography of the wind diviner Li Nan 李南. He had transmitted his skills to his daughter, and she used the techniques in a domestic context. His biography also relates how he passed his skills on to her:

南女亦曉家術，為由拳縣人妻。晨詣爨室，卒有暴風，婦便上堂從姑求歸，辭其二親。姑不許，乃跪而泣曰：「家世傳術，疾風卒起，先吹灶突及井，此禍為婦女主爨者，妾將亡之應。」因著其亡日。乃聽還家，如期病卒。

Nan's daughter also understood the arts of her family, and she was the wife of a man from Youquan prefecture. One morning as she entered the kitchen, there was a

[77] *SJ* 79.2418, cf. *Xunzi* 5.72 and *Qianfu lun* 27.311.

[78] "Physiognomizing spirit qi" (*Xiang shen qi* 相神氣) and "Secret exposition of the wonders of spirit" (*Xuantan shenmiao jue* 玄談神妙訣), in *Shenxiang quanbian* 神相全編 (*Gujin tushu jicheng*, chs. 631–44), chs. 1 (ch. 631, juan 473, ce 4 p. 1) and 7 (ch. 637, juan 473, ce 30 p. 1). With no continuity, this attribution cannot be taken at value, but it does indicate her status as a legendary figure.

[79] *LSCQ*, 1414 ("Guan biao" 20.8), translated in Chapter 4.

[80] *HHS* 10A: 418–19. She is discussed further in Chapter 8.

[81] *SJ* 105.2805. He correctly predicts that she has a fatal illness, despite apparent health.

> sudden burst of wind, and she rushed to her mother-in-law and sought to return [home] in order to bid farewell to her parents. When her mother-in-law would not permit it she knelt weeping and said: "My family has transmitted its arts through the generations. When an ill wind blows up suddenly and blows through the kitchen as far as the well, this is a sign of disaster for the woman in charge of the kitchen, and it is a sign of my impending death." She disclosed the day of her death, and was allowed to return home. She fell ill and died in just such a way.[82]

In this story Nan's daughter used her mantic access on her own behalf to predict her fate and see her family before her death.

In summary, Warring States and Han texts portray women as mantic objects of both official and private queries. But they also show women as having mantic access as subjects. They depict women as competent in a range of techniques, prognosticating in both official and domestic contexts, and using their expertise to persuade others of what they consider the right course of action.

Chinese women as consultors

The *Lienü zhuan* gives one very brief account of a woman who prognosticates on her own behalf. When Jiang Yuan, the mother of Houji, is distressed at her miraculous pregnancy and seeks to end it, she consults turtle shell and milfoil and offers sacrifice.[83] She is effectively using divination to attempt an abortion. The story is all the more striking because it portrays a commoner with access to the elaborate techniques of turtle shell divination.

Another possible area of significant difference between men and women as mantic subjects lies in possession of mantic instruments. The cord and hook motif appears in the tombs of both men and women in late Warring States and Western Han tombs. Men's tombs contain mantic astrolabes and *liubo* game boards. In addition to the odd *liubo* set, elite women's tombs frequently contain TLV mirrors (introduced in Chapter 2) inscribed with variations of the cord and hook pattern. These mirrors are not mantic instruments, but they are cosmographic representations that draw on the same body of knowledge and interest.[84]

A richer discussion of women as mantic objects appears in the Shuihudi daybooks. Auspicious days for marriage are described as "taking a wife" (*qu fu* 娶婦) or "giving a daughter in marriage" (*jia zi* 嫁子), from the viewpoint

[82] *HHS* 82A.2717, trans. after Ngo Van Xuyet 1976: 94–95.
[83] 卜筮禋祀. *LNZ* 1.2a, cf. GY, 518–19 (Zheng 1.1), *SJ* 4.147–49.
[84] *Changsha Mawangdui er, san hao Han mu* 2004: 165. Cord and hook: Harper 1999b.

of a prospective husband or father, never from the perspective of the bride. Most predictions of a wife's temperament or prospects are also from the husband's viewpoint, for example predictions that the wife will be jealous, poor, ferocious, talkative, or become a *wu*. One entry may be read that a girl born on the day *renyin* will become a physician; if this reading is correct, it indicates the possibility that a woman could be a physician.[85]

The daybooks also give some evidence for women as at least indirect consultors. The content of the predictions suggests that the daybooks were used by both men and women (or their families), since their predictions reflected the interests and expectation of both parties. Some predictions, like the wealth or temperament of a prospective wife, seem addressed to a potential husband or his family. Others, such as the chances of the woman's death in childbirth or the systematic prognostications of the future of a newborn child, clearly concerned both husband and wife. But a few questions seem to specifically reflect the interests and concerns of a woman or her family. Will her husband abandon her? Will the husband love the wife (as distinct from the wife loving the husband)?

Richard Smith has argued that in late imperial China gender distinctions probably affected mantic technique, and his observation probably applies to early China as well. Male and female horoscopes were calculated differently. Palm-reading and pulse-taking, presumably on the model of physicians, used the left (*yang*) hand for a man and the right (*yin*) for a woman. Illustrations in physiognomy manuals made sharp gender distinctions in their portrayal and interpretation of physical features. Gender-based social roles also affected the interpretation of mantic evidence. A man's fate calculation would predict his official position or wealth; the same calculation for a woman would typically predict her husband's prospects.[86] Prediction about her own future would typically be limited to auspicious dates for marriage or predictions about childbirth. Overall, these observations apply to the childbirth predictions in the Shuihudi daybooks.

Comparisons and conclusions

An important but neglected aspect of the relation between state and private divination is the way in which divination was used to mediate relations between individuals and groups. A number of Greek examples focus on the

[85] *SHD* (Daybooks): slips 140–49. See Appendix F.
[86] See Chao Wei-pang 1946: esp. 314 and R. J. Smith 1991: 198–99.

use of private divination for public purposes. Socrates' advice to Xenophon to consult Delphi about Cyrus' expedition is explicitly intended to deflect Athenian criticism of an association with a foe of Athens. Xenophon may have been genuinely troubled by his dreams after embarking with Cyrus, but he uses them to initiate a debate among the army. In the first case Xenophon uses Delphi to protect himself against criticism before the fact. In the other he uses a spontaneous sign to initiate a debate on important decisions.

Chinese accounts, by contrast, tend to focus on divination initiated by the state. In some cases it is criticized by anonymous individuals. For example, the *Shi jing* poem "First Month" laments the incompetence of court diviners, possibly an indirect criticism of the throne itself. The detailed *Shu jing* accounts of how to address disagreements about prognostication explicitly address disagreements between the state and an unnamed populace. Other Chinese examples show rulers initiating prognostication to preempt or mediate disagreements with official advisors. For example, King Jianzi of Zhao summons an independent physiognomist to advise him on the choice of succession. Emperor Wu cannot get clear advice from his prognosticators because their theories disagree.

Consultor and practitioner

Both Chinese and Greek accounts of mantic sessions take up complex and sometimes conflicting interests between consultor and practitioner, but they describe these interactions in very different ways. Several Greek accounts address situations where consultor and diviner have immediate conflicts of interest. An obvious and not infrequent case pitted generals' desire to attack against *manteis*' desire to await favorable sacrifices. Examples include Herodotus' account of the battle of Plataea and Xenophon's account of *sphagia* in *Anabasis* 4.

By contrast, Chinese accounts of difficult mantic encounters typically describe the independence and accuracy of the prognosticator who must negotiate a consultation initiated and nominally controlled by a ruler. For example, in King Jianzi's consultation of the physiognomist Gubu Ziqing, King Jianzi presumably wanted Ziqing to choose one of his sons as heir. But Ziqing rejects them all and chooses a commoner, whom he diplomatically identifies as a (true) son of King Jianzi. The remainder of the anecdote goes on to justify this judgment. The blind physiognomist's prediction to Lü Zhi is an after-the-fact justification of the rule, first of Han Gaozu and then of Empress Lü. But it also justifies the skills of Lü Zhi's father, the physiognomist who gave her in marriage to the commoner Liu Bang. In these stories the empowered individual is not the consultor but the prognosticator.

The mantic encounters described in this chapter portray what could be called satisfactory consultations, both in outcome and in management of the process. But what happens when the consultor is not satisfied with the results? Or when a consultation is inappropriate? Another type of difficult interaction between consultor and practitioner occurs when the response is just impossibly bad.

The most famous example in Greek history is the first part of the "Wooden Wall" oracle to the Athenians of 481. The Athenians had sent envoys to Delphi and followed the normal rituals for consultation. As they were entering and taking their seats, which is to say before they had asked a question, the Pythia Aristonikē spontaneously enjoined them to fly to the ends of the earth and prepare for destruction. Here the account takes an interesting turn. The Athenian envoys were completely downcast. Seeing their distress, an eminent citizen of Delphi advised them to return to the oracle as suppliants and request a second consultation. The Athenians returned as suppliants and requested a better oracle, threatening to remain in the *adyton* for the rest of their lives (7.140–41). Whereupon the Pythia gave Athens a second oracle: that Zeus had granted to Athena a "wooden wall" (Hdt. 7.140–41). This oracle is discussed further in Chapter 8.

In Herodotus' account, the Athenian consultors intercede to request another consultation in an unsatisfactory session. But Delphi, unlike an independent *mantis*, had no immediate need to please clients, and little motive to modify an unwelcome oracle. Interestingly, the recommendation to return as suppliants comes from a Delphian: the well-respected Timon. By approaching the oracle as suppliants, the Athenians emphasize their own subordination to the will of the god, but invite him to reconsider. The Pythia is at liberty to soften the blow without undermining Delphic authority. I know of no Chinese textual example of a similar response, but fieldwork on contemporary divination and my own observations indicate that Chinese temple diviners may also find ways to repeat and thus mitigate a truly unsatisfactory divination.

Finally, both the Greek and Chinese evidence indicates that skilled practitioners used divination to diagnose the psychological needs of their clients. Xenophon's account of his own interaction with Eucleides attests to the psychological skills of a *mantis* who knows his client well. Eucleides diagnoses both Xenophon's psychological state and his material problems, and offers an astute remedy. Xenophon's obstacle is himself: specifically the neglect of his family's habitual sacrifices. This is a fundamental difference between oracular and independent divination. Oracles were not interested in their clients' histories, and derived their authority from entirely different notions of truth. Accounts of Qing and contemporary Chinese temple divination have more in common with the Greek independent *mantis*, who has the self-confidence, keen observation, and astuteness of street and temple diviners.

Another difference between official and independent practitioners is in the choice of method available to consultors. Both Chinese state and Greek "dependent" consultation generally followed set methods. For example, specific offices such as the *Taibu* or *Taishi* used set procedures. Oracles also used set procedures, and in the case of public consultation, *poleis* had deliberate methods for authorizing an envoy or *theopropos*, and recording and safeguarding the response until it was delivered to its proper audience.

Greek private consultation may have been more flexible. For example, if a bean oracle was offered at Delphi, the choice may have been determined by the calendar, or possibly by the consultor's place in the order of *promanteia*. The oracle of Zeus at Dodona may also have used a range of methods, but there is insufficient evidence to know the options at any given time. Choice of method is a conspicuous feature of contemporary Chinese temple oracles. Many advertise a range of skills, and their first question to the prospective client is a choice of method.

Gender

The paucity of sources makes it difficult to assess the use of divination by women. It could be argued that, both as objects of divination and as practitioners, Greek women functioned as possessions (*ktēmata*). There is ample evidence of Greek women as priestesses or *manteis*, but female *manteis* were lower in status than their male counterparts. In received accounts, their inspiration was invasive and was associated with madness arising from divine possession. Greek oracular institutions were centered on the pronouncements of female priestesses, but their activities were at some level managed and interpreted by male priestly lineages such as the Selloi at Dodona and the Branchidae at Didyma.[87] There may be no lexical distinction between a male and female *mantis*, but descriptions of their activities and the lexicon used of them indicate a vast difference between their perceived activities, mode of divination, and social status.

[87] Invasive madness: Padel 1983. Didyma: Catherine Morgan 1989: 27.

There is evidence of women as consultors at Dodona and Epidaurus, but many of their questions and concerns seem to have reflected the interests of their families (as did many queries by men). In a few cases, priestesses put questions to oracles on their own initiative, but these questions arose from their office. The striking exception is queries by female slaves on flight and manumission, which reflect a purely individual interest.

The lack of mantic access by Greek women seems less "normal" when it is contrasted with what we know of women in early China as objects, subjects, and consultors of the mantic arts. As mantic officials, their functions seem to have mirrored those of their male counterparts. Chinese sources mention female consultors and practitioners of turtle shell, milfoil, and dream divination as well as female *wu* and practitioners of *fang* arts.

As in Greece, Chinese women appear frequently as mantic objects in both the received tradition and excavated texts, especially in the contexts of marriage and progeny. But we find substantial evidence of Chinese women as mantic subjects. In fact, an area of difference between early China and the late imperial period is the relative lack of gender segregation and greater access of female consultors to a range of technical experts, including physicians and diviners. Examples include male physicians treating female patients and male physiognomists "reading" female consultors.[88]

Overall, the Chinese evidence suggests a higher degree of mantic access by women in early China than in Greece. From very early times, women had ritual status to practice divination. Their status as mantic consultors is complex because we know of few cases in which women were empowered to choose the questions put to a diviner.

Finally, comparison of Chinese and Greek mantic encounters offers a different perspective than comparisons between African oracles and Delphi, which juxtapose primarily official consultation (at Delphi) with primarily private consultation in much of the African fieldwork. It makes possible a separate comparison of official and private consultations, and tells us something about what respective concerns affected both kinds of mantic consultation.

In the Chinese case, we can supplement this picture with rich and ongoing evidence from temple oracles, which remain an active source of mantic consultation in many areas of Greater China.

[88] Male physicians treating female patients: Raphals 1998b.

Appendix 7.1: Women consultors to Epidaurus

(latter half of fourth century, after *IG* 4^2.1.121–22, cf. EE 1.221–23, Stele 2, nos. 1–42)

No.	Name	Problem	Vision and cure
1	Cleo	five-year pregnancy	Birth of a son old enough to wash himself and walk.
2	Ithmonice of Pellene	to bear a daughter	Asclepius agrees to make her pregnant with a daughter.
		three-year pregnancy	Asclepius asks if she had not obtained her desire (pregnancy), and what else she wishes. Birth of a daughter.
4	Ambrosia of Athens	blind in one eye	Asclepius cuts the sick eyeball and pours in a drug.
21	Arata of Lacedaemon	dropsy	(To her mother, who slept in the temple.) Asclepius cut off the daughter's head, emptied it of fluid, and refit it.
23	Aristagora of Troezen	tapeworm	Asclepius' sons tried to cut off her head, but couldn't refit it; he returned and reattached her head.
25	Sostrata of Pherae	pregnant with worms	No dream. Asclepius appeared to her on her homeward journey, and cut worms out of her abdomen.
31	Andromache of Epirus	for children	Asclepius touched her with his hand and she bore a son.
34	woman of Troezen	for children	Asclepius asked her whether she wished for a son or daughter (a son). He was born within the year.
39	Agameda of Cos	for children	A serpent lay on her belly. Five children born.

No.	Name	Problem	Vision and cure
41	Erasippe of Caphyiae	swollen abdomen, fever, vomiting	Asclepius massaged and kissed her, gave her a drug, and ordered her to vomit the contents of her stomach.
42	Nicasibula of Messene	for children	Asclepius came to her with a serpent; she had intercourse with it. Two sons within the year.

8 Mantic narratives

> I know the number of grains of sand and the measure of the sea;
> I understand the speech of the dumb; I hear those who do not speak.
>
> (Apollo to Croesus, Hdt. 1.47.3)[1]

> [Under the reign of a virtuous ruler] priests and historiographers can set forth the truth, and [a virtuous ruler] has nothing to be ashamed of in his mind. The spirits accept his offerings and the state receives their blessing, in which the priests and scribes share.
>
> (*Zuo zhuan*, Zhao 20.6)

In the previous chapters I have made an ongoing distinction between mantic questions and responses that are historically factual and transparent and narratives about mantic encounters that are of dubious historicity. In this chapter I take up problems of mantic narratives with significant didactic, literary, ideological, or other narrative content. In order to be plausible, such accounts must give recognizable representations of mantic practitioners, methods, questions, and consultations; and are valuable as such. Nonetheless, these accounts are motivated by a range of ideological and literary concerns that affect the content and form of mantic responses.

An obvious but important point about both Chinese and Greek mantic narratives is that they occur within literary sources, rather than in inscriptions or excavated texts. I begin with an overview of the genres of Greek and Chinese mantic narratives and the problems involved in comparing them. The second section consists of a series of comparisons. In three sets of examples, the common genres of narratives about warfare, historiography, and biography motivate the comparison. A fourth example compares narratives about portents from different genres (Greek biography and Chinese memorials).

The third section takes up two sets of Chinese and Greek mantic narratives that seem completely incommensurable. The first set examines very different literary representations of human–divine communication in Greek tragedy and Chinese poetry. The second set examines mantic ambiguity as

[1] Hdt. 1.47.3, trans. after Godley (Loeb) and Kindt 2006: 36.

an expression of very different views of the relations between humans and gods. I suggest that there were two very different kinds of moral judgment in Greek narratives about mantic ambiguity and Chinese narratives about sagely prescience.

A unified genre of mantic narrative?

Vernant makes a distinction between two models of divination. Oracular divination as actually practiced in the Classical period (oracular practice) gives advice about the present by answering binary (yes–no) questions; it does not make predictions about the future or offer open-ended advice. A second model of divination is its theoretical representations. According to Vernant, the prophetic function of divination manifests as an irruption of divine immutability and omniscience into the flux of human existence. But if the oracle announced the future, it would undermine the radical difference between humans and gods.[2] It is this second, theoretical model of divination that informs Delphic oracle stories.

Julia Kindt argues persuasively that Delphic oracle stories are a distinct topos or genre of Greek reflective literature. She describes these stories as unique narratives by which the Greeks reflected on the world and their human place within it. Although Delphic oracle stories changed over time, they had common features, including divine foreknowledge, the human desire to predict, the obscurity and difficulty of oracular language, and finally the expectation that, properly understood, oracular predictions come true.[3]

She argues that, in the Athenian late fifth century especially, these stories addressed a need for orientation during a time of rapid social, cultural, and political change, where the present and future little resembled the past. In fifth-century Athens, they appear in historiography, tragedy, and comedy. For the historian, Delphic oracle stories introduce the authority of an oracle to back up the authority of the historian. The most extensive source for Delphic oracle stories is probably the *Histories* of Herodotus. Accounts of oracular consultation also occur in Thucydides and Xenophon, but for Herodotus oracles are a historiographical strategy: they structure narrative, introduce authority, render moral judgments, and serve as a mode of religious reflection.

Mantic narratives also figure importantly in tragedy and comedy, which rely heavily on oracles and predictions, but respond less directly than history

[2] Vernant 1991: 303–17, esp. 314–15, cf. Manetti 1993: 18–19.
[3] On these points see Kindt 2003: 32–46.

to a need for orientation in time.[4] Tragedy retells the mythical past in ways that shed light on the present, and comedy compares a corrupt present to a better past. Aeschylus and Sophocles center their recreations of ancient myths on Delphic oracles. Delphic oracles are central to the plots of Aeschylus' (*c.* 525–*c.* 456) *Eumenides* and *Seven against Thebes*, Sophocles' (*c.* 496–406) *Oedipus Tyrannus*, and Euripides' (*c.* 480–406) *Ion*. Other plays feature the predictions of Amphiaraus and Tiresias. Diviners and chresmologues are objects of derision in the comedies of Aristophanes (*c.* 448–380), especially in the *Birds* and *Knights*. Tragedies typically hinge on correct predictions; comedies gain their jest from incorrect ones.[5] In drama, oracular utterances play very different roles than in historiography or biography. No omniscient narrator establishes mantic authority; the utterances are always spoken by a character within the play, both to an internal audience and to the play's spectators. They structure plot and produce suspense. They appear at times of critical uncertainty – sometimes in response to crises such as famine or impending warfare – and introduce the theme of human knowledge and its limits, and the omniscience of the gods, especially Zeus and Apollo.[6]

Oracle stories also appear in narratives about colonization, the rise of tyrants, and warfare. These accounts first appear during the Archaic period (*c.* 750–480), when Greeks engaged in far-flung colonization of foreign territories. Colony foundation accounts significantly include colonization oracles, and suggest that Delphi was an important element in the Archaic colonization movement. These oracles show how Greeks represented colonization to themselves in a coherent system of cultural meaning.[7]

Tyrant stories reproduce crises in meaning and orientation that emerged around the usurping power of a tyrant. Obscure oracles about war concern crucial questions in dangerous situations: the outcome of battle, the best strategy, etc. In all three contexts, oracular obscurity is a textual strategy to communicate the "openness" of the future to the audience.

Finally, mantic narratives become an important structuring element in some biographical narratives in Plutarch's *Lives*, especially the lives of Alexander, Cimon, Nicias, and Pericles.

[4] For instances of divination in Greek and Roman drama see Staehlin 1912. See also the indices in Fontenrose 1978: 451–57.

[5] For accounts of divination in tragedy see Hamilton 1978 (Euripides), Dodds 1966, Vellacott 1964, and Burkert 1991 (Sophocles, especially *Oedipus Tyrannus*). For Aristophanic comedy see N. D. Smith 1989. For discussion see Kindt 2003: 12–13.

[6] Kindt 2003: 60–64.

[7] Colonization narratives are introduced in Chapters 4, 6, and 7. See also Dougherty 1992, 1993, 1994.

Oracular obscurity is also significant as a religio-philosophical concept, which asserts the ontological difference between humans and gods. In Delphic oracle stories, human knowledge arises out of insight into the true meaning of an obscure oracle. It is closely linked to the use and correct understanding of language and reference. Delphic oracle stories also reflect strong notions of order, justice, and morality.

Kindt argues that these stories were popular for several reasons. First, they were "good to think with," reflecting old and new and human and divine. Second, their sustained reflection on time emphasized the openness of the future, and supplied new historical narratives to bridge gaps between the past and an obscure future. They share a distinct narrative pattern of question and answer, problem and solution. The human consultor asks Apollo a question about the past, present, or future and receives a response which usually answers the question and implied request. Oracular obscurity complicates the basic pattern by delaying understanding of the answer. Obscure oracles describe future contingencies, in indirect and difficult ways. They are like detective stories insofar as both are built around blocked information, a "case" to be solved. The withholding of key information sets a hermeneutic task for the audience, who are linked to the protagonist, facing obscure oracular language. Apollo and the narrator know what will happen; the protagonist and the reader do not know the meaning of the oracle until the end of the narrative. The stories use three main techniques to "block" the advice they give: ambiguity, metaphor, and vagueness.[8]

Kindt's study raises important questions that invite comparison.[9] What is the status of mantic narratives as a possible transcultural genre or topos, somewhere between history and literature? Several problems complicate the application of Kindt's findings to Chinese material.

In a different context, Marc Kalinowski describes predictive discourse in the *Zuo zhuan* as "a literary genre halfway between the discursive arguments of counsellors and the oracular pronouncements in divinatory consultations."[10] Kalinowski argues that *Zuo zhuan* predictions have a consistent structure and perform significant narrative functions throughout the text. An interlocutor (usually a prince) incites an "author" (usually a

8 Kindt 2003: esp. 75–81 (fifth-century Athens), 85–89 (narrative patterns).

9 Kindt (2003) has argued that "Delphic oracle stories" are an important part of a Greek reflective discourse on the world and the place of humans within it. She argues that they have three key features: obscurity of responses, special oracular language, and problems of human interpretation.

10 Kalinowski 1999: 38. Other studies of divination in the *Zuo zhuan*: Imai Usaburō 1969, Li Jingchi 1978, Gao Heng 1979, Seiwert 1979, K. Smith 1989.

minister) to make a prediction about another individual or situation (the subject), often accompanied by an explanation or argument. Predictions occur in a set narrative sequence. An anecdote describes the context of the divinatory event, followed by one or more predictions about it. Arguments before or after the prediction are strongly didactic in tone. Some involve a second prediction that confirms or elaborates the first. The arguments analyze the event and transform the prediction into a reasoned anticipation of future events, sometimes including a recommendation or warning. Arguments draw on the ritual comportment of the subject, analysis of facts about preceding occurrences, citations from the *Shi jing*, and analyses of political behavior. Finally, the prediction is verified; as in the *Histories*, fulfillment of a prediction may take months or even years (the more distant the event, the more "divination-like" the prediction).

These cycles of prediction, argument, and verification perform several narrative functions, which differ in important ways from the predictions of Delphic oracle stories. First, like Delphic oracle stories, they render ethical judgments and oppose the predictive wisdom of the text's authors to the failings of its narrative subjects. Second, they anticipate the mandate or decrees of heaven (*tian ming* 天命, also translated as the "Heavenly mandate") and actors' obedience to or disrespect for them. As such, *Zuo zhuan* predictions are never themselves objects of criticism. Finally, prescience (*xian zhi* 先知) is often presented as a cognitive process of a superior order that is independent of, and at times opposed to, predictions by the mantic arts.

The warfare narratives and historiography of Herodotus' *History* and the *Zuo zhuan* present a clear context for comparison of mantic narratives. However, an immediate difference is that Greek mantic narratives are overwhelmingly attributed to one source – the oracle of Apollo at Delphi – while Chinese mantic narratives are very diverse in both genre and attribution. They appear in texts that describe incidents of prognostication and divination (introduced in Chapter 2). These include historical narratives, biographies, poems, philosophical works, and memorials in dynastic histories.

A second problem lies in the role of obscurity and the creation of meaning. Vernant and Kindt argue that oracle stories create meaning by reiterating a fundamental dichotomy between human and divine perspectives, especially in the perception of time.[11] But that dichotomy does not exist in Chinese narratives, where the line between mortals and immortals is

[11] Vernant 1991, Kindt 2003: 116. In Delphic oracle stories, human success is linked closely to the balance between the human and divine spheres.

more fluid. Ancestors become immortals, as do virtuous individuals under certain circumstances. Greek Delphic oracle stories thus problematize how Chinese mantic narratives create meaning.

Chinese and Greek mantic narratives

I now turn to four sets of mantic narratives of varying comparability, across several genres. Mantic obscurity and ambiguity provide a powerful tool for reflection in Greek mantic narratives, for both protagonists and audience. But obscurity and ambiguity are not defining features of Chinese mantic narratives, which emphasize different notions of cosmic order and human morality.

Historiography: the Croesus cycle and predictive cycles in the *Zuo zhuan*

The story of Croesus and the battle of Plataea mark respectively the beginning of Persian hostilities toward the Greeks and the key land battle that ended Persian invasion of Greek territory. Herodotus' accounts of both prominently feature mantic encounters: between Croesus and the oracle of Apollo at Delphi, and between the predictions of the *manteis* employed by the Greek and Persian armies.

Herodotus specifically designates Croesus as the first to behave unjustly (*adika*) toward the Greeks, the first foreigner to subdue Greeks (1.6.3), and thus responsible (*aitios*) for the ultimate conflict between the Greeks and the Persians.[12] The rise and fall of Croesus takes up most of Book 1 of the *Histories*; that account prominently features Delphic oracles.[13] The cycle begins with the usurpation of the throne of Lydia by Croesus' ancestor Gyges. Delphi confirms his kingship, but also predicts vengeance on his posterity in the fifth generation.[14]

Before making extensive use of the oracle, Croesus attempts an empirical test by sending the same question to seven different oracles. Only Delphi

[12] Hdt. 1.1.1, 1.2.2, and 1.2.7–8. For a detailed account of these oracles see Crahay 1956: 185–207.

[13] Scholars have given many accounts of Croesus' role in the *Histories*. For example, Jean Defradas (1954: 208–28) reads the entire sequence as Delphic apologetics. François Hartog (1988, 1999, 2000) and Julia Kindt (2003: 132–53, 2006: 34–35) argue that Herodotus used Delphic oracles to establish the authority of a text written in a new genre.

[14] Hdt. 1.13.1, 1.14.3–4, 11, and 16. Croesus' father Alyattes inquires about his illness, and receives a response only after repair of the temple of Athena he destroyed (1.19–21 and 25).

answers to his satisfaction.[15] Yet Croesus consistently fails to profit from oracular advice. He begins by transgressing the norms of consultation: by asking a question to which he knows the answer and by appropriating the obscurity proper to a god. Croesus falsely assumes that Apollo is speaking to him transparently, and repeatedly misinterprets his oracles.[16]

He questions Delphi on war with Persia, and is advised that if he crosses the Halys he will destroy a great empire.[17] He famously misunderstands the oracle to refer to the Persian empire, rather than his own. The other part of the response – on whether to take an ally – prompts an account of oracles to Sparta during the Messenian Wars (740–680).[18] In these stories, misinterpretation is key to oracular failure. Non-interpretation of an oracle does not necessarily result in failure, but misinterpretation does. Why? Croesus and other heroes of misinterpretation stories are consistently over-confident. By assuming the oracle's language to be straightforward, they never acknowledge differences between mortal and divine knowledge and perceptions of time and causality.

Croesus receives another obscure oracle: when he asks Delphi if his rule would be long-lasting. He is told to beware the day that a mule becomes lord of the Medes. He misunderstands this to mean that he has nothing to fear, since a mule cannot rule a kingdom. But the mule is a metaphor for an event that has already happened. Cyrus is a "mule": he is the hybrid offspring of a Persian father and Median mother. He already rules Persia, and thence the Medes.[19]

Finally, when questioned by Cyrus as to why he had invaded Persia, he tried to put the blame on Apollo. He even sends to Delphi to ask whether the god was not ashamed at having encouraged him with misleading oracles. The Pythia replies that not even a deity can escape destiny (*moira*), and that Croesus has expiated in the fifth generation the crime of his ancestor. Apollo wanted to postpone the fall of Sardis to the time of Croesus' sons, but could

[15] Hdt. 1.47.3 (Q99, PW no. 52). The oracles were Delphi, Abae (in Phocis), Dodona, Miletus, Amphiaraus, Trophonius, and Ammon. On the hundredth day after his departure from Sardis, each messenger was to ask what Croesus was doing at that time. Herodotus quotes only the response. Croesus was satisfied and made lavish offerings to Delphi. See Klees 1965.

[16] On these points see Kindt 2006: 34–40. [17] Hdt. 1.53–54 and 1.87, Q100, PW no. 53.

[18] Messene was located in the southwest Peloponnese near the Messenian plain and Mount Ithome. It withstood sieges by both Sparta and Macedon, and was absorbed by Philip II of Macedon after the battle of Chaeronea in 338. For example, when Sparta asked about conquering Arcadia, they were told that they would measure out the Tegean plain in fetters, presumably the chains of their conquered opponents. The Spartans misunderstood and attacked Tegea, only to suffer defeat and themselves measure out the Tegean plain in fetters (Hdt. 1.66.2, Q88, PW no. 31).

[19] Hdt. 1.55, Q101, PW no. 54. See Kindt 2006: 39–40.

not divert the course of destiny (*paragagein Moiras*). He had given Croesus as much as the Fates allowed, and had even saved him from the sacrificial pyre of Cyrus. Herodotus concludes:

> As to the oracle, Croesus had no right to find fault with it: the god had declared that if he attacked the Persians he would bring down a mighty empire. After an answer like that, the wise thing would have been to send again to inquire which empire was meant, Cyrus' or his own. But as he misinterpreted what was said and made no second inquiry, he must admit the fault to have been his own.[20]

On hearing this, Croesus admits that he alone is to blame. In realizing his previous errors, Croesus moves closer to the knowledge of Apollo, and even assumes a quasi-oracular voice, as does Herodotus himself.[21]

Mantic narratives of the *Zuo zhuan* present a different structuring of time and prediction. *Zuo zhuan* prognostications provide a positive judgment on powerful figures, often by means of narratives that are considered to be later interpolations. Some are predictions by mantic specialists (turtle shell and milfoil diviners); others are spontaneous predictions by non-specialists, sometimes women, from dreams or physiognomy.

One repeated pattern is the double-edged prediction that an unborn or newborn son will flourish, but only as his home state declines. He will be illustrious, but only elsewhere. The (chronologically) first of these concerns Gongzi Wan of Chen 陳公子完 (b. 762, also known as Jing Zhong 敬仲), the eventual founder of the Tian 田 lineage of the state of Qi 齊. The story begins with his exile to Qi, when the people of Chen 陳 killed the heir to the throne. The marquis of Qi wanted to make him a minister of state, but he declined because of his status as an exile. The marquis then appointed him to a lesser office.[22]

The *Zuo zhuan* introduces a detailed assessment of his character. In one account, he hosted the marquis with wine. When his guest asked for candles to continue their drinking, he avoided excess, and declined politely, on grounds that he has not prognosticated about drinking at night.[23] This passage establishes his character by demonstrating his willingness and ability to remonstrate with a superior and his concern (depending on emphasis) for the details of ritual or for mantic completeness. The point of either reading is to highlight Jing Zhong's character. This moral judgment is then justified by two retrospective predictions and their fulfillment. The first is a query by his father-in-law on whether to give his daughter in

20 Hdt. 1.91.1–5, Q103, PW no. 56, trans. after Godley (Loeb) and Kindt 2006: 42.

21 Hdt. 1.91.6; Kindt 2003: 147–49.

22 Zuo, 220 (Zhuang 22.1), Legge 103.

23 Zuo, 220 (Zhuang 22.1), Legge 103.

marriage to Jing Zhong. His wife interprets the prognostication as auspicious, and adds that Jing Zhong's posterity will flourish in Qi: in five generations they will attain the highest office, and in eight, no one will compare with them.[24] The second is a prognostication from Jing Zhong's childhood by a scribe from Zhou who possesses a copy of the *Zhou yi*. Jing Zhong's father requested a prognostication about the boy's future; the *Yi* divination foretold that he would flourish, but only as the fortunes of his home state of Chen declined. His descendants would be illustrious, but elsewhere.[25] This prediction uses the mantic authority of the *Zhou yi* to augment the *Zuo zhuan* authors' positive assessment of Jing Zhong and his descendants.[26]

One series of mantic narratives illustrates the moral superiority of Duke Wen of Jin 晉文公 (697–628), culminating in the battle of Chengpu 城濮. The text establishes the moral faults and ritual impropriety of Viscount of Chu (楚子) through accounts of his transgressive behavior toward women.[27] It describes the virtues of Duke Wen through accounts of his exile in Chu and his return to power after twenty years.[28] In a key incident, as a guest of King Cheng of Chu (Chu Cheng Wang 楚成王, 671–626), he promises goodwill to Chu; should there ever be war between Jin and Chu, he promises to order his troops to retreat three *she* 舍 (about thirty miles), and only fight if there could be no reconciliation.[29]

In 635 Duke Wen prognosticates on whether to ally with Qin to restore King Xiang of Zhou 周襄王 (d. 619), who had been ousted by his brother. This narrative features a disagreement over the meaning of the cracks. Diviner Yan 卜偃 reads them as auspicious and urges Duke Wen to unify the states. He cautiously replies that the auspice is too good; he orders a milfoil divination, which is equally auspicious.[30] Only then does Duke Wen agree to lead the alliance that ultimately restores King Xiang. This decision brings Jin into conflict with Chu.

[24] Zuo, 221 (Zhuang 22.1), cf. Legge 103. See Kalinowski 1999: 52 and Pines 2002: 22–26.

[25] Zuo, 222 (Zhuang 22.1), Legge 103.

[26] In another double-edged prediction about progeny dated to 660, Duke Huan of Lu orders a childbirth prognostication and learns that his son Cheng Ji's 成季 fortunes would be inverse to those of Lu. See Zuo, 263–64 (Min 2.4), Legge 129.

[27] He improperly brings women into the domain of warfare by displaying captives and the ears of the slain to the wives of the earl of Zheng. Feasted in Zheng and showered with gifts, he again violates propriety by taking the earl's wives back with him as his concubines. See Zuo, 399–401 (Xi 22.9), Legge 183.

[28] Zuo, 401–29 (Xi 23–24), Legge 184–92.

[29] Zuo, 409 (Xi 23.6), Legge 187.

[30] Zuo, 431–32 and 435 (Xi 25.4), Legge 195–96.

Subsequent developments underscore the virtues of Jin and the faults of Chu. The Chu commander mistreats his own soldiers and is so rude that the Jin officers predict his defeat.[31] In 632 the Jin and Chu troops meet in battle. Faithful to his earlier promise, Duke Wen orders his troops to retreat three *she*. But the Chu commander, unaware of Duke Wen's prior promise to King Cheng, misunderstands his withdrawal and gives chase. At that point, no reconciliation is possible. Duke Wen orders the Jin troops to retaliate, inflicting a crushing defeat on Chu at the battle of Chengpu. The *chengyu* idiom "retreating three *she* as a condition for peace" (*tuibi sanshe* 退避三舍) derives from this incident.[32]

These few incidents illustrate the didactic nature of the *Zuo zhuan*, and how mantic predictions underscore the moral and historiographical judgments of its authors. They introduce the authority of turtle shell and milfoil divination, structure the text, and confer a deductive style on the text as a whole. Kalinowski argues that these divinations were not fabricated by the *Zuo* authors, but rather that the mantic narrative structure was the main stylistic device of early Chinese historiography.[33] It created an artifice of narrative unity, and the doctrinal content of the text was articulated by the argument within the divinations.[34]

The dangers of war: Plataea and Han

Herodotus brings the resolution of the war between the Greeks and the Persians to a head in Book 9, with the Persian defeat at the battle of Plataea. Here the mantic locus is not Delphic oracles, but the activities of *manteis*, especially battle-line *hiera* and *sphagia* sacrifices on both sides. These incidents frame the entire account, beginning on the second day after all the troops were arrayed, when both armies offered sacrifice. Herodotus recounts the sacrifices and interpretations of the two highly paid Elean *manteis* performing *hiera* on behalf of the Greeks and the Persians. Each interprets the sacrifices the same way: auspicious for defense but ominous for attack. As a result, neither side was willing to initiate an attack, and for ten days no major action occurred (9.33–36).

[31] Zuo, 444–45 (Xi 27.4, Legge 201–2) and 457–59 (Xi 28.3, Legge 208–13).

[32] Zuo, 458 (Xi 28.3), Legge 210. *Chengyu* 成語 ("proverbial idioms") are four-character idiomatic expressions, usually derived from Classical literature, and widely used both in Classical Chinese and in contemporary language. In the latter context they differ from proverbs in that they are Classical Chinese phrases embedded in contemporary language.

[33] For further discussion of the philosophical background of the *Zuo zhuan* see Schaberg 2001.

[34] Kalinowski 1999: 39–48 and 56–65. His analysis focuses on ninety-six narratives, spread throughout the reigns chronicled in the *Zuo zhuan*.

This narrative is nuanced by Herodotus' account of the character and history of each *mantis*. Tisamenus of Elis, the *mantis* employed by Sparta (9.35), had consulted Delphi about offspring (a standard form of mantic query), but had received the unusual response that he should win five great victories. He misunderstood these victories to refer to athletic competitions. The Spartans understood them correctly as military victories, and recruited Tisamenus at the uniquely high price of full Spartan citizenship for himself and his brother. He helped Sparta win five great victories at Plataea, Tegea, Dipaea, Ithome, and Tanagra. By contrast (9.37–38), the Elean *mantis* Hegesistratus had been condemned by the Spartans. He escaped from prison by cutting off his own foot, and took refuge in Tegea. An open enemy of Sparta, he worked for Mardonius both for pay and for revenge.

As more Greek forces poured in, the Persians debated their course of action. Mardonius argued vehemently and without moderation to ignore the divinations of Hegesistratus and to fight, in the Persian manner, before more Greek troops arrived (9.41). He prevailed by asking whether anyone knew an oracle predicting the Persians' defeat. He himself offered an oracle predicting Persian defeat after plundering the temple at Delphi, and proposed to avoid defeat by avoiding the temple (9.42).

On the Greek side, Alexander of Macedon forewarned the Greeks, predicting that Mardonius would disregard the *hiera* and attack (9.45). The Spartans and Tegeans performed *sphagia* again to improve their chances against Mardonius, but the results were still unfavorable, and many were killed and wounded. Finally, the Spartan commander Pausanias prayed to Hera; the sacrifices turned favorable, Mardonius was killed, and the Spartans defeated.[35] Herodotus concludes:

> On that day, according to the oracle [*khrēstērion*], the Spartans received full justice for Leonidas from Mardonius, and also the finest of victories, which we all know was won by Pausanias.[36]

[35] Hdt. 9.61–63. They thus achieve a victory that celebrates the two Homeric heroic values of force and guile. See Detienne and Vernant 1978 and Raphals 1992.

[36] Hdt. 9.64, trans. after Godley. This passage refers to a Delphic oracle to Sparta, which consulted Delphi after receiving a request to aid the Greek forces against Persia. The Spartans received a prediction in verse that they either would be sacked by the Persians or must mourn the death of a king descended from Heracles (7.220). In 480, Leonidas went to Thermopylae with 300 men, to take command of the Greek forces. Vastly outnumbered, he repulsed an initial Persian attack. Leonidas sent away the allied Greek troops and remained with a small force of Spartans to defend the pass at Thermopylae, where he died with his men.

Although this sequence ends with the fulfillment of a Delphic oracle, it also prominently includes debates about *sphagia* sacrifice and predictions by *manteis*. These predictions feature some of the ambiguity of Delphic oracle stories, and, like them, introduce moral judgments by Herodotus. The rhetorical force of these accounts of opposed *manteis* is to contrast the moral probity of Tisamenus and the astuteness of the Spartans with the criminality and vindictiveness of Hegesistratus. The contrast is underscored by a further difference between the arrogance, hubris, and short-sighted view of time of Mardonius and the piety of Alexander and Pausanias.

In summary, Herodotus' account of both oracles and the predictions of *manteis* plays on a combination of consultors' misinterpretations and Herodotus' own political and moral judgments.

Zuo zhuan predictive cycles prominently feature military campaigns and the circumstances that cause and justify them. Battles are often presented as the culmination of complex chains of prediction and moral judgment. They sometimes include arguments over strategic decisions based on disagreements about the interpretation of military divinations, not unlike the arguments by *manteis* in Herodotus and Xenophon. As an example, I take a cycle of *Zuo zhuan* predictions about Duke Xian of Jin 晉獻公 (r. 676–651) and his second and third sons: Chong'er 重耳, subsequently Duke Wen of Jin, and Yiwu, subsequently Duke Hui of Jin 晉惠公 (d. 637).[37] These events culminate in the battle of Han 韓 in 645 and the battle of Chengpu in 632. In particular, the stories contrast the rise to power and eventual death of the malevolent Yiwu and the subsequent rise and virtuous reign of Chong'er (mentioned above).

The cycle begins in 656 with an incident and a prediction that describes the moral failings of Duke Xian. They begin with his committing incest and violating generational taboos by his marriage to Qi Jiang 齊姜, formerly the concubine of his father Duke Wu of Jin 晉武公 (r. 679–677). After her death, he prognosticates about marriage to his concubine Li Ji 驪姬. After an inauspicious divination by turtle shell and an auspicious divination by milfoil, Duke Xian opts to "follow the milfoil," which accords with his own wishes. The diviner disagrees, but Duke Xuan ignores advice, and

[37] Duke Xian had five sons by six wives. The first, Jia Jun 賈君 of the State of Jia 賈, bore no heir. Next was his father's concubine Qi Jiang, the mother of Shensheng. He then married two women from the Rong 戎 tribe: Hu Ji 狐姬, the mother of Chong'er 重耳, and her younger sister Xiao Rongzi 小戎子, the mother of Yiwu 夷吾. Finally he married two women from the Li Rong tribe: Li Ji, the mother of Xiqi 奚齊, and her younger sister Shao Ji 少姬, the mother of Zhuozi 卓子. See Zuo, 239 (Zhuang 28.2), Legge 114.

establishes Li Ji as his wife.[38] This account uses the prognostication to criticize Duke Xian on several counts. First, he succumbed to an infatuation, despite mantic advice. Second, he engaged in the profound impropriety of promoting a concubine to the role of wife.[39] Finally, all these faults are compounded by the duke's attempt to manipulate mantic authority to his own purposes. Li Ji engineers a series of events that force Duke Xian's heir, the virtuous prince Shensheng 申生, to commit suicide in 656. She also uses her influence to turn Duke Xian against his other two sons Yiwu and Chong'er, who are forced into exile. Later, Prince Yiwu is established as Duke Hui.[40]

The battle of Han resolves a long series of predictions that establish the moral and military inferiority of Duke Hui to his opponent: Duke Mu of Qin 秦穆公 (d. 621).[41] The sequence culminates in the fulfillment of the predictive cycle. Forced into a defensive engagement at the Han River, Duke Hui consults the turtle shell to select a leader for the impending battle. But he rejects the officer selected by the procedure, and ignores the advice of his own officers. In the final battle, his chariot becomes stuck in the mud and he appeals for help to the very officer he had rejected. The man replies that since Hui has "rejected counsel and defied divination" (*bi jian wei bu* 愎諫違卜), his defeat is inevitable.[42] The *Chunqiu* records that the marquis of Jin was captured in the battle of Han in the eleventh month.[43] This statement verifies the entire sequence of predictions and divinations on both sides, which justify the Qin victory. All three predictions justify the Qin invasion because of Yiwu's faults of character. In the narrative construction of the

[38] Zuo, 295 (Xi 4.6), Legge 141. She gives birth to Xiqi and her younger sister to Zhuozi.

[39] For Shensheng and Li Ji see Zuo, 358–59 (Xi 15.4), Legge 168. For a different account of the same events see *LNZ*, chapter 7, story 7. The story of Li Ji is one of a type of Warring States legends about women who cause destruction by influencing royal succession or retaining power after their husbands' deaths. For discussion see Raphals 1998a: 37 and 62–63.

[40] After Duke Xian's death, she placed her son Xiqi on the throne. Li Ji, Xiqi, and Zhuozi were killed by the official Li Ke 里克, who invited Chong'er to return as Duke of Jin. When Chong'er declined, Li Ke established Prince Yiwu as Duke Hui, who immediately forced Li Ke to commit suicide.

[41] They begin in 650, with an epiphany of the ghost of Shensheng (Zuo, 335 (Xi 10.3), Legge 157). Four years later, after an anomaly (the collapse of a hill), the Jin official Diviner Yan 卜偃 predicts a great calamity before the year's end (Zuo, 347 (Xi 14.3), Legge 162). In 645 Duke Mu performs a milfoil divination to decide whether to launch a retributive invasion against Duke Hui, and receives the auspicious prediction that after three defeats he would capture his foe (Zuo, 353 (Xi 15.4), Legge 167). Duke Hui had denied Qin grain relief in a famine, against the advice of his own officials, and despite famine relief from Qin the previous year.

[42] Zuo, 356 (Xi 15.4), Legge 168.

[43] Zuo, 350 (Xi 15.12), Legge 166. The *Chunqiu* is introduced in Chapter 2.

Zuo zhuan, Yiwu's disregard for mantic authority helps establish him as a man marked for defeat.

The *Histories* and the *Zuo zhuan* share several features in their account of oracles, predictions, and prognostications. Both use predictions and the dynamics of mantic encounters to assess the moral character, wisdom, and success or failure of their protagonists. Croesus and Mardonius fail to understand the nature of oracular language. Instead of puzzling out the real meaning of oracles or signs, they jump at the interpretations that suit their own desires and consistently misinterpret to their own advantage. They even try to subvert divine predictions with actions intended to make them invalid, for example Mardonius' proposal to spare the temple at Delphi. Similarly Duke Xian chooses the mantic result that suits his desires and marries Qi Jiang. Duke Hui ignores mantic advice completely. In both sets of stories, failure turns on misinterpreting mantic results to one's own advantage through a combination of over-confidence and moral shortcomings.

Biographical narratives: Alexander and Empress Deng Sui

Divination is also a prominent feature in biographies of rulers. Plutarch uses mantic encounters and beliefs about divination as key elements in his portrayals of Alexander and Nicias. The Han Standard Histories include predictions about future rulers, told as dreams or encounters with physiognomists. The Treatise sections include memorials that use portents and anomalies to justify the dynasty or to criticize emperors.

Plutarch's sources for the *Life of Alexander* are obscure, and his reasons for using mantic narratives are complex, but several points can be made nonetheless. First, at the beginning of the *Life of Alexander*, Plutarch compares himself to the painter who captures a person's spirit by concentrating on the eyes, and omitting less revealing details; in a brief "life," he abbreviates and selects, choosing points he considers essential. For Alexander, these appear to have included his religiosity and belief in a quasi-divine destiny.

Second, Plutarch is a moralist. He is interested in Alexander's virtues and vices, and how the balance of virtue (*aretē*) and chance or fortune (*tukhē*) informs the course of his life, and its effect on the rest of the world. That interest emerges clearly in the Orations. In *On the Fortune or Virtue of Alexander*, Plutarch presents Alexander as a man of virtue, despite the adverse influence of chance. That antithesis also appears in *On the Fortune of the Romans*, where Plutarch asks whether virtue or fortune predominated in Rome's success, and argues that fortune played the greater role. In particular, Rome was fortunate in the early death of Alexander, who would have invaded Italy (326a).[44] Here it is significant that in the parallel lives, Plutarch juxtaposes Alexander with Caesar.

Third, the *Lives* were probably written while Plutarch was a priest at Delphi, and clearly reflect his high regard for Apollo and his shrine.[45] But he describes the rise and fall of Alexander with a combination of mantic narratives, consisting of both oracles from Delphi and Ammon and of interpretations of dreams and portents. The oracles reveal his rise and potential. The portents are more mixed, and eventually presage his early death.

Plutarch's *Life of Alexander* repeatedly uses predictions by oracles and dreams and portents interpreted by *manteis* to affirm Alexander's divine descent and imperial destiny. Elsewhere, Plutarch uses portents to prefigure momentous events, such as the rise of Athens and the death of Caesar.

Almost all known Macedonian oracular responses are historically problematic, but they make powerful claims for a destiny preordained for the Macedonian kings Philip II and Alexander III and Macedonian queries about Alexander's entry into Asia in 334. They begin with a clearly legendary colonization oracle requesting Delphic sanction to found an Argive colony in Macedon. It supports Macedonian claims of descent from Argive Greeks, claims Philip used in attempts to stabilize Greece through diplomatic means.[46]

The first oracle to Alexander himself occurs on the eve of the Persian campaign, about 335. It turns on a linguistic ambiguity. Alexander receives an oracle that he would be guided by a wolf (*lukos*, genitive *lukiou*). His guide turns out to be the son of a Lycian (*Lukios*, genitive *Lukiou*). Here the ambiguous language of the oracle turns on a homonym.[47]

A second oracle from Delphi assures Alexander that he is invincible. According to Plutarch, Alexander declared that he had got the answer he wished for, and had no further need to consult Delphi.[48]

[44] For the speeches see Wardman 1955: esp. 98–100.

[45] Plut. *Alex.* 1.2. For details on Plutarch and his methods see Wardman 1955 and 1971, Opsomer 1996, Bosworth 2003.

[46] L50, PW nos. 225 and 227; Euphorion ap. Schol. in Clem. *Alex.* Protr. 11P. Euripides had been a guest of the Macedonian king Archelaus, who had made peace with Athens and Hellenized his court. Such claims begin with Herodotus' account of Alexander I's descent from exiled Argive descendants of Temenus (8.137–39, cf. 9.45, 5.22). At the time of the Persian invasions, this story allowed Alexander to ingratiate himself with the Greeks without undermining his status as an ally and subject of Persia. See Hammond and Griffith 1979, Borza 1982, Hammond 1993.

[47] Plut. *Alex.* 37.1, Q217, PW no. 271. Animal guide motif: Fontenrose 1978: 73–74. Homonyms in Delphic oracles: Kindt 2003: 90–91.

[48] Plut. *Alex.* 14.4, Q216, PW no. 270.

At this point Alexander's mantic engagements leave the genre of Delphic oracle stories and continue elsewhere. After he gained control of Egypt in 332, his first move was to sacrifice to Apis at Memphis and assume the title of Pharaoh, with implied descent from the god Ammon. The next year he visited the sanctuary of Ammon at Siwah.[49] This visit is controversial because of its role in his claims to divine descent and its bearing on broader assessments of his character, ambitions, and intentions.[50]

Most portents in the biography are interpreted by the *mantis* Aristander of Telmessus, beginning with a dream about the birth of Alexander.[51] Other oracles predict a quasi-divine destiny.[52] For example, Aristander interprets sweat on a cypress statue of Orpheus to mean that Alexander would force future bards to work and sweat to describe his deeds (14.8–9). Subsequent portents become increasingly dire. Aristander interprets a bird flying over

[49] E.g. Plut. *Alex.* 27.4. According to Arrian (3.4.5), he stated that he had received the answers his heart desired, possibly instructions for sacrifices while on campaign. Arrian also reports (3.9.6) that before setting out for Asia, he performed a great sacrifice to Zeus Basileus, which would have obeyed the oracle to Philip to sacrifice to Ammon. This sequence also explains Alexander's neglect of Delphi; he had inherited his father's war and perhaps believed he had also inherited his prognostication. See Fredricksmeyer 1991: 202.

[50] W. W. Tarn (1930: 377–78) plays down the incident on grounds that consulting Ammon in this way was normal and traditional; as Pharaoh, Alexander was considered the son of Ammon. Other scholars stress the singularity of the visit on grounds that Pharaohs did not normally journey from Memphis to Siwah, Alexander was not Egyptian, and the visit to Siwah was one of Alexander's few diversions from the most strategic route, suggesting its importance to him. See Bosworth 1977: 75, 1994: 810–11, and Fredricksmeyer 1991: 199–201. For a detailed account of the Egyptian context see Lane Fox 1973: 202–10.

[51] Shortly after his marriage to the Epirote princess Olympias, Philip dreams that a snake enters her bed and seals her body with a seal bearing the figure of a lion. Some of Philip's court *manteis* take the dream as a warning against Olympias, but Aristander argues that its meaning is that Olympias would bear a son with a lion's courage. Philip sends to Delphi, and is advised to sacrifice to Ammon, and also that he would lose sight in the eye that spied on Zeus lying with his wife in the form of a serpent. See Plut. *Alex.* 2.5 and 3.1, Q211, PW no. 269. The instruction to worship Ammon is a standard response to the cult query concerning which god to worship for best advantage. The prediction that Philip would lose an eye for spying on Zeus is not; it introduces the claim of Alexander's descent from Zeus.

[52] Other oracles predicting the destiny of Alexander also combine conventional and quasi-fictional elements. In an oracle Parke and Wormell consider genuine, Philip asks whether he can prevail against Persia, and is told: "the bull is garlanded; he comes to an end; the sacrificer is at hand," which Philip apparently took as a sign of victory (Paus. 8.7.6, Diod. 16.91.2, Q213, PW no. 266). Less probably, the question "Who will become king after me?" receives an ambiguous response suggesting that his successor would rule the world (Ps.-Callisthenes, *Historia Alexandri Magni*, Raabe 36, Q212, PW no. 507). Two other historically dubious oracles promise Philip military victories (Q214 and 215, PW nos. 267 and 268, Posidonius in Cic. *Fat.* 3.5 and *Suda* A3788, *c.* 350 and *c.* 340). The questions are not reported, but one response advises Philip to "fight with silver spears and you will win everything"; the other to "secure safety from the violence of a chariot." Aelian (3.44) reports that the assassin who killed Philip had the figure of a chariot engraved on his sword hilt.

Alexander's head and becoming trapped in the nets of a battering ram to mean that he would be wounded at Gaza, but would take the city nonetheless.[53]

In other accounts, Aristander performs hieroscopy. Some results, like Delphic oracle stories, depend on correct interpretation for their fulfillment. For example, during the siege of Tyre in 331, Aristander predicted that Alexander would take Tyre that month. It was the last day of the month, and Alexander's troops made fun of the prediction. Alexander intervened and set the calendar back a week, counting the thirtieth day of the month as the twenty-third. He then ordered the attack, and so inflamed his forces that they took Tyre that very day, thereby bringing Aristander's prediction to pass.[54]

Some modern scholarship has dismissed these accounts as fictional. Lowell Edmunds argues that recent scholarship tends to overlook or trivialize Alexander's religiosity (including his attitudes toward divination), either by reducing it to debates about whether he believed himself to be divine or by representing religiously motivated actions as political propaganda.[55] Edmunds argues that Alexander's devotion to the gods was widely recognized, and that his heroism and emulation of mythical heroes were aspects of a Macedonian religiosity that had more in common with sixth-century or even Homeric values than with the values of fourth-century Greece. As he puts it: "Homeric kingship lived on in Macedon. The king was preeminent amongst the aristocratic chiefs on account of his own wealth and power. His power consisted in his own *aretē*."[56] And Macedonian kingship, like Homeric kingship, was deeply religious; Macedonian kings were priests who could, for example, purify the army at need.[57] They were deeply involved with divination, and retained mantic seers such as Aristander and Demophon as advisors.

Dynastic histories and other narratives use predictive dreams to justify dynastic change. According to the *Guo yu*, Moxi 妹喜, the concubine of the

[53] Plut. *Alex.* 25.4–5. See Brenk 1977: esp. 194–200.

[54] Plut. *Alex.* 25.1–3. Aristander also performed *sphagia* sacrifice before the battle of Gaugamela in 331. At the start of the battle, Aristander pointed out an eagle that soared over Alexander and flew toward the enemy, effectively encouraging the army to charge Darius' troops (*Alex.* 33.1–3). Aristander disappears from the record in 328, but another *mantis* named Demophon appears briefly in the accounts of Diodorus and Curtius (e.g. Diod. 17.93, Curt. 9.4.27–29). By contrast Arrian (*An.* 6.9.1–11.8) and Plutarch (*Alex.* 63) do not mention him. Arrian does mention that Demophon was one of a group of men who slept in the temple of Babylonian Serapis to inquire about Alexander's health at the end of his life (7.26.2).

[55] Arrian, for example, refers to him as "the most attentive with respect to the gods" (*An.* 7.28.2).

[56] Edmunds 1971: 370. [57] E.g. Curt. 10.9.11–12.

last Xia king, dreamed of two suns fighting in the sky. She interpreted the dream as a warning that King Xia Jie's 夏桀 mandate to rule was at an end. Subsequently, his nobles rebelled, his soldiers abandoned him, and King Tang 湯 (r. 1617–1588) established the Shang dynasty.[58]

Other narratives justify the reign of a ruler through predictions of a commoner's royal destiny. Eastern Han rulers, whose power was increasingly undermined by powerful landed families, used accounts of the royal destiny of the Han founder Han Gaozu (originally the commoner Liu Bang) to justify the legitimacy of the Eastern Han through its roots in the Western Han. In the *Han shu* "Discourse on the Mandate of the King" (*Wangming lun* 王命論), Ban Biao goes to great lengths to justify Han Gaozu's accession to the throne, claiming that Heaven selects upright rulers for their virtue. His qualifications include extraordinary physiognomy and other "signs" of royal destiny.[59]

Another account of imperial destiny concerns one of the few female rulers of China: Empress Deng Sui 鄧綏 (81–121 CE), the wife of Han He Di 漢和帝 (79–105 CE) and eventually Empress Deng. The force of these stories is to predict and justify her rule as regent. According to the *Hou Han shu*, her father died at the time when she otherwise would have been admitted to the women's apartments of the palace (92 CE). At this time, she dreamed that she touched the heavens in the form of a stalactite, and drank the drippings. She consulted a dream interpreter, who told her that the sage kings Yao 堯 and Tang had similar dreams before they became rulers.[60]

Later she met a physiognomist, who remarked on her resemblance to Tang. The biography reports that her family privately rejoiced, but did not dare to spread it about. Her uncle explained it in this way:

常聞活千人者，子孫有封。兄訓為謁者，使修石臼河，歲活數千人。天道可信，家必蒙福。

58 See GY 255 (7.2 Jin 1), *LSCQ*, 844 ("Shen da" 慎大 15.1), *LNZ* 7.1a, cf. Raphals 1998a.

59 *HS* 100A.4207–12, cf. *HHS* 40A.1324. The latter passage includes claims for descent from Emperor Yao, character, skill at managing subordinates, and the appearance of divine signs when he assumed rule. Ban Biao argues that Heaven's mandate for rule (*tian ming*) depends on two equal factors: merit arising from ancestral line and auspicious destiny. See Y. K. Lo 2010: 327. As Michael Nylan (2009: esp. 56) has observed, this essay is a work of theology rather than logic, insofar as it offers no concrete or rational support for the legitimacy of the Eastern Han. For Empress Lü see *LH*, 113–15 ("Gu xiang" 3.11), translated in Chapter 7. Han Gaozu is introduced in Chapters 4 and 7.

60 斯皆聖王之前占，吉不可言。 *HHS* 10A.419. He also warned her against speaking of these auspicious omens. In these accounts, she is analogized to a male ruler, but is a mantic object nonetheless.

It is often heard that someone who saves a thousand lives has descendants who are ennobled. My brother Shun [her late father] held the office of Imperial Messenger [*ye zhe*]. When he was ordered to make repairs at the Shijiu River, in one year he saved several thousand lives. The way of Heaven is trustworthy; reward and good fortune are certain to come to his family![61]

On this interpretation, Deng Sui's subsequent rule over China is not a woman over-reaching herself, but Heaven's reward to her family for the virtue of her father.

The *Hou Han shu* reports that, in 95 CE, she again was chosen to enter the palace. After the dethronement and death of He Di's first empress Yin Hou 陰后, Deng was proclaimed empress.[62] He Di died in 105, and his son died a year later. Because there was no male heir, Deng Sui became regent as Empress Dowager Hexi (Hexi Huang Hou 和熹皇后). She was one of the few women rulers of China, and perhaps one of the last effective rulers of the Eastern Han, a role sufficiently controversial to require justification.

In summary, Plutarch's accounts of oracles and interpretations of portents by *manteis* are central to his assessment of Alexander.[63] Some scholars have read the mantic narratives in the *Life of Alexander* as politically motivated, but that reading fails to take full account of Alexander's own religious views or Plutarch's stylistic methods. The Alexander of the *Lives* is a man of great religiosity and virtue, but is also cursed by adverse fortune, revealed in increasingly adverse portents toward the end of his life. The dream of Deng Sui explains Deng Sui's destiny as the action of *dao* and Heaven, rewarding her family for the past virtuous actions of her father. In both cases, predictions of an imperial or quasi-divine destiny provide justifications for the authority of a controversial ruler.

Manipulating portents

The opposite of using divination and portents to legitimate authority is using them to manipulate political or military decisions. I take up two examples: the use of memorials on portents to criticize Han emperors and

[61] *HHS* 10A.419, trans. after Swann 1931: 140. For *ye zhe* see Loewe 2000: 763.

[62] Yin Hou was dethroned in 102 CE after accusations of using witchcraft against other members of the imperial household, probably including Deng Sui.

[63] Nor is there a contradiction between Philip and Alexander retaining a traditional *mantis* and revolutionizing the practice of warfare in ways that left little room for battlefield divination. Battle rituals: Pritchett 1974–79: 1.87–89; Hellenistic warfare: Garlan 1975, Bosworth 1994, Chaniotis 2005.

the role of divination and portents in the Athenian decision to launch the disastrous Sicilian Expedition.

Mantic narratives could also influence political opinion and decision-making, and arguments about portents provide a powerful example. Plutarch's *Life of Nicias* is structured around the lunar eclipse of 413, which provides a striking example of the deliberate manipulation of mantic information to influence public decisions.

Plutarch portrays the conflict between Nicias and Alcibiades and his faction as a struggle between young men who wanted war and elderly men who wanted peace.[64] Their disagreement came to a head in 413, when Alcibiades contrived a divination to persuade the Athenians to support an expedition against Syracuse, the most powerful polis on the island of Sicily. His private diviners and chresmologues found (or manufactured) an oracle predicting an Athenian victory. They reported only the parts of an oracle from Ammon that predicted the capture of Syracuse, concealing conflicting and negative utterances (*Nic.* 13.1). Under the influence of Alcibiades, the Athenians disregarded other signs, such as the mutilation of the herms, the appearance of ravens on Athenian dedications at Delphi, and an oracle from Delphi to consult a priestess of Athena from Clazomenae named Irene ("Peace," 13.3).

Nicias was elected as general of the expedition. Nevertheless, he continued to oppose the war, and he and others used oracular arguments to make their case. The astrologer Meton pretended to be mad and set his house on fire, possibly to free his son from a disastrous command. According to Socrates, his *daimonion* had told him that the expedition would lead to the ruin of Athens (13.5).

Even on his arrival in Sicily, Nicias held back from military action. After losses at Syracuse, he decided to return to Athens, only to be confronted by the phenomenon of a lunar eclipse (23.2). Here Plutarch digresses with a brief account of Anaxagoras and the history of Greek knowledge of the phases of the moon. He remarks that lunar eclipses were broadly understood at the time, but that most people still considered them uncanny, and a divine sign portending great calamities.

The effect of the digression is to underscore Nicias' ignorance and superstition (*deisidaimonia*). Plutarch describes him as terrified, all the more so because his *mantis* Stilbides had just died and he was without advice. Plutarch also describes Stilbides as the one man who was able to release Nicias from his superstitions (23.5). Afraid to proceed, Nicias persuaded the

64 Plut. *Nic.* 11.3.

Athenians to delay a month, hoping for a sign of the restoration of normalcy to the heavens (23.6). But the Syracusans attacked while he was frantically praying and divining; they were encouraged by their own diviners' predictions of victory in a defensive battle (25.1). The Syracusans thus repelled the Athenian naval expedition – in a defensive battle – and the Athenians were forced to withdraw by land (26.1). Most of the expeditionary force, an appreciable amount of Athens' military resources, surrendered or were killed on the island of Sicily. This defeat also proved to be the turning point for Athens in the Peloponnesian War.

Plutarch structures the account of Nicias around a sequence of divinations and portents, interpreted and misinterpreted. He praises Nicias for his courage and morality: he leads the Sicilian Expedition despite his disapproval. But Nicias (like Alexander) is ultimately undone by fortune, in a combination of the eclipse, his own superstition, the untimely death of Stilbides, and his fatal misinterpretation of the significance of the eclipse.

During the Western Han, the study of portents became a recognized form of political discourse and critique. Scholars such as Dong Zhongshu 董仲舒 (*c.* 179–*c.* 104) and Liu Xiang 劉向 (77–6 BCE) argued that the will of Heaven manifested in omens and portents. Portent theory (*zaiyi shuo* 災異說) was based on the premise of a bond between Heaven and humanity, and held that Heaven uses natural phenomena to communicate its will to humanity out of concern for human wellbeing. Portent studies gained influence over the course of the Western Han. Emperors resisted it because of its potential to criticize them. Nonetheless, portent interpretation became a powerful tool in political struggles, and court factions used natural disasters – which did occur regularly – to attack their rivals. By the Eastern Han, portents had become a recognized part of political discourse and portent studies were considered an orthodox form of intellectual inquiry.[65]

Han discourses on omens also reflected new tensions between rulers who claimed to maintain the cosmo-moral order and the officials who prescribed it. Scholar-officials who created imperial legitimacy through omens and correlative cosmology used the same hermeneutics to criticize the government: if not the ruler himself, then those close to him and in power.

The most important portents were solar eclipses. For example:

[65] For a concise account of the development of portent theory see Hinsch 2006. For further discussion see Chang Ch'uan-ts'ai 1995: 136–51 and Huang Zhaoji 1998: 16–27. For portent studies in Han politics see Wang Baoding 1997: 104–8.

冬十二月戊申朔，日有蝕之。夜，地震未央宮殿中。詔曰：「...君道得，則草木昆蟲咸得其所；人君不德，謫見天地，災異婁發，以告不治。」

In the winter, during the twelfth month on [the day] *wushen* [January 5, 29 BCE], the first day of the month, there was an eclipse of the sun, and in the night there was an earthquake in the Weiyang Palace. The imperial edict said: "... when the way of a true prince is obtained, even grasses, trees, and insects find their proper places. But when the prince of men is not virtuous, a reproach appears in Heaven or Earth, and there are frequent anomalies in order to inform him that he is not governing rightly."[66]

This entry includes both the account of an eclipse, which had been memorialized to Emperor Cheng Di, but also the emperor's edict and response to the report.

There were many kinds of portent. Astral portents included comets, meteors, shooting stars, double moons, and other strange astral phenomena. Weather-related portents included prolonged rain, storms, fog, droughts, and abnormal weather such as unseasonable rain, frost, snow, or thunderstorms, or winters without ice. Other portents were terrestrial: earthquakes, avalanches, floods, fires, plagues of locusts or other insects, famines, and other anomalous behavior of plants or animals, including monstrous births of animals and human beings.[67]

In what has become a classic survey of this material, Wolfram Eberhard argued that many of these accounts of portents were inserted for political reasons, primarily as a method of criticizing the emperor or more broadly the government as represented by him. Eberhard compared astronomical records of the solar eclipses visible in China during the Western Han with records of eclipses in the *Han shu*. He realized that many clearly visible eclipses were not recorded, and argued that eclipses were recorded primarily for political, rather than astronomical, purposes. In some cases of particularly unpopular reigns, negative portents were even manufactured. He identified several peaks in accounts of solar eclipse portents over the course of the Han, and argued that negative interpretations of these and other portents were directed, sometimes against the emperor himself, but often against other political actors.[68] Eberhard used this evidence to argue that

66 *HS* 10: 307, trans. after Dubs 1938–55: 2.382, cited by Bielenstein 1950: 135.

67 See Bielenstein 1950: 127–28.

68 For example, portents between 195 and 185 are directed, not against Emperor Hui 漢惠帝 (r. 194–188), but against the "usurpation" of his mother Empress Lü. Portents from 180 to 170 criticized not Emperor Wen 漢文帝 (r. 179–157), but a series of revolts by princes. Portents from 115 to 110 warned against the excessive wars of Han Wu Di. Peaks on the number of portents in the latter half of the first century CE refer to the rise to power of Wang Mang and the Wang clan.

portents were a powerful political method for officials and moralists to exercise institutional checks on the power of the emperor.

Eberhard attributed these criticisms to Ban Gu (the main author of the *Han shu*). Homer Dubs thought they came from the people, who "looked for portents whenever things began to go wrong, and found a portent in any strange event."[69] In other words, reporting portents became a "safe" outlet for people's criticism, which was forwarded to the emperor by the government.

Eberhard's findings are nuanced in a subsequent study by Hans Bielenstein, who compared accounts of other portents: comets, meteors, earthquakes, etc. – events that occur more frequently than do solar eclipses. Bielenstein agreed with Eberhard that portent reports were high in unpopular reigns and low in popular ones, but differed in his account of the identity of the critics. Like Dubs, Bielenstein argued that Ban Gu accurately reported portents that were (in some cases, fabricated and) memorialized to Han emperors by others, along with the imperial edicts that announced them.

In Bielenstein's view, the criticisms came from officials, especially officials in the capital who had their own reasons for dissatisfaction with the government.[70] He argued that officials adapted or elaborated empirical records of eclipses and other anomalies to voice criticisms that were otherwise unavailable to them. During the reigns of emperors who were popular, or receptive to direct criticism, these devices were unnecessary. In other words, the rhetorical use of mantic discourse – rhetorical in the sense that it was driven by political imperatives – was by no means the sole province of rulers. It could be used both to control subordinates and to criticize superiors.

In summary, Chinese and Greek mantic narratives about political power were both dramatic and influential.[71] For example, legendary, fictional, and quasi-historical accounts (from the broad sample) of Delphic consultations by future kings begin with standard questions, but end with dramatic and historically improbable responses. Mantic narratives may legitimate a weakened dynasty through its founding ruler (such as Han Gaozu) or a controversial or unpopular ruler (such as Empress Lü or Deng Sui). Dreams particularly lend themselves to mantic narratives of this kind, since dreams are inherently private experiences that cannot be witnessed or verified.

See Eberhard 1957: esp. 57–58, which attempts a statistical analysis of the information in all three sources. For another view see Sivin 1978. For a useful review see M. Kern 2000.

69 Dubs 1938–55: 2.375. 70 Bielenstein 1950: 137–42.

71 Maurizio (1995: 312) has argued that written records of Delphic oracles stand at the end of a long process of oral performances, and should be analyzed as oral literature, rather than by modes of authorship and authenticity appropriate to written texts.

Humans, gods, and mantic hermeneutics

The narratives presented above are all more or less comparable in genre and structure. In other cases, Chinese and Greek mantic narratives do not mesh. The key difference seems to be different views of the relations between humans and gods, with very different implications for mantic discourse.

Divination appears in both Chinese and Greek literary texts, but in different contexts and for different purposes. Accounts of prognostication are prominent in Chinese poetic writing in several ways that have no Greek counterpart. The three major modes of early Chinese poetic writing – the *Odes* (*Shi jing*), *Songs of Chu* (*Chu ci*), and the *fu* poetry of the Western and Eastern Han – all include accounts of divination. The *Shi jing* and *Chu ci* give critical accounts of mantic procedures that fail, and some *fu* poetry mentions divination in a (successful) ritual context.

Chinese poems of failed divination

Beginning in early imperial China, poetry became the mode of writing most identified with self-expression and the individual authorial voice. Warring States poetry falls into three major categories.[72] Two – the *Shi jing* and *Chu ci* – describe failed divination as a form of protest or persuasion.[73] *Fu* poetry is also linked to mantic procedures.[74]

[72] The first consisted of songs from the Zhou preserved and collected in the *Shi jing*. The second consisted of anonymous verse incorporated into philosophical works such as the *Daode jing*, *Guanzi*, *Zhuangzi*, and *Xunzi*. (Other works, especially the *Lunyu* and *Mengzi*, contain many quotations from *Shi jing* verses.) A third group was verses derived from ritual songs, mantic rituals, and the activities of *wu*, collected in the *Chu ci*. See Lewis 1999: 147.

[73] Poems also appear in *Zuo zhuan* accounts of diviners improvising divination rhymes (*zhou* 繇). See Zuo 264 (Min 2.4), 295–96 (Xi 4.6), 885 (Cheng 16.5), 978 (Xiang 10.5), and 1709–10 (Ai 17.5). For discussion see Schaberg 2001: 342 n. 39.

[74] Ban Gu begins the preface to the "Fu on the Two Capitals" ("Liang Du Fu" 兩都賦) with the statement that the genre of ancient poetry is *fu* (賦者古詩之流也, *Wen xuan* 1.1, cf. Knechtges 1987: 1.93). He describes the revival of ancient practices during the reigns of the Han emperors Wu and Xuan, including collecting music and harmonizing pitch pipes, with the result that the people were content and auspicious omens (*fuying* 福應) were plentiful. The passage ends with the statement that "officials in attendance for their skill with words" offered compositions, presumably by recording and presenting auspicious omens (言語侍從之臣, *Wen xuan* 1.2, cf. Knechtges 1987: 1.95).

The "Fu on the Gaotang Shrine" (*Gaotang fu* 高唐賦) includes a passage that recalls the language of the divinatory sacrifices from Baoshan: "They made oblations to all the spirits, and performed rites to Taiyi. The invocations were all prepared, the words and phrases [*yanci*] were all complete" (醮諸神，禮太一。顏傳祝已具，言辭已畢。 Song Yu (fl. third century BCE), *Gaotang fu* 高唐賦, *Wen xuan* 2.881, trans. Knechtges 1987: 3.325–27). See *Baoshan* 1991, slips

Shi jing mantic consultations typically fail, but the language of the poems celebrates the skills associated with prognostication, and may reflect the perspectives of mantic practitioners. Other poems criticize the mantic arts and may reflect the perspectives of dissatisfied consultors. These poems complain of the failure of divination from several points of view, ranging from individual laments against the deaf heavens to broader complaints of the breakdown of the cosmo-moral order.

Several *Shi jing* poems lament the state of the Zhou kingdom. The causes vary: corrupt officials, degenerate queens, ministers without political will, or the ancestors or even the emperor himself failing to aid the people. But at the root of these laments is the failure of the cycle of divination and sacrifice, itself a sign of the Zhou dynasty's loss of the heavenly Mandate (*tian ming*). One poem describes a solar eclipse as a baleful sign in which the swerves of the sun and moon from their proper paths mirror the missteps of a corrupt government.[75] Another describes the failure of divination to reach political consensus or take decisive action:

> 我龜既厭、不我告猶。
> 謀夫孔多、是用不集。
> 發言盈庭、誰敢執其咎。
> 如匪行邁謀、是用不得于道。
>
> Our turtle shells are exhausted, but tell us no plans;
> Strategists everywhere, nothing ever done.
> Speakers fill the hall, who dares risk calamity?
> Like planning a journey without taking a step, so no step is ever taken.[76]

A third poem describes a situation in which the ancestors are unable or unwilling to help. Laments about an unjust Heaven describe the breakdown of the sacrificial basis of political order. A fourth poem describes an unrelieved drought as a sign of the end of the Zhou mandate.[77]

The theme of the inadequacy of divination also appears throughout the *Chu ci*. Its first poem, the *Li sao*, is partially structured around two failed divinations. The diviner Ling Fen 靈氛 sends the narrator on a failed quest;

202v and 215, cf. slips 210, 213, 237, and 243. Here the court *fu* poets seem to combine the roles of the Great Incantator (*Taizhu*) and Director of Astronomy (*Taishi*) from the *Zhou li* (both discussed in Chapter 4). Divination remains a subject for *fu* poetry long after the Eastern Han, for example in a *fu* by the eighth-century poet Liu Yuxi 劉禹錫 (772–842) titled "Why Prognosticate?" (*Hebu fu* 何卜賦). I am grateful to Robert Neather for calling this text to my attention.

[75] "Shiyue zhe jiao" 十月之交, Mao 193. [76] "Xiao min" 小旻, Mao 195.

[77] "Si yue" 四月, Mao 204 and "Yun han" 雲漢, Mao 258.

Wu Xian 巫咸, a famous Shang *wu*, sends the narrator on a second voyage. Neither comes to anything.[78] In "Summoning the Soul," Wu Yang 巫陽 consults the milfoil on the narrator's behalf. After failing at both milfoil and dream divination, he uses an incantatory ritual to summon the soul.[79] The Nine Songs (*Jiu ge*) depicts failed human–divine communication in the failures of spirit mediums to summon divinities and the failures of spirits to attract worshippers or lovers.

The theme of failed divination is most prominent in two poems explicitly concerned with fate and divination. One of the Nine Songs, "Great Director of Destinies" (Da Si Ming 大司命), begins as a praise poem to the power of the god and his control of human destinies and lifespans.[80] But it ends as a lament for human failure to influence him; the speaker laments that old age has crept upon him and the god is no longer close. The last two couplets almost mirror the first; but here the abandoned devotee laments that his life is at the mercy of fate:

固人命兮有當。孰離合兮可為。

Every human fate is set; meeting, parting, who can choose?[81]

In another poem titled "Divination" (*Bu ju* 卜居), Qu Yuan consults the *Taibu* of the state of Zheng. He asks what is auspicious, what is not; what to avoid, and what to follow. But the *Taibu* replies that divination is inadequate to answer such questions. He throws away his stalks and excuses himself because, at times:

物有所不足。智有所不明。數有所不逮。
神有所不通。用君之心。
行君之意。龜策誠不能知事。

Instruments are not enough; knowledge cannot clarify; numbers cannot snare.
Spirits cannot engage it. For someone of My lord's mind
and resolution, shells, and stalks cannot reveal it.[82]

78 Ling Fen: *Chu ci bu zhu*, 35 ("Li sao" 1), trans. Hawkes 1985: 75, lines 257–58. Wu Xian: *Chu ci bu zhu*, 36–37 ("Li sao" 1), trans. Hawkes 1985: 76–77, lines 279–80 and 333–34. Failure: *Chu ci bu zhu*, 46–47 ("Li sao" 1), Hawkes 1985: 78, lines 363–68. For failed divination in the *Chu ci* see Lewis 1999: 182–90.

79 *Chu ci bu zhu*, 197–98 ("Zhao hun" 9), Hawkes 1985: 224, lines 7–9. Each form of divination appears once in the *Chu ci*: dream and milfoil divination here, and turtle shell divination in the poem *Bu ju*, discussed below. The *Tian wen* asks a question about *wu* bringing Gun back to life after he is transformed into a bear (*Chu ci bu zhu*, 100 ("Tian wen" 3), trans. Hawkes 1985: 129, lines 74–75).

80 *Chu ci bu zhu*, 68–69 ("Jiu ge" 2, Da Si Ming), cf. Hawkes 1985: 110, lines 1–8.

81 *Chu ci bu zhu* 71 ("Jiu ge" 2, Da Si Ming), cf. Hawkes 1985: 111, line 28.

82 *Chu ci bu zhu* 176–78 ("Bu ju" 6), cf. Hawkes 1985: 204–5.

In these poems the activities of *wu* and diviners are a poor show. They are ineffectual and divination simply does not work.

These examples from different poetic genres all describe – and protest – a discontinuity between Heaven and humanity. They are political because mantic procedures fail as a result of human misrule, which disrupts the harmony between Heaven and humanity. Although the poems describe gods and spirit journeys, they are not theological in nature, and they do not comment on correct relations between humans and gods.

Oracular narratives in Pindar, Aeschylus, and Sophocles

By contrast, some oracular narratives in fifth-century poetry and tragedy use the ancient legend of Oedipus to present a rhetoric of inexorable fate. The Oedipus legend is one of a series of myths of identical structure that center on the Delphic oracles. They all begin with a prediction: usually an oracle but sometimes the interpretation of a dream or prodigy. It foretells the birth of a malefic child – usually an unborn son of the consultor, but sometimes a nephew or descendant – who will cause the death of the consultor or the ruin of his city. The consultor takes vain precautions, but the oracle is inevitably fulfilled. Both the consultor and the malefic child end badly, sometimes with a curse on their descendants. The paradigmatic tale is the legend of Oedipus, but similar narratives occur in the myths of Jason, Paris, and Perseus.[83] They also have analogues in history, for example Herodotus' account of Croesus' attempts to save his son from death predicted in a dream (1.34–45).

These stories could not be more different from Chinese *Zuo zhuan* narratives predicting the fortunes of unborn or infant sons. They succeed by leaving their natal homes, or despite them. The Greek versions teach us that destiny is inescapable, and this rhetoric of infallible divination is linked to the rise of Delphi as a panhellenic shrine.[84]

Early treatments of the Oedipus story focus on family conflicts, especially the conflict between Oedipus' sons Eteocles and Polynices.[85] Pindar

[83] Moreau 1990, Liu Chun 2010.

[84] Moreau (1990: 276–78) speculates that, at some point between the sixth and fifth centuries, when the prestige of the oracle was at its height, a choice was made to put these myths at the service of Apollo: misinterpreted oracles could reveal the subtlety of the god and the foolishness of mortals.

[85] The story of the incest of Oedipus is clearly ancient. It first appears in the *Odyssey* when Odysseus describes his meeting in Hades with the mother of Oedipus, Epicaste [Iocasta], who married her own son in ignorance (Hom. *Od.* 11.271–74, cf. Paus. 9.5.1.10 and Apollod. *Epit.* 3.5.8). Of the

presents the key elements in his summary of the legend in the second Olympian ode: Moira (fate), the oracle to Laius, Oedipus' murder of his father, and the fulfillment of the oracle:

> Thus does Moira, who holds
> kind destiny for patrimony, at other times
> bring pain and reversal with god-given prosperity,
> ever since his fate-apportioned son killed Laius
> when their paths crossed, and the Pythian oracle
> spoken of old, was fulfilled.[86]

Less than ten years later, the oracle to Laius also appears in Aeschylus' *Seven against Thebes* (467 BCE). There it is not inevitable, but is part of the moral machinery of tales of crime and punishment. The chorus describes Apollo's three oracular warnings to Laius, who could have saved himself and his city by following oracular advice. Instead, he marries Jocasta, and Aeschylus describes the newlyweds as united by madness (*Sept.* 742–57). Like Duke Xian of Jin, Laius cannot follow mantic advice, and gives in to his appetites instead. (In Duke Xian's case, disregarding mantic advice is his second transgression, since it is never acceptable to appropriate a father's concubine or promote a concubine to wife.) *Seven against Thebes* presents a universe of moral choice, transgression, and retribution, through the devices of curses and oracles.

In *Oedipus Tyrannus* (429 BCE), Sophocles reworks the legend by removing most of the family context and centering the drama on Oedipus himself. The new focus is a series of mantic consultations. These begin when Oedipus consults Delphi to save Thebes from the plague. Second, he consults the *mantis* Tiresias about the response that the plague is due to blood pollution from the unsolved murder of Laius.[87] Only at this point do we learn from Iocasta of the oracle to Laius that he would be killed by a son born to the two of them (*OT* 711–15). She impugns its genuineness and describes Laius' attempts to avert it (*OT* 721–25), but this oracle is not advice or a warning, but an inevitable prediction. Finally, in a key detail manufactured by Sophocles, a drunken insult alerts Oedipus to his uncertain paternity with the result that he himself consults Delphi. He tries to

two extant fragments of a lost *Oedipodeia* (preserved by Pausanias), one concerns the Sphinx and the other his marriage to Euryganeia (Paus. 9.5.11). For this history see Liu Chun 2010: 56–61.

86 Pind. *Ol.* 2.35–42. The poem was written to celebrate a chariot race victory by Theron of Acragas, a purported descendant of Oedipus, in 476 BCE.

87 Tiresias makes a brief appearance of 150 lines, and does not offer mantic advice. He does, however, play the important role of setting Oedipus off on the search for his own origins. See Liu Chun 2010: 61–65.

avert his own disastrous oracle by fleeing Corinth for Thebes, only himself to bring about the oracle's prediction that he would kill his father and marry his mother (*OT* 790–93). The curse extends to his children: Polynices kills Eteocles, and ten years later an Argive expedition conquers Thebes.[88]

This new version of the story problematizes human free will. Human actions seem to lack moral significance if Oedipus and Iocasta are guilty of nothing worse than hasty temper and disrespect for oracles. Other commentators argue that Oedipus knew what he was doing, and was punished by just retribution.[89] Yet others take Oedipus as an exemplar of free will. E. R. Dodds takes Oedipus as a good man, driven by loyalty to Thebes and the will to discover the hidden meaning of past events.[90]

Mantic ambiguity in Greek Delphic oracle stories

Ambiguity is central to Greek mantic narratives (and the religious discourse they imply), but has no Chinese equivalent. If Delphic oracle stories delineate a clear line between human (mortal) and divine (immortal) perspectives, they suggest a major difference in the theological underpinnings of Chinese and Greek accounts of mantic activity.[91]

In colonization oracles, Delphic ambiguity represents the foundation of a colony as an ongoing process of interpretation. Lillian Dougherty argues that Delphic ambiguity – particularly in puns – creates a new vision of reality that transforms and translates the phenomena of the new locale into Greek language and experience. Like solving a puzzle, the colony restores order to an unfamiliar or disordered landscape. Riddles, like metaphors, often use paradoxes or puzzles to make improbable but ultimately sound

[88] By contrast, the oracle is not central to Euripides' account of the same story in the *Phoenician Women* (408 BCE), where the Delphic oracle appears only in passing (lines 34ff.).

[89] Vellacott (1964) argues that Oedipus and Iocasta were guilty and responsible parties who had every means to deduce the truth, but chose to ignore it.

[90] As Dodds (1966: 38–46) puts it, attempts to account for the *hamartia* ("tragic flaw") of Oedipus reflect the values of later Greek and Christian commentators, for whom piety required a just god alien to the quasi-Homeric sensibility of Sophocles.

[91] Kindt (2008: 27) argues that they help to situate human agency and the human condition in: (1) an ontological opposition between the human and divine spheres, (2) an epistemological opposition between divine knowledge and human ignorance, and (3) a continuum of past, present, and future. The ambiguity of oracular languages provides a mode of reflection on all three.

comparisons. Colonial riddles use this technique to describe colonization sites as impossible landscapes.[92]

An example is Thucydides' account of the founding of Acarnania. Alcmaeon the son of Amphiaraus was told by the oracle that he could rest only when he found a place that had not been seen by the sun and was not land at the time of his mother's death. The solution he discovers is the deposits at the mouth of the Achelous river: at the time of her death, they were insufficient to be called land. He settled there and named the country after his son Acarnan. As Dougherty points out, in examples of this kind, the oracle seems to send colonists to impossible places that cannot exist in the real world. But the solution to the riddle or code "reclassifies the categories of nature" and restores a Greek sense of order to the natural world.[93]

The solution of the riddle also underscores the hermeneutic skills of the Greek colonists and their right – through divine command – to the land colonized. Dougherty also points out that the substitution of an ambiguous oracular response for the uncertainty of human existence shifts indeterminacy from the gods to the human world of interpretation, providing an illusion of control over events that are both uncertain and dangerous. In these oracles, the answer to the riddle is less important than the hermeneutic process. Colonial oracles exploit the structure of riddles to represent the colony's foundation as the restoration of normal order. They thus impose Greek boundaries, distinctions, and notions of civic order on the new site, including division of land and the creation of city walls.[94]

Mantic narratives provide important authoritative voices for the historian, but comparison shows that those voices have different registers. Herodotus uses oracles, predictions, and omens to establish the authority of the *Histories*; and also to present a "panoptic" view of time that encompasses past, present, and future, in a way that speaks directly to the actors of the text.

In some stories the right human reaction is an essential precondition for an oracle's fulfillment. Here the oracle does not predict; it makes the desired outcome of the events dependent upon human action. Perhaps the strongest example is Herodotus' account of the "Wooden Wall" oracle to Athens in 481. After an initial prediction of disaster (already mentioned in Chapter 7),

[92] Dougherty 1992. [93] Thuc. 2.102.5–6; Dougherty 1992: 37.
[94] A. J. Graham 1964: 29–39, Malkin 1987: 135–86, Dougherty 1992.

the Pythia gave Athens a second oracle: that Zeus had granted to Athena a "wooden wall" (*teikhos xulinon*):

> it alone will stand unsacked, and help you and your children.
> But do not wait quietly for horsemen and footmen
> to come from the land, but withdraw
> and turn your backs. The day will come when you will face them.
> O Divine Salamis, you will bring death to the sons of women
> either when Demeter scatters the corn or gathers the harvest.[95]

The passage is problematic in many ways, including the spontaneous prophecy, two oracles in hexameter verse, and the ensuing debate in Athens. It is also clearly inconsistent with other accounts of the normal function of the oracle in state consultations. In his extensive discussion of this passage, Bowden speculates that the actual question took a more conventional form: whether or not it was permissible to abandon the city of Athens (and with it the temples of the gods). If so, the verses quoted by Herodotus may have been composed after the fact and "published" by Delphi itself, possibly in a single consultation which Herodotus divided into two for dramatic purposes.[96]

The point for the present discussion is that Herodotus portrays the oracle and its fulfillment as a series of interactions. First, the Athenians were able to intercede with the oracle; by taking the role of suppliants, they obtained a revision or even reversal of an initially hopeless prediction. Second, the oracle's fulfillment depended on correct reception and interpretation by its ultimate audience. Herodotus continues:

> These seemed to them to be gentler than the previous response, so they wrote them down and went back to Athens. But when the *theopropoi* returned and reported the message to the people, there were many opinions about the interpretation of the oracle.[97]

Some thought the wooden wall referred to the Acropolis, and that the oracle was advising them to save it. Others thought it referred to the Athenian ships, which should be prepared for a sea battle. But the chresmologues argued that "Salamis bringing death" signified a naval defeat at Salamis. Themistocles argued persuasively that they had misunderstood, that the lines referred not to Athens but to her enemies. The Athenians followed Themistocles' advice and won a great sea battle at Salamis.

[95] Hdt. 7.141.3–4, Q147, PW no. 95, cf. Godley. [96] Bowden 2005: 102–7.
[97] Hdt. 7.142.1, trans. after Godley.

This story turns on interactions between humans and gods. Zeus, as ruler of the human and divine worlds, decides to give them a chance at victory: giving Athena a "wooden wall" to protect the Athenians. But his help comes in the form of a test. Apollo, as the god of prophecy, gives them a key, but one that they must understand properly to use correctly.

Moral order and sagacity in the *Zuo zhuan*

The *Zuo zhuan* authors give their own accounts of moral success and failure. Most contemporary scholars take the *Zuo zhuan* to be a multi-authored text that assumed its final form in the fourth century, and actively promulgated a broadly Confucian vision of religion, politics, and morality, with its emphasis on the human virtues of ritual propriety (*li* 禮), rectitude or appropriate behavior (*yi* 義), benevolence or humanity (*ren* 仁), and wisdom (*zhi* 智). These values are laid out in many speeches throughout the text. These values include: (1) principles for the correct relations between humans and spirits (*shen*), including proper rituals for sacrifice, but these relations do not involve direct human–divine interactions. Instead, their direct focus is on social and political relations, including: (2) social hierarchies in human relations, states, lineages, and social classes, as well as relations between states; (3) a vision of Zhou kingship in which an ideal ruler maintains correct relations with both the spirits and his officials and people; and finally (4) "just" hegemons, who maintain correct relations to the (declining) Zhou throne and to the rulers of other states.

A few examples illustrate the straightforward nature of these judgments. One comes from a series of anecdotes describing the rise and fall of King Ling of Chu 楚靈王 (r. 540–529) between 547 and 529 through a series of predictions about him. They begin with predictions of prosperity and success.[98] Then they shift to predictions that he will become a great lord, but will ultimately fall.[99] The following year, he kills the king of Chu and usurps the throne.[100] Some ten subsequent predictions foresee his downfall.[101] The series culminates with his suicide after a popular rebellion against him. In the final prediction, he himself performed turtle shell divination in the hope to acquire all under heaven. The divination was inauspicious, and he cast down the shell and cursed heaven, threatening to take what heaven would not give. The people were distressed at

98 Zuo, 1193–94 (Xiang 31.13), 1202–4 (Zhao 1.1), 1207–8 (Zhao 1.3), and 1223 (Zhao 1.13).

99 Zuo, 1193–95 (Xiang 31.13). 100 Zuo, 1123–24 (Zhao 1.13).

101 Zuo, 1252 (Zhao 4.3), 1254 (4.4), 1267 (5.4), 1279 (6.7), 1322–24 (11.2), 1327 (11.8), 1327–29 (11.10), and 1240 (12.11).

his instability and rebelled against him.[102] An early speech in the series presents him as the complete antithesis of the virtues of the Zhou founder, King Wen.[103]

The *Zuo zhuan* authors contrast morally deficient individuals like King Ling to the wisdom of sages, who understand the workings of heaven. Some passages attribute predictions of the fate of states and the end of their ruling lines to Confucius.[104] Others introduce tension between mantic and non-mantic prediction by recommending prediction based on moral assessment, rather than divination. Some stories explicitly reject mantic expertise as a source of wisdom.[105] For example, Duke Xiang of Shan 單襄公 (*c.* 590) uses his observation of the behavior of officials at the Jin court to predict civil war there. When asked how he knows this, he replies:

吾非瞽，史，焉知天道？吾見晉君之容，而聽三郤之語矣，
殆必禍者也。夫君子目以定體，足以從之，是以觀其容而知其心矣。

I am no blind musician or astrologer [*shi*]: how can I understand the Dao of Heaven? But I observed the looks of the lord of Jin and listened to the words of the three Xi [nobles]: they are dangerous and must lead to disaster. Now a *junzi* [gentleman] uses his eyes to position his body and the feet follow; therefore if you observe his looks, you can understand his heart-mind.[106]

This passage argues that the attitude of the body is an index to moral character. Although the assessment he describes is closely related to some aspects of physiognomy, Duke Xiang emphasizes that he is not a mantic specialist. He is making the stronger claim that assessment of character based on close observation is a more powerful predictor than mantic expertise.

102 Zuo, 1347–50 (Zhao 13.2). For detailed analysis of this series see Schaberg 2001: 30–34 and 193–95.

103 Zuo, 1193–95 (Xiang 31.13), cf. Schaberg 2001: 31–35.

104 Examples include the rise of Wei (1496, Zhao 28.3), the fall of Jin (1504–5, Zhao 29.5), chaos in the Zhao lineage (1573, Ding 9.3), and the outcome of a civil war in Wei (1696, Ai 15.5). See Lewis 1999: 138–39.

105 Zuo, 131 (Huan 11.2) and 1721 (Ai 23.2). For the importance King Wu attached to military divination see *SJ* 128.3224. In another case, Mu Jiang prognosticates about her imprisonment and rejects an auspicious prediction obtained through divination in favor of her own interpretation of her compromised moral circumstances (Zuo, 965–66, Xiang 9.3). For another passage that opposes these two modes of prediction see Zuo, 1096 (Xiang 25.2). For other moral prognostications by Chen Wenzi see Zuo, 1077 (Xiang 23.4), 1090–91 (Xiang 24.5), and 1146 (Xiang 28.9).

106 GY 3, Zhou yu xia, pp. 90–91. Elsewhere (GY 3, Zhou yu xia, p. 98) Duke Xiang predicts that a Jin hostage in his court will eventually rule Jin because he has the culture and virtues associated with King Wen. For another version of this story see Zuo, 782 (Cheng 1.3 or 1.4), Legge 337.

Several points are important. First, the perspective of the text is often that of ministers who must contend with royal power and its excesses. Their emphasis is on the human virtue, and especially the Confucian virtues of ritual propriety, righteousness, humanity, wisdom, loyalty, and trustworthiness.[107]

These virtues also apply to the writing of history. An important difference between Chinese and Greek historiography is the ceremonial and even quasi-religious role of the scribe or scribe-historian (*shi*), who brings that authority to the writing of history. The role of the *shi* traditionally included prayer, divination, regulation of the calendar, and the recording and interpretation of anomalies and calamities (discussed in Chapter 4). For example, the Qi minister Yanzi puts scribes alongside priests and declares their sacred responsibility:

若有德之君。外內不廢。上下無怨。動無違事。其祝史薦信。無愧心矣。
是以鬼神用饗。國受其福。祝史與焉。 . . .

If there is a virtuous ruler, who neglects nothing within or without, where high and low are without dissatisfaction, and his movements are never contrary to circumstances, his priests and scribes can set forth the truth, and he has nothing to be ashamed of in his mind. Therefore the spirits accept his offerings, and the state receives their blessing, in which the priests and historiographers share.[108]

Second, the spirits are fundamentally important to the *Zuo* authors' vision of a natural and social order, but the spirit world is mostly opaque to human perception and more distant from their concerns. The spirits are satisfied through correct human action. Given this very different set of relations between humans and divine powers, it is not surprising that ambiguity and obscurity are not a central feature of *Zuo zhuan* mantic narratives.[109]

Finally, Mark Edward Lewis has argued that divination was one of the major sources for the images, theories, and practices by means of which rulership was reinvented through the Warring States ideal of the sage ruler, who was the ultimate interpreter of both natural phenomena and human action. Lewis argues that the growth of new forms of administration in the Warring States built on, rather than eliminated, earlier Shang and Zhou models of the ruler as diviner. The ability to perceive patterns underlying change and to respond appropriately to changing circumstances became the hallmark of the leader, variously described in Warring States texts as sage, ruler, or general. As he observes, this kind of predictive talent figured

[107] See Schaberg 2001: esp. 125–45. [108] Zuo, 1416 (Zhao 20.6), trans. after Legge 683.

[109] For Chinese views of the boundaries between the human and divine see the essays in Lagerwey and Kalinowski 2009. For a controversial view see Puett 2002.

in all the politically definitive roles of the Warring States but was the particular hallmark of the ruler.[110]

Mantic narratives compared

Comparisons of mantic narratives in historical writing – Herodotus, the *Zuo zhuan*, Plutarch, and dynastic histories – suggest that mantic narratives may be a transcultural topos or genre. By contrast, the obscurity and ambiguity of Greek oracular language seems culturally specific and closely linked to Greek religious views of the relations between humans and gods. Chinese mantic narratives theorize those relations very differently.

Chinese and Greek mantic narratives are both deeply grounded in religious and cosmological reflection. As such they cannot be read as a binary comparison. The Apollo of Herodotus' Croesus cycle inhabits a different cosmos from the benign divinity of the Stoics of Plutarch's time. While Plutarch may have opposed the Stoics on many points, he was thoroughly familiar with their views, and may have espoused some of them.[111] The Chinese cosmologies of the late Warring States and Han do not stress human–divine communications, and their moral judgments and messages are very different from those of Delphic oracle stories or of Plutarch.

Of the brief sample discussed here, the strongest case for comparability is between the *Histories* of Herodotus and the *Zuo zhuan*. Both use mantic narratives to structure and explain relations and hostilities between states that can take many years to resolve. Both use mantic narratives to make moral judgments on the actions or character of their narrative subjects in several broadly similar ways.

First, they use cycles of divination, portents, and prediction to comment on (or justify) the rise and fall of rulers, lineages, dynasties, and kingdoms in a long vision of human history. Chinese dynastic histories are organized around different structuring principles. This difference is all the more striking because the pattern for dynastic histories was largely set by the structure of the *Shi ji*, a text written by a father and son who both held the office of scribe-historian (*shi*). Chinese dynastic histories did use mantic information in a way that has no exact Greek equivalent: to criticize the government in memorials on portents. But accounts of omens, anomalies, and prodigies are not mantic narratives in the above sense. They do not use

110 Lewis 1999: 38–49.

111 Plutarch and the Stoics: Babut 1969. For a different view see Long 1972.

prediction as a mode of historical reflection, and they are not structured on the role of human agency in the fulfillment of predictions.

Second, the mantic narratives of Herodotus and the *Zuo* authors in particular introduce distinctive forms of historical reflection. Herodotus creates a mode of reflection that contrasts and arguably competes with the authority of epic. He devises a new method of demonstration (*apodeixis*) as a mode of public performance. It combines the skills of the Homeric bard who is a master of song (*aoidos*) and the skills of the historian, who is a master of speech and explanation (*logos*). The bard reveals what is hidden and utters riddles. Herodotus does the same thing through the use of a poetic register, provided by the quotation of Delphic oracles. In this sense, historians resemble diviners (and take on aspects of their authority). At one level, accounts of successful and failed divination and tropes of destiny fulfilled highlight the moral qualities of their protagonists.

Oracles also perform the narrative role of introducing poetic forms to frame prose descriptions of events and actions based on human will. This confers meaning on the narrative action and infuses elements of poetry and epic into historical prose narrative. Repeated reference to oracles and divination allows Herodotus to blend prose narratives into the traditions of epic poetry, substituting oracles for the plan of Zeus and the divine interventions of epic narrative. By claiming the ability and authority to *semainein*, Herodotus indirectly asserts claims to mantic modes of knowledge. Both *semainein* and *historein* thus emerge as intellectual processes for dealing with the invisible.[112]

Several of these points also apply to the structure of the *Zuo zhuan*. Both use mantic narrative structure as a main stylistic device. Both use the combination of embedded mantic narratives and moral judgments to create a subtle artifice of narrative unity. Both use divinations and arguments within them to convey moral judgments and doctrinal content. Finally, although the *Zuo zhuan* uses different methods of demonstration and moral analysis than the *Histories*, these devices give particular deductive styles to both works.

Nonetheless, the hermeneutic problems of the two texts differ considerably. Delphic oracle stories present problems of reference, either between words and things, or of homonymy between words that sound the same.

[112] See Nagy 1990 (esp. 273), Calame 1996 (esp. 151–53), and Hartog 1996 (esp. 702–8), 1999 (esp. 186–94), and 2000 (esp. 394). Nagy (1996: 329) describes two parallel appropriations of the authority of epic: the lyric "authoritative speech" (*ainos*) of Pindar and the "inquiry" (*historia*) of Herodotus. Herodotus combines prose and the "poetry of oracles" to convey the same kind of message as Pindaric lyric.

Problems such as whether the "wooden wall" denotes a building or ships, *who* will measure out the Tegean plain in fetters, and *whose* mighty empire will be destroyed by Croesus' invasion are not culturally specific. By contrast, problems of homonymy are linked to language. Some arise through human misunderstanding of the will of the gods or because of human attempts to appropriate divine knowledge or perspectives. Many require human ingenuity in solving the problem of the oracle.

As readers culturally conditioned to expect the ambiguity of oracular language, we may be surprised to discover that it is both absent in and unnecessary for comparable Chinese narratives. Most *Zuo zhuan* prognostications do not turn on ambiguities of reference or language, but they do require human moral agency for their fulfillment. Success depends on the moral character of the narrative subjects, rather than hermeneutic failure to interpret a prediction correctly.[113] The absence of ambiguous language based on homonymy is striking for two reasons. One is the prominence of homonymy in both Classical and modern Chinese. The other is a long history of homonyms and "riddling" in later fate calculation techniques based on homonymy, especially between two distinct written characters with the same pronunciation.[114]

There are also important differences between Herodotus' and the *Zuo* authors' accounts of moral failure. For Herodotus, moral failure lies in the failure to recognize differences between mortal and immortal perspectives. Herodotus' Delphic oracle stories strongly reflect the dichotomy between the human and the divine, and human success is linked to respecting and preserving that difference. The moral judgments of the *Zuo* authors in these narratives do not involve direct human–divine communication or differences between human and divine perspectives on time or reality. Rather, the text is concerned with whether its narrative subjects follow the "decrees of Heaven" (*tian ming*). By contrast, ambiguous Delphic oracle stories can take the form of a kind of moral "test," in which solving the riddle of the oracle correctly is a test of the consultor's ingenuity and character.

[113] Some predictions are made directly to their narrative subjects, for example Duke Mu's divination on whether to invade Jin and Duke Wen's prognostication on whether to restore the king of Zhou. Others are delivered to third parties. For example, Shensheng's ghost appears to his charioteer, not to Yiwu; here the *Zuo* reader has access to the prediction but Yiwu does not.

[114] See Fuehrer 2006.

9 | Divination and systematic inquiry

Where were the areas of significant interaction between divination and systematic philosophical or scientific thought and inquiry? In what sense did divination represent a coherent system of knowledge and belief, and of what kind?

From its beginnings, Chinese divination prominently featured the use of symmetry, number, and a complex and nuanced model of cosmic change. Most important were the early articulation of: (1) a cosmic *yin–yang* polarity, which was (2) elaborated into all possible combinations of *yin* and *yang* into the sixty-four hexagrams of the *Zhou yi*, and (3) represented by numbers that abstracted patterns of change to a discrete number of types. Much Han theorizing about *yin–yang*, *qi*, and eventually *wuxing* developed from the ideas and methods of the technical specialties, especially medicine, astronomy, and the mantic arts.

Most Greek divination was oriented toward communication between the realms of humans and gods. A "*do ut des*" economy of sacrifice first appears in the Homeric poems, and remains prominent in both inscriptions and historical writing. In Hellenistic Greece, divination became part of a discourse of causation and moral responsibility, but even then it was not divorced from notions of direct divine agency.

This chapter takes up areas of relation between the mantic arts and Chinese and Greek systematic thought and inquiry. I begin with two directly comparable developments: the role of divination in the development of medical thought and the relations between physicians and mantic specialists. The remaining sections present developments that are not directly comparable. The role of the mantic arts in the development of Chinese astronomy and cosmology has no Greek counterpart; changing Greek views of divination and the understanding of causation have no direct Chinese counterpart. I conclude with brief remarks on very different Chinese and Greek understandings of divination as a semiotic system.

Medicine

We can distinguish two shared tendencies in Chinese and Greek iatromancy. One is apotropaic. If illness is caused by invasive entities and divine displeasure, the function of diagnosis is to identify the entity behind an illness and bring about a cure through prayer, sacrifice, or exorcism of the invasive entity. The other is naturalistic. Here the goal of mantic activity is prognosis of the course of a disease: when it will diminish, end, or cause death. Unlike apotropaic divination, such predictions can be verified or falsified. Importantly, the relationship between these two types of iatromancy is not a straightforward one of evolution.

Hemerological and naturalistic medicine

Comparison of the Baoshan and Wangshan Illness divinations, daybooks, and the *Huangdi neijing* illustrates the coexistence of apotropaic and naturalistic iatromancy and medicine.[1] The Baoshan divinations are clearly apotropaic. The daybooks introduce a new naturalistic theory of the cause of disease. Auspicious days for treatment are determined by a typology of illness according to *yin–yang* and *wuxing* schemata. In the daybook from Jiudian, all illnesses that begin on the same day have the same etiology and prognosis: respite, recovery, or death.[2] One section gives auspicious and inauspicious aspects of the Twelve Earth Branches, and associates each with the onset of a particular illness.[3] The Shuihudi daybooks are better preserved, with more extensive sections on stem and branch iatromancy and more systematic correlations to *wuxing* theory. For example, the "Illness" section of Daybook A links the day of onset of an illness to both a divine and a material cause:

甲乙有疾父母為祟。得之於肉。從東方來。裹以桼（漆）器。戊己病庚有閒辛酢（作）。若不酢（作），煩居東方，歲在東方，青色死。

[1] The *Huangdi neijing* 黃帝內經 (Inner Classic of the Yellow Lord) is divided into two sections: the *Suwen* 素問 (Basic Questions) and the *Lingshu* 靈樞 (Spiritual Pivot). These also contain an earlier section, the *Taisu* 太素 (Grand Basis). There are serious questions concerning the authenticity and dating of the *Huangdi neijing*. See Sivin in ECTBG and Unschuld 2003.

[2] For the Baoshan and Wangshan Illness divinations and the Jiudian and Shuihudi daybooks see Chapters 2, 5, and 6 and Appendices E and F.

[3] For example, if an illness begins on a *chen* day, respite will occur on a *you* day, recovery on a *xu* day, and death on a *zi* day. If the onset is on a *wei* day, respite will be on a *zi* day, recovery on a *mao* day, and death on a *yin* day, etc. Jiudian 52–53, slips 64 and 67, cf. Harper 2001: 105–6.

If there is illness on a *jia* or *yi* day [stems 1 and 2], father and mother are the calamity. It is obtained from meat; comes from the east; and is placed in a lacquer container. It manifests on a *wu* or *ji* day [stems 5 and 6], there will be some respite on a *geng* day [stem 7] and recovery on a *xin* day [stem 8]. If there is no recovery, Fever will dwell in the east quarter, Sui [Year or Jupiter] will be in the east quarter; and the color azure [*qing*] [portends] death.[4]

According to this formula, an illness manifests after four days, with a respite on the fifth or sixth day and recovery on the sixth or seventh. If the illness does not resolve during this one-week period, it is attributed to Fever (*fan* 煩), associated with the star Year (*Sui* 歲). Year travels over the four directions four times a year in a cycle of: east (months one, five, and nine), south (months two, six, and ten), west (months three, seven, and eleven), and north (months four, eight, and twelve).[5] The illness is fatal if both Fever and Year are in the quadrant associated with its origin, here east.

Daybook B links illness to Earth branch correlations for auspicious activities, after a description of the circumstances that can produce illness:

以有疾，<辰>少翏　(瘳)，午大翏(瘳)，死生在申，黑肉從北方來，把者黑色，外鬼父葉（世) 為姓(眚)，高王父譴適（謫)。

If there is illness, slight respite will occur on a *chen* day [branch 5], great respite [recovery] on a *wu* day [branch 7], and death on a *shen* day [branch 9]. Black meat comes from the north; the bearer is black in color. External demons and father's brothers are the calamity; great-grandfather is the calamity.[6]

These passages indicate a new reliance on the inevitability of the sexagenary cycle. As Donald Harper has shown, this approach totally changed the iatromantic encounter by introducing a new kind of predictability. Prognosis and cure occur, not by divine intervention, but by the mechanical operation of the sexagenary cycle. Invasive entities are still considered responsible for the origin of illness, but in the daybooks, prognosis is determined solely through the sexagenary cycle, without intervention from the spirit world or medical art.

Iatromantic materials are conspicuously absent from a group of medical manuscripts excavated from Mawangdui.[7] An exception is the Book of the

4 *SHD* (Daybooks): 193, slips 68–69, after Harper 2001: 110.

5 See Kalinowski 1991: 105, Liu Lexian 1994: 116–22, Harper 2001: esp. 105–13.

6 *SHD* (Daybooks): 245, slips 157–58. The commentary to this passage cross-references the Heaven Stem predictions for a *jia* or *yi* day, immediately above.

7 The Mawangdui medical manuscripts consist of seven manuscripts written on three sheets of silk, recovered from Mawangdui Tomb 3. Original publication: *Mawangdui Han mu boshu* (*MWD*) vol. 4 (1983); translation and commentary: Harper 1998.

Generation of the Fetus (*Taichan shu*), which includes a diagram used to determine a child's fortune based on the branch sign associated with its date of birth. The same technique appears in more detail (and with a better-preserved diagram) in the daybooks from Shuihudi (Figure 6.2).[8]

Some scholars push hemerological medicine back as far as the Baoshan and Wangshan prognostications. Yang Hua argues that the illness onset days and prognostications from Baoshan and Wangshan are consistent with the respite, recovery, and death predictions of the daybooks. He speculates that the Baoshan and Wangshan diviners used some kind of *wuxing*-based daybook like those found at Jiudian and Shuihudi.[9] In either case, the relation of apotropaic medicine to the hemerological medicine of the daybooks is not one of straightforward evolution, because apotropaic medicine did not disappear with the rise of *yin–yang wuxing* medical theory. It coexisted with the systematic theories of the *Huangdi neijing* and later *yin–yang wuxing* medical texts.

Both apotropaic and naturalistic explanations appear in the *Huangdi neijing* account of directional winds, which in Warring States iatromancy were associated with the origin and onset of diseases. Prognostication based on the eight winds appears in *Huangdi neijing* chapters whose content probably dates to the Warring States. They describe diseases as arising from malevolent directional winds at particular times of the year, linked to the transits of the star god Taiyi.[10]

One passage, now preserved in the *Lingshu* chapter "Predicting the Eight Regularities by Observing the Winds" (*Bazheng fenghou* 八正風候) in the *Huangdi neijing*, uses directional winds to explain why large numbers of people suffer from the same disease in some years but not others. It links variations in "epidemic" years to a mantic account of the regular movements of Taiyi through the Nine Palaces and also to naturalistic notions of depletion and repletion (*xu shi* 虛實). The movements of Taiyi were marked by eight transits: the two equinoxes, the two solstices, and the first days of the four seasons. At any of these times, a wind from the direction occupied by Taiyi was considered an auspicious "repletion" wind; a wind from the opposite direction was an inauspicious "depletion" wind. According to the *Lingshu*, in a year of harmonious climate with few depletion winds, few people would fall ill and die; by contrast, many would sicken in a year with

8 *MWD* 4.133, after Harper 1998: 35, 372–77 and Harper 2001; *SHD* (Daybooks): 202–6, accompanying text, slips 140–54.

9 Yang Hua 2003. Field (n. 119, below) holds a similar view.

10 This material appears in the *Taisu* chapters, which are believed to date from the late Warring States, and are now preserved in the Western Han compilation in the *Lingshu*.

frequent depletion winds.[11] Particular illnesses were also associated with directional winds at different times of the year: for example, heart and abdomen ailments with lack of wind in the second month, heat and cold ailments with lack of warm weather in the third, jaundice with lack of hot weather in the fourth, and sudden death with lack of cold weather in the tenth.

This theory of Taiyi iatromancy is elaborated in the chapter titled "Nine Palaces and Eight Winds" (*Jiugong bafeng* 九宮八風). It links the weather at the transits of Taiyi to the condition of the people, crops, and the country overall. For example, wind and rain on the day of the transit mean an auspicious year of peace and good health. On the day before the transit they signify abundant rainfall; on the day after, drought. Particular transits also signify. Winds on the day when Taiyi dwells in the palace of the winter solstice predict the future of the ruler; the palace of the spring equinox, his ministers; the central palace, his officials; the palace of the autumn equinox, his generals; and the palace of the summer solstice, the future of the people overall.[12]

Other chapters give purely naturalistic explanations for wind-borne illness. The *Suwen* section of the *Huangdi neijing* describes wind as a source of malevolent or heteropathic *qi* (*xie qi* 邪氣) that causes disease.[13] Several *Suwen* chapters describe wind as the cause of the hundred diseases, but with no reference to directional winds or hemerology.[14] The "Discourse on Yao Illnesses" (*Yao lun* 瘧論, *SW* 35) attributes quasi-malarial illnesses to seasonal winds and *yin-yang* influences. The "Discourse on Winds" (*Feng lun* 風論, *SW* 42) explains why wind causes different kinds of illnesses with different names and locations in the body. These texts focus on the effects of wind's progressive penetration of the body. Some accounts of wind pathology draw on *wuxing* correlations.[15] Others focus on the depth of entry or the nature of blockage if the wind is trapped in the skin, stomach, or muscles. These accounts emphasize the diversity of symptoms caused by invasive winds. Physicians used directional winds to explain both individual ailments and illnesses in populations.

[11] *LS* 79: 599–600, cf. Unschuld 1985: 263–71, 2003: 186–87, Yamada Keiji 1980.

[12] *LS* 77: 562–73, trans. Unschuld 1985: 265–67. [13] *Xie qi fa bing* 邪氣發病. *SW* 4: 34.

[14] *SW* 3: 27, 19: 165, 42: 324, 60: 440.

[15] For example, *SW* 42: 323–24 describes the penetration of the liver wind in spring, heart wind in summer, spleen wind in midsummer, lung wind in autumn, and kidney wind in winter. It describes winds associated with the brain, eyes, head, and intestines and how they enter the body. The account is not systematic and includes discrepancies resulting from the joining of what, in the earlier *Huangdi Taisu*, had been two separate chapters.

Another innovation of the *Huangdi neijing* was the naturalization of dream diagnosis, in detailed typologies that diagnosed *qi* excesses and deficiencies in the organs of the body. These theories linked dream content to *yin–yang* and *wuxing*. Dreams were understood to manifest conflict between internal and external *qi* on the "battlefield" of the dreamer's body. They indicated either the presence of pathogenic *qi* or the body's vulnerability to heteropathic *qi* during sleep. The "Treatise on the Essence of the Pulses" (*Maiyao jingwei* 脈要精微, *SW* 17) explains dream interpretation as a diagnostic of the balance of *yin* and *yang qi* in the body.[16] A separate chapter on oneiromancy titled "Dreams from Heteropathic *Qi*" (*Yin xie fa meng* 淫邪發夢, *LS* 43) amplifies this description. During sleep the body is especially permeable to the influence of external *qi*, and dreams and restlessness occur when this external *qi* encounters the defensive *qi* of the dreamer's internal organs. This dream typology describes the effects of excess *yin* and *yang qi* in the organs of the body.[17]

In summary, Chinese iatromantic methods run a gamut. The oldest are purely apotropaic, but starting in the fourth century, substantial attention is given to recording symptoms. There is no clear demarcation between the apotropaic texts of fourth-century tombs and the mechanical sexagenary correlations of the daybooks. The *Huangdi neijing* and other Western Han medical literature include both iatromantic elements and systematic explanations of the causes of illness that deployed (not necessarily together) theories of *qi*, *yin–yang*, and *wuxing*.

Greek medical oracles and physicians

We also find a coincidence of apotropaic and naturalistic medicine in fifth- and fourth-century Greece. Geoffrey Lloyd has emphasized the paradox that Asclepian temple healing and Hippocratic naturalistic medicine were historically concurrent developments, and not an evolutionary process as

[16] For example, fearful dreams of great waters or fires indicate excesses of *yin* and *yang*; dreams of murder and harm indicate excess of both. Flying and falling indicates excess *qi* in the upper and lower body. Dreams of giving or taking indicate excess or lack of food. Dreams of anger or weeping indicate excess liver or lung *qi*. Dreams of crowds or violence indicate short or long worms in the bowels. See *SW* 17.136–37.

[17] Like the typology of "Harmonizing *Yin* and *Yang*," it associates excess liver *qi* with anger and excess lung *qi* with fear and tears. It also gives dream diagnostics for excess *qi* in the heart, spleen, and kidneys; and for deficient *qi* in the heart, lungs, liver, spleen, kidneys, urinary bladder, stomach, large and small intestines, gall bladder, genitals, neck, shins, limbs, and womb. See *SW* 43.330–31.

represented by positivist historians of medicine.[18] Testimonies from Epidaurus provide examples:

> A man came as a suppliant to the god. He was so blind that of one of his eyes he had only the eyelids left – within them was nothing, but they were entirely empty. Some of those in the Temple laughed at his silliness to think that he could recover his sight when one of his eyes had not even a trace of the ball, but only the socket. As he slept a vision appeared to him. It seemed to him that the god prepared some drug, then, opening his eyelids, poured it into them. When day came he departed with the sight of both eyes restored.[19]

This account is rhetorical insofar as it advertises a successful cure, but it also emphasizes the medical expertise and therapeutic powers of the god.[20]

An initial problem is that much of our knowledge of iatromancy comes through the texts of its opponents, the authors of the Hippocratic Corpus.[21] For example, the authors of *On the Sacred Disease* (late fifth to fourth century) reject the view that "the sacred disease" is sent by the gods. The text argues that epilepsy has a natural cause and is no more sacred than any other disease. Its unique status is due to false claims by *magoi*, purifiers, vagabonds, and charlatans, whom the text accuses of ignorance, fraud, and impiety.[22] Nonetheless, the treatments of Hippocratic physicians sometimes resembled those of their opponents. For example, the author of *Prorrhetic* emphasizes that he will not engage in divination (*ou manteusomai*) but will record signs (*sēmeia de graphō*) that bear witness to future health.[23] *Regimen in Acute Diseases* sets up a hostile analogy between divination and medicine. Physicians differ so greatly in their prescriptions

[18] Lloyd 2003. In addition to the major centers at Epidaurus and Pergamum, incubation was practiced by Boeotian medical oracles of Amphiaraus and Trophonius. There were also Boeotian medical oracles at Sarapis and at Oropus in the Hellenistic and Roman periods. See Bloch 1984: 18–19, Flacelière 1965: 21–24, and Bonnechère 1990.

[19] IG 4^2.1.121–22, Stele 1, no. 9, trans. EE 1.231–32.

[20] Another testimony records that a man named Hegestratus suffered from headaches and insomnia. He dreamed that the god cured him and even taught him the lunge used in the *pankration*. Not only was he cured of his headaches, he also won the *pankration* at the Nemean games. IG 4^2.1.121–22, Stele 2, no. 29, trans. EE 1.235.

[21] The thirty-four books attributed to Hippocrates of Cos were probably composed between the sixth and fourth centuries. Hippocratic physicians propounded theories of the natural cause of disease: that every disease has a cause (*ekaston de ekhei physin*, *Aer.* 22.8; L 2.77–78) and no disease occurs apart from its cause (*kai ouden aneu physios gignetai*, *Aer.* 22.9; L 2.78–79). Cf. *Morb. sacr.* 1.2–3, L 6.352–53 and *De arte* 8.8–9, L 6.12–17.

[22] Hippoc. *Morb. sacr.* 1.8, 1.29, 1.93; L 6.352–65.

[23] Hippoc. *Prorrh.* 2 1.2–22, L 5.510–72 and 9.6–9. The philology of the root *mant** is discussed in Chapter 4.

for acute diseases that people consider the art of medicine "no better than divination":

Diviners think that the selfsame bird is a good omen if it appears on the left and a bad one if on the right, and others think the opposite. And in hieroscopy there are similar differences of opinion.[24]

Yet Hippocratic physicians used the language, imagery, and methods of their predecessors and contemporaries, including prayer, amulets, and divination. *On Regimen* 4 ("On Dreams") criticizes prayer as a cure for disease, but gives instructions to determine which gods should be the object of prayer.[25]

Hippocratic texts consistently advocate prognosis. *Articulations* admonishes the physician to forewarn (*katamanteusasthai*) patients in cases where a shoulder dislocation may return.[26] *On Prognosis* stresses that not all patients can be cured, and that the effective physician must be able to recognize those who could. Hippocratic prognosis differed from divination in its emphasis on physical signs and critical days.[27]

Nonetheless, there were important similarities between prognosis and divination. One was the common use of oneiromancy. *On Regimen* 4 is a text on dreams that provides both a theoretic basis and detailed instructions for dream interpretation.

In the cases of such dreams as are divine and presage good or bad fortune to *poleis* or to private individuals, those who know how to judge them have a precise art [or "science," *akribēn tekhnēn*]. But in cases where the soul presages disease of the body – surfeit, depletion, excess of something natural, or change to something unaccustomed – those who judge these things sometimes get it right but sometimes miss the mark.[28]

On Regimen 4 indicates the medical significance of a wide range of dreams. It criticizes temple healers; prescribes regimens; and uses microcosm–macrocosm analogies to correlate signs in the heavens (revealed in dreams) to corresponding conditions of the body. It refers to specialists at interpretation of "God-given dreams" and stresses the importance of accurate knowledge of dream signs. Finally, it gives an explanation for the diagnostic

24 *Acut.* 3.20, L 2.238–45, trans. after Littré. 25 Hippoc. *Vict.* 4.87, 4.89, and 4.90, L 6.640–59.

26 Hippoc. *Art.* 9.3–4, L 4.100–1.

27 Such as facial appearance, posture, gestures, breathing, sweating, swellings or edema, cold, and the appearance of excreta. The significance of symptoms was dependent on critical days; for example, sweating or fever were good signs on critical days but bad signs at other times.

28 *Vict.* 4.87, L 6.640–42, trans. after Littré.

power of dreams: in sleep the soul achieves a comprehensive perception because it is freed from the body and the distraction of physical sensations.

It is noteworthy that the prescriptions in *On Regimen* 4 always include prayer. The text also distinguishes between dreams that reflect daily activities and those that indicate illness or imbalance. Dreams of the latter type portray conflict or victory in the context of daily activities, where the seriousness of the conflict indicates the seriousness of the condition. Significant dream elements included the appearance of celestial bodies, mists, clouds, and other atmospheric phenomena, land and water formations, free or constrained movement, and clothing.

In general, normality indicates freedom from disturbing influences. Changes in position indicate disease, with the details of the anomaly indicating its nature. The presence and position of the stars, sun, or moon indicated specific treatment regimens of exercise and diet. Abnormal conditions, such as a fiery atmosphere or the wandering of the heavenly bodies, indicate mental disturbance. Direction of motion also signified. For example, bright stars moving east indicated health; dim stars moving west or downward presaged illness. Direction of movement also indicated the location of the illness in the body: upward movement indicated a head ailment; seaward movement, the bowels; earthward movement, tumors.

Other signs of health included clear sight and hearing; free movement, walking or running; fertile earth, good fields, and normal water flow. Disturbances in normal patterns indicated particular diseases, for example:

Dream element	Location of ailment
poor sight and hearing	the head
rough land	the flesh
stunted trees or flooded land	fluids or semen
abnormal rivers	blood
springs and wells	bladder
the sea	bowels

Dreams of normal clothing of the correct size, white color, and good shoes indicated health (and vice versa). Similarly, the appearance of the dead was a sign of health if they appeared in clean, white clothes, or gave the dreamer something clean. Conversely, dreams of the dead naked, in dark clothes, or taking anything from the house were bad signs. Other dire signs included monstrous creatures, drinking impure water, flight in fear, fighting, injury, being bound, fording rivers, or enemy soldiers. An impending change of health (positive or negative) was indicated by dreams of earthquakes or new clothing.[29]

The chapter includes treatment recommendations for all these conditions. They all included prayer, determined by the nature of the dream. Positive signs indicated prayers to Zeus, Athena, Hermes, and Apollo: all gods of sky, medicine, and wisdom. Negative signs indicated prayers to protector gods, gods of the earth, and heroes.

Despite these similarities, there is a crucial difference between divination and medical prognosis: the Hippocratic authors insist that diseases have natural causes. For example, in *On the Sacred Disease*, belief in natural causation is a key distinction between Hippocratic physicians and the temple practices they attack. The "naturalists" (*phusikoi*) drew on the idea of the "nature" (*phusis*) of things and their causes (*aitia*) as the hallmark of their own expertise: the ability to elucidate the natural causes of phenomena. In this area, diviners and physicians (as well as other naturalists) stand at opposite poles in the development of systematic inquiry into nature. The naturalists' idea of nature as a type of explanation was entirely new, even if their actual explanations were little removed from those of their competitors.

Finally, although the Hippocratic authors freely attack independent purifiers and magicians – their direct competitors – they never attack the cults of Asclepius or Apollo. In summary, the relations between Hippocratic and Asclepian medicine were complex. They share the use of diagnostic oneiromancy, interest in prognosis (often for illnesses neither could treat), and notions of purification (*katharsis*), understood as ritual purification or physical purgatives.[30]

Comparable contexts for iatromancy and medicine

In summary, in the development of systematic Chinese and Greek medical thought, the relationship of the mantic arts and systematic medicine was one of coexistence, rather than opposition or evolution.

First, illness remained an ongoing topic of both Greek and Chinese mantic consultation, even after some kind of systematic medicine offered other options. We see evidence of this in fourth-century records from Dodona and Delphi and the proliferation of Asclepian oracles; Hippocratic naturalistic medicine and Asclepian temple healing coexisted. An analogous situation exists in second-century China. The period between

[29] *Vict.* 4.88–93, L 6.642–62. [30] Lloyd 2003: esp. 47–53.

the medical casebook of Chunyu Yi and the formation of the *Huangdi neijing* coincides with the medical and mantic texts from Mawangdui. The *Hou Han shu* biographies of *fang* experts make it clear that medicine was an important area of *fang* practice, and indicate the importance of illness as a topic of mantic consultation.[31] Contemporary studies of temple medicine indicate the ongoing importance of iatromancy and its coexistence with biomedicine. For example, the Hong Kong Huang Daxian, famous for its medical oracles, opened a medical clinic in 1980 so consultors could fill prescriptions on-site. An official offshoot of the temple opened in New York in 1985.[32]

Second, both Chinese and Greek physicians incorporated (and modified) mantic rhetoric and procedures, especially oneiromancy and prognosis. Chunyu Yi combined the prognostic language of mantic consultation with *yin–yang*-based medicine, and criticized the "incorrect" prognoses of competing physicians with inferior methods. Although Hippocratic physicians made rhetorical targets of purifiers and priests, both used a common language of pollution and purification.[33] Temple healers and purifiers offered cleansing rituals to private consultors. Hippocratic physicians advocated "catharsis" (*katharsis*) through physical purgatives and diuretics that rectified imbalances and eliminated external pathogens.

Robin Yates has argued that a discourse of purity and pollution in early China paralleled, but was distinct from, discourses of good and ill auspice. One of its foci was identifying the cause of invasive maladies and exorcizing the invading entity.[34] By contrast, Greek notions of pollution and purification were pervasive and explicit in law and ritual. Blood pollution was a consideration in legal cases of murder, sacrilege, and profanation, as was the inheritance of guilt for the crimes of parents or ancestors.[35] Chinese evidence on this point helps show the force and singularity of Greek notions of miasma and catharsis.

31 E.g. Guo Yu 郭玉 (*HHS* 72B.2735) and Hua Tuo 華佗 (*HHS* 72B.2736–41; *Sanguo zhi* 29.799–801, "Wei shu" 魏書).

32 Strickmann 2005: esp. 44–45, Carole Morgan 1987.

33 *On the Sacred Disease* explicitly takes as its opponents "mages, purifiers (*katharmoi*), charlatans, and quacks" (Hippoc. *Morb. sacr.* 1.8; L 6.354). Hippocratic texts conspicuously do not attack religion, Delphi, or Asclepian sanctuaries (Lloyd 2003: 52).

34 Yates (1997) identifies it in music, colors, various practices of everyday life concerning sacrifice, spirits, medicine, warfare, crime, and punishment. He also argues that warfare was understood as a means of eliminating pollution, and divination was the first step in identifying the polluting agent.

35 *Poleis* institutionalized purifying practices such as the regular expulsion of the *pharmakos* and the use of scapegoats. Pollution was also a focus in Greek tragedy. Versions of the story of Oedipus prominently inform several tragedies, yet there is debate about his role as a *pharmakos* in the purification of Thebes. See Vernant 1978.

Finally, although Greek medical writers used iatromantic elements, their formulation of explicit notions of nature (*phusis*) and cause (*aitia*) distanced them from mantic practitioners in ways that have no Chinese counterpart.

The Chinese mantic arts and systematic cosmology

Unlike the case of medicine, the role of the mantic arts in the development of Chinese systematic cosmology has no Greek equivalent and is in this sense a "non-comparable." We find in pre-Han and Han China a continuous and consistent interest in thinking systematically about the cosmos and how mantic knowledge fits into cosmic patterns. Central to that discourse was the use of number, symmetry, astronomy, and hemerology, as well as evolving theories of three key concepts: *qi*, *yin–yang*, and *wuxing*.

Despite some efforts to date cosmological thinking in China to the Shang or even earlier, it is now widely agreed that the bases of cosmological speculation first appeared in the ideas and methods of Warring States technical specialists, whose terms and techniques were later incorporated into the *yin–yang* and *wuxing* theories of correlative cosmology. This view was first argued by A. C. Graham some twenty years ago, and excavated texts on technical arts have reinforced it by supplementing the sparser evidence of the received tradition.[36]

Qi, yin–yang, wuxing

Fundamental to discussion of Chinese systematic inquiry is a distinction between cosmology and so-called "correlative cosmology." Correlative cosmology was based on a fusion of three originally distinct concepts: *qi*, *yin–yang*, and *wuxing*, all terms of considerable importance to mantic discourse.

The term *qi* resists easy definition. It refers to invisible energies that inform everything. These energies were not distinct from matter. The term was also used in medical literature (for example, in the previous section) to describe the circulation of energy in the body. *Qi* also manifested as vapor, shapes, or perceptible movement.[37] By the fourth century, the primary manifestations of *qi* were understood to be of two types: *yin* and

[36] A. C. Graham 1991: esp. 225–35. For attempts to attribute a Shang or even Neolithic origin to cosmological thinking see n. 89.

[37] These terms are introduced in Chapter 1. Several techniques for observing *qi* are discussed in Chapter 5.

yang. These terms date to the *Zhou yi*, and refer to a profound original polarity, originally understood as the complementary and cyclic alteration of the seasons.[38] The meaning of *wuxing* also changed according to time and context. Between the fourth and second centuries *wuxing* could refer to five agents or processes, five courses (of planetary motion), five materials, five powers, or five modes of conduct. As A. C. Graham pointed out, the meaning of *wuxing* changed over time from "Five Agents" or processes to the "Five Phases" of correlative cosmology, probably at some point in the Han. The "Five Phases" referred to several set sequences of transformation of *qi*.[39] To further complicate matters, *wuxing* correlations were widely used by mantic specialists, Ru, and other textual specialists, who may have adapted these categories to their own purposes. Those purposes may have included competition with technical experts for patronage and imperial favor.[40]

Sinologists since the 1950s have used the term "correlative cosmology" to describe a vast pre-Han or Han system of correlations between *yin* and *yang*, *qi*, *wuxing*, and various orders in the natural or human world.[41] The term has become so influential that it is virtually impossible to consider early Chinese cosmology or systematic inquiry without it. Correlative cosmology sought to explain a universe composed of *qi* in constant transformation by means of categories based on *yin–yang* and *wuxing*.[42] It classified various aspects of the human body, the body politic, the natural world, and dynastic change by grouping these phenomena into categories derived from combinations of *yin–yang* and *wuxing*, especially in fives (colors, sounds, tastes, cardinal directions, etc.).

The concepts of *qi* and *yin–yang* clearly appear together as early as the fourth century BCE, but the identification of *qi* and *wuxing* is more difficult to date, and with it, the emergence of correlative cosmology.[43] There is

[38] For changing understandings of the meaning of *qi* and *yin–yang* see A. C. Graham 1986: 91–92, Xu Fuguan 1969, and Raphals 1998a: 139–68.

[39] A. C. Graham 1991: 225–30, cf. Major 1993: esp. 5–15, Nivison, in Loewe and Shaughnessy 1999: esp. 809–12. The term also had specialized meanings in astronomy (see n. 73). One example of these cycles is the "conquest" cycle, described in Chapter 5, n. 117.

[40] This issue is discussed in Chapter 4. See also Nylan 2010.

[41] For accounts of correlative cosmology see Needham and Wang Ling (1956: 280–81), Henderson (1984: 1), A. C. Graham (1986: 319–20), Major (1993: 28), and Wang Aihe (2000b: 2). For detailed discussion of this issue see Nylan 2010.

[42] Sivin (1995) has argued that, for a given time period, any "systematic" theory of *qi* based on *yin–yang* and *wuxing* must meet three criteria of being relational, aspectual, and processual: (1) These terms must describe relationships rather than substances. (2) Classifications based on them must refer to particular *aspects* of the things being classified. (3) They must refer to non-static "processual" aspects of *qi*.

[43] *Qi* and *yin–yang* appear together in the *Zuo zhuan* and the *Zhuangzi*. Several examples are discussed in Chapters 2 and 5.

considerable debate about when these three concepts were joined into a cosmological system. Some scholars have dated the fusion to some time between 300 and 100 BCE, but others argue that there is little positive evidence for any such fusion before the late Western Han.

Debates about correlative cosmology and the dating of the first coincidence of *yin–yang*, *qi*, and *wuxing* tend to obscure the more important question of the origins of Chinese *cosmological* speculation. By cosmological speculation I mean speculations or theories of the ultimate constituents of the universe and explanations for cosmic change. This simpler criterion is met by the combination of theories of *qi* and *yin–yang*. My interest is to ask how mantic practices contributed to the development of systematic cosmology. In other words, Chinese theories about *qi*, *yin–yang*, and *wuxing* individually can be cosmological, and important examples of systematic inquiry, without being correlative in the senses discussed above.

Several elements contributed to the systematic and cosmological orientation of the Chinese mantic arts. Important aspects of pre-Han Chinese divination include: (1) an interest in symmetry, already visible in the oracle bone inscriptions; (2) the articulation of a *yin–yang* polarity, abstracted as patterns of change, represented by numbers (these patterns were elaborated and nuanced in the hexagrams of the *Zhou yi*); and (3) an interest in astronomy and calendrics as systematic models of space and time. They all were based on observation of natural phenomena. Eventually *yin* and *yang* were elaborated into *wuxing* methods and applied systematically (and perhaps arbitrarily) to a wide range of phenomena.

Symmetry: the Shang oracle bone inscriptions

The earliest manifestation of systematic and cosmographic thinking is in the inscription of divination records in symmetrical layouts (Figure 9.1) and the association of numbers with divination statements. Some scholars argue for the beginnings of cosmological thought in the oracle bone inscriptions, and much scholarly debate has surrounded the question of their purpose and their careful preparation and symmetry. David Keightley ascribes a significant metaphysical aspect to the symmetrical placement of positive and negative "complementary charges" in late Shang inscriptions, beginning with the reign of Wu Ding 武丁 (r. 1250–1192). In his view, the symmetry of the charges reflects deliberate and careful placement in which the balance of the calligraphy and deliberate placement of the cracks create a virtual mirror image. He describes the Shang worldview as a "proto-*yin–yang* metaphysics," a balanced, dualistic symbiosis of good and ill auspice and

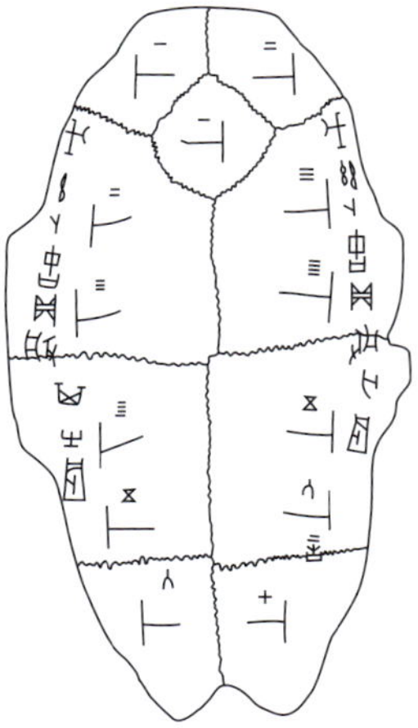

Figure 9.1 Symmetrical layout of a turtle shell divination (Heji 4264).

good and bad fortune. That dualism is echoed in the binary structures of the *Zhou yi*.[44] Other scholars see a "*sifang*" 四方 (four-direction) cosmology in which a circular heaven superimposed on a square earth creates a five-element, cruciform shape resembling the character *ya* 亞: a central square surrounded by four squares pointing to each of the cardinal directions.[45]

These explanations are suggestive, but speculative, and go well beyond what we know about the Shang. Two points are important. One is the assumption that humans could communicate with extra-human powers. This belief was part of a common Shang–Zhou religious heritage, based on the assumption of an inseparable connection between the human and extra-human worlds, visible in signs that could reveal information about the future and be used to enhance personal welfare. In sum, they shared a belief in predictability and in the mutability of fate.[46] The other is what Léon Vandermeersch has called a Shang "rationalisme divinatoire." He suggests that the symmetrical structures of early plastromancy had a profound influence on later Chinese notions of parallelism in poetics, rhetoric, and styles of reasoning and philosophical exegesis.[47]

Numeric representations of hexagram lines

Oracle bone divination (like many Delphic oracles) answers a yes–no question. Recent archaeology has revealed a clear link between Shang and

[44] Keightley 1988: esp. 373–74, 386–87. Other examples: *Heji* 776r, 5658r, 6473, 6647r, 14198r.
[45] Allan 1991: esp. 75–77, Wang Aihe 2000b: 26–34. [46] See Raphals 2003.
[47] Poo Mu-chou 1998: 27–29; Vandermeersch 1974, 1977–80: 2.285–316, 1994.

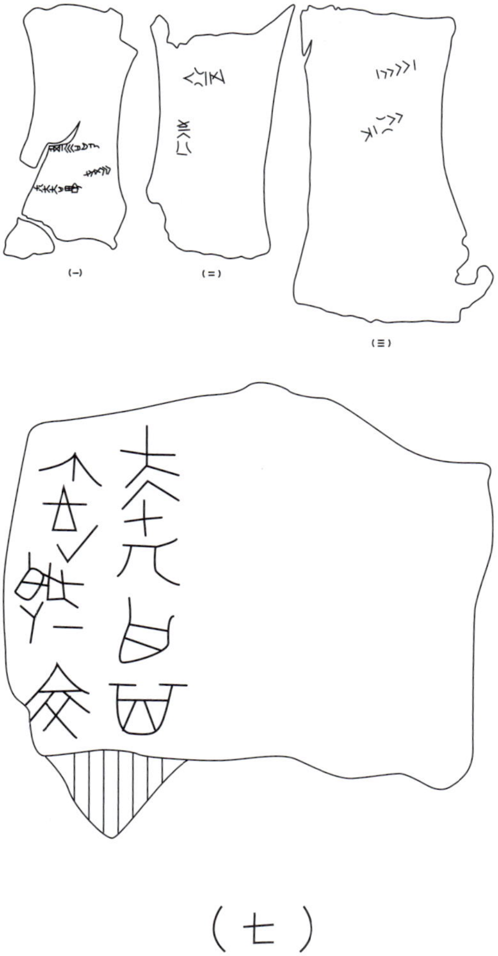

Figure 9.2 Inscribed bones from Sipanmo and Qishan.

Western Zhou metaphysics in the early association of sequences of numbers with mantic statements in Shang and Western Zhou scapulae and plastrons. The oldest are from Sipanmo 四盤磨 (Anhui, late Shang).[48] The left-hand bone in the upper row (Figure 9.2) has two sequences of numbers, each followed by the word *yue* 曰 ("says") and an additional character. Numbers also appear on the so-called "Zhouyuan oracle bones" from Qishan 岐山 (Shaanxi) at what may have been the ancestral temple of the Western Zhou. Here, sequences of numbers are associated with statements, and some contain sequences of numbers in groups of six, resembling *Yi jing*

48 Sipanmo: Zhang Zhenglang 1980: 81 n. 4 and 404 (dating), trans. Huber et al. 1980: esp. 87. Original report: Li Xueqin 1956: 16–17. Milfoil: Zhang Yachu and Liu Yu 1981.

hexagrams.[49] These six-number sequences suggest some kind of divination by lots (cleromancy) using a more complex sortition than the binary results of oracle bone divination.

The sequences were not initially recognized as numbers, and these "strange graphs" were thought to be lineage emblems. While leading the restoration of the Mawangdui *Yi* fragments, Zhang Zhenglang noticed that these marks appeared consistently in the context of *Yi* divination, and identified the numeric sequences as milfoil divinations. These numbers are now understood as hexagram lines in the earliest representations of the hexagrams, as numbers.[50] Milfoil divination records from Baoshan, Wangshan, and Wangjiatai also give sequences of six numbers that resemble the number sequences of the Zhouyuan oracle bones. None of these early records of milfoil divination make any reference to a mantic text.[51]

The Zhouyuan oracle bones also suggest the concurrent use of pyromancy and milfoil divination. Five of the nine bones inscribed with numbers also show signs of cracking, either from cracks on the front of the bone or hollows incised in the back.[52] The presence of cracks and hollows on bones inscribed with numbers suggests the use of a number-based mantic technique in conjunction with pyromancy.[53] One bone has five number sequences: one on the front and four on the rear.[54] Another (Figure 9.2, lower row) associates a number sequence with a statement:

[49] Numerical inscriptions appear on nine bones: H11:7, 81, 85, 90, 91, 108 (which has four numbers inscribed on the reverse side), 177, 235, and 263. See Cao Wei 2002: 7, 61, 65, 67, 76, 105, 123, and 130, cf. Chen Quanfang 1988: 145–48. Magnified transcriptions (back matter): 58 and 107–8. Qishan: These three hundred were out of a total of 17,000 bones. See Wang Yuxin 1984, Chen Quanfang 1988, Xu Xitai 1989, Shaughnessy 1985–87. Hexagrams: Zhang Zhenglang 1979, 1980: 81 nn. 5–10, and 1984.

[50] Numeric representations of the hexagrams by the numbers one 一, five 㐅, six 六, seven 七, and eight 八 continue well into the Warring States. One, five, and seven were *yang*; six and eight were *yin*. Zhang Zhenglang 1980, trans. Huber et al. 1980; Harper 1999b: 857–59.

[51] The appearance of *yue* 曰 after the number sequences suggest that what follows is a mantic text. See Field 2000.

[52] Bones (without numeric inscriptions) whose reverse sides have square cracking hollows: H11:47, 48, 50, 52, and 69, reproduced in Cao Wei 2002: 38–40, 42, and 47. The undersides of the bone show hollows in a carved square shape, which is different from the *bu*-shaped cracks at Anyang. There are also round hollows on the bone (e.g. FQ1 in Cao Wei 2002: 142) and square hollows on turtle plastrons (e.g. FQ2 in Cao Wei 2002: 144–45).

[53] Four bones (H11:7, 81, 90, and 91) show cracks on the surface and one (H11:7) also appears to have hollows for cracking incised on its reverse side. One (H11:81) has a visible crack on the surface of the bone to the right of the inscribed number sequence 766766. Another (H11:90) is cracked just below the inscribed number 667. See Cao Wei 2002: 7, 61, 67; Chen Quanfang 1988: 58, 107–8. Chen Quanfang 1988: 107 has a magnified transcription of H11:90 (5x).

[54] Chen Quanfang 1988: 106, H11:108. Front: 161668. Left rear: 18685 and 5684; right rear 698186 and 9365.

七六六七一八 曰 : 其 . . . □ 既魚

766718 says: "will . . . a gift of fish."[55]

Additional inscribed scapulae from the late Western Zhou were discovered in 1956 at Zhangjiapo 張家坡 near present-day Xi'an.[56]

The Baoshan records of milfoil divinations also record sequences of numbers. Each prognostication is a pair of six-number sequences, indicating the transformation of the right sequence into the left (Figure 9.3). For example, slip 201 (upper left) represents the transformation of the right-hand sequence 666166 (read bottom to top) into the sequence 116116 (also bottom to top). In the received tradition this corresponds to the transformation of Hexagram 19 (Yu 豫) into Hexagram 58 (Dui 兌).[57] The Baoshan records never mention the *Zhou yi* or the name of any hexagram.

In summary, interest in symmetry dates back to the Shang dynasty. We also see, starting in the late Shang, and developing further in the Western Zhou and Warring States, the association of numbers, first with *yin* and *yang* and then with hexagram lines.

Yin–yang and *yi* divination

A second aspect of systematic thought is explicit cosmology. The four excavated *Yi* ("Changes") texts (introduced in Chapters 2 and 6) help us see the development of the *Yi* as a cosmological text. (1) The oldest version, the so-called Shanghai Museum text – fragments of thirty-four hexagrams on bamboo slips – indicates that a stable version of something like the received *Zhou yi* was in circulation by 300, and that mantic interpretations associated with it were still flexible at this time.[58] (2) A different *Yi* text

55 Cao Wei 2002: 65 (Bone H11:85), cf. Chen Quanfang 1988: 108 and Zhang Yachu and Liu Yu 1981: 156, Bone 7.

56 Zhangjiapo: Zhang Zhenglang 1980: 81 nn. 1–3, *Zhangjiapo xi Zhou mu di, Zhongguo tianye kaogu baogaoji* 1999. *Yi* divination in the oracle bones: Rao Zongyi 1982 and Li Xueqin 1992: 218–55.

57 *Baoshan*: 32, slip 201. The other hexagram number sequences occur in slips 210, 229, 232, 239, and 245. Zhang Zhenglang (1980) explains the numbering system: 1, 5, and 7 were *yang*; 6 and 8 were *yin*. The sequence in slip 229 is particularly difficult to read. The *Baoshan* editors take it as Gu 蠱 (18) transforming into Bo 剝 (23), through transformation of the two *yang* lines to *yin*, despite the *yang* 5 in the left-hand sequence, which would indicate Jin 晉 (35). See *Baoshan*: 57 n. 454.

58 Ma Chengyuan et al. (2001–8), vol. 3: photographs 11–70, transcription 131–260. It consists of bamboo slips or fragments of thirty-four hexagrams. It is unique in that each hexagram picture is divided into two trigrams, and square black or red symbols appear immediately after each

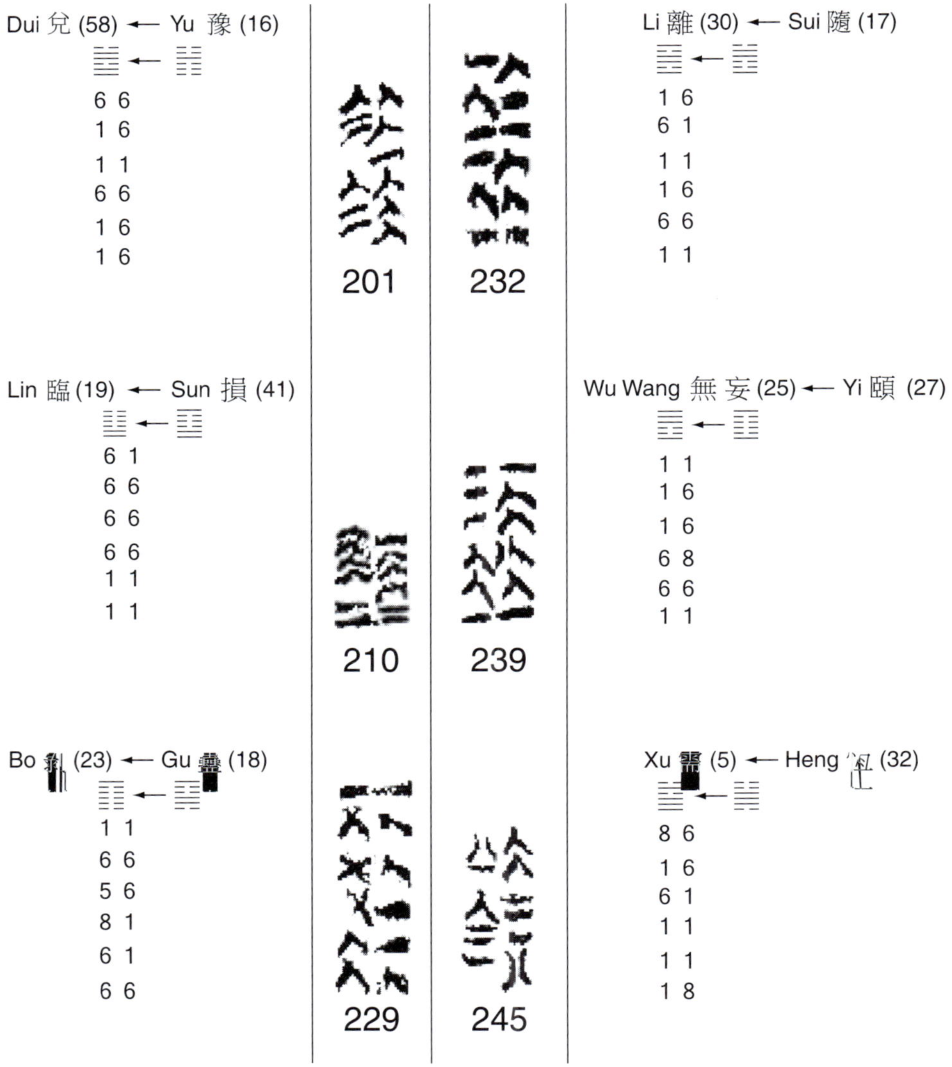

Figure 9.3 Hexagram number graphs from Baoshan.

associated with the Shang dynasty, the *Guicang* 歸藏 (Returning to the Treasury), has been excavated from Wangjiatai 王家台 Tomb 15 (Jiangling 江陵, Hubei, 278–207). (3) The so-called Fuyang *Zhou yi* was excavated from Shuanggudui 雙古堆 Tomb 1 (Fuyang 阜陽, Anhui, 165). These two versions indicate the association of omens with numbers in early versions of

hexagram name. There are many *variora*, including characters seen in texts from Chu 楚 and other differences from the received text. Even so, it corresponds to the received text in many ways. See Liao Mingchun 2000a, 2000b: 21–31; Liao Mingchun and Zhu Yuanqing 2002; Pu Maozuo 2006; Shaughnessy 2005–6: esp. 23–24.

the text. (4) The most complete version was excavated from a tomb at Mawangdui 馬王堆 (Changsha, Hunan, 168). It also uses numbers (one and eight) to represent the hexagrams. Importantly, it includes the *Xi ci* commentary.[59]

The Wangjiatai *Guicang* and Fuyang *Zhou yi* provide evidence of the earlier evolution of the *Yi* or of alternative *Yi* traditions. Both group omen statements under the headings of the hexagrams and lines, and use the numbers one (*yang*) and eight (*yin*) to represent hexagram lines.[60] The Fuyang version also adds brief statements after each line statement that indicate the importance of the line for a particular topic, such as weather, punishment, warfare, illness, marriage, residence, pregnancy, birth, bureaucratic service, administration, travel, hunting, and fishing – the categories of the daybooks.[61] The Mawangdui text includes copies of the *Zhou yi* and *Xi ci* commentary as well as four hitherto unknown commentaries, but does not include the stalk-casting procedure found in the received version of the *Xi ci*. It also differs from the received version in the order of the hexagrams (which are organized by constituent trigrams) and the hexagram names.[62]

The *Zuo zhuan* provides additional information on the hexagrams as abstractions of processes of change. It contains some two dozen accounts of

[59] "Mawangdui boshu 'Liushisi gua' shiwen" in *WW* 1984.3: 1–8; Deng Qiubo 1987; Zhang Liwen 1991; Ikeda Tomohisa 1994: 111–207 and 1995: 1–105; Shaughnessy 1996.

[60] The *Guicang Yi* text from Wangjiatai includes fifty-three hexagrams followed by the word *yue*, each followed by an example of a divination from the distant past. Most of the hexagram names correspond to the names of received text of the *Yi jing*; the exceptions resemble the hexagram names of the Mawangdui *Zhou yi*. It closely resembles extant portions of the *Guicang*. The extant fragments were preserved by Ma Guohan (1794–1857) and others in Ma Guohan 1883: 1.1–23. Although "reconstituted redactions" (*jiben*) of the *Guicang* had long been considered problematic, the Wangjiatai fragments are believed to be genuine. See Wang Mingqin 2004: 441–43 and Chapter 6 nn. 15–17.

[61] The Fuyang *Zhou yi* consists of fragmentary bamboo slips of some fifty-two hexagrams and line statements. It also contains a text on physiognomy ("Moving *Qi*" 行氣), daybooks, and texts similar to the *Xingde* texts from Mawangdui. Initial publication: Hu Pingsheng 1998. Transcription: Han Ziqiang 2000a, 2000b: esp. 127–32. Texts found in the tomb: Shaughnessy 2001: esp. 15–18. Warring States and Chu context: Li Ling 1993: 271–78; Loewe 1994: 160–90, 214–35. See also Chapter 6 n. 10.

[62] Variant Han readings prior to the Mawangdui version: Xu Qinting 1975. Other Mawangdui *Yi* texts: *Ersan zi wen* 二三子問 ("Several Disciples Asked") is a collection of quotations on the *Yi* attributed to Confucius. *Yi zhi yi* 易之義 ("Properties of the *Yi*") discusses *yin*, *yang*, and many hexagrams. They resemble the *Wenyan* (Words on the Text) and *Shuo gua* commentaries of the received tradition. *Yao* 要 ("Essentials") gives indications of social and political attitudes toward mantic practices. For example, Confucius compares himself to mantic experts who use the same means for different ends. Other studies: Chen Songchang and Liao Mingchun 1993, Liao Mingchun 1993 and 2000a, Wang Bo 1995, Xing Wen 1995, Wang Baoxian 1995.

Yi divination. While the entries themselves cannot be taken at face value, they show a shift of form that may reflect changes in the practice of *Yi* interpretation. Accounts of incidents that pre-date 604 show the *Yi* being used exclusively as a mantic text.[63] The *Zuo zhuan* also indicates that as early as the fourth century, the *Yi* had the status of a source of moral expertise and was no longer primarily regarded as a mantic text.[64] In later entries, the *Yi* is cited as an authority, but without the immediate context of actual divination.

The *Xi ci* commentary in the *Yi jing* changes its scope entirely. It explains the organization of the hexagrams by numerical correlations between the *Zhou yi* and the structure of the world:

天一。地二。天三。地四。天五。地六。天七。地八。天九。地十。

Heaven is one; earth is two; heaven is three; earth is four; heaven is five; earth is six; heaven is seven; earth is eight; heaven is nine; earth is ten.[65]

By linking odd numbers to heaven and even numbers to earth, the *Xi ci* asserts that numbers order the world by dividing it into quantified, measurable units.[66] It ascribes the invention of the hexagrams to the legendary sage ruler Fu Xi 伏犧 (along with writing and record-keeping). It claims that he invented the eight trigrams (*bagua* 八卦) from the images and models of Heaven and Earth and the patterns (*wen* 文) of birds and beasts.[67] In this account of the origins of divination, the trigrams are the first form of written record and the *Zhou yi* is a comprehensive microcosm of the universe.[68] The *Xi ci* thus describes the cosmos and the *Zhou yi* as two parallel systems of signs whose correspondences allow the *Zhou yi* to reveal hidden meanings

63 These early accounts identify hexagrams by a combination of the hexagram name and the line that is most important for the particular prognostication. For example, the phrase "Mingyi's Qian" 明夷之謙 (Zuo, 1263 (Zhao 5.1), Legge 603) refers to the first (bottom) *yin* line of the hexagram Qian 謙 (no. 15). Changing this line to *yang* generates the hexagram Mingyi 明夷 (no. 36). Similarly, the phrase "Kun's Bi" 坤之比 refers to the generation of the hexagram Kun 坤 (no. 2) when the fifth (from the bottom) *yin* line of the hexagram Bi 比 (no. 8) is reversed, to generate the *yang* fifth line of Kun (Zuo, 1337 (Zhao 12.10), Legge 640).

64 Imai Usaburō 1969: 51–97; Toda Toyosaburō 1957: 1–11; Li Jingchi 1978; Gao Heng 1979: 70–110.

65 *ZY* 7.26b ("Xi ci shang"), Legge 365.

66 Quantification: Raphals 2002. Numbers as signs of learning: Lloyd 1994: 155.

67 *ZY* 8.5a–8a ("Xi ci xia"), cf. *BHT*, 51–52 ("San huang wu di san wang wu bo" 三皇五帝三王五伯 2.1).

68 Other legends depict the Duke of Zhou as a turtle-shell diviner who communicates with gods and spirits, and is associated with the development of the *Yi jing*. E.g. *Shang shu* 13.8a–10a ("Jin teng" 金縢, Legge 351–61); 13.15a–20b ("Da gao" 大誥, Legge 362–74); 15.15b–18a ("Luo gao" 洛誥, Legge 434–37). See Lewis 1999: 211–13 and 241–86.

and establish fate.[69] The *Xi ci* even describes the process of *Yi* divination as a literal physical analog to the processes of the universe when it states that the trigrams are square and the milfoil round.[70]

It is important to stress that *Zhou yi* itself contains none of these cosmological analogies. The *Zhou yi* eventually attained the full status of a canonical wisdom text or "classic" (*jing*) as the *Yi jing*.[71] The point for present purposes is that the *Zhou yi* itself does not include the cosmological interpretations of these commentaries, which represented the hexagrams as a microcosm and analog of cosmic processes.

Finally, the *Yi jing* combined the use of writing, number, calculation, and a new distance from any active human–divine encounter. The authors of the *Yi jing* commentaries reinterpreted the *Zhou yi* as a philosophical theory of signs, images, numbers, and systematic analogies that articulated cosmic principles in a concise vocabulary of visual signs.[72] In the process, the text was transformed from a mantic text into a classic of moral expertise.

Astronomy and astrocalendrics

A wide range of Chinese astrocalendric methods (discussed in Chapter 5) bespeak an early interest in the systematic mapping and observation of the heavens.[73] The *Zhou li* mentions several astronomical officials (discussed in

69 The *Xi ci* also makes the moral and political claim that the *Zhou yi* is the product of sages, a model for gentlemen, and the basis of ritual (*ZY* 7.28b–32b, "Xi ci shang"). These texts indicate the existence of professional *Yi* diviners and ambivalent attitudes of Ru toward them. They suggest the early existence of a Confucian *Yi* tradition, including a new mythology of the origins of the *Yi* in the *Xi ci* (*ZY* 7.26b and 28b–30a, "Xi ci shang" 繫辭上 and 8.5a–6a, "Xi ci xia" 繫辭下).

70 *ZY* 7.26b ("Xi ci shang").

71 This shift is difficult to date because much controversy remains over the dating of *Yi jing* commentaries. See Shaughnessy, in Loewe 1993.

72 Gao Heng 1979: 70–110; Lewis 1999: 241–43, 284–86; Nylan 2001a: 202–52, esp. 224–28.

73 The antiquity of Chinese astronomy and the question of possible external influences remain controversial. Shang oracle bones with astronomical records place its origins at least to the first half of the second millennium (Ho Peng Yoke 1985: 116–18). According to a late chapter of the *Shu jing*, Yao commanded his officials to compute and delineate the sun, moon, and stars, to make measurements of the rising sun and the Lunar Lodges at the spring and fall equinox and summer and winter solstices (2.9a–10b (*Yao dian* 堯典), trans. Karlgren 3). However, since this chapter probably dates from the Qin unification or later (Nylan 2001a: 134–35), its force is to legitimize the astronomical interests of the Qin or Western Han. More recent studies argue that, regardless of when the *Yao dian* was compiled, it nonetheless includes content dating to the second millennium, including the names of the gods of the four quarters as attested in the oracle bone inscriptions. The discovery of the Taosi and Yaoshan solar observation altars indicates that astronomical observations of the kind necessary to create the calendar described

Chapter 4), and Sima Qian describes astronomical observations recorded during the Qin and Han.[74] It would appear that only with the political order of the Qin and Han were attempts at regular astronomical observations possible.

Systematic interest in astrocalendrics is attested by mantic astrolabes (diviner's boards), by hemerological texts excavated from tombs (e.g. at Zhoujiatai, Fuyang, and Mawangdui), and by Western Han astronomical treatises. The increasingly official character of Chinese astronomy becomes apparent with the creation of court institutions in the Western Han and in the consolidation of power in the Astronomical Bureau in the Eastern Han.[75] As in the case of Mesopotamia, the reasons for patronage of astronomy were political and pragmatic.

These methods depend on comprehensive and systematic representations of time (the sexagenary cycle) and space (correlative divisions of heaven and earth), expressed in terms of *yin-yang* and *wuxing*.[76] We find evidence of these representations in several types of source: (1) star prognostication; (2) mantic astrolabes and cosmographic imagery; and (3) *wuxing*-based cosmic systems.

Star prognostication methods became increasingly complex in the Han. Accounts of them come from the astrocalendric treatises in the *Shi ji* and *Han shu*, which refer to mantic astrolabes (diviner's boards), the Lunar Lodges, and the gods associated with them.[77] In the first systematic description of the heavens, the *Shi ji* Astronomical Treatise

in the *Yao dian* were underway in the third millennium. See Liu Qiyu 2004, Pankenier et al. 2009, and Pankenier 2010.

[74] *SJ* 27.1348–49.

[75] That official character is also evidenced by the official status of the individuals whose tombs contain astrocalendric instruments. The occupant of the Zhoujiatai tomb seems to have been a petty official aged less than thirty. Some of the bamboo slips buried with him are official in nature, for example a calendar of the sexagenary cycle for the thirty-fourth year of Qin Shihuang's reign period (the year 213). The occupant of the tomb at Shuanggudui, Fuyang was Xiahou Zao (d. 165), the second marquis of Ruyin and a high Chu official whose tomb contained *Liuren* and *Jiugong* mantic astrolabes. The occupant of Mawangdui Tomb 3 (the source of the manuscripts) was a Han official, Li Cang (d. 168), chancellor of Changsha and marquis of Dai. His tomb also contained astrocalendric and meteorological texts and instruments. Although there is too little evidence to generalize, the presence of astrocalendric texts and instruments in combination with other official documents in the tombs of state officials also suggests state sponsorship of astrocalendric observation. See Nylan and Loewe 2010: 117–20.

[76] From the fourth to second centuries, *wuxing* referred to several different things. In an astronomical context, it referred to the "Five Courses" (*wuxing* 五行) of planetary motion. In other contexts it referred to other groupings of five categories. See Nylan 2010: 403.

[77] *HNZ* 3 (*Tianwenxun* 天文訓, trans. Major 1993: 55–139), *SJ* 127.3218, *HS* 99B.4190.

gives a detailed account of the stars and constellations of the Five Palaces (the four directions and the Circumpolar region), of planetary motion, and of the Twenty-eight Lunar Lodges, which it correlates with regions of the earth. It includes sections on prognostication by the sun and moon (including eclipses of both), stars, clouds, and mists, and prognostications about harvests.[78] Excavated texts and instruments provide additional information. An astrocalendric text from Mawangdui titled *Wuxing zhan* 五星占 (Five Stars Divination) correlates the "Five Courses" (*wuxing*) of the planets Jupiter (Sui or "Year"), Venus, Mars, Saturn, and Mercury to five spirits, to the sexagenary cycle, and to omens for each period.[79]

Mantic astrolabes (*shi* 式 or *shi pan* 式盤) model the cosmos for purposes of mantic calculation.[80] They have been excavated from tombs at Wangjiatai, Zhoujiatai (a text), and Fuyang.[81] Different types have different elements and organizations, but they all superimpose a round Heaven plate which can be rotated over a square, stationary Earth plate. Han instruments such as those excavated from Fuyang make explicit use of *yin–yang* and *wuxing*.

The earliest known example may have been used to determine the orientation of the handle of the Northern Dipper among the Twenty-eight Lunar Lodges. It is a square wooden board with a handle, excavated from Wangjiatai Tomb 15, and dated to a period between 278 BCE and the late Qin. According to the archaeological report, it consists of a cruciform figure with the names of the Five Agents inscribed in the four cardinal directions and center. A surrounding circle contains the names of the twelve months and the Lunar Lodges are inscribed in the four directions.[82]

78 *SJ* 27.1331–42, Chavannes 3.385–401. The *Han shu* Astronomical Treatise (*Tianwenzhi* 天文志, *HS* 26.1273–1314) was probably written by Ma Xu 馬續 and finished by Ban Gu's sister Ban Zhao 班昭. It follows the organization of the *Shi ji*, but contains more detailed astronomical information, including of eclipses.

79 Li Ling 1993: 36–39. It also lists the yearly position of each planet from the years 246 to 177 (from the year of Qin Shihuang's accession to the Qin throne to the third year of the reign of Han Wen Di). The *Wuxing zhan* is transcribed in *WW* 1974.11: 37–39 and *Zhongguo tian wen xue shi wen ji* 1978. It is discussed in Cullen 2011.

80 Mantic astrolabes are instruments for calculation; they are not models of the cosmos beyond the limited sense required by their function.

81 The definitive study of Han *Liuren* boards is Kalinowski 1983: esp. 309–419. Recent archaeology: Yan Dunjie 1978, Kalinowski 1996: esp. 62–64 and 69–72. Later history: Kalinowski 1991 and 2003, Ho Peng Yoke 2003.

82 Described (without illustration) in *WW* 1995.1: 42.

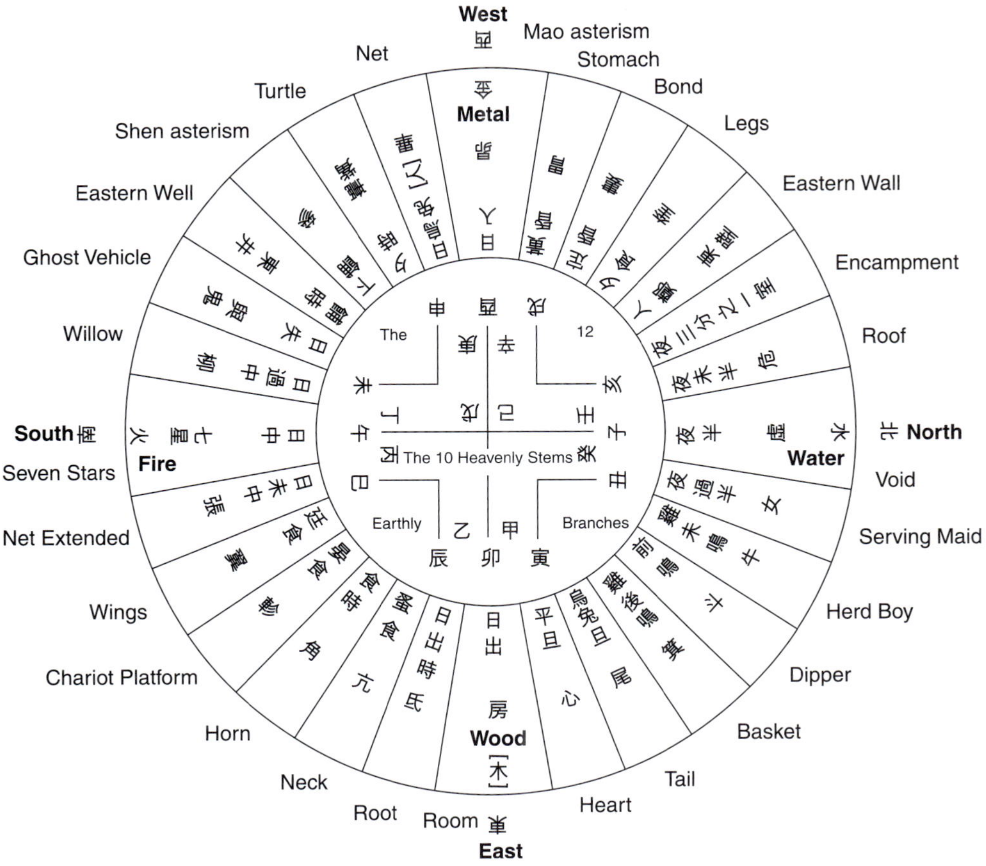

Figure 9.4 The Zhoujiatai diagram.

Several Western Han instruments and texts about them have been excavated from tombs. An illustrated text from Zhoujiatai (Guanju, Hubei) discusses the use of the Dipper astrolabe and shows its structure. At its center is a cord and hook pattern with the Ten Heaven Stems at the center of the cruciform figure and the Twelve Earth Branches in order along its four cardinal directions (Figure 9.4).[83] The outer circle associates the four cardinal directions with the Five Agents of *wuxing* and the names of the Lunar Lodges in counter-clockwise order, starting from Horn in the southwest. Each lodge is also correlated with an observation or prognostication, such as "Sun emerges" (Room, East), "Sun at the center" (Seven Stars, South), "Sun enters" (Mao, West), and "Night Halfway" (Void, North). To obtain a prognostication, the

[83] *ZJT* 107. I am indebted to unpublished material by Marc Kalinowski on this material. Archaeological report: *WW* 1999.6: 26–47.

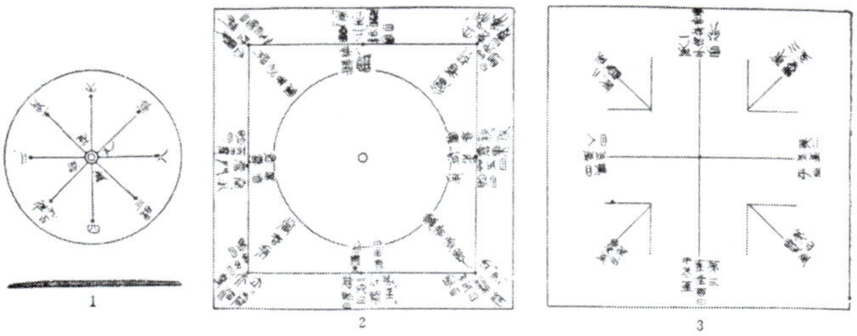

(1) Heaven Plate (2) Earth Plate, front view (3) Earth Plate, back view

The Nine Palaces

Spirit	Trigram	Palace	Influence
Tian Yi	li	south	crops and harvest
Tai Yi	kan	north	drought and flood
Tian Fu 天符		central	famine and scarcity
She Ti 攝提 Suppliants	kun	southwest	illness and suffering
Xuan Yuan 軒轅	zhen	east	storms and rain
Zhao Yao 招搖 Shining	xun	southeast	winds and clouds
Qing Long 青龍 Green Dragon	qian	northeast	frost and hail
Xian Chi 咸池 Vast Pond	dui	west	warfare and pillage
Tai Yin 太 陰 Supreme Yin	gen	northeast	intrigues and plots

Figure 9.5 *Jiugong* mantic astrolabe from Fuyang.

Heaven plate (not shown in the text) was keyed to the month of the solar calendar or "solar lodge" associated with the time of the prognostication. Once it was correctly positioned, the Dipper handle pointed to a Lunar Lodge and a prognostication associated with it.

Most excavated Han mantic astrolabes are of two types: *Jiugong* 九宮 (Nine Palaces) and *Liuren* (Six *Ren* Days). *Jiugong* mantic astrolabes divide the Heaven plate into nine "palaces," consisting of eight directional degree markers (governed by eight celestial gods) and a central point, governed by the star god Taiyi. The Lunar Lodges are arrayed in the four cardinal directions, each containing seven lodges. The Earth plate is divided into eight corresponding directional regions. It correlates solstices and equinoxes with references to auspicious and inauspicious times. The Fuyang tomb contained a *Jiugong* board (Figure 9.5), which may have been used to calculate the movements of Taiyi.[84]

Liuren astrolabes (Figure 9.6) have a more complex organization, and use a system of calculation based on the six *ren* days (*Liuren*) of the sexagenary cycle.[85] The Heaven plate shows the Northern Dipper at the

84 Fuyang board: Kalinowski 1983: 323–52 and 1996: 71–72. Original report: Wang Xiangtian and Han Ziqiang 1978: 12–31. Taiyi: Qian Baocong 1932, Li Ling 2000b, trans. Harper 1995–96.

85 That is, the six days denoted by a combination of *ren* (the ninth of the Ten Stems) and six of the Twelve Branches: Day 9 (*renshen* 壬申), Day 19 (*renwu* 壬午), Day 29 (*renchen* 壬辰), Day 39 (*renyin* 壬寅), Day 49 (*renzi* 壬子), and Day 59 (*renxu* 壬戌).

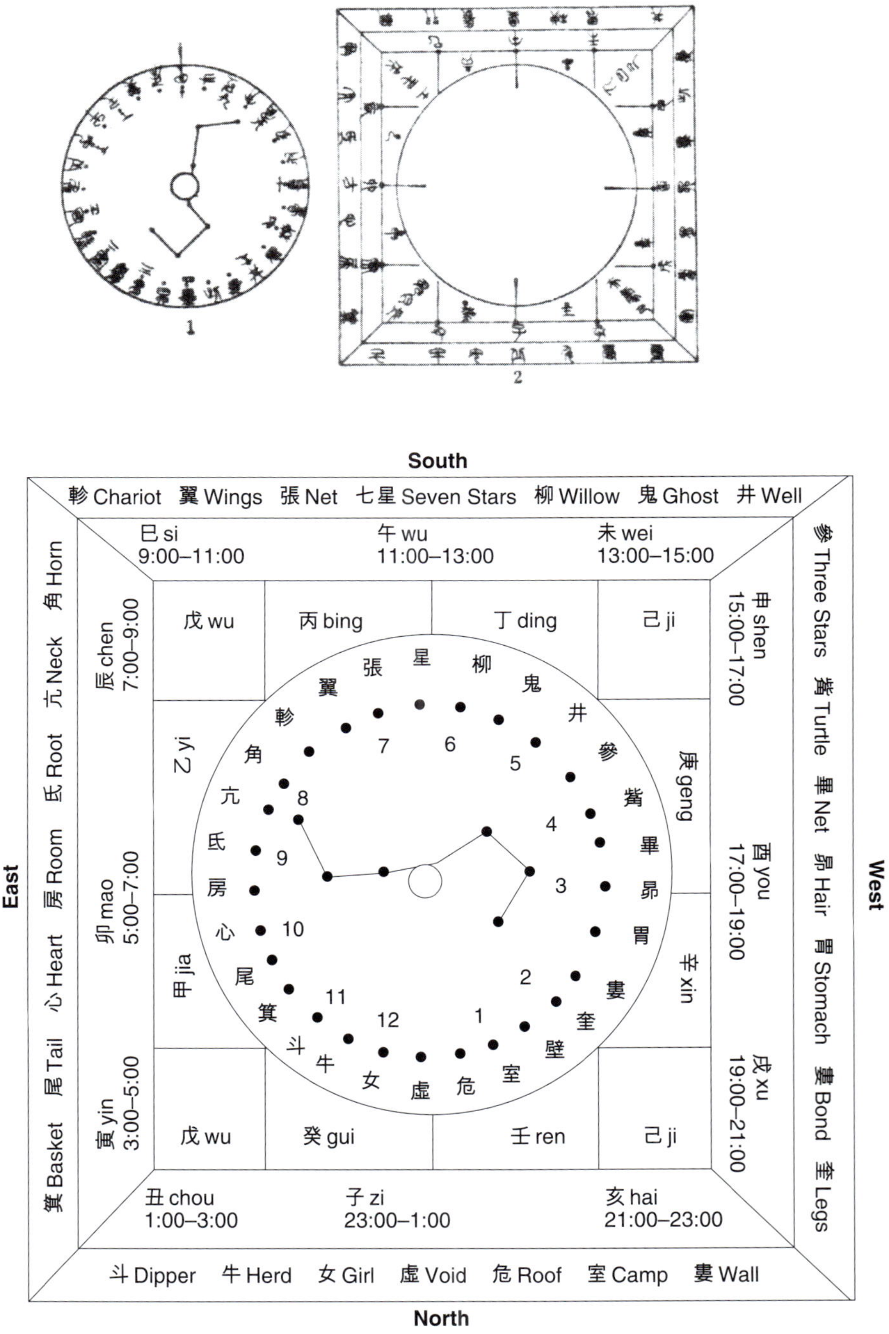

Figure 9.6 The Fuyang *Liuren* mantic astrolabe and schematic diagram.

center, surrounded by the Twenty-eight Lunar Lodges at the periphery of the circle. They are aligned with the numbers one through twelve, signifying the twelve months of the solar calendar or "solar lodges" (Figure 9.6, left side). The Heaven plate thus correlates the lunar and solar calendars. The Earth plate also contains an intermediate square of twelve degree markers (corresponding to twelve divisions of time and their corresponding gods) and the Twenty-eight Lunar Lodges at the outer periphery of the square (Figure 9.6, right side). As Donald Harper points out, the perspective of the diagram is to show the Dipper from above. Rotating the Heaven plate imitates the movement of the Dipper handle around the celestial equator over the year. The Dipper handle was used in two ways: as an astrocalendric instrument to determine the position of the sun to orient the board and as a mantic instrument to point to a segment of the Earth plate.[86]

In the schematic diagram in Figure 9.6, the Dipper handle points to the Lunar Lodge Horn (*jiao*) in the southeast (the upper left-hand corner), associated with the eighth month. The Earth plate consists of three concentric rectangular bands. Outermost are four cardinal directions (with south facing up) and the Twenty-eight Lunar Lodges, seven in each direction. The middle band contains the Twelve Earth Branches. As described in Song sources, they are markers for twelve double-hour time segments (*shi* 時), a division of the day that dates to the Late Zhou.[87] The inner band contains the Ten Heaven Stems, with *wu* and *ji* duplicated to make twelve numbers to correspond to the Twelve Earth Branches. The Dipper handle can be rotated to point to a Lunar Lodge, stem–branch combination, or marker on the Earth plate.

Scholars have also attributed an early interest in cosmology to excavated objects whose decorative motifs have been interpreted to have mantic or cosmographic significance. The first is the "cord and hook pattern" described by the *Huainanzi* as "two cords and four hooks" (*er sheng si gou* 二繩四鉤), derived from the Twelve Earth Branches.[88] Some scholars trace this motif back to the Shang or even the Neolithic, claiming a resemblance to the pattern of a Neolithic jade from Hanshan (Anhui) and to a Shang dynasty cosmology.[89] The motif of a circular heaven and a *ya*-shaped earth produces a design

[86] Harper 1979a. For a different view see Pankenier 2010. [87] Needham 1959: 322.

[88] *HNZ* 3.10b, cf. Major 1993: 84. The two cords are *ziwu* (branches 1 and 7) and *maoyou* (branches 4 and 8); the four hooks are *chouyin* (branches 2 and 3), *chensi* (branches 5 and 6), *weishen* (branches 8 and 9), and *xuhai* (branches 11 and 12).

[89] It is inscribed with a rectangle superimposed by a circle; in the center is a smaller circle containing the image of the sun. Between the circles are eight arrows pointing to the eight directions. Li Xueqin (1992–93) argues that the rectangle represents the earth and the circle the heavens and the cycle of the seasons. Archaeological report: *WW* 1989.4: 1–9; Chen Jiujin and Zhang Jingguo 1989. Direction and

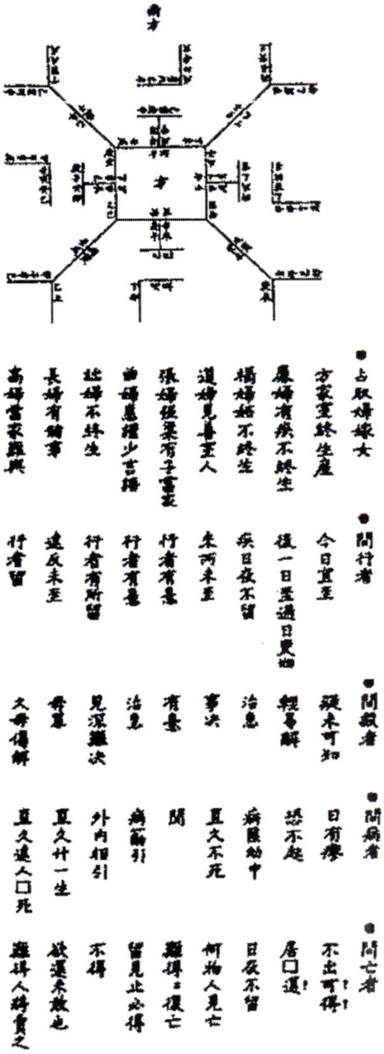

Figure 9.7 *Liubo* text from Yinwan.

that resembles both the cord and hook pattern and "TLV" design found on *liubo* boards and certain bronze mirrors. (The board for the game *liubo* should not be confused with the *Liuren* diviner's board, a mantic astrolabe, discussed above.)

On the *liubo* board, superimposing a round Heaven plate onto the square board generates the vertical component of the "L"s and the right angles of the "V"s from the cord and hook pattern of the lower square plate. When

Shang cosmology: Hu Houxuan 1944 and 1956; Allan 1991: 74–111; Wang Aihe 2000b: 23–74, esp. 54–56. Cosmograph: Major 1993: 329–43; Harper 1999a: 833–43 and 1999b: 836–39.

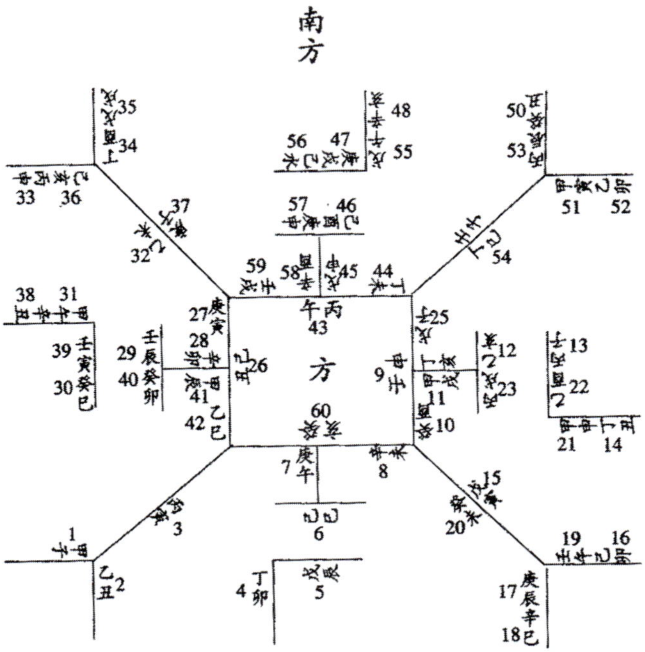

Figure 9.8 The upper register of the Yinwan diagram.

used for divination, the moves on the *liubo* board were linked to the sexagenary cycle.[90] The earliest known *liubo* sets, from Tianxingguan, Yutaishan and Pingshan (discussed on p. 43), are incomplete and provide little information, but more complete sets from Shuihudi, Fenghuangshan, Mawangdui, and Yinwan give some indication of how the game was played and how it was used for divination.[91]

Players seem to have moved pieces along the paths of the lines of the board, with moves determined by casting six bamboo counting rods (reminiscent of the six hexagram lines of *Yi* divination).[92] The set from

[90] *Yinwan*, esp. 125–26. Original report and transcription: *WW* 1996.8: 4–25, Teng Zhaozong 1996a and 1996b. Use in divination: Liu Lexian 1997; Li Xueqin 1997; Zeng Lanying 1999 and (as Lillian Lan-ying Tseng) 2002 and 2011; Li Jiemin 2000. Bronze mirrors and TLV pattern: Cammann 1948, Hayashi Minao 1973, Loewe 1979.

[91] *Liubo* boards: Yang Lien-sheng 1945 and 1952. Tianxingguan: *Jingzhou Tianxingguan er hao Chu mu* 2003: 167–68 and plate 58. Yutaishan: *Kaogu* 1980.5: 399. Pingshan: *WW* 1979.1: 1–31, esp. 26, figure 33; Watson 1995: 58–59.

[92] Two *liubo* sets excavated from Shuihudi each contained six counting rods. A set excavated from Fenghuangshan (Jiangling, Hubei) contained six counting rods and an eighteen-sided die marked with numbers. Another set from Mawangdui contained dice but no rods, suggesting that the movements could be determined either by rods or by dice. Shuihudi: *Yunmeng Shuihudi Qin mu* 1981: 55–56. Fenghuangshan: *WW* 1974.6: 50–51. Mawangdui: *Changsha Mawangdui er, san hao Han mu* 2004: 163–66.

Wangjiatai includes dice that may have been used for generating hexagrams. The link between *liubo* and prognostication is clear in a set excavated from Yinwan, which contains a mantic text on a wooden slip (as well as an eighteen-sided die). It is possible that the user identified the day of interest by the labels from the sexagenary cycle on the upper register of the diagram (Figure 9.7), starting in the lower left-hand corner. The lower register consisted of a chart of five rows and nine columns. A tenth column on the right, headed by the character *zhan* (prognostication), lists five topics: marriage (*qufu jianü* 取婦嫁女), travel (*xing* 行), imprisonment (*xi* 繫), illness (*bing* 病), and desertion (*wang* 亡). Each day of the cycle was associated with one of the headings of the columns in the lower register. The consultor could then look up the topic of interest in one of the five rows of the table. It is not known exactly how the days were identified with the nine columns of the lower register. The exact relation of the normal use of the board to this divinatory use is also not known.

The upper register of the *liubo* text from Yinwan shows the TLV-shaped paths of the board (Figure 9.8). The character *fang* (square) is at the center and the phrase *nanfang* (south) on one side. Most of the straight or L-shaped lines are inscribed with notations indicating day type in the sexagenary cycle.

Hemerology and *wuxing*

Another type of systematic thought about the cosmos uses *wuxing* in a range of contexts. The most comprehensive are hemerological texts: almanacs, daybooks, and monthly ordinances. These are all accounts of cosmic time. (By contrast, mantic astrolabes are spatial models of the cosmos.) Their methods differ, but hemerological texts all represent cosmic time and link cycles of time with human action, expressed either as good and ill auspice or as permitted and prohibited activities.

The hemerologies of the *Lüshi chunqiu* and *Huainanzi* introduce systematic correlations of *qi*, *yin–yang*, and *wuxing* in an astrocalendric context, and are often credited with the introduction of correlative cosmology. There is considerable doubt whether this attribution is apt.[93] What is important for the present discussion is that *wuxing* appears in astrocalendric

[93] For example, only three titles in the "*Wuxing*" section of the *Han shu* Bibliographic Treatise specifically mention *wuxing*: the Subterranean Five Courses of Shen Nong (*Shen Nong da you wuxing* 神農大幽五行), the Classic of the Four Seasons and Five Courses (*Sishi wuxing jing* 四時五行經), and Seasonal Commands for *Yin–yang* and *Wuxing* (*Yin–yang wuxing shiling* 陰陽五行時令). See *HS* 30.1767–68. Most titles concern astrocalendrics, hemerology, yin–yang, baleful omens (*zaiyi* 災異), prognostication by pitch pipes, the star Taiyi, and "Sanctions and Virtues" (*xingde*).

instruments and texts on hemerology, cloud and wind divination, iatromancy (discussed above), and physiognomy. However, not all hemerological systems use *wuxing* theory as their organizing principle. A few examples illustrate some of these variations.

The oldest known hemerological text is the Chu Silk Manuscript. It shows images of the gods of the months grouped by season around the perimeter of the outer circle. Statements next to each figure name permitted and prohibited activities and unlucky days. The central portion of the diagram contains two texts: a cosmogonic myth and a text on astrology and the calendar.[94] Daybooks (extensively introduced in Chapter 6) divide the year into types of day. Some base their typologies on *wuxing* theory, but other calendric sections use other systems. For example, the *jianchu* calendar in Shuihudi Daybook A is a calendar for a *chu* 除 year in the *jianchu* 建除 (Establishment and Removal) cycle (discussed in detail in Appendix F).[95]

Almanac texts correlate the months of the year to the Lunar Lodges and the days of the year to the Five Agents. *Wuxing* correlations structure the *Yue ling* calendars (Monthly Ordinances), which appear in almost identical form in the *Guanzi*, *Lüshi chunqiu*, *Huainanzi*, and *Li ji*.[96] Their presentation is rigid and formulaic.[97] The ordinances for the month cover such topics as state activities (fortification, planting, etc.) and the consequences of incorrectly performing activities appropriate to different times. These are the first texts in the received tradition to link the Twenty-eight Lunar Lodges to the months, associating each month with the lodge occupied by the sun for that period. They draw on mantic astronomical traditions based on the observation of the Lunar Lodges.

Several texts from Mawangdui refer to the Five Agents, beginning with the "Treatise on the Five Agents" (*Wuxing zhi*). Other texts describe methods for plotting calendric cycles on a spatial grid defined by the cord and hook pattern. Two versions of a text titled "Sanctions and Virtues" (*Xingde* 刑德, A and B) map sixty-year cycles of Sanctions (*xing*) and

94 See Li Ling 1985, 1993: 168–79, 180–85; Li Xueqin 1985a: 435–40; Harper 1999b: 845–47.

95 *Jianchu* oracles are so named because they follow variants of the series *jian* 建, *chu* 除, *ying* 盈, *ping* 平, *ding* 定, *zhi* 執, *bo* 柀, *wei* 危, *cheng* 成, *shou* 收, *kai* 開 and *bi* 閉. See Loewe 1994: 220–26, Harper 1999b: 848–49.

96 *Guanzi*: 3.8 (*Youguan*) and 3.9 (*Youguan tu*), trans. Rickett 1.148–92. *LSCQ*: Books 1.1 etc. for books 1–12, trans. Knoblock and Riegel 59–273. *HNZ* 5 (*Shixiun*), trans. Major 1993: 217–68. *LJ* 14 and 15 (trans. Legge 1.249–310 and Couvreur 1.330–411), cf. Bodde 1975: 16 and Loewe 1994: 184, 223–24, 228.

97 For the pattern of the *Huainanzi* version see *HNZ* 5.1a–2b, trans. Major 1993: 220–25.

Virtues (*de*), linking them to the sexagenary cycle and the Five Agents.[98] These hemerological systems cluster around three or four lodges, but they all link divinatory formulae to regular spatial representations of time.

Wuxing also informs divination by subcelestial phenomena, especially winds and clouds.[99] The *Lüshi chunqiu* describes the movement of clouds and mists from east to west.[100] Another passage correlates four cloud shapes (vegetation, fish scales, smoke or fire, and waves) to four types of origin (mountains, water, drought, and rain).[101]

The first systematic account of clouds and mists is in the *Shi ji* Astronomical Treatise, which describes "observing the *qi* of clouds" (*wang yun qi* 望雲氣) and correlates their five colors to *wuxing*.[102] It describes clouds by color, topographical origin (arising over mountains, rivers, etc.), size, and height. It also gives rules of thumb for judging their distance, and states that the most important clouds are those with the shapes of animals.[103] Nonetheless, the discussion that follows does not focus on clouds with animal shapes:

徒氣白。土功氣黃。車氣乍高乍下，往往而聚。騎氣卑而布。卒氣摶。前卑而後高者，疾；前方而後高者，兌[銳]；後兌[銳]而卑者，卻。其氣平者其行徐。前高而後卑者，不止而反。

The *qi* of convict laborers is white; the *qi* of building activities is yellow. *Qi* [emanations indicative of] chariots are now high, now low, and they repeatedly assemble. Cavalry *qi* is low and wide. Infantry *qi* is bent; if low in front and high behind, they are hurrying, if square and high in front and pointed and low behind, they are retiring. If the *qi* is flat, they are proceeding slowly; if high in front and low behind, they are turning without stopping.[104]

98 Mawangdui *Xingde* B: Transcription: Fu Juyou and Chen Songchang 1992: 132–41. Discussion: Kalinowski 1998–99. Twelve monthly lodges: Yamada Keiji 1985: 1–44, esp. 1–2, 36–37. The Virtues (*de*) cycle is also correlated to the movements of the star Tai Yin 太陰 (correlate of Jupiter). The Tianyi method is described in a Mawangdui manuscript titled *Yin–yang wuxing* 陰陽五行 or *Shifa* 式法, transcribed in *WW* 2000.7: 85–94. See also Chen Songchang 2000 and 2001.

99 The earliest references to prognostication by clouds and vapors (*yunqi*) are in *Zuo zhuan* (Xi 5.1) and *Mozi* 68: 574–75. See Chapter 5 n. 18.

100 *LSCQ*, 72 ("Yuan dao" 圜道 3.5), Knoblock and Riegel 110.

101 *LSCQ*, 677–88 ("Ying tong" 應同 13.2), Knoblock and Riegel, 283–84. Kuroda Genji (1977: 165–72) has argued that Warring States thinkers had two distinct views of cloud *qi*: one as simple natural phenomena, the other as instruments for prognostication. Cf. Loewe 1994: 194.

102 *SJ* 27.1336–39; Chavannes 3.393–97, cf. *HSBZ* 26.43a, trans. Hulsewé 1979: 40–49 and *LSCQ*, 1412 ("Guan biao" 觀表 20.8), Knoblock and Riegel 540.

103 *SJ* 27.1336; Chavannes 3.393.

104 *SJ* 27.1337, trans. after Hulsewé 1979: 43, cf. *HSBZ* 26.43b and Chavannes 3.394. Both Chavannes and Hulsewé translate *qi* as "vapors," but here I think the term refers to the manifestation of *qi* as vapors or clouds. Hulsewé's translation is informed by the versions in *Jin shu* 12 and *Sui shu* 21, which closely parallel this *SJ* (and *HS*) passage.

稍雲精白者，其將悍，其士怯。其大根而前絕遠者，當戰。青白，其前低者，戰勝；其前赤而仰者，戰不勝。

In the case of sleet-bearing clouds that are blue–green and white, their general is fierce, but his soldiers are cowards. If it has a large root and it is cut off faraway in front, there will be battle. If blue and white with a low front, the battle will be victorious; if the front is red and raised, the battle will not be victorious.[105]

The chapter states that cloud prognostication conforms to the five colors, but that all cloud divination is based on clouds' forms. The examples are military: the clouds and vapors of northern barbarians resemble the shapes of domestic animals and tents; those of southern barbarians resemble the shapes of boats and military banners. There are further variations based on geography: the presence of mountains, water, etc. The chapter also links thunder, lightning, and rainbows with *yang qi*, which manifests in spring and summer and is hidden in winter and fall. Sima Qian describes recording clouds and vapors as an official duty of the *Taishi*.[106]

This passage is also consistent with the text on clouds from Mawangdui. The techniques are clarified further by nearly identical passages in standard histories of the Jin (*Jin shu*) and Sui (*Sui shu*). It also resembles a manuscript found at Dunhuang, probably dating from the tenth century.[107] These texts list types of clouds, classified by the names of pre-Han Chinese states and by images such as cloth, ox, carriage, rat, crimson clothing, and dragon. Each has an illustration and associated prediction. Specifically military prognostications were associated with different types of cloud formation. These texts mention the five colors, but *wuxing* theory does not seem to be the fundamental organizing principle.

The *Han shu* Bibliographic Treatise also classifies wind divination under *wuxing*. The Five Agents were correlated to eight directional winds, measured by "watching for *qi*" (*hou qi*) by the use of pitch pipes (introduced in Chapter 5). The *Huainanzi* associates each of the eight winds with a period of forty-five days. It lists the winds' names, the most appropriate activities for each period, and the gods and spirits born from each wind.[108] The twelve notes (six male and six female) were correlated with the twelve months, and it was believed that the note of each pipe would sound spontaneously during its month.[109]

105 *SJ* 27.1337, trans. after Hulsewé 1979: 43.

106 *SJ* 27.1353; Chavannes 3.409–10. For duties of the *Taishi* 太史 or *Taishi ling* 太史令 see Chapter 4 n. 13.

107 *Jin shu* 12.317; *Sui shu* 20.576; cf. Ho Peng Yoke 1966; Ho Peng Yoke and Ho Koon Piu 1985.

108 *HNZ* 3.8b, 4.2a, 4.15b, trans. Major 1993: 77–78, 145, 208–9.

109 *HNZ* 3.21a, trans. Major 1993: 110.

The *Shi ji*, *Han shu*, and *Hou Han shu* give more detail on both methods. The Treatise on the Pitch Pipes (*SJ* 25) correlates the eight winds to the Twenty-eight Lunar Lodges and their domains of activity.[110] The *Tianguan* chapter of the *Shi ji* uses the winds for prognostication about harvests. The five notes of the musical scale and their *wuxing* correspondences were correlated to five types: good harvest, warfare, drought, floods, and poor harvest. The chapter describes the wind diviner Wei Xian, who interpreted the winds at the beginning of each year. He correlates the eight winds with eight types of condition. Wind from the south or southwest indicated great or minor drought, respectively. Wind from the west presaged military uprisings; if from the northwest, it indicated ripening beans, few rains, and moving armies. Winds from the north presaged an average harvest, from the northeast an exceptional one. East winds meant floods, and southeast winds presaged epidemics and bad harvests.[111]

Physiognomy texts demonstrate another variant on *wuxing*: the use of color apart from its "Five Colors" schema. This point is illustrated by "Physiognomy" (*Xiang shu* 相書), the earliest known systematic exposition of the principles of physiognomy. It is attributed to the woman physiognomist Xu Fu (discussed in Chapter 4), and is extant in a manuscript from Dunhuang. It surveys the human body and explains the significance of each feature. Most important are the form, proportions, and appearance of the body and face.

The most auspicious forms are associated with symbols of plenty and stability, especially the circle (heaven) and square (earth), for example a face that is round like the full moon, or a square chin or chest. Other forms derive from the appearance of animals: the turtle, lion, tiger, sheep, buffalo, horse, elephant, eagle, bird, dragon, duck, silkworm, etc. A third type of form derives from writing, for example the shapes of the character *shan* 山 (mountain) or *si* 四 (the number four).[112] Finally, there is aspect and

110 *SJ* 25.1243–48, Chavannes 3.300–13.

111 *SJ* 27.1340 (Chavannes 3.396–97), cf. Loewe 1994: 202–3. See also *HSBZ* 26.46a, Bodde 1975: 45. The winds are described more briefly in the *Han shu* Astronomical Treatise (*HS* 26.1299) and in *BHT*, 341 ("Ba feng" 八風 7.32, Som 2.534). A forthcoming book by D. W. Pankenier includes a new translation of *SJ* 27. As Field (2008: 107–9) points out, Wei Xian's prognostications may have some basis in empirical observation. Sea winds from the maritime northeast would be likely to bring strong rains, and winds from the semi-arid Tibetan plateau in the southwest would bring drought. But Five-phase correlations are also involved. South correlates to fire, which predicts drought. West correlates to metal, the element of weapons, and predicts warfare. West is also the direction of most Han dynasty barbarian incursions. East (and southeast) correlate to wood, and predict poor harvests.

112 The *Xiang shu* survives in three manuscript versions (P. 2572, P. 2797, P. 3589) found at Dunhuang. See Despeux 2003: esp. 521–23. These texts can be accessed at the International Dunhuang Project: www.idp.bl.uk.

fineness of shape, especially of the teeth and hair. This criterion includes the length of the nose, tongue, and chest, and the harmony of body proportions. Brilliance and luminosity – especially of the face, eyes, and hair – signify good health and good fortune.

The *Xiang shu* uses color for prognostication, but not the standardized colors of correlative cosmology. For example, the section titled "Physiognomizing the Face" specifies that someone with a face the color of a green melon (*qing gua* 青瓜) will achieve great riches. According to "Physiognomizing Women's Breasts and Abdomens," a breast (or nipples) of a variegated black color (*hei ru lan se* 黑如斓色) signifies honors.[113] Birthmarks were important in certain parts of the body, in particular on the face, in the hair, above the eyebrows, below the nose, and on the back, penis, or vagina. Finally, certain lines and figures inscribed on the face were significant, especially below the nose, on the tongue, and on the forehead, as well as on the hands or fingers, the soles of the feet, and the palms of the hands.

Like the early omen statements, the physiognomic prognostications in the *Xiang shu* are not systematic, and are grouped under headings such as face, eyes, nose, etc. Color attributes appear among the statements, but with no systematic significance. Like the cloud divination sections of the *Shi ji*, color seems to take second place to form, including forms derived from animals.

Some Masters texts use skill in physiognomy as a metaphor for broader perception of the human condition or cosmos. A passage in the *Zhuangzi* uses dog and horse physiognomy.[114] The *Lüshi chunqiu* uses the example of sword physiognomy to make an argument about limited and broad perspectives.[115] Another passage compares the famous horse physiognomist Bo Le 伯樂 to Pao Ding 庖丁, the skillful butcher of *Zhuangzi* 3: "When Bo Le studied horse physiognomy he saw nothing except horses, and this was because he was focused completely on horses" – a paraphrase of Pao Ding's account of how he learned mastery of the Way.[116] These examples use

113 *Xiang shu*, P. 2572, *Xiang mian bu* 相面部 (section 5), col. 13 and *Xiang nai du qi* 相妳肚臍 (section 22), col. 74. Accessed at the International Dunhuang Project: www.idp.bl.uk.

114 *Zhuangzi* 24.819. The passage actually describes their behavior, rather than their structure, and makes a subtle shift in the meaning of physiognomy to further its philosophical points. Burton Watson's translation (1968: 261–62) omits any mention of physiognomy.

115 *LSCQ*, 1642–43 ("Bie lei" 別類 25.2), Knoblock and Riegel 628. Another passage describes a man from Qi who was an expert in dog physiognomy. See *LSCQ*, 1689–90 ("Shi rong" 士容 26.1), cf. Knoblock and Riegel 644–45.

116 伯樂學相馬，所見無非馬者，誠乎馬也。 *LSCQ*, 507 ("Jing tong" 精通 9.5), after Knoblock and Riegel 220. For discussion see Raphals 2008–9: 72–76.

physiognomy as a metaphor for a comprehensive (though not necessarily systematic) perspective. Their interest in physiognomy is purely rhetorical.

Wang Chong uses physiognomy to articulate the earliest systematic theory of fate. He argues that human destiny is embodied in the face and body during the course of gestation. He gives the example of King Wen, whose endowment included a "dragon countenance" and four nipples.[117] Elsewhere he argues that fate is visible in the body and bones. His example is Han Gaozu, including the story that his extraordinary looks caused a physiognomist to give him his daughter in marriage.[118] Wang Chong gives many other examples of remarkable physiognomies and predictions of destiny, and uses the predictions of Shu Ji of Jin (introduced in Chapter 7) to argue against Mencius' claim that original nature is good.

In summary, the preceding discussion of late Warring States and Western Han mantic discourse on number, *yin–yang*, astronomy, hemerology, and a range of *wuxing* systems illustrates a consistent interest in thinking systematically about the cosmos and how mantic knowledge fits into cosmic patterns. Their variations from the grand unification of correlative cosmology are especially interesting. Scholars disagree about whether the daybooks from Jiudian and Shuihudi use the *wuxing* systems of correlative cosmology, but no correlations are ever made explicit.[119] Cloud divination and physiognomy show that "five colors" are not necessarily the "Five Colors" of correlative cosmology. The important point is that the ongoing interest in applying cosmological speculation to thinking of this kind is distinct from the correlative cosmologies of the Eastern Han and their imperial motivations and preoccupations. It also has no clear Greek counterpart. Greek systematic theorizing about divination took a very different turn.

[117] *LH*, 125–26 ("Chu bing" 初禀 3.12), Forke 1.131–32. Kalinowski's (2011) translation of the *Lun heng* chapters concerned with fate and divination does not include this chapter.

[118] *LH*, 113–15 ("Gu xiang" 骨相 3.11), Forke 1.305. See Chapter 7 for Empress Lü.

[119] Kalinowski 1986: esp. 222–24, cf. Yang Hua 2003, discussed above. Kalinowski argues that some of the Shuihudi correlations seem to represent a system of "Three Harmonies" (*Sanhe* 三合), rather than Five Phases. By contrast, Stephen Field (2008: 120–22 and personal communication) argues that the cycle of Heaven Stems, which determines good and ill auspice in the daybooks, corresponds to the mutual generation and conquest orders of the Five Agents and their directional correlates, as well as the logic of the sequence. Thus in the example illness days from Shuihudi in Chapter 6, stems 1 and 2 produce stems 3 and 4 because wood feeds fire, etc. Thus illnesses linked with stem 7 and 8 days come from the west because those stems correlate to the direction west and the agent Metal. Metal cuts Wood, the agent correlated to stems 1 and 2, and the illness worsens on those days. Fire, the agent correlated to stems 3 and 4, melts Metal, bringing about the end of the illness.

Divination and Greek systematic inquiry

The nature and implications of mantic activity become a topic of Greek systematic philosophical speculation, but in ways that are very different from its role in Chinese expertise traditions. Greek reflection on divination focused on problems of determinism and causality, and their ethical implications. Stoic responses to Aristotle made divination an important site of philosophical debate in Hellenistic Greece. Pre-Hellenistic references are scattered, beginning with references to divination and the Pythia in Presocratic fragments. Thales (*c.* 624–546), Xenophanes (*c.* 570–475), Heraclitus (*c.* 535–*c.* 475), and others express a range of opinions on divination.

Philosophical debates about divination

Greek mantic discourse recognized that knowledge of the future somehow implied its preexistence. Tension between belief in the efficacy of divination and belief in inexorable fate first appears in Homer. The problem of the poets was to reconcile divination (which sought to "change" the future) with belief in the plan of Zeus. The philosophers had an opposite problem: to theorize divination in ways that reconciled traditional religion with new theories of nature, cause, and so forth.

Most philosophers before Socrates either affirmed some kind of belief in divination, or held beliefs compatible with it, including Thales, Anaximander, Anaximenes, and Anaxagoras, whose *nous* can be converted into attentive Providence.[120] Democritus based his notions of prediction on laws of mechanical movement of atoms in space. Yet even he believed in the possibility of presentiment of future events because he considered the universe to be ordered by divine will according to providence.[121]

The two major Presocratic critics of divination were Xenophanes and Heraclitus. Xenophanes repudiated divination in its entirety, attacking the immorality of the Homeric gods and the anthropomorphism of Greek religion (frs. 11–12, 14–16). The god postulated by Xenophanes would have no motive to provide divinatory knowledge to humans, nor would humans understand it. Heraclitus criticized the religious conventions of his

[120] *Nous* refers to "mind," or "intellect," the innate faculty of intellectual apprehension, as distinct from wisdom (*sophia*), theoretical intelligence (*epistēmē*), and practical intelligence (*phronēsis*).

[121] Cic. *Div.* 1.5, cf. fr. 166 and Plut. *Quaest. conv.* 735a–b, *Conv. sept. sap.* 3.2.

day in order to advance new notions of flux and the union of opposites. He rejected technical divination, oneiromancy, and ritual purifications after murder, but accepted the divination of the Sibyl and Pythia (frs. 92–93), and asserted that the Delphic oracle offers signs to humankind, and "neither speaks nor hides, but signifies."[122]

Other Presocratics may have been diviners. The Purifications of Empedocles begins with a claim to be in high demand everywhere, to: "some seeking mantic arts, others seeking healing oracular speech for all kinds of diseases" (fr. 112, Clem. *Strom.* 6.30).

Several sources report that Pythagoras (*c.* 570–*c.* 495) practiced augury and divination, staring with Cicero.[123] Diogenes (8.32) reports that he instructed his students to "honor every kind of divination"; and that he was called "Pyth-agoras" because he outdid the Pythia in the truth of his public pronouncements in the *agora* (8.21). More details emerge in the biographies of Porphyry (234–*c.* 305 CE) and Iamblichus (*c.* 245–*c.* 325 CE):

> While at the Olympic Games, he was discoursing with his friends about auguries, omens, and divine signs, and how men of true piety do receive messages from the gods. Flying over his head was an eagle, who stopped, and came down to Pythagoras. After stroking her awhile he released her.[124]

Iamblichus reports that Pythagoras also developed a method of divination by numbers as an alternative to blood sacrifice, which he opposed:

> instead of divining by the entrails of beasts, he revealed to him [Abaris] the art of prognosticating by numbers, conceiving this to be a purer and more divine method, more adapted to the celestial numbers of the Gods.[125]

Some details of this system have emerged from Byzantine manuscripts, which describe a numerological procedure for medical prognosis that probably dates to early Hellenistic times, and is attributed to Pythagoras and others. The person's name was converted to a number, by correlating the letters of the Greek alphabet to a series of numbers from 1 (α) to 800 (ω). This number was related to the phase of the moon at the onset of the illness. The resulting number was applied to a (modular) circle, which predicted an outcome of life, death, or fast or slow recovery or decline, using a series of

[122] *Oute legei oute kruptei alla sēmainei*, fr. 93, Plut. *Pyth. orac.* 404d8.

[123] Cic. *Div.* 1.5. Cicero also notes his refusal to sacrifice animal victims (*Nat. Deor.* 2.88, *Leg.* 2.26). He even accounts for the Pythagorean aversion to beans as a preparation for trustworthy dreams during sleep (*Div.* 2.119).

[124] Porph. *Pyth.* 25, trans. after Guthrie 1987. See also Barton 1994a: 207 and Riedweg and Rendall 2008: 3.

[125] Porph. *Iambl.* 19, trans. after Guthrie 1987.

numbers from 1 to 30, which were arrayed on a circle ("the circle of Petosiris") or two- or three-line tables.[126] This method does not seem to have ever been in widespread use for state or private consultation.

Did Socrates believe in divination? The question becomes an important element in his trial, because the moral status of his philosophical activities and his claim that these pursuits are grounded in divination are central to his defense. He describes the oracle to Chaerephon – that no man is wiser than Socrates – as the source of his philosophical mission, and repeatedly affirms his trust in his *daimonion* to warn him against error.[127] Commentators typically disregard this apparent trust in divination as a source of truth, as they do the implication that Socrates' moral and philosophical convictions are religious in origin. But, as Brickhouse and Smith have argued, the *daimonion* provides him with certainty that he must serve the god by practicing philosophy in Athens, but not about anything else, including the nature of virtue, which must be understood from the *elenchus*.[128] This leaves Socrates in the position of being certain that his philosophical activities are virtuous but unable to offer a *logos* to explain their virtue.[129] So in recommending the mantic arts he was not advocating laziness or shortcuts, because he did not consider divine knowledge a substitute for human knowledge.

And Socrates did recommend them, as attested by Plato and Xenophon. Socrates thus brought divination into the purview of philosophy; and Plato and his successors continued that approach. Plato enjoins the city to consult the oracle on religious and moral issues. He incorporates respect for Delphi into his own philosophical claims, most notably in his distinction between divine madness and the *tekhnē* of interpreting signs. The distinction is part of Plato's broad epistemological agenda to contrast the self-conscious reflection of the philosopher with the inferior, unreflective activity of the seer and bard. They work not by wisdom (*sophia*) but by nature (*phusis*), and are ignorant of what they create. They can describe sword and shield but cannot wield them. Plato needs to

126 Bouché-Leclercq 1899. For more details of these procedures see Neugebauer and Salibah 1988.

127 Pl. *Ap.* 22c. The term *daimonion*, literally something "*daimōn*-like," is often described as his "divine sign," what in earlier English might have been called his *weird*.

128 Brickhouse and Smith 1984. The *elenchus* (Greek *elenkhos*, "refutation") is a method of argument that refutes a proposition by proving the opposite of its conclusions. Socrates in particular used it to show that the consequences of a position or argument contradict some accepted position. The word derives from *elenkhein*, "to put to shame or refute."

129 Pl. *Ap.* 20e, 22c, 31d, 40a–b.

deny seers and bards self-conscious reflection about their art in order to reserve this ability for philosophers.[130]

Divination, causality, and responsibility

A positive Greek consensus on divination always coexisted with *ad hominem* attacks against individual practitioners. But divination itself became an object of heated and systematic debate in Hellenistic Greece because of its key role in new arguments about fate, causality, necessity, and determinism. These arguments had ethical implications, both for Stoic advocates of divination and for their Epicurean and skeptical critics. That debate, as in China, had both epistemological and ethical ramifications.

From Plato to Aristotle there is a sudden and brutal transition. Aristotle rejects most divination. As Bouché-Leclercq puts it, Plato tried to absorb science in revelation; Aristotle sought to absorb revelation in science.[131] Chrysippus (*c.* 279–*c.* 206) and the Stoic defenders of divination claimed empirical efficacy but denied any causal link between the "signs" of divination and their signifiers. Causal explanation would make divination a science like any other; it would lose its privileged metaphysical status as a hermeneutic for divine knowledge and agency.

The most significant epistemological element in these debates was skepticism, asserted and denied. A second critique was purely empirical: does divination work? Empirical arguments figure unevenly in Greek debates, and it is noteworthy that recorded accounts of tests of the reliability of oracles come from foreigners; Greeks seemed to consider such tests both unnecessary and impious.[132]

Aristotle addresses the meaning and validity of divination in "On Divination through Dreams" (*De Divinatione per Somnia*), a work of medical oneiromancy, where he emphasizes their clinical significance. Yet Aristotle's major effect on the philosophical history of divination was his view of choice as central to notions of human responsibility. Reactions to his analysis of responsible human action were the starting point for Hellenistic debates about determinism and freedom. As a result, the question of divination also becomes linked to other late Greek debates on fate, necessity, and causality.

[130] Xenophon: Xen. *An.* 3.1. Consultation: Pl. *Rep.* 427b; *Leg.* 738b–d. Inspired divination: *Phdr.* 244c–e, cf. *Tim.* 71b–e, discussed in Chapter 3.

[131] Bouché-Leclercq 1879–82: 1.57.

[132] Notably the "test" oracle of Croesus (Hdt. 1.46–55). Herodotus reports two other comments on the accuracy of oracles by non-Greeks: Amasis (2.174) and Xerxes and Mardonius (8.133–36).

Hellenistic ethical debates about divination were driven by the ethical implications of fate, causality, necessity, and determinism. Efforts to reconcile determinism and moral responsibility (called soft determinism or compatibilism by contemporary philosophers) became a major issue in Stoic attempts to refute attacks by skeptics and Epicureans. These attacks include the so-called Master Argument and Lazy Argument.[133] They also informed a broad debate on modality and modal logic that preoccupied many Hellenistic philosophers. The ethical problem of human responsibility for events foretold by gods first appears in Homer, but early texts do not emphasize these difficulties. For example, the mechanistic atomism of Democritus raises issues of human responsibility for a modern reader, but not, apparently, for Democritus. Plato touches on the relation of destiny and human choice in *Republic* 10, but destiny and determinism are not a central issue. It was Aristotle who first suggested that determinism threatens human choice and human freedom. It thus precludes morality and agency, which were central to his concept of the good life.

Aristotle treated cause as a matter of explanation, and did not connect the notions of cause and necessity. He viewed events not as chains of cause and effect but as ripples from a stone in a pond. He thus denied that all events are determined by necessary chains of causation. He held that some events result from chance rather than necessity, but his treatment of chance and coincidence did not rule out determinism. His primary interest was in the problem of explanation (the possibility that there are chance events with no scientific explanation), without recourse to indeterminism.[134] Hellenistic debates about determinism and freedom began as reactions to Aristotle's incomplete analysis of causation, determinism, and responsibility. The question of whether the future can be known is logically distinct from the question of whether the universe is deterministic, but in antiquity arguments about fate and prediction were considered related, perhaps because individual fate was so often the object of prediction.[135]

But there was general agreement that for a future event to be knowable, it must in some sense be caused. The Stoics treated prediction under the rubric of divination and used divination to argue theories of fate. Their account of prediction and divination was part of an integrated systematic

[133] For discussion of these arguments see Hankinson 1998 and Bobzien 1998: 87–96.

[134] Arist. *Metaph.* 1027a20–b14. For details see Sorabji 1980.

[135] Here I follow Sorabji's (1980: ix) definition of determinism as the view that whatever happens has all along been necessary in the sense of fixed or inevitable. His definition uses necessity, rather than causation, and does not deny moral responsibility, as do "hard" determinists. Causal determinism is the idea that every event is necessitated by antecedent events and conditions.

theory that included ethics, theology, and metaphysics. These debates begin with Chrysippus, the third head of the Stoic school. He attempted to prove that "all things happen according to fate" (*heimarmenē*) and devised a "syllogism" to prove that the gods exist and reveal the future:

> If there are gods and they do not declare the future to mortals, then either they do not love humans, or they do not know the future, or they think that knowledge of the future will not benefit humanity, or they think it against their own majesty to presignify to mortals what the future will be, or they themselves are not able to determine it.[136]

Chrysippus tried to develop new accounts of possibility and necessity that were consistent with both moral responsibility and the Stoic "fate principle."[137] (He was thus a soft determinist in that he asserted both determinism and moral responsibility.) He described his modal theory as a proof, but also made or implied empirical claims for divination.

Posidonius attempted to theorize divination by *sumpatheia*, the benevolent interest of divine powers. He claimed that nature gives signs of future events, which unfold over time like a cable unwinding.[138] Epicurean critics argued that chance rather than fate controlled events. Skeptics refused to acknowledge any role for providence. Plutarch defended inspired divination and the reputation of the Delphic oracle, but attacked Chrysippus for contradictions between his theories of possibility and fate.[139] In Plutarch's own theory of moral agency, fate mixed and intertwined with chance. In this and other middle Platonic views, moral choice is not fated, but fate affects the consequences of moral choice. These arguments, Stoic notions of co-fated events, and notions of events contrary to fate attempted to solve the moral dilemma by incrementally ramifying the concept of fate to soften its deterministic edges. They are reminiscent of some of the anti-fatalist arguments of Wang Chong, who also introduced new categorizations of fate and placed a new emphasis on the role of chance in human events.

Much of the Stoic account of divination comes through unfriendly sources, especially Cicero's *De Divinatione*, which reflects Cicero's own hostility to Stoicism and bias toward the views of Epicurus and the Academic skeptics. *De Divinatione* is set up as a dialogue between a skeptic (Cicero or Marcus) and a Stoic (his brother Quintus). Cicero defines divination as prediction and knowledge of future events; at issue is the

136 Cic. *Div.* 2.101. For Chrysippus see Diog. Laert. *Vit.* 7.149 and Cic. *Fat.* 20.
137 Theodoretus 6.14 = *SVF* 2.916, Diogenianus, in Eus. *Praep. Evang.* 6.261c = *SVF* 2.925.
138 Posidonius (*c.* 135–*c.* 50): Diog. Laert. 7.149. Critique by Cicero: *Fat.* 5–7.
139 Plut. *Comm. not.* 1075e.

proposition that knowledge of the future is possible (1.1). The first book is a defense of the mantic arts. Quintus presents the Stoic position that divination is communication from the gods, without whose existence and interest it is impossible. After an initial exposition, it largely consists of anecdotal examples that rely on example and appeal to experience, including accounts of the importance of divination in Roman myth and history.

Cicero explicitly excludes from natural divination both the use of reason and predictions by "natural law."[140] By contrast, technical divination (hepatoscopy, portents, lots, astrology, and augury) required rationality (*ratio*) and intelligence (*intelligentia*) to interpret signs from the gods in natural phenomena (1.70). The admittedly hostile defense of divination in Book 1 is strikingly theological, and in this sense the logically systematic account of divination ends here. The important point about natural divination, the highest form of the mantic art, is that it comes from the gods. Cicero rejects technical divination, based on reason.

Book 2 is Cicero's skeptical refutation of the Stoic position. He argues that there is no causal connection between signs and communication from the gods (2.29). He gives empirical examples (2.45) and argues that Quintus' account lacks logical consistency and is obscure in many details. He dismisses divination as superstition and stresses its empirical failures and the many disagreements between diviners. More seriously, he argues that Stoic fatalism itself undermines divination, since a fixed future cannot be changed or avoided. Whether or not Cicero had the last word, Hellenistic debates on divination center on problems of ethics and metaphysics. They did not inform inquiry into nature, nor were they linked to systematic theories of causation or change. One tendency in Greek divination that may help account for this marginal position is the relative lack of interest in astronomy.

The relative absence of astronomy in Greek (and later Roman) theorizing about divination is striking: in contrast with China, with Mesopotamia, and with the prominent role of philosophical debate. Early Greek interest in astronomy is difficult to reconstruct. Plato gives an obscure description of astronomy and cosmology in the *Timaeus*. Contact with Babylon may have increased after the Persian wars. Babylonian methods may have influenced attempts to reform the Athenian calendar about 432, and descriptions of the constellations by Eudoxus of Cnidus (408–355). In addition, various individuals were credited (or blamed) for bringing "eastern" astrology into Greece, including the atomist philosopher Democritus of Abdera

[140] E.g. predictions by physicians, pilots, and farmers and predictions of eclipses and earthquakes (Cic. *Div.* 1.49.111–1.50.112, also discussed in Chapter 3 n. 5).

(*c.* 460–370), Berossus (350–280), a Babylonian priest who settled in Cos, and the Babylonian diviner Sudines (fl. *c.* 240).[141]

The Hellenistic period marked the beginning of extensive Greek interest in astronomy, astrology, and calendrics, but that interest did not take the form of state sponsorship. Increased contact after Alexander's conquest of Persia (330) brought Greeks into contact with Mesopotamian ideas of the zodiac and the methods and data of Babylonian astronomy and astrology. These had profound effects on astronomy and astrological cosmology. Hellenistic Alexandria became the cradle of Greek astrology.

Greek astrology was also incorporated into Roman politics. Astrology entered Rome as a component of Greek high culture, but it was only taken up by elite Romans in the first century BCE, when generals began to listen to astrologers. The rise of astrology in Rome coincided with the beginning of the fall of the Republic, a coincidence which, Tamsyn Barton argues, was no accident. Under the Republic, the college of augurs and the *haruspices* were official state diviners. They were in charge of extispicy, weather divination, and prodigies. They were expected to warn the senate of signs of the gods' (dis)favor and to advise on ritual action, but the power of decision was always held by the senate. The custodians of the books of Sibylline prophecy were also drawn from the senate. The constitution put power in the hands of the senate, and limited the power of diviners to set policy.[142]

Astrology by contrast was the province of a ruler who held sole power. The "portent" of a comet during the mourning for Julius Caesar was used to justify his deification by the Roman senate. Caesar's adopted son Octavian then used its image, and the linked images of father and son, to provide legitimacy to his own rule as Caesar Augustus. During this period, official diviners were effectively replaced by unofficial advisors close to the ruler. Anonymous college augurs were replaced by famous astrologers and other diviners who increasingly focused on the fates of individuals, rather than questions of divine approval for a particular course of action. Astrology helped to move the individual and individualized prediction to the center of the divinatory agenda. Astrology was suited to monarchy in that astrologers, unlike republican state augurs, had no obligation to report their findings publicly and could pick and choose their clients.

[141] Berossus wrote an extensive account of astrology in a history of Babylon, written in Greek and dedicated to King Antiochus I of Syria (Cic. *Div.* 1.19, 2.36). For Sudines, see Strabo 16.1.6. See Barton 1994a: 9, 23, 215 n. 1, and 216 n. 26. Greek astrology: Bouché-Leclercq 1899.

[142] Barton 1994a: esp. 21–23, 30–31, 38–41. They were elements of an earlier Etruscan tradition which had been absorbed into Roman life.

Although Augustus had used astrology to legitimate his position as the first emperor, by the end of his life he forbade private astrological consultations. Later emperors followed the pattern set by his successor Tiberius: belief in the infallibility of astrology, a kind of astrological paranoia about potential rivals to the throne, and strict regulation of astrology by law. Decrees banned astrologers from Rome and Italy and astrologers and their clients were put on trial. This period also saw skepticism about astrology, but it manifested not in politics but in philosophical debates about free will and determinism.[143]

Dissimilar institutions seem to leave nothing to compare between Chinese and Greek patronage of astronomy and astrocalendrics. Chinese state interest in astronomy and astrocalendrics culminated in systematic sponsorship and control in the Western and Eastern Han, where (as in Mesopotamia) astronomical observation and astrological theory were key elements in mantic discourse and consultation. Because Chinese omenology was used both to legitimate the dynasty and to criticize the throne, astronomy became an important locus of debate on state policy.

This situation presents no Greek equivalent. Interest in astronomy developed late and never became an object of state patronage. Hellenistic astronomy developed through private uses of astrology. (Astrology took a different turn in Rome, where Roman rulers used horoscopes to help establish their own legitimacy.) State-supported astronomy and official consultation or oracles or *manteis* seem to have provided two alternative modes of "official" divination in the ancient Mediterranean. Both could confer authority and legitimacy, but not at once. A fundamental difference was that oracles and *manteis* preserved the relative independence of state power, which was impossible for state-sponsored astronomy. (Even primarily local oracles such as Didyma were never monopolized or controlled by state patrons.)

Greek divination as a hermeneutic system

Chinese and Greek mantic specialists shared the core idea that divination was not transparent. Hidden patterns could be studied, interpreted, and systematized by those with the correct expertise. These practices resulted from different assumptions, led in different directions, and changed over time within each culture. They had very different effects on the growth of abstraction, systematic thought, and exegesis. There were different approaches to the manipulation of mantic information at different points in its generation,

[143] Cramer 1954, Barton 1994a: 62–63.

transmission, performance, and authorization. Two differences are particularly important. One was in attitudes toward divination as a hermeneutic system. The other was in the complex interactions of orality and writing.

Early Chinese and Greek texts give very different accounts of how signs are encoded, transmitted, and interpreted. As Cicero makes clear, Greek divination is significantly premised on the assumption of divination as human–divine communication. To put it another way, the philosopher Nicholas Denyer argues that technical divination is "dotty" as a science, but makes perfect sense if it is understood as a system of direct communication from the gods.[144] Here, the arbitrariness of these systems reinforces their "objectivity" and their divine nature. Yet the very characteristics that make them theologically robust make them intellectually unsatisfactory. They do not rely on empirical observation or systematic thought, and Cicero emphasizes this point.

We can see the role of communication in Greek views of divination more clearly by distinguishing between the transmission and interpretation of mantic signs.[145] In most cases, humans initiate the encounter, but there are also accounts of divine epiphanies. This communication comes in a coded form, but the code is not regular or systematic. It does involve a message, its transmission, and its interpretation.

Under what circumstances did such messages occur? Epiphanies are the most straightforward; a god or hero speaks directly, either in person or in a dream. Quasi-historical epiphanies include spontaneous Delphic oracles and battlefield epiphanies.[146] Here, the initiative for communication comes from the gods. By contrast, ritual, prayer, sacrifice, and magic allow humans to initiate communication in order to persuade the gods to speak. In these cases, communication is direct, with no divinatory sign and no hermeneutics.

There are also Chinese legendary accounts of divine epiphanies in dreams and in legends of recognition, in which divine entities take human form and reward humans who recognize their extraordinary qualities.[147] Human

[144] Ahern 1981: esp. 53; Denyer 1985.

[145] It is based on a Prague School account of signification, introduced in Chapter 1.

[146] In many Homeric examples gods appear in human form: Athena as Mentor to Telemachus (*Od.* 2.260–85), to Odysseus (*Od.* 22.205–54); Hermes as a youth to Odysseus (*Od.* 5.28–96).

[147] For example, the legends associated with the transmission of military strategy manuals, in which a hero gains unique abilities from soteric instruction by a god or spirit whom he "recognizes." For example, the Yellow Emperor defeats Chi You with the help of a divine woman. See *Huang Di xuan nü zhan fa* 黃帝玄女戰法 in *Taiping yulan* 15.9b and 79.3b. Another legend, reported in the *Shi ji* (55.2033–49), relates the receipt of esoteric military instruction by Zhang Liang 張良 by a mysterious old man; he used that knowledge to help Liu Bang establish the Han dynasty. See Lewis 1990: 98–103 and Raphals 1998a: 114–16.

form allows the gods to hide their identity, to address one person in the presence of others, or to "test" a chosen individual. Here the precondition is that the intended audience will recognize the divinity or at least the divine nature of the communication. These accounts present a different problem than Greek epiphanies; the hermeneutic problem is to identify the speaker (not the message), but there are no semiotics and no interpretation is required. There is also no ritual. In other situations, such as spirit medium divination, where a god speaks through an intermediary in response to a question, the communication may or may not be direct.

In a second type of human–divine communication, the god speaks through a spirit medium to a third party, for example in Greek oracular divination. The spirit medium is the *promantis*, a role that implies neither passivity nor mania, and is consistent with the ability to make coherent, articulate, and informed utterances. Coherence in fact indicates divine inspiration and is analogous to Greek accounts of the inspiration of bards. In Plato's account of the divine inspiration of a bard or a *mantis*, the transmission of the god's message is simultaneous with, and inextricable from, its interpretation.[148] Chinese *wu* are also spirit mediums, but our sources are ambiguous about their roles in the transmission and interpretation of divinatory messages. The *Zhou li* describes them as interacting closely with mantic officials. Here *wu* seem to have no hermeneutic role, but other texts portray them as healers with their own special techniques.[149] Accounts of both *promanteis* and *wu* are fragmentary and indirect; both may have greater roles in mantic hermeneutics than most accounts credit.

The third type of communication, most relevant to systematic thought, is semiosis, in which the gods speak through coded messages or omens. Here the sender relies on the recipient's ability to recognize that a message is being sent and to interpret it correctly. The three major Greek modes of semiosis were bird sign, weather omens, and hieroscopy. Recipients knew that bird and weather signs were associated with particular gods. The semiotic system (like the linguistic sign of semiotic theory) was arbitrary, but omens were understood to systematically reflect divine intentions. (By analogy, language systematically uses an individually arbitrary system of linguistic signs.) The mechanism of transmission was divine possession of the object. This possession is what makes the bird's flight or the clap of thunder an omen and distinguishes it from the ordinary behavior of birds and weather. The god's possession of the object also ensures that the result

148 Maurizio 1995: esp. 72, 79.

149 Falkenhausen 1995a: 290–93; Boileau 2002: 357–61. *Wu* are discussed in Chapter 4.

of the divination is beyond the control of either diviner or consultor; it thus ensures the integrity of the process.

For all three, the distinctions between signs are qualitative, rather than quantitative. They did not lend themselves to measurement, quantification, or abstraction.

Greek medical authors take oneiromancy in a different direction by interpreting natural patterns without direct connection to or communication from the gods. Hippocratic oneiromancy and Stoic accounts of divination may use the same codes (eagles, eclipses, thunder, etc.), but there is an important difference. The sender is all but absent and the focus of the process is on the ability of the recipient to decode the sign.

Here Aristotle's views are distinctive because Aristotle effectively denies the code. Aristotle disagreed with earlier accounts of the meaning of dreams and explicitly rejected the theory that dreams come from the gods. His argument comes from the dreams of animals. If animals dream – and he observed physical signs that they did – dreams cannot come from the gods or be intended to reveal the future (*Div. somn.* 463b12–16). Aristotle tries to explain dreams as the result of physical and psychic processes and residual sense perception.[150] This biological explanation allows him to balance empirically plausible accounts of dream divination against the lack of a clear cause or explanation, adding that even physicians advise careful attention to dreams.[151] But Aristotle like Plato focuses on the second phase of dream signification: the "scientific" interpretation of the dream's biological significance. This approach is carried farther by Galen, who develops a humoral theory of dream diagnosis. Most Chinese methods discussed in Chapter 5 also focus on the interpretation of natural phenomena without direct involvement of gods. They focus on the message, and not on how it may have been encoded or transmitted.

Orality and writing

The transmission and interpretation phases of mantic activity partially correspond to a distinction between oral and textual aspects of mantic procedures. Ritual and performance are oral, and are all part of the

[150] Arist. *Div. somn.* 462b12–26, *Insom.* 459a1–22, 461a18–20, 462a29–31, cf. *Div. somn.* 456a30–b11, 456b17, 457a33–b26. Animals' dreams: Arist. *HA* 536b27–30. Cicero (*Div.* 2.128, 239–40) used these arguments in his own claim that dream divination was based on false assumptions about the gods.

[151] Arist. *Div. somn.* 462b13f and 463a5.

transmission phase. The creation of written records is an addendum to interpretation.

Greek divination seems to have been pervasively oral, beginning with the language used to refer to it. Many ordinary words connected with speech were used as technical terms in a mantic context.[152] It is also undisputed that the Pythia gave verbal responses. Some temples retained divination records, and writing clearly played an important role in some consultations. For example, at Dodona, writing was an integral part of the transmission phase of consultation.[153] At Epidaurus, what appear to be carefully selected records were displayed on stone stelae but not as part of the consultation process.

Vernant too emphasizes the Greek preference for oral divination in a civilization where writing was recent and phonetic.[154] Oracular divination relied upon and emphasized transparent public performance, especially in the transmission and performance of oracles in the home territory of state consultors. Such performance put into public view a kind of knowledge that the possessors of mantic records and interpretations reserved for a closed and privileged group. The growth of Greek written literature that replaced traditional modes of oral expression corresponded to the growth of political, historical, scientific, and philosophical systems of thought that assimilated and sought to displace divination in a new discourse of rationality.

There is some evidence for the existence of Greek divination books. According to Isocrates, the seer Polemainetos (a generation later than Aeschylus) bequeathed his divination books to a friend, who was thereafter able to earn a good living, including from consultation by women seeking advice about children.[155] Divination results were also recorded and became objects for independent exegesis, for example, the oracle collections Athenian chresmologues. But these few references only underscore the importance of oral divination.

For all the importance of writing and record-keeping to Chinese mantic practices, there are compelling reasons to believe that Chinese divination also had strong verbal (and ritual) elements. For example, in Shang divination we can distinguish oral and performative mantic processes from the

[152] E.g. *hupokrinesthai*, to respond or interpret an oracular response; *epeirōtān ta khrēstēria*, to interrogate omens (Hdt. 1.53.2); *keleuein*, to order (Hdt. 1.167.9, 4.15.15); and *anairein*, to prescribe or emit an oracular response (Hdt. 9.33.6–8). Other words reflect the oral nature of mantic speech: *manteuein*, to utter mantic speech; *thespizein*, to speak in divine words; *theopropein*, to render an oracle. See Crahay 1974: esp. 203–6. Other terms reflect symbolic, visual, or semiotic aspects of divination: *klēdon* (Latin *omen*), *sēmeion*, divinatory signs; and *phainein* (to appear), *prophainein* (to manifest), and *prophanton* (the thing manifested).

[153] Roberts 1880: 229–30; Nicol 1958: 138–41. [154] Vernant 1974b: 18.

[155] See Isocrates 19 (*Aegineticus* 5–6). Titles of mantic works: Pritchett 1974–79: 3.73.

subsequent creation of written records. The large number of bones and plastrons that are cracked but not inscribed suggests oral prognostication without written records. Thus communication with spirits (with its ritual demands) seems to have been distinct from the creation of written records for whatever purpose of collective memory.[156] Olivier Venture has argued that the content of the inscriptions was spoken aloud within a sacrificial and ritual context. The inscriptions themselves repeatedly state that "the king prognosticated and spoke" (*wang zhan yue* 王占曰). Robert Bagley suggests that the oracle bone inscriptions may be summaries of longer series of queries, since a binary (yes–no) divination method may require a series of questions. Some Western and Chinese scholars have questioned the traditional view that the oracle bone inscriptions were questions at all, and read them as predictions. Either way, one possibility is that diviners orally either asked questions or made predictions about each day before making a crack, with the diviner keeping track of the whole process, and the king interpreting the accumulated evidence.[157]

Another point that becomes clear once we distinguish oral, ritual, and written aspects of Shang divination is that the oracle bone inscriptions were not created as physical media for messages addressed to gods or ancestors. In other words, they did not form part of the transmission phase of messages from humans to divine powers. By contrast, Shang and Western Zhou bronze inscriptions (which are contemporaneous with the oracle bones) were created at the same time as the vessels of which they are an integral part. The bronze vessels, then, probably were messages, but to whom? Venture argues that the intended audience was not the spirits but future human generations, sent via the bronze vessel, with the transmission of the message being an important function of the vessel. Venture also argues that, from the Han on, there is compelling evidence for the preeminence of writing as a means of communication with the spirit world, whereas there is far less evidence for earlier periods.[158]

[156] It is widely accepted that the oracle bone records were inscribed after the actual divination. See Keightley 1978b: 45–56, Djamouri 1999: esp. 11–12, Venture 2002a, Bagley 2004.

[157] Bagley 2004: 196–200. Venture (2002a: 36 n. 12) suggests that the formulae introducing some predictions clearly indicate the oral nature of the questions, e.g. *Heji* 24126 and 23002. For a summary of the "question" question see Qiu Xigui 1989.

[158] Venture 2002a: esp. 35–49. There was thus a fundamental evolution in this aspect of the role of writing from the period when writing was associated with a small group of scribes at the Shang court at Anyang to the wide diffusion of writing in the Han period. Even in the fifth-century texts excavated from Houma and Wenxian, writing is not a substitute for the spoken word. By contrast, one text from Fenghuangshan is a letter to the ruler of the dead. See *Houma meng shu* 1976.

Zhou accounts of plastromancy also contain clear oral elements. *Zuo zhuan* divinations refer to otherwise unknown omen verses (*zhou*).[159] There may even be an oral component in early milfoil divination. The multiple procedures of the Baoshan records clearly indicate a ritual context, with written records presumably created afterwards.

If Shang divination was primarily oral, how do we explain the oracle bone inscriptions? Vandermeersch has argued that Shang plastromancy manifested a specifically Chinese attitude toward the universe, articulated and systematized much later, in which the visual form and longevity of the turtle are models of the cosmos. Keightley proposes a political rationale: that written records provided legitimacy by validating ancestral sacrifices; the Shang kings used them to legitimate political choices and royal supremacy.[160] Both explanations emphasize the separation between mantic procedures (transmission) and written records (hermeneutics).

Yet in *Yi jing* hermeneutics both consultation and interpretation depend on the explicitly *written* character of the text. Jacques Gernet has described it as *deductive* in the sense that it purports less to know the will of gods than to analyze situations; its logic of a system of signs assumes prominence over individual, isolated declarations. Nor is the term "quasi-mathematical" a figure of speech. According to Vandermeersch, the early introduction of symbol systems and principles of order allowed prediction of the future, not by intuition, but by the systematic interpretation of complex and varied signs, which in turn facilitated the early proliferation of experimental techniques. Detailed claims have been made for specifically mathematical aspects of *Yi* divination. Both Mark Elvin and the statistician Persi Diaconis have argued that different hexagram lines had very different mathematical probabilities.[161] But even the *Yi jing* seems to have had oral antecedents. Omen statements from Fuyang suggest that, at an earlier stage, collections of what may have been oral statements were organized under the headings of the hexagrams.

There are important differences between Chinese and Greek written divination records. Greek records do not focus on the act of writing itself, or its intellectual implications. Chinese written records over a long historical span show interest in the possibilities afforded by writing. Shang inscriptions were carefully and symmetrically laid out. The *Zhou yi* that emerged from collected omen statements was abstract, visual, and symbolic. Its

159 E.g. the prognostication of Sun Wenzi in Xiang 10.5, discussed in Chapter 7.

160 Vandermeersch 1974 and 1992; Keightley 1978a.

161 J. Gernet 1974: 54; Vandermeersch 1974: 28–30; Elvin, n.d.; Diaconis 1985, also discussed in Appendix 5.2.

system of written signs offered the prospect, not only of predicting individual events but of decoding the "text" of the universe itself. Nor was visuality confined to turtle and milfoil. Astrocalendric texts are schematic in form and many contain diagrams and other visual representations. Some methods focus on various aspects of writing itself: the analysis of written characters, spirit writing, and even perhaps the pervasive use of written memorials in Daoist ceremonies.[162]

What is comparable?

We are now in a position to reconsider the contributions of the mantic arts to the growth of systematic thought in both China and Greece in the areas of medicine, astrocalendrics, and understandings of causality.

Symbolic systems

In the first section of this chapter I showed that illness remained a topic of both Chinese and Greek mantic consultation, even when systematic medicine offered an alternative. In both contexts, iatromancy and systematic medicine coexisted. They were not opposed, nor did one evolve into the other.

It might still be argued that the mantic arts did not advance medical knowledge in fundamental ways. There are two areas of which mantic discourse made unequivocal contributions to Chinese and Greek systematic thought. In China the contribution was in an early and ongoing interest in symmetry, number, and abstraction combined with empirical observation, especially in the areas of astronomy and hemerology. In several areas of mantic practice – omen texts, daybooks, and physiognomy – we find what may have been initially unsystematic and possibly empirical observations grouped under classificatory headings that became progressively systematic and abstract.

Thus Chinese divination broke away from the notions of either a determined future or a future dependent on divine powers; instead it sought to eliminate accident and tragic uncertainty by anticipating temporary conjunctions of cosmic forces. In this sense, destiny was "decodable," and, as Gernet argues, could be acted on by choosing actions appropriate to the circumstances as determined by judicious choices of names and of signs.

[162] R. J. Smith 1991: 201–5 and 221–33, Lang and Ragvald 1998.

In the words of Vandermeersch, the quasi-mathematical symbolic patterning of *Yi* divination displaced older ideas of a world governed directly by divine will.[163]

Elements from the mantic arts were systematized in a comprehensive cosmology based on *yin–yang* and *wuxing*, but it is not obvious that the cosmological step was an advance. The empirical basis of these theories in particular is open to question, and invites the charge of arbitrariness and superstition that has been leveled against traditional mantic practices, as well as certain aspects of traditional Chinese medicine. But it is worth noting that these early interests in symmetry, number, abstraction, and observation had no clear Greek counterpart. An exception is the Pythagoreans, who used a form of numerological divination (discussed above). However, their system never came into widespread use. (For example, I know of no report of an actual account of its use, either for state or for private purposes.) Further, its correlation with calendrics was only slight, and it does not seem to have been correlated with any observational astronomy.[164]

Divination was central to comprehensive Stoic cosmologies and theories of causation and fate. It was also an important impetus to the growth of skepticism. Neither had a Chinese equivalent.

The use of symbols in Greek mantic speech took a very different direction: in informing the development of the poetic devices of symbol, metaphor, and allegory.[165] Plutarch notes that, in the past, oracles were characterized by riddles (*ainigmata*) and allegories, which people held in awe as manifestations of divine power. Later, they censured poetic language in oracles as obstructing true meaning and introducing vagueness and obscurity; and became suspicious of metaphor, enigma, and ambiguity as refuges for errors in prophecy.[166] Peter Struck argues that the "darkness" of oracular and poetic language reveals a tension in Greek views of language and literary criticism between proponents of "dark" language and advocates of clarity. The one view takes the obscurity of oracular language, riddles (*ainigmata*), symbols, and allegories as a necessary means to work around the inherent limitations of language, especially to express knowledge of the divine.[167] The other view, of Aristotle and of the rhetoricians, prized clarity

163 Gernet 1974: 54 and 67. Vandermeersch 1974: 28–30 and 50.

164 Neugebauer and Salibah (1988: 205) are emphatic on this point. They explain that the lunar data took into account a waxing or waning moon, but that they could find no astrological motivations for the system.

165 Struck 2004, esp. 180–90. 166 Plut. *Mor.* 407a–b.

167 E.g. Heraclitus (DK 22 B1, B48, and B67), Plato's banishment of the poets from the Republic (*Rep.* 10 598b, 599a, 599d, 601b, 605c).

and transparency.[168] If Struck is right, the legacy of the Greek mantic arts lies in an opposite direction from the scientists and systematizers.

Vernant has argued that in all the great "scriptural civilizations," graphic combinations and symbolic configurations oriented the early progress of rationality and science.[169] The records of early Chinese divination seem to bear out this argument far more than their Greek equivalents. This situation contrasts markedly with that of late imperial China, where the practitioners of mantic arts may have been less likely to embrace new knowledge or rationalist scientific systems.

By contrast, Greek divination records did not take a systematic form that encouraged the development of symbolic systems for interpretation. Greek divination was in this sense culturally conservative, and became a source of opposition to the new techniques and claims of the *physiologoi* (although those oppositions have been greatly exaggerated). Indeed, Greek written language carried a very different legacy from mantic speech into poetic language.

Intellectual debate

The process of intellectual debate itself is also an impetus to the development of philosophy and science. Divination was an object of debate in both Greece and China, but the debates were very different in kind. Both are significantly epistemological. In each case divination is rejected as an inferior mode of knowledge. The early Daoists used this rejection rhetorically to argue for the superiority of understanding of *dao*; Plato used it rhetorically to argue for the superiority of philosophy. Greek critiques of divination were significantly and self-consciously skeptical, whereas skepticism is not a central argument in Chinese debates about divination.

Ethics was a significant factor in both Chinese and Greek debates, but in culturally very particular ways. Some Chinese critiques associated divination with acquisitiveness and inauthenticity; others rejected it as inferior to prediction on the basis of moral character. Greek ethical debates focus on divination as a concomitant of determinism, and the perceived conflict between the key value of moral choice and the determinism implied in certain accounts of necessity and causality. The extremely elaborate logical debate that ensued is peculiarly Greek, and goes hand in hand with other features of Greek debate, including emphasis on proof and the use of quasi-

[168] Arist. *Poet.* 1458a18, cf. Struck 2004: 23–24 and 59–68. [169] Vernant 1974b: 24.

legal modes of argumentation. These debates honed logical skills that were an important contribution to Greek systematic thinking.

Finally, both traditions shared the broad view that valid and authentic prognostication or divination derived from the skill and virtue (sagacity, wisdom, insight) of the seer. We find in both traditions the notion of a "right" reading of the "text" of the cosmos. Accounts of that "text" varied both between and within these two traditions, but both understood it to be hermeneutic and, in this sense, fundamentally the same as textual interpretation. (In other words, a "correct" reading is correct semiosis, however understood.)

10 | Conclusions

I have argued that the early history of Chinese mantic practice presents important contrasts to Greek modes of divination and to comparative studies based on anthropological fieldwork. Vernant's key insight – that divination must be studied through the dual aspects of intellectual and social operations – arose through comparative study and specifically through the study of African divination. However, several problems attend this insight. One is that the problems motivating his comparison arose primarily from the study of Greek divination, especially of the Delphic oracle. They inevitably tend to privilege issues that arise from the Greek material, with the risk of universalizing issues that may be culturally specific. Another problem is that comparable contexts were not always employed. For example, comparing oracular divination at Delphi and various modes of African divination often juxtaposes official or "state" and private queries. In all these cases, the wealth and multiplicity of the Chinese evidence offers an unparalleled opportunity.

Any comparison must address substantial differences in both sources and theoretical accounts. Chinese sources far outnumber the Greek; this presents both an opportunity and a problem. The opportunity is the prospect for using the Chinese evidence to address some lacunae in the Greek record. The extent, continuity, and multiplicity of Chinese sources even in the limited historical period considered here allows us to see important changes and debates within as well as between cultural traditions; and attention to these internal changes and debates helps avoid over-generalization. Detail and multiplicity also help us problematize the choice of "comparables" across cultures. To do so we must consider historically specific and concrete comparanda in their contexts. This is a necessary preliminary to any attempt to define comparables.

The Chinese evidence also offers the advantage of historical continuity. Mantic activity remains widely practiced in greater China; the Chinese evidence thus offers the prospect of both historical and ethnographic materials within one tradition. In both these areas, the present study has only begun to sketch the possibilities.

Yet not all aspects of Chinese and Greek divination are equally comparable. One difficulty is the comparability of genres. In some areas, such as medicine or historiography, the textual genres and interpretive problems are readily comparable. In others, they are not, for example in the huge institutional differences between Greek oracular consultation and Chinese court-sponsored mantic activity.

There is also a question of different strengths. A history of engagement between Classics and anthropology, and the efforts of Finley, Vernant, Detienne, and others to establish comparative methods in these disciplines, have created a wealth of theoretical perspectives that have no clear Chinese equivalent.

An engagement between Hellenist methods and Sinological evidence might also usefully parochialize ultimately Greek categories and taxonomies that have dominated the historical study of divination. And I have argued here that we need to question the received categories under which divination is studied. For example, the distinction between inspired and technical divination is a legacy of Plato and Cicero that simply does not fit the Chinese mantic picture. The distinction was turned on its head by historians of science in order to privilege empirical, rational prediction (technical divination) over superstition (inspired divination). Yet the Chinese evidence emphasizes the pervasive coexistence of religio-ritual and technical aspects of divination.

This study began with the questions and problems originally posed by Vernant, but with some differences that, I hope, will advance the discourse. My conclusions begin again with articulation of the problem of the dual intellectual and social roles of divination; the treatment is divided between intellectual and social and institutional aspects of divination. What kind of rationality and intellectual operations informed Chinese and Greek divination and how does a comparison help us understand them better? What functions did each society assign mantic knowledge at different times? What kind of mantic access was available? How was it gendered or otherwise constrained? How did mantic knowledge change within these respective cultural traditions, and what debates and shifts highlight those changes? Finally, how should we, as contemporary students of these practices in the past (and present), classify and understand the phenomenon of divination, past and present?

Social and institutional comparables

Let me review five comparable social and institutional contexts of divination.

(1) The contrast between official and independent practitioners. The problem of Chapter 4 was to reconcile a Greek distinction between "dependent" oracular diviners and their independent counterparts (*manteis*) with a Chinese distinction between "official" and independent mantic specialists. In both cases we can distinguish between official and independent practitioners (even though states consulted both). However, Greek and Chinese official and independent mantic specialists practiced under very different conditions. Chinese official divination was bureaucratic, specialized, and closely connected with writing and record-keeping from an early period. That organization underwent important changes, especially in the Western and Eastern Han.

Both Greek and Chinese independent practitioners seem to have enjoyed lower status than their official counterparts. (Some Han *fang* experts enjoyed high status in their *official* capacities, which were distinct from their mantic expertise.) We also know less about them, since few records of these consultations survive. What accounts for their lower prestige? One possibility is the prevalence of *ad hominem* criticism, which did not threaten belief in divination overall. Another possibility is that their procedures were perceived as less objective and less safe from bias or tampering. Here again, the Chinese evidence parochializes a Greek perspective because in many cases official and independent diviners used the same methods (turtle and milfoil, diviner's boards, hemerology). But one "guarantee" offered by official practice was the rationalization of procedures for the selection of mantic personnel, such as the requirements specified in statutes from Shuihudi and Zhangjiashan.

(2) The roles of mantic lineages. Both sides of the comparison underscore the importance of family lineages, but for very different reasons. Greek *manteis* derived competitive advantage from claims for descent from a mantic family, and oracles were managed by priestly clans. There may have been a lineage element in the appointment of priestesses, if we are to judge from some inscriptions from Didyma. And without institutional procedures for selecting and training mantic specialists, claims of mantic descent provided at least some assurance of competence. Procedures for the

selection of official personnel in China made such claims less necessary (though some offices were at least partially hereditary). But for independent diviners, family lineages provided vehicles for both oral instruction and the transmission of (usually secret) texts. In some cases family transmission included daughters as well as sons.

(3) Competition. A third comparable is competition between mantic expertise and other kinds of technical, textual, or ritual mastery in both China and Greece. The relative independence of mantic experts and the absence of central political power in both Warring States China and fifth- and early fourth-century Greece led to intense competition, political and intellectual, among and between mantic and other intellectual specialists. The extent of state control of mantic activity in Shang and Western Zhou China is a matter of debate, and no such control existed in Archaic Greece. In Warring States China, social and geographic mobility probably helped diffuse mantic activity from the courts of kings. Mantic experts sought, and competed for, employment by local courts and wealthy families. Rulers did not monopolize mantic expertise, and by the third century, it was claimed by competing groups of experts including *shushu* specialists (mantic, medical, and other technical experts), the textual masters of the philosophical traditions, and emergent bureaucracies of local officials and administrators. Nonetheless, the official character of divination persisted through its links to state ritual. Even when performed in local courts or families in practice, it drew its authority in principle from connection to state ritual.

A striking result of that competition, in the Chinese case, is the pervasive *absence* of mantic texts from the received textual tradition. The titles in the technical sections of the *Han shu* Bibliographic Treatise show the importance of these texts, but with the exception of the *Zhou yi* in the *Yi jing*, none survive in the received tradition. By contrast, mantic texts – especially daybooks – are widespread among texts excavated from tombs.

Greek mantic activity was competitive at several levels. Independent *manteis* needed quick wits, flexibility, and a great deal of personal charisma, possibly a result of a "cultural translation" of Mesopotamian mantic practices to Greece. In China, by contrast, the two types of practitioner coexisted, interacted, and often used the same methods.

The competitive ethos of fifth-century Greek intellectual and political life has been widely noted. Mantic practitioners competed with physicians and masters of other *tekhnē*.

The history of this period has been written by the victors, and the received history of science contains the views of the naturalistic thinkers whose texts have come down to us. They highlight the competition of new naturalistic methods both with older mantic practices and with each other. It is less clear whether diviners felt impelled to compete with the new specialists, since they traditionally gained legitimation through membership in specialist families or teaching lineages.

By contrast, the limited evidence of Chinese excavated texts shows the consultation of multiple experts, some drawing on the results of their colleagues and predecessors in mantic sequences such as the Baoshan records. We do not know how high-level administrators selected the diviners they employed, or on what if any basis they attempted to compare their skills or results.

How significant or unique was the Greek ethos of competition, criticism, and debate, which has been linked to the rise of Greek science? The social mobility of the Warring States period affected the development of the mantic arts through internal and external competition, especially between technical specialists and the textual specialists of the Masters traditions. That competition seems to have been instrumental in the development of the Masters traditions, rather than in naturalistic inquiry. Finally, the Chinese mixture of official and freelance specialists provides a very different comparandum to Greek practices than do Mesopotamian court astrologers.

The rise of oracles also underscored a polarization between the status and activities of male and female mantic practitioners that has no equivalent in China. Female *manteis* were of lower status than their male counterparts. Even discrediting extreme accounts of invasive possession and madness, priestesses were under the management of the male priestly lineages. Female independent *manteis* lacked access to the key role of military advisor and ritualist, with its tangible power and rewards.

(4) Mantic consultation. A fourth comparable is mantic questions and the dynamics of interaction between consultor and practitioner. Initially, Chinese and Greek divination question topics seem strikingly similar. States sought mantic advice on warfare, alliances, rainfall and harvests, disasters, choice of personnel, major plans and policies, and on ritual, sacrifice, and other matters of state religious cult. Private consultors asked about domestic matters – especially marriage, children, prosperity, and illness – and about intended actions, including travel, changes of residence, and decisions about livelihood or financial decisions. Importantly, most questions are not predictive; they ask what will be advantageous, pleasing to the gods, or auspicious. Such questions do not invite verification.

But there are important differences. Chinese questions and methods attempt to map good and ill auspice onto chronological cycles. The result is a model of the operation of good auspice that is not immediately dependent on divine goodwill. The focus of risk and doubt becomes temporal, and questions of this kind ask not what to do but when to do it.

State and private consultations involve different relations (and potential tensions) between the political authority and legitimacy of powerful consultors and the mantic authority of practitioners. Chinese and Greek accounts from different periods highlight some of these. For example, *Zuo zhuan* accounts and early prescriptive texts describe divination to preempt or resolve disagreements. Han memorials engage in detailed arguments on the meaning of anomalies. Greek accounts are fullest for the consultation of independent *manteis*. Xenophon shows one case of conflict of interest between individual consultor, practitioner, and the broader beneficiary group.

Both Chinese and Greek materials indicate the possibility of negotiation between consultor and practitioner when the results are undesirable. Both Chinese and Greek accounts indicate the psychological interactions between client and practitioner. Contemporary fieldwork shows Chinese temple diviners and itinerant practitioners finding ways to mitigate truly disastrous results without undermining their own authority. Xenophon's account of his meeting with the *mantis* Eucleides also attests to the importance of a skilled *mantis* knowing his client. Accounts of both temple diviners and Greek independent *manteis* stress their combination of astute observation and self-confidence. We see these skills equally clearly in the hostile accounts of "reformed" PRC fortune-tellers revealing the tricks of their trade. In this they differ from "official" practitioners, whose choice of method was at least partially determined by their office. By contrast, a choice of methods is good for business.

The consultors we know least about are women and slaves, who frequently appear as objects of consultation, but less often as subjects. There is evidence that both consulted the oracles of Dodona and Epidaurus, and flight and manumission were topics of consultation. The Chinese evidence shows women using mantic expertise, especially in physiognomy. This expertise would have become increasingly invisible with the institutionalization of the mantic arts in the Western Han and its shift toward court astrocalendrics.

(5) Mantic consultation and risk. A fifth comparable is the way in which mantic consultation reflects perceptions of risk. Mantic consultation by

private individuals tells us something about the personal concerns and perceived dangers of ordinary people. While contemporary fieldwork can address this issue in contemporary China, the archaeological record offers fewer opportunities. Because of the very different institutions and methods of mantic consultation, it is very difficult to find comparable Chinese and Greek sources. The Shuihudi daybooks and Dodona lead tablets both present explicit categories of mantic query. Juxtaposed, these two corpora give us a comparative window on the perception of risk in everyday life. Despite differences of methods, both types of consultor sought advice in choosing between, usually two, alternatives, described respectively as "better" or "more good" (*lōion*, *ameinon*) and "auspicious" (*ji*). As with many of the mantic questions described in Chapter 6, these queries optimize, rather than predict.

We also find perceptions of risk in topics of official or "state" divination. The most dangerous was warfare, initially understood as a ritual activity in both cultures. Both Hellenistic Greek and late Warring States Chinese warfare were transformed by the emergence of large armies and new technologies, yet criticisms of military divination underscore that it was still performed. Astronomy is a very different case. Astronomy became politically charged, especially during the Eastern Han and the Roman empire, because of its potential to affirm or question the legitimacy and future of the ruling house. (Physiognomy also had ideological and rhetorical uses, but it did not become an object of the same kind of imperial patronage or debate.) Official interest in divination also coexisted with the expanding use of personal or private divination. This situation provided both advantages and disadvantages for diviners and their consultors.

Chinese perspectives: oracular divination and mantic authority

The Chinese evidence challenges received opinion on the nature of divination and oracles in several ways. The origins of oracular divination and the Delphic oracle have vexed Greek scholarship on divination for decades. By the sociological account, new problems of emerging Greek *poleis* required new institutions to address new social tensions at the end of the Greek "Dark Age." Oracular divination offered a way to reconcile social change and community values in the face of crises of authority and unprecedented problems and conflicts.

Comparative evidence has been used to claim that, in other societies, oracles also provided ways to address social change, attain consensus, and diffuse blame. The Chinese evidence contributes to a transcultural understanding of the origins of oracles, their roles in periods of social and political upheaval, and their contemporary functions. For example, the establishment of Confucian chairs in the Western Han arguably undermined mantic and other technical expertise as a path to political or intellectual authority. Yet many Han mantic experts were Ru, including two of the most famous Confucian exegetes of the time: Liu Xiang (an expert on the *Yi jing*) and Dong Zhongshu (an expert on omens). Indeed, the ability to prognosticate becomes part of the definition of a "successful" Ru. Nor did mantic experts disappear in the Eastern Han, for example the biographies of many experts in *fang* arts appear in the *Hou Han shu* (discussed in Chapter 4).

Chinese evidence also offers new perspectives on the nature of mantic authority. The rise of Greek oracular divination in the eighth century was a new phenomenon. Delphi and other oracles derived their authority from the claim to speak with the voice of the god. In a society in which mantic activity was never abstracted or distanced from the gods, it is not surprising that inspired, communicative divination may have had more appeal than methods based on technical competence alone.

A key to the success of Delphi in particular was a reputation for political neutrality. When the reputation declined, the oracle's specifically political reputation declined with it, and oracles and chresmologues increasingly became targets for the barbs of Attic comedy. If oracular divination drew authority from its independence of the state, Chinese mantic activity drew its authority from its connection with it, however indirect. Community and family rituals drew authority by analogy to state ritual. Even in the social mobility of the Warring States, turtle and milfoil divination and hemerology were the official methods of the Zhou court, and lent corresponding authority to any marketplace diviner who could use them.

Consensus and prediction

Comparison of the Chinese and Greek materials also makes it clear that mantic queries provided three very important kinds of response. There is an immediate distinction between requests for predictions and requests for normative advice, religious or political. Both are distinct from the political consensus or construction of authority stressed by sociological accounts. The Chinese evidence thus invites reconsideration of the sociological argument that divination was less concerned with prediction than with social regulation and consensus.

The Chinese evidence clearly does support the view that social consensus was an important social function of divination. A range of genres describe the use of divination to resolve disagreements, and detailed instructions in several texts suggest the importance of consensus as an important goal of mantic activity. Sociological accounts of Greek oracles do not address the topic of debate and disagreement. Nor do they address instances of Pythias being suborned or Greek skepticism about both oracles and *manteis*.

But the Chinese evidence also shows us that we cannot reduce the role of divination and prognostication to social consensus and regulation. Clear interest in prediction – and verification of predictions – dates back to the oracle bone inscriptions. Chinese normative questions on good and ill auspice did not seek predictions, but they were centrally concerned with regularity in cycles of time. We see ongoing Chinese interest in both predictability and regularity in official uses of divination to manage agriculture, in astronomy (whether truly observational or idealized models for hemerological purposes), in hemerology of all kinds, and in the very idea of anomalies. But portents and anomalies were also fabricated (or suppressed) for political reasons.

In summary, we can identify two coexisting tendencies in Chinese and Greek divination. One was toward empirical procedures that relied on observation, and were refined by experience. Their pragmatic value was predictive. The other was toward a symbolic mode of discourse whose pragmatic value was rhetorical: to provide normative advice or social consensus. Its procedures were religious and ritual, and observed phenomena were understood as correspondences between the macrocosm of the universe and the microcosm of the body or body politic, or as communications from the gods. Its pragmatic value was social and political. Both modes of divination could provide social protection from the burden of individual responsibility for predictions, recommendations, or decisions. Both also could involve technical skills.

It should also be stressed that these two aspects do not map onto any simple antinomy between "proto-science" and its imagined opposite. It would be easy but misplaced to associate only the predictive aspects of divination with the rise of scientific thought and systematic inquiry. But the idea of a comprehensive symbolic system that encompassed all potential mantic signs also implies a systematizing attitude toward the world.

The intellectual operations

In both China and Greece, as elsewhere, divination left its mark on a wide range of intellectual domains. Both Chinese and Greek metaphysical assumptions led to beliefs in semiosis and hermeneutics: that mantic signs manifested hidden patterns, and could be read and interpreted by those with the correct expertise. But these beliefs (and debates about them) resulted from different assumptions, led in different directions, and changed over time. These practices affected the growth of systematic thought and abstraction. They led to a perceived need for techniques for validating or rejecting interpretations, including in the context of oral performance. Divination also was associated with, and at times polemicized by, a wide range of technical disciplines and empirical knowledge. In China, the perceived need to record or verify divinations was closely associated with the development of writing. The ambiguity that was so central to Greek reflective narratives about divination is virtually absent in China, where theorizing cosmic regularity was a key goal of mantic activity.

Divination, gods, and hermeneutics

Both Chinese and Greek metaphysics assumed the existence of gods or divine powers and the possibility of communicating with them. Within both traditions there is disagreement over whether they had some benign interest in human affairs. In both traditions there are examples of economies of human–divine relations based on prayer and sacrifice. The ancient practices of Greek bird and weather divination and Chinese oracle bone divination offered ways for diviners to effectively negotiate with the gods by means of repeated questions. Both traditions also include ethical frameworks for divination, based on presumed correlations between cosmic and human orders. Both Chinese and Greek philosophers emphasized the ethical role of divination in defining divine concepts of justice and retribution.

But Chinese and Greek understandings of the nature of these interactions were very different. Chinese models of divine–human relations were genetic (gods as royal ancestors) or bureaucratic (gods as a hierarchy of rulers and officials). Some Chinese mantic techniques addressed particular gods responsible for specific time periods and modes of activity, but they progressively de-emphasize direct communication or negotiation with divine powers.

Greek assumptions about the benevolence and interest of the gods in humanity are more equivocal. Greek bird and weather diviners associated a wide range of phenomena with communications from particular gods and predictions of particular kinds, and omens were understood to systematically reflect divine intentions. These practices persisted into Hellenistic Greece, but the legacy of Plato and Cicero privileged oracular divination. The gods of Greek myth were notoriously fickle; the arbitrariness of human fates and the indifference of the gods are recurring themes from Homeric epic to Attic tragedy. Later Greek divinatory reflection shifted to the idea that the future was somehow predetermined and thence predictable. One result was a systematic and abstract reflection on problems of cause, necessity, and the logical preconditions that made divination possible and legitimate.

Starting in the late Warring States period, competing schemata began to link *yin* and *yang* (variously described) to phenomena in space (the directions), time (the calendar), notions of good and ill auspice, and the body. The eventual hermeneutics of Han correlative cosmology focused on elaborate microcosm–macrocosm correspondences between the three realms of Heaven, Earth, and humanity, and used numbers to express these symbolic correlations. Chinese correlative cosmology also provided "natural" explanations for the establishment and expansion of the Han dynasty. Scholar officials also used correlative cosmology and discourses on omens to define (and circumscribe) royal power through admonition.

Writing and visuality

Another intellectual problem was the need for techniques to validate or reject interpretations. In China this was intimately associated with the development of writing, but there is significant evidence that the oral aspects of mantic ritual were also important. By contrast, the Greek and African mantic practices compared by some Hellenists share a bias toward oral and aural divination. But other problems arise when speech and writing interact in complex ways in mantic rituals and practices. Chinese mantic practitioners developed a strongly visual, "inscribed," and symbolic practice that has no counterpart in Greek divination, which was predominantly oral and performative from its beginnings. This visuality includes turtle and milfoil techniques, *qi* observation (including wind and cloud divination), and physiognomy. Later methods focus on aspects of writing itself.

Vernant emphasized a Greek preference for spoken divination. But, as written literature replaced traditional modes of oral expression, new political, historical, scientific, and philosophical systems of thought assimilated and sought to displace divination in a new discourse of rationality. This picture can be nuanced in certain ways. Early mantic techniques relied on visual signs: the flight of birds, the details of the sky, the direction of smoke. Oracular procedures, especially for state queries, introduced more complex sequences of consultation, response, transmission (by the *theōros* from the oracular shrine to his home polis), and performance of the response to the original consultors. These procedures were oral and performative but also involved writing.

The oral orientation of both *manteis* and oracles did not encourage the development of systematic or symbolic systems for decoding and interpreting omens. By contrast, the basis of Chinese divination in a system of written signs offered the prospect, not only of predicting individual events, but of decoding the "text" of the universe itself; in this sense Greek divination was culturally conservative. Although traditional Chinese emphasis on ritual has often been described as counterproductive to progress or rationalist thought, the early history of divination suggests a very different possibility.

Finally, there was no Greek equivalent to Chinese ritual classics, which provided the theoretical and practical foundations for ritual practice. The Greeks never made the connection between divination, ritual, writing, and record-keeping that so characterized early Chinese divination and intellectual development. Why were mantic and ritual texts compiled in China but not in Greece? Divination by both bones and milfoil predate mantic texts of any kind by hundreds or thousands of years. Stylization occurred even in the oracle bone inscriptions over the course of the Shang.[1] Similar questions concern possible reasons for the creation of the omen collections that eventually became the *Zhou yi* and the daybooks.

Divination and systematic thought

Where do we place the Chinese and Greek mantic arts in the development of systematic inquiry? Did mantic theories and practices advance or impede intellectual experimentation and inquiry? Did they encourage political experimentation, mobility, or tyranny? The picture is mixed, and subject

[1] Discussed in Chapters 2 and 6. Michael Loewe (1994) has speculated that stylized ritual procedures displaced the spontaneous actions and reactions of earlier mantic experts, and that even the original motives for mantic procedures may have been lost by the time ritual texts were written down.

to intellectual and political microclimates. At times divination was a conservative and stultifying influence, but it cannot be dismissed as intellectual superstition or political or religious conservatism. A comparative perspective shows the areas in which it was linked to the observation of regularity, the development of techniques for observation and verification, and analyses of cause and effect. It was also a major vehicle for early speculation about cosmology and for the development of theories of hermeneutics and semiosis. Finally, it gave rise to the systematic expression of abstract concepts in formal systems. The particular concepts and systems are, in many cases, not ones we would use today, despite the ongoing popularity of divination, but the importance of the ability to articulate such systems cannot be overstated.

It is immediately striking that many Chinese mantic techniques simply do not fit into Bouché-Leclercq's system of intuitive and inductive divination. Greek methods address the will of the gods, mediated through natural phenomena, but through no system of signs. Most Chinese methods keep a "respectful distance" from divine powers, and are abstract, systematic, and significantly based on number and calculation. Most Greek procedures presupposed a direct divine origin for divinatory signs that privileged spontaneous events, especially the movements of birds, thunder and lightning, involuntary motion, and dreams. Given these fundamental differences, it is no surprise that apparently similar techniques were understood very differently. Wind divination, physiognomy, and cleromancy are cases in point.

Chinese and Greek divination methods also diverge in relation to naturalistic thinking. Again the key difference is the perceived proximity and involvement of divine powers. Chinese mantic methods and attitudes were compatible with naturalistic inquiry and offered opportunities for it. By contrast, a tension between naturalistic thinking and mantic practices that involved the gods directly seems peculiarly Greek. Although Greek medicine and mantic practices coexisted, the Greek formulation of explicit notions of nature and cause set them apart in a way that has no Chinese counterpart. Some of those practices became targets of invective for the *physiologoi*, a competition that became central to the positivist historiography of Greek science. Here again, comparison underscores the danger of broad historical generalization from limited and culturally specific Greek evidence.

An enduring intellectual legacy of the Western Han was the selective canonization and official sponsorship of some texts and modes of knowledge and the marginalization of others. Earlier competition between technical specialists and Masters textualists was transformed. Non-orthodox textual specialists still practiced their crafts – and many were prominent Ru – but their arts were marginalized from official ideology and institutions. For example, the *Yi jing* became a privileged form of moral knowledge. Many of these developments were intellectually conservative, marginalizing systematic thought and empirical observation, and constraining the kind of systematic and abstract thought often linked to the development of science and philosophy. An exception to this general trend was astrocalendrics. The evidence of both the standard histories and excavated texts shows the increasing complexity of astronomical observation or theory and the development of new astrocalendric instruments during the Qin and Han. By contrast, Greek interest in astronomy, astrology, and calendrics did not take the form of state sponsorship.

In summary, Chinese and Greek mantic practice contributed to systematic thought in different ways. Chinese notions of symmetry, number, and abstract patterns of change were central to the development of systematic medicine, astronomy, and cosmology. Greek debates about divination were central to the development of skepticism, logic, and theories of causation.

This analysis has highlighted repeatedly a contrast between the lack of tension between human and divine realms in China and a strong tension between them in Greece. This contrast also informs a defining issue in twentieth-century discussions of Chinese thought, namely the cultural uniqueness of Chinese cosmology or its commensurability with "Western" cosmologies. At one pole of the debate, Weber argued that the Chinese were limited by the lack of a notion of transcendence or tension between the human and divine realms.[2] At the other, Marcel Granet argued for the distinctiveness of Chinese cosmology because of the lack of demarcation of human and divine realms, including a notion of transcendence.[3] Granet's work in turn has informed (in very different ways) several important studies, especially the work of Joseph Needham, K. C. Chang, A. C. Graham, and David Hall and Roger Ames.[4] These studies all argue that radically different cosmologies distinguish China and the West. A different view is presented by Michael Puett, who argues that the term *shen* 神 ("spirit") refers both to spirits who reside in the extra-human world and hold power over natural phenomena and to

[2] Weber 1951: esp. 152–53, 196–200, 226–27, and 235–48. [3] Granet 1934.

[4] Needham and Wang Ling (1956: esp. 216–17, 280–82), K. C. Chang (1963), A. C. Graham (1986 and 1991), and Hall and Ames (1995: xviii, 257). For discussion of this issue see Puett 2002: 8–22.

refined forms of *qi* within the human body.[5] My study also points toward a contrast between relations between humans and gods in China and Greece, but (like Puett) I reject the dichotomy between evolutionist and cultural-essentialist models. In both China and Greece we see changing and contested relations between mantic practitioners and theories and the practitioners of science and philosophy. In both cases we see complex coexistence, negotiation, and mutual influence. Methodologically, the present study also ends by recommending nuanced approaches that are historically contextualized.

Future directions

Finally, what new directions of study does a comparison of Chinese and Greek divination suggest? Another function of comparison is to suggest areas for future research, and I end with a few of them. One is the striking absence of explicit theories of divination in early Chinese or Greek accounts. In China we find cosmological theories (in the sense articulated in Chapter 9) underlying mantic practices, but without a specific mantic theory. The first Chinese and Greek theories of divination – Cicero's *De Divinatione* and Wang Chong's *Lun heng* – are relatively late and relatively hostile.

The entire area of mantic narratives warrants further study. For example, in the *Shi ji* and later works, individuals are specifically treated as members of groups, and biographies classify and describe them as such. How do diviners fit into taxonomies of groups?

In particular, the role of women as mantic practitioners wants further study. Biographies of diviners list very few women.[6] By contrast, as this study has shown, Chinese historical narratives mention a fair number of women with mantic expertise who are not "professional" diviners, and who do not appear in biographies of diviners.[7]

Finally, how do divination practices bear on fundamental ideas of personhood, destiny, and autonomy?

In conclusion, this study shows the tremendous – arguably universal – interest in the problem of the future and the diverse influence of mantic practices, as well as a pervasive need for some kind of extra-human

[5] Puett 2002: 21–22 and passim. However, rather than taking this wide semantic field as evidence of a smooth and porous boundary between humans and gods, he takes that relationship as point of contestation to be examined historically.

[6] E.g. Yuan Shushan 1926 and 1948. [7] I am indebted to Richard Smith for this point.

authority or explanation for how and why things come out as they do. The Chinese and Greek mantic practices surveyed in this book all involve extra-human agency and regularity in nature, but articulated through widely differing methods, human interactions, and hermeneutics. Indeed, the more extensive Chinese evidence shows major differences between historical periods or even individual reign periods in the details of mantic questions and the use and reportage of anomalies as a mode of political critique.

Thus the comparative evidence suggests many things, including new areas of future study, but I believe that it argues for neither the cultural unity nor diversity of mantic practices, nor does comparison suggest a unified, transcultural theory of divination.

How should cultural comparison be undertaken? In the case of social practices, the important point is the comparison of concrete particulars embedded in their social contexts and institutions. In the case of ideas, comparative context is provided by a history of change and debate within each culture. Cultural comparison, undertaken in concrete situations and on questions subjected to debate in each particular context, can bring new and unexpected insights to help us to improve our understanding of concepts and practices which, because of their universality, can easily lead us to partial and reducing generalizations.

Glossary

Chinese

Bu 卜. Turtle shell divination.

Chunqiu 春秋 (literally "Springs and Autumns"). The *Chunqiu* was an official chronicle of events in the state of Lu between the years 722 BCE and 481 BCE. The events are arranged by year, month, and day on annalistic principles.

Cord and hook pattern. A Han dynasty cruciform decorative motif representing four directions and a center.

Correlative cosmology. A late Western or Eastern Han cosmological system that classified aspects of the human body, the body politic, and the natural world by grouping them in categories based on combinations of *yin-yang* and *wuxing*, especially in fives (colors, sounds, tastes, cardinal directions, etc.).

Daybook. See *Rishu*.

Divination rods. See *Qian*.

Diviner's board. See *Shi* or *shi pan*.

Earth Branches. See *Ganzhi*.

Fangshi 方士 (recipe masters). First mentioned prominently during the reign of Han Wu Di.

Ganzhi 干支. The traditional Chinese calendric system, a cyclic numeral system of the sixty possible combinations of Ten Heaven Stems and Twelve Earth Branches. It was used in divination and astrology, and was also used to number days and years in China, Japan, Korea, and Vietnam.

Heaven Stems. See *Ganzhi*.

Hexagram (*gua* 卦). A (bottom to top) vertical sequence of six *yin* or *yang* "lines."

Huangdi neijing 黃帝內經 (Inner Classic of the Yellow Lord). First major Chinese medical work (*c.* 100 BCE). It is divided into two sections: the *Suwen* 素問 (Basic Questions) and the *Lingshu* 靈樞 (Spiritual Pivot).

Illness divination (*jibing* 疾病). Divinations from Baoshan and elsewhere that punctuate a normal sequence of Year divinations after the appearance of a health problem.

Incantator (*zhu* 祝). Mantic official in the *Zhou li*, whose function was to invoke the spirits. They worked in conjunction with diviners (*bu*) and recording officials (*shi*).

Intercalary month. An "extra" month inserted into the Chinese (and other) lunisolar calendars every thirty-third month to rectify differences between the solar and lunar calendars, because the solar year is not evenly divisible by an exact number of lunations.

Jiaguwen 甲骨文. See Oracle bone inscriptions.

Jing 經. Bibliographic classification as "classic" (classification of textual genres).

Jiugong 九宮. Nine Palaces board. Type of mantic astrolabe.

Li 禮. Ritual propriety.

Liubo 六博. An ancient Chinese board game, played by two players. The board was also used for divination.

Liuren 六壬 (Six *Ren* Days). Astrocalendric divination method. See Appendix 5.3.

Lunar Lodges (*xiu* 宿). See Twenty-eight Lunar Lodges.

May Fourth Movement. A Chinese intellectual, cultural, and pro-independence political reform movement that began on May 4, 1919, as a protest against the government's (lack of) response to the Treaty of Versailles. More broadly, it refers to a cultural reform movement from 1915 to 1921.

Milfoil (yarrow), *shi* 筮. Method of divination using stalks of the plant Achillea millefolium, used in "stalk casting" divination method of *Yi* divination.

Nine Palaces. See *Jiugong*.

Oracle bone inscriptions (*jiaguwen* 甲骨文). Inscriptions on turtle plastrons or bones used for divination, especially during the Shang dynasty.

Pitch pipes (*lü* 律). A form of divination using pipes of different lengths, filled with ash, believed to detect subtle movements of *qi*.

Qi 氣 (also spelled *ch'i*). Matter, energy, breath, the vital energy that constitutes and organizes matter and makes growth possible, and also the force in living matter that influences other things.

Qian 籤. Rods with numbers inscribed on them, used for divination.

Rishu 日書. A collection of short hemerological texts that provided guidance for selecting auspicious times for a range of everyday activities. Daybooks have some resemblance to European almanacs but they do not provide systematic treatment of the entire calendar.

Ru 儒. A textual specialist, scholar, or literatus. The term is also used of specifically Confucian scholars.

Sanctions and Virtues (*Xingde* 刑德). Title of a divination text from Mawangdui. It plots calendric cycles on a spatial grid, and was used for military divination.

Sexagenary cycle. See *Ganzhi*.

Shi 史. Astronomer/astrologer/scribe.

Shi 筮. See Milfoil.

Shi 式 or *shi pan* 式盘. Mantic astrolabe or diviner's board. This device was used for astrocalendric calculation. A round "Heaven plate" in the center of a square, stationary "Earth plate" could be rotated to model cosmological data, somewhat in the manner of a slide rule. (In this sense it is not a board.) It has also been called a cosmograph insofar as it models cosmological information.

Taiyi 太乙. "Great One." A star and the divinity (in anthropomorphic form) associated with it.

TLV mirror. A type of bronze mirror with a distinctive "TLV"-shaped decorative motif, first appearing in Han tombs, and excavated from tombs as late as the Tang.

Twenty-eight Lunar Lodges (*Ershiba xiu* 二十八宿). Division of the celestial equator around the pole star. The Lodges were grouped into four palaces, each containing seven lodges.

Wang qi 望氣. Observing vapors/*qi*. Cloud divination technique.

Wu 巫. "Spirit medium," sometimes incorrectly called shamans, usually women.

Wuxing 五行. Five Agents, Five Phases. Its meaning changed over time from five processes ("Five Agents") to the five transformations of *qi* ("Five Phases") associated with correlative cosmology. In an astronomical context it refers to the "five courses" of planetary motion. In other contexts it refers to other groupings of five categories.

Xi ci 繫辭. An important commentary in the *Yi jing*.

Yao 爻. The six "lines" of a *Yi jing* hexagram.

Year divination (*sui* 歲). At Baoshan and in other excavated texts, a quasi-formulaic type of mantic query that sought to ascertain (or establish) the consultor's overall success in official service to the king during the ensuing year. See Illness divination.

Yi jing 易經. In its present form the *Yi jing* consists of the *Zhou yi* and seven commentaries.

Yin and yang 陰陽. Two complementary and fundamental forces, whose constant interactions create change in the universe.

Yue ling 月令 (monthly ordinances). Chapters in the *Lüshi chunqiu* and *Huainanzi*. They are calendric texts that prescribe particular activities for each month.

Yunqi 雲氣 (literally "cloud vapors" or "clouds and vapors"). The *qi* (vital energy) that is inherent in the clouds and recognizable in their shapes, which are interpreted in cloud divination.

Zhanbu 占卜. Prognostication.

Zhou 繇 (also written 籀). A divination omen verse associated with turtle shell divination.

Zhou yi 周易. "Zhou Changes." The core of the *Yi jing*.

Zi 子. "Masters." Classification of textual genres.

Greek and modern English

Adyton. "Inaccessible" restricted area in a Greek or Roman temple, reserved for oracles, priests, or acolytes, and forbidden to the general public. At Delphi, the *adyton* was reserved for the Pythia.

Asylia. A decree that a person or place was considered "sacred and inviolable" by the tutelary god of the polis.

Catharsis. "Cleansing," "purging," or "purification." The term applies to both ritual or moral cleansing or purification from some form of pollution and to the medical use of purgatives.

Chresmologue. Compiler or collector of oracles.

Cledonomancy. Divination based on involuntary or unconscious speech.

Cleromancy. Divination by the casting of lots, coins, or similar chance procedures.

Daimonion. The "divine guide" whose advice Socrates claimed that he always followed.

Extispicy. Divination by examination of the entrails or livers of sacrificial animals. See Hieroscopy.

Hemerology. Literally the understanding of days. Calendrics.

Hepatoscopy. Divination by examination of the livers of sacrificial animals.

Hiera. "Normal" methods of sacrifice by armies on the move, typically including animal sacrifice and hieroscopy.

Hieroscopy. Divination by examination of the entrails or livers of sacrificial animals (see Extispicy).

Iatromancy. Medical divination.

Khrēstērion. The seat of an oracle. By extension, an oracle or an offering to an oracle.

Lusis kakōn. Release from evils.

Mantis (pl. *manteis*). Individual Greek seer or diviner, frequently a specialist in military divination.

Miasma. "Pollution" of a person or polis.

Oikist. The founder of a colony, designated as such by the founding polis.

Oneiromancy. Dream divination.

Ornithomancy. Divination by the calls or movements of birds.

Pelanos. Nominal "fee" to consult the oracle of Apollo at Delphi.

Polis (pl. *poleis*). Greek city-state.

Promanteia. Grant of priority of access to the oracle of Apollo, bypassing the normal use of lots to decide order of access.

Prophētēs (fem. *prophētis*). "Prophet." Used by the oracle at Delphi as a mantic spokesperson (male or female) for the god.

Pyromancy. Divination by fire.

Pythia. The priestess of Apollo at Delphi.

Sortition. Casting lots, for mantic or other purposes. In a political context, the use of lots to select political officials or decision-makers from a group of candidates.

Sphagia. Blood sacrifice, used in military divination.

Tekhnē. "Art" or "Science."

Theopropos. An authorized envoy sent to Delphi by a polis to consult the oracle and bring back the response.

Thuoskoos (Lat. *haruspex*). A "sacrifice diviner," who inspects sacrificial offerings.

Appendix A | Inscriptional evidence for Delphic oracles

PW	Font	Consultor	Topic	Inscription	Date
89	Q052	Megarians	construction of tomb for Orsippus	*IG* 7.52	*c.* 700
123	H01	Athenians	public maintenance in Prytaneion	*IG* I2 77.11	440–430
124	H02	Athenians	honoring Moirai, Zeus, Ge	*IG* I2 80	430–420
164	H09	Athenians	offering first fruits at Eleusis	Tod 1 no. 74	421–415
165	H10	Athenians	cult of Apollo exegete to Athenians	*IG* I2 78	*c.* 420
260	H19	Chalcidice, Macedon	treaty between Chalcidice and Philip	Tod 2 no. 158	356
262	H21	Athenians	letting lands in Eleusinian *orgas*	*IG* 2 I2 204	352–351
277	H23	Halieis	appearance of sacred snake of Asclepius	*IG* 4^2.122	pre-320
278	H24	Athenians	Demon's house dedicated to Asclepius	*IG* 2–2.4969	*c.* 350
279	H25	Isyllus the poet	whether to compose a paean to Apollo	*IG* 42 1.128.1.32	338–335
280	H26	Cyrene	adoption of a code of ritual regulations	*SEG* 9.72	*c.* 325
281	H27	Athens or Acharnae	erection of altars of Athena & Ares	Robert 293ff	400–300
284	H31	Amphictyony	work on temple	Diehl 2.255	344–343
285	H33	Athenians	proposal to improve *kosmoi* of goddess	*IG* 22 33.c.11.24ff	335–334
330	H35	Amphictyony	*sōtēria* after Gaul victory	Delph 3.(1).483	*c.* 275
334	H34	a husband	children	Delph 3(1). 560.11 1 and 2	*c.* 360
335	H36	Poseidonus of Halicarnassus	family welfare	B Mus 4.1.896	*c.* 250?
336	H37	Unknown	sanction to honor Artemidorus	*IG* 12(3)863	*c.* 250?

PW	Font	Consultor	Topic	Inscription	Date
339	Q243	Cretans	not stated, on purification	*IM* no. 215	*c.* 200?
340	H53	King Dropion of Paines	personal?, dedicate statue	*BCH* 76 1952	*c.* 240
341	H38	Cyzicenes	*sōtēria* festival for Kora Soteria	Delph 3.(3).342	300
342	H39	Cyzicenes	decision to honor certain gods	Delph 3.(3).343	200–100
343	H40	Cyzicenes	decision to honor certain gods	Delph 3.(3).344	200–100
346	H43	Antichus of Chrysaoreis	declaring city *asylon*	*OGI* 1.234	210–200
347	H45	Magnesia-on-Maender	establish festival in honor of Artemis	*IM* no. 16	221–220
348	H46	Teos	to declare the city *asylon*	*IC* 1.19.2	201
349	H52	Hellespont Dionysiast society	*asylia* of Dionysiac artists	*IG* 11.(4).1061	pre-176
350	H71	Megara	specification of *asylia*	*IG* 7.16	*c.* 200
351	H47	Eretrians	legislation voted by demos	*IG* 12.(9).213	210–200
378	L163	Magnesians	on return to Magnesia	*IM* no. 17	
379	L164	Magnesians in Crete	return to Magnesia after omens	*IM* no. 17	
380	L165	Magnesians in Crete	where to go and how	*IM* no. 17	
381	L166	Magnesians in Crete	where to go and how	*IM* no. 17	
382	L167	Leucippus	confirmation of preceding oracles	*IM* no. 17	
426	H50	Rhodian garrison on Tenos	sacrifice to various gods	*IG* 12.(5).913	*c.* 177
427	H54	Timotheus of Anaphe	building a temple of Aphrodite	*IG* 12.(3).248	110–100
429	H56	Parians	what god sacrifice for colony wellbeing	*IG* 12.suppl. 200	*c.* 180
432	H57	Athenians	Pythiad procession to Delphi to sacrifice	Delph 3.(2).47.11.4	Bef. 128
437	H58	Genos of Athens	appointment of priest of Zeus	*IG* 2.2.1096	37–36
457	H59	Athenians	not stated	*IG* 2.2.3177	
458	H64	Athenians	concerning Dodecad	Delph 3.(2).66.1.14	

PW	Font	Consultor	Topic	Inscription	Date
459	H60	Parians	not stated	*IG* 12.(5).155	
460	H61	uncertain	uncertain	Delphi *BCH* VI 1882 p. 88	
466	H66	Athenians	not stated	*IG* 2.2.5006	
467	H67	not stated	where to appease Hera	*IM* no. 228	

Appendix B | The sexagenary cycle

The Ten Heaven Stems and Twelve Earth Branches

1	2	3	4	5	6	7	8	9	10		
甲	乙	丙	丁	戊	己	庚	辛	壬	癸		
jia	*yi*	*bing*	*ding*	*wu*	*ji*	*geng*	*xin*	*ren*	*gui*		
子	丑	寅	卯	辰	巳	午	未	申	酉	戌	亥
zi	*chou*	*yin*	*mao*	*chen*	*si*	*wu*	*wei*	*shen*	*you*	*xu*	*hai*
1	2	3	4	5	6	7	8	9	10	11	12

The Sexagenary Cycle

1甲子 *jiazi*	2乙丑 *yichou*	3 丙寅 *bingyin*	4丁卯 *dingmao*	5 戊辰 *wuchen*	6 己巳 *jisi*	7 庚午 *gengwu*	8 辛未 *xinwei*	9 壬申 *renshen*	10癸酉 *guiyou*
11甲戌 *jiaxu*	12乙亥 *yihai*	13丙子 *bingzi*	14丁丑 *dingchou*	15戊寅 *wuyin*	16己卯 *jimao*	17庚辰 *gengchen*	18辛巳 *xinsi*	19壬午 *renwu*	20癸未 *guiwei*
21甲申 *jiashen*	22乙酉 *yiyou*	23丙戌 *bingxu*	24丁亥 *dinghai*	25戊子 *wuzi*	26己丑 *jichou*	27庚寅 *gengyin*	28辛卯 *xinmao*	29壬辰 *renchen*	30癸巳 *guisi*
31甲午 *jiawu*	32乙未 *yiwei*	33丙申 *bingshen*	34丁酉 *dingyou*	35戊戌 *wuxu*	36己亥 *jihai*	37庚子 *gengzi*	38辛丑 *xinchou*	39壬寅 *renyin*	40癸卯 *guimao*
41甲辰 *jiachen*	42乙巳 *yisi*	43丙午 *bingwu*	44丁未 *dingwei*	45戊申 *wushen*	46己酉 *jiyou*	47庚戌 *gengxu*	48辛亥 *xinhai*	49壬子 *renzi*	50癸丑 *guichou*
51甲寅 *jiayin*	52乙卯 *yimao*	53丙辰 *bingchen*	54丁巳 *dingsi*	55戊午 *wuwu*	56己未 *jiwei*	57庚申 *gengshen*	58辛酉 *xinyou*	59壬戌 *renxu*	60癸亥 *guihai*

Five-Phase Correlations of the Stems and Branches

(after Needham with Wang Ling 1956: 2.262–63)

1	2	3	4	5	6	7	8	9	10		
甲	乙	丙	丁	戊	己	庚	辛	壬	癸		
jia	*yi*	*bing*	*ding*	*wu*	*ji*	*geng*	*xin*	*ren*	*gui*		
wood	wood	fire	fire	earth	earth	metal	metal	water	water		
1	2	3	4	5	6	7	8	9	10	11	12
子	丑	寅	卯	辰	巳	午	未	申	酉	戌	亥
zi	*chou*	*yin*	*mao*	*chen*	*si*	*wu*	*wei*	*shen*	*you*	*xu*	*hai*
water	earth	wood	wood	earth	fire	fire	earth	metal	metal	earth	water

The Twenty-four Solar Nodes (after *Huainanzi* 3)

Sexag. Cycle Branch	Solar Lodge Stem	Dates (approx.)	Month	Solar Node	English Name
wu 戊 3 *yin* 寅	*wu* 戊	5 Feb–19 Feb 19 Feb–4 Mar	1 1	*Li chun* *Yu shui*	4 Start of Spring 5 Rain
jia 甲 4 *mao* 卯	*jia* 甲	5 Mar–20 Mar 21 Mar–4 Apr	2 2	*Jing zhe* *Chun fen*	6 Awakening of Insects 7 Spring Equinox
yi 乙 5 *chen* 辰	*yi* 乙	5 Apr–19 Apr 20 Apr–4 May	3 3	*Qing ming* *Gu yu*	8 Bright Wind Maximum 9 Grain Rain
wu 戊 6 *si* 巳	*wu* 戊	5 May–20 May 21 May–5 Jun	4 4	*Li xia* *Xiao man*	10 Start of Summer 11 Lesser Fullness
bing 丙 7 *wu* 午	*bing* 丙	6 Jun–20 Jun 21 Jun–6 July	5 5	*Mang chong* *Xia zhi*	12 Grain in Ear 13 Summer Solstice
ding 丁 8 *wei* 未	*ding* 丁	7 July–22 July 23 July–6 Aug	6 6	*Xiao shu* *Da shu*	14 Lesser Heat 15 Great Heat
ji 己 9 *shen* 申	*ji* 己	7 Aug–22 Aug 23 Aug–6 Sep	7 7	*Li qiu* *Chu shu*	16 Start of Autumn 17 End of Heat
geng 庚 10 *you* 酉	*geng* 庚	7 Sep–21 Sep 22 Sep–7 Oct	8 8	*Bai lu* *Qiu fen*	18 Descent of White Dew 19 Autumn Equinox
xin 辛 11 *xu* 戌	*xin* 辛	8 Oct–22 Oct 23 Oct–6 Nov	9 9	*Han lu* *Shuang jiang*	20 Cold Dew 21 Descent of Hoar Frost

ji 己 12 *hai* 亥	*ji* 己	7 Nov–21 Nov 22 Nov–6 Dec	10 10	*Li dong* *Xiao xue*	22 Start of Winter 23 Lesser Snow
ren 壬 1 *zi* 子	*ren* 壬	7 Dec–21 Dec 22 Dec–4 Jan	11 11	*Da xue* *Dong zhi*	24 Great Snow 1 Winter Solstice
gui 癸 2 *chou* 丑	*gui* 癸	5 Jan–19 Jan 20 Jan–3 Feb	12 12	*Xiao Han* *Da Han*	2 Lesser Cold 3 Greater Cold

Appendix C | Narrow Sample of Delphic responses

The Broad Sample (330 responses) is based on Fontenrose's H and Q responses, eliminating responses with no clear question topic. It consists of 71 H oracles (eliminating H55, H61, H70, and H72) and 259 Q oracles (eliminating Q108, Q195, Q197, Q199, Q227, Q238, Q244, Q261, and Q264). Queries listed as multiple entries by Parke and Wormell but as single entries by Fontenrose are consolidated according to Fontenrose.

The Narrow Sample (100 responses) eliminates all quasi-historical oracles Fontenrose considers not genuine from the Broad Sample.

< before   > after   K. King   P personal query

PW	Font.	Consultor	Topic	Date	Type
123	H1	Athenians	public maintenance in Prytaneion	440–430	govt.
124	H2	Athenians	honors to Moirai, Zeus, Ge	430–420	cult
134	H3	Chaerophon	Is anyone wiser than Socrates?	< 430?	P other
136	H4	Epidamnians	war with Illyria	433	war
137	H5	Spartans	war with Athens	431	war
159	H6	Spartans	foundation of Heracleia	426	govt. colony
160	H7	Spartans	[bring back seed of Zeus' son]	427	cult
162	H8	Athenians	military defeats, restoration of Delians	421	war
164	H9	Athenians	first fruits at Eleusis	421–415	cult
165	H10	Athenians	cult of Apollo, exegete to Athenians	*c.* 420	cult
172	H11	Xenophon	to what god to sacrifice for safe return	401	P wellbeing
174	H12	Xenophon	tithe for Artemis left with him	394	cult
175	H13	K. Agesipolis of Sparta	*hosion* to accept preemptive truce	388	war cult
177	H14	Parians	authority to found a colony	> 385	govt. colony

PW	Font.	Consultor	Topic	Date	Type
178	H15	Clazomenae, Cyme	possessor of Leuke	> 383	cult
182	H16	Ionian league	transfer of Panionia to Ephesus	> 373	cult
256	H17	Delphians	Jason's presiding at Pythian games	370	cult
259	H18	Callistratus of Athens	after exile, obtaining law in Athens	*c.* 356	wellbeing
260	H19	Chalcidians, Macedon	treaty between Chalcidice and Philip	356	govt. treaty
261	H20	Philomedes of Phocis	Third Sacred War	> 355	war
262	H21	Athenians	letting lands in Eleusinian *orgas*	352/1	cult
265	H22	Unknown	prodigies, Philip's war against Amphissa	*c.* 340	war
277	H23	Halieis	epiphany of sacred snake of Asclepius	< 320	cult
278	H24	Athenians	Demon's house dedicated to Asclepius	*c.* 350	cult
279	H25	Isyllus the poet	whether to compose a paean to Apollo	338–335	P cult
280	H26	Cyrene	adopting a code of ritual regulations	*c.* 325	cult
281	H27	Athens or Acharnia	altars of Athena and Ares	4c	cult
282	H28	Athenians	welfare and prosperity of state	< 348	wellbeing
283	H29	Athenians	what god, after portent, for wellbeing	< 340	wellbeing
	H30	Athenians	proposal to honor Pluto	330	cult
284	H31	Amphictyony	work on temple	344/3	cult
	H32	Philodamus of Scarpheia	sanction for composition of hymn	344/3	P cult
285	H33	Athenians	improving *kosmoi* of goddess	335/4	cult
334	H34	a husband	personal, for children	*c.* 360	P domestic
330	H35	Amphictyony	*sōtēria* after victory against Gaul	*c.* 275	cult
335	H36	Poseidonus of Halicarnassus	family welfare	*c.* 250?	P wellbeing
336	H37	Unknown	sanction to honor Artemidorus	*c.* 250?	cult
341	H38	Cyzicenes	*sōtēria* festival for Kora Soteria	300	cult

PW	Font.	Consultor	Topic	Date	Type
342	H39	Cyzicenes	decision to honor certain gods	2c	cult
343	H40	Cyzicenes	decision to honor certain gods	2c	cult
344	H41	Tenus	honors to Poseidon	*c*. 250	cult
345	H42	Smyrna	*asylia* of city and Aphrodite sanctuary	246 or 242	cult
346	H43	Antichus (Chrysaoreis)	*asylia* of city	210–200	cult
	H44	Erythrai	establishing cults of several gods	< 250	cult
347	H45	Magnesia-on-Maender	festival in honor of Artemis	221/0	cult
348	H46	Teos	*asylia* of city	201	cult
351	H47	Eretrians	legislation voted by demos	210–200	govt.
354	H48	Rome	what god to pray for victory	216	*lusis* war
	H49	Anthister assoc.	on worship of Antitheter	210–200	cult
426	H50	Rhodian garrison, Tenos	sacrifice to various gods	*c*. 177	cult
416	H51	Dionysius	cult	176/5	cult
349	H52	Dionysiast society	*asylia* of Dionysiac artists	< 176	cult
340	H53	K. Dropion of Paines	personal?, dedicating a statue	*c*. 240	cult
427	H54	Timotheus of Anaphe	building a temple of Aphrodite	110/00	cult
429	H56	Parians	sacrifice for wellbeing of colony	*c*. 180	wellbeing
432	H57	Athenians	procession to Delphi for sacrifice	< 128	cult
437	H58	Genos of Athens	appointment of priest of Zeus	37–36	cult
457	H59	priest of Zeus, Palladion	a seat for Pallas at his own expense	27–14 CE	cult
459	H60	Parians	founding a cult of Asclepius Soter	+1–200	cult
462	H62	Dion Chrysostomos	on his course of life after exile	+85	P wellbeing
464	H63	priest of Heracles	absolution for violation of vows	+50–*c*. 100	P action
458	H64	Athenians	envoys to Delphi for ox-face sacrifice	+100–99	cult
465	H65	Emperor Hadrian	Homer's birthplace and parentage	+117–38	P other

PW	Font.	Consultor	Topic	Date	Type
466	H66	Athenians	on sanctuary of Demeter	+125	cult
467	H67	Unknown	appeasing Hera	+190–200	cult
471	H68	Cleitosthenes of Tralles	affliction of the land	+250	cult
473	H69	Amelios, Neo-Platonist	where soul of Plotinus has gone	+262	P other
350	H71	Megara	specification of *asylia*	*c.* 200	cult
176	H73	Tiribazus	revolt against Artaxerxes	>385	war
	H74	Mnesiepes	on cult	350–325	cult
274	H75	Athenians	refusal of Olympic misconduct fine	332–330	cult
21	Q8	Lycurgus	adoption of Lycurgan laws	700	govt.
561	Q11	Spartans	swearing oaths by Heracles	<500?	cult
539	Q12	K. Charilaus, Archelaus	allotting land to Apollo	*c.* 750?	cult
269	Q22	Messenians	bring Aristomes' bones to Ithome	>4c	cult
13	Q65	Athenians	*lusis*, plague	596	*lusis*
326	Q69	Solon of Athens	directions on sacrifices	*c.* 570	war cult
62	Q111	Athenians	colonizing Thracian Chersonese	*c.* 560	govt. colony
79	Q124	Spartans	any Spartan question [free Athens]	*c.* 510	war
80	Q125	Cleisthenes of Athens	eponyms for 10 tribes	510–509	govt.
87	Q137	Spartans	legitimacy of King Demaratus	*c.* 491	govt.
90	Q142	Athenians	apparition at the battle of Marathon	490	war cult
96	Q148	Delphians	Persian threat to all Hellas	480	*lusis* war
102	Q154	Athenians	for help against Mardonius	479	*lusis* war
104	Q156	Greeks	sacrifices after victory at Plataea	479	cult
105	Q157	Greeks	first fruits after Salamis	480/79	cult
117	Q167	Epizephyrian Locrians	omen, lightning striking statues	*c.* 470	cult
119	Q178	Delphians	Pindar's share of Apollo offerings	442–440	cult
132	Q187	Thurians	*oikist* [Apollo]	*c.* 433	cult
125	Q189	Athenians	Plague after Peloponnesian War	*c.* 430	*lusis*
158	Q190	Cleonaeans	relief from plague	430	*lusis*
253	Q205	Thebans	battle at Leuctra	371	war

PW	Font.	Consultor	Topic	Date	Type
555	Q222	Spartans	on cult	< 300?	cult
356	Q237	Rome	Sybilline oracle promising victory	205	war *nikē*
337	Q241	Methymnaeans	what god or hero is found image	*c.* 200?	P cult
430	Q244	K. Perseus of Macedon	portents or omens	174	cult
549	Q266	Spartans	[establish a foot race]	< 300?	cult
550	Q267	citizens of Alea	[flog women at Dion festival]	< 300?	cult

Appendix D | Selected *Zuo zhuan* prognostications

Military divinations

- 563. *Zuo* 978–79 (Xiang 10.5, Legge 447) and 1013 (Xiang 14.4, Legge 465–66, cf. *LNZ* 1.5b). Prognostication by Sun Wenzi of Wei (see Chapter 7) reveals the wisdom of the dowager Lady Ding Jiang and the moral failings of her stepson Duke Xian. The Wei minister Sun Wenzi accepts her crack-reading and her predictions of military and political ruin in Wei; the *Zuo zhuan* verifies her predictions with a detailed account of Duke Xian's loss of Wei.
- *Zuo* 885 and 890 (Cheng 16.5, Legge 397–98), cf. 860–67 (Cheng 13, Legge 379–83), 872–77 (Cheng 15, Legge 385–89), and 885. The Marquis of Jin consulted milfoil after crossing the Yellow River and unexpectedly encountering a force from Chu. He reversed an earlier disinclination to fight because he interpreted the auspicious hexagram Fu 復 (no. 24) as a prediction of victory (Jin's defeat of Chu in the battle of Yanling in 575).
- 536. *Zuo* 1271 (Zhao 5.8), Legge 606. The king of Wu consults the turtle shell about an impending invasion by Chu. Wu sends a messenger to observe the Chu forces in order to prepare appropriately. Chu forces capture the Wu prince, and the Chu king's fury and execution of his captive show Chu's true colors. The prince emphasizes that the consultor was the state, not himself personally. His capture and death were part of the recommended action, and in no way contradicted the result.
- 524. *Zuo* 1392 (Zhao 17.6), Legge 668. Wu had invaded Chu in 524, twelve years after Chu's capture of the Wu prince (discussed above). The Chu minister had prognosticated the battle (*bu zhan* 卜戰) and received an inauspicious result. The commander Ziyi objected that their strong military position *should* yield a victory. He requests to take control of the procedure, on grounds that, in Chu custom, the Sima (his own office) has charge of the turtle shell. Ziyi then reprognosticates, with a differently phrased question. This time the response is that victory is possible if the army persists, even if Ziyi and his followers are killed. This incident resembles a situation described in Chapter 6, in which a temple diviner

deflects an unacceptably negative result by finding a ritually appropriate way to repeat the procedure. But it is noteworthy that Ziyi does not reject the divination (as did Duke Hui, above). There is no guarantee that the second outcome will be any more to his liking than the first. In other words, as in the personal consultations described in Chapter 7, there is a negotiation of the results. Interestingly, the *Zuo zhuan* narrative also finds a way to negotiate the contradiction between the two results. It reports that Ziyi and his men did die, but Chu won a great victory, including the capture of a sacred vessel, confirming the second response. However, when the Wu forces tried to retrieve the sacred vessel, the Chu army became confused and were routed, confirming the first response. Thus both prognostications were fulfilled.

- 487. *Zuo* 1653 (Ai 9.6), Legge 819. Jin used turtle and milfoil to decide whether to attack Song (they were dissuaded).
- 473. *Zuo* 1721 (Ai 23.2), Legge 854. Jin had invaded Qi. On the eve of battle, Chang Wuzi of Jin wanted to read the cracks. The Jin commander replied that the king of Jin had already performed turtle shell divination in the ancestral temple with the shell reserved for that purpose. It was propitious so there was no need to divine further.

Dreams

- The *Zuo zhuan* describes some two dozen accounts of oneiromancy, performed by physicians, *wu* spirit mediums, and astrologers (*shi*), sometimes with the aid of other methods.[1] Most appear to rulers, princes, or ministers, and concern five topics: (1) divine epiphanies, (2) premonitions of illness or death, (3) the meaning of past events, (4) questions about royal succession, and (5) military victory. The few reported dreams of commoners also address state concerns. Some *Zuo zhuan* dreams predict illness or impending death or transmit advice or information from the dead. A spirit or ancestor may appear to request sacrifice. Others explain the meaning of past events, use puns or anomalies to alert the dreamer to important signs of future events, or predict the fortunes of progeny and recommend the choice of succession. Some make specific requests of the dreamer, for example an order to secure the succession for a particular individual. In some accounts, women's dreams predict the fortunes of as yet unborn children.

[1] Early Chinese dream divination: *Siku quanshu zongmu* 111.53b–55a; Strickmann 1988; Ong 1985: esp. 2–5, 11–20, 35–36, 40–41, 74–108; Brennan 1993. *Zuo zhuan*: Yang Jianmin 1993.

- Dreams about warfare predict military outcomes or give advice, but oneiromancy seems to play a small role in military divination.[2] By contrast, a Ming military encyclopedia contains a section on dream omens, but it is part of a comprehensive catalog of all types of military divination.[3] Dream divination seems to assume greater importance in later periods.[4]

Divine epiphanies

- *Zuo* 295–300 (Xi 4.6), Legge 142. The stepmother of Prince Shensheng of Jin claims that his father Duke Xian has dreamed of his dead mother. Her request that Shensheng offer sacrifices to his mother's spirit is the beginning of the plot that ends in his betrayal and suicide. She poisons the sacrificial meat he sends to his father; the discovery of the poisoned meat forces his suicide.

Illness or impending death

- *Zuo* 849 (Cheng 10.4), Legge 374. Duke Huan of Jin dreamed that a demon accused him of murdering its descendants, broke into the palace, and pursued him from the chamber of state. He consults a spirit medium, who recounts the entire dream and predicts his death. He became ill and sent for a physician from Qin. Before his arrival, Duke Huan had another dream in which his illness manifests as two boys debating how to evade the skilled physician. The physician also predicts death.

Explanations of past events

- *Zuo* 763–64 (Xuan 15.5), Legge 328. Prince Ke 顆 of Wei 魏 dreamed of an old man whose skillfully made ropes had helped him win a victory against Qin. The man explains that this victory is a recompense for Ke's

[2] There is one reference in the *Jin shu* (1:10) to using dream omens (*meng zhao* 夢兆) for military prognostication. The *Song shi* recounts a discussion of dream omens and their political import (455.13,373) and an incident in which a dream omen identifies a murderer (460.13,484).

[3] Fan Jingwen, *Zhan shou quan shu* 18: 37ab, cf. Yates 2005: 22–24. The omens vary by both the status of the dreamer and the content of the dream. Like some techniques of cloud divination, they link figural dream elements with specific predictions. For example, a dream of violent water in turbid waves is a sign to refrain from fighting (no. 8), but soldiers dreaming of water portends good auspice at the start of battle (no. 1) and a general dreaming of entering the sea portends the marching of troops (no. 2).

[4] See R. J. Smith 1991, Chen Meiying et al. 1995, Huang Yi-Long 1998, Liu Wenying 2000, and Drettas 2007.

saving the life of his daughter, the king's favorite concubine. Ke had disregarded instructions to sacrifice her after his father's death, and had found her a suitable husband instead.

Portents and anomalies

- *Zuo* 1256–59 (Zhao 4.8), Legge 599. In 538 Shusun Bao 叔孫豹 of Lu 魯 was forced into exile. He slept with a woman and dreamed that the sky came down on him and he could not hold it up. He was saved by a dark hump-backed man with a pig's mouth named Ox (*niu* 牛). There was no such man among his followers, but he recorded the description. Many years later, when he had returned to Lu, the woman sent him their son Niu (ox), who prevented his stepbrothers from starving their father to death for opposing them.[5]
- *Zuo* 1644–45 (Ai 7.5), Legge 814. In 488, shortly before Song forces were besieging the capital of Cao, a commoner from Cao dreamed that several men were consulting in the temple of Cao about the ruin of the state. One was the first earl of Cao, who begged them to wait for Gongsun Jiang 公孫彊. The next day the man sought for anyone named Gongsun Jiang, but could find no such person. He warned his son to flee Cao if he ever heard of an official of that name. Years later, a Gongsun Jiang became minister of works, and the son fled Cao, which was invaded by Song. Cf. *Zuo* 1513–14 (Zhao 31.6, Legge 738) and 1709–10 (Ai 17.5, Legge 850).

Royal succession

- *Zuo* 1286–87 (Zhao 7.3), Legge 616–17; 535. Kong Chengzi 孔成子 of Wei 衛 dreamed of Duke Xiang 襄 (r. 543–535 BCE), the first marquis of Wei. At the time of his death, his wife was childless but his favorite concubine had a son, and in the dream Duke Xiang ordered Kong Chengzi to secure the succession for the concubine's yet unborn grandson. When the boy was born, Kong used *Yi* divination to verify his superiority to a less meritorious prince.
- *Zuo* 1297–98 (Zhao 7.15), Legge 619–20. After the death of Duke Jing of Song 宋景公 (r. 516–469), one of his ministers usurped the throne. His adopted son has a dream that was interpreted to mean that he would succeed to the state.

5 See Li Wai-yee 1999: 35.

- *Zuo* 674–75 (Xuan 3.6), Legge 294. A concubine dreams that Heaven presented her with a *lan* 蘭 flower and foretold a brilliant future for a son named Lan.
- *Zuo* 1217–23 (Zhao 1.12), Legge 580. The wife of King Wu dreams of a spirit who predicts the birth of her son (King Yu) and even names his minister (Cheng Tang).
- *Zuo* 1324–25 (Zhao 11.4), Legge 634. An unnamed commoner dreams of making a tent for the Meng family temple out of her curtains. She seeks out the Lu nobleman Meng Xizi 孟僖子, who makes her an assistant to his concubine, and eventually has two sons by her.

Dreams about military victory

- *Zuo* 467–68 (Xi 28.4), Legge 209–10. Before the battle of Chengpu in 632 both antagonists dream of the impending battle. Duke Wen of Jin dreams that his rival Ziyu beats him and sucks out his brains. Ziyu of Chu dreams that the Yellow River offers him victory in exchange for his jewelled cap. He refuses, and loses.
- *Zuo* 793–95 (Cheng 2.3), Legge 345. Before the battle of An in 589 Han Jue of Jin dreamed that his father told him what strategy to use in the impending battle. He used it and defeated the forces of Qi.
- *Zuo* 1389–90 (Zhao 17.4), Legge 668. Xuanzi 宣子 of Jin dreamed that Duke Wen gave him victory over Lu Hun 陸渾, who had sworn allegiance to Chu.
- *Zuo* 886–87 (Cheng 16.5), Legge 397. Lu Qi 呂錡 dreamed that he hit the moon with an arrow but became caught in a mire while returning. He shot the king of Chu in battle, but was himself killed.

Appendix E | The Baoshan divinations

Formulaic structure

According to Li Ling, the Baoshan prognostications use a formulaic structure that dates back to the oracle bone inscriptions. Like Shang and Western Zhou prognostications, they use structured mantic formulae, including a preface, charge or topic, and prediction or prognostication.

1. Preface (*xuci* 序辭): date of the divination and the name of diviner.
2. Charge (*mingci* 命辭): purpose or topic of the divination, which resulted in:
3. Prognostication (*zhanci* 占辭) and
4. Verification (*yanci* 驗辭) or postface (*houci* 後辭): place and date of events in the lunar calendar and liturgic cycle.

Additional charges and prognostications specified detailed sacrifices to Chu gods and ancestors, and instructions for future prognostications.[1]

Year divinations

The Year divinations from Baoshan take the general form:

自 X 之月以庚 X 之月，出入事王， 盡卒歲，盡集歲躬身尚毋又(有)咎。

From month X [this year] to month X of next year, for the whole of the year, coming and going [lit. exiting and entering] in service to the king, for the entire year, may his [physical] person be without calamity.[2]

For example, the first Year divination from Baoshan occurs in 318:

自刑 尸之月以庚刑尸之月，出入事王，盡卒歲，躬身尚母又(有)咎。

[1] Oracle bone formulae: Keightley 1978b: 37; Zhang Bingquan 1960, 1967: 868–70. On Chu inscriptions: Li Ling 1990: 81, 1993: 259–61.

[2] Slips 197–98, 199–200, and 201–4 in 318; slips 209–11, 212–15, and 216–17 in 317; slips 230–31, 232–33, 234–35, 236–38, and 239–40 in 316.

From [this year's month] Xingyi up to the next Xingyi, coming and going [lit. exiting and entering] in service to the king, for the entire year, may his [physical] person be without calamity.[3]

Illness divinations

The Baoshan Illness divinations begin:

傍腹疾，以少氣，尚毋又(有)咎。占之，貞吉，少未已，以其古(故)祝之。薦於野地主一豭，宮地主一豭，賽於行一白犬、酒食，占之曰：吉，刑尸且見王。

There is an illness near the abdomen with shortness of breath; may there be no calamity. He prognosticated about it: the prognostication is auspicious; it is slight but it has not stopped; get rid of it according to its cause. He made offerings: one billy goat to the Lord of the Wild Lands, one billy goat to the Lord of the Grave. He performed *sai* [repayment] sacrifice to the Lord of the Path [Xing] with one white dog and wine oblations. He prognosticated about it: it is auspicious. In the month *xingyi* he [Shao Tuo] will have an audience with the king.[4]

Subsequent prognostications indicate a worsening condition, possibly (but not necessarily) deriving from the initial ailment:

(2) [傍]心疾，少氣，不内(入)食 . . . 尚毋有恙。
There is an ailment in the lower abdomen with shortness of breath; he is not able to take in food. May there be no concern (slips 221 and 223).

(3) 既腹心疾，以上氣，不甘 食，舊不瘥。
There is an ailment of the abdomen and heart along with rising *qi* and a bad taste [to food]; and there has been no improvement for a long time (slips 236, 239, 242, 245, 247).[5]

(4) 以其有瘴病，上氣，尚毋死。
There is a miasmal illness and rising *qi*; may he not die (slip 249).[6]

[3] *Baoshan*, slips 197–98. This passage presents many complications and controversies. I primarily follow Li Ling 1990 and 2000c, Chen Wei 1996, and Cook 2006, which contains an excellent and accessible account of the philological issues. I follow the *Baoshan Chujian* transcription as much as possible. In some cases I have used modern orthography to render what in the original were compound graphs (e.g. 之月, 躬身) or have used later equivalents of Chu script characters (e.g. *xing* 刑 for a Chu graph consisting of *xing* 刑 with the element *tian* 田 under it and *shi* 尸 for the Chu graph consisting of *shi* 尸 with the element *shi* 示 under it). My translation follows Chen Wei (1996: 231). He transcribes *geng* 庚 as *di* 帝 and reads it as *shi* 適, "to go."

[4] *Baoshan*, slips 207–8. This repeats in four entries dated to the eleventh month of the same year (month *cuan*, day *jiyou*, slips 218 and 220).

[5] These five entries are from the fourth month of 316 (month *xingyi*, day *jimao*).

[6] This entry is from the fifth month of that year (month *xiayi*, day *jihai*). For *zhang* 瘴 see Chen Wei 1996: 154.

At one point (2), there is disagreement on whether to perform an exorcism. Five months later (3), five diviners performed Year and Illness divinations alternating between turtle and milfoil. They specify elaborate sacrifices; all consider the ailment due to the influence of ghosts or spirits, but they disagree on which. One attributes it to the god Year, others to curses: of war dead, flood victims, or the innocent dead. A month later (4), after a crisis, a new diviner is introduced. The final entry records Shao Tuo's date of interment.

Appendix F | Selections from the Shuihudi daybooks

Calendar Table for a *chu* 除 year, *SHD* (Daybook A), slips 1–25 (pp. 180–81)

Trans. after Poo Mu-chou 2009, cf. Liu Lexian 1994: 21–27 and Loewe 1994: 219–20.

- The far right column of the upper register gives the months of the year by their position in the Twenty-eight Lunar Lodges for that year. The first row lists the twelve characters of the *jianchu* series from right to left, starting with *jian*. (In some cases the text uses variant graphs for elements of the series.)
- The lower register of each column contains a phrase for that column. It describes that type of day as broadly auspicious (*ji*), inauspicious (*xiong*), or suitable for some particular activity such as travel, marriage, etc. The table lists the days of the sexagenary cycle, ordered by the Twelve Earth Branches, starting with *zi* in the upper right-hand corner. (1r through 13r in the last row of the table: in the Chinese original these entries are written vertically.)
- A prognostication for a *zi* day illustrates the use of the chart. A *zi* day in the eleventh month would take the prognostication for the *kai* 開 column (no. 1). But a *zi* day in the twelfth month would use the *shou* 收 column (no. 12); in the sixth month it would use the *ping* 平 column (no. 6), in the ninth month, the *jian* 建 prognostication (no. 3), and in the first month the prognostication from the *cheng* 成 column (no. 11). Similarly a *hai* day would take the prognostication from the *ping* column in the fifth month (no. 6), etc. However, because the days in the table are identified only by the Earth Branch (rather than by a stem–branch combination), each branch day occurs several times in any month. An additional table would be used to determine which earth branches corresponded to each day of the month. Other sections of the daybooks are organized around particular activities.

Upper register

shou 收 [甬]	*cheng* 成	*wei* 危 [蓋]	*bo* 柀 [坐]	*zhi* 執 [空]	*ding* 定 [寧]	*ping* 平	*ying* 盈 [彼]	*chu* 除 [陷]	*jian* 建	*bi* 閉 [羸]	*kai* 開 [濡]	Month & Lunar Lodge
12 *hai* 亥	11 *xu* 戌	10 *you* 酉	9 *shen* 申	8 *wei* 未	7 *wu* 午	6 *si* 巳	5 *chen* 辰	4 *mao* 卯	3 *yin* 寅	2 *chou* 丑	1 *zi* 子	11 斗 Dipper
1 *zi* 子	12 *hai* 亥	11 *xu* 戌	10 *you* 酉	9 *shen* 申	8 *wei* 未	7 *wu* 午	6 *si* 巳	5 *chen* 辰	4 *mao* 卯	3 *yin* 寅	2 *chou* 丑	12 女 Girl
2 *chou* 丑	1 *zi* 子	12 *hai* 亥	11 *xu* 戌	10 *you* 酉	9 *shen* 申	8 *wei* 未	7 *wu* 午	6 *si* 巳	5 *chen* 辰	4 *mao* 卯	3 *yin* 寅	1營 Camp
3 *yin* 寅	2 *chou* 丑	1 *zi* 子	12 *hai* 亥	11 *xu* 戌	10 *you* 酉	9 *shen* 申	8 *wei* 未	7 *wu* 午	6 *si* 巳	5 *chen* 辰	4 *mao* 卯	2 奎 Legs
4 *mao* 卯	3 *yin* 寅	2 *chou* 丑	1 *zi* 子	12 *hai* 亥	11 *xu* 戌	10 *you* 酉	9 *shen* 申	8 *wei* 未	7 *wu* 午	6 *si* 巳	5 *chen* 辰	3胃 Stomach
5 *chen* 辰	4 *mao* 卯	3 *yin* 寅	2 *chou* 丑	1 *zi* 子	12 *hai* 亥	11 *xu* 戌	10 *you* 酉	9 *shen* 申	8 *wei* 未	7 *wu* 午	6 *si* 巳	4 畢 Net
6 *si* 巳	5 *chen* 辰	4 *mao* 卯	3 *yin* 寅	2 *chou* 丑	1 *zi* 子	12 *hai* 亥	11 *xu* 戌	10 *you* 酉	9 *shen* 申	8 *wei* 未	7 *wu* 午	5 東 East
7 *wu* 午	6 *si* 巳	5 *chen* 辰	4 *mao* 卯	3 *yin* 寅	2 *chou* 丑	1 *zi* 子	12 *hai* 亥	11 *xu* 戌	10 *you* 酉	9 *shen* 申	8 *wei* 未	6 柳 Willow

Upper register (contd.)

8 *wei* 未	7 *wu* 午	6 *si* 巳	5 *chen* 辰	4 *mao* 卯	3 *yin* 寅	2 *chou* 丑	1 *zi* 子	12 *hai* 亥	11 *xu* 戌	10 *you* 酉	9 *shen* 申	7 張 Extend
9 *shen* 申	8 *wei* 未	7 *wu* 午	6 *si* 巳	5 *chen* 辰	4 *mao* 卯	3 *yin* 寅	2 *chou* 丑	1 *zi* 子	12 *hai* 亥	11 *xu* 戌	10 *you* 酉	8 角 Horn
10 *you* 酉	9 *shen* 申	8 *wei* 未	7 *wu* 午	6 *si* 巳	5 *chen* 辰	4 *mao* 卯	3 *yin* 寅	2 *chou* 丑	1 *zi* 子	12 *hai* 亥	11 *xu* 戌	9 氐 Root
11 *xu* 戌	10 *you* 酉	9 *shen* 申	8 *wei* 未	7 *wu* 午	6 *si* 巳	5 *chen* 辰	4 *mao* 卯	3 *yin* 寅	2 *chou* 丑	1 *zi* 子	12 *hai* 亥	10 心 Heart
no. 12	no. 11	no. 10	no. 9	no. 8	no. 7	no. 6	no. 5	no. 4	no. 3	no. 2	no. 1	
Lower Register												
13r	12r	11r	10r	9r	8r	7r	6r	5r	4r	3r	2r	1r

1r 不可用者，秋三月辰，冬三月未，春三月戌，夏三月亥〈丑〉。
Days [branch types] that cannot be used: autumn, *chen* days in the third month; winter, *wei* days in the third month; spring, *wu* days in the third month; summer, *hai* [*chou*] days in the third month.

2r 結日，作事不成，以祭閵（吝）。生子無弟，有弟必死。以寄人，寄人必奪主室。
Jie day [no. 1]: Doing matters of business is not successful. For making sacrifice, not auspicious. If a son is born he will have no younger brothers; if he has a younger brother he [the brother] will be sure to die. If you permit a guest into your house, the house guest will be sure to occupy your house by force.

3r 陽日，百事順成。邦郡得年，小夫四成。以祭，上下群神饗之，乃盈志。
Yang day [no. 2]: All affairs succeed without obstacle. Country and prefecture achieve yearly harvests; ordinary people successful in every way. For sacrifice, above and below all the spirits will be nourished and they will be satisfied.

4r 交日，利以實事。鑿井，吉。以祭門行、行水，吉。
Jiao day [no. 3]: Beneficial for matters of commerce. Digging a well: auspicious. For sacrifice to the gods of the Door, the Path, and the Boat: auspicious.

5r 害日，利以除凶（厲），說不祥。祭門行，吉。以祭，最眾必亂者。
Hai day [no. 4]: Beneficial for driving out inauspicious demons and for expelling inauspicious things. For making sacrifice to the [gods of the] Door and the Path: auspicious. When sacrificing: if crowds gather there will surely be disorder.

6r 陰日，利以家室。祭祀、家子、 娶婦、入材，大吉。以見君上，數達，無咎。
Yin day [no. 5]: Beneficial for family matters. Ancestral sacrifice, marrying daughters, taking a wife, bringing in materials: greatly auspicious. For an audience with a superior, many successes and no harm.

7r 達日，利以行師出征，見人。 以祭，上下皆吉。生子，男吉，女必出於邦。
Da day [no. 6]: Beneficial for marshalling troops, marching out the army, audiences with others. For sacrifice: above and below, all auspicious. If a son is born: auspicious, if a daughter, she will be sure to depart from the country.

8r 外陽日，利以建野外，可以田邋（獵）。以亡，不得，□門。
Waiyang day [no. 7]: Beneficial for going to the fields, it is permissible to hunt in the fields. For desertion, he will not be caught . . . the door.

9r 外害日，不可以行作。之四方野外，必耦（遇）寇盜，見兵。
Waihai day [no. 8]: It is not permissible to do work, when you arrive in the countryside in any direction you will be sure to meet with robbers and see soldiers.

10r 外陰日，利以祭祀。作事、入材，皆吉。不可以之野外。
Waiyin day [no. 9]: Beneficial for sacrifice. Doing business, bringing in materials: all auspicious. It is not permissible to go to the countryside.

11r □□□□□ 可名曰□（擊）日，以生子，窶孤。□人，不得。利以說盟詛、百不祥。
[*Jueji* day] [no. 10]: . . . can be named a "contest" day: if a son is born, he will be poor and an orphan. In . . . people there will be no gain. Beneficial for exorcizing curses and all kinds of inauspicious things.

12r 夬光日，利以登高、飲食、獵四方野外。居有食，行有得。以生子，男女必美。
Jueguang day [no. 11]: Beneficial for climbing mountains, feasting, hunting in the countryside in the west. There is food in the house, if you travel there will be gain. If a child is born, boy or girl, it will be beautiful.

13r 秀日，利以起大事。大祭，吉。冠，掣車，折衣裳，服帶吉。生子吉，弟凶。
Xiu day [no. 12]: Beneficial for commencing great matters. Grand sacrifice: auspicious. Capping ceremony, pulling chariots, folding garments, and wearing belts: auspicious. If a child is born: auspicious, for a younger brother, inauspicious.

From "Stars and Constellations" (*Xing*), *SHD* (Daybook A), slips 68–94 (pp. 191–92)

Trans. after Poo Mu-chou 2009, cf. Liu Lexian 1994: 109–16.

68 角，利祠及行，吉。不可蓋屋。取妻，妻妒。生子，為吏。
Horn: beneficial for ancestral sacrifice and also for travel, auspicious. It is not permitted to roof buildings. For marriage: the wife will be jealous. Children will become officials.

70 氐，祠及行、出入貨，吉。取妻，妻貧。生子，巧。
Root: for sacrifice and travel, for commerce: auspicious. Marriage: the wife will be poor. Children: skillful.

71 房，取婦、嫁女、出入貨及祠，吉。可為室屋。生子，富。
Room: for taking a wife, giving a daughter in marriage, commerce, or sacrifice: auspicious. Construction is permitted. Children: wealthy.

72 心，不可祠及行，凶。可以行水。取妻，妻悍。生子，人愛之。
Heart: it is not permitted to sacrifice or travel: inauspicious. Travel by water is permitted. For marriage: the wife will be ferocious. Children: people will love them.

74 箕，不可祠。百事凶。取妻，妻多舌。生子，貧富半。
Basket: sacrifice is not permitted. Business matters: inauspicious. For marriage: the wife will be talkative. Children: half will be poor, half rich.

75 斗，利祠及行賈、賈市，吉。取妻，妻為巫。生子，不盈三歲死。可以攻伐。
Dipper: beneficial for sacrifice, also for business travel, markets: auspicious. For marriage, the wife will become a *wu*. Children: within three years they will die. Invasions are permitted.

80 營室，利祠。不可為室及入之。以取妻，妻不寧。生子，為大吏。
Encampment: beneficial for sacrifice, construction and entering buildings not permitted. For marriage, the wife will be restless. Children: great officials.

91 柳，百事吉。取妻，吉。以生子，肥。可以寇〈冠〉，可請謁，可田獵。
Willow: auspicious for business. For marriage, auspicious. Children will be fecund. Permissible for capping ceremony, requesting an audience, hunting in the fields.

94 翼，利行。不可藏。以祠，必有火起。取妻，必棄。生子，男為覡，女為巫。
Wings: beneficial for travel. Storing away is not permitted. For sacrifice, the fire will flare up. Marriage, she is sure to be abandoned. Children: a boy will become a *xi* [spirit medium], a girl will become a *wu*.

From "Taking a Wife or Marrying a Daughter," *SHD* (Daybook A), slips 2v–9v (pp. 208–9)

Trans. after Poo Mu-chou 2009, cf. Liu Lexian 1994: 204–12.

2v 癸丑、戊午、己未，禹以取梌山之女日也，不棄，必以子死。
Days *guichou*, *wuwu*, *jiwei*: "Yu married the Tushan girl" days. If she is not abandoned, she will be sure to die in childbirth.

3v 戊申、己酉，牽牛以取織女而不果，不出三歲，棄若亡。
Days *wushen* and *jiyou*: the Herd Boy tried to wed the Weaver Girl and did not succeed. Before three years have passed, she will be abandoned or dead.

4v 壬辰、癸巳，囊婦以出，夫先死，不出二歲。[1]
Days *renchen* and *guisi*: he will reject his wife and throw her out; if she does not die first, she will die before two years have passed.

5v 庚辰、辛巳，敝毛之士以取妻，不死，棄。
Days *gengchen* and *xinsi*: a shabby-haired official takes a wife; if she does not die, she will be abandoned.

6v 凡取妻、出女之日，冬三月奎、婁吉。以奎，夫愛妻；以婁，妻愛夫。
Days for taking a wife or marrying a daughter: in the third month of winter the Lunar Lodges *Kui* [Legs] and *Lou* [Bond] are auspicious. With *Kui* the husband will love the wife, with *Lou* the wife will love the husband.

7v 壬申、癸酉，天以震高山，以取妻，不居，不吉。
Renshen and *guiyou*: Heaven shakes the high mountains; for marriage, no dwelling, not auspicious.

8v 甲子、午、庚辰、丁巳，不可取妻、嫁子。
Jiazi, *wu*, *gengchen*, *dingsi*: it is not permitted to take a wife or marry a daughter.

9v 甲寅之旬，不可取妻，無子。雖有，無男。
The *Jiayin* decad: it is not permitted to take a wife, there will be no children, or if there are there will be no boys.

2v 直參以出女，室必盡。
Through [the lodge] *Shen*: for marrying a daughter the dwelling will be depleted.

[1] Reading *nang* 囊 as *rang* 攘, cf. *SHD* (Daybooks): S 209 n. 4.

3v 直營室以出女，父母必從居。
Through [the lodge] Encampment: for marrying a daughter, the parents will be sure to move from the dwelling.

4v 直牽牛、須女出女，父母有咎。
Through [lodges] Herdboy and *Xunü*: marrying a daughter, the parents will have calamities.

6v 凡參、翼、軫以出女，丁巳以出女，皆棄之。
If you marry a daughter in the [lodges] Shen, Wings, and Chariot Platform or on the day *dingsi*, in all these cases she will be abandoned.

Childbirth Prognostications, *SHD* (Daybook A), slips 140–49 (pp. 202–5)

Trans. after Poo Mu-chou 2009, cf. Liu Lexian 1994: 179–86.

Day 1	甲戌生子，飲食急。 A child born on *Jiaxu*: hasty in food and drink.
Day 2	乙亥生子，穀而富。A child born on *Yihai*: happy and wealthy.
Day 3	丙子生子，不吉。A child born on *Bingzi*: inauspicious.
Day 4	丁丑生子，好言語，或生（眚）於目。A child born on *Dingchou* will love to talk and . . . will grow on his eye.
Day 5	戊寅生子，去父母南。A child born on *Wuyin* will leave his parents and go south.
Day 6	己卯生子，去其邦。A child born on *Jimao* will leave his home.
Day 7	庚辰生子，好女子。A child born on *Gengchen* will love women.
Day 8	辛巳生子，吉而富。A child born on *Xinsi*: auspicious and wealthy.
Day 9	壬午生子，穀而武。A child born on *Renwu*: happy and martial.
Day 10	癸未生子，長大，善得。A child born on *Guiwei*: very tall, good at success.
Day 11	甲申生子，巧，有身事。A child born on *Jiashen*: skilled, he will have an occupation.
Day 12	乙酉生子，穀，好樂。A child born on *Yiyou*: happy, he will love pleasure.
Day 13	丙戌生子，有事。A child born on *Bingxu* will have an occupation.
Day 14	丁亥生子，工巧，孝。 A child born on *Dinghai*: a skilled worker, filial.
Day 15	戊子生子，去其邦北。 A child born on *Wuzi* will leave his home and go north.

Day 16	己丑生子，貧而疾。A child born on *Jichou*: poor and sickly.
Day 17	庚寅生子，女為賈，男好衣佩而貴。 A child born on *Gengyin*: a girl will become a merchant; a boy will love clothes and ornament and will receive honors.
Day 18	辛卯生子，吉及穀。A child born on *Xinmao*: auspicious and also happy.
Day 19	壬辰生子，武而好衣劍。A child born on *Renchen*: martial and will love clothes and swords.
Day 20	癸巳生子，穀。A child born on *Guisi*: happy.
Day 21	甲午生子，武有力，少孤。A child born on *Jiawu*: martial and strong, orphaned young.
Day 22	乙未生子，有疾，少孤，後富。A child born on *Yiwei*: he will be sickly, orphaned young, later wealthy.
Day 23	丙申生子，好家室。A child born on *Bingshen* will love family.
Day 24	丁酉生子，嗜酒。A child born on *Dingyou*: a tippler.
Day 25	戊戌生子，好田野邑屋。A child born on *Wuxu* will love fields and houses.
Day 26	己亥生子，穀。A child born on *Jihai*: happy.
Day 27	庚子生子，少孤，污。A child born on *Gengzi*: orphaned young, filthy.
Day 28	辛丑生子，有（心）終。A child born on *Xinchou* will have a heart and . . .
Day 29	壬寅生子，不吉，女為醫。A child born on *Renyin*: inauspicious, a girl will become a physician.
Day 30	癸卯生子，不吉。A child born on *Guimao*: inauspicious.
Day 31	甲辰生子，穀，且武而利弟。A child born on *Jiachen*: happy, he will also be martial and will benefit a younger brother.
Day 32	乙巳生子，吉。 A child born on *Yisi*: auspicious.
Day 33	丙午生子，嗜酒而疾，後富。A child born on *Bingwu*: a tippler and sickly, later wealthy.
Day 34	丁未生子，不吉，無母，必嘗繫囚。A child born on *Dingwei*: inauspicious, no mother, sure to be imprisoned.
Day 35	戊申生子，寵，事君。A child born on *Wushen* will be adored, will serve a lord.
Day 36	己酉生子，穀，有商。A child born on *Jiyou*: happy, he will have a business.
Day 37	庚戌生子，武而貧。A child born on *Gengxu*: martial and poor.
Day 38	辛亥生子，不吉。A child born on *Xinhai*: inauspicious.
Day 39	壬子生子，勇。A child born on *Renzi*: brave.

Day 40	癸丑生子，好水，少疾，必為吏。A child born on *Guichou* will love water, sickly when young, sure to be a clerk.
Day 41	甲寅生子，必為吏。A child born on *Jiayin*: sure to be a clerk.
Day 42	乙卯生子，要 (腰) . . . A child born on *Yimao* will . . .
Day 43	丙辰生子，有疵於（體）而勇 。 A child born on *Bingchen* will have a mole on [the body] and will be brave.
Day 44	丁巳生子，穀而美，有 . . . A child born on *Dingsi*: happy and beautiful and will have . . .
Day 45	戊午生子，嗜酒及田獵。 A child born on *Wuwu* will love wine and hunting in the fields.
Day 46	己未生子，吉。A child born on *Jiwei*: auspicious.
Day 47	庚申生子，良。A child born on *Gengshen*: good.
Day 48	辛酉生子，不吉。 A child born on *Xinyou*: inauspicious.
Day 49	壬戌生子，好家室。 A child born on *Renxu* will love his family.
Day 50	癸亥生子，無終。 A child born on *Guihai* will have no . . .
Day 51	甲子生子，少孤，衣污。 A child born on *Jiazi*: orphaned young, filthy clothes.
Day 52	乙丑生子，武以工巧。A child born on *Yichou*: martial and will become a skillful artisan.
Day 53	丙寅生子，武以聖。A child born on *Bingyin*: martial and will become sagely.
Day 54	丁卯生子，不正，乃有疵前。A child born on *Dingmao*: not upright and will have a mole on the forehead.
Day 55	戊辰生子，有寵。A child born on *Wuchen* will be adored.
Day 56	己巳生子鬼，必為人臣妾。A child born on *Jisi*: ghostly, sure to become a servant.
Day 57	庚午生子，貧，有力，先〈□〉冬（終）。. . . A child born on *Gengwu*: poor, strong, will . . . before . . .
Day 58	辛未生子，肉食。 A child born on *Xinwei* will eat meat.
Day 59	壬申生子，聞。A child born on *Renshen*: famous.
Day 60	癸酉生子，先〈□〉冬（終）。 A child born on *Guiyou* will . . . before . . .

Bibliography

(Abbreviations and conventions are listed on pp. xvi–xxv.)

Ahern, E. M. (1981) *Chinese Ritual and Politics*. Cambridge.

Ai Lan 艾蘭 (S. Allan) and Xing Wen 邢文 (eds.) (2004) *Xin chu jian bo yan jiu* 新出簡帛研究 [Studies on recently discovered Chinese manuscripts]. Beijing.

Allan, S. (1991) *The Shape of the Turtle: Myth, Art, and Cosmos in Early China*. Albany.

Amandry, P. (1939) "Convention religieuse conclue entre Delphes et Skiathos," *BCH* **63**: 86–119.

(1950) *La Mantique apollonienne à Delphes: Essai sur le fonctionnement de l'Oracle*. Paris.

Ames, R. T. and D. L. Hall (2001) *Focusing the Familiar: A Translation and Philosophical Interpretation of the Zhongyong*. Honolulu. See Hall and Ames 1995.

Anagnost, A. S. (1987) "Politics and magic in contemporary China," *Modern China* **13**: 41–61.

Arnush, M. (2005) "Pilgrimage to the oracle of Apollo at Delphi: patterns of public and private consultation," in *Pilgrimage in Graeco-Roman and Early Christian Antiquity: Seeing the Gods*, ed. J. Elsner and I. Rutherford. Oxford: 97–110.

Babut, D. (1969) *Plutarque et le stoïcisme*. Paris.

Bagley, R. (2004) "Anyang writing and the origin of Chinese writing," in *The First Writing: Script Invention as History and Process*, ed. S. D. Houston. Cambridge: 190–249.

Baihu tong 白虎通 [Testimonies on the White Tiger Hall]. By Ban Gu 班固 (32–92 CE), in *Baihu tong shu zheng* 白虎通疏證, ed. Chen Li 陳立 (1809–69). Beijing, 1994. [*BHT*]

Baoshan Chu jian 包山楚簡 [The Chu Inscribed Bamboo Slips from Baoshan]. Beijing, 1991. [*Baoshan*]

Baoshan Chu mu 包山楚墓 [The Chu Tombs at Baoshan] (2 vols.). Beijing, 1991.

Barnard, N. (1973) *The Ch'u Silk Manuscript: Translation and Commentary*. Canberra.

Barton, T. (1994a) *Ancient Astrology*. London.

(1994b) *Power and Knowledge: Astrology, Physiognomics, and Medicine under the Roman Empire*. Ann Arbor.

Beard, M. (1986) "Cicero and divination: the formation of a Latin discourse," *JRS* **76**: 33–46.

Betz, H. D. (ed.) (1986) *The Greek Magical Papyri in Translation, Including the Demotic Spells*. Chicago.
Bielenstein, H. (1950) "An interpretation of the portents in the Ts'ien-Han-shu," *BMFEA* **22**: 127–43.
(1980) *The Bureaucracy of Han Times*. Cambridge.
Biot, E. (1851) *Le Tcheou-li: ou, Rites des Tcheou* (3 vols.). Paris, rpt. Taipei, 1975.
Bloch, R. (1984) *La divination dans l'antiquité*. Paris.
(1991) *La divination: essai sur l'avenir et son imaginaire*. Paris.
Bobzien, S. (1998) *Determinism and Freedom in Stoic Philosophy*. Oxford.
Bodde, D. (1959) "The Chinese magic known as watching for the ethers," in *Studia Serica Bernhard Kargren dedicata*, ed. S. Egerod and E. Glahn. Copenhagen: 14–35; rpt. in LeBlanc and Borei (1981): 351–72.
(1975) *Festivals in Classical China: New Year and Other Annual Observances during the Han Dynasty 206 B.C.–A.D. 220*. Princeton and Hong Kong.
(1981) "Myths of ancient China," in LeBlanc and Borei (1981): 45–84. Originally published in *Myths of the Ancient World*, ed. S. N. Kramer, New York, 1961.
Boileau, G. (2002) "Wu and shaman," *BSOAS* **65.2**: 350–78.
Bonnechère, P. (1990) "Les oracles de Béotie," *Kernos* **3**: 53–65.
Bonnet-Bidaud, J.-M., F. Praderie, and S. Whitfield (2009) "The Dunhuang Chinese sky: a comprehensive study of the oldest known star atlas," *Journal of Astronomical History and Heritage* **12**: 39–59.
Borza, E. N. (1982) "Athenians, Macedonians, and the origins of the Macedonian royal house," in *Hesperia Supplements*, vol. 19. Athens: 7–13.
Bosworth, A. B. (1977) "Alexander and Ammon," in *Greece and the Eastern Mediterranean in Ancient History and Prehistory: Studies Presented to Fritz Schachermeyr on the Occasion of his Eightieth Birthday*, ed. K. H. Kinzl. Berlin: 51–75.
(1994) "Alexander the Great" parts 1 and 2, in *The Cambridge Ancient History Volume 6: The Fourth Century BC*, ed. D. M. Lewis, J. Boardman, S. Hornblower, and M. Ostwald. 2nd edn. Cambridge: 791–875.
(2003) "Plus ça change . . .: ancient historians and their sources," *CA* **22**: 167–98.
Bottéro, J. (1974) "Symptômes, signes, écritures en Mésopotamie ancienne," in Vernant (1974): 70–197.
(1992) *Mesopotamia: Writing, Reasoning, and the Gods*. Chicago.
(2001) *Everyday Life in Ancient Mesopotamia*. Baltimore.
Bouché-Leclercq, A. (1879–82) *Histoire de la divination dans l'antiquité* (4 vols.). Paris, rpt. New York, 1975.
(1899) *L'astrologie grecque*. Paris.
Bowden, H. (2003) "Oracles for sale," in *Herodotus and his World: Essays from a Conference in Memory of George Forrest*, ed. P. Derow and R. Parker. Oxford: 256–74.
(2005) *Classical Athens and the Delphic Oracle: Divination and Democracy*. Cambridge.

Bremmer, J. (1993) “Prophets, seers, and politics in Greece, Israel, and early modern Europe,” *Numen* **40**: 150–83.

(1996) “The status and symbolic capital of the seer,” in *The Role of Religion in the Early Greek Polis: Proceedings of the Third International Seminar on Ancient Greek Cult, Organized by the Swedish Institute at Athens, 16–18 October 1992*, ed. R. Högg. Stockholm: 97–109.

Brenk, F. E. (1977) *In Mist Apparelled: Religious Themes in Plutarch's Moralia and Lives*. Leiden.

Brennan, J. (1993) “Dreams, divination and statecraft: the politics of dreams in early Chinese history and literature,” in *The Dream and the Text: Essays on Literature and Language*, ed. C. S. Rupprecht. Albany: 73–102.

Brewitt-Taylor, C. H. (1925) *San kuo or Romance of the three kingdoms*. 2 vols. Shanghai, rpt. North Clarendon, VT, 2002.

Brickhouse, T. C. and N. D. Smith (1984) “The paradox of Socratic ignorance in Plato's Apology,” *HPhQ* **1**: 125–31.

Bridgman, R. F. (1955) *La Médecine dans la Chine antique: Mélanges chinois et bouddhiques*. Brussels.

Brown, D. (2000) *Mesopotamian Planetary Astronomy-Astrology*. Cuneiform Monographs, no. 18. Groningen.

Burkert, W. (1985) *Greek Religion*, trans. J. Raffan. Cambridge, MA.

(1991) *Oedipus, Oracles and Meaning: From Sophocles to Umberto Eco*. Toronto.

(1992) *The Orientalizing Revolution: Near Eastern Influence on Greek Culture in the Early Archaic Age*, trans. M. E. Pinder and W. Burkert. Cambridge, MA.

(2005) “Signs, commands, and knowledge,” in Johnston and Struck (2005): 29–49.

Buxton, R. (ed.) (1999) *From Myth to Reason? Studies in the Development of Greek Thought*. Oxford.

(ed.) (2000) *Oxford Readings in Greek Religion*. Oxford.

Cabanes, P. (ed.) (1993) *L'Illyrie méridionale et l'Épire dans l'antiquité, 2: Actes du IIe colloque international de Clermont-Ferrand, 25–27 octobre 1990*. Paris.

Calame, C. (1996) *Mythe et histoire dans l'antiquité grecque: La création symbolique d'une colonie*. Lausanne.

(2003) *Myth and History in Ancient Greece: The Symbolic Creation of a Colony*, trans. D. W. Berman. Princeton.

Cammann, S. (1948) “The ‘TLV’ pattern on cosmic mirrors of the Han dynasty,” *JAOS* **68.4**: 159–67.

Cao Wei 曹瑋 (2002) *Zhouyuan jiaguwen* 周原甲骨文 [The Zhouyuan Oracle Bone Inscriptions]. Beijing.

Caquot, A. and M. Leibovici (1968) *La divination: Études recueillies* (2 vols.). Paris.

Carapanos, C. (1878) *Dodone et ses ruines*. Paris. [C]

Cartledge, P. (1994) “The Greeks and anthropology,” *Anthropology Today* **10.3**: 3–6.

Casevitz, M. (1992) “‘Mantis’: le vrai sens,” *REG* **105**: 1–18.

Ceci, S. J. and M. Bruck (1993) “Suggestibility of the child witness: a historical review and synthesis,” *Psychological Bulletin* **113**: 403–39.

Chan, Wing-tsit (1967) "The individual in Chinese religion," in *The Chinese Mind: Essentials of Chinese Philosophy and Culture*, ed. C. Moore. Honolulu: 286–306.

Chang Ch'uan-ts'ai 章權才 (1995) *Liang Han jing xue shi* 兩漢經學史 [History of Western and Eastern Han Study of the Classics]. Taipei.

Chang, K. C. (1963) *The Archaeology of Ancient China*. 4th edn. New Haven, 1986.

(1980) *Shang Civilization*. New Haven.

(1982) *Zhongguo qing tong shi dai* 中國青銅時代 [The Bronze Age of China]. Hong Kong.

(1983) *Art. Myth and Ritual: The Path to Political Authority in Ancient China*. Cambridge, MA.

(1994) "Shang shamans," in *The Power of Culture: Studies in Chinese Cultural History*, ed. W. J. Peterson, A. H. Plaks, and Yu Ying-shih. Hong Kong: 10–36.

Changsha Mawangdui er, san hao Han mu 長沙馬王堆二,三號漢墓 [The Han Tombs Numbers 2 and 3 from Changsha, Mawangdui]. Beijing, 2004.

Changsha Mawangdui yi hao Han mu 長沙馬王堆一號漢墓 [The Han Tomb Number 1 from Changsha, Mawangdui] (2 vols.). Beijing, 1973.

Chaniotis, A. (2005) *War in the Hellenistic World: A Social and Cultural History*. Oxford.

Chantraine, P. (1968–80) *Dictionnaire étymologique de la langue grecque: histoire des mots* (4 vols.). Paris.

Chao Wei-pang (1946) "The Chinese science of fate calculation," *Folklore Studies* **5**: 279–315.

Chavannes, E. (1895–1905) *Les mémoires historiques de Se-ma Ts'ien* (5 vols.). Paris, rpt. with vol. 6, Paris, 1969.

Chemla, K., D. Harper, and M. Kalinowski (eds.) (1999) Divination et rationalité en Chine ancienne. *EO* **21**.

Chen Cheng-Yih (1996) *Early Chinese Work in Natural Science: A Re-examination of the Physics of Motion, Acoustics, Astronomy and Scientific Thoughts*. Hong Kong.

Chen Jiujin 陳久金 and Zhang Jingguo 張敬國 (1989) "Hanshan chu tu yu pian tu xing shi kao" 含山出土玉片圖形試考 [Preliminary Examination of the Jade Pieces Excavated from Hanshan], *WW* **1989.4**: 14–17.

Chen Meiying 陳美英 et al. (1995) *Zhonghua zhan meng shu* 中華占夢術 [The Art of Chinese Dream Divination]. Taipei.

Chen Mengjia 陳夢家 (1936) "Shang dai de shen hua yu wu shu" 商代的神話與巫術 [Shang Dynasty Mythology and Magic], *Yanjing xuebao* **20**: 485–576.

Chen Ning (1997) "The genesis of the concept of blind fate in ancient China," *JCR* **25** (Fall): 141–67.

Chen Quanfang 陳全方 (1988) *Zhouyuan yu Zhou wen hua* 周原與周文化 [Zhouyuan and Zhou Culture]. Shanghai.

Chen Songchang 陳松長 (2000) "Mawangdui boshu 'xingde' jia, yi ben de bi jiao yan jiu" 馬王堆帛書《刑德》甲，乙本的比較研究 [Research comparing Books A and B of the Mawangdui silk manuscript "Xingde"], *WW* **2000.3**: 75–85.

(2001) *Mawangdui bo shu "xing de" yan jiu lun gao* 馬王堆帛書《刑德》研究論稿 [Discussion of Studies of the "Xingde" Text from the Mawangdui Silk Manuscripts]. Taipei.

and Liao Mingchun 廖名春 (1993) "Boshu 'Er san zi wen,' 'Yi zhi yi,' 'Yao' shiwen" 帛書《二三子問》，《易之義》，《要》釋文 [Transcriptions of silk manuscripts: "Two or three disciples question," and "Meaning of the Changes," and "Essentials"], *DJ* **3**: 424–35.

Chen Wei 陳偉 (1996) *Baoshan Chu jian chu tan* 包山楚簡初探 [A First Exploration of the Baoshan Chu Bamboo Slips]. Wuhan.

(1997) "Wangshan Chu jian suo jian de bu shi yu dao ci – yu Baoshan Chu jian xiang dui zhao" 望山楚簡所見的卜筮與禱祠 – 與包山楚簡相對照 [Comparison of turtle shell and milfoil divination and prayer as seen in the Wangshan and Baoshan Chu bamboo slips], *JHKG* **1997.2**: 72–75.

(1999) "Hubei Jingmen Baoshan bu shi Chu jian suo jian shen zhi xi tong yu xiang ji zhi du" 湖北荊門包山卜筮楚簡所見神祇系統與享祭制度 [The spirit veneration system and funerary sacrifice rules as seen in the Chu bamboo slips on turtle shell and yarrow divination from Baoshan, Jingmen, Hubei], *Kaogu* **1999.4**: 51–59.

Chen Zungui 陳遵嬀 (1980–89) *Zhongguo tian wen xue shi* 中國天文學史 [History of Chinese Astronomy] (4 vols.). Shanghai.

Cheng, A. (2001) "What did it mean to be a Ru in Han times?," *AM*, 3rd series, **14.2**: 101–18.

Christidis, A.-Ph., S. Dakaris, and I. Vokotopoulou (1999) "Magic in the oracular tablets from Dodona," in *The World of Magic: Papers from the First International Samson Eitrem Seminar at the Norwegian Institute at Athens 4–8 May 1997*, ed. D. R. Jordan, H. Montgomery, and E. Thomassen. Bergen: 67–72. [CDV]

Chu ci bu zhu 楚辭補注 [Supplementary Notes to the Songs of Chu], ed. Hong Xingzu 洪興祖 (1090–1155). Taipei 1995, rpt. 2004.

Chunqiu fan lu 春秋繁露 [Luxuriant Dew of the Spring and Autumn], att. Dong Zhongshu 董仲舒 (2nd cent. BCE), in *Chunqiu fan lu jin zhu jin yi* 春秋繁露今註今譯, ed. Lai Yanyuan 賴炎元. Taipei, 1984.

Chunqiu Zuo zhuan zhu 春秋左傳注 [Commentary on the Spring and Autumn Annals and Zuo Transmissions], ed. Yang Bojun 楊伯峻. Gaoxiong, 1991. [Zuo]

Ciraolo, L. and J. Seidel (eds.) (2002) *Magic and Divination in the Ancient World: Proceedings of the Conference on Magic and Divination in the Ancient World Held at the University of California at Berkeley in February 1994*. Leiden.

Clement of Alexandria (*c.* 150–*c.* 205 CE). *Stromata* (3 vols.). Berlin, 1960.

Connor, W. R. (1987) "Tribes, festivals and processions: civic ceremonial and political manipulation in ancient Greece," *JHS* **107**: 40–50, rpt. in Buxton (2000): 56–75.

(1988) "'Sacred' and 'secular': *hiera kai hosia* and the classical Athenian concept of the state," *Ancient Society* **19**: 161–88.

Cook, C. (1995–96) "Scribes, cooks, and artisans: breaking Zhou tradition," *EC* **20**: 241–77.

(2006) *Death in Ancient China: The Tale of One Man's Journey*. Leiden.

Couvreur, S. (1913) *Li Ki: ou mémoires sur les bienséances* (2 vols.). Ho Kien Fou.

(1916) *I-li, Cérémonial*. Ho Kien Fou.

Crahay, R. (1956) *La littérature oraculaire chez Hérodote*. Paris.

(1974) "La bouche de la vérité," in Vernant (1974): 201–19.

Cramer, F. H. (1954) *Astrology in Roman Law and Politics*. Philadelphia.

Crespigny, R. de (1976) *Portents of Protest in the Later Han Dynasty: The Memorials of Hsiang K'ai to Emperor Huan*. Canberra.

Csikszentmihalyi, M. (2004) *Material Virtue Ethics and the Body in Early China*. Leiden.

and M. Nylan (2003) "Constructing lineages and inventing traditions through exemplary figures in early China," *TP* **89.1–3**: 59–99.

Cullen, C. (2011) "Understanding the planets in ancient China: prediction and divination in the *Wu xing zhan*," *Early Science and Medicine* **16.3**: 218–51.

Curnow, T. (2004) *The Oracles of the Ancient World: A Comprehensive Guide*. London.

Dakaris, S. (1970) *Das Heiligtum von Dodona: Tempel und Stätten der Götter Griechenlands*. Cologne.

(1971) *Archaeological Guide to Dodona*, trans. E. Kirk-Defterou. Ioannina.

(1993) *Dodona*. Congleton, 2nd edn. Athens, 1996.

Dakaris, S., A.-Ph. Christidis, and I. Vokotopoulou (1993) "Les lamelles oraculaires de Dodone et les villes de l'Épire dans l'antiquité," in Cabanes (1993): 55–60. [DCV]

De Boer, J. Z., J. R. Hale, and J. Chanton (2001) "New evidence of the geological origins of the ancient Delphic oracle," *Geology* **29**: 707–10.

Defradas, J. (1954) *Les thèmes de la propagande Delphique*. Paris.

(1968) "La Divination en Grèce," in Caquot and Leibovici (1968) 1: 157–95.

Delbrück, H. (1904) "Theologische Philologie," *Preussische Jahrbücher* **116**: 209–40.

[1920] (1975) *History of the Art of War within the Framework of Political History*. Vol. I, trans. W. J. Renfroe. London.

Deng Qiubo 鄧球柏 (1987) *Bo shu Zhou yi jiao shi* 帛書周易校釋 [Translation and Critique of the Zhou yi of Silk Manuscripts]. Changsha.

Denyer, N. (1985) "The case against divination: an examination of Cicero's *De Divinatione*," *PCPhS* **31**: 1–10.

Despeux, C. (2003) "Physiognomie," in Kalinowski (2003): 513–55.

Detienne, M. (1981) *L'invention de la mythologie*. Paris, trans. M. Cook as *The Invention of Mythology*. Chicago, 1986.

(2000) *Comparer l'incomparable*. Paris.

(2001) "Back to the village: a tropism of Hellenists?," *HR* **41.2**: 99–113.

(2002) "Murderous identity: anthropology, history, and the art of constructing comparables," trans. A. Noor, *Common Knowledge* **8.1**: 178–87.

Detienne, Marcel, and J.-P. Vernant (1978) *Cunning Intelligence in Greek Culture and Society*, trans. J. Lloyd. Atlantic Highlands, NJ.

(1989) *The Cuisine of Sacrifice among the Greeks*, trans. P. Wissing. Chicago.

DeWoskin, K. J. (1983) *Doctors, Diviners and Magicians of Ancient China: Biographies of the Fang-shih*. New York.

Diaconis, P. (1985) "Theories of data analysis: from magical thinking through classical statistics," in *Exploring Data Tables, Trends and Shapes*, ed. D. Hoaglin, F. Mosteller, and J. Tukey. New York: 1–36.

Diels, H. and W. Kranz (eds.) (1951–52) *Die Fragmente der Vorsokratiker* (3 vols.). 6th edn. Dublin and Zürich: 1966.

Dietrich, B. C. (1965) *Death, Fate, and the Gods: The Development of a Religious Idea in Greek Popular Belief and in Homer*. London.

(1990) "Oracles and divine inspiration," *Kernos* **3**: 157–74.

(1992) "Divine madness and conflict at Delphi," *Kernos* **5**: 41–58.

Dillery, J. (2005) "Chresmologues and manteis: independent diviners and the problem of authority," in Johnston and Struck (2005): 167–231.

Dirlik, A. (1995) "Confucius in the borderlands: global capitalism and the reinvention of Confucianism," *Boundary* 2, **22.3**: 229–73.

Djamouri, R. (1999) "Écriture et divination sous les Shang," *EO* **21**: 11–35.

Dobson, M. (1979) "Herodotus 1.47.1 and the Hymn to Hermes: a solution to the test oracle," *AJPh* **100.3**: 349–59.

Dodds, E. R. (1951) *The Greeks and the Irrational*. Berkeley.

(1966) "On misunderstanding the Oedipus Rex," *G&R*, 2nd ser. **13**: 37–49.

Dong Zuobin 董作賓 (1965) *Jiagu xue liu shi nian* 甲骨學六十年 [Sixty Years of Oracle Bone Studies]. Taipei.

(1967–68) *Dong Zuobin xue shu lun zhu* 董作賓學術論著 [Collected Scholarship of Dong Zuobin] (2 vols.). Taipei.

Doolittle, Justus (1865) *Social Life of the Chinese*. New York.

Dougherty, C. (1992) "When rain falls from the clear blue sky: riddles and colonization oracles," *CA* **11**: 28–44.

(1993) "It's murder to found a colony," in Dougherty and Kurke (1993): 178–98.

(1994) "Archaic Greek foundation poetry: questions of genre and occasion," *JHS* **114**: 35–46.

Dougherty, C. and L. Kurke (eds.) (1993) *Cultural Poetics in Archaic Greece: Cult, Performance*. Cambridge, paperback edn., Oxford, 1998.

(eds.) (2003) *The Cultures Within Ancient Greek Culture: Contact, Conflict, Collaboration*. Cambridge.

Douglas, M. (1985) *Risk Acceptability According to the Social Sciences*. New York.

(1992) *Risk and Blame: Essays in Cultural Theory*. Rpt. London, 2002.

Drège, J.-P. and D. Drettas (2003) "Oniromancie," in Kalinowski (2003): 369–403.

Drettas, D. (2007) "Le Rêve mis en ordre. Les traités onirologiques des Ming, à l'épreuve des traditions divinatoire, médicale et religieuse du rêve en Chine" [Dreams Put in Order: Ming Oneirological Treatises as Evidence of Divinatory, Medical, and Religious Traditions of the Dream in China]. Ph.D. Dissertation. École Pratique des Hautes Études.

Dubs, H. H. (1938–55) *History of the Former Han Dynasty* (3 vols.). Baltimore.

(1958) "The beginnings of Chinese astronomy," *JAOS* **78.4**: 295–300.

Durand, J.-L. (1989a) "Greek animals: toward a topology of edible bodies," in Detienne and Vernant (1989): 87–118.

(1989b) "Ritual as instrumentality," in Detienne and Vernant (1989): 119–28.

Eberhard, W. (1957) "The political function of astronomy and astronomers in Han China," in *Chinese Thought and Institutions*, ed. J. K. Fairbank. Chicago: 37–70.

(1970) *Studies in Chinese Folklore and Related Essays*. Bloomington.

Edelstein, E. J. and L. Edelstein (eds.) (1945) *Asclepius: A Collection and Interpretation of the Testimonies* (2 vols.). Baltimore, paperback edn. (1 vol.), 1998. [EE]

Edmunds, L. (1971) "The religiosity of Alexander," *GRBS* **12.3**: 363–91.

Eidinow, E. (2007a) *Oracles, Curses, and Risk among the Ancient Greeks*. Oxford.

(2007b) "Why the Athenians began to curse," in *Debating the Athenian Cultural Revolution: Art, Literature, Philosophy and Politics 430–380 BC*, ed. R. Osborne. Cambridge: 44–71.

Elman, B. (1984) *From Philosophy to Philology: Intellectual and Social Aspects of Change in Late Imperial China*. Cambridge, MA.

Elvin, M. (n.d.) "Personal luck: why premodern China – probably – did not develop probabilistic thinking." Manuscript.

Evangelidis, D. (1929) "Ἀνασκαφὴ τοῦ Ἱεροῦ τῆς Δωδώνης," *PAAH*: 104–29.

(1931) "Ἀνασκαφὴ τοῦ Ἱεροῦ τῆς Δωδώνης," *PAAH*: 192–260.

(1932) "Ἀνασκαφὴ τοῦ Ἱεροῦ τῆς Δωδώνης," *PAAH*: 47–52.

(1935) "Ἠπειρωτικαι Ἔρευναι," *Ep. Chron.* **10**: 192–260.

(1952) "Ἀνασκαφὴ τοῦ Ἱεροῦ τῆς Δωδώνης," *PAAH*: 279–306.

(1958) "Ἀνασκαφὴ τοῦ Ἱεροῦ τῆς Δωδώνης," *PAAH*: 103–6.

(1965) "Ἀνασκαφὴ τοῦ Ἱεροῦ τῆς Δωδώνης," *PAAH*: 53–65.

(1967) "Ἀνασκαφὴ τοῦ Ἱεροῦ τῆς Δωδώνης," *PAAH*: 33–54.

(1968) "Ἀνασκαφὴ ἐν Δωδώνη," *PAAH*: 42–59.

(1973) "Ἀνασκαφὴ τοῦ Ἱεροῦ τῆς Δωδώνης," *PAAH*: 87–98.

Evans, E. C. (1945) "Galen the physician as physiognomist," *TAPhA* **76**: 287–98.

(1969) "Physiognomics in the ancient world," *TAPhA* **59**: 5–97.

Evans-Pritchard, E. E. (1976) *Witchcraft, Oracles and Magic Among the Azande*. Oxford, paperback edn. First published in 1937.

Falkenhausen, L. von (1993a) "On the historiographical orientation of Chinese archaeology," *Antiquity* **67**: 839–49.

(1993b) *Suspended Music: Chime Bells in the Culture of Bronze Age China*. Berkeley.

(1995a) "Reflections on the political rôle of spirit mediums in early China: the *wu* officials in the *Zhou li*," *EC* **20**: 279–300.

(1995b) "The regionalist paradigm in Chinese archaeology," in *Nationalism, Politics and the Practice of Archaeology*, ed. P. L. Kohl and C. Fawcett. Cambridge: 198–217.

(2003) "Social ranking in Chu tombs: the mortuary background of the Warring States manuscript finds," *MS* **51**: 439–526.

(2004) Review of M. J. Puett, *To Become a God: Cosmology, Sacrifice, and Self-Divinization in Early China*, *HJAS* **64.3**: 465–79.

(2006) *Chinese Society in the Age of Confucius (1000–250 BC): The Archaeological Evidence*. Los Angeles.

Fan Jingwen 范景文 [1587–1644] (2000) *Zhan shou quan shu* 戰守全書 [Complete Texts on Attack and Defense]. 18 juan. Rpt. *Ming Chong zhen ke ben, Beijing tushuguan cang* 明崇禎刻本, 北京圖書館藏. *Siku jin hui shu congkan* 四庫禁燬書叢刊. Beijing: 195–592.

Fan Yuzhou (1989) "Military campaign inscriptions from YH 127," *BSOAS* **52.3**: 533–40.

Farmer, J. M. (2001) "The World of the Mind in Early Medieval Sichuan: The Life and Works of Qiao Zhou." Ph.D. Dissertation. University of Wisconsin-Madison.

Feng Shi 馮時 (1994) "Yin bu ci si fang feng yan jiu" 殷卜辭四方風研究 [A study of the four directions and winds from them recorded in Yin [Shang] oracle bone inscriptions], *KGXB* **1994.2**: 131–54.

Feuchtwang, S. (1989) "The problem of 'superstition' in the People's Republic of China," in *Religion and Political Power*, ed. G. Benavides and M. Daly. Albany: 43–68.

Field, S. L. (1992) "Cosmos, cosmograph, and the inquiring poet," *EC* **17**: 83–110.

(2000) "Who told the fortunes? The speaker in early Chinese divination records," *AM* **13.2**: 1–14.

(2008) *Ancient Chinese Divination*. Honolulu.

Finley, M. I. (1954) *The World of Odysseus*, 2nd edn. New York, 1979.

(1975) "Anthropology and the Classics," in *The Use and Abuse of History*, ed. M. I. Finley. London: 102–19.

Fiskesjö, M. (2001) "Rising from blood-stained fields: royal hunting and state formation in Shang China," *BMFEA* **73**: 49–191.

Flacelière, R. (1965) *Greek Oracles*, trans. D. Garman. New York.

Flad, R. K. (2004) "Specialized Salt Production and Changing Social Structure at the Prehistoric Site of Zhongba in the Eastern Sichuan Basin, China." Ph.D. Dissertation. UCLA.

(2008) "Divination and power: a multiregional view of the development of oracle bone divination in early China," *Current Anthropology* **49.3**: 403–37.

Flower, M. A. (2008) *The Seer in Ancient Greece*. Berkeley.

Foerster, R. (ed.) (1893) *Scriptores Physiognomonici Graeci et Latini*. Leipzig.

Fontenrose, J. E. (1959) *Python: A Study of Delphic Myth and Its Origins*. Berkeley, rpt. 1980.

(1968) "The hero as athlete," *California Studies in Classical Antiquity* **1**: 73–104.

(1978) *The Delphic Oracle: Its Responses and Operations with a Catalogue of Responses*. Berkeley.

(1988) *Didyma: Apollo's Oracle, Cult, and Companions*. Berkeley.

Forke, A. F. (1911) *Lun Heng: Essays of Wang Chong* (2 vols.), rpt. New York, 1962.

Förster, R. (1893) *Scriptores Physiognomonici Graeci et Latini* (2 vols.). Leipzig.

Fouilles de Delphes, see T. Homolle et al.

Fredricksmeyer, E. A. (1991) "Alexander, Zeus, Ammon and the conquest of Asia," *TAPhA* **121**: 199–214.

Fu Juyou 傅舉有 and Chen Songchang 陳松長 (1992) *Mawangdui Han mu wen wu* 馬王堆漢墓文物 [The Cultural Relics Unearthed from the Han Tombs at Mawangdui]. Changsha.

Fuehrer, B. (2006) "Seers and jesters: graph analysis between punning and predicting the future," *EASTM* **25**: 47–68.

Furth, C. (ed.) (1976) *The Limits of Change: Essays on Conservative Alternatives in Republican China*. Cambridge, MA.

Fustel de Coulanges, N. D. (1864) *La Cité antique: Étude sur le culte, le droit, les institutions de la Grèce et de Rome*. Paris, rpt. 1947.

Gadd, C. J. (1966) "Some Babylonian divinatory methods and their interrelations," in *La divination en Mésopotamie ancienne et dans les régions voisines*, ed. J. Nougayrol et al. Paris: 21–35.

Gao Heng 高亨 (1947) *Zhou yi gu jing jin zhu* 周易古經今注 [Contemporary Notes on the Ancient Classic the Zhou Changes]. Shanghai, rpt. Beijing, 1984.

(1958) *Zhou yi gu jing tong shuo* 周易古經通說 [General Explanation of the Ancient Classic the Zhou Changes]. Beijing.

(1979) "Zuo zhuan Guo yu de Zhou yi shuo tong jie" 左傳國語的周易說通解 [Explanation of collected Zhou yi accounts in the Zuo zhuan and Guoyu], in *Zhou yi za lun* 周易雜論. Ji'nan.

Garlan, Y. (1975) *War in the Ancient World: A Social History*, trans. J. Lloyd. London.

Geertz, C. (1983) *Local Knowledge: Further Essays in Interpretive Anthropology*. New York.

Gernet, J. (1974) "Petits écarts et grands écarts," in Vernant (1974): 52–69.

Gernet, L. (1955) "Delphes et la pensée religieuse en Grèce," *Annales, Économies, Sociétés, Civilisations* **10**: 526–42.

(1981) *The Anthropology of Ancient Greece*, trans. B. Nagy and J. Hamilton. Baltimore.

Giddens, A. (1990) *The Consequences of Modernity*. Palo Alto.

Giele, E. (2003) "Using early Chinese manuscripts as historical source materials," *MS* **51**: 409–38.

Ginzburg, C. (1979) "Clues: roots of a scientific paradigm," *Theory and Society* **7.3**: 273–88.

Goh Thean Chye [Wu Tiancai] (1967) "The History of the Astronomical Bureau." M.A. Thesis. University of Malaysia.

Graham, A. C. (1986) *Yin-Yang and the Nature of Correlative Thinking*. Singapore.

(1991) *Disputers of the Tao: Philosophical Argument in Ancient China*. LaSalle.

Graham, A. J. (1964) *Colony and Mother City in Ancient Greece*. New York.

(1982) "The colonial expansion of ancient Greece," in *The Cambridge Ancient History: The Expansion of the Greek World, Eighth to Sixth Centuries B.C.*, Part 3: Vol. III, ed. J. Boardman and N.G. L. Hammond. 2nd edn. Cambridge: 83–162.

Granet, M. (1934) *La penseé chinoise*. Paris.

Griffin, J. (1977) "The epic cycle and the uniqueness of Homer," *JHS* **97**: 39–53.

Gu Jiegang 顧頡剛 et al. (eds.) (1926–41) *Gu shi bian* 古史辨 [Debating Ancient History] (7 vols.). Vols. 1–5: Beijing, 1926–35; vols. 6–7: Shanghai, 1938–41, rpt. Hong Kong, 1962–63.

Gu Tiefu 顧鐵符 (1978) "Mawangdui bo shu 'T'ian wen qi xiang za zhan nei rong jian shu'" 馬王堆帛書天文氣象雜占內容簡述, *WW* **2**: 1–4. Trans.: see Harper (1979a).

Guanju Qin Han mu jian du 關沮秦漢墓簡牘 [Written Records from the Qin and Han Tombs at Guanju]. Beijing, 2001. [*ZJT*]

Guanzi 管子. *SBBY* edn.

Guo Moruo 郭沫若 and Hu Houxuan 胡厚宣 (eds.) (1978–82) *Jiaguwen heji* 甲骨文合集 [Collected Oracle Bone Inscriptions] (13 vols.). Beijing.

Guo yu 國語 [Discourses of the States]. Att. Zuo Qiuming 左丘明 (5th cent. BCE). Shanghai, 1978. [GY]

Guodian Chu mu zhu jian 郭店楚墓竹簡 [Bamboo Slips from the Chu Tombs at Guodian] (1998). Beijing. [*Guodian*]

Guthrie, K.S. (1987) *The Pythagorean Sourcebook and Library: An Anthology of Ancient Writings which relate to Pythagoras and Pythagorean Philosophy*, ed. D.R. Fideler. Grand Rapids.

Gwynn, A. (1918) "The character of Greek colonisation," *JHS* **38**: 88–123.

Hacking, I. (1975) *The Emergence of Probability*. Cambridge.

(1990) *The Taming of Chance*. Cambridge.

Hale, J.R., J.Z. de Boer, J.P. Chanton, and H.A. Spiller (2003) "Questioning the Delphic Oracle," *Scientific American* (August): 66–73.

Hall, D.L. and R.T. Ames (1995) *Anticipating China: Thinking Through the Narratives of Chinese and Western Culture*. See Ames and Hall 2001.

Hall, J.M. (1997) *Ethnic Identity in Greek Antiquity*. Cambridge.

(2002) *Hellenicity: Between Ethnicity and Culture*. Chicago.

(2003a) "How 'Greek' were the early western Greeks?," in *Greek Identity in the Western Mediterranean*, ed. K. Lomas. Leiden: 35–54.

(2003b) "Culture or cultures? Hellenism in the late sixth century," in Dougherty and Kurke (2003): 23–34.

Halliday, W.R. (1913) *Greek Divination: A Study of Its Methods and Principles*. London.

Hamilton, R. (1978) "Prologue, prophecy and plot in four plays of Euripides," *AJP* **99**: 277–302.

Hammond, N.G.L. (1993) *Sources for Alexander the Great: An Analysis of Plutarch's Life and Arrian's Anabasis Alexandrou*. Cambridge.

(1998) "The Branchidae at Didyma and in Sogdiana," *CQ*, n.s. **48.2**: 339–44.

and G. T. Griffith (1979) *A History of Macedonia, II, 550–336 B.C.* Oxford.

Han jian shi wen. See Wu?Jiulong (1985).

Han shu 漢書 [Standard History of the Han], by Ban?Gu 班固 (32–92 CE). Beijing, 1962. [*HS*]

Han shu bu zhu 漢書補注 [Collected Commentaries on the Han shu]. By Wang Xianqian 王先謙. Changsha 1900, facs. repr. Beijing, 1995. [*HSBZ*]

Han Ziqiang 韓自強 (2000a) "Fuyang Han jian Zhou yi shi wen" 阜陽漢簡周易釋文 [Transcription of the Fuyang Han bamboo slips of the Zhouyi], *DJ* **18**: 15–62.

(2000b) "Fuyang Han jian Zhou yi yan jiu" 阜陽漢簡周易研究 [Research on the Fuyang Han bamboo slips of the Zhouyi], *DJ* **18**: 63–132.

Hankinson, R. J. (1998) "Stoicism, science and divination," *Apeiron* **21.2**: 123–60.

Hanson, M. (2008) "Hand mnemonics in classical Chinese medicine: texts, earliest images, and arts of memory," *AM*, 3rd ser., **21.1**: 325–57.

Harper, D. (1979a) "The Han cosmic board (*shih* 式)," *EC* **4**: 1–10.

(1979b) "A summary of the contents of the Ma-wang-tui silk-scroll book 'Assorted astronomical and meteorological prognostications,'" *Chinese Studies in Archaeology* **1.1**: 56–74.

(1985) "A Chinese demonography of the third century B.C.," *HJAS* **45.2**: 459–98.

(1995) "The bellows analogy in Laozi V and early Chinese macrobiotic hygiene," *EC* **20**: 381–91.

(1995–96) "An archaeological study of Taiyi (Grand One) worship," *Early Medieval China* **2**: 1–39.

(1997) "Warring States, Qin and Han manuscripts related to natural philosophy and the occult," in Shaughnessy (1997): 223–52.

(1998) *Early Chinese Medical Literature: The Mawangdui Medical Manuscripts.* London and New York.

(1999a) "Physicians and diviners: the relations of divination to the medicine of the *Huangdi neijing* (Inner Canon of the Yellow Thearch)," *EO* **21**: 91–110.

(1999b) "Warring States natural philosophy and occult thought," in Loewe and Shaughnessy (1999): 813–84.

(2001) "Iatromancy, prognosis, and diagnosis in early Chinese medicine," in *Innovation in Chinese Medicine*, ed. E. Hsu. Cambridge: 99–120.

(2010) "The textual form of knowledge: occult miscellanies in ancient and medieval Chinese manuscripts, fourth century B.C. to tenth century A.D.," in *Looking at it from Asia: The Processes that Shaped the Sources of History of Science*, ed. F. Bretelle-Establet, *Boston Studies in the Philosophy of Science* **265**: 37–80.

Harrison, J. E. (1903) *Prolegomena to the Study of Greek Religion*. Cambridge, 2nd edn. 1908, rpt. Princeton, 1991.

Harrist, R. E., Jr. (1997) "The legacy of Bole: physiognomy and horses in Chinese painting," *Artibus Asiae* **57.1/2**: 135–56.

Hartog, F. (1988) *The Mirror of Herodotus: The Representation of the Other in the Writing of History*, trans. J. Lloyd. Berkeley.

(1996) "Hérodote," in *Savoir Grec Dictionnaire Critique*, ed. J. Brunschwig and G. E. R. Lloyd. Paris: 702–8.

(1999) "'Myth into logos': The case of Croesus, or the historian at work," in Buxton (1999): 183–96.

(2000) "The invention of history: the pre-history of a concept from Homer to Herodotus," *History and Theory* **39.3**: 384–95.

Hawkes, D. (1985) *Songs of the South: An Ancient Chinese Anthology of Poems by Qu Yuan and Other Poets*. New York and London.

Hayashi Minao 林巳奈夫 (1973) "Kan kyō no zugara ni, san ni tsuite" 漢鏡の圖二, 三について [On some designs in Han bronze mirror decoration], *Tōhō gakuhō* 東方學報 [Kyoto] **44**: 1–65.

He Shuangquan 何雙全 (1989a) "Tianshui Fangmatan Qin mu chu tu di tu chu tan" 天水放馬灘秦墓 出土地圖初探 [Preliminary study of the maps excavated from the Qin tombs at Fangmatan, Tianshui], *WW* **1989.2**: 12–22.

(1989b) "Tianshui Fangmatan Qin jian zong shu" 天水放馬灘秦簡綜述 [Summary of the Qin bamboo books from Fangmatan, Tianshui], *WW* **1989.2**: 23–31.

(1989c) "Tianshui Fangmatan Qin jian jia zhong 'rishu' kao shu" 天水放馬灘秦簡甲種《日書》考述 [An examination of the first "Daybook" from the Qin slips from Fangmatan, Tianshui], in *Qin Han jian du lun wen ji*. Lanzhou: 7–28.

Heintz, J.-G. (ed.) (1997) *Oracles et prophéties dans l'antiquité: actes du colloque de Strassbourg, 15–17 juin 1995*. Paris.

Henderson, J. (1984) *The Development and Decline of Chinese Cosmology*. New York.

Herzog, R. (1931) *Die Wunderheilungen von Epidauros. Philologus*, suppl. 22 fasc. 3. Leipzig.

Hignett, C. (1963) *Xerxes' Invasion of Greece*. Oxford.

Hinsch, B. (2006) "The criticism of powerful women by Western Han dynasty portent experts," *Journal of the Economic and Social History of the Orient (JESHO)* **49.1**: 96–121.

Ho Peng Yoke (1966) *Astronomical Chapters of the Chin Shu*. Paris.

(1985) *Li, Qi and Shu: An Introduction to Science and Civilization in China*. Seattle and London.

(2003) *Chinese Mathematical Astronomy*. London.

[He Bingyu] 何丙郁 and Ho Koon Piu [He Biaoguan] 何冠彪 (1985) *Dunhuang can juan Zhan yun qi shu yan jiu* 敦煌殘卷占雲氣書研究 [Research on the Dunhuang manuscript "Divining by cloud qi"], *Wen shi* **25**: 67–94.

Hoffman, O. (1899) "Die Orakelinschriften aus Dodona," in *Sammlung der Griechischen Dialekt-Inschriften*, vol. II, ed. H. Collitz and F. Bechtel. Gottingen, nos. 1557–98. [*SGDI*]

Hollis, M. and S. Lukes (eds.) (1982) *Rationality and Relativism*. Oxford.

Hollman, A. (2005) "The manipulation of signs in Herodotus' Histories," *TAPhA* **135**: 279–327.

Homolle, T. et al. (eds.) (1906–) *Fouilles de Delphes* (5 vols.). Paris.
Hong Anquan 洪安全 (1990) "Bo Le yu qian li ma" 伯樂與千里馬 [Bo Le and the thousand-li horse], *Gugong Wenwu Yuekan* 故宮文物月刊 **82**: 60–69.
Hornblower, S. (1992) "The religious dimension to the Peloponnesian War, or, what Thucydides does not tell us," *HSPh* **94**: 169–97.
Hou Han shu 後漢書 [Standard History of the Later Han], by Fan Ye 范曄 (398–445) (1962). Beijing. [*HHS*]
Houma meng shu 候馬盟書 [The Houma Oath Texts] (1976). Shanghai.
Howe, L. and A. Wain (eds.) (1993) *Predicting the Future*. Cambridge.
Hu Houxuan 胡厚宣 (1944) "Jiaguwen si fang feng ming kao zheng" 甲骨文四方風名考證 [Verification of the names of the winds of the four directions in the oracle bone inscriptions], in *Jiagu xue Shang shi lun cong chu ji* 甲骨學商史論叢初集 vol I. Chengdu.
(1956) "Shi Yindai qiu nian yu si fang he si fang feng de ji si" 釋殷代求年于四方和四方風的祭祀 [An explanation of the Yin [Shang] Dynasty asking about the year by means of the four directions and ancestral sacrifices to the four directions], *Fudan xuebao* 復旦學報 **1956.1**: 49–86.
Hu Pingsheng 胡平生 (1989) "'Ma ta fei niao' shi xiang ma fa shi" 馬踏飛鳥是相馬法式 [The "horse stepping on a flying bird" is a model for horse physiognomy], *WW* **1989.6**: 75–83.
(1998) "Fuyang Han jian Zhou yi gai shu" 阜陽漢簡周易概述 [Summary of the Fuyang Han slips of the Zhouyi], *Jianbo yan jiu* **3**: 248–66.
Huainanzi 淮南子 [Huainan Annals], by Liu An 劉安 (d. 122 BCE). *SBBY*. [*HNZ*]
Huang di nei jing ling shu yi jie 黃帝內經靈樞譯解 [The Inner Classic of the Yellow Lord: Spiritual Pivot], ed. Yang Weijie 楊維傑. Taipei, 1984.
Huang di nei jing su wen yi jie 黃帝內經素問譯解 [The Inner Classic of the Yellow Lord: Basic Questions] (1984), ed. Yang Weijie 楊維傑. Taipei.
Huang Yi-Long 黃一龍 (1998) *Zhongguo ren de meng* 中國人的夢 [The Dreams of the Chinese People]. Shanghai.
and Chang Chih-Ch'eng (1996) "The evolution and decline of the ancient Chinese practice of watching for the ethers," *CS* **13**: 82–106.
Huang Zhaoji 黃肇基 (1998) "Han dai Gongyang xue zai yi li lun yanjiu" 漢代公羊學災異理論研究 [Research on the Theory of Anomalies in Han Dynasty Gongyang Studies]. Taipei.
Huang Zhengjian 黃正建 (2001) *Dunhuang zhan bu wen shu yu Tang Wudai zhan bu yan jiu* 敦煌占卜文書與唐五代占卜研究 [Research on the Dunhuang Divination Documents and on Tang and Five Dynasty Divination]. Beijing.
Huber, H., J. R. Ching, S. Davis, S. R. Weld, and R. D. B. Yates (1980) "An interpretation of the divinatory inscriptions on early Chou bronzes," trans. of Zhang Zhenglang (1980), *EC* **6**: 80–96.
Hulsewé, A. F. P. (1979) "Watching the vapours: an ancient Chinese technique of prognostication," *Nachrichten der Gesellschaft für Natur- und Volkerkunde Ostasiens* **125**: 40–49.

(1985) *Remnants of Ch'in Law: An Annotated Translation of the Ch'in Legal and Administrative Rules of the 3rd Century B.C. Discovered in Yün-meng Prefecture, Hu-pei Province, in 1975*. Leiden.

(1990) "Fragments of Han law," *TP* **76**: 208–33.

Humphreys, S. C. (1974) "Classics and anthropology," *Didaskalos* **4**: 425–41. Rpt. and cited in Humphreys (1978): 17–30.

(1978) *Anthropology and the Greeks*. London.

Ikeda Tomohisa 池田知久 (1994) "Maōtai Kan bo hakusho Shūeki Yō hen no kenkyū" 馬王堆漢墓帛書周易要篇の研究 [Studies on Zhou yi and Yao texts from the Mawangdui silk manuscripts]. *Tōyōbunka Kenkyūsho Kīyō* **123**: 111–207.

(1995) "Maōtai Kan bo hakusho Shūeki Yō hen no shisō" 馬王堆漢墓帛書周易要篇の思想 [Ideas of the Zhou yi and Yao texts from the Mawangdui silk manuscripts], *Tōyōbunka Kenkyūsho Kīyō* **126**: 1–105.

Imai Usaburō 今井字三郎 (1969) "Saden, Kokugo zeisen kō" 左傳國語筮占考 [Research on turtle shell and yarrow divination in the Zuo zhuan and Guo yu], *Kokubungaku Kanbungaku Ronsō* **14**: 51–97.

Jameson, M. H. (1991) "Sacrifice before battle," in *Hoplites: The Classical Greek Battle Experience*. London: 197–227.

Jeyes, U. (1978) "The 'Palace Gate' of the liver: a study of terminology and methods in Babylonian extispicy," *Journal of Cuneiform Studies* **30.4**: 209–33.

Jiangling Jiudian dong Zhou mu 江陵九店東周墓 [The Eastern Han Tombs at Jiudian, Jiangling] (1995). Beijing.

Jiangling Wangshan Sha zhong Chu mu 江陵望山沙塚楚墓 [The Chu Tombs at Wangshan and Sha zhong, Jiangling] (1986). Beijing. [*Wangshan*]

Jiangling Yutaishan Chu mu 江陵雨台山楚墓 [The Chu Tombs at Yutaishan, Jiangling] (1984). Beijing.

Jin Chunfeng 金春峯 (1993) *Zhou guan zhi chengshu ji qi fanying de wenhua yu shidai xinkao* 周官之成書及其反映的文化與時代新考 [New Examination of the Composition of the Zhou Guan and the Culture and Age Reflected in It]. Taipei.

Jin shu 晉書 [Standard History of the Jin]. By Fang Xuanling 房玄齡 (578–648 CE) (1990). Taipei.

Jin Weinuo 金維諾 (1974) "Tan Changsha Mawangdui san hao Han mu bo hua" 談長沙馬王堆三號漢墓帛畫 [Discussion of paintings in the Han silk manuscript from Tomb no. 3, Changsha, Mawangdui], *WW* **1974.11**: 40–44.

Jingzhou Tianxingguan er hao Chu mu 荊州天星觀二號楚墓 (2003) [The Chu Tomb Number 2 at Tianxingguan, Jingzhou]. Beijing.

Jiudian Chu mu 九店楚墓 [The Chu Tombs at Jiudian] (1999). Beijing. [*Jiudian*]

Johnston, S. I. (2001) "Charming children: the use of the child in ancient divination," *Arethusa* **34**: 97–117.

(2008) *Ancient Greek Divination*. Oxford.

and P. T. Struck (eds.) (2005) *Mantikē: Studies in Ancient Divination. Religions in the Graeco-Roman World*. Leiden.

Jules-Rosette, B. (1978) "The veil of objectivity: prophecy, divination, and social inquiry," *American Anthropologist* **80**: 549–70.

Juyan xin jian: Jiaqu Houguan yu di si sui 居延新簡: 甲渠候官與第四燧 [New Bamboo Slips from Juyan: Jiaqu Houguan and the Fourth Beacon] (1990). Beijing.

Kalinowski, M. (1983) "Les instruments astro-calendériques des Han et la méthode Liuren," *BEFEO* **72**: 309–419.

(1986) "Les traités de Shuihudi et l'hémérologie Chinoise a la fin des Royaumes-Combattants," *TP* **72.4/5**: 175–228.

(1989–90) "La littérature divinatoire dans le Daozang," *Cahiers d'Extrême-Asie* **5**: 83–110.

(1991) *Cosmologie et divination dans la Chine ancienne: le Compendium des cinq agents (Wuxing dayi, VIe siècle)*. Paris.

(1996) "The use of the Twenty-eight Xiu as a day-count in early China," *CS* **13**: 55–81.

(1998–99) "The Xingde texts from Mawangdui," *EC* **23–24**: 125–202.

(1999) "La rhétorique oraculaire dans les chroniques anciennes de la Chine: une étude des discours prédictifs dans le Zuozhuan," *EO* **21**: 37–65.

(ed.) (2003) *Divination et société dans la Chine médiévale: Etude des manuscrits de Dunhuang de la Bibliothèque Nationale de France et de la British Library*. Paris.

(2004) "Technical traditions in ancient China and shushu culture in Chinese religion," in *Religion and Chinese Society. Volume I: Ancient and Medieval*, ed. J. Lagerwey. Hong Kong: 223–48.

(2005) "Divination et astrologie dans l'empire Han: sources historiographiques et découvertes archéologiques récentes," *Cahiers Glotz* **16**: 275–96.

(2010) "Divination and astrology: received texts and excavated manuscripts," in Nylan and Loewe (2010): 339–66.

(2011) *Wang Chong, Les traités sur la divination, la providence et le destin dans la "Balance de discours" (Lunheng)*, trans. M. Kalinowski. Paris.

Kaltenmark, M. and Ngo Van Xuyet (1966) "La Divination dans la Chine ancienne," in Caquot and Leibovici (1996), vol. 1: 333–56.

Kane, R. L. (1975) "Prophecy and perception in the Oedipus Rex," *TAPhA* **105**: 189–208.

Kaogu **1975.1**: 47–61. "Mawangdui er, san, hao Han mu fajue de zhuyao shou huo" 馬王堆二、三號漢墓發掘的主要收獲 [Major results from the brief report of the excavations of Han tombs number 2 and 3 at Mawangdui].

Kaogu **1980.5**: 391–402. "Jiangling Yutaishan Chu mu fajue jianbao" 江陵雨台山楚墓發掘簡報 [Brief report on the slips excavated from the Chu tombs at Yutaishan, Jiangling].

Kaogu **2003.6**: 3–6. "Jinan shi Daxinzhuang yizhi chutu Shangdai jiaguwen" 濟南市大辛莊遺址出土商代甲骨文 [Inscribed oracle bones of the Shang period unearthed from Daxinzhuang, Jinan City].

Kaogu xuebao **1982.1**: 71–116. "Jiangling Tianxingguan yi hao Chu mu" 江陵天星觀一號楚墓 [The Chu tomb number one at Tiangxingguan, Jiangling].

Karlgren, B. (1950a) *The Book of Documents*. Stockholm.

(1950b) *The Book of Odes*. Stockholm.

Keegan, D. J. (1988) "The 'Huang-ti Nei-ching': The Structure of the Compilation; the Significance of the Structure." Ph.D. Dissertation. University of California, Berkeley.

Keightley, D. N. (1978a) "The religious commitment: Shang theology and the genesis of Chinese political culture," *HR* **17**: 211–24.

(1978b) *Sources of Shang History: The Oracle-bone Inscriptions of Bronze Age China*. Berkeley.

(1983) "The late Shang state: when, where, and what?," in *The Origins of Chinese Civilization*, ed. D. N. Keightley. Berkeley: 523–64.

(1984) "Late Shang divination: the magico-religious legacy," in *Explorations in Early Chinese Cosmology*, ed. H. Rosemont, Jr. *Journal of the American Academy of Religion Studies* **50.2**: 11–34.

(1988) "Shang divination and metaphysics," *PEW* **38.4**: 367–97.

(1997) "Shang oracle-bone inscriptions," in Shaughnessy (1997): 15–55.

(1998) "Shamanism, death, and the ancestors: religious mediation in Neolithic and Shang China (ca. 5000–1000 B.C.)," *Asiatische Studien* **52.3**: 763–831.

(1999a) "At the beginning: the status of women in Neolithic and Shang China," *NN* **1**: 1–62.

(1999b) "The Shang: China's first historical dynasty," in Loewe and Shaughnessy (1999): 232–91.

(2000) *The Ancestral Landscape: Time, Space and Community in Late Shang China (ca. 1200–1045 B.C.)*. Berkeley.

(2006) "Sacred waste – theirs or ours?," in *Studies in Chinese Language and Culture: Festschrift in Honour of Christoph Harbsmeier on the Occasion of His 60th Birthday*, ed. C. Anderl and H. Eifring. Oslo: 3–12.

Kekule von Stradonitz, R. and H. Winnefeld (1909) *Bronzen aus Dodona in den Königlichen Museen zu Berlin*. Berlin.

Kern, M. (2000) "Religious anxiety and political interest in Western Han omen interpretation: the case of the Han Wudi period (141–87 B.C.)," *Chūgoku shigaku* **10**: 1–31.

(ed.) (2005) *Text and Ritual in Early China*. Seattle.

Kern, O. (ed.) (1900) *Die Inschriften von Magnesia am Maeander*. Berlin.

Kindt, J. C. (2003) "The Delphic Oracle: A Poetics of Futures Past Between History, Literature and Religion." Ph.D. Dissertation. University of Cambridge.

(2006) "Delphic oracle stories and the beginning of historiography: Herodotus' Croesus logos," *CPh* **101**: 34–51.

(2007) "Apollo's oracle in Euripides' Ion: ambiguous identities in fifth-century Athens," *Ancient Narrative* **6**: 1–30.

(2008) "Oracular ambiguity as a mediation triple," *Classicum* **334**: 23–27.
(forthcoming) *Futures Past in Fifth-Century Athens.*

Kinney, A. B. (1991) "Predestination and prognostication in the Ch'ien-fu lun," *JCR* **19**: 27–45.

Klees, H. (1965) *Die Eigenart des griechischen Glaubens an Orakel und Seher: Ein Vergleich zwischen griechischer und nichtgriechischer Mantik bei Herodot.* Stuttgart.

Kleinman, A. (1980) *Patients and Healers in the Context of Culture: An Exploration of the Borderland between Anthropology, Medicine and Psychiatry.* Berkeley.

Knechtges, D. R. (1987) *Wen Xuan or Selections of Refined Literature.* 3 vols. Princeton, rpt. 1996.

Knoblock, J. and J. Riegel (2000) *The Annals of Lü Buwei: A Complete Translation and Study.* Palo Alto.

Kohn, L. (1986) "A textbook of physiognomy: the tradition of the 'Shenxiang quanbian,'" *Asian Folklore Studies* **45.2**: 227–58.

Konstan, D. (2001) "To Hellēnikon ethnos: ethnicity and the construction of ancient Greek identity," in Malkin 2001: 29–50.

Ku T'ieh-fu. See Gu Tiefu.

Kuriyama, Shigehisa (1999) *The Expressiveness of the Body and the Divergence of Greek and Chinese Medicine.* New York.

Kuroda Genji 黒田源次 (1977) *Kino kenkyū* 氣の研究 [Research on Qi]. Tokyo.

Labat, R. (1951) *Traité Akkadien de diagnostics et pronostics médicaux.* Leiden.

Lagerwey, J. and M. Kalinowski (eds.) (2009) *Early Chinese Religion. Part One: Shang through Han (1250 BC–220 AD)* (2 vols.). Leiden.

Lane Fox, R. (1973) *Alexander the Great.* London and New York, paperback edn., 2004.

Lang, G. and L. Ragvald (1998) "Spirit-writing and the development of Chinese cults," *Sociology of Religion* **58.14**: 309–22.

Langholf, V. (1990) *Medical Theories in Hippocrates: Early Texts and the "Epidemics."* Berlin.

Lau, D. C. (1970) *Mencius.* London and New York.

LeBlanc, C. and S. Blader (eds.) (1987) *Chinese Ideas about Nature and Society: Studies in Honour of Derk Bodde.* Hong Kong.

LeBlanc, C. and D. Borei (eds.) (1981) *Derk Bodde: Essays on Chinese Civilization.* Princeton.

Legge, J. (1885a) *The Chinese Classics, Volume III: The Shoo King, or The Book of Historical Documents.*
(1885b) *The Chinese Classics, Volume IV: The She King, or The Book of Poetry.*
(1885c) *The Chinese Classics, Volume V: The Ch'un Ts'ew with the Tso Chuen.* 2nd edn. Oxford, rpt. Hong Kong, 1960.
(1885d) *Li Chi: Book of Rites. Sacred Books of the East*, vols. 27 and 28. Oxford, rpt. New York, 2 vols., 1967.

Legrand, P. E. (1900) "Questions oraculaires: 1. la promanteia," *REG* **13**: 281–301.

Leibovici, M. (1966) "Introduction," in Caquot and Leibovici (1966), vol. I: v–xix.

Lévi-Strauss, C. (1963) *Structural Anthropology.* New York.

Lévy, E. (1997) "Devins et oracles chez Hérodote," in Heintz (1997): 345–65.

Lewis, M. E. (1990) *Sanctioned Violence in Early China*. Albany.

(1999) *Writing and Authority in Early China*. Albany.

L'Hôte, E. (2006) *Les Lamelles Oraculaires de Dodone*. Geneva.

Li ji zhu shu 禮記注疏 [Commentary and Subcommentary to the Book of Rites]. *SSJZS*.

Li Jiemin 李解民 (2000) "'Yinwan Han mu "Bo ju zhan" mu du shijie' ding bu" 《尹彎漢墓〈博局占〉木牘試解》訂補 [Explanation of the restoration of the TLV divination diagrams of the Han tombs at Yinwan], *WW* **2000.8**: 73–75.

Li Jingchi 李鏡池 (1978) "Zuo Guo zhong Yi shi zhi yan jiu" 左國中易筮之研究 [Research on Yi and yarrow divination in the Zuo zhuan and Guoyu], in *Zhou yi tan yuan* 周易探源. Beijing.

Li Ling 李零 (1985) *Changsha Zidanku Zhanguo Chu bo shu yan jiu* 長沙子彈庫戰國楚帛書研究 [Research on the Warring States Chu bamboo slips from Zidanku, Changsha]. Beijing.

(1990) "Formulaic structure of Chu divinatory bamboo slips," trans. W. G. Boltz, *EC* **15**: 71–86.

(1993) *Zhongguo fang shu kao* 中國方術考 [A Study of the Occult Arts of China]. Beijing.

(1995) "Zhanguo Qin Han fang shi liu pai kao" 戰國秦漢方士流派考 [The sects of Warring States, Qin, and Han fangshi], *Chuantong wenhua yu xiandai hua* 傳統文化與現代化 **1995.2**: 34–48.

(2000a) "Ru shan yu chu sai" 入山與出塞 [Entering mountains and crossing borders], *WW* **2000.2**: 87–95.

(2000b) "Taiyi chong bai de kao gu yan jiu" 太乙崇拜的考古研究 [An archaeological study of the worship of Taiyi], in Li Ling (2000): 207–38, trans. as Harper (1995–96).

(2000c) *Zhongguo fang shu xu kao* 中國方術續考 [Supplementary Studies of the Occult Arts of China]. Beijing.

(2011) "Beida Han jian zhong de shu shu shu" 北大漢簡中的數朮書 [Books on numbers and techniques in the Western Han bamboo slips collected by Peking University], *WW* **2011.6**: 80–83.

Li Xueqin 李學勤 (1956) "Tan Anyang Xiaotun yiwai chutu de you zi jiagu" 談安陽小屯 以外出土的有字甲骨 [Discussion of the characters in oracle bones excavated from Xiaotun, Anyang], *Wenwu cankao ziliao* 文物參考資料 **1956.11**: 16–17.

(1985a) *Eastern Zhou and Qin Civilizations*. New Haven.

(1985b) "Shuihudi Qin jian 'rishu' yu Chu Qin shehui" 睡虎地秦簡《日書》與楚秦社會 [The Qin bamboo slip daybooks from Shuihudi and Chu and Qin society], *JHKG* **4**: 60–64.

(1990) "Fangmatan jian zhong de zhi guai gu shi" 放馬灘簡中的志怪故事 [A ghost story in the bamboo slips from Fangmatan], *WW* **1990.4**: 43–47.

(1992) *Zhou yi jing zhuan su yuan* 周易經傳溯源 [Tracing the Sources of the Classics and Commentaries of the Zhouyi]. Changqun.

(1992–93) "A Neolithic jade plaque and ancient Chinese cosmology," *National Palace Museum Bulletin* **27.5/6**: 1–8.

(1997) "Bo ju zhan yu gui ju wen" 博局占與規矩文 [Divination by gambling and the TLV design], *WW* **1997.1**: 49–51.

and Xing Wen 邢文 (2001) "New light on the early-Han code: a reappraisal of the Zhangjiashan bamboo-slip legal texts," *AM* **14.1**: 125–46.

Li Wai-yee (1999) "Knowledge and skepticism in ancient Chinese historiography and philosophy," in *The Limits of Historiography: Genre and Narrative in Ancient Historical Texts*, ed. C. S. Kraus. Leiden: 27–54.

Liao Mingchun 廖名春 (1993) "Bo shu 'Yao' jian shuo" 帛書《要》簡說 [Explanation of the "Yao" bamboo strips from the silk manuscripts], *DJ* **3**: 202–6.

(2000a) "Cong Guodian Chu jian lun xian Qin Ru jia yu 'Zhou yi' de guanxi" 從郭店楚簡論先秦儒家與《周易》的關係 [A study of the relationship between the Book of Changes and pre-Qin Confucianism based on the Guodian bamboo slips], *Han xue yan jiu* **18.1**: 55–72.

(2000b) "Guodian Chu jian yin Shu lun Shu kao" 郭店楚簡引書論書考 [Investigation of materials on the Shangshu in the Chu slips from Guodian], in *Guodian Chu jian Guoji xue shu yan tao hui lun wen ji* 郭店楚簡國際學術研討會論文集. Wuhan: 111–27.

and Zhu Yuanqing 朱淵清 (eds.) (2002) *Shang bo guan cang Zhanguo Chu zhu shu yan jiu* 上博館藏戰國楚竹書研究 [Research on the Warring States Chu Bamboo Documents in the Treasures of the Shanghai Museum]. Shanghai.

Liddell, H. G. and R. Scott (1883) *Greek–English Lexicon*. 7th edn. New York. Retrieved from www.books.google.com/books?id=IEQQAAAAYAAJ.

Lienü zhuan jiao zhu 列女傳校注 [Collected Commentaries on the Collected Life Stories of Women] (1983), att. Liu Xiang 劉向, ed. Liang Duan 梁端. Taipei. [*LNZ*]

Lippiello, T. (2001) *Auspicious Omens and Miracles in Ancient China: Han, Three Kingdoms, and Six Dynasties*. Sankt Augustin.

Littré, E. (1844) *Oeuvres complètes d'Hippocrate* (10 vols.). Paris, rpt. Amsterdam, 1962. [L]

Liu Chun 劉淳 (2010) "The Motif of Fate in Homeric Epics and Oedipus Tyrannus." Ph.D. Dissertation. University of California, Riverside.

Liu Lexian 劉樂賢 (1994) *Shuihudi Qin jian rishu yan jiu* 睡虎地秦簡日書研究 [A Study of the Qin Daybooks from Shuihudi]. Taipei.

(1996) "Jiudian Chu jian rishu yan jiu" 九店楚簡日書研究 [Research on the Chu daybooks from Jiudian], *Hua xue* **2.12**: 61–71.

(1997) "Yinwan Han jian 'Xing dao ji xiong' chu tan" 尹灣漢簡《行道吉凶》初探 [A preliminary study of the "Xingdao jixiong" Han slips from Yinwan], *Zhongguo shi yan jiu* **1997.4**: 50–53.

Liu Qiyu 劉起釪 (2004) "Yaodian Xi He zhang yanjiu" 堯典羲和章研究 [Research on the memorial of Xi He in the Yaodian], *Zhongguo shehui kexue yuan lishi yanjiusuo xuekan* 中國社會科學院歷史研究所學刊 **2**: 43–70. Beijing.

Liu Shu-hsien (1991) "A critical review of contemporary Neo-Confucian thought with a view to modernisation," in *The Triadic Chord: Confucian Ethics, Industrial Asia, and Max Weber*, ed. Tu Wei-ming. Singapore: 377–96.

Liu tao 六韜 [The Six Tactics]. *SBCK*.

Liu Wenying 劉文英 (1995) *An Oriental Interpretation of Dreams*, trans. Zhang Zhixiang 張致祥 and Pan Chuanfa 潘傳發. Beijing.

(2000) *Meng de mi xin yu meng de tan suo* 夢的迷信與夢的探索 [Dream Superstitions and the Exploration of Dreams]. Beijing.

Liuren daquan 六壬大全 [Complete Book of Liuren]. Anon. Ming dynasty. *SKQS*.

Lloyd, G. E. R. (1979) *Magic, Reason and Experience: Studies in the Origins and Development of Greek Science*. Cambridge.

(1983) *Science, Folklore and Ideology: Studies in the Life Sciences in Ancient Greece*. Cambridge.

(1987) *The Revolutions of Wisdom: Studies in the Claims and Practice of Ancient Greek Science*. Cambridge.

(1990) *Demystifying Mentalities*. Cambridge.

(1994) "Learning by numbers," *EO* **16**: 153–67.

(1996) *Adversaries and Authorities: Investigations into Ancient Greek and Chinese Science*. Cambridge.

(1999a) "Divination: traditions and controversies, Chinese and Greek," *EO* **21**: 156–65.

(1999b) "Mythology: reflections from a Chinese perspective," in Buxton (1999): 145–68.

(2002) *The Ambitions of Curiosity: Understanding the World in Ancient Greece and China*. Cambridge.

(2003) *In the Grip of Disease: Studies in the Greek Imagination*. Oxford.

(2007) *Cognitive Variations: Reflections on the Unity and Diversity of the Human Mind*. Oxford.

and N. Sivin (2002) *The Way and The Word: Science and Medicine in Early China and Greece*. New Haven.

Lloyd-Jones, H. (1976) "The Delphic oracle," *G&R* **23**: 60–73.

Lo, V. (2005) "Self-cultivation and the popular medical traditions," in Lo and Cullen (2005): 207–25.

and C. Cullen (eds.) (2005) *Medieval Chinese Medicine: The Dunhuang Medical Manuscripts*. London.

Lo, Y. K. (2010) "Destiny and retribution in early medieval China," in *Philosophy and Religion in Early Medieval China*, ed. A. K. L. Chan and Y. K. Lo. Albany: 319–56.

Loewe, M. (1979) *Ways to Paradise: The Chinese Quest for Immortality*. London.

(1981) "China," in Loewe and Blacker (1981): 38–62.

(1982) *Chinese Ideas of Life and Death: Faith, Myth, and Reason in the Han Period (202 BC–AD 220)*. London and Boston, rpt. Boston 2005 as *Faith, Myth and Reason in Han China*.

(ed.) (1993) *Early Chinese Texts: A Bibliographical Guide*. Berkeley. [ECTBG]

(1994) *Divination, Mythology and Monarchy in Han China*. Cambridge.
(1997) "The physician Chunyu Yi and his historical background," in *En suivant La voie royale*, ed. J. Gernet, M. Kalinowski, and J.-P. Dièny. Paris: 297–313.
(2000) *A Biographical Dictionary of the Qin, Han and Xin Dynasties*. Leiden.
(2004) *The Men who Governed China in Han Times*. Leiden.
(2006) *The Government of the Qin and Han Empires: 221 BCE–220 CE*. Cambridge, MA.
and C. Blacker (eds.) (1981) *Oracles and Divination*. London and Boston.
and E. L. Shaughnessy (eds.) (1999) *The Cambridge History of Ancient China: From the Origins of Civilization to 221 B.C.* Cambridge.
Long, A. A. (1972) "Plutarch and Stoicism," review of Babut (1969), *CR*, n.s. **22.1**: 27–29.
Lonis, R. (1979) *Guerre et religion en Grèce à l'époque classique: Recherches sur les rites, les dieux, l'idéologie de la victoire*. Paris.
Lü shi chunqiu jiao shi 呂氏春秋校釋 [Springs and Autumns of Master Lü], by Lü Buwei 呂不韋 (291?–235 BCE), ed. Chen Qiyou 陳奇猷. Shanghai, 1984. [*LSCQ*]
Lun heng 論衡 [Weighing Discourses], by Wang Chong 王充 (27–97) (1990), in *Lun heng jiao shi* 論衡校釋, ed. Liu Pansui 劉盼遂, Beijing. [*LH*]
Lunyu zheng yi 論語正義 [Standard Edition of the Analects], ed. Liu Baonan 劉寶楠. *ZZJC*.
Luo Fuyi 羅福頤 (1974) "Linyi Han jian gai shu" 臨沂漢簡概述 [Notes on the Han bamboo slips from Linyi], *WW* **1974.2**: 32–35.
Lupke, C. (ed.) (2005) *The Magnitude of Ming: Command, Allotment, and Fate in Chinese Culture*. Honolulu.
Lynn, R. J. (1994) *The Classic of Changes: A New Translation of the I Ching as Interpreted by Wang Bi*. New York.
Ma Chengyuan 馬承源 (2002) "Ma Chengyuan xian sheng tan Shang bo jian" 馬承源先生談上博簡 [Mister Ma Chengyuan discusses the Shanghai Museum slips], in Liao and Zhu (2002): 1–8.
et al. (2001–8) *Shanghai Bowuguan Cang Zhanguo Chu Zhu Shu* 上海博物館藏戰國楚竹書 [The Shanghai Museum Warring States Chu Bamboo Texts] (7 vols.). Shanghai.
Ma Guohan 馬國翰 (1883) *Yuhan shan fang ji yi shu* 玉函山房輯佚書 [A Collection of Lost Books from the Yuhan Studio]. Changsha, rpt. Shanghai, 1999.
Major, J. S. (1993) *Heaven and Earth in Early Han Thought*. Albany.
Malinowski, B. (1954) *Magic Science and Religion*. New York.
Malkin, I. (1987) *Religion and Colonisation in Ancient Greece*. Leiden.
(ed.) (2001) *Ancient Perceptions of Greek Ethnicity*. Cambridge, MA.
Manetti, G. (1993) *Theories of the Sign in Classical Antiquity*, trans. C. Richardson. Bloomington, IN.
Mansvelt-Beck, B. J. (1990) *The Treatises of Later Han: Their Author, Sources, Contents and Place in Chinese Historiography*. Leiden.
Maspéro, H. (1924) "Légendes mythologiques dans le Chou king," *JA* **204** (Jan.–Mar.): 1–100.

Maurizio, L. (1993) "Delphic Narratives: Recontextualizing the Pythia and her Prophecies." Ph.D. Dissertation. Stanford University.
(1995) "Anthropology and spirit possession: a reconsideration of the Pythia's role at Delphi," *JHS* **115**: 69–86.
(1997) "Delphic oracles as oral performances: authenticity and historical evidence," *CA* **16.2**: 308–34.
(2001) "The voice at the center of the world: the Pythias' ambiguity and authority," in *Making Silence Speak: Women's Voices in Greek Literature and Society*, ed. A. Lardinois and L. McClure. Princeton: 38–54.
Mawangdui Han mu bo shu 馬王堆漢墓帛書 [The Silk Manuscripts from the Han Tombs at Mawangdui] (1980–) (6 vols.). Beijing. [*MWD*]
Mawangdui Han mu wen wu. See Fu Juyou and Chen Songchang.
McLeod, W. E. (1961) "Oral bards at Delphi," *TAPhA* **92**: 317–25.
Mengzi zhengyi 孟子正義 [Standard Edition of Mencius], ed. Jiao Xun 焦循 (1763–1820). Beijing, 1987.
Merriam, A. C. (1884) "On an inscription of Dodona," *AJPh* **5.1**: 85–86.
Mikalson, J. (2003) *Herodotus and Religion in the Persian Wars*. Chapel Hill.
Milet: Ergebnisse der Ausgrabungen und Untersuchungen. See Wiegand et al. (1906–).
Monro, D. B. (1884) "The poems of the epic cycle," *JHS* **5**: 1–41.
Moore, O. K. (1957) "Divination – a new perspective," *American Anthropologist* **59**: 69–74.
Moreau, A. (1990) "Déjouer l'oracle ou la précaution inutile," *Kernos* **3**: 261–79.
Morgan, Carole (1987) "A propos des fiches oraculaires de Huang Daxian," *JA* **275**: 1–2.
Morgan, Catherine (1988) "Corinth, the Corinthian gulf and western Greece during the 8th century BC," *Annual of the British School at Athens* **83**: 313–38.
(1989) "Divination and society at Delphi and Didyma," *Hermathena* **147**: 17–42.
(1990) *Athletes and Oracles: The Transformation of Olympia and Delphi in the Eighth Century BC*. Cambridge.
(2001) "Ethne, ethnicity and early Greek states, ca.1200–480: an archaeological perspective," in Malkin (2001): 75–112.
Morris, I. (1987) *Burial and Ancient Society*. Cambridge.
(1989) "Attitudes toward death in archaic Greece," *CA* **8**: 297–320.
(1992) *Death Ritual and Social Structure in Classical Antiquity*. Cambridge.
(1993) "Poetics of power: the interpretation of ritual action in archaic Greece," in Dougherty and Kurke (1993): 15–45.
Morrison, J. I. (1993) "Predicting the future," review of Howe and Wain (1993), *British Medical Journal* **306.6886** (May 1): 1216.
Mozi 墨子, in *Mozi jian gu* 墨子閒詁, ed. Sun Yirang 孫詒讓 (1895), rpt. Xinbian Zhuzi jicheng.
Murray, O. (2007) "Jean-Pierre Vernant: resistance leader and Hellenist," *The Independent*. 11 January. Online edn. www.independent.co.uk/news/obituaries/jeanpierre-vernant-431606.html.

Nagy, G. (1990) *Pindar's Homer: The Lyric Possession of an Epic Past*. Baltimore.
(1996) *Poetry as Performance: Homer and Beyond*. Cambridge, MA.
Nakayama, Shigeru (1966) "Characteristics of Chinese astrology," *Isis* **57.4**: 442–54.
Needham, J. (1959) *Science and Civilisation in China*, vol. 3: *Mathematics and the Sciences of the Heavens and the Earth*. Cambridge.
and Wang Ling (1956) *Science and Civilisation in China*, vol. 2: *History of Scientific Thought*. Cambridge.
(1962) *Science and Civilisation in China*, vol. 4, part 1: *Physics and Physical Technology*. Cambridge.
Neer, R. T. (2001) "Framing the gift: the politics of the Siphnian treasury at Delphi," *CA* **20**: 273–336.
(2004) "The Athenian treasury at Delphi and the material of politics," *CA* **23.1**: 63–93.
Netz, R. (2002) "Counter culture: towards a history of Greek numeracy," *History of Science* **40.3**: 321–52.
Neugebauer, O. (1975) *A History of Ancient Mathematical Astronomy*. Berlin.
and G. Saliba (1988) "On Greek numerology," *Centaurus* **31**: 189–206.
Nevius, J. L. (1869) *China and the Chinese*. New York.
Newton, C. T. and F. H. Marshall (eds.) (1874–1916) *The Collection of Ancient Greek Inscriptions in the British Museum* (4 vols.). Oxford. [*AGIBM*]
Ng, On-cho (2003) "The epochal concept of 'early modernity' and the intellectual history of late imperial China," *Journal of World History* **14.1**: 37–61.
Ngo Van Xuyet (1976) *Divination, magie et politique dans la Chine ancienne*. Paris, rpt. You-feng, 2002.
Nicol, D. M. (1958) "The oracle of Dodona," *G&R*, 2nd ser. **5.2**: 128–43.
Nilsson, M. P. (1940) *Greek Popular Religion*. New York.
Nivison, D. (1982) "The 'question' question." Paper for the international conference on Shang civilization, University of Hawaii, East–West Center. Honolulu.
Nock, A. D. (1972) *Essays*, ed. Z. Stewart (2 vols.). Oxford.
Nylan, M. (2001a) *The Five "Confucian" Classics*. New Haven.
(2001b) "On the politics of pleasure," *AM* **14.1**: 73–124.
(2005) "Towards an archaeology of writing: text, ritual, and the culture of public display in the classical period (475 B.C.E.–220 C.E.)," in Kern (2005): 3–49.
(2009) "The rhetoric of 'empire' in the classical period in China," in *Conceiving the Empire: China and Rome Compared*, ed. F.-H. Mutschler and A. Mittag. Oxford: 39–64.
(2010) "Yin–yang, five phases, and qi," in Nylan and Loewe (2010): 398–414.
and M. Loewe (eds.) (2010) *China's Early Empires: A Re-appraisal*. Cambridge.
and N. Sivin (1987) "The first Neo-Confucianism: an introduction to the 'Canon of supreme mystery' (T'ai hsuan ching, ca. 4 B.C.)," in LeBlanc and Blader (1987): 41–99.
Ong, R. (1985) *The Interpretation of Dreams in Ancient China*. Bochum.
Oppenheim, A. L. (1977) *Ancient Mesopotamia: Portrait of a Dead Civilization*. Chicago.

Opsomer, J. (1996) "Divination and Academic 'scepticism' according to Plutarch," *Studia Hellenistica* **32**: 165–94.

Osborne, M. J. (1981–82) *Naturalization in Athens* (2 vols.). Brussels.

Osborne, R. (1989) "A crisis in archaeological history? The seventh century B.C. in Attica," *British Studies in Archaeology* **84**: 297–322.

(1991) "Olympia and Delphi," review of Morgan (1990), *CR*, n.s. **41.2**: 439–40.

(1997) *Greece in the Making c.1200–479 BC*. London.

Padel, R. (1983) "Women: models for possession by Greek daemons," in *Images of Women in Antiquity*, ed. A. Cameron and A. Kuhrt. London: 3–19.

Pang Pu 龐樸 (1988) *Langyou ji* 稂莠集 [A Collection of Weeds and Grass]. Shanghai.

Pankenier, D. W. (2010) "Cosmic capitals and numinous precincts in early China." *Journal of Cosmology* **9**: 2030–40.

Ciyuan Y. Liu, and S. de Meis (2009) "The Xiangfen, Taosi site: a Chinese Neolithic 'observatory'?" *Archaeologica Baltica* **10**: 141–48.

Park, G. K. (1963) "Divination and its social contexts," *Journal of the Royal Anthropological Institute* **93**: 195–209.

and R. A. Gilbert (2003) "Divination," *Encyclopedia Britannica*. Encyclopedia Britannica Online. www.search.eb.com/eb/article?eu=114999.

Parke, H. W. (1939) *A History of the Delphic Oracle*. London.

(1943) "The days for consulting the Delphic oracle," *CQ* **37**: 19–22.

(1967) *The Oracles of Zeus: Dodona, Olympia, Ammon*. Cambridge, MA.

(1984) "Croesus and Delphi," *GRBS* **25.3**: 209–32.

(1988) *Sibyls and Sybilline Prophecy in Classical Antiquity*, ed. B. C. McGing. London.

and Wormell, D. E. (1956) *The Delphic Oracle* (2 vols.). Oxford. [PW]

Parker, R. (1983) *Miasma: Pollution and Purification in Early Greek Religion*. Oxford.

(2000a) "Greek states and Greek oracles," in Buxton (2000): 76–108. First published in *Crux: Essays in Greek History presented to G. E. M. de Ste Croix on his 75th Birthday*, eds. P. A. Cartledge and F. D. Harvey. London: 298–326.

(2000b) "Sacrifice and battle," in *War and Violence in Ancient Greece*, ed. H. van Wees and P. Beston. London: 299–314.

Parpola, S. (1993) *Letters from Assyrian and Babylonian Scholars*. Helsinki.

Peek, P. M. (ed.) (1991) *African Divination Systems: Ways of Knowing*. Bloomington.

Pines, Y. (2002) *Foundations of Confucian Thought: Intellectual Life in the Chunqiu Period, 722–453 B.C.E.* Honolulu.

Pokora, T. (1987) "Shih chi 127: the symbiosis of two historians," in LeBlanc and Blader (1987): 215–34.

Polyaenus. *Stratagems*, in *Polyaenus Stratagems of War*, ed. and trans. P. Krentz and I. L. Wheeler (2 vols.). Chicago, 1994.

Poo Mu-chou (1993) "Popular religion in early imperial China: observations on the almanacs of Shui-hu-ti," *TP* **79**: 225–48.

(1998) *In Search of Personal Welfare: A View of Ancient Chinese Religion*. Albany.
(2009) "Popular belief in ancient China." The China Mirror. Center for Chinese Studies. University of Michigan. www.lsa.umich.edu/chinamirror/moduleview_5.asp?MID=5&PID=1.
See Pu Muzhou.
Popp, H. (1957) "Die Einwirkung von Vorzeichen, Opfern und Festen auf die Kriegführung der Griechen im 5. und 4. Jahrhundert v. Chr." Ph.D. Dissertation. Erlangen.
Posidonius. *Die Fragmenta*. Berlin, 1982.
Postgate, N., T. Wang, and T. Wilkinson (1995) "The evidence for early ceremonial writing: utilitarian or ceremonial?," *Antiquity* **69**: 459–80.
Powell, A. (1979) 'Thucydides and divination," *BICS* **26**: 45–50.
Preisendanz, K. and A. Henrichs (eds.) (1973–74) *Papyri Graecae Magicae: Die griechischen Zauberpapyri* (2 vols.). Stuttgart.
Price, S. (1985) "Delphi and divination," in *Greek Religion and Society*, ed. P. E. Easterling and J. V. Muir. Cambridge: 128–54.
(1999) *Religions of the Ancient Greeks*. Cambridge.
Pritchett, W. K. (1974–79) *The Greek State at War* (3 vols.). Berkeley.
Pu Maozuo 濮茅左 (2006) *Chu zhu shu Zhou yi yan jiu* 楚竹書周易研究 [Research on the Chu Bamboo Texts of the Zhou yi] (2 vols.). Shanghai.
Pu Muzhou 蒲慕州 (1992) "Shuihudi Qin jian rishu de shijie" 睡虎地秦簡日書的世界. *BIHP* **62.4**: 623–75. See Poo Mu-chou.
Puett, M. J. (2001) *The Ambivalence of Creation: Debates Concerning Innovation and Artifice in Early China*. Palo Alto.
(2002) *To Become a God: Cosmology, Sacrifice and Self-Divinization in Early China*. Cambridge, MA.
Qian Baocong 錢寶琮 (1932) "Taiyi kao" 太一攷 [An Examination of Tai Yi]. *Yanjing xuebao* **12**: 2449–78.
Qianfu lun 潛夫論 [Comments of a Recluse], by Wang Fu 王符 (ca. 90–165), in *Qianfu lun jian jiao zheng* 潛夫論箋校正, ed. Peng Duo 彭鐸. Beijing, 1997.
Qin ding gu jin tu shu ji cheng 欽定古今圖書集成 [Imperial Edition of the Complete Collection of Past and Present Illustrations and Writings]. 1726, ed. Jiang Tingxi 蔣廷錫. Beijing, 1985.
Qin jian jian du lun wen ji 秦簡簡牘論文集 [Collected Essays on Qin Bamboo Slips]. Lanzhou, 1989.
Qiu Xigui 裘錫圭 (1989) "An examination of whether the charges in Shang oracle-bone inscriptions are questions," *EC* **14**: 77–114.
(2000) *Chinese Writing* (文字學概要), trans. G. L. Mattos and J. Norman. Berkeley.
Rao Zongyi 饒宗頤 (1982) "Yin dai yi gua ji you guan zhan bu zhu wen ti" 殷代易卦及有關占卜諸問題 [Various questions on Shang dynasty Yi hexagrams and their relation to divination], *Wen shi* **20**: 1–13.

(1993) "Tan Yinqueshan jian 'tian di ba feng wu xing ke zhu wu yin zhi ju'" 談銀雀山簡天地八風五行客主五音之居 [Discussion of the Yinqueshan bamboo text "Gathering together of heaven and earth, the eight winds, the five phases, guest and host, and the five tones"], *Jianbo yan jiu* **1**: 113–19.

and Zeng Xiantong 曾憲通 (1982) *Yunmeng Qin jian rishu yan jiu* 雲夢秦簡日書研究 [A Study of the Qin Bamboo Daybooks from Yunmeng]. Hong Kong.

Raphals, L. A. (1992) *Knowing Words: Wisdom and Cunning in the Classical Traditions of China and Greece*. Ithaca.

(1998a) *Sharing the Light: Representations of Women and Virtue in Early China*. Albany.

(1998b) "The treatment of women in a second-century medical casebook," *CS*: 7–28.

(2002) "A 'Chinese Eratosthenes' reconsidered: Chinese and Greek calculations and categories," *EASTM* **19**: 10–61.

(2003) "Fate, fortune, chance, and luck in Chinese and Greek: a comparative semantic history," *PEW* **53.4**: 537–74.

(2004) "Notes on the Baoshan medical manuscripts," in Ai Lan 艾蘭 (S. Allan) and Xing Wen 邢文 (eds.) (2004): 388–408.

(2005) "Divination and medicine in China and Greece: a comparative perspective on the Baoshan illness divinations," *EASTM* **24**: 78–103.

(2008–9) "Divination in the *Han shu* Bibliographic treatise," *EC* **32**: 45–102.

(2009) "Thirteen ways of looking at the self in early China," *HPhQ* **26.4**: 315–36.

Riedweg, C. and S. Rendall (2008) *Pythagoras: His Life, Teaching, and Influence*. Ithaca.

Rehm, A. and R. Harder (eds.) (1958) *Didyma: Die Inschriften* (2 vols.). Berlin. [DI]

Reiner, E. and D. Pingree (1975) *Bibliotheca Mesopotamica Vol II Fasc.1. Babylonian Planetary Omens: Part 1, Enuma Anu Enlil, Tablet 63: The Venus Tablet of Ammisaduqa*. Malibu, CA.

Rhodes, P. and R. Osborne (2003) *Greek Historical Inscriptions, 404–323 BC*. Oxford. [RO]

Ricci, M. (1910–13) *Opere storiche* (2 vols.), ed. Fr. Tacchi Venturi. Macerata.

Rickett, W. A. (1985–98) *Guanzi: Political, Economic and Philosophical Essays from Early China* (2 vols.). Princeton.

Robert, L. (1938) *Études épigraphiques et philologiques*. Paris.

Roberts, D. H. (1984) *Apollo and his Oracle in the Oresteia*. Göttingen.

Roberts, E. S. (1880) "The oracle inscriptions discovered at Dodona," *JHS* **1**: 228–41.

(1881) "Inscriptions from Dodona II," *JHS* **2**: 102–21.

Robertson, N. (1978) "The myth of the First Sacred War," *CQ*, n.s. **28.1**: 38–73.

Robinson, T. L. (1981) "Theological Oracles and the Sanctuaries of Claros and Didyma." PhD dissertation, Harvard University.

Rochberg, F. (2000) "Babylonian horoscopy: the texts and their relations," in *Ancient Astronomy and Celestial Divination*, ed. N. M. Swerdlow. Cambridge, MA: 39–60.

(2004) *The Heavenly Writing: Divination, Horoscopy, and Astronomy in Mesopotamian Culture*. Cambridge.

Rosenberger, V. (1999) "Die Ökonomie der Pythia oder: Wirtschaftliche Aspekte griechischer Orakel," *Laverna* **10**: 153–64.

(2001) *Griechische Orakel: Eine Kulturgeschichte*. Darmstadt.

Roth, P. (1982) "Mantis: The Nature, Function, and Status of a Greek Prophetic Type." Ph.D. Dissertation. Bryn Mawr College.

(1984) "Tiresias as mantis and intellectual in Euripides' Bacchae," *TAPhA* **114**: 59–69.

Roux, G. (1976) *Delphes: son oracle et ses dieux*. Paris.

Sanguo yanyi 三國演義 [Romance of the Three Kingdoms], by Luo Guanzhong 羅貫中. Hong Kong, n.d., trans. as *Romance of the Three Kingdoms* by C. H. Brewitt-Taylor (2 vols.). Rutland and Tokyo, 1959, paperback edn. 1990.

Sawyer, R. D. (1993) *The Seven Military Classics of Ancient China*. Boulder.

Schaab-Hanke, D. (2003–4) "Did Chu Shaosun contribute to a tradition of the scribe?'" *Oriens Extremus* **44**: 11–26.

Schaberg, D. (2001) *A Patterned Past: Form and Thought in Early Chinese Historiography*. Cambridge, MA.

Schilling, D. (2009) *Yijing: Das Buch der Wandlungen*. Frankfurt and Leipzig.

Seiwert, H. M. (1979) *Orakelwesen und Zukunftsdeutung im chinesischen Altertum: Eine Religionsgeschichtliche Untersuchung zur Entwicklung des Welt- und Menschenbildes während der Zhou-Dynastie*. Bonn.

Shang Chengzuo 商承祚, comp. (1995) *Zhanguo Chu zhu jian hui bian* 戰國楚竹簡匯編 [Compendium of Warring States and Chu Bamboo Slips]. Shandong.

Shangjun shu 尚君書 [The Book of Lord Shang]. *ZZJC*.

Shaughnessy, E. L. (1981–82) "Some observations about milfoil divination based on Shang and Zhou *bagua* numerical symbols," trans. of Zhang Yachu and Liu Yu (1981) *EC* **7**: 46–54.

(1983) "The Composition of the Zhouyi." Ph.D. Dissertation. Stanford University.

(1985–87) "Zhouyuan oracle-bone inscriptions: entering the research stage?," *EC* **11–12**: 146–63.

(1996) *I Ching, The Classic of Changes: The First English Translation of the Newly Discovered Second-Century B.C. Mawangdui Texts*. New York.

(ed.) (1997) *New Sources of Early Chinese History: An Introduction to the Reading of Inscriptions and Manuscripts*. Berkeley.

(2001) "The Fuyang *Zhou yi* and the making of a divination manual," *AM*, 3rd ser. **14.1**: 7–18.

(2005–6) "A first reading of the Shanghai Museum bamboo-strip manuscript of the *Zhou yi*," *EC* **30**: 1–24.

Shen Gua 沈括 (1086) *Meng xi bi tan jiao zheng* 夢溪筆談校證 [Dream Pool Essays, variorum edition], ed. Hu Daojing 胡道靜 (2 vols.). Shanghai, 1956.

Shi ji 史記 [Annals], by Sima Qian 司馬遷 (?145–?86) and others. Beijing, 1959. [*SJ*]

Shi Qi 施杞 (1994) *Zhong yi bing an xue* 中醫病案學 [The Study of Case Histories in Chinese Medicine]. Shanghai.

Shils, E. (1965) "Charisma, order, and status," *American Sociological Review* **30.2**: 199–213.

Shisan jing zhushu 十三經注疏, comp. Ruan Yuan 阮元, 1815, facs. rpt. Taipei, 1980.

Shuihudi Qin mu zhu jian 睡虎地秦墓竹簡 [The Inscribed Books from the Qin Tombs at Shuihudi]. Beijing, 1990. [*SHD*]

Sibu beiyao 四部備要. Shanghai, 1927–35. [*SBBY*]

Sibu congkan 四部叢刊. Shanghai, 1919–36. [*SBCK*]

Siku quanshu zongmu 四庫全書總目 [Annotated Catalog of the Complete Collection of the Four Treasuries]. 1782, rpt. Beijing, 1965.

Sinn, U. (1991) "Olympia: die Stellung der Wettkämpfe im Kult des Zeus Olympios," *Nikephoros* **4**: 31–54.

Sivin, N. (1978) "Cosmos and computation in early Chinese mathematical astronomy," *TP* **55**: 1–73.

(1995) "The myth of the naturalists," in *Medicine, Philosophy and Religion in Ancient China: Researches and Reflections*. Aldershot: 1–33.

Smith, K. (1989) "Zhouyi interpretation from accounts in the *Zuozhuan*," *HJAS* **1989.2**: 421–63.

(2003) "Sima Tan and the invention of Daoism, 'Legalism,' et cetera," *JAS* **62.1**: 129–56.

Smith, N. D. (1989) "Diviners and divination in Aristophanic comedy," *Classical Antiquity* **8.1**: 140–58.

Smith, R. J. (1991) *Fortune-tellers and Philosophers: Divination in Traditional Chinese Society*. Boulder.

(2008) *Fathoming the Cosmos and Ordering the World: The Yijing (I-Ching, or Classic of Changes) and Its Evolution in China*. Charlottesville.

Snodgrass, A. M. (1971) *The Dark Age of Greece: An Archaeological Survey of the Eleventh to the Eighth Centuries B.C.* Edinburgh.

(1980) *Archaic Greece: The Age of Experiment*. London.

(1986) "Interaction by design: the Greek city-state," in *Peer Polity Interaction and the Development of Socio-Cultural Complexity*, ed. A. C. Renfrew and J. F. Cherry. Cambridge: 47–58.

(1987) *An Archaeology of Greece*. Berkeley.

Som, T. T. (1949–52) *Po Hu T'ung, the Comprehensive Discussions in the White Tiger Hall* (2 vols.). Leiden.

Song Zhenhao 宋鎮豪 (1999) "Zai tan Yinxu bu yong jiagu de laiyuan" 再談殷墟卜用甲骨的來源 [A reconsideration of Shang divination on the basis of recently discovered oracle bones], in *Sandai wen ming yan jiu (1): 1998 nian Hebei Xingtai-Zhongguo Shang Zhou wen ming guo ji xue shu yan tao hui lun wen ji* 三代文明研究（一）1998年河北邢台中國商周文明國際學術研討會論文集. Beijing: 392–98.

(2000) "Yinxu jiagu zhanbu chengshi de zhuisuo" 殷墟甲骨占卜程式的追索 [An exploration of the formulae of Shang oracle bone divination], *WW* **2000.4**: 35–45.

Song shi 宋史 [Standard History of the Song] (1345), by Tuo Tuo 脫脫 (1313–55). Beijing, 1977.

Sorabji, R. (1980) *Necessity, Cause, and Blame: Perspectives on Aristotle's Theory*. London.

Sourvinou-Inwood, C. (1987) "Myth as history: the previous owners of the Delphic oracle," in *Interpretations of Greek Mythology*, ed. J. Bremmer. London: 215–41.

(1990) "What is polis religion?," in *The Greek City from Homer to Alexander*, ed. O. Murray and S. Price. Oxford: 295–322.

Spence, J. (1990) "Western perceptions of China from the late sixteenth century to the present," in *Heritage of China: Contemporary Perspectives on Chinese Civilization*, ed. P. S. Ropp. Berkeley: 1–18.

Spiegel, M. and Human Rights Watch Asia (1997) "Appendix IV: Regulations of the Shanghai Religious Affairs Bureau." In *China: State Control of Religion, Issue 1 Human Rights Watch*, October, 90–99.

Spiller, H. A., J. R. Hale, and J. Z. de Boer (2002) "The Delphic oracle: a multi-disciplinary defense of the gaseous vent theory," *Journal of Clinical Toxicology* **40.2**: 189–96.

Staehlin, R. (1912–13) "Das Motiv der Mantik im Antiken Drama," *Religionsgeschichtliche Versuche und Vorarbeiten* **12**: 1–233.

Steele, J. (1917) *The I li or Book of Etiquette and Ceremonial* (2 vols.). London.

Strickmann, M. (1988) "Dreamwork of psycho-Sinologists: doctors, Taoists, monks," in *Psycho-Sinology: The Universe of Dreams in Chinese Culture*, ed. C. Brown. Lanham, MD and London.

(2005) *Chinese Poetry and Prophecy: The Written Oracle in East Asia*. Palo Alto.

Struck, P. T. (2004) *Birth of the Symbol: Ancient Readers at the Limits of Their Texts*. Princeton.

Su Bingqi 蘇秉琦 (1983) *Su Bingqi kao gu xue lun shu xuan ji* 蘇秉琦考古學論述選集 [Selected Works of Archaeology by Su Bingqi]. Beijing.

Su Rongyu 蘇榮譽 (2004) "The reception of 'archaeology' and 'prehistory' and the founding of archeology in late imperial China," in *Mapping Meanings: The Field of New Learning in Late Qing China*, ed. M. Lackner and N. Vittinghoff. Leiden: 423–49.

Sui shu 隋書 [Standard History of the Sui], by Wei Zheng 魏徵 (580–643). Beijing, 1982.

Swann, N. L. (1931) "Biography of the empress Têng: a translation from the Annals of the Later Han Dynasty," *JAOS* **51.2**: 138–59.

Sweek, J. (2002) "Inquiring for the state in the ancient Near East: delineating political location," in Ciraolo and Seidel (2002): 41–56.

Swerdlow, N. M. (1998) *The Babylonian Theory of the Planets*. Princeton.

Taigong liu tao 太公六韜 [The Six Tactics of Taigong], in *Taigong liu tao jinzhu jinyi* 太公六韜今註今譯, ed. Xu Peigen 徐培根. Taipei, 1976.

Taiping yu lan 太平御覽 [Imperially Reviewed Encyclopedia of the Taiping Era], ed. Li Fang 李昉 (925–96). Beijing, 1983.

Tan Weisi 譚維四 (2003) *Zeng hou Yi mu* 曾侯乙墓 [The Tomb of Marquis Yi of Zeng]. Beijing.

T'ang Chün-yi (1962) "The Tien-ming (Heavenly Ordinance) in Pre-Ch'in China," *PEW* **11.4**: 195–218.

(1963) "The T'ien-ming (Heavenly Ordinance) in Pre-Ch'in China – II," *PEW* **12.1**: 29–42.

Tang Junyi 唐君毅 (1957) "Xian Qin sixiang zhong zhi tian ming guan" 先秦思想中之天命觀 [The concept of tian ming in Pre-Ch'in China], *Xinya xuebao* 新亞學報 **2.2**: 1–33. See T'ang Chün-yi.

Tanner, J. (2009) "Ancient Greece, early China: Sino-Hellenic studies and comparative approaches to the classical world. A review article," *JHS* **129**: 89–109.

Tarn, W. W. (1930) "Alexander: the conquest of Persia," in *The Cambridge Ancient History VI: Macedon: 401–301 B.C.*, ed. J. B. Bury, S. A. Cook, and F. E. Adcock, 1st edn. New York: 352–86.

Teng Zhaozong 滕昭宗 (1996a) "Yinwan Han mu jian du shi wen xuan" 尹灣漢墓簡牘釋文選 [Transcription of the inscribed slips from Han tombs at Yinwan], *WW* **1996.8**: 26–31.

(1996b) "Yinwan Han mu jian du gai shu" 尹灣漢墓簡牘概述 [A general account of the inscribed slips from Han tombs at Yinwan], *WW* **1996.8**: 32–36.

The Collection of Ancient Greek Inscriptions in the British Museum. See Newton and Marshall 1874–1916.

Thomas, R. (1992) *Literacy and Orality in Ancient Greece*. Cambridge.

Thorp, R. L. (1981) "The Sui Xian tomb: re-thinking the fifth century," *Artibus Asiae* **43.1/2**: 67–110.

Tianshui Fangmatan Qin jian 天水放馬灘秦簡 [The Qin Bamboo Slips from Tianshui, Fangmatan] (2009). Beijing.

Tod, M. N. (ed.) (1933–48) *Greek Historical Inscriptions* (2 vols.). Oxford. [Tod]

Toda Toyosaburō 戸田豐三郎 (1957) "Sa Koku no Ekizei kiji kanken" 左國の易筮記事管見 [Stalk-casting in the *Zuo zhuan*, *Guo ya* and *Yi jing*], *Shinagaku kenkyū* 支那学研究 **16**: 1–11.

Tong Enzheng 童恩正 (1995) "Thirty years of Chinese archaeology," in *Nationalism, Politics, and the Practice of Archaeology*, ed. P. L. Kohl and C. Fawcett. Cambridge: 177–97.

(2002) "Magicians, magic and shamanism in ancient China," ed. L. von Falkenhausen, *Journal of East Asian Archaeology* **1.4**: 27–73.

Tseng, Lillian Lan-ying (2002) "Divining from the game Liubo: an explanation of a Han wooden slip excavated at Yinwan," *China Archaeology and Art Digest* **4.4**: 55–62.

(2011) *Picturing Heaven in Early China*. Cambridge, MA.

Tuchelt, K. (1980) "Didyma: Bericht über die Arbeiten der Jahre 1975–1979," *Istanbuler Mitteilungen* **30**: 99–197.

Turner, V. (1975) *Revelation and Divination in Ndembu Ritual*. Ithaca.

Twitchett, D. and M. Loewe (eds.) (1986) *The Cambridge History of China: Ch'in and Han*. Cambridge.

Unschuld, P. U. (1985) *Medicine in China: A History of Ideas*. Berkeley.

(2003) *Huang Di nei jing su wen: Nature, Knowledge, Imagery in an Ancient Chinese Medical Text*. Berkeley.

(2011) *Huang Di Nei Jing Su Wen: Annotated Translation of Huang Di's Inner Classic – Basic Questions*. Berkeley.

Vandermeersch, L. (1974) "De la tortue à l'achillée," in Vernant (1974): 29–51.

(1977–80) *Wang dao ou la voie royale* (2 vols.). Paris.

(1992) "Le rationalisme divinatoire," *EO* **11**: 285–315.

(1994) *Études sinologiques*. Paris.

Vellacott, P. H. (1964) "The guilt of Oedipus," *G&R*, 2nd ser., **113**: 137–48.

Venture, O. (2002a) "L'écriture et la communication avec les esprits en Chine ancienne," *BMFEA* **74**: 35–65.

(2002b) "Étude d'un emploi ritual de l'écrit dans la Chine archaïque (XIIIe–IIIe siècle avant notre ère): Réflexion sur les matériaux épigraphiques des Shang et des Zhou occidentaux." Ph.D. Dissertation. University of Paris 7–Denis Diderot.

Vernant, Jacques (1948) "La divination: contexte et sens psychologique des rites et des doctrines," *Journal de Psychologie* **1**: 299–325.

Vernant, J.-P. (ed.) (1974a) *Divination et rationalité*. Paris.

(1974b) "Parole et signes muets," in Vernant (1974a): 9–25.

(1977) "Inaugural address at the College de France, 5th December 1975," *Social Science Information* **16.1**: 5–24. Republished as "Greek religion, ancient religions," in *Mortals and Immortals: Collected Essays by Jean Pierre Vernant*, ed. F. Zeitlin. Princeton, 1991: 269–89.

(1978) "Ambiguity and reversal: on the enigmatic structure of Oedipus Rex," trans. P. duBois, *New Literary History* **9.3**: 475–501.

(1981) "Preface," in Gernet (1981): vii–xi.

(1982) *The Origins of Greek Thought*. Ithaca.

(1983) *Myth and Thought among the Greeks*, trans. J. Lloyd with J. Fort. London and Boston.

(1991) "Speech and mute signs," in *Mortals and Immortals: Collected Essays*, ed. F. Zeitlin. Princeton: 303–17.

Vidal-Naquet, P. (1986) *The Black Hunter: Forms of Thought and Forms of Society in the Greek World*, trans. A. Szegedy-Maszak. Baltimore.

Vogel, H. U. (1994) "Aspects of metrosophy and metrology during the Han period," *EO* **16**: 135–52.

Vokotopoulou, I. (1992) "Dodone et les villes de la grande Grèce et de la Sicile," in *La magna Grecia e i grandi santuari della madrepatria,* atti del Trentunesimo Convegno di Studi sulla Magna Grecia 4–8 Ottobre 1991. Taranto: 64–90. [V]

Wang Aihe (2000a) "Antiquity, modernity, and social theory," *Journal of East Asian Archaeology* **2.1**: 363–81.

(2000b) *Cosmology and Political Culture in Early China*. Cambridge.

Wang Baoding 王保頂 (1997) "Han dai zai yi guan lüe lun" 漢代災異觀略論 [A brief discussion of Han dynasty views of portents]. *Xueshu yuekan* 學術月刊 **1997.5**: 104–8.

Wang Baoxian 王葆玹 (1995) "Boshu 'Yao' yu 'Yi zhi yi' de zhuanzuo shidai ji qi yu 'Xi ci' de guanxi" 帛書《要》與《易之義》的撰作時代及其與《繫辭》的關係 [The time of composition and authorship of the silk manuscripts "Yao" and "Essence of the Yi" and their relation to the Xici], *DJ* **6**: 350–66.

Wang Bo 王博 (1995) "'Yao' pian lüe lun" 《要》篇略論 [Essentials of the "Yao" silk manuscript], *DJ* **6**: 320–28.

Wang Jianmin 王健民 and Liang Zhu 梁柱 (1979) "Zenghou Yi mu chutu de ershiba xiu qinglong baihu tuxiang" 曾侯乙墓出土的二十八宿青龍白虎圖象 [The images of the Twenty-eight Lunar Lodges, the azure dragon, and the white tiger excavated from the tomb of Marquis Yi of Zeng], *WW* **1979.7**: 40–45.

Wang Mingqin 王明欽 (2004) "Wangjiatai Qin mu zhujian gaishu" 王家台秦墓竹簡概述 [A survey of the bamboo slips from the Wangjiatai Qin tomb], in Ai Lan 艾蘭 (S. Allan) and Xing Wen 邢文 (eds.) (2004): 26–49, English summary: 439–45.

Wang Xiangtian 王襄天 and Han Ziqiang 韓自強 (1978) "Fuyang Shuanggudui Xi Han Ruyin hou mu fajue jianbao" 阜陽雙古堆西漢汝陰侯墓發掘簡報 [Brief report on the excavations of the Western Han tomb of Duke Ruyin at Shuanggudui, Fuyang], *WW* **1978.8**: 12–31.

Wang Yuxin 王宇信 (1984) *Xi Zhou jiagu tan lun* 西周甲骨談論 [A Discussion of the Western Zhou Oracle Bones]. Beijing.

Wardman, A. E. (1955) "Plutarch and Alexander," *CQ*, n.s. **5.1/2**: 96–107.

(1971) "Plutarch's methods in the Lives," *CQ*, n.s. **21.1**: 254–61.

Watson, B. (1968) *The Complete Works of Chuang Tzu*. New York.

Watson, W. (1995) *The Arts of China to AD 900*. New Haven.

Weber, M. (1951) *The Religion of China: Confucianism and Taoism*, trans. and ed. H. H. Gerth. New York.

(1978) *Economy and Society: An Outline of Interpretive Sociology* (2 vols.), ed. G. Roth and C. Wittich. Berkeley.

Weld, S. (1999) "Chu law in action: legal documents from Tomb 2 at Baoshan," in *Defining Chu: Image and Reality in Ancient China*, ed. C. A. Cook and J. S. Major. Honolulu: 77–97.

Weniger, L. (1915) "Die Seher von Olympia," *Archiv für Religionswissenschaft* **18**: 53–115.

West, M. L. (1997) *The East Face of Helicon: West Asiatic Elements in Greek Poetry and Myth*. Oxford.

Whittaker, C. R. (1965) "The Delphic oracle: belief and behaviour in ancient Greece – and Africa," *Harvard Theological Review* **58**: 21–47.

Wiegand, T., A. Rehm, R. Harder et al. (1906–) *Milet: Ergebnisse der Ausgrabungen und Untersuchungen seit dem Jahre 1899* (4 vols.). Berlin.

Wilamowitz-Moellendorff, U. von (1893) *Aristoteles und Athen* (2 vols.). Berlin.

Wilhelm, R. (1950) *The I Ching or Book of Changes*, trans. C. F. Baynes. Princeton.

Winkler, J. J. (1990) *The Constraints of Desire: The Anthropology of Sex and Gender in Ancient Greece*. New York.

Woronoff, M. (1999) "Pouvoir et divination dans l'*Iliade*," in *Pouvoir, divination, prédestination dans le monde antique*, ed. E. Smadja and E. Geny. Besançon: 175–83.

Wu Hong (1989) *The Wu Liang Shrine: The Ideology of Early Chinese Pictorial Art*. Palo Alto.

Wu Jiulong 吳九龍 (ed.) (1985) *Yinqueshan Han jian shi wen* 銀雀山漢簡釋文 [Transcription of the Han Bamboo Slips from Yinqueshan]. Beijing.

Wuwei Han dai yijian 武威漢代醫簡 [The Han Medical Bamboo Slips from Wuwei]. Beijing, 1975.

Wuwei Han jian 武威漢簡 [The Han Bamboo Slips from Wuwei] (1964), ed. Chen Mengjia 陳夢家. Beijing.

WW 1974.6: 41–61. "Hubei Jiangling Fenghuangshan Xi Han mu fajue jianbao" 湖北江陵鳳凰山西漢墓發掘簡報 [Brief report on the excavation of the Western Han tombs at Fenghuangshan in Jiangling, Hubei].

WW 1974.11: 37–39. "Wuxing zhan fubiao shiwen" 五星占附表釋文 [Transcription of the chart attached to Divination by the Five Stars].

WW 1977.8: 17–22. "Mawangdui Han mu boshu Xiangma jing shiwen" 馬王堆漢墓帛書相馬經釋文 [Transcription of the silk manuscript "Horse Physiognomy Classic" excavated from the Han tomb at Mawangdui].

WW 1979.1: 1–31. "Hebei sheng Pingshan xian Zhanguo shi qi Zhongshan guo mu zang fajue jianbao" 河北省平山縣戰國時期中山國墓葬發掘簡報 [Brief report on the excavations of the Warring States period tombs of the Prince of Zhongshan at Pingshan, Hebei].

WW 1984.3: 1–8. "Mawangdui boshu 'Liushisi gua' shiwen" 馬王堆漢墓帛書《六十四卦》釋文 [Transcription of the silk manuscript "64 Hexagrams" excavated from Mawangdui].

WW 1988.5: 35–38. "Hubei Jiangling Yutaishan ershiyi hao Zhanguo Chu mu" 湖北江陵雨台山二 十一號戰國楚墓 [The Warring States Chu tomb 21 at Yutaishan, Jiangling, Hubei].

WW 1989.2: 1–11. "Gansu Tianshui Fangmatan Zhanguo Qin Han mu qun de fajue" 甘肅天水放馬灘戰國秦漢墓群的發掘 [Excavation of the Warring States, Qin, and Han tombs at Fangmatan, Tianshui, Gansu].

WW 1989.4: 1–9. "Anhui Han shan Lingjia tan xin shiqi shidai mudi fajue jianbao" 安徽含山凌家灘新石器時代墓地發掘簡報 [Brief report on the excavations from the Neolithic cemetery at Lingjiatan, Hanshan, Anhui].

WW 1995.1: 37–43. "Jiangling Wangjiatai shiwu hao Qin mu" 江陵王家台15號秦墓 [The Han tomb number 15 at Wangjiatai, Jiangling].

WW 1996.8: 4–25. "Jiangsu Donghai xian Yinwan Han mu qun fajue jianbao" 江蘇東海縣尹灣漢墓群發掘簡報 [Excavation of some Han tombs at Yinwan, Donghai, Jiangsu].

WW 1999.6: 26–47. "Guanju Qin Han mu qingli jianbao" 關沮秦漢墓清理簡報 [Brief report on the excavation of the Qin and Han tombs at Guanju, Jingzhou, Hubei].

WW 2000.5: 27–45. "Dunhuang Xuanquan Han jian shiwen xuan" 敦煌懸泉漢簡釋文選 [Selected transcription of the Han slips from Dunhuang, Gansu].

WW 2000.7: 85–94. "Mawangdui boshu 'shi fa' shiwen zhaiyao" 馬王堆帛書《式法》釋文摘要 [The silk book Shi Fa from Mawangdui].

WW 2001.9: 4–21. "Hubei sheng Jingzhou shi Tianxingguan er hao mu fa chu jianbao" 湖北省荊州市天星觀二號墓發出簡報 [Brief report on the excavation of Tomb Number 2, Tianxingguan, Jingzhou, Hubei].

WW 2011.6: 49–56. "Beijing Daxue cang Xi Han zhu shu gai shuo" 北京大學藏西漢竹書概說 [A general survey of the Western Han bamboo slips collected by Peking University].

*Xiaotun nandi jiagu kaoshi. S*ee Yao Xiaosui.

Xie Chengxia 謝成俠 (1977) "Guanyu Changsha Mawangdui Han mu boshu Xiangma jing de tantao" 關於長沙馬王堆漢墓帛書相馬經的探討 [Discussion of the silk manuscript "Horse Physiognomy Classic" from the Han tomb at Mawangdui], *WW* **1977.8**: 23–26.

Xing Wen 邢文 (1995) "Heguanzi yu boshu 'Yao'" 鶡冠子與帛書《要》 [Yao in the Heguanzi and the silk manuscripts], *DJ* **6**: 336–49.

(2000) "Qin jian 'Guicang' yu 'Zhou yi' yong shang" 秦簡《歸藏》與《周易》用商 [The Qin bamboo Guicang and Zhou yi references to Shang divinatory texts], *WW* **2002.2**: 58–63.

(2003) "Hexagram pictures and early Yi schools: reconsidering the Book of Changes in light of excavated Yi texts," *MS* **51**: 571–604.

(2004) "Pictoral arrangements of early Chinese manuscripts," in Ai Lan 艾蘭 (S. Allan) and Xing Wen 邢文 (eds.) (2004): 420–31.

Xu Fuguan 徐復觀 (1963) *Zhongguo renxing lun shi – xian Qin pian* 中國人性論史: 先秦篇 [History of Chinese Theories of Human Nature: Pre-Qin Period]. Taipei.

(1969) "Yinyang, wuxing, ji qi youguan wenxian de yanjiu" 陰陽五行及其有關文獻的研究 [Yin–yang, wuxing, and research on texts concerned with them], *Zhongguo renxinglun shi* 中國人性論史. Taipei, 509–87.

(1980) "Yuan shi – you zongjiao tongxiang renwen de shixue de chengli" 原史-由宗教通向人文的史学的成立 [The original scribe – from a religious toward the establishment of a humanistic historiography], in *Zhongguo shi xue shi lun wen xuan ji* 中國史学史論文選集 [A Collection of Essays on the History of Chinese Historiography] III, eds. Tu Weiyun 杜維運 and Chen Jinzhong 陳錦忠. Taipei: 1–72.

Xu Qinting 徐芹庭 (1975) *Zhou yi yiwen kao* 周易異文考 [Examination of Alternative Graphs in the Zhou yi]. Taipei.

Xu Xitai 徐錫台 (1989) *Zhou yuan jiaguwen zongshu* 周原甲骨文總述 [Summary of the Zhouyuan Oracle Bones]. Xi'an.

Xu Zhentao, D.W. Pankenier, and Jiang Yaotiao (2000) *East Asian Archaeoastronomy: Historical Records of Astronomical Observations of China, Japan and Korea*. Amsterdam.

Xunzi jijie 荀子集解 [Collected commentaries on the Xunzi] by Xun Qing 荀卿 (ca. 313–238), ed. Wang Xianqian 王先謙. Beijing, 1988.

Yamada Keiji 山田慶兒 (1979) "The formation of the Huang-ti Nei-ching," *Acta asiatica* **36**: 67–89.

(1980) "Kyū-ku hachi-fu setsu to Shōshiha no tachiba" 九宮八風說と少師派の立場 [The theory of the nine palaces and eight winds and the position of the followers of Shaoshi], *Tōhō gakuhō* 東方學報 [Kyoto] **52**: 199–242.

(ed.) (1985) *Shin hatsugen Chūgoku kagakushi shiryō no kenkyū* 新發現中國科學史資の研究 [Researches on Newly Found Manuscripts from the Viewpoint of the History of Science in China]. Kyoto: 1–44.

Yan Dunjie 嚴敦傑 (1978) "Guanyu Xi-Han chuqi de shi pan he zhanpan" 關於西漢初期的式盤和占盤 [On early Western Han *shi* boards and their use in divination], *KGXB* **1978.5**: 334–37.

(1985) "Shi pan zongshu" 式盤綜述 [Summary account of the *shi* board], *KGXB* **4**: 445–64.

Yang Hua 楊華 (2003) "Chutu rishu yu Chu di de jibing zhanbu" 出土日書與楚地的疾病占卜 [Excavated daybooks and disease divination in the Chu area], *Wuhan daxue xuebao* **56.5**: 564–70.

Yang Jianmin 杨建民 (1993) "Zuo zhuan jimeng de mengxiang leixing ji zhanmeng tedian" 《左傳》記夢的夢象類型及占夢特點 [Types of dream imagery and characteristics of oneiromancy in the Zuo zhuan], *Fudan lun tan* **3**: 34–40.

Yang Lien-sheng (1945) "A note on the so-called TLV mirrors and the game Liu-po," *HJAS* **9.3/4**: 202–6.

(1952) "An additional note on the ancient game Liu-bo," *HJAS* **15.1/2**: 124–39.

Yao Xiaosui 姚孝遂 and Xiao Ding 肖丁 (eds.) (1985) *Xiaotun nan di jiagu kaoshi* 小屯南地甲骨考釋 [The Oracle Bones from Nan Di, Xiaotun]. Beijing.

Yates, R. D. S. (1988) "New light on ancient Chinese military texts: notes on their nature and evolution, and the development of military specialization in Warring States China," *TP* **74.4/5**: 211–48.

(1994) "An introduction to and a partial reconstruction of the yin-yang texts from Yinqueshan: notes on their significance in relation to Huang Lao Daoism," *EC* **19**: 75–144.

(1995) "State control of bureaucrats under the Qin: techniques and procedures," *EC* **20**: 331–66.

(1997) "Purity and pollution in early China," *Integrated Studies of Chinese Archaeology and Historiography*. Symposium series of the Institute of History and Philology, Academia Sinica, no. 4 (July): 479–536.

(2005) "The history of military divination in China," *EASTM* **24**: 15–43.

Yinqueshan Han mu zhujian 銀雀山漢墓竹簡 [The Bamboo Slips from the Han Tombs at Yinqueshan]. Beijing, 1985, rpt. 1989.

Yinwan Han mu jiandu 尹灣漢墓簡讀 [Reading the Bamboo Slips from the Han Tombs at Yinwan]. Beijing, 1977. [*Yinwan*]

Yuan Shushan 袁樹珊 (1926) *Shu bu shi xing xiang xue* 述卜筮星相學 [Studies of the Transmission of Divination, Spirit Mediumship, Astrology, and Physiognomy] (4 vols.). Shanghai.

(1948) *Zhongguo li dai bu ren zhuan* 中國歷代卜人傳 [Biographies of Diviners in Chinese History by Periods]. Shanghai, rpt. Taipei, 1985.

Yunmeng Shuihudi Qin mu 雲夢睡虎地秦墓 [The Qin Tombs from Shuihudi, Yunmeng] (1981). Beijing.

Zeng Lanying 曾藍瀅 (1999) "Yinwan Han mu 'Bo ju zhan' mu du de shijie" 尹彎漢墓'博局占'木牘的試解 [An explanation of the TLV diagram for divination from Yinwan], *WW* **1999.8**: 62–65. See Tseng, Lillian Lan-ying.

Zeng Qinliang 曾勤良 (1993) *Zuo zhuan yin shi fu shi zhi shi jiao yan jiu* 左傳引詩賦詩之詩教研究 [Studies of Poetic Education through Zuo zhuan Quotations of *shi* and *fu*]. Taipei.

Zenghou Yi mu. See Tan Weisi 2003.

Zhang Bingquan 張秉權 (1960) "Lun chengtao buci" 論成套卜辭 [A theory of sets of oracle bone inscriptions], *Zhongyang yanjiuyuan lishi yuyan yanjiusuo jikan waibian* **4.1**: 389–401.

(1967) "Jiaguwen de faxian yu gubu xiguan de kaozheng" 甲骨文的發現與骨卜習慣的考證 [The discovery of the oracle bone inscriptions and the custom of bone divination], *BIHP* **37.2**: 827–79.

Zhang Liwen 張立文 (1991) *Zhou yi boshu jin zhu jin yi* 周易帛書今注今譯 [Commentary and Contemporary Translation of the Silk Manuscripts of the Zhou yi] (2 vols.). Taipei.

Zhang Longxi (1988) "The myth of the other: China in the eyes of the West," *Critical Inquiry* **15.1**: 108–31.

Zhang Quancai. See Chang Ch'uan-ts'ai 1995.

Zhang Yachu 張亞初 and Liu Yu 劉雨 (1981) "Cong Shang Zhou bagua shu zi fuhao tan shi fa de jige wenti" 從商周八卦數字符號談筮法的幾個問題 [Some observations about milfoil divination based on Shang and Zhou *bagua* numerical symbols]. *Kaogu* **1981.2**: 154–63, trans. Shaughnessy (1981–82).

Zhang Zhenglang 張政烺 (1979) "Shaanxi Qishan Fengchucun faxian Zhou chu jiaguwen" 陝西岐山鳳雛村發現周初甲骨文 [The discovery of early Zhou oracle bone inscriptions at Fengchucun, Qishan, Shaanxi], *WW* **1979.10**: 27–37.

(1980) "Shishi Zhou chu qingtongqi mingwen zhong de Yi gua" 試釋周初青銅器銘文中的易卦 [An explanation of the Yi hexagrams inscribed in early Zhou bronzes], *KGXB* **1980.4**: 403–15.

(1984) "Boshu 'liushisi gua' ba" 帛書《六十四卦》跋 [The "Sixty-four Hexagrams" in the silk manuscript], *WW* **1984.3**: 9–14.

Zhangjiapo xi Zhou mu di 張家坡西周墓地 [The Western Zhou Tombs at Zhangjiapo] (1999). Beijing.

Zhangjiashan Han mu zhujian (ersiqi hao mu) 張家山漢墓竹簡 (二四七號墓) [The Bamboo Strips Excavated from the Han Tomb 247 at Zhanjiashan]. Beijing, 2001. [*ZJS*]

Zhao Kuifu 趙逵夫 (1989) "Mawangdui Han mu chutu 'Xiangma jing, Da guang po zhang, Gu xun zhuan' fawei" 馬王堆漢墓出土《相馬經·大光破章, 故訓傳》發微 [Investigation of the silk manuscript "Horse Physiognomy Classic" from the Han tomb at Mawangdui], *Wen xian* 文獻 **1989.4**: 262–68.

Zhao Zhenhua 趙振華 (1985) "Luoyang liang Zhou bu yong jiagu de chubu kaocha" 洛陽兩周卜用甲骨的初步考察 [Initial investigation of oracle bone divination at Luoyang during the Eastern and Western Zhou], *Kaogu* **1985.4**: 371–79.

Zhong Zhaopeng 鍾肇鵬 (1993) *Chen wei lun lüe* 讖緯論略 [A Brief Discussion of Apocrypha and Weft Texts]. Shenyang.

Zhongguo tian wen xue shi wen ji 中國天文學史文集 (1978): 1–13. "Mawangdui Han mu bo shu 'Wuxing zhan' shiwen" 馬王堆漢墓帛書《五星占》釋文 [Transcription of the silk manuscript "Divination by the Five Stars" excavated from the Han tomb at Mawangdui]. Beijing.

Zhongguo wenwu 中國文物 **1** (1979): 26–29. "Xi Han boshu Tianwen qixiang zazhan shiwen" 西漢帛書天文氣象雜占釋文 [Transcription of the Western Han silk text miscellaneous prognostications by celestial patterns and qi configurations].

"Zhongxian Zhongba yizhi fajue baogao" 忠線中壩遺址發掘報告 [Excavation report on the Zhongba site in Zhongxian] (2001), in *Chongqing kuqu kaogu baogaoji – 1997 juan* 重慶庫區考古報告集 – 1997 卷 [Compilation of Reports from the Chongqing Reservoir Area – 1997 Season]. Beijing: 559–610.

Zhou Yimou 周一謀 (1994) "Cong zhujian 'Shi wen' deng kan daojia yu yang-sheng" 從竹簡《十問》等看道家與養生 [From the Bamboo texts' "Ten Questions" to Daoism and nurturing life], *DJ* **5**: 239–46.

Zhuangzi jishi 莊子集釋 [Collected Explanations of the Zhuangzi], ed. Guo Qingfan 郭慶藩 (1844–96). Beijing, 1961.

Zuesse, E. M. (1987) "Divination," *Encyclopedia of Religion*, ed. M. Eliade. New York: 375–82.

Zufferey, N. (1998) "Erudits et lettrés au début de la dynastie Han," *Études Asiatiques* **52.3**: 915–65.

(2003) *To the Origins of Confucianism: The Ru in Pre-Qin Times and during the Early Han Dynasty*. Berne.

Index